Information Systems for Management
Planning and Control

**The Irwin Series in Management and
The Behavioral Sciences**

Consulting Editors
L. L. CUMMINGS AND E. KIRBY WARREN
Advisory Editor
JOHN F. MEE

INFORMATION SYSTEMS FOR MANAGEMENT PLANNING AND CONTROL

THOMAS R. PRINCE, Ph.D.

Professor and Chairman
Department of Accounting and Information Systems
Graduate School of Management
Northwestern University

226738

Third Edition   1975

RICHARD D. IRWIN, INC.   Homewood, Illinois   60430

Irwin-Dorsey International   London, England   WC2H 9NJ
Irwin-Dorsey Limited   Georgetown, Ontario   L7G 4B3

Third Edition

First Printing, May 1975

ISBN 0-256-01647-X
Library of Congress Catalog Card No. 74–29748
Printed in the United States of America

*To
Eleanor*

Preface

THIS BOOK examines the information dimensions of decision-making processes in diverse organizational settings. The characteristics of the expanded managerial or decision-making functions are determined through study of organizations from the perspective of the systems analyst. The systems analyst is concerned with the specification of information requirements associated with a given decision-making process, the identification of data sources, the matching of information requirements with data sources into information flows, and the evaluation, modification, and integration of information flows into information systems.

The sequence of topics in the text material emphasizes the evolution of highly developed systems from a balanced level of advancement in a multidimensional setting. Eight common dimensions of computer-based networks are analyzed, compared, and contrasted in each of the generalized models of management information systems. These dimensions are (*a*) models of the administrative process, (*b*) organizational structure, (*c*) identification of decision maker, (*d*) nature of activities supported by network, (*e*) degree of interaction by decision maker with computer-based network, (*f*) time cycle, (*g*) interface of network with other networks, and (*h*) data structure. In addition to these dimensions at each balanced level of advancement, four other issues are examined as overall considerations in the movement from simple computer-based networks to advanced information systems. These other issues are (*a*) management control, (*b*) internal control, (*c*) security and confidentiality of data, and (*d*) committee structures for planning, implementing, maintaining, and modifying large-scale computer-based networks.

A formal program is presented for planning, designing, and implementing an information system. As this framework is repeatedly applied to each balanced level of advancement, the reader is challenged to think scientifically about the information dimensions of decision-making activities throughout an organization. The text materials reinforced by the case studies provide the reader with the opportunity for a systematic analysis of increasingly complex organizational settings that can be studied from the common threads of this formal program.

This Third Edition of *Information Systems for Management Planning and Control* reflects the significant changes and developments in information systems and the systems analyst's functions in recent years. Flowcharts are included to clarify the specific elements and interrelations in the five generalized models of information systems. These flowcharts serve a unifying and integrating function of pulling together the conceptual aspects of the *information systems approach*.

The coverage of the book has been expanded to include nonprofit organizations, especially health care institutions. There has also been extensive revision of some materials and deletion of others to reflect recent developments in the field. Four case studies included in the revised edition have been deleted, and eight case studies have been added to strengthen the coverage in new areas. Explanatory materials have been added to 7 of the 25 case studies that are included from the revised edition; the purpose of these additional notes and flowcharts is to provide the reader with a better understanding of the problem situation. Other explanatory material have been added to the text so a student does not need a prerequisite course in administrative policy before taking a course in information systems.

Machine manufacturer's names and model numbers have been omitted, where possible, from the Third Edition. Instead, computer equipment is referred to by its generation (such as, third generation large-scale computer system, fourth generation minicomputer system, and fourth generation large-scale computer system). Amoco Chemicals Corporation, Mead Corporation, and Mercantile Financial Corporation and Subsidiaries are three case studies which have not been updated so as to preserve their respective representations of an organization in which third generation systems philosophy, second generation systems philosophy, or first generation systems philosophy is being applied.

Part I of this book presents the foundation and overview for the information systems approach and serves as the frame of reference for the other five parts. The subsequent parts of the book contain general descriptions of information systems in each of the functional areas, the progress toward total information systems encompassing all functional areas, and the special concerns with information systems. Thus, the book is a broad survey of many diverse areas within an organization that are viewed from the perspective of the systems analyst. From another standpoint, it can be described as a special method for (*a*) identifying information flows associated with decision-making activities throughout an organization, (*b*) evaluating information flows, and (*c*) designing new information flows.

The material in this book was developed for use in both graduate and undergraduate courses at Northwestern University, and these courses were scheduled near the end of the formal academic program, during the spring session of the senior year for undergraduate students and during the spring session of the second year for graduate students. By scheduling this type of course late in the formal academic program, the material will serve as a consolidating and integrating device.

The book intentionally reexamines areas with which the reader may already be familiar, such as PERT and inventory-control models. However, these areas are reexamined from a new slant that emphasizes the information dimensions of decision-making activities throughout an organization. Thus, the contents are similar to the policy type of management course, except that where the policy type of course focuses upon the decision process of executive management, the information systems approach focuses upon the information used in the decision process and the information flow associated with each decision process throughout the organization.

The case studies and technical notes included in this book do not require the reader to have familiarity with any given computer programming language. However, I have discovered from experience that it is desirable for the reader to complete instruction in some computer programming language before beginning to study the material in this book. This latter instruction should be in sufficient detail that the reader has actually programmed a rather complicated administrative problem. In the process of developing and testing this program, the reader will gain an increased awareness of the capabilities and limitations of electronic computers.

As far as other prerequisites, the reader should have the equivalent of an introductory course in cost accounting which includes (*a*) an appreciation of the nature of costs, (*b*) an understanding of what is meant by the statement, "different costs for different purposes," and (c) a general orientation toward the operation of integrated standard cost- and budgetary-control systems. The reader should have a general understanding of the administrative process and an appreciation of the application of mathematical methods to administrative activities. In this latter area, the minimum exposure would include a familiarization with the linear programming technique. All other prerequisites will typically be achieved by scheduling this instruction during the last session of the formal academic program.

The research and analyses encompassed within this book are drawn from the author's professional activities while receiving financial support from six organizations, agencies, and foundations: Arthur Andersen & Co., Northwestern University, the Ford Foundation, the Office of Naval Research, the Department of Health, Education, and Welfare, and the Kellogg Foundation. Two specific contracts must be cited for some of the research: Office of Naval Research Contract N00014–67–A–0356–0015 and Department of Health, Education, and Welfare Contract HSM–110–70–368 (Supplemental Agreement no. 2) .

I am grateful to the many organizations that cooperated in making available their experience in the area of information systems. Many organizations elected to use disguised names; however, in all other respects, the case description is the actual company, firm, or institution. I acknowledge the permission of the Technical Association of the Pulp and Paper Industry to include material in Chapter 6 from my earlier publication with the association. The comments, questions, and discussions of the many students who studied earlier drafts of this book have significantly influenced this Third Edition. The author is indebted to George R. Bruha of the University of Michigan, Howard W. Melton of the University of Illinois, Ronald D. Picur of the University of Illinois, and James B. Thies of Northwestern University for their ideas and constructive comments. I am also indebted to Robert E. Malcom of Pennsylvania State University for his detailed comments on an earlier draft of this edition of the book. I appreciate the editorial assistance of Betty Powell and Barbara Gunner. A final word of gratitude must be said to my wife for her encouragement and understanding during the lengthy period of time I worked on this book.

April 1975   THOMAS R. PRINCE

Contents

ing System. Responsibility Accounting Reports. Coding Pattern. Accounting Statistical Data. Reporting Guidelines.

8. Profitability Accounting Systems   240

Basic Concept. The General Model. Comparison with Other Models. Systems Analyst's Perspective. Coding Pattern. Summary. A Note on the Industrial Chemical Industry.

9. Critical Path Planning and Scheduling Information Systems   265

Benefits from This Approach: *History. Comparison. CPM Terminology. Illustrative Examples of CPM Technique. Advantages of the Method. Other Considerations.* The Method from the Perspective of the Systems Analyst.

Part III
PRODUCTION AND OPERATION
INFORMATION SYSTEMS

10. Operations Management Information Systems   293

The General Model. TYPE 2 Information System. The Eight Common Dimensions. Coding Patterns and Programs for the Coordination Phase. Illustration of Coordination Phase. Systems Analyst's Perspective of Coordination Phase. Level of Service.

11. Inventory Management Information Systems   318

Diverse Objectives: *The Cost of Carrying Inventory. The Cost of Not Carrying Inventory.* Identification System for Inventory Items. Reorder Quantity: *Costs Varying with the Number of Lots Processed. Costs Varying*

PART **I**

FOUNDATION AND OVERVIEW

CHAPTER 1

The Information Systems Approach

COMPUTER-BASED SYSTEMS have assisted humans in probing outer space, landing on the moon, adjusting the speed and direction of manned space vehicles, photographing the surface of Mars, monitoring hospital patients in intensive care units, performing medical multiphasic screening, forecasting national elections, and eliminating many of the clerical and routine tasks in numerous diverse fields. Television, newspapers, and other mass media have highlighted many of these applications of computer-based systems. This communication coverage has been so thorough that it is unusual today to find an adult in the United States who has not heard something about computers.

Although the mass media will occasionally describe a mammoth mistake created by a computer-based system, the layman continues to have untempered expectations about the capabilities of these systems. If computers can assist us in landing on the moon, then ". . . there are no limits to what a computer can do." This position toward computers appears to be pervasive. Recent attitudinal tests in five hospitals (including samples of physicians, administrators, nurses, technicians, and clerical employees) revealed the same attitude of unreasonable expectations that had also been identified in business organizations.

This over-optimistic layman's attitude toward computer-based systems can be contrasted with the experienced business administrator's bourgeoning suspicions of computer-based systems. Many managers and administrators have had unsatisfactory experiences with these systems. In some cases the proposed objectives of a planned computer-based system were never realized. In other cases a poorly conceived network was abandoned after considerable personnel and financial resources were committed to the project. Executives with these unfortunate experiences become more pessimistic about the size and scope of a computer-based system that can be implemented within a given period.

Systems analysts engaged in designing and implementing computer-based information systems must cope with both of these attitudes—the unreasonable expectations of laymen and the pessimistic perspective of experienced executives. While these opposing attitudes create some additional excitement in the organization under scrutiny, the systems analyst must seek a balanced perspective that includes an active management participation in planning and designing the computer-based system. The systems analyst desires to nurture the enthusiasm of supervisors, technicians, chiefs, and clerks without losing primary focus on the decision makers whom the proposed computer-based system is intended to support.

The purpose of our study here is to help the systems analyst design, for individual organizations, computer-based systems. The objective is for these information systems to use the minimum time and personnel to process the required information which management needs to make intelligent decisions regarding the welfare of its particular organization. Our study extends beyond systems design and includes strategies for implementation of systems, strategies for evaluation of systems, and approaches for management of systems efforts.

THE OBJECTIVE OF A COMPUTER-BASED SYSTEM

Although a computer-based system must do more than just capture the existing manual flow of data in an organization, a *faster transmission* of existing data flows may be a helpful first step for management. However, if this first step is directly pursued, then it may be part of an approach in which there is no second step. *The basic objective of a computer-based system is to assist management in its decision-making activities.*

In planning and designing a system to support specific decision-making activities, the systems analyst's first step is to understand the broader "environment" in which these decision-making activities occur. The second step is to comprehend in detail the purpose, function, scope, and operation of these decision-making activities. The level of understanding that is required for the successful accomplishment of the second step is typically greater than that possessed by anyone other than a decision maker. Thus, direct participation by management in planning and designing a computer-based system is a common feature of a network that supports the decision-making activities.

There is no acceptable substitute for executive management's participation in planning and designing a computer-based system. Though supervisors, technicians, and administrative assistants will have a thorough grasp of specific current data being used by management in the decision-making process, these individuals probably will not comprehend the total decision-making process. For example, from management's perspective, the current data collection and processing may not even be a satisfactory short-term arrangement for providing relevant data. Instead, management may have a new set of information requirements that has emerged from a reevaluation of the environment and the decision-making activities. This reevaluation will include those organizational factors that are controlled by management and which may be scheduled to change in the near future, thus yielding different data needs and processing requirements.

In addition to the role of a unique data source, active participation by management in planning and designing a computer-based system is an essential part of the commitment and organizational support required to sustain a new network. Otherwise, the proposed network will never be fully implemented in the sense of supporting the decision-making activities.

COMPONENTS OF A DECISION

Management in its decision-making activities must select among alternative courses of action and must possess the capability for implementing, administering, and monitoring the selected alternative. In a large, complex organization, the personal manual efforts required to administer a selected alternative may be more than a full-time job. Many new organizational arrangements and management control procedures have been developed to assist management by delegating these administrative tasks and responsibilities to subordinates while maintaining overall control of them. Programmed decision rules incorporated in electronic control devices and in computer programs have frequently been employed by management as part of these revised management control networks.

But where does the information come from that management uses in selecting among alternatives? What additional information would management like to have regarding these alternatives? Is this information available? If not, is it economically feasible to make it available? What is the time lag between the initial accumulation and the subsequent transmission of information to management? Is all information transmitted to management, or is some screening device employed so that only exceptional information (according to the management-by-exception procedures) is transmitted to management? What additional data should be currently accumulated for possible use by management in a predictable "new set" of decision-making activities in the future?

The previous questions relate only to some aspects of the "information dimensions" of the decision-making processes of management in the current, complex environment. Another series of questions might relate to the manner in which management has used electronic computers, communication equipment, or mathematical tools and techniques in coping with different information flows associated with the decision-making process.

This book is primarily concerned with *the information dimensions of the decision-making process throughout the enterprise* and presents a special approach for viewing and analyzing these information dimensions. Before this special approach is described, attention is given to the historical and environmental changes that permit and support it.

THE ORGANIZATION AS A SET OF INFORMATION NETWORKS

An organization can be viewed as a series of large information networks which connect the information requirements in each decision-making process with the data sources. These networks extend throughout all of the administrative processes and extend down to actions of information users. In large complex organizations, the different operations of a given division or organizational unit can be described as separate information networks, with one giant overall information network superimposed on the individual information systems.

This idea of viewing an organization as a series of information networks has been expounded by teachers of management for many years. Until recently, however, this idea was relegated to the general discussions of the administrative processes. Any attempt to systematically examine different aspects of each information network was obstructed by the overwhelming requirements for (*a*) information determination, (*b*) information collection, (*c*) information processing, (*d*) information analysis, (*e*) information transmission, and (*f*) information interpretation. In spite of these practical constraints, the concept continued to have appeal to members of management. In several organizations management provided economic support for the application of methods, tools, techniques, and processing equipment to implement this concept. Eventually, this management concept which had only been a vision was achieved in practice.

These recent developments in studying administrative processes within an organization were extensions from interdisciplinary approaches taken during the 1950s. The professional literature of the 1940s contains numerous examples of discipline-oriented analysis in the specific areas of accounting, finance, manufacturing, marketing, and personnel. Combined analyses, such as accounting-manufacturing or finance-marketing, were indicative of the first types of extended studies. Gradually, the focus during the 1950s shifted from *discipline areas* to *problem areas,* and the membership of a study team might include representatives from each of the functional fields within the organization as well as outside consultants. The formal education of these consultants began to include some individuals with advanced work in behavioral science, political science, and economics.

Once the focus on problem areas became the dominant type of analysis, an array of interdisciplinary approaches were undertaken in various organizations. During this same period of the late 1950s, other developments were occurring in the economic environment regarding techniques, procedures, processing equipment, and communication equipment. It is difficult to classify individually each of these developments of the 1950s because each tends to overlap other developments. For purposes of this discussion, however, these dynamic changes are classified according to four movements.

FOUR MOVEMENTS WITHIN ECONOMIC
ENVIRONMENT

First, the behavioral science approach toward studying an organization combined psychological and sociological inquiries to emphasize the human motivational aspects of each area. The interdisciplinary studies of the early 1950s were merged with these behavioral science approaches and resulted in team studies being made of organizations and of the various departments and operations within organizations. These teams consisted of representatives from different functions and departments within organizations but with psychologists and sociologists playing dominant positions. These dominant roles included the area of the team's analysis, the specification of methodology employed, and the content of the team's report.

Second, extensive studies were made of data flows within the organization and of the feasibility of installing data processing and communication equipment for coping with these flows. This type of study is in response to the change occurring in the economic environment which made the electronic computer a familiar tool. The capabilities and applications of this equipment were significantly expanded in the late 1950s. Simultaneous developments in electronic computers and communication equipment provided the necessary means for rapid accumulating, calculating, processing, summarizing, reporting, and transmitting of information.

Third, mathematical tools and techniques were applied to the study of management events. Many of these techniques have been in existence for years, but were not employed because there was no rapid means by which this information could be processed. For example, the ideas of reorder points and reorder quantities (providing the critical controls around which the integrated inventory control and production control system operates) were developed earlier; however, they were only widely applied in the late 1950s as these processing capabilities became available. The mathematical approach to studying and solving administrative processes and problems has produced new management control devices and management tools for coping with the various functions and organizational activities.

Fourth, scientific methodology has been applied to the study of organizational situations. Mathematical, descriptive, analytical, or simulated models have been developed to represent critical dimensions of this analysis. There are many common features between the third and fourth movements. While mathematical analyses were dominant in the third approach, organizational theory has a major role in the fourth approach.

GENERAL SYSTEMS THEORY

During the formative stages of the above four movements, a different type of concept was being developed in academic research centers. Interdisciplinary studies possessing some characteristics of each of the four movements cited above were being conducted under a new banner called the "General Systems Theory."[1] The father of general systems theory, Ludwig von Bertalanffy, contends that studies of this type have five common features:

1. They focus on problems characteristic of the behavioral and biological sciences which are not explained in conventional physical theory.
2. They introduce concepts and models from physics as a basis for comparison, like comparing information with energy.
3. They concern complex, multivariate problems.
4. They are multidisciplinary in nature.
5. They consider such "unscientific" concepts like wholeness, organization, teleology and directiveness legitimate subjects for scientific analysis.[2]

As a result of developments in general systems theory, scientific analysis of biological, behavioral, and social phenomena became "acceptable," thus enabling us to use theoretical constructs to explain general relationships in the empirical world. From another perspective, a set of associated relationships was viewed as an entity and an appropriate subject of analysis. Thus, the study of systems became a familiar type of scientific analysis.

During the late 1950s the methodologies of general systems theory were cited in the professional literature as the rationale for selected studies of organizations. Some studies were primarily along func-

---

[1] Ludwig von Bertalanffy, "General Systems Theory: A New Approach to Unity of Science," *Human Biology*, vol. 23 (December 1951) , pp. 303–61.

[2] Ludwig von Bertalanffy, "General System Theory—A Critical Review," *General Systems*, vol. 7 (1962) , pp. 1–20.

tional fields, such as "A General Systems Theory Approach to Financial Management" or "A General Systems Theory Approach to Marketing Management." Other studies were broader in scope and contained dynamic elements, such as, "A General Systems Theory Approach to Integrated Inventory Procurement, Manufacturing, and Shipping."

The set of associated relationships within an organization that was viewed as the entity varied significantly even among studies in the same organization. One study might focus on physical products and their movement within the organization. Another might examine the "paper flow" within the organization. A third study might map the verbal and written communications within a given organization. For example, in one organization tape recordings were made of the chief executive officer's telephone calls, and all conference meetings were filmed by hidden cameras and taped. Schematic diagrams were made of the origin, flow, and destination of each verbal and written communication.

Prof. Kenneth Boulding added to general systems theory a framework for arranging empirical fields in a hierarchy according to their complexity. This framework was based on the organization of underlying or "individual" or unit behavior in the various empirical fields.[3] Boulding's approach leads toward a "system-of-systems" which he outlined as nine levels of theoretical analysis where each level was a different type of system.

Scientists engaged in the development of general systems theory during the 1950s envisioned the establishment of a set of systematic theoretical constructs to explain relationships in the empirical world. These systematic theoretical constructs can be described as analytical and communication vehicles that connect two or more specific disciplines. For example, the common areas of concern in biological sciences and chemistry were interfaced and described as biochemistry. Another example is the development of cybernetic models which combine constructs from the nervous system, control theory, electrical engineering, and information theory. Thus, the long-term objective of general systems theory is to develop a set of these analytical and communication vehicles that will connect and interrelate all disciplines.

---

[3] Kenneth E. Boulding, "General Systems Theory—The Skeleton of Science," *Management Science*, vol. 2 (April 1956), pp. 197–208.

Although the goal of general systems theory has not yet been realized in practice, this conceptual development has had a significant impact upon the understanding and expansion of scientific knowledge. Special studies have been made in the management of organizations which brought into focus behavioral and social aspects of empirical phenomena that had not previously been highlighted. The empirical phenomena examined in some of these models and constructs frequently "behaved" in a manner different from that suggested by physical theory.

The approach presented in this book for studying the information dimensions of decision-making processes throughout an organization draws heavily upon some of the basic ideas associated with general systems theory. Specifically, the approach transcends the physical science constraints of existing technology and management "know-how." It incorporates the "system-of-systems" or "hierarchy-of-complexity" concept to highlight the limitations of the analysis of an isolated system. This latter feature provides a useful framework for viewing a given model on an enlarged scale. Our approach also uses the general systems theory concept of coordination—cyclical and harmonious action within an observed unit—as part of the scientific model dealing with dynamic interaction.

The approach subsequently described, however, differs in many instances from general systems theory. While general systems theory has an inclusive perspective toward sets of associated relationships within an organization, the special approach followed in this book will be restricted to relationships associated with decision-making processes. Alternatively, the special approach followed in this book contains a priority system for ordering sets of associated relationships after benefiting from the breadth of the dimensions brought into focus by a general systems theory approach. In addition, the approach of this book is in the direction of increasing management's understanding of the practical, decision-making processes within an organization. While the latter approach emphasizes applied understanding, general systems theory is more concerned with theoretical expansions of scientific knowledge.

DESCRIPTION OF APPROACH

The special approach presented in this book for studying the information dimensions of decision-making processes is called the *information systems approach.* This can be described as a systematic method for observing, analyzing, evaluating, and modifying an organization or any part of an organization. From another perspective, the information systems approach can be described as a special method for (*a*) identifying information flows associated with decision-making activities throughout an organization, (*b*) evaluating information flows, and (*c*) designing new information flows.

The term "systematic method" implies that items are viewed from a special point of view guided by specific theories. For purposes of this book, the term "systems analyst" is used to identify an individual who possesses (or at least is supposed to adhere to) the point of view characterized by the information systems approach. This qualification is necessary because some of the case studies included in this book describe systems analysts who may not always fully comply with the information systems approach.

A human being can perceive more sense impressions than he can intelligently organize and classify. The systems analyst seeks theoretical models which intentionally permit some aspects of reality to escape observation so that those aspects which are noted can be precisely organized within their specific limitations. Each of the models that the systems analyst selects will feature information dimensions of decision-making processes at some level of system. Thus, decision-making processes, decision makers, and information flows that support these decision-making activities are the dominant items in the systems analyst's perspective of an organization.

Figure 1.1 presents the general model of a simple organizational setting featuring a decision maker (symbol A6) whose information requirements have been specified and translated into online computer programs that retrieve selected data. The data sources are depicted by the general purpose flowcharting notation (symbol A1) that represents all types, forms, and mediums of data inputs. The matching of information requirements with data sources is represented by a series of four processing and reporting operations (symbols A2 to A5). Online computer programs (symbol A2) contain the detailed instructions for editing, filtering, and screening the coded data, and these activities are performed within the central processing unit (symbol A3). The screened and processed data are placed in online storage (symbol A4) where the decision maker (symbol A6) has the capability of online inquiring and monitoring (symbol A5).

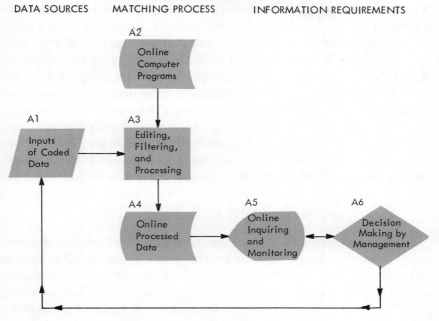

FIGURE 1.1
Matching of Information Requirements with Data Sources
in an Organizational Setting

The network incorporated in Figure 1.1 is an extremely simple system which was included for purposes of depicting how information requirements can be matched with data sources in providing relevant information to decision makers. The specification of information requirements, identification of data sources, and the design of the matching process are three key elements in the information systems approach.

This type of inquiry—the information systems approach—is especially appropriate for coping with the current economic environment. Concurrent developments in electronic computers, communication facilities, mathematical tools and techniques, and management technology have significantly changed both the economic environment and the manner in which most organizations conduct their operations. Furthermore, these developments have influenced some organizations to completely change the nature of their administrative processes. In these cases, the organizations are currently engaged in totally new types of economic activities.

The information systems approach is an attempt to get a "handle" on the administrative processes in diverse economic environments. The applicability of this approach to diverse economic environments is illustrated in the case studies included in this book. These case studies and technical notes are intentionally arranged so that there is a gradual transition from the simple, familiar economic environment to the more complex economic environment. In other words, in these case studies, the only constant is the approach—the information systems approach; all other aspects are variables.

The relevance of the information systems approach to cope with these diverse organizational settings is illustrated in the next section where a sequence of formal information systems are presented. These systems cover the gamut from the simple to the complex network.

FORMAL INFORMATION SYSTEMS

In the formative stages of the four movements discussed previously and during the early phases of general systems theory, there was a major overall development in information systems within organizations. During the past two decades there has been a significant change in the role and nature of *Formal Information Systems* (FIS) within an organization. While the financial accounting system represented the only FIS in most organizations in 1950, this type of network now has been joined by a series of other types of FISs. In this context, a FIS is a specified network of data sources, matching and processing procedures, and data outputs; these operations may be performed on either a manual or an electronic basis.

Figure 1.2 presents the financial accounting network as a formal information system in 1950. This illustrative network presents the simplest version of FIS in which Manual Operation A, Manual Operation B, and Manual Operation C are connected by informal lines to the financial accounting network. This type of representation is made to reflect the general case of 1950 before data processing procedures were widely used in industrial and service organizations, governmental agencies, and health care institutions.

Manual Operation A represents an informal inquiry from an external source including, for instance, a verbal sales order from a customer or a written sales order that is not recorded by the organization receiving this document, a request for service from a citizen, or a pre-admission request to a hospital from a scheduled patient. The

FIGURE 1.2
The Financial Accounting Network as a Formal Information System

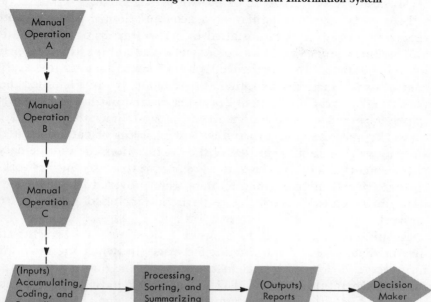

details of these inquiries are not recorded, and formal documents are not forwarded to the organizational units that will provide the goods or services.

Within the organization, there are divisions or departments that perform specific operations. The information request from the organizational unit designated by Manual Operation A is respectively communicated to the organizational units designated Manual Operation B and Manual Operation C. There is no detailed *recording* of the message that is communicated from A to B to C.

Eventually, an informal communication is given to the financial accounting network from Manual Operation C verifying that specific services or goods have been provided; the details of this transaction are recorded. This accumulating, coding, and recording operation represents the *only complete* capture of the economic transaction that is being inputted into the financial accounting network. Within the financial accounting network, these data are processed, sorted, summarized, and reported in the format requested by the decision maker or external user. The outputs, therefore, from the financial accounting network include all the formal external reports prepared by the organization as well as special reports for management.

During the 1950s, modular data accumulation, processing, and reporting operations were installed in many organizations. The initial modular units were limited in scope and complexity and primarily supported a prescribed operational area, such as inventory control or production scheduling. These modular units handled the prescribed set of data inputs, processing, accumulating, and reporting operations associated with a given function. Since these modular networks were designed to handle common types of data associated with a given function regardless of the organization, the unique data requirements of a decision maker were not provided by this network. In other words, simple, common data were provided by these modular units; unique, special data were not included within these networks.

In this gamut of simple to complex FISs, Figure 1.3 presents an intermediate series of information networks in which the modular units serve as formal inputs to the financial accounting network. Manual Operations A, B, and C in Figure 1.2 have been replaced with three modular data accumulation, processing, and reporting

FIGURE 1.3
An Intermediate Series of Formal Information Networks Interfaced
with the Financial Accounting Network

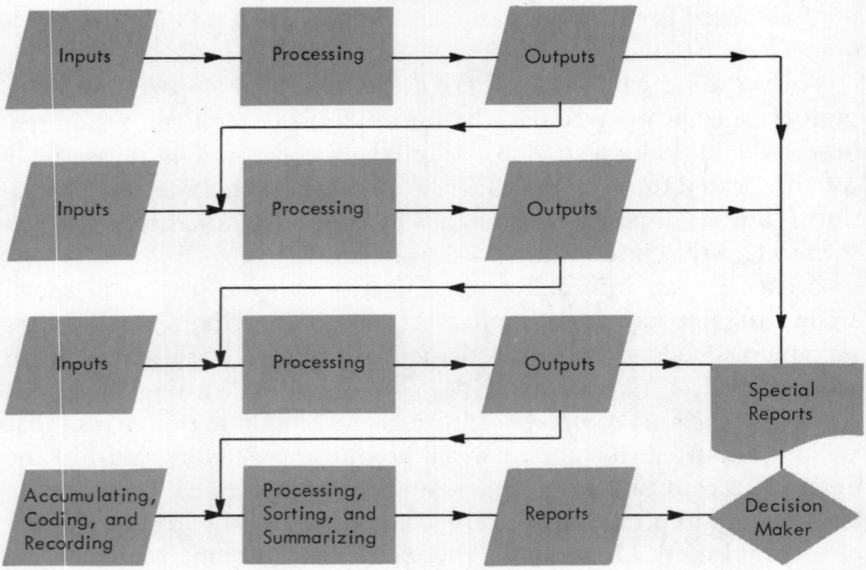

operations. In this schematic representation, the decision maker may obtain some special reports from each of the modular units. The main source of information, however, continues to be the financial accounting network.

In the early 1960s these modular data accumulation, processing, and reporting operations expanded the scope and range of information flows encompassed within the module. Online data storage capabilities were incorporated within each module, and computer generated special reports were now available from a given module without any computer processing requirement being placed upon the central processor supporting the financial accounting network. Some of these storage and processing capabilities were incorporated in the minicomputers of the late 1960s and 1970s.

Organization-wide information systems studies were conducted by management during the mid 1960s, and these management studies were responsible for changing the configuration of the formal information networks. The modular operation ceased being primary inputs to the financial accounting network. Instead, each modular unit was a formal information system, and each FIS was online to other FISs.

Figure 1.4 presents this series of FISs. Since each of the four FISs in this schematic representation is online to the central processing unit, a decision maker may obtain information from the common

FIGURE 1.4
A Series of Formal Information Systems

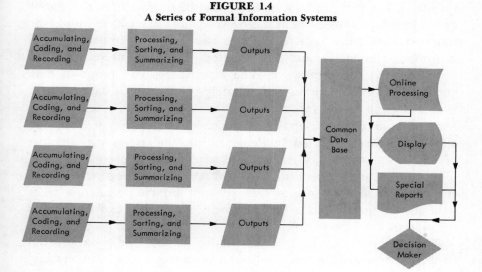

data base without disrupting any of the scheduled activities within a FIS. This capability represents a significant change within the organization; the decision maker is no longer dependent upon the financial accounting network as the information source. The user (decision maker) may interact directly with the FIS, obtaining detailed data in the format and at the desired levels of aggregation, accuracy, and currency. The user may also have the option of specifying or limiting the accessibility of the data to other potential users within the FIS.

By comparing Figure 1.2 with Figure 1.4, the magnitude of this development in the aggregate becomes apparent. First, large segments of activities have become highly formalized as an information system. Second, the *distance* (physical) of the economic event from the FIS has disappeared. Remote terminal capabilities permit the *initial* entry of the economic event at its origin (including a direct communication link to the customer as the purchase order request is being initially specified). Third, the need for duplicate recording of economic events has been eliminated. The initial capture of the event serves all remote terminal users as well as the overall data management system.

Fourth, complete data are now captured at the point of origin, and these data are available for the full system. This type of data—*complete*—was not previously available at the detailed level. All supporting aspects of an economic event are available (such as the full specifics from the invoice) at the point of origin; now the major question is the amount of machine readable data which should be retained. Previously, only partial data were available in the informal information networks, and only selected data were entered into the financial accounting network. The type, scope, and range of data entered into the system have completely changed—full data with all the supporting details are captured.

Fifth, a decision maker has a choice of the source of data; the choice is between detailed data entered into the system at the points of origin and summary data stored after having been processed. The decision maker may use a special set of computer programs to generate the desired information without informing anyone what data are being retrieved. These expanded capabilities increase the decision maker's interactive role with the common data base.

The changes incorporated in Figure 1.4 can be viewed from another perspective. There has been a blending of needs, processing,

and sources. There has been a *quality* increase in the kind of transactions captured in the FIS. There has been a *quantity* increase in
the data available due to the capture of internal data, statistics, and
related events as part of the recording of an economic event at the
point of origin. There has been an integration of functions and data
files into an overall common data base as a result of the management
information systems studies. And, finally, the capability for direct
interaction of the user with the data system has been established,
since the filter that previously separated the user from the data bank
has been eliminated. These developments have resulted in a change
in the location and overall nature of the information systems functions within the organization.

The series of FISs encompassed in Figure 1.4 is indicative of the
level of integration of the simplest computer-based system that will
be examined in this book. The network included in the first case
study in this book (Case 2–1, Lakewood Service Corporation) is
significantly more advanced than the simple model represented in
Figure 1.4. In Chapter 2 attention is given to explaining flowcharting symbols and computer-based terminology so Exhibit A in Case
2–1 will be understood by all readers.

This series of three FISs was presented to emphasize the magnitude of the operational changes in information processing which
have occurred over the past two decades. As indicated, this book will
begin with an examination of decision-making operations in organizational settings where the information flows will be more complex
than that represented by the model in Figure 1.4. The studies
performed by systems analysts of these organizational settings must
include several dimensions. They must encompass (*a*) the dynamic
interactions between the FISs and the decision makers, (*b*) the
evolving organizational arrangements that emerge from these interactions, and (*c*) the sets of information requirements that are imposed upon the networks after management gains experience with
computer-based networks. To these complexities, the systems analyst
must add the planned improvements and modifications that are
incorporated in the current systems planning and design efforts.

As previously discussed, the information systems approach is a
method of analysis that is compatible with these multidimensions in
changing organizational settings. With a dominant focus on the
information dimensions of decision-making processes in an organization, this approach is applicable (*a*) in gaining an understanding of

the existing organizational arrangement and decision-making processes, (*b*) in evaluating existing information flows, (*c*) in designing new information flows, and (*d*) in planning a revised organizational arrangement. Therefore, the information systems approach is a multidisciplinary, scientific method of analysis that permits interpretation of empirical phenomena in complex settings through an underlying emphasis on information for decision-making processes.

CHARACTERISTICS OF APPROACH

The information systems approach represents a new approach toward studying an organization or any part of an organization. Basically, the systems analyst attempts to group major decisions that management must make (both formally and informally, explicitly and implicitly—thus, all decisions) into categories which are a combination of (*a*) the general area that the decision concerns, (*b*) the time dimension of the decision process, and (*c*) the general area and time dimensions for *information* in the decision process.

A group of decisions possessing these three characteristics is the nucleus of an *information system*. The systems analyst is concerned with tracing all information flows associated with this group of decisions and with the decision-making processes involved, regardless of the organizational boundaries that must be penetrated. This network of information flows that has been traced and charted for each group of related decisions constitutes a *system*. Since the focus of each network or *system* is upon "information flows," each network is called an *information system*.

Thus, the information systems approach is a special method for viewing and analyzing an organization or any part of an organization so that the systems analyst can perceive each major information system within the administrative process. If the systems analyst is to perceive each major information system, then each major information flow must be identified. An information flow results from an organization's matching information requirements with data sources for each major decision. This matching process is accomplished by management and frequently involves the employment of various management science tools and techniques.

In the above description of how an information system is formed, one of the fundamental ideas is the matter of *information requirements*. The information systems approach as presented in this book is different from the approach recommended in most other contemporary systems references in that the emphasis is on *information requirements,* not on *information uses.* Therefore, the systems analyst is not concerned with the current "paper flow" and other aspects of existing information uses. Instead, the systems analyst focuses upon the decision-making activities involved and the requirements for information of the decision maker (which may be a team) in each of these decision-making activities.

From another viewpoint, the practical concept of an information system has assumed a new meaning because of the changes that have occurred in the economic environment. These changes are the result of the interaction of the previously cited four movements: advancements in behavioral science; developments in electronic computers and communication equipment; developments in mathematical tools and techniques; and the application of the scientific method to the study of management. As a result, the practical concept of an information system has shifted from a traditional *accounting system* to an *economic activity system* which encompasses all types of economic data.

Recognizing that this degree of change has occurred in the economic environment and that a state of continuous change is forecast for the immediate future, the systems analyst needs an approach to studying the administrative process which transcends the existing flow of documents and the existing processing and communication equipment. Or, from another perspective, the systems analyst needs an approach enabling him or her to make a diagnosis of the patient rather than treatment of the symptoms. The information systems approach is a systematic method for accomplishing these objectives.

Although systems analysis in a given organization must include the task of treating the symptoms, this important area of concern is reserved for other systems references, and no attention is given in this book to the patchwork approach of trying to improve the document flow within a given department or division of an organization.

In summary, the systems analyst attempts to identify, observe, analyze, and specify information requirements in decision-making activities throughout the business organization; to determine data sources; and to match the information requirements with the appropriate data sources, by employing some of the current management science tools and techniques. The systems analyst follows a systematic method in the performance of each of these steps. In order to understand this systematic method, it is necessary to know (1) the special point of view and (2) the theory that guides the observations by the systems analyst. Chapter 2 presents a general frame of reference in which these two aspects, along with other facets of the information systems approach, are fully examined. However, before considering this general frame of reference, special attention is given to the underlying objective of this book.

OBJECTIVE

The overall objective of this book is to teach the systems analyst to think scientifically about the information dimensions of decision-making activities throughout an organization and to acquire an approach toward establishing criteria for information flows. A four-step method is followed in teaching the systems analyst to think scientifically about information systems.

The first step is to give the system analyst a conception of the entire organization and all of its segments. In other words, the systems analyst must possess the ability to view simultaneously the overall organization and the individual parts or segments of this overall organization. Chapter 2 presents a general frame of reference for assisting the systems analyst in achieving this proper perspective for viewing the process and for identifying, measuring, and evaluating information flows. Chapter 6 describes the extensions of the information systems approach from studying information flows to studying a total organization or studying major types of activities within an organization.

The second step in teaching the systems analyst to think scientifically about information systems is to instill within the analyst an understanding of model construction and the ability to formulate models that represent decision-making activities throughout the organization. This second step is achieved in several ways. First, various parts and chapters of this book are described as being models. At appropriate points in the book, selected models are compared and contrasted with other models. The case studies and topics for class discussion specifically require the reader to express an interpretation of some relation in model form. After these decision-making activities have been expressed in model form, the reader is required to interpret and to justify the model. Furthermore, the reader must make certain types of extensions from the model. Thus, the second approach is accomplished and reinforced again and again throughout this book.

The third step is to assist the systems analyst in bridging the gap between the ideal, model information system and the operational, practical information system. The selected case studies are presented in an appropriate order so that the variance between the ideal and the operational system is magnified in each successive case study. As this variance increases, the systems analyst must evaluate the various alternative methods, and must select those methods which will be used for reducing this variance.

The fourth step in the development of scientific thinking about the information system is to instill in the systems analyst the ability to draw a conclusion and make a decision from the analysis. The systems analyst has to learn to choose among alternatives; the information system that is best for one set of conditions may not provide appropriate information for another set of conditions. In searching for the "right" conclusion, the systems analyst may be forced to return to the first step and begin the analysis again. This is especially applicable where the systems analyst's interpretation of the management situation—upon further study—is discovered to be erroneous. Or, if the economic environment has changed (for example, a new method of processing information at a lower cost is introduced by a machine manufacturer), a new analysis may be required. This re-examination process is part of the dynamic dimension of the information systems approach. This fourth step, of course, is achieved by the various case studies that require the reader to draw a conclusion and to make a decision from that analysis.

While the systems analyst is achieving this overall objective, the contents of this book are so developed that an important secondary objective is also achieved. Various electronic computer equipment, transmission and communication facilities, operations research techniques, management control systems, and information retrieval systems are presented in the selected case studies. The systems analyst views each of these items not from the standpoint of a tool or technique but as a *user, processor,* or *consumer* of information. Emphasis is placed on information sources, information processing means, scientific tools and techniques for analyzing information, information flows in a control network, and information retrieval. Thus, the systems analyst examines each item from the perspective of the information system, and the concept *information* permeates each analysis.

As the systems analysts perform these analyses, they are also acquiring an orientation to some of the recent developments in management science. These developments are presented as part of the economic environment in the different case studies and, as such, represent occurrences with which the systems analyst must have at least some familiarization. In other case studies, the problem situations occurring in the application of these management science tools and techniques are featured in an economic environment where the systems analyst is asked to respond to the situation. Thus, the systems analyst responds to these case studies and is acquiring an appreciation of the *use* of some of these recent developments in management science rather than acquiring a mere description of what some of these recent developments are. This type of orientation to the recent developments in management science is the secondary objective of this book.

TOPICS FOR CLASS DISCUSSION

1. During the past decade, many colleges and universities have added a business policy course which is offered at the end of the formal educational experience. The business policy course is an interdisciplinary inquiry of the business enterprise which transcends the functional lines of business and emphasizes the impact that a given policy type decision has on the total activities of the business organization. Or, from a different perspective, the business policy approach toward studying a business organization emphasizes the necessity for business management to consider the numerous factors in several functional areas of business before reaching a decision on a given policy type of question. How does the business policy approach toward studying an organization differ from the information systems approach? Contrast and differentiate between the two approaches.

2. What is the difference between the objective of general systems theory and the objective of the information systems approach?

3. With the integration of formal information systems into large-scale, computer-based networks, members of management in an organization have new sets of choices regarding the scope, content

and origin of data within each network. They have other new choices as to timeliness and currency of data. Explain why these choices are *new* to members of management.

4. The evolving changes in formal information systems have resulted in a change in the location and overall nature of the information systems function within the organization. Explain these changes.

CHAPTER 2

Establishing a General Frame
of Reference

THE INFORMATION SYSTEMS approach has previously been described as a systematic method for observing, analyzing, evaluating, and modifying an organization or any part of an organization. Alternatively, the information systems approach was described as a special method for (a) identifying information flows associated with decision-making activities throughout an organization, (b) evaluating information flows, and (c) designing new information flows.

Before examining this special method, consideration is first given to describing the general characteristics of those individuals who claim to adhere to the information systems approach—the systems analysts. After examining the systematic method, an overvew is given to computer science terminology for purposes of specifying terms and symbols that are frequently used in describing information systems.

THE SYSTEMS ANALYST AS A TRAINED OBSERVER

There are numerous ways an individual may observe an object, event, activity, or relationship. Each observer perceives the item through a filter composed of experience, education, and training. Some observers have been trained and conditioned so that they are capable of "role playing." These observers can assume a special perspective for viewing an item for a given purpose and can comply with the particular theories associated with this special perspective. This procedure creates designed observations for a given purpose.

Trained observers capable of role playing are able to eliminate much of their personal bias by compensating in their designed observations for the unique filter through which they perceive an item. They follow a three step sequence in designing observations. These steps are indicated by the following questions: What is it that is being observed? For what purpose is this item being observed? What theories are associated with the design of observations?

This latter question can be restated: How is the item being observed?

A systems analyst is a trained observer who performs designed observations of the information flows associated with decision-making processes throughout the organization to evaluate existing information flows and design new information flows. A description of the above three steps will permit us to comprehend what is meant by this definition of a systems analyst.

1. What Is Being Observed?

Although the description of the information systems approach states "an organization or any part of an organization" is being observed, this is not really correct. An organization or an enterprise is an invisible creature and, as such, cannot be *directly* observed. However, different manifestations of it can be perceived.

A trained observer may study a given manifestation from several positions, depending on the set of theories that govern the planned observations. The profession contains many types of trained observers, and each type of trained observer may be guided by a slightly different set of theories regarding the nature of this invisible creature. Therefore, different trained observers respond to varying sets of designed observations.

For example, the financial accountant is a trained observer who has been taught to see in an organization all of those economic activities and events that relate to the measurement of the organization's financial condition, reported income, flow of funds, and so forth. After the financial accountant has perceived an economic activity or event, a decision must be made whether the *identified* economic activity meets the given organization's rules for inclusion in its regular published financial statements (alternative procedures may be employed at the discretion of the organization's management). Finally, the analyst must determine what measurement rules to follow in expressing this *identified* economic activity that has been *selected* for inclusion in the published financial reports.

Other traditional types of trained observers include the financial manager, the sales manager, and the production manager. The financial manager's view of an organization emphasizes the relation of the various activities of the enterprise to the external price of stock, to the credit classification of the organization's long-term securities, and so forth. The sales manager's view emphasizes the markets, the products, and the customers. The production manager's view emphasizes the physical units of output, raw materials, assembly lines, scheduling operations, and selection of alternative inputs.

The systems analyst, like the financial accountant, the financial manager, the sales manager, and the production manager, is concerned with designing observations of certain manifestations of an organization. But unlike these other trained observers, the systems analyst does not respond to any traditional set of theories associated with a functional area. Instead, the systems analyst assumes a new, interdisciplinary perspective for viewing specific manifestations of an organization.

What manifestations does the systems analyst observe? The answer to this question has been implied in other discussions. The systems analyst is concerned with the information dimensions of decision-making activities throughout the organization, and must be trained and conditioned to identify the information flows within the organization. This completes the first phase of the systems analyst's work.

Assuming the term "information" refers to relevant data for a given decision-making process, the systems analyst must first be conditioned to perceive *data* only when viewing an organization or any segment of that organization. Next, the systems analyst groups "data" into three categories: (*a*) data that are currently used in some decision process, (*b*) data that are not currently used in some decision process, but are accumulated for possible use in some predictable future decision-making processes, and (*c*) data that are not now used nor scheduled for future use in decision-making processes. Data that are classified by this latter grouping are referred to as "noise."

Data have special meaning to the systems analyst. Data are the symbols of the analyst's perception of economic activity. These symbols must be at least at an ordinal scale of measurement, which means that the item can be compared with a similar item by the notation of "more than" or "less than." We have arbitrarily elected to exclude from the "data label" those items which can only be identified at the nominal scale of measurement.

Now, let us examine the systems analyst's view of "economic activity." The systems analyst sees economic activity from an "organization theory" perspective. To an organization theorist, an enterprise is a group of people united by some common objective in the production and distribution of goods and services. Beyond this general statement, organization theorists will differ as to the identification of the specific objectives, missions and goals for the particular enterprise under scrutiny.

While the teacher of management takes this concept of the enterprise as a point of departure and emphasizes the administrative process of working with and through people in the pursuit of the organization's objectives, the systems analyst focuses on the *information dimension* of this concept. Furthermore, the systems analyst sees economic activity as the observed results of people in the organization responding and interacting through time to the underlying goals, objectives, and missions of the organization. As previously stated, this concept of observed results has been arbitrarily restricted in this book to being at least at the ordinal scale of measurement.

The previous descriptions of data and economic activity are important for purposes of emphasizing that aspect of the organization seen by the systems analyst. Specifically, the systems analyst does not see the existing document flow within the organization, but views the organization from a more conceptual perspective. A subsequent discussion of the steps involved in the information systems approach will clarify what the systems analyst observes when viewing "an organization or any part of an organization." Attention is now focused on the second question.

2. For What Purpose Is This Item Being Observed?

The primary focus of the systems analyst is the information dimension of an organization's decision-making process. The systems analyst needs this knowledge to carry through the "information systems approach," which was described as a special method for (1) identifying information flows associated with decision-making activities throughout an organization, (2) evaluating information flows, and (3) designing new information flows.

The "information flow" associated with each decision-making activity can be described as the network that connects information requirements with data sources. The numerous networks are classified on the basis of a combination of (*a*) general area that the decision concerns, (*b*) time dimension of the decision process, and (*c*) general area and time dimensions for information in the decision process. Each formal group of related networks is called an "information system."

The systems analyst desires to establish the ideal set of information systems that is compatible with the major decision-making requirements in the existing unique environment of a particular organization. This ideal set of information systems in one organization may make extensive use of computer equipment, communication facilities, and operations research techniques; however, in another organization, limited use may be made of these items. Thus, the systems analyst does not try to develop a standard set of information systems for every organization, but instead tries to develop that unique set of information systems that is most appropriate for the existing conditions in each organization.

Why does the systems analyst desire to establish the ideal set of information systems for each organization? The answer to this question is self-evident. The ideal set will be a balance of the most timely, most efficient, and most economical arrangement of information flows for that specific organization. As a result of such systems, management will have better information for particular decision-making activities, management control devices will establish that management be notified of recurring decisions only on an exception basis, and management's understanding of the operation of its own organization will generally increase. Thus, these systems will give management more time for handling unpredicted activities and for short- and long-term planning activities.

In the common situation of an organization prior to the establishment of this ideal set of information systems, management has too large a quantity of certain types of information and has voids in reference to other required information. The systems analyst, therefore, views the manifestations of the organization from the perspective of the information dimension of the major decision-making activities. This view allows the systems analyst to evaluate existing information flows and, where appropriate, design new information flows.

3. How Is the Item Being Observed?

This question can be restated: What are the theories associated with designing "observations" for evaluating these existing information flows and, where appropriate, designing new information flows?

Today, many management scientists have training and experience in the biological and physical sciences, and these management scientists use expressions and concepts from these areas in their discussions regarding the information network of an organization. For example, analogies are frequently made between physical control systems and business information systems. The nervous system of the human being is compared with the information system of a business organization. Other comparisons are made between the ability of the human body to maintain a balanced blood chemistry and the regulatory and control functions in the organization. Others suggest that the principles of organization theory can be observed in the behavior of very simple animals.

While these analogies and interdisciplinary comparisons are useful generalizations, the systems analyst is cautioned against over-reliance on any such simplified explanations of information systems. On the other hand, the systems analyst can use these interdisciplinary analogies to improve personal understanding of this intangible being— the organization. But systems analysts must confront the sobering fact that they must cope with the information dimension of decision-making activities if they are to achieve the objective.

As implied in the previous discussion of data, the systems analyst guides personal designed observations with organization theory. At all times, the systems analyst is conscious that the business organization is a group of *people* united by some common objective in the production and distribution of goods and services. Management's role is to coordinate the personnel, money, materials, machinery, and technology in such a way that it is possible to realize the organization's long-term, common objective.

The systems analyst is concerned with each major decision-making activity and with the decision maker (including both individuals and teams). The systems analyst desires to study and analyze each major decision-making activity according to a systematic method. The systematic method employed by the systems analyst will vary based on the educational background and training of the analyst.

The systematic method presented in this book is not the *definitive* method for performing such analyses, for the current state of the art does not permit students of the administrative process to know when the definitive method has been specified. Instead, the systematic method presented here is a practical scheme that we have successfully employed in several diverse environments.

THE SYSTEMATIC METHOD

This systematic method represents a special point of view, guided by theory, for observing the administrative process and is equally applicable to analysis at any organizational level. For example, the administrative process under study might be at any of five levels: (*a*) a decision-making activity that directly involves only a given problem area in one department, (*b*) a decision-making activity that directly involves only a given functional area in one department, (*c*) a decision-making activity that directly involves only a given department, (*d*) a decision-making activity that directly involves only a given division, and (*e*) a decision-making activity that directly involves the total organization (such as a major policy question with organization-wide implications).

This systematic method will be examined from an abstract position, and the decision-making activity under scrutiny will be assumed to represent the single, major decision-making activity in the organization.

As an overview, the systems analyst attempts to specify the information requirements in this decision-making activity, to determine the data sources, and to match the information requirements with the appropriate data sources by employing current management science tools and techniques. Each of these phases is examined in the following discussion.

Information Requirements

Specifying the information requirements is the last step in a three-step sequence. The first step is understanding the administrative process for the whole organization under study. The second step is understanding the administrative process for the particular *segment* of the overall organization under study. We will examine each of these steps separately. The first step—understanding the administrative process for the whole organization—requires a familiarization with the unique industry characteristics and practices as well as an appreciation of the general environment of the organization. This appreciation will include a general insight into how the organization reacts to its environment.

Before considering how the first step is accomplished, reexamine the wording of this initial step, specifically, "understanding the administrative process for the whole organization." In other words, what are the general nature and characteristics of the environment in which this decision-making activity takes place?

While there are unusual circumstances in which any scheme must be modified, generally the systems analyst should not immediately go to the physical place of operations and observe the activities. Instead, the analyst who does not understand the economic environment should go to a public or private business library and make a preliminary review of the professional literature regarding the general nature of the environment in which the decision-making activity under scrutiny is located.

After the systems analyst has this limited familiarization with the environment, then the operations on location can be observed more intelligently and more enlightened and relevant questions can be asked. While a checklist of questions may assist the systems analyst in performing this first step, there is no substitute for experience. The experienced systems analyst possesses a "feel" for the environment— has perfected the "art" of sensitivity to surroundings.

The inexperienced systems analyst should not be discouraged by a personal lack of perception. Instead, view such shortcomings as a challenge to exert additional efforts and use the library facilities in researching this environment. This advice is also applicable to the case studies in this book; if the reader does not have a "feel" for the environment after reading and studying the descriptive material in the case study, then use the library facilities *before* responding to case situations.

In the second step in our three-step sequence, the systems analyst expands her or his understanding of the administrative process for that particular segment selected for study within the overall organization's operations. The systems analyst must determine the exact missions, goals, and objectives for this administrative process. In this step as in the first step, experience is a key factor. There is no cook-book approach that is always applicable. The systems analyst observes and asks questions, and evaluates replies and observations while gaining a general "feel" for the environment. Thus, the successful accomplishments of the second step will demand all of the systems analyst's analytical abilities.

For example, in a recent consulting engagement, we eventually realized that the objective of a small manufacturing company was not to produce a small group of products in such a manner that they could be sold at a profit. Instead, this particular manufacturing company was primarily engaged in a financing operation. Almost all of the profit was derived from the interest charges on accounts receiv-able rather than from the margin between cost and selling price of each product. When this general observation was discussed with the company's president, he commented that his organization had been primarily a "financial institution" for the past two years. Further-more, because of the competitive situation, the future of this organi-zation appears to be directly dependent upon the successful continuation of these financing activities.

In the third and last step of our sequence, the systems analyst must specify the exact requirements for information that are needed for achieving the objective. As in the other steps, it is easier to state what the systems analyst should not do rather than what should be done. Do not begin by asking the decision maker: What information are you currently using? Likewise, do not begin by asking the deci-sion maker: What information do you need?

The systems analyst approaches this third step from another per-spective by asking the decision maker: Will you please describe what occurs in the decision-making process? The analyst is concerned with identifying the various questions that must be resolved in the par-ticular decision-making activity. Expedite this step by asking the decision maker: Please cite the issues or questions that must be resolved in this administrative process. However, the analyst is cau-tioned against over-reliance on this technique. For example, the decision maker may fail to cite some questions, feeling that the answers to these questions are taken as "givens," when, in fact, they may be the most significant issues in the total decision process under scrutiny. In other words, these "givens" are assumptions about the frame of reference in which the administrative process is being per-formed; in a management science modelling context, these givens are the parameters for the variables in the decision process. These givens and parameters in most organizational settings do change, and most strategic planning efforts are directed toward modifying one or more of these givens or parameters.

There is another aspect of this third step which merits attention. The systems analyst can view the decision-making process from an abstract perspective, or can view the same process with a concurrent focus on the unique capabilities and characteristics of the decision maker. The inexperienced systems analyst should remember: The decision maker must be capable of understanding and using the relevant data transmitted to the decision maker before these data can properly be classified as "information." Frequently, the analyst spends more time "educating" the decision maker and "informing" subordinates than in designing a new information system. This educational instruction is one of the major parts of the implementation phase of a new information system.

A different aspect of this third step relates to the matter of electronic computer equipment, communication facilities, operations research techniques, and technology. Are the organization's current capabilities in these areas considered as a "given" for purposes of this analysis? Or, should the analysis include resources planned to be available in the near future? The answers to these questions are dictated by the purpose and scope of the investigation.

In summary, the attention given to specifying the information requirements for a particular decision-making activity marks the difference between the systems analyst and those practitioners who do not follow the information systems approach. Because of this attention, this phase of the systems analyst's work is similar to an organization review.

This discussion of information requirements was presented from the standpoint of the inexperienced systems analyst. We also discussed in the first step the experienced systems analyst's advantage in being able to "feel" the environment. In addition, the experienced analyst may already have a good background appreciation of the environment, and thus, will only give brief attention to the first step.

The experienced systems analyst also has a significant advantage in the third step. As soon as the decision maker begins to concentrate on the nature of the decision-making process, the experienced analyst will quickly gain a general appreciation of the nature of this process.

For example, the analyst who believes that the basic problem is in the area of inventory forecasting already knows the significant variables or the typical questions that must be resolved in a normal inventory forecasting activity. If this diagnosis is correct, then the analyst will change the focus of the discussion with the decision maker to determine what unique variables are present in the current situation that are not in the typical situation. Furthermore, the experienced analyst will be equally concerned with why some typical variables associated with this general type of problem are not present in the current situation.

Finally, though specifying an organization's information requirements is second nature to the experienced systems analyst, the inexperienced analyst must make a conscious effort to follow each step carefully.

Data Sources

The systems analyst begins to consider the data sources even before completing the process of specifying the information requirements. In fact, it would be more appropriate to describe these two actions as overlapping.

The systems analyst first prepares a "tentative list of information requirements." Next, the analyst looks (a) at the various books, records, documents, and reports within the organization and (b) at the external published statistical data (including both industry statistics and general economic data), and then indicates what data sources are available for coping with each requirement on the list. For many requirements, there may be a choice of several possible data sources. Although the systems analyst may not know of any existing data sources for a few items on the list, further inquiry frequently reveals sources for most items.

We will not examine individually the items on the "tentative list of information requirements" for which there is no specified data source. The systems analyst indicates by each of these requirements either (a) a new source which might be established for providing data or (b) that there is no known source for the data.

Next, the systems analyst performs an economic evaluation of each requirement. Does the estimated benefit from using each "tentative requirement" in a decision-making process exceed the cost of accumulating, processing, and transmitting the data that will directly

satisfy that requirement? Of course, there may be overlapping requirements for the same type of data in different decision-making
activities. In any case, the systems analyst must decide which of the
items on the "tentative list" are considered valid requirements for
the current time frame.

Matching Process

These "valid" information requirements are matched with the
indicated data sources. This matching frequently takes the physical
format of a matrix diagram with the information requirements
enumerated along one axis and the data sources specified along the
second axis. Figure 2.1 depicts the matching of information requirements and data sources associated with a sales invoice for a small
manufacturing company. The columnar headings in this figure represent general types of decision-making activities; if these activities
were explicitly stated, a series of columns would specify each set of
information requirements now represented by a single column.

How far beyond the matrix diagram the systems analyst will go
depends on the nature of the decision-making activity under scrutiny
and the purpose of the study. While planning and designing an
information system, the analyst will participate with management
personnel in describing its operations in detail and representing
these operations by a series of flowcharts. By using the standard flowchart symbols, the detailed data flows can be easily represented and
specified in a multidimensional framework.

In matching information requirements and data sources, there are
levels of aggregation and varying time cycles. The timeliness of data
in one flow may be a two-minute response while the same data in
another flow may be a twenty-minute response. The currency of data
between flows varies significantly; for example, the two minute
response may be using yesterday's data while the twenty minute
response uses one-hour-old data. Within this matching activity, the
processing mode, transmission mode, data base arrangement (series
of subsystems or an integrated network of files), and types of interaction (such as offline, online, or online and real-time) are also
important dimensions of the detailed specification of data flows.

From another perspective, a significant part of this matching
activity is determined by the existing capabilities in electronic computer equipment, communication facilities, and management science

FIGURE 2.1
Matching Process for Information Requirements and Data Sources

SALES INVOICE	Shipping Department					Marketing Department				Production Department			Finance and Accounting Department		
	Scheduling	Warehousing	Packaging	Routing	Distribution	Product Management	Pricing	Advertising	Sales Management	Inventory Management	Forecasting	Planning	Accounts Receivable Mgt.	General Ledger Accts.	Managerial Accounts
Invoice Number	1C	1C	1C	1C	1C	1C	1C	1C	1C	1C	1C	1C	1C	1C	1C
Customer Code	1C	1C			1C	1D	1C		1D				1D		1D
Product Code			1D		1C	1D				1D					1D
Total Amount						2D	2D	2D	1D		2D	2D	1D	2C	2C
Quantity	1D	1D	1D	1D	1D	1D	2D		2D	1D	2D		1D		1D
Unit of Measure		1D	1D			1D				1D			1D		1D
Price per Unit						2D	1D	2D	2D		2D	2D	1D		1D
Packaging Code		1D	1D	1C	1C										
Shipped to and Ship from	1D	1D			1C								1C		
Location Code and Cost Center						1C			1C						1C
Sales Channel and Territory						1C			1C						1C
Salesperson Code						1D			1D						1C
General Ledger Account														1D	1C
Subaccount															1C
Division															1C
Customer Name		1D	1D	1C	1C	1C			1C				1C		1C
Customer Address	1D	1D		1D	1D										1C

1 = Detailed Data
2 = Summary Data
C = Management Control and Identification
D = Decision

tools and techniques. Another part of this process is determined by the availability of the data sources; for example, there may be two matchings. During the current time frame this source will be matched with a certain requirement, but concurrently, a new data source is being created so that in a future time frame (12 months from now, 18 months, etc.) a new matching will occur.

This matching process is further examined in the context of each of the case studies in this book. In addition, much of the material subsequently presented in this book might be labeled *descriptions of applied management science tools and techniques in the matching of information requirements with data sources.*

Summary

The information systems approach is a special perspective for viewing the administrative process in order to identify existing information flows, evaluate these information flows, and to design, where appropriate, new information flows. It does not matter which purpose the systems analyst is coping with—identifying, evaluating, or designing—the general method remains constant. The systems analyst specifies the information requirements in each decision-making activity (or in resolving each problem area), lists the data sources that are available or could be made available in satisfying these requirements, and matches the information requirements with the data sources utilizing selective management science tools and techniques.

COMPUTER SCIENCE TERMINOLOGY

The systems analyst maintains a unique perspective when viewing the electronic capabilities, transmission equipment, and software facilities supporting the computer-based system. He or she is concerned with the impact that technological advancements have on service, performance, dependability, efficiency, and cost of a network. The specific electronic and engineering features of the equipment are not of primary interest to the systems analyst.

In completing the establishment of a general frame of reference, this final part of the chapter examines selected computer science capabilities from the perspective of the analyst. This examination includes the similarities and differences between related computer science facilities. The overview is at the conceptual level without indicating the specific manufacturer or model of the equipment.

Selected standard flowcharting symbols are described and illustrated as part of the overview, and many of these symbols are included in the figures and exhibits subsequently presented in this book. The American National Standards Institute, Inc., and the International Organization for Standardization are two bodies that specify, define, and illustrate flowchart symbols for information processing. These symbols are multidimensional representations of data capture, flow, processing, storage, transmission, display, and output. Four dimensions encompassed in many symbols are (1) general class of function, (2) specific operation, (3) mode of interface, and (4) medium.

Input and Output Capabilities

The traditional arrangement for inputs to a computer-based system is a *batch processing operation*. Punched cards, punched paper tape, magnetic tape, magnetic ink characters, mark sense cards, console light, switch settings, push buttons, magnetic disk, or other medium are used for the periodic entering of data into the computer-based system. The input equipment reads these data and interprets them into a binary form of representation; after the data have been represented in binary code they can be edited, processed, summarized, stored, and reported by the computer-based system.

Under batch processing operations, the input equipment for reading specific data is *periodically* connected to the computer. This periodic connection may be on a time-cycle arrangement (which is the case of most time-sharing networks) or on a computer operator's request. If several hundred data cards or records are being inputted, the mechanical, time-cycle arrangement will frequently require a series of episodes of "electronic connections" to the computer; however, the overall lapsed time in which these data are serially inputted may be a very few minutes. The speeds at which these episodes occur is such that the layman is given the illusion that the batch processing terminal is operating continuously.

After the batch or series of data is inputted, the electronic interface is terminated. Where a series of remote terminals is used for inputting data, mechanical equipment is typically employed for handling the episodes of "electronic connections." This equipment called a *"multiplexor"* is used for querying a terminal and establishing the electronic interface. In most networks and in all large-scale, computer-based systems, this multiplexor switching operation is sup-

ported by a set of buffers. These buffers serve as an intermediate
storage of data until they are transmitted to the computer.

At the other extreme from batch processing is *online processing*.
In the pure usage of the word, online processing occurs when a
terminal is continuously connected to the computer. But since remote terminals are typically constrained by some activities to human
speeds, the computer would be used very inefficiently if it were
limited by a set of terminals engaged in "pure" online processing.
Therefore, with the possible exception of the computer operator's
console (which is often not an exception), *serial* online processing
rather than "pure" online processing is the arrangement that is
employed. The multiplexor and supporting buffers may make frequent queries of the remote terminals to capture all input data. The
speed and frequency of these queries are such that the layman is
given the illusion that each remote terminal is really online with the
computer, when in fact, seven or eight remote terminals may all be
sharing a single access or channel to the computer and operating in a
serial online processing mode.

The sharp distinctions between batch processing and serial online
processing tend to become a blur to the layman as the number of
remote terminals is increased. There are some differences in the
transmission equipment, communication system, and multiplexor
arrangement depending on the processing mode. However, these
electronic and communication differences are not of primary concern
to the systems analyst. The time-sharing system under either processing mode for 50 to 60 remote terminals tends to have similar
capabilities. Figure 2.2 presents a flowchart of a time-sharing system
that is applicable to either mode of processing.

Symbol B6 in Figure 2.2 is the multiplexor arrangement that is
self-contained and is not under the direct control of the computer.
Symbol B7 represents the supporting buffers that provide intermediate storage of data which are under the control of the auxiliary
equipment (symbol B6). Symbols B8 to B12 represent equipment
and operations that are directly controlled by the computer. Symbols
B1 to B5 should be interpreted not as five terminals, but as a series of
remote terminals; an overall network containing many series of
remote terminals can be thought of as flowing into symbol B6.

Most of the standard symbols for input and output are included in
Figure 2.2; however, four typical symbols omitted here represent
punched cards, magnetic tape, punched tape, and document me-

FIGURE 2.2
Flowchart of a Time-Sharing System

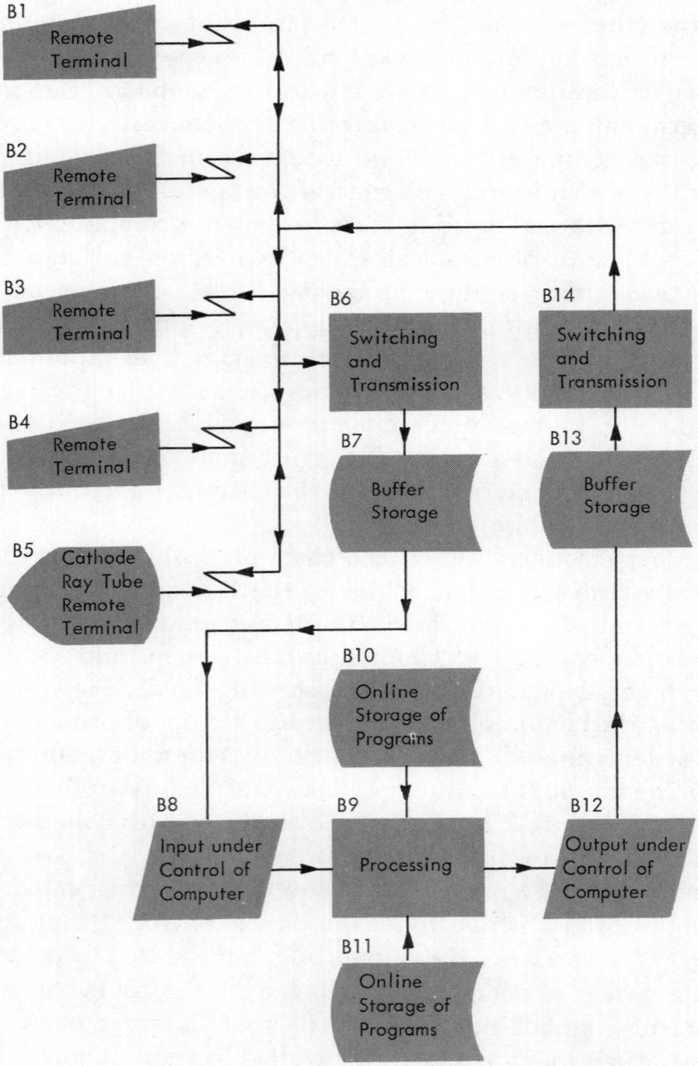

diums of input or output. Figure 2.3 presents selected standard input/output, processing, and storage symbols which are used subsequently in this book. Symbols C2, C3, C4, and C5, respectively, depict the punched card, magnetic tape, punched tape, and document mediums of input.

FIGURE 2.3

Selected Standard Input/Output, Processing, and Storage Symbols

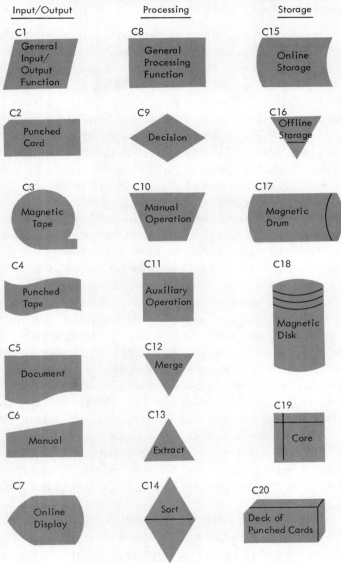

Processing and Storage Capabilities

The vacuum tubes of the first generation computers, the transistorized machines for the second generation, and the attempts to use integrated circuits in the third generation computers provided convenient physical features for differentiating among equipment in the mid-1960s. It was also easy to contrast hardware (the physical equipment and devices forming a computer and supporting peripheral equipment) with software (programs and routines used to extend the capabilities of computers, such as, compilers, assemblers, routines, subroutines, functions, and packages).

The fourth generation computers introduced in the late 1960s and early 1970s contained complete use of Large Scale Integration (LSI) in the circuitry of entire networks. This LSI technique has been widely used in expanding the functions of peripheral equipment and auxiliary facilities. LSI networks have been used to incorporate within the hardware former subroutines (available as software) and to incorporate within the software computational capabilities that were previously included in the computer. These advancements have resulted in the creation of *firmware* which are a combination of previous hardware and software capabilities. Because of these developments, today it is impossible for the systems analyst to draw fine distinctions between categories of facilities. For example, a minicomputer may be used as a remote terminal, as a central processor, or as a switching and transmission facility. Recent advancements in disk, drum and file storage and retrieval systems have created the situation where there are more similarities than differences among these systems. Thus, the systems analyst is primarily concerned with the functions performed by the network rather than attempting to assign labels to the equipment and facilities included within the network.

The systems analyst perspective with regard to processing and storage capabilities is similar to that of the remote terminal user in a time-sharing system. Primary concerns are with the (1) response rate (the speed with which the systems analyst can interact with the system), (2) guarantee of access time per day (such as, 23 hours per day), (3) types of online programs for processing, sorting, and manipulating data, (4) types of interactive languages in the system, (5) the extent to which online storage is made available on a restricted basis to each user, (6) security and confidentiality of data procedures employed, (7) quality of supporting software capabilities, and (8) overall level of service provided by the computer center. In addition to these positive features, he is interested in backup facilities and procedures to be employed during machine failure and periods of disaster.

In summary, these technological developments and management science advancements have eliminated many of the traditional distinctions between various types of equipment, processing facilities, and storage capabilities. What is important to the systems analyst is that management has an ever-expanding list of alternatives and choices that were not previously available. Each unit of equipment or facility is a multidimensional selection whose primary function in the overall computer-based network may be used in many different ways over time. This period's central processor may be next period's front-end equipment (input capability) and the subsequent period's remote terminal. This period's online storage equipment may be next period's buffer for the switching and transmission facility and the subsequent period's dedicated storage for a minicomputer serving as a remote terminal. The advancements in technology coupled with significant reductions in cost have created a challenging environment with major problems in the areas of systems design and information systems specification rather than in the areas of storage, processing, and retrieval.

TOPICS FOR CLASS DISCUSSION

1. If an individual were to analyze a given decision-making process in an organization, she would identify many uses of information. Explain the difference from both a practical and a conceptual standpoint between the expressions "uses of information" and "information requirements."

2. The financial accountant, the financial manager, the sales manager, and the production manager represent, respectively, the four traditional trained observers for studying a business organization. Explain how the approach followed by the systems analyst differs from the approach followed by each of these traditional trained observers.

3. Explain the perspective that the systems analyst assumes for viewing the organization. Be specific.

4. Explain the difference between an "information flow" and an "information system."

5. An individual following the ideas of general systems theory might describe the information flows associated with each major activity of the business organization as a "system." The horizontal information flows between a selected group of major activities would also be a "system." The horizontal information flows between the various selected groups of major activities would be a "system" at a higher level. The adherence to this approach would result in the development of a "system-of-systems" or a hierarchy of systems for the business organization under scrutiny. Explain the difference in the grouping of "information flows" for a general systems theory type of "system" versus the information systems approach type of "information system."

CASE 2–1. LAKEWOOD SERVICE CORPORATION

Representatives of two financial institutions and three insurance companies have been formally organized into a team for purposes of studying the information storage and retrieval problems in each organization as related to the decision-making processes of investment account managers. At present, each organization has its own business library where an up-to-date card system is maintained of the financial statements, reports, and professional articles for most business organizations in the United States whose capital stock is listed on a major stock exchange or regularly sold over-the-counter.

In addition, three of the organizations have selected financial and statistical data for some of these corporations stored in the computer facilities. In each of these three organizations, special computer programs have been developed for selecting for further study those companies that appear to meet certain criteria as to investment opportunity.

During the past year, the investment account managers in these five participating companies were severely criticized for failing to invest in several corporations that experienced tremendous growth. These investment account managers were also criticized for slowly responding to the published statistical data for several major corporations.

As a result of these developments, several investment account managers in the organizations began to respond to this criticism by seeking employment with other similar organizations. Gradually it became apparent to these investment account managers that the problem they were facing was not an individual problem or even a company problem but was an industry problem. Several investment account managers from different business organizations informally met and pondered their common problem. After much discussion within the various organizations and between these organizations, this team of representatives from five participating companies was formally organized.

A preliminary investigation of the financial costs involved versus the estimated benefits from different types of information storage and retrieval systems indicated that it was economically feasible to establish a utility type of online information system for the five participating organizations. The planned system will be financed by the formation of a new corporation, the Lakewood Service Corporation. The capital stock of this latter firm will be sold exclusively to the five participating corporations.

An electronic computer system will be installed at the Lakewood Service Corporation, and a series of communication lines will connect this electronic computer system with inquiry equipment that will be located on the desk of each investment account manager in the five participating corporations. As statistical and financial data are stored in the electronic computer system, they will become available for use by the investment account managers. In this proposed system there is no time delay between the point that the investment account manager commences to use the inquiry equipment and the point that this action is recognized in the electronic computer system (thus, it will be "online").

The preliminary plans call for three different information systems containing relevant data for investment account managers who are serviced by a single computer-based network. Exhibit A indicates the proposed arrangement of information services to be provided by Lakewood Service Corporation to investment account managers at the five participating organizations. Each investment account manager (symbols A1, A4 and A7) will have an online display capability (symbols A2, A5 and A8) that retrieves selected data from each of the three information systems (symbols A12, A13 and A15) according to either the general retrieval computer program stored online in Lakewood Service Corporation's computer system (symbol A14) or a special retrieval procedure that the investment account manager has

EXHIBIT A
Arrangement of Information Services to Be Provided by Lakewood Service Corporation

Five Participating Organizations   Lakewood Service Corporation

specified through the data entry and transmission capabilities of that remote terminal (symbols A3, A6 and A9).

Entering a complete computer program into the system via a remote terminal is a very slow operation, and this tends to discourage special remote terminal use of the network. Therefore, the proposed arrangement of information services includes the feature of permitting a remote terminal user to store in the computer memory special personal computer programs, processing and sorting routines, and special data to be used as criteria or factors in computer-based analyses (symbol A11). This feature is referred to as a "personalized data base," since the content of assigned storage location is directly under the control of each remote terminal user. Thus, this allocated portion of the central memory represents an individual or personalized data storage location.

Information System No. 1 (symbol A12) is proposed as an online type of system for the retrieval of financial and statistical data for a selected group of active companies. This system will also contain coded statistical data that are based on significant articles, papers, speeches and other releases appearing in professional sources (such as *The Wall Street Journal, Business Week,* and *Barron's*) which relate to these selected business organizations. Since all of the financial and statistical data in Information System No. 1 will be online, the investment account manager will receive an immediate display of the selected data requested.

Information System No. 2 (symbol A13) is planned to contain financial and statistical data for all other companies. These two systems (Information System No. 1 and Information System No. 2) will contain data on every business corporation listed on any recognized stock exchange in the United States or commonly traded over-the-counter. The detailed data for Information System No. 2 will be stored offline in magnetic tape units (symbols A17 and A18), and these units will be connected periodically to the computer system so that all inquiries of financial and statistical data stored in a given tape unit can be answered. In Information System No. 2 there will be a time delay in securing answers to inquires, and these delays will probably be from 15 to 20 minutes.

The online storage symbol that is labeled "Online Information System No. 2" (symbol A13) is really an online storage of information requests for the financial and statistical data stored in the magnetic tape units (symbols A17 and A18). Periodically, as the information requests (stored in symbol A13) are satisfied by the processing, sorting and reporting of selected data (represented by symbol A16), the timely display of selected data will occur at the desk of the investment account manager.

Information System No. 3 will represent a common business library for the five participating organizations. An up-to-date index will be maintained within the computer system (symbol A15) of the professional literature and releases relating to each corporation included in Information System No. 1 and Information System No. 2. Except for this online index (symbol A15), the specific library data will be stored offline (symbol A19), and these library data will not enter Lakewood Service Corporation's computer system. An investment account manager will be provided with one-day service on copies of any requested article, paper, speech or release, and these copies will be hand delivered by a messenger service.

In this proposed arrangement of information services, there are several time sharing capabilities that must be maintained. Exhibit B represents a network of the data processing, updating and systems maintenance activities at Lakewood Service Corporation. The manual aspects of the business library function associated with proposed Information System No. 3 are represented by symbols A29, A19 and A30. After the articles, papers, speeches and releases have been catalogued in the business library, then data regarding these must be transmitted to the input location (symbol A20) for the computer system so that the online index (symbol A15) is updated.

Most of the data processing operations will occur at Lakewood Service Corporation; some limited data entry operations will be performed by the investment account managers through their remote terminal capabilities. In Exhibit B, symbols A20, A21, and A22 represent these coding, key punching, verifying, correcting, editing, sorting and data processing operations using the online set of computer programs (symbol A23). As indicated previously, these input

EXHIBIT B
Data Processing, Updating and Systems Maintenance Activities at Lakewood Service Corporation

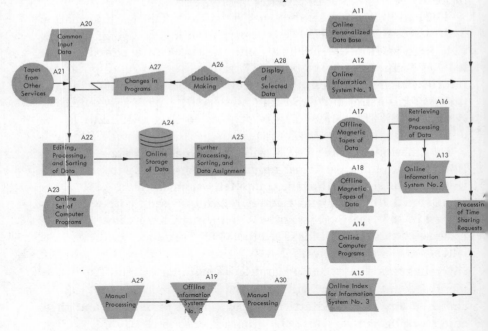

operations will include the update data on the index of library data (symbol A15).

After the new sets of data have been screened, filtered and edited, they are accumulated in an online storage location (symbol A24). Periodically, these new data are processed, sorted, summarized and assigned to selected online data files (symbols A12 and A15) and offline files (symbols A17 and A18). Most of the data for the online personalized data base (symbol A11) will enter the computer system through the investment account managers' remote terminal units.

The set of online computer programs available on call by the remote terminal users is an important feature in this proposed arrangement. These online programs (symbol A14) will be the focus of continuous software development activities by the systems personnel at Lakewood Service Corporation. Most of the improvements in these online programs will be processed by the group of operations represented by symbols A27, A26 and A28. These latter symbols also represent the systems maintenance and monitoring activities that are required for an effective network of time sharing services.

There is another essential feature in this proposed arrangement that is not separately specified in either exhibit. There is a monitoring of the time sharing requests (symbol A10) with restrictions being placed on access to the personalized data base (symbol A11). These security measures and other control procedures will provide the investment account manager with assurance of confidentiality of data access.

The five participating organizations have agreed to the tentative plans for the Lakewood Service Corporation and have asked the coordinating team to continue to study the project. Furthermore, the coordinating team has been asked to submit, as soon as possible, the formal, complete plans covering the general details of the proposed system.

After further study, the coordinating group for the Lakewood Service Corporation has decided on the following approach for designing the information retrieval systems. A survey will be made of the current uses that investment account managers are making of financial statements and statistical data regarding the listed corporations, and a model will be developed which includes a list of all of these uses.

Next, a list will be prepared representing a sample of those business organizations that will be included in the proposed information systems. For each company in this sample, the published annual reports and appropriate statistical data from the professional literature will be accumulated and used as inputs into a computer program. The computer programmers will prepare the appropriate flow charts and the resulting computer program necessary for matching these uses of information (per the list of uses developed from the survey of investment account managers) with the sources of data stored in the program.

This computer program will be run using various sequencing of uses of information, and a close scrutiny of this simulation model will serve a twofold purpose: (1) the uses and data sources will be matched to see that all uses of information are satisfied by data sources and (2) a coding pattern will be developed to facilitate the retrieval of information based upon the traditional methods the investment account managers are accustomed to following. While this latter step is being performed, consideration will also be given to the matter of selecting the exact computer equipment and communication facilities that should be purchased as well as determining the financial rate that should be charged for the information retrieval service.

REQUIRED:

1. From the perspective of the information systems approach, evaluate the approach that the coordinating group has decided to follow.
2. Explain step-by-step how a systems analyst would develop the three information systems.

CASE 2–2.   MIDWEST ADHESIVE COMPANY

The Midwest Adhesive Company is a relatively small manufacturer of adhesives for industrial purposes, with annual sales of approximately $3,500,000. Frank Martin, president of the Midwest Adhesive Company, was concerned about recent complaints regarding finished goods inventory and asked his new administrative assistant to determine what was required to improve the control of inventories and the writing of resulting production orders.

Dave Miller, the new administrative assistant, had recently graduated from college and was employed at Midwest Adhesive Company earlier in the week. Therefore, the above project was the first significant task that Dave Miller had been assigned.

Dave interviewed the inventory control manager and his associates. During the next few days, Dave talked with sales personnel, production supervisors, and the chief accountant. After these discussions, Dave decided that operations research techniques should be employed in developing a system of sales forecasting and inventory control over adhesive inventories. The basic objectives of this proposed system are to:

1. Maintain customer service.
2. Maintain a minimum, balanced inventory.
3. Provide a means for forecasting future sales and inventories by months.

Later that same week, Dave prepared a one-page report for Frank Martin, which stated the above recommendation.

REQUIRED:

1. Evaluate Dave's recommendation.
2. Explain step-by-step how a systems analyst would cope with the president's request.

CHAPTER 3

Using Systems for Planning and Control

IN THE OVERVIEW of computer science terminology presented in the previous chapter, brief attention was given to recent advancements in input and output, processing, and storage capabilities. This chapter examines the typical types of planning and control computer-based networks that have been designed incorporating some of these technological advancements.

INTRODUCTION

During the past two decades systems analysts have designed and implemented an extremely wide range of computer-based networks in various types of organizational locations, and these systems analysts have witnessed a continuing evolution of what was considered a highly developed information system. In 1956 a computer-based network which was considered a highly developed information system encompassed reorder points and reorder quantities for perpetual inventory combined with a computer-generated purchase order. In 1962, a computer system that incorporated an inventory control and management system with a production scheduling system was considered highly developed.

By 1965, the highly developed information system had evolved to encompass quality mathematical models and sophisticated management science techniques which were represented by programmed decision rules within computer-based networks.

Integration of information systems began to occur in the late 1960s, and this type of integration was the hallmark of what was then envisioned as a highly developed information system. These evolutionary developments in information systems are the results of a series of internal and external influences which prevailed in the 1950s and 1960s.

The primary thrust of this discussion is to identify information systems developments and associated organizational arrangements which have been created in the 1970s in response to internal and external influences on management information systems. These developments, based on extensions from companies with highly developed information systems, indicate a new level of adaptation to and awareness of the environment.

While the focus of this presentation is on the advancement incorporated in this latest type of highly developed information system, systems analysts should not expect that the computer-based network in a given organization will necessarily progress in an evolutionary manner to this ideal stage of adaptation and awareness. The progress of a network towards this most advanced stage is being constrained by an array of organizational, administrative, economic, environmental, and technological factors which may limit further multidimensional development. These factors can be viewed as interactive forces constraining the advancement of information systems. An alternative perspective is to view these constraints as barricades limiting further evolutionary advancement.

Many of the organizational and administrative factors constraining the evolving structure of highly developed systems are explained in Chapter 4. The current examination of information systems developments is divided into three parts. First, the evolution of highly developed information systems is examined. This analysis runs the gamut from a simple system featuring a computer program to an advanced information system encompassing a series of online and interactive capabilities. Second, the move from an operating system to an information system is examined in detail, and the problem areas encountered in this movement are highlighted. Third, criteria for evaluating computer-based networks are examined for each level of progression from a computer program to an advanced information system.

EVOLUTION OF HIGHLY DEVELOPED
INFORMATION SYSTEMS

The phrase "highly developed information system" implies that a given electronic network is operating at about the optimum "state of the art" for the specified time period. This means that the computer-based network incorporates the latest in available technology which can be supported on a cost-benefit basis for hardware, firmware, software, communication facilities and systems design.

The "latest in available technology"—as qualified in the above statement—is not the same as the "most advanced technology." There are many demonstration networks and prototype systems designed under significant research support from the federal government, and many of these special networks do not currently meet the cost-benefit test, primarily because they are not a *balanced* development. While a prototype system may possess extraordinary capabilities in several areas, often the supporting software and integrated computer facilities currently available are not capable of overall operation at the same level.

If it is not completely developed, it is not balanced; however, the future *balanced* advancements in highly developed information systems will be built upon the insights gained from working with these special, prototype systems.

The scope, nature, and contents of a highly developed information system for a given period represent an overall balance of available technology, management abilities, systems analysis efforts and management science models. A specific configuration in this evolutionary process is a response or adaptation to a given set of internal and external factors.

As these evolutionary changes occurred, networks possessing significantly different sets of characteristics were identified by similar words in the professional information systems literature. Because of this confusion in terminology, a brief description is given for each general type of computer-based network, including comparisons and distinctions among computer-based networks. Thus, from this presentation, the reader should gain an appreciation of the terminology as well as the balanced set of evolving characteristics encompassed within highly developed information systems.

There is some uncertainty within the professional information systems literature over the exact meaning of the word "system" because of the many diverse contexts in which the word is used. In this book, an adjective will be used with the word "system" to denote the applicable context. The typical adjectives that will be used with "system" are *operating* system, *information* system and *advanced information* system. These three types of systems represent fairly sophisticated online capabilities for handling data processing, sorting, data file assignment, storage, and retrieval operations. The exact meaning of each of these systems is explained after presenting a brief sketch of more elementary networks which may be integrated into these systems.

Simple Systems

In the context of computer-based networks, a simple system is an electronic capability for handling data inputs, data processing, and data outputs. The data processing function in this simple case is accomplished by a set of instructions which are incorporated into a computer program. Figure 3.1 depicts these three functions with the appropriate standard flowcharting symbols.

In a simple system, the set of instructions contained in the computer program is straightforward and limited in scope and complexity. One type of simple system at the computer program level is an

FIGURE 3.1
Model of a
Simple System

electronic capability for data inputs, data processing, and data outputs which is based on a set of programmed responses to a specified array of questions that were previously handled manually by clerical personnel, superiors, supervisors, and middle management. An example of this type of system is a perpetual inventory system that daily prints, for each item of inventory, an updated balance based on the beginning balance, daily issues, daily receipts, returns, and adjustments.

Expanded Systems

As the scope and complexity of this electronic capability are increased, the resulting networks pass through a series of modified simple systems. This concept of a series of networks is represented in Figure 3.2 by a continuum showing the relative complexity of programs and systems.

FIGURE 3.2
A Continuum Showing Relative Complexity of Programs and Systems

Computer Program	Activity Program	Functional Program	Operating System	Information System	Advanced Information System
1			5		10

The position of a simple system featuring a *computer program* is presented in Figure 3.2 as the extreme primitive position on a continuum running from 1 to 10. The data processing function is expanded in scope and complexity as the evolving network progresses to the expanded systems of the *activity program* and the *functional program*. There are also parallel increases in the capabilities for data inputs and data outputs in these expanded systems. But the primary distinction is in the nature of the online capability for data processing.

An *activity program* is an integrated network of the computer programs designed to handle typical events or transactions identified with a given organizational unit. As the computer programs in a given organizational unit are integrated and clustered together into a single network, the resulting activity program represents the online capability for handling all of the typical transactions and events which were previously manually handled by personnel within the organizational unit. This shift from manual processing to an integrated, electronic capability results in significant personnel labor savings within the organizational unit. The labor savings increases as the computer networks become more complex.

An example of an activity program is a perpetual inventory system which is integrated with a procurement system. In this network when the perpetual inventory position reaches the reorder point, a purchase order request for that item's reorder quantity is generated by the computer system. This automatic preparation of a requisition request for inventory eliminates the manual interfacing efforts between the perpetual inventory network and the reorder quantity data.

A *functional program* is a larger and more encompassing network of integrated computer programs than is an activity program. Organizationally, a functional program accommodates the information processing requirements for a major set of decision-making activities. Alternatively, it represents a series of integrated computer programs which handle the data processing requirements encompassed in a major delegation of management's responsibility. A functional program is frequently established by integrating a series of computer programs with an activity program. The labor savings efforts achieved with this integration are normally identified with the middle management personnel directly responsible for the functional area.

If the activity program previously described for an integrated perpetual inventory and procurement system was expanded to include, for each item of inventory, the suppliers' names, prices, shipping terms, billing instructions, and other procurement details, then the resulting online system would be classified as a functional program. As two or more activity programs are integrated into a functional program, the set of computer programs within this designed integrated network will be involved, highly integrated, relatively closed, and self-contained. In other words, there is a restructuring of the computer programs to achieve a maximum degree of online integration and operating control. The labor savings efforts realized from a functional program include a reduction in management's time for monitoring internal control, since some of the electronic capabilities assist in this area.

In summary a simple system as well as an expanded system uses a set of programmed instructions incorporated in an online package to capture the essence of an array of decision-making responses. The result of this effort is the capability for quickly handling by electronic means a large volume of data inputs, data processing, and data outputs. Where these types of systems have been established, there are significant savings in the personnel costs previously associated with manual processing efforts. In the expanded system there are also savings in management's efforts for monitoring the operations for internal control purposes. Many of the computer-based systems installed in large organizations during the late 1950s and early 1960s were indicative of these simple systems and expanded systems. The intermediate series of formal information networks interfaced with the financial accounting network, depicted by Figure 1.2 in Chapter 1, is a good representation of an integrated network of functional programs in the late 1950s and early 1960s.

Operating Systems

An operating system is an integrated network of computer programs designed to handle most information flows associated with a significant grouping of the organization's activities. The computer programs encompassed in an operating system are self-contained, closed, and capable of responding to a predetermined set of inputs; in other words, these integrated programs have been designed to process a predetermined set of inputs in a prescribed manner and are capable of operating on a continuous basis with no human intervention. The set of programmed decision rules incorporated in an operating system tends to be fixed because the designed integration was in response to coding of inputs, and little attention was given to outputs. This fixed structure and lack of flexibility in an operating system are in marked contrast to the features incorporated in an *information system* or in an *advanced information system*.

As indicated by the relative position on the continuum in Figure 3.2, an operating system is a more advanced network than a functional program. An operating system will frequently consist of an expanded network developed by integrating two or more functional programs. Thus, the operating system is an electronic capability for the efficient handling of a high volume of diverse types of data inputs, data processing, and data outputs. While the scope of activities accommodated by an operating system is vast, only limited efforts are made to include any nonprogrammed activities within this network.

An operating system is a self-contained, computer-based unit that may monitor and control a complex operation. The only requirement is that the complex operation must be able to be represented by an integrated set of programmed decision rules. An example of such an operation is the use of a production and control computer system for operating a $15 million paper machine which fully handles the manufacture of paper from raw materials to a finished product state. The operating system may be designed so that there can be human intervention in the network permitting a manual override of the programmed set of decision rules. The capability of human intervention in the network is an added feature that is not part of the general model of an operating system; however, this feature is normally present in this type of complex production and control system as a means of minimizing any product or service loss generated during a partial systems failure.

The main feature in the general model of an operating system is a perpetual capacity for handling a defined set of operations in a prescribed manner. A generalized model of this type of network is presented in Figure 3.3. The heart of the operating system is the set of online computer programs which filter, edit, process, sort, summarize, assign, and store selected data that flow through the network. In handling inputs, the operating system may respond to changes in other operating systems, and this information is transmitted by tape. The more typical method of inputting data into an operating system is through regular data cards which might be generalized to include punched tape and magnetic-tape types of inputs. The third type of input symbol for the generalized model represents another type of activity. The online keyboard would serve where the operating system is quickly responding to changes in inventory position, changes in production orders, and other status information that is transmitted from an online keyboard situated at a remote location.

The outputs from an operating system cover the gamut of communication devices; from documents and reports, to magnetic tape, microfilm, or any other type of filing. In an analysis of an operating system it is important to consider the form of the major missing ingredient. Specifically, there is no return "information flow" from the documents, reports, and other outputs that intersects or connects

FIGURE 3.3
A Generalized Model of an Operating System

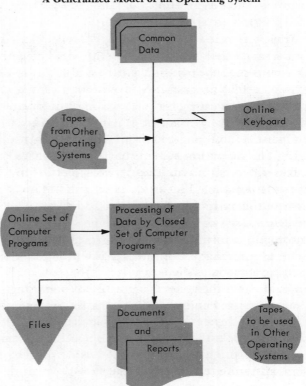

the input locations. Overall, the operating system, as indicated above, serves to process a volume of transactions. The set of computer programs stored within the computer can be described as programmed-decision rules. However, the overall operating system does not contain any human decision makers as an integral part of the system. An information system will always have human decision makers, and this point will be further developed in the subsequent section.

Evolution. Operating systems have evolved out of the integration of related computer programs. For example, an operating system in personnel might consist of the integration of the following three computer programs related to personnel planning: (1) a payroll-computer program, (2) a personnel-record computer program, and

(3) an employee performance computer program. These three computer programs require the same data for inputs.

The daily time and attendance report for each employee is the common input for these three programs. When these three computer programs are integrated into an operating system, the newly created operating system should be designed so that it performs the following activities: (1) reads the common input—the daily time and attendance report for each employee, (2) processes these data, (3) stores selected data for payroll purposes, (4) stores selected data for subsequent use in the cost and performance reports, and (5) stores selected data for use in preparing special reports for governmental agencies. It is suggested that the reader mentally re-label the symbols in the generalized model of an operating system (Figure 3.3) so as to indicate where these five activities are accomplished.

Characteristics.   The operating system is a closed network of computer programs for processing a large volume of transactions or inputs. These programs are both closed and self-contained, which means that parameters and variables within this network of computer programs have been specified and continue to operate until management elects to change these values. If no change is initiated, then theoretically this network of computer programs can be employed continuously to process this same set or type of transactions on a perpetual basis.

It is important to grasp the concept of an operating system, as a network of computer programs capable of being stored within the computer system, operating on a perpetual basis, and handling a large volume of activity. Since the emphasis in an operating system is on being self-contained and closed, this type of system is typically not designed to permit change. Lack of features for implementing executive management decisions is one of the elements that differentiates an operating system from an information system. This point is described in detail in the next section of this discussion.

Ideally, an operating system should encompass within its set of online computer programs the capability for processing all recurring transactions and events which are organizationally identified with a major part of management's responsibility. Unusual transactions and events that occur on an exceptional basis are intentionally excluded from the operating system by screens on data inputs to the network. In this high-volume system, the exclusion of these exceptional items as well as the exclusion of nonprogrammed activities results in significant savings in processing speeds and computer systems costs. Since the operating system electronically handles all regular, recurring transactions, members of management can devote their time and efforts to coping with the unusual and exceptional events.

A highly developed information system of the early 1960s would be classified as an operating system in the 1970s The series of formal information systems presented in Figure 1.3 in Chapter 1 is representative of this level of complexity and online processing capability.

The systems analyst's interest in operating systems extends beyond this evolutionary classification. *Operating systems serve as the backbone of an information system.* A generalized model of an information system is presented subsequently, and this discussion will indicate the special power that an information system obtains through harnessing an operating system and through the continuous monitoring of the system.

Information System

An information system is a computer-based network containing two or more operating systems. It provides relevant data to management for decision-making purposes and contains also the necessary mechanism for implementing changes or responses made by management. A generalized model of an information system containing three operating systems is presented in Figure 3.4. The diamond, denoting the decision-making process by management, is the first of the three key features in an information system. The decision maker or a decision-making group is formally recognized as the user of the relevant data provided by the network. Note that the three operating systems provide relevant information to management for decision-making processes. Management also uses other input locations for important planning information. The results of the management decision-making process are translated into changes in parameters and variables. These parameters and variables refer to the closed set of computer programs contained within each operating system. Note that the data flow for changes in parameters and variables is a closed loop, going from the decision-making process by management, and connecting with the input terminals to each operating system. In the subsequent paragraphs, we will see how difficult it is to design

FIGURE 3.4
A Generalized Model of an Information System Containing Three
Operating Systems

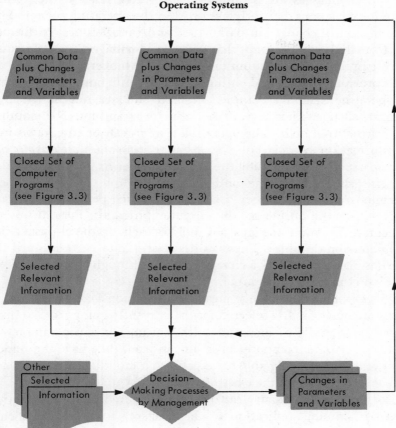

operating systems that permit changes in parameters and variables. This closed set of computer programs contains all the features that were present in the generalized model of an operating system presented in Figure 3.3.

The second feature in an information system is the establishment of a formal feedback loop from data outputs through the decision maker to the data inputs, and this arrangement is an integral part of the network. The third feature in an information system utilizes the second feature, the formal feedback loop; this third feature is the capability for implementing the results of the management decision-making process. As indicated in Figure 3.4, these results are translated into changes in parameters and variables for the online computer programs currently used within the operating system. This transmission of changes in parameters and variables occurs through the formal feedback loop that connects management's decision-making process with the input terminals to each operating system.

As previously explained, online computer programs stored within an operating system are *input oriented* and are not designed to facilitate change. Therefore, these online programs must be modified and restructured *before* the operating systems can be integrated into an information system. The systems analyst assumes an *output oriented* perspective in assisting the decision maker in forecasting which elements should have the online capability for change. As these elements are identified, they become unspecified parameters or variables within the online set of computer programs. Periodically an "executive program" assigns a value to each of these unspecified parameters or variables. These values continue to be used until the decision maker transmits a change in value through the formal feedback loop to the input terminal.

This capability for change means that decision makers can almost instantaneously modify selected factors currently being used to process online data. They incur no delay waiting for a programmer to modify the online computer program; instead, they have the important capability of being able to respond to a modified situation or to a revised assessment of the existing situation.

The concept of a change capability represented in an information system is simple; application of the concept, however, is difficult. There are numerous elements (parameters and variables) in a series of programmed decision-rules that must be incorporated into an online computer program for a single operating system. Only a few of these elements can be selected for identification as *unspecified*. The decision maker must anticipate which of these elements need to be specified as *change values*. Except for the unspecified elements, the variables and parameters within the online sets of computer programs can only be changed by interrupting operations, taking the online programs offline, making changes in the elements, testing and validating the changes, and then placing the modified programs online. This lengthy procedure is typical of the generalized model of an information system. If the procedures are more advanced, then the network to which they are being applied is probably an advanced information system.

By comparing Figure 3.4 with Figure 3.1, a systems analyst can quickly identify some of the major evolutionary developments in computer-based networks over the past two decades. The magnitude of this change is similar to that seen by contrasting a 747 luxury space craft that cruises at 650 miles per hour and comfortably accommodates over 400 passengers with a propeller-driven aircraft that cruises at 80 miles per hour and accommodates five passengers. This change is so enormous that individual measures of the change are almost meaningless.

An increase in cruising speed by a factor of 8 and an increase in passenger accommodations by a factor of 80 miss the major considerations. Safety, dependability, comfort, economy, luxury, and capability for operating during severe inclement weather are some indicators of the balanced improvement that has occurred in air transportation. A composite index is needed to express this balanced improvement in all of these areas (please note the similarity between this analysis and that for general systems theory as discussed in Chapter 1).

Similarly, when comparing Figure 3.4 with Figure 3.1, the systems analyst seeks an index that expresses the overall ability of the network to provide management with relevant, current data in a timely manner. This overall accomplishment is possible because of the fantastic improvements in computing capacity, size, and speed of online storage capabilities, processing speeds, communication capabilities, hardware, firmware, and software. These overall improvements have occurred with concurrent reductions in cost.

As indicated previously, the role of the decision maker, the feedback loop, and the capability for change in the online processing activities are three features in an information system that are not present in an operating system. The information system obtains its special power from adding these three features to the "stand-alone" capabilities of operating systems. Though the generalized model in Figure 3.4 contains three operating systems, there can be several operating systems within a given information system. Each of these operating systems has significant electronic capabilities, and each module is able to efficiently and effectively process a high volume of diverse data.

Advanced Information System

An advanced information system is a large-scale, computer-based network with online communication facilities and interactive capabilities for remote terminal users in two or more departments within an organization. The series of operating systems encompassed within the advanced information system contains a set of online computer programs that (*a*) handles the data processing requirements for two or more departments and (*b*) accommodates the online response or change mechanism as a result of management's actions. One or more of these operating systems may possess a special remote terminal for monitoring selected changes in the external environment (such as specific prices of raw materials or demands for products in a highly fluctuating market). This monitoring feature will also have the capability of reexamining the current assignment of resources and, if appropriate, specifying immediate changes in resource assignment for the duration of the ongoing cycle. Though these monitoring, reexamination, and revised assignment tasks are online within the computer system, there is usually a human review of the "suggested" revisions before the "actual" revised assignment occurs.

In the 1970s, an information system that is highly developed enough to be classified as an advanced information system must have a common data base that supports decision makers in two or more departments. The nature of this support is important; the decision makers not only must be engaged in an online, interactive arrangement with the data base, but also must have appropriate software to permit quick sorting, processing, manipulating, and retrieving of selected data. These capabilities are meaningful only when the decision makers have experience in operating within this type of interactive arrangement.

Today, there are balanced levels of advancement beyond an information system. From an analysis of 38 organizations with computer-based systems, the author of this book has identified specific features for five major stages of development. From this study, generalized models of advanced information systems have been designed for each of these five evolving levels, and these models will be examined later in this book. These levels of balanced advancement are dated, of course, and will probably be superseded by future technological developments.

For purposes of the current discussion, attention is focused again on Figure 3.2 with a specific emphasis on operating systems and information systems. Consideration is now given to moving from operating systems to information systems.

MOVEMENT FROM AN OPERATING SYSTEM TO AN INFORMATION SYSTEM

As previously indicated operating systems have evolved from the integration of activity or functional computer programs. Therefore, it would appear logical that systems analysts could move one step further and progress from an operating system to an integrated set of operating systems which would serve as the base for an information system. Unfortunately, this is not the case.

A step-by-step, building block, or modular approach toward the design of an information system is not always possible. Systems efforts do not necessarily move a computer-based network to higher levels of computer application merely by adding additional computer personnel, expanding the systems department, or acquiring more computer or communication equipment. These additional investments may occur without changing the composite classification of the network from the operating systems level. There are six reasons for this constraint on advancement from an operating system to an information system.

First, a systems analyst may determine from studying the organization that the activities surrounding various operating systems represent noncompatible segments which are not capable of being merged. For instance, each operating system has a defined time frame and cycle in which the overall network processing is performed. These closed loop operations may be performed in a two-minute time interval or, at the other extreme, in a monthly time interval. Most operating systems will use a time interval between the two-minute and the monthly cycle. If two operating systems' time periods are not identical, it is frequently impossible to merge the two networks unless one of the operating systems is reprogrammed.

Second, a systems analyst designs each operating system to respond to or process a defined set of inputs. Two operating systems in the same general area will frequently require different types of inputs. The only way such systems can be merged is for one of them to be reprogrammed. Even if executive management requests this reprogramming, the systems analyst should not start at this point in designing an integrated network. Instead, the analyst should perform an administrative type of organization review to gain an overview of the decision-making processes that are to be serviced by the integrated set of operating systems. This point is further developed in a discussion of the five phases in the design and implementation of an information system which is presented in Chapter 6.

Third, there are optimal locations for obtaining information from an operating system, and there are limitations on the volume of data that can be transmitted by communication equipment. This may mean that a plant manager and a department manager at the home office cannot fully use the same operating system. The department manager may hourly use information provided by the operating system. The plant manager may be limited to mailed daily reports. Limitations on integrating operating systems (because of the location of the decision maker) are not restricted to the plant and home office arrangements. This same type of problem may apply to decision makers in different departments of the central office where the organization does not have extensive online computer terminals.

Fourth, two operating systems handling related problems may be based on incomplete or incompatible coding patterns which are not capable of being expanded into a complete coding structure. For example, a given inventory identification code may be excellent for use with the ABCD Method of Inventory Control; however, items of inventory classified by this system may not be appropriately identified for the marketing management system. The latter system is more sensitive to varying markup rates than it is to dollar price and volume. If a systems analyst desires to integrate these two networks, then each item of inventory may have to be recoded.

Fifth, a systems analyst working with a single operating system will probably not have a "big picture" perspective for the overall organization. The "system-of-systems" within his or her limited perspective may not contain the appropriate hierarchy of networks seen from a broader initial viewpoint. Also, the systems analyst is confronted with many optional values that must be specified within any computer program, and after these values are specified, they become constraints in the computer programs. If the analyst does not possess a broad perspective of the organization's decision-making activities, then it is likely that many of these constraints will be incompatible with the requirements of an expanded, integrated set of operating systems.

Sixth, the design of an information system in a dynamic setting may not be a feasible objective. It was previously explained how a series of operating systems can serve as a foundation for an information system. One important element within the information system is the capability for responding to management's decision-making activities. This capability is represented by variables or parameters in those decision models which are stored online within the computer system and whose unspecified values can be quickly changed. In a dynamic setting it may not be feasible for a systems analyst to design this capability for online processing of change.

If an organization is located in an environment where there are significant changes in the mission during the short term (which is typically the case in the public administration area), then it may not be feasible to establish an information system. Where there are frequent changes in mission or organizational goals, it is almost futile to update the online variables and parameters which will permit executive management an online response to changes in the environment or overall assessment. About the time the systems analyst has established channels for responding to executive management's decisions and incorporated these channels in the closed set of online computer programs, the organization's change in mission will make the predicted channels inappropriate. If significant changes in mission do occur, it might then be necessary to compartmentalize this large-scale computer network and to keep only a series of operating systems for the subsequent period. The other operating systems would then have to be replaced with new networks more appropriate to the new assigned mission.

In a highly dynamic environment, management's objectives can usually be better served through the establishment of a series of specific operating systems. In this case, management teams and committees can link these different operating systems forming a "human" information system, but one with no online capability for change. In this situation, the management team serves in place of the integrated computer programs that link operating systems together.

In regard to this final point, the systems analyst does not always work toward the establishment of an information system, but instead strives to design appropriate sets of programmed decision rules for handling recurring types of transactions. Then, depending upon the environment, the organizational structure, the decision makers and their capabilities, and the anticipated short-term objectives of the organization, this systems analyst determines what type of network might be established. This, along with other related matters pertaining to planning and designing an information system are discussed in Chapter 6.

In summary, systems analysts cannot always move step-by-step to higher levels of computer applications in a systems context. Noncompatible time frames and cycles may not permit the integration of two related operating systems. The content of the network and the input requirements may be such that two related operating systems are really totally different types of networks that must be redesigned and reprogrammed if they are to be integrated. The organizational location of various decision makers may be such that an integrated set of operating systems cannot fully service these managers through the online computer terminals. Many optional values in a computer program later become constraints which may prohibit the integration of two existing operating systems. Finally, in a dynamic setting with changes in organizational goals and mission, the establishment of an information system may not be a feasible objective.

One way the systems analyst can avoid these constraints is to gain a broad perspective of the decision-making activities before specifying these optional values in a computer program and planning a coding structure. The second phase (discussed in Chapter 6) in the five phases for planning and implementing an information system is designed to provide this perspective. The shortcomings of the building block or modular approach are also resolved when the systems analyst employs the five phases in planning and designing an information system.

CRITERIA FOR EVALUATING COMPUTER-BASED NETWORKS

The continuum showing relative complexity of programs and systems (Figure 3.2) can be interpreted from the perspective of total cost for planning, designing, and implementing the computer-based network exclusive of capital expenditures for hardware. The labeled positions along the continuum—computer program, activity program, functional program, operating system, information system, and advanced information system—can be envisioned as six steps with the cost of each level being equal to double the combined cost of all previous levels. Alternatively, the incremental cost of each level is equivalent to the combined cost of all previous levels. Figure 3.5

FIGURE 3.5
Illustration of the Comparative Cost of Planning, Designing, and Implementing the Computer-Based Network
(exclusive of capital expenditures for hardware)

Scale* and Description		*Incremental Cost per Level*	*Total Cost†*
1.0	Computer program	$ 60,000	$ 60,000
2.4	Activity program	60,000	120,000
4.3	Functional program	120,000	240,000
5.8	Operating system	240,000	480,000
7.0	Information system	480,000	960,000
10.0	Advanced information system	960,000	1,920,000

° Per Figure 3.2.
† These total cost values are for illustration purposes only.

illustrates the comparative cost of planning, designing, and implementing computer-based networks at these six levels.

The planning, designing, and implementing cost data for each level in the computer-based network as presented in Figure 3.5 are for illustrating purposes only. The actual cost will vary with the scope and complexity of activities encompassed within the network as well as with the economic size of the organization and its administrative arrangement. In addition to these qualifications, the illustrative cost data in Figure 3.5 are based on the assumption of minimum expansion in the scope and complexity of the integrated network at each level. If, for example, 4 operating systems are to be integrated into an information system instead of 2 operating systems (by definition, an information system consists of at least 2 operating systems), then the cost for this level may be double the minimal cost—such as, an incremental cost of $960,000 instead of $480,000.

Recognizing these constraints in generalizing from these illustrative data, another dimension can be used to examine the incremental activities in planning, designing, and implementing a computer-based network. The work, analyses, and software requirements at each level are significantly different. These illustrative data are used for indicating the changing nature of these components at each level. Figure 3.6 presents the component cost at selected levels at both the incremental and cumulative positions.

FIGURE 3.6

Illustration of the Components of the Comparative Cost of Planning, Designing, and Implementing the Computer-Based Network at Selected Levels, Using Data Constraints of Figure 3.5

Description	Incremental Cost per Level	Cumulative Cost
Computer program for record keeping	$ 60,000	$ 60,000
Clerical coding activities	$ 25,000	$ 25,000
Data processing	15,000	15,000
Systems planning and design—management	10,000	10,000
Terminals and data communications	5,000	5,000
Other software capabilities.	5,000	5,000
Activity program for operating control	$ 60,000	$120,000
Program packages	$ 10,000	$ 10,000
Systems planning and design—management	10,000	20,000
Terminals and data communication	10,000	15,000
Other software capabilities	10,000	15,000
Machine coding activities	7,500	7,500
Data processing	7,500	22,500
Clerical coding activities	5,000	30,000
Functional program for administrative coordination . . .	$120,000	$240,000
Program packages	$ 35,000	$ 45,000
Exception reporting routines	20,000	20,000
Monitoring and display equipment	19,000	19,000
Systems planning and design—management	15,000	35,000
Systems coding	10,000	10,000
Machine coding	10,000	17,500
Terminals and data communication	5,000	20,000
Data processing	5,000	27,500
Clerical coding	1,000	31,000
Other software capabilities.	-0-	15,000
Information system for planning and control	$480,000	$960,000
Systems planning and design—staff	$120,000	$135,000
Systems planning and design—management	100,000	175,000
Systems planning and design—consultants	80,000	80,000
Editing, screening and monitoring	60,000	120,000
Program packages	30,000	110,000
Monitoring and display equipment	10,000	49,000
Retrieval systems	40,000	40,000
Modelling capabilities	40,000	40,000
Exception reporting routines	-0-	80,000
Clerical coding	-0-	31,000
Data processing	-0-	27,500
Terminals and data communication	-0-	20,000
Systems coding	-0-	20,000
Machine coding	-0-	17,500
Other software capabilities.	-0-	15,000

As previously indicated, the cost data presented in Figure 3.6 are only for illustrative purposes. The *components* included at each level are of more importance than the specific cost data. In evaluating a proposal to plan, design, and implement a computer-based network, attention should be given to the nature of the dominant activities and processes at each incremental level being considered. The incremental cost changes of components by level indicate the relevant dimensions of analysis with a weighing of significance among components.

Each dominant component may require a unique method of evaluating the cost and benefits. The cost part of this evaluation may be generalized; in other words, the same analytical method for incremental cost analysis is applicable at each level for this component. The benefit part, on the other hand, varies significantly between levels of computer-based networks; therefore, the relevant factors for evaluating the benefits are different at each level.

Using the dominant component of incremental cost at a given level as the basis for drawing a distinction, a unique label can be ascribed to the evaluation approach for the cost and benefit study employed at each stage. Figure 3.7 presents the six levels of computer-

FIGURE 3.7
**Relation of Dominant Analytical Methods to Level of
Computer-Based Networks**

Level	Description	Dominant Analytical Method*
Computer program	Record keeping	Time and motion analysis
Activity program	Operating control	Operational analysis
Functional program	Administrative coordination	Economic analysis
Operating system	Management control	Managerial analysis
Information system	Planning and control	Decision analysis
Advanced information system	Strategic planning and control	Environmental analysis

* Classified on the basis of the relevant analytical method for the dominant component of incremental cost at the respective level.

based networks with an indication of the relevant approach for evaluating the dominant components of incremental cost by level. The reader is cautioned not to generalize from the labels presented in Figure 3.7; each component at each level may require a specific analytical approach. The "dominant" approach at a given level may be a completely inappropriate method for the evaluation of the other incremental cost components at the specified level.

In moving from a manual system to the initial level of a computer program for record keeping (see Figure 3.6), the dominant effort is clerical coding activities. From Figure 3.7 we see that time and motion analysis is the relevant method for evaluating the cost portion of clerical coding activities. However, please note (per Figure 3.6) that the clerical coding activities is the dominant component of cost only at the computer program level.

Alternatively, if the move is from an operating system to an information system, systems planning and design accounts for $300,000 of the $480,000 of incremental cost. Decision analysis is specified in Figure 3.7 as the dominant analytical method for evaluating the cost portion of these incremental changes.

The systems analyst is frequently confronted with a situation where the proposed computer-based network will be the result of spanning two or more levels. In these cases, the dominant evaluation method for each respective level must be separately applied to the situation; otherwise, the designed computer-based network may include the "wrong" balance of software, firmware, program packages, transmission facilities, and input and output capabilities. The application of the dominant evaluation method on a level-by-level study may have resulted in the creation of a different configuration of computer science capabilities.

As an example, a move from a manual system to a functional program spans *three levels*. Economic analysis is the dominant evaluation method for *incremental* cost at the functional program level (per Figure 3.7) ; however, there are other significant components of *cumulative* cost that must be considered in this proposed three-level move. Time and motion analysis and operational analysis are two other evaluation methods that must be fully applied to this situation. In addition, the relevant evaluation methods for the other components of cost also merit close scrutiny by the systems analyst.

In summary, the systems analyst views the evaluation of computer-based networks from a six-level frame of reference in which the relevant, incremental components of cost are a function of the change in the domain of the proposed network. At each level within the framework, there is a dominant evaluation method associated with the incremental changes in activities and processes, and the systems analyst will apply this dominant evaluation technique as well as the application evaluation methods called for by the other incremental components of cost. When more than one level is being spanned by a proposed network, the systems analyst's study will expand correspondingly with separate attention being given to the dominant evaluation method and other supporting analysis suggested by the situation at each level. Although the evaluation of incremental cost data by component tends toward generalization across the six-level framework, the study of benefit data by component assumes different characteristics depending on the level. Thus, the evaluation methods for benefits are unique by level.

TOPICS FOR CLASS DISCUSSION

1. Management of the CDR Manufacturing Company is considering the purchase of a set of program packages for purposes of establishing an activity program in place of the current manual system. Assuming that the non-hardware expenditures are $120,000 (see Figure 3.6 for the cost components), indicate the types of evaluation methods which should be applied in this situation. Explain your choice of evaluation methods.

2. Figure 3.2 presented a continuum showing the relative complexity of programs and systems. In determining the assigned value for a specific network, what attributes are being quantified?

3. When a study team is analyzing a computer-based management system over a period of time, it is sometimes said, "this cycle's information system will become an operating system in the future." What does this general expression mean from an information systems standpoint? Explain your answer.

4. Since the majority of all data processing and clerical coding activities is incurred in the first two levels of advancement, these components can be ignored if the organization is considering a proposed network that moves from an activity program to a functional program. Do you agree? Explain your position.

5. In a governmental agency we have a quarterly change in the assigned mission of the agency. Sometimes the mission may change monthly. In this type of dynamic setting, is it possible to design and implement an information system? Explain your response.

6. Select some part of a business organization, describe the activities within this organizational unit, and explain how these activities can be handled by a *functional program*. Next, modify the organizational unit and indicate what is necessary for an *operating system*. Finally, expand the context and explain what might be encompassed in an *information system* for this same area.

7. A systems analyst stated: "It is inappropriate to use the evaluation method of decision analysis at the manual to computer program

level; likewise, it is inappropriate to use time and motion analysis at the operating system to the information systems level." Do you agree? Explain in operational terms the meaning of the above statement as well as your position.

CASE 3–1. TKS HEALTH SYSTEMS, INC.

TKS Health Systems, Inc., your employer, was awarded a subcontract by Carol Health Service to perform an external evaluation of shared modular hospital information systems at the four Carol Health Service hospitals. A national foundation which annually awards millions of dollars for research and teaching in health care and the health sciences selected the latter group of hospitals as the demonstration site for testing the application of shared modular hospital information systems. A major two-year foundation grant to Carol Health Service provided the necessary financial support for this demonstration and evaluation project.

You are assigned to this project by TKS Health Systems—a consulting firm that specializes in analyzing, planning, designing, monitoring and evaluating health care delivery systems. You have been involved with this project from the inception, and you assisted TKS Health Systems in developing the initial proposal that resulted in the subcontract to perform external evaluation services.

Subsequent to the awarding of the subcontract, you prepared a 60-page Master Research Design report for TKS Health Systems' portion of the total project. The latter report contains a detailed outline of the steps to be followed in analyzing and evaluating shared modular hospital information systems at the four Carol Health Service hospitals. The time schedule in the foundation's contract (and TKS Health Systems' subcontract) calls for the preparation of the Master Research Design within 60 days of the effective date of the contract. The four hospitals have some flexibility as to which "on the shelf" hospital computer applications they will use; moreover, there are choices as to the scope of specific applications. Therefore, you are in the precarious situation of developing the 60-page Master Research Design before the four hospitals reach a final decision on which computer applications will be installed.

Carol Health Service also entered into a subcontract with a commercial vendor to provide the computer service on a time sharing basis that is required for the shared modular hospital information systems project. During the same 60-day period, the commercial vendor worked with the four Carol Health Service hospitals in selecting the particular application areas for which time sharing services were to be provided and in developing a schedule of installation of applications. The Admission and Bed Census application area at Community Hospital (the largest Carol Health Service hospital) was selected as the initial demonstration area.

During the third month of the project, systems analysts from the computer services vendor are working with the admission personnel, hospital administrators and nursing staff in determining the exact features of the Admission and Bed Census application to be implemented at Community Hospital. One of the computer services vendor's computer programmers has begun to make adjustments to the Admission and Bed Census application package so that it can accommodate the unique requirements of personnel at Community Hospital. The computer services vendor is responsible for training operating personnel at Community Hospital who will be directly involved with the application, and this training program is scheduled to start at the beginning of the next month.

At this point in time, the national foundation, as part of its ongoing administrative and research monitoring efforts, appointed a team of three consultants to review the overall shared modular hospital information system project with Carol Health Service. TKS Health Systems' Master Research Design became the focus of a major portion of this review. The team of consultants was critical of several parts of your Master Research Design including (*a*) using post implementation analyses as a basis for describing the prior to implementation situation, (*b*) focusing on information flows within an area without accumulating objective time and motion data on manual processing procedures associated with a set of operations, and (*c*) planning on generalizing from the experience at Carol Health Service Hospitals on the basis of economic benefits *realized* rather than the *projected* savings that could have been achieved if all time and motion efforts had been utilized in an ideal manner.

You are requested by management of TKS Health Systems to respond to these three charges. After reflecting on these criticisms, you recognize that the team of consultants was really questioning the total information systems approach which you have incorporated in the Master Research Design report. This latter realization encourages you to review that total project before beginning to prepare your written response to these charges.

Purpose of Overall Project

The objective of this project is to establish, demonstrate and evaluate *Shared Modular Hospital Information Systems* (SMHIS) utilizing computer applications based on the *Massachusetts General Hospital Utility Multipurpose Programming* System (MUMPS) language within a consortium of hospitals, namely the Carol Health Service hospitals in Florida. A significant part of this study is to demonstrate if commercially available MUMPS-based computer services can be provided to a hospital without requiring technical expertise with these computer programs or supporting computer facilities within the hospital. The evaluation of this project will be in terms of cost containment, manpower utilization, quality of care, public acceptance, and extent to which the system can be generalized.

The foundation's desire for an objective evaluation of hospital information systems utilizing the MUMPS-based language permeates this total project. MUMPS is a high level, interpretive, user-oriented, general purpose programming language designed for interactive time-shared systems with an emphasis on the capabilities to manipulate character strings and data files. This language was developed at the Laboratory of Computer Science of Massachusetts General Hospital under sponsored research projects from the National Center for Health Services Research and Development and the National Institute of Health.

The MUMPS language was initially developed to support clinical data management applications; however, MUMPS special properties of combining algebraic and Boolean expression handling capabilities with the ability to handle string information were recognized as being applicable to many hospital and medical problems. A series of Public Health Service grants was made to the Laboratory of Computer Science of Massachusetts General Hospital for the design, development and demonstration of MUMPS-based applications, including (*a*) computer-based automated medical history, (*b*) medication system, (*c*) computer program to assist acute respiratory care, (*d*) intensive care unit records, (*e*) computer-based examination, (*f*) clinical data management system, (*g*) ambulatory patient medical record system, (*h*) sequential problem solving programs for use in teaching, and (*i*) laboratory test reporting system.

The latter demonstrations have been encouraging in that they have illustrated in operational form the relevance of MUMPS-based applications to a wide range of health care activities. Moreover, this special high level time-sharing language can operate on a medium and small computer. However, there has not been a full scale, objective evaluation of these applications, and the purpose of the current project is to support this type of evaluation in an unbiased setting.

Hospital Information System

The function of a computerized hospital information system is to integrate and automate many of the communications, ordering, reporting, accounting and control activities of a hospital. To date, a completely successful total hospital information system has not been achieved. This is due to the difficulties which arise in attempting to design a system that: (*a*) reflects the linkages and interactions among the various departments and (*b*) interfaces appropriately with a wide variety of users within the hospital.

Previous approaches to the problem have been to design a total, integrated, dedicated computer system to serve this purpose. The total hospital information systems approach requires a significant financial commitment in technical personnel and computer facilities which is prohibitive for most small and medium size hospitals. Moreover, the lack of a completely successful hospital information system indicates that even if the financial and personnel resources are available, there is no guarantee of success with this approach at the present time. With the advent of commercial time-shared computers, a new approach to this problem is possible.

Shared Modular Hospital Information System

This new approach to the problem features a group of cooperating hospitals which share the cost, according to use, of a computer facility without requiring that a hospital have the technical personnel to support such a facility. The service to be offered by this facility will be modular in nature, allowing automation of departments and functions within the hospital on a selective basis, such as Bed Census and Admissions, Clinical Laboratory, and Scheduling and Treatment Planning for Radiation Therapy. As each of these applications are brought into use, their appropriate linkages with existing modules will be implemented.

As implied by these comments, there are several advantages of the SMHIS approach over previous approaches; these include:

1.   Minimal capital investment in computer equipment on the part of the participating hospitals.
2.   Avoidance of the mass disruptions that the implementation of a total system would have.
3.   Opportunity for department by department preparation for automation.
4.   Fostering of cooperation and standardization by participating hospitals in other areas.

Because of the relatively low cost of telephone communications between user terminals and a remote computer, the shared use of such a system can quite feasibly occur over relatively long distances.

Other benefits emerge from the five types of *sharing* encompassed within the SMHIS approach:

1.   Time sharing within the computer system, such that each remote terminal operator appears to have its own computer.
2.   Sharing the cost of the computer system on a "utility" basis according to use by the remote terminal operators.
3.   Sharing state of the art medical programs as they become available to the system.
4.   Sharing new administrative techniques based on information provided by the computerized system.
5.   Sharing the cost of the development of new computer applications which may be of special interest to a group of cooperating hospitals.

The SMHIS approach has only recently been applied to the design and implementation of computer services for the health care field by commercial vendors. The evaluation of the SMHIS approach for purposes of this contract will be restricted to a set of those commercially available computer modules in the MUMPS-based language.

TKS Health Systems' Master Research Design

In developing your Master Research Design report, you gave special attention to (a) the operational problems associated with the introduction and use of the SMHIS system in a hospital environment and (b) the maintenance of an unbiased setting for this project. This focus on the analysis and evaluation of SMHIS demonstration was incorporated in six special studies which highlighted various dimensions of these problems and issues. These six studies are:

1. Analysis of SMHIS Usage.
2. Analysis of Computer System Failures.
3. Evaluation of the Maintenance of an Unbiased Setting.
4. Evaluation of Aggregate Cost Effectiveness of SMHIS System.
5. Analysis of Computer Access Sharing.
6. Analysis of Effectiveness of Computer Applications.

These latter studies were part of the Analysis and Evaluation of SMHIS Demonstration part of the Master Research Design report, and this was the second major part of the report being preceded by the Implementation Plan.

The third major part of the Master Research Design was titled Evaluation of Computer Applications. This is a comprehensive analysis of each application site within a hospital as well as comparative studies of applications at different sites. Some of the computer-based applications are intentionally implemented at all four Carol Health Service hospitals so as to provide comparative data on different organizational settings. The research plan for performing this comprehensive analysis includes a systems analysis and flowcharting of each application:

1. Prior to implementation.
2. One month after implementation.
3. Six to nine months after implementation.
4. Termination of provider of computer service's contract.

Attitudinal scaling of application acceptance will be performed both six weeks and six months after implementation. Computer-based accumulation procedures will be incorporated in the network to provide multidimensional operational data for quantitative evaluation.

After these detailed evaluations of the applications at the Carol Health Service hospitals, the last part of the Master Research Design—"General Evaluation"—represents a shift in perspective. The focus is on the general insights gained from this demonstration and evaluation which can assist regional and national health care efforts.

Consultants Criticism

You reviewed the three major criticisms of the team of consultants and you acknowledged that each of these criticisms represents a valid difference of opinion. Before formally responding to these charges, you decide to briefly outline the affirmative and negative positions with respect to each criticism.

A. *Using post implementation analyses as a basis for describing the prior to implementation situation.*

Affirmative position
1. After a computer system has been installed, it is impossible to exactly capture the before situation.
2. Many relevant volume, operating and environmental data can only be obtained on a direct basis; these data are not accumulated and retained for regular use in management planning and control activities.

Negative position
1. There is considerable flexibility in the set of computer-based operations that are incorporated in a specific MUMPS-based application. Before the fact, it is impossible to specify the exact scope and parameters of the application, unless TKS Health Systems, Inc. was also to perform the systems analysis and systems design activities. For example, the admission and bed census program must handle the operations associated with the scheduling of preadmit patients, the admission activities, transfer of patients between beds, and discharge of patients. However, will the estimated length of stay (an estimate provided by the admitting physician) feature be incorporated into the computer program? Which of the following lists will be used: ward report, doctor list, baby list, medicare recertification list, surgical reservation list, obstetrics reservation list, admissions list by hospital location, bed availability list, alphabetical list

of today's admissions by patient's name, bad accounts list, business office summary, and patient charges for charity cases? What other special features will be included in the computer-based application?

2. If you talk with hospital personnel prior to implementation of the computer system, there is a high risk that you will negate the unbiased setting by increasing hospital personnel's expectations in areas where computer-based services will probably not be made available to them.

B. *Focusing on information flows within an area without accumulating objective time and motion data on manual processing procedures associated with a set of operations.*

Affirmative position

1. Objective, time and motion data are needed for the manual operating procedures employed prior to the implementation of the computer system as well as comparable data for the operations after implementation of the computer system.

2. Economic benefits from time and motion savings provide objective measures which can be further analyzed by a wide range of statistical tests. In addition, this approach gives a definitive basis for another extensions.

Negative position

1. It is only in the case of labor intensive operations with tremendous volume that a computer system can be economically justified on a labor savings basis for a single set of operations; it is more common to have significant manpower savings in several related areas. These labor related benefits are usually supplemented by direct economic benefits from reducing the time dimensions of data (for example, faster processing of patient accounts may result in a reduction in the float of accounts receivable). In more advanced systems, many of the benefits are in the area of new decision-making activities that are possible under the computer-based system but were not possible previously.

2. The typical computer-based system produces a series of changes in the organization—some immediate and others deferred. The latter delayed effects tend to have greater economic benefits because they are of a more sophisticated nature (from the position of management planning and control ac-

tivities). It is only through a flowcharting of information flows which are cross referenced to individuals, organization positions and responsibility areas that it is possible to get a handle on the economic benefits attributed through time to the introduction, implementation and modification of a computer-based system.

C. *Planning on generalizing from the experience at Carol Health Service hospitals on the basis of economic benefits realized rather than the projected savings that could have been achieved if all time and motion efforts had been utilized in an ideal manner.*

Affirmative position
1. Economic benefits derived from objective time and motion data provide a useful basis for extending this study to other hospitals of varying size.
2. The potential benefits are the primary concern of this SMHIS study; otherwise, the evaluation of these MUMPS-based applications would be limited by the level of management competence present at the Carol Health Service hospitals.

Negative position
1. The purpose of this SMHIS study is to determine if time-sharing capabilities written in MUMPS-based language can be made available on an economic basis to small and medium size hospitals. The primary focus of this economic justification is on what was actually achieved, not on what is theoretically possible.

REQUIRED:

Prepare the report requested by management of TKS Health Systems to respond to these three charges.

CASE 3–2.   TURNER PRECISION ENGINEERING CORPORATION

Turner Precision Engineering Corporation is a Chicago-based manufacturer of high quality electronic parts that are components in major equipment, machinery and systems. Recently this precision manufacturing company with annual sales of $8 million has purchased and implemented a minicomputer; the applications to date include invoicing, accounts receivable management, purchasing, disbursements, payroll, and monthly departmental cost reports. You were engaged to review the installation and to suggest a program of new applications.

The Company

Turner Precision Engineering Corporation was established in 1942 as a manufacturer of specialized military parts. During the next three decades, the company's major product line has changed every 5 to 8 years because of technological developments. Most of the product changes required major redesign of the manufacturing equipment, and Turner's plant engineers have designed and supervised the construction of the equipment used to manufacture these new products. The nature of the precision parts manufactured by Turner has significantly changed with these technological developments; currently the primary products are electronic components.

Turner is the original manufacturer of components for medical equipment, environmental monitoring systems, heat treatment equipment, aircraft onboard computers, and radar systems. These original equipment sales account for less than 35 per cent of Turner's annual dollar sales; replacement part sales in other areas are responsible for the remaining 65 per cent.

Products

The six-month schedule of prices contains a list of 106 items manufactured by Turner Precision Engineering Corporation. Sixty-two of the items are in the latter years of their respective life cycle and, therefore, in total, account for less than 20 per cent of annual dollar sales. Many of these items are replacement parts for components in equipment and machinery, and, frequently, the original equipment manufacturing company will market Turner's replacement part instead of producing any replacement parts of its own. In these cases the distribution channels of the original equipment manufacturing company are used for selling Turner's products.

The remaining 44 items accounting for over 80 per cent of annual dollar sales include items of varying degrees of activity. For example, 16 of the 44 items tend to have only average dollar sales volumes; 20

tend to have good sales volumes; and the remaining 8 tend to have outstanding sales volumes. Some of these 8 items with outstanding sales volumes are sold to many customers; most of the 20 items with good sales volumes can be classified as more than a "one-customer product."

Because of the diversity of products manufactured by Turner, the largest customer might be interested in 16 of the 44 active items and 8 or 9 of the 62 slow items. There are 26 customers who account for over 65 per cent of annual dollar sales.

Raw Materials

There are significant variations in the short-term cost of selected raw materials used in some parts or items, but, on the average, a six-month price can be established for the finished part using this material without incurring any significant losses. In addition to the inflationary pressures on raw materials, supply shortages may necessitate the use of a substitutable material that is more expensive. Fortunately, Turner has not experienced many such supply shortages, and it is estimated that not more than 10 per cent of the annual material cost is for the purchase of substitutable items.

Turner does not maintain a perpetual inventory costing system for raw materials. An engineering study is made of each part or item, and an "average material cost" is determined for that part. This average material cost for each part is stored in the computer system. On the monthly financial reports, the cost of materials within the cost of goods manufactured is determined by multiplying the number of units processed by the "average material cost." A physical inventory is annually taken, and the appropriate adjustments are made to the cumulative cost account.

Computer-Based Applications

A time and motion evaluation was made of the cost and benefits of replacing the present manual system with a series of activity programs supported by a minicomputer. As a result of this study, a minicomputer was purchased 8 months ago, and a series of 6 applications has been implemented. Before any of the applications was designed, a chart of accounts and code structure were developed for the 14 departments so cost, expense, and performance data could be accumulated. This code structure consisted of six digits—four digits for the type of cost, expense and performance statistics and two digits for specifying the organizational unit.

The six applications that have been fully implemented are (*a*) accounts payable and invoice register (includes data on purchases by department, cost and expense distribution by department, and a routine for retrieving selected data), (*b*) cash disbursements and check writing, (*c*) payroll program (a total system for factory workers, hourly employees, and salary personnel; including taxes, deductions, state and federal reports), (*d*) accounts receivable and sales (balance by account, billing, collections related to invoice, and aging), (*e*) collection and cashier activities, and (*f*) report generator for trial balance, general ledger, and departmental reports.

An order entry application has been designed and is in the process of being implemented. The order entry program will accommodate partial shipments and maintain residual balances. It will also maintain continuous data on (*a*) unfilled orders by customer, (*b*) unfilled orders by part or item (which can be used in the manual scheduling of production), and (*c*) month and year-to-date data on order by part or item. After the order entry application has been fully implemented, then inventory control data on shipments can be obtained from the computer system.

In addition to these applications, the Production Department schedules parts or items daily on a manual basis in 100-unit lots. Since the manufactured units are small, metal racks containing space for 25 units have been designed for use in storage and in physical movement of a 100-unit lot through the plant. The work flow in the 6 processing departments within the factory is organized so that each 100-unit lot (or the items on 4 metal racks) is separately handled; performance and quality control data are manually accumulated on a card that is placed in the card holder attached to the metal rack. The latter data are used for manually determining yield and performance.

REQUIRED:

1. Specify the types of evaluation methods that you would apply in reviewing the present applications and in developing a program of proposed applications. Justify the evaluation methods selected.

2. As a systems analyst, review the present system. Present a brief summary of your findings and specify the critical problem areas that appear to require further study.

3. Develop a program of proposed applications and indicate the critical activities (non-dollar cost components) that are incrementally required to implement each proposed application. Explain the reasons for your selection.

CHAPTER 4

Organizational and Administrative Arrangements That Support Computer-Based Networks beyond the Operating System

A COMPUTER-BASED network at the planning, designing, and initial implementing stages is an entity that is separate and distinct from the organization in which the network is being established. A simple system supported by a computer program or an expanded system containing either an activity program or a functional program (see Figure 3.2) may be tolerated by administrative and management personnel without any "complete" acceptance of these networks. The scope and impact of the networks do not encompass all activities within a functional area; thus, there are still nonconstraining activities in which administrative and management personnel can express themselves. Although some individuals may feel threatened by any type of computer-based network, the majority of the administrative and management personnel will have a positive attitude toward such networks.[1]

---

[1] Recent attitudinal studies of administrative, medical, and management personnel at four hospitals which were conducted by the author and his colleague, Dr. James B. Thies, indicate that the positive perspective toward computer-based networks is very strong (for more information on the study, see James B. Thies, "Hospital Personnel and Computer-Based Systems: A Study of Attitudes and Perceptions," *Hospital Administration*, vol. 20 [1975], pp. 17–26). Separate analyses were made of individuals who attended college, graduated with a bachelor's degree, graduated with a master's degree, and graduated with other advanced degrees. In addition, consideration was given to whether or not the

The attitudes of administrative and management personnel as well as the general environmental setting at the computer program, activity program, and functional program levels tend to be conducive to the successful installation of a computer-based network. This environmental reaction of the organization to the network might be interpreted as being analogous to the medical reactions of the human being to simple transplants from other parts of the individual's body. A skin transplant might be analogous to a computer program; hair transplants might be compared with an activity program; and the transplant of a slice of a tissue might be equated with a functional program. The medical probabilities of success in all of these are very high; occasionally, there are complications, but they can be corrected by medical treatment and medical care. (In this series of analogies all the medical transplants were between locations on the same individual's body; therefore, the reader should note that "environmental" reactions of a transplant from another human being were not considered.)

At the operating system level and beyond, administrative and management personnel as well as the environmental setting are not as open and supportive of planning, designing, and implementing

---

individual had worked with computer-based networks before, years of professional employment, years with current employer, years in current position, and the extent of any previous educational training with computer-based networks. There were very strong positive attitudes among personnel in all categories and in all composite groups. Second and third sets of attitudinal instruments were administered, respectively, 6 weeks and 6 months after these personnel had worked with the computer-based networks which were in the process of being designed and implemented. In all of these analyses, a strong positive attitude toward computer-based networks persisted; however, the measured attitudes did deteriorate significantly over the project. This downward shift in attitudes is understandable in part because there were periods of extensive computer-failures and downtimes which disrupted regular operations; many of the personnel being measured had to work overtime in reestablishing the computer-based data.

In addition, a disaster destroyed the computer system and most of the machine-readable records. In spite of this shift in attitudes over the 22 month project, two thirds of the personnel at the end of the project indicated that they would still recommend that similar departments in other hospitals should implement such computer-based networks. (It is acknowledged that some behavioral scientists will attribute some of this positive attitude to the mere fact that individual's opinions and feelings are being studied—the "Hawthorne effect.")

The most advanced of the computer-based networks included in this project might be classified as a functional program; however, most of the applications were at the activity program level. Thus, these findings are only generalizable at that level.

computer-based networks. Continuing with the medical analogies, the transplant of a tissue might be compared with an operating system; the transplant of part of a minor organ might be related to an information system; and the transplant of a minor organ might be equated with an advanced information system. The latter two transplants would, by definition, be from another human being; therefore, the human body's reaction to the "foreign" element is a major concern. Occasionally, the human body will not accept a specific, minor organ transplant, and the surgical process must be repeated. Currently, there is over an 85 per cent probability of success without any complications on a minor organ transplant, and most of those cases with complications are corrected either through medical treatment or by repeating the surgical process.

There are limitations with drawing analogies, for the reader may desire to pursue each dimension of the comparison. The main point in this series of medical analogies is that *a computer-based network beyond an operating system is the transplant of a foreign element and there are environmental reactions to this situation.* This point is especially applicable in the planning, designing, and initial implementation stages for computer-based networks.

The systems analyst views the proposed computer-based network beyond the operating system as a foreign transplant, and, therefore, very carefully monitors the administrative and organizational reactions to this *new* element. The systems analyst knows also that administrative techniques, organizational arrangements, and political approaches can assist in the establishment of a conducive environment in which the new network can grow and mature. Alternatively, these items can be perceived as organizational and administrative factors constraining the evolving structure of information systems or as stopping rules which limit further advancement.

The current discussion is divided into three parts. First, the organizational arrangements of the information systems department are examined. Second, a multidimensional analysis is made of the information systems function as related to computer-based networks at the operating system level and beyond; after examining the concept of management by systems, attention is focused on eight common dimensions of the administrative process and organizational arrangements encompassed in these networks. Third, the administrative arrangements for planning and coordinating a series of computer-based networks are explored. This composite analysis is presented in the description of the role, function, and membership of four committees: code structure identification and maintenance committee, data management committee, information systems coordinating committee, and confidentiality of data committee.

ORGANIZATIONAL ARRANGEMENTS OF THE INFORMATION SYSTEMS DEPARTMENT

There is a significant difference between the information systems *department* and the information systems *function*. The latter is examined in the second part of this chapter; the information systems department as well as the areas within the department are analyzed in this part of the chapter. This inquiry consists of three parts: (*a*) the shifting title of the chief executive officer responsible for the information system department, (*b*) the data processing and computer center activities, and (*c*) the overall activities of the information systems department are contrasted with the activities of the computer systems center.

Title of Chief Executive Officer Responsible for Department

There is no uniform location for the information systems department in organizations. The centralization or decentralization of information systems activities varies somewhat by size of organization (both in annual dollar volume of sales or quantity of services and in the average dollar value per customer order or constituent's service), geographical dispersion of organization, and the degree to which there are physical similarities among items in various product lines or groups of services. The current location of this department is also influenced by whichever officer or administrator was primarily responsible for initially introducing large-scale computer systems into the organization, when this occurred, the extent to which these efforts tended to service the needs of the organization, and the present political status of the individual or successor who initially introduced the systems. Power struggles, personnel conflicts, and other organizational considerations are continuously changing the location of these activities.

For example, in one major corporation included within the top 100 companies of *Fortune* magazine's list of industrial enterprises, there was an administrative services group at the assistant vice president level that was organizationally independent and had total corporate responsibility for the information systems activities. Two years later, the corporate controller has assumed this total corporate responsibility, and the former members of the administrative services group are part of the controller's staff.

In another major corporation within this same list of industrial enterprises, the information systems activities are performed by an information systems group on the staff of the corporate controller. Two years later, this group has been elevated to the vice presidential level, which is the same level as the corporate controller and the treasurer. However, as far as status is concerned, the Vice-Prsident— Information Systems is higher than either the corporate controller or the treasurer. Since the president and the chairman of the board are inactive positions in this company, the only active positions with higher status are those of the Executive Vice President—Manufacturing and the Senior Executive Vice President.

With these types of changes occurring in major companies, it is impossible to present any single, dominant organizational reaction to information systems activities. Moreover, agencies, bureaus, associations, services, hospitals, and institutions have implemened computer-based systems, and the organizational location of the information systems department includes all of the variations as those experienced by business enterprise. The five major current arrangements are briefly described.

Under the Corporate Controller.   One of the most common organizational reactions is for the information systems department to be under the corporate controller. There tends to be a strong correlation between the classification of the computer-based network (per Figure 3.2) and the location of the information systems department. The impetus for computer-based networks frequently emerged in the areas of accounting and finance; therefore, the corporate controller is often involved in directing the shift from manual systems to computer-based networks at the activity program and the functional program levels. Because of the impetus and leadership, financial and accounting data are well represented in these networks, and marketing and environmental data are only given minimal representation.

Under the Vice President—Finance.   As the size and scope of the computer-based networks expand, the information systems activities tend to be part of the responsibility of the vice president for finance. A scenario applicable to many organizations which computerized their activities five years previously (the actual time may be the late 1950s, early, mid, or late 1960s, or early 1970s, and this tendency includes all types of institutions—business, hospitals, and health services, and public administration) is the timing of the shift from the controller's staff to the staff of the vice president for finance. This expansion in size and scope of computer-based networks reaches a critical mass between the third to the fifth year following computerization; as a result, there is an organizational elevation of the information systems department.

There are, of course, exceptions to the above statement, but in the majority of the organizations that computerized operations five years previously, the information systems department is not today under the controller. It has been elevated. The other type of exception is that this elevation occurs in some organizations during the second year following computerization.

Administrative Services Group. A few organizations have established an independent administrative services group at either the vice presidential or assistant vice presidential level to act as management consultants to the other organizational units. This particular arrangement has been extremely successful in some companies. Under this type of arrangement, it is typical for the other organizational units to be billed at some predetermined cost rate for both "consulting" types of assistance and for "information services" provided by the group.

The project manager for an advanced information system who is operating under this arrangement of an administrative services group will tend to be comparable with a product brand manager for marketing operations. The project manager's personality, temperament, and abilities are significant factors in influencing the scope and breadth of the advanced information system being designed.

Vice President of Information with Decentralized Operations. This position and the next arrangement are at the vice presidential level. If the information systems activities are organizationally located at this level, then there is a strong tendency for the entity to have one or more advanced information systems. Conversely, if the computer-based network is only classified as an information system (per Figure 3.2), it is unusual for these activities to be elevated to the vice presidential level.

If we have a computer-based system that is classified as an information system and if the administration of the support for this network is not under the vice president for finance, then we would expect this administration to be performed by the staff of an assistant vice president or by the assistant vice president. But as soon as the computer-based network can be classified as an advanced information system, there is ordinarily an elevation of the information systems activities. Alternatively, the advanced information system encompasses various management planning and control networks that are interfaced with strategic planning; organizationally, this level of interface demands a vice presidential position.

Under this arrangement at the vice presidential level, there is a small central staff that provides the basic expertise for the information systems activities. This central staff typically includes operations researchers, statisticians, system designers, programmers, management accountants, and management scientists. However, each division or department has its own "information systems controller." This individual serves as the organizational unit's communication link with the central staff, and is responsible for appropriately representing the special interests of that organizational unit when any advanced information system is being designed and implemented. After the advanced information system has been installed, the controller has the responsibility for understanding the system and being able to explain the system, when appropriate, to the other management members of the organizational unit. For example, the system may prohibit certain types of comparisons and operations from being performed; if so, the information systems controller is supposed to know about that because these restrictions may have an effect on the functions of the organizational unit.

Vice President of Information with Centralized Operations. This type of organizational arrangement is similar to that described above for the vice president for information with decentralized operations, except that with a centralized operation the division or department information systems controllers do not formally exist. Various members of the central staff perform these services; in fact, there may be a regular *assignment* of responsibility for the various divisions to specific members of the central staff.

Incidentally, this "vice president of information" is not a new title substituted for either the corporate controller or the treasurer. Both of these latter positions continue to exist concurrently with the vice president of information.

At this point in time there are too many organizational pressures for change regarding the information systems activities and their administration for an individual to predict with a high degree of confidence what the typical organizational response will be a decade from now. However, we believe that there will be a substantial increase in the number of corporate officials with the position of "vice president for information systems." This position is also represented, sometimes, by the following titles: "vice president—operations," "vice president—planning," "vice president—administration," and "vice president—information services."

Data Processing and Computer Center Activities

There are several distinct sets of activities within the information systems department, and each of these sets is explained in the next part of this discussion. One of these sets is the data processing and computer center activities which are collectively referred to as "facilities operations" or "facilities management." This set usually encompasses computer operations, communications, computer software, applications programming, systems improvement and maintenance, and standards and documentation.

The manager of facilities operations or the director of facilities management is typically a computer scientist, and this individual will have formal education in most of the following areas: file design, dynamic storage arrangements, retrieval languages, interactive programming languages, machine languages, simulation languages, and advanced programming. One of the professional problems confronting the computer scientist is the need to stay abreast of technological advancements in hardware, software, and firmware while, at the same time, keeping informed of the unique features being incorporated in applications maintained and updated by the computer center's staff.

Within the facilities operations, there are staff members who schedule jobs, equipment, and machines. These include switching and communication equipment, remote terminals and cathode ray tubes, remote processors, high-speed card readers, magnetic tape readers, magnetic drum, magnetic core, high-speed printers, plotters, other graphic display equipment, and software facilities. In addition, there are, of course, key punches and peripheral equipment.

The formal education of the computer scientist is significantly different from that of the systems analyst. The latter will have only one or two survey courses in computer science for purpose of gaining an appreciation of "what is possible." Within the information systems department, the profile (background, formal education, skills, abilities, and experience) of the computer scientist is in marked contrast to the systems analyst, the management scientist, the operations researcher, and the other professional members of the information systems department. Moreover, an experienced computer scientist is not typically envisioned by others as a career path en route to the position of chief executive officer for the information systems department. Because of promotion and staffing considerations, a significant number of small and medium-size organizations have begun to have the facilities operations or the facilities management performed by outside concerns.

Without commenting on the latter trend, it is sufficient to state that facilities management can be separated from information systems. Facilities management is an essential feature of a computer-based network, but the administration of these activities as well as the physical location of the computer center do not have to be restricted to the organization. Either or both can be performed outside the organization.

Information Systems Department

From the previous discussion, we see that the formal education and professional experience of the computer scientist is different from that of the systems analyst. Figure 4.1 presents a typical arrangement of the information systems department, and the computer scientist will be the Manager, Facilities Operations. The Manager, Operations Research will frequently have, at least, one advance degree in mathematics, management science, or operations research; in a large organization some of the members of this group may have doctoral degrees. The other three groups—Manager, Commercial Systems and Applications; Manager, Education and Technical Services; and Manager, Scientific and Control Applications—are career paths of systems analyst.

Within the information systems department, there will be a group of application programmers or systems programmers. These are the initial positions of the computer scientist. In those organizations where the application programmers and systems programmers are not part of the facilities operations, these individuals will frequently have some type of professional relation with the computer scientist

FIGURE 4.1
Information Systems Department

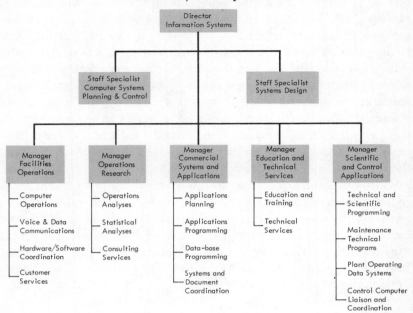

serving as manager, facilities operations. In a larger organization there may be a committee of computer scientists (systems programmers, application programmers, and manager, facilities operations) who meet at regular intervals for professional education and association purposes. In a very large organization, the major differences are titles; we may be talking about an executive vice president of information systems with a corresponding elevation in the titles of staff personnel.

In the information systems department less than 40 percent of the regular work load relates to maintenance and housekeeping activities. The major portion of the department's activities pertains to planning and designing new computer-based systems. The two staff assistants are barometers of this orientation: (*a*) Staff Specialist— Computer Systems Planning and Control and (*b*) Staff Specialist— Systems Design.

The organizational arrangement of the information systems department is primarily for identifying responsibilities and for administrative purposes. During the systems planning and designing efforts, it is unusual for a study team to be staffed by members from any one group or unit. Housekeeping and systems maintenance activities are, on the other hand, primarily performed by members of one group.

The study coordinator for each major information systems project (those projects that involve planning, designing, implementing, and documenting of the new systems) is usually selected from among the managers in the information systems department. Typically, the manager from one of the following three groups will be selected as study coordinator: commercial systems applications, operations research, and scientific and control applications. The two staff specialists may also be selected as study coordinators; alternatively, the staff specialists may serve as ex officio members on the study team for each major information systems project.

From this brief statement we can see the expertise available in the information systems department. These personnel serve not only as staff resources for special projects but may participate as team members on large-scale information systems studies. The membership of such teams and their organizational and administrative relationships are examined in the last part of this chapter.

Summary

The first part of this chapter has focused on the information systems department or with the activities identified with the professional staff normally associated with this department. The organizational unit comprising this set of personnel may be elevated to a division or group status depending upon the size of the organization and its internal structure. However, in the interests of simplicity, the information systems *division* or the information systems *group* will be referred to subsequently in this book as an information systems *department*.

This analysis of the information systems department has consisted of three areas. First, an overview was made of the changing title of the chief executive officer responsible for the information systems department. Second, a brief description was given of the tasks performed by the computing center or the facilities management unit, and some consideration was given to the formal education of the computer scientist who typically manages a computing center. Third, the facilities management operations of the computing center were compared and contrasted with the broader set of activities performed by the information systems department's professional staff.

The *information systems department* was presented as an organizational unit with clearly specified responsibilities for providing computer-based support and facilities management as well as providing staff assistance in planning, designing, implementing, documenting, and maintaining computer-based applications. Resource personnel in operations research and management science are frequently assigned to this department for administrative purposes.

In the next part we shall examine broader sets of activities than those identified with the professional staff in the information systems department. Our expanded frame of reference will be the *information systems function* in which the above activities comprise only a small portion of the total.

INFORMATION SYSTEMS FUNCTION

An examination of the information systems function within an organization is somewhat analogous to an examination of the management or administration of the organization. Both concepts permeate the total organizational structure and all of the activities that are encompassed within the structure. Because of the pervasiveness of these two concepts, specific dimensions of each concept must be identified before there is a high degree of communication and understanding of what is the objective of the analysis.

Alternatively, we can approach these two related concepts from the definition of common terms previously presented in this book. The term "information systems" has been uniquely described as possessing a special meaning relating to the decision-making process:

> . . . the information systems approach can be described as a special method for (*a*) identifying information flows associated with decision-making activities throughout an organization, (*b*) evaluating information flows, and (*c*) designing new information flows.[2]

From a different perspective, we can describe the information systems process as the set of activities encompassed with identifying

---

[2] *Supra,* p. 12.

information needs, specifying information requirements, locating data sources, and designing information networks that effectively and efficiently match data sources with information requirements. This process can be applied to designing new networks or to evaluating existing networks.

These information needs, information requirements, and information networks are all predicated upon the existence of decision-making activities. These activities or decision-making models are representations of the management or administration process, and they draw upon the tools of management science and systems analysis in bringing structure to the models. Thus, the concept of the information systems function is subordinate to a concept of management or administration that permeates the total organization.

Within the professional literature, there is a difference of opinion over what is "management" versus "administration." *Management* is sometimes described as the art of *administering* the human and economic resources of the organization in an efficient and effective manner in pursuit of its goals and objectives. The activities so administered are identified with the production and distribution of economic goods and services. In the above statement, some professional writers will substitute the words "administration" and "managing," respectively, for the words "management" and "administering." The perspective taken on the choice of words between *management* and *administration* tends to be based on the orientation of the formal education of the writer. The term administration tends to be preferred by professional writers in public management, health care, and education. The term management tends to be the dominant word used by professional writers in business. We will use both terms in a dominant position, depending upon the institutional setting being described.

For purposes of this discussion, management or administration identifies the underlying process that is being represented in the decision-making models. As previously stated, the concept of the information systems function is subordinate to the concept of management or administration, and this concept of the information systems function draws heavily upon the alternative frameworks provided by decision-making models.

Within this context, the information systems function is an attempt to develop a framework of the management or administration process in organizations which have undergone systematic analysis of resources, operations, demands, opportunities, and plans. The latter includes the organizational and administrative arrangements required in planning, coordinating, controlling, and evaluating activities in pursuit of organizational goals.

In examining the information systems function in organizations possessing computer-based networks at the operating system level and beyond (see Figure 3.7 for a refresher on the levels of complexity in programs and computer-based networks), there are certain common dimensions of the function which merit attention. For example, the sets of integrated transactions handled by these electronic capabilities for computer-based networks at the operating system and beyond were all directed toward management control; the more advanced networks had also incorporated various aspects of planning into the system. We will view these common dimensions for these three levels of complexity in computer-based networks after considering the concept of *management by systems* which is a prerequisite for the three levels.

Management by Systems

Implicit in the design of the operating system (which was described as serving as the backbone of an information system) is the capability of handling a large volume of recurring transactions in a management controlled setting. This can be presented from an alternative perspective as the first phase of management by systems. Specifically, a set of programmed decision rules has been developed for monitoring performance, controlling assets, evaluating accomplishments, and suggesting corrective action on an exception basis. Thus, as we examine computer-based networks at the operating system level and beyond, we are viewing some facets of the concept of management by systems.

Other facets of this concept were encompassed in the need for management's participation in analyzing the environment, designing programmed decision rules, and specifying alternative decision-making activities. Part of this analysis included the separation of activities between programmed and nonprogrammed, the further consideration of activities so classified, and the reevaluation of these classifications after programmed decision rules had been implemented to represent selected activities.

There are many factors which influence the degree to which members of management are able to fully apply the concept of management by systems. Some of our recent studies have indicated that the formal education, previous experience, awareness of management science techniques, familiarization with computer science capabilities, and age of the decision maker are among the relevant factors.[3]

Some members of management are not able to fully accept the concept of management by systems. Others will go through the process of developing programmed rules and delegating to subordinates the tasks of administering these rules in coping with daily activities. However, many members of management in this second group are not philosophically and emotionally able to direct their efforts to the unusual transaction or toward the strategic planning opportunities. Instead, they direct their attention toward monitoring subordinates' handling of typical transactions. On the other hand, some members of management are able to fully accept the concept of management by systems including the desire to focus their attention on nonrecurring transactions and strategic planning issues.

Thus, education or the reorientation of members of management is one of the major steps in planning, designing, implementing, and documenting a computer-based network. This educational program or professional development session must assist in reorienting members of management to apply the systems concept in more successfully carrying out their duties and responsibilities. This desire on the part of management to fully apply the concept of management by systems is a prerequisite for the implementation, maintenance, and improvement of computer-based networks.

In applying the concept of management by systems to organizational settings containing computer-based networks, members of management must directly or indirectly use some framework of the administrative process. Although the labels in the framework vary by professional writer, there are common threads in each framework. These aspects of the administrative process are used for highlighting important facets of the information systems function in organizations possessing computer-based networks at the operating system level and beyond.

---

[3] *Supra,* p. 92.

Operating System

This computer-based network is designed to handle a large volume of recurring transactions in a prescribed manner with a set of programmed decision rules incorporated in online computer programs (see Figure 3.3 for a generalized model of an operating system). We will examine eight dimensions of the administrative process and the organizational arrangements encompassed in the typical operating system.

1. Models of the Administrative Process. Implicit in the generalized model of the administrative process is a simple model of the administrative process consisting of two phases: a planning phase and a control phase. The results of the planning phase are incorporated in the set of online computer programs used for processing the high volume of transactions. The control phase accumulates data on performance, compares actual with planned accomplishments, and prepares exception reports when a high variation exists between actual versus planned activities.

After the planning phase has been performed, there are three levels of outputs: (*a*) a restatement of the overall *policy* issues for the organization that directly pertain to the model (including any changes in organizational structure, organizational assets, and other resources necessitated by the modified policy), (*b*) a statement of specific strategic plans which give short-term guidance as to priorities with regard to the utilization of the organization's assets, and (*c*) operational plans of tasks and activities to be performed immediately. The latter normally includes intermediate measures of these tasks and activities which can be used in evaluating performance and coordinating efforts.

The control phase in an operating system is at an intermediate level of sophistication. Physical control over resources and technical control over performance and activities are key features in the models of the administrative process of more primitive computer-based networks. Many of the traditional measures of performance are based on models of technical control for specification of objectives, tasks, and activities; these are usually supplemented with exception sorting criteria and reporting programs for preparing management-by-exception reports. If it were not for these well-developed models of technical control over operations, members of management would have to direct their major attention at the technical control level rather than focusing on planning and strategic planning issues. But these models do exist, and management by systems at the operating systems level assumes the computer-based network contains an effective arrangement for monitoring physical control and technical control. (The latter models are assumed to be a prerequisite for a computer-based network at the operating system level and beyond; therefore, the online computer programs that perform the monitoring and reporting functions for physical control and technical control are taken as given and are not individually discussed in this book.)

In addition to physical control and technical control, the control phase in an operating system also features *management control*. The concept of management control has been one of the primary areas of interest of managerial accountants for the past two decades, and Robert N. Anthony was one of the earlier writers who developed a detailed framework for the concept.[4] According to Anthony:

> Management control *is the process by which managers assure that resources are obtained and used effectively in the accomplishment of an organization's objectives.*[5]

This concept of management control in the operating system is the same as Anthony's framework; both are predicated upon the existence of technical and physical control. Beyond these elements, management control adds to the control phase a monitoring capability over activities that have been delegated most frequently in a responsibility center context. (The latter arrangement is examined in detail in Chapter 7 of this book.) For the present consideration, the management control dimensions of the control phase provide monitoring, comparison, and exception reporting over performance exerted in carrying out the objectives set forth by the planning phase. Thus, the planning phase and the management control part of the control phase both relate to the same integrated framework.

---

[4] Robert N. Anthony, *Planning and Control Systems: A Framework for Analysis* (Boston: Division of Research, Graduate School of Business Administration, Harvard University, 1965). A preliminary report of this framework appeared in the initial issue of *Management Services* (March-April 1964, vol. 1, pp. 18–24).

[5] Robert N. Anthony, *Management Accounting: Text and Cases,* 4th ed. (Homewood, Illinois: Richard D. Irwin, Inc., 1970), p. 414.

2. Organizational Structure.   There is a close relationship between the models of the administrative process and the organizational structure that are supported by a computer-based network. The planning phase and the control phase in an operating system are matched with a traditional organizational structure that tends to be along functional lines. The delegation of authority and the scope of responsibility possessed by a given decision maker associated with an operating system are representative of a traditional arrangement of line and staff personnel.

From an alternative perspective, the compartmentalization of data for the operating system is compatible with the grouping of data by organizational unit. This commonality of the parameters of the entity for which data are accumulated facilitates multiuses of these data within that entity.

3. Identification of Decision Maker.   The decision maker directly associated with a given operating system may be any one of a number of middle managers in the organization. Typically, the individual in question will have the title of manager or be in charge of a traditional department. There is no inherent reason why this decision maker must be physically located near the computer center; conversely, there may be a major geographical separation between the location of the decision maker and the location of the computer center. As implied above, there is a wide range of feasible locations of the decision maker associated with a given operating system within the organization; this wide range exists not only for title and organizational level but also for geographical location.

4. Nature of Activities Supported by Network.   There are almost as many classifications of activities supported by computer-based networks as there are professional writers. However, there are some attempts to classify—using various labels—the administrators into three groups. The policy makers specify the parameters that are taken as given in decision-making activities utilizing these constraints. The decision makers accept the policy makers' parameters (such as organizational structure, resources available for commitment, fixed assets, personnel constraints, and assessment of priorities in meeting short-term organizational objectives), and they determine which of the competing alternative strategies will be employed. After the course of action has been selected by the decision makers, the planners decide among alternative methods and arrangements for achieving a selected course of action.

In a decision theory context, the policy makers' outputs are parameters for subsequent models. The decision makers use the policy makers' parameters and select among variables which are courses of action. The planners take as given the policy makers' parameters and the decision makers' variables, and within these narrow areas of movement, the planners decide how a given short-term course of action is to be accomplished.

Using this classification of policy makers, decision makers, and planners, the activities associated with an operating system tend to be, at best, associated with planners. Even in these specialized cases, an operating system is usually not as encompassing as the whole array of activities and options open to a given planner associated with the network; instead, the operating system tends to relate to only a portion of the activities. Using the models of the administrative process described previously, most operating systems are primarily concerned with management control issues and the associated specifications from the planning phase.

This classification of the administrators will be used in describing the nature of the activities supported by more advanced computer-based networks. In general as these networks advance in complexity they tend to progress from planners to decision makers to policy makers in terms of the primary focus of the activities associated with the network.

5. Degree of Interaction by Decision Maker with Computer-Based Network. This fifth dimension of the administrative process and organizational arrangements encompassed in the typical operating system is almost at the start of a continuum of interaction in which an advanced information system would be at the other end of the continuum. The decision maker associated with an operating system typically does not have any online interaction with the computer-based network or with any data base created by the set of online computer programs encompassed within the network. Typically, an operating system does not contain any personalized data base for the decision maker associated with the network. However, as implied above, each of these types of interaction will be present in the subsequent networks that are classified at a higher level.

6. Time Cycle. The outputs of the planning phase are for the duration of the control phase that commences with the termination of the planning phase. The life of the organization consists of the summation of the control phases. If the control phase is for several days or weeks, then typically the planning phase will not really start until toward the end of the control phase. To add to the complexity, the planning phase in a more advanced network is partitioned among short-term planning, strategic planning, and long-range planning. There are also arrangements for partial adjustments while the control phase is underway, and this latter will be referred to as the coordinating phase. In other words, while the planning phase and the control phase represent the two phases of the administrative process in an operating system and either phase could be used equally to explain the life of the organization, this approach is not valid for more advanced networks. The life cycle of the organization based on the summation of control phases is the only applicable approach for more advanced networks that encompasses all periods of time.

The time cycle of the control phase in an operating system tends to be for an extended period, such as a week or a month. The online programs within the operating system monitor performance and prepare relevant exception reports under the previously described concepts of physical control, technical control, and management control. Therefore, the decision maker associated with the operating system is up-to-date on performance, and the range of responses taken by the decision maker tends to be toward taking corrective action with the individuals or events which caused the variation rather than changing the criteria in any online computer program. Thus, from a conceptual standpoint, it is only when there is a need to change the online computer programs (which are inserted as the outputs of the planning phase) that there is a need for terminating and starting again a control phase. Otherwise, there can be a lengthy period of time covered by a control phase in an operating system.

While the time cycle in an operating system is not a dominant factor which constrains the network, it is a dominant factor in the more advanced computer-based networks. The capability of handling multi-time cycles will also be discussed.

7. Interface of Network with Other Networks. The computer programs in an operating system are designed to handle a large volume of recurring transactions, and most of such programs fully handle all facets of the set of transactions. Therefore, there is a minimum amount of reprocessing of data, and only limited benefit from linking operating systems. On the other hand, there are many negative costs associated with linking operating systems (both in terms of computer processing time and efforts required to update given computer programs).

In general, there is a high degree of interface of the functional programs into an operating system. However, the interface stops at that level, unless an information system is to be designed. It is unusual to have two or more operating systems interfaced in an environmental setting in which an information system is not in the process of being designed and implemented.

8. Data Structure. This final dimension of the administrative process and the organizational arrangements encompassed in the typical operating system tends to be comparable to the fifth dimension. The data structure of a computer-based network at the operating system level is almost at the beginning of a continuum that extends to the position of an advanced information system. Currency and timeliness of data are two aspects of this eighth dimension which will be examined in the more advanced computer-based networks.

Information System

An information system is a computer-based network containing two or more operating systems, provides relevant data to management for decision-making purposes, and contains the necessary mechanism for implementing changes or responses made by management (see Figure 3.4 for a generalized model of an information system). We will examine the same eight dimensions of the administrative process and the organizational arrangements encompassed in the typical information system as were applied to the examination of operating systems in the previous section.

1. Models of the Administrative Process. The information system has a planning phase and a control phase; however, each of these phases is expanded in scope over its arrangement in the operating system. The integrated framework of the planning and control phases is more action oriented, and this computer-based network has the capability for implementing management's responses.

In addition to the planning phase and control phase, models of the administrative process in an information system also contain an editing and filtering phase. This is primarily a data processing function that screens input data before they are accepted by the computer-based network. Since the editing and filtering phase has programmed decision-rules based on anticipated characteristics of data inputs, a high degree of stability must exist for a sufficient period of time to permit the identification, design, implementation, documentation, and maintenance of these decision rules.

2. Organizational Structure.   The traditional, functional organizational structure that is typical of an agency, association, company, or institution possessing an operating system tends to be modified before the information system is fully implemented. The decision maker or the team of decision makers associated with a given information system will frequently have some unique authority for coping with the opportunities provided by the change capabilities in the online computer programs. This latter type of expanded authority which exceeds that normally provided by the traditional organizational structure is referred to as a *matrix organizational arrangement.* In a matrix organizational structure an individual may have multilines of authority and levels of responsibility depending upon the issue.

3. Identification of Decision Maker.   The decision maker directly associated with an information system will frequently be a major department head, a division head, or the vice president in charge of a functional area. While the decision maker can use the change capabilities incorporated in an information system for implementing action, the use of this feature does not necessitate any physical proximity of the decision maker with the physical location of the computer center. As was the case of this dimension in an operating system, there may be a major geographical separation between the location of the decision maker and the location of the computer center. As implied above, the decision maker associated with an information system will be a higher organizational level with more authority than that possessed by a decision maker associated with an operating system.

4. Nature of Activities Supported by Network.   Using the same decision theory context as explained for the previous discussion of operating systems, the scope of activities supported by an information system encompasses all of the management control and planning efforts that were associated with the operating system. In addition the action aspects of the change capabilities encompassed within an information system require that the manager associated with the information system must select among variables. In other words, part of these efforts must be fully classified as "decision-making activities" if the computer-based network is an information system with its defined characteristics (per Figure 3.4). Because of the flexibility provided by the matrix organizational arrangement, an individual may be classified as a planner for most activities while he or she is classified as a decision maker for purposes of directing the action aspects of the information system.

5. Degree of Interaction by Decision Maker with Computer-Based Network. The decision maker associated with an information system typically does not have an online interaction with the computer-based network or with any data base created by the set of online programs. An information system does not typically possess any personalized data base for this decision maker. However, the decision maker must have some convenient mode of interaction so that the change capabilities within an information system can be activated and modified by his or her processing actions. These latter change capabilities frequently are designed to be handled by a minimum amount of inputs from the decision maker; therefore, a slow speed remote terminal is an acceptable mode of interaction.

6. Time Cycle. The outputs of the planning phase initiate the changes in the online programs that are to operate during the control phase. Alternatively, these online capabilities for implementing management's decision-making activities are not processed in a simple information system until the start of a new control phase. It is not unusual in a large organization for the control phase to be restricted to 24 hours; in several organizations the control phase is of an 8 hour duration.

The critical point in the time cycle is not that the control phase is limited to a day. Instead, management has the daily capability of modifying online criteria used in processing volumes of transactions. Of course, many times the outputs of the planning phase will be to repeat the previous control cycle; however, management did have the opportunity of making a change in the online computer programs.

7. Interface of Network with Other Networks. The data processing and exception reporting activities in an information system are more sophisticated than that present in an operating system. Selected management data are present in the system as change criteria, and there is a monitoring function which suggests when these change criteria should be modified. Thus, there are more management-oriented data in an information system than that present in an operating system; therefore, there is more of a tendency to interface one or more information systems so management-oriented data from one information system can be used in a second information system.

8. Data Structure.   This final dimension of the administrative process and the organizational arrangements encompassed in the typical information system is concerned with both the currency of data and the timeliness of data. As indicated in the discussion of time cycle, the control phase is frequently operating on a one day basis. Each day the outputs of the planning phase may change the online criteria encompassed in various computer programs. In this dynamic setting, the data which management uses must be up-to-date, and there must be an effective arrangement for retrieving stored data so management has access to the latest data during the planning phase.

Advanced Information System

An advanced information system is a large-scale, computer-based network with online communication facilities for remote terminal users in two or more departments within an organization. Beyond these features, there are special characteristics that are possessed by the more advanced computer-based networks. In subsequent chapters we will examine five discrete models of information systems and advanced information systems which represent certain integrated levels of complexity. For purposes of this discussion, we will examine an elementary model of an advanced information system.

1. Models of the Administrative Process.   The planning phase, control phase, and editing and filtering phase which were encompassed in an information system have been strengthened by three additional phases—systems processing phase, coordination phase, and monitoring and inquiring phase. The systems processing phase and the editing and filtering phase both relate to the data processing function and the screening of data. The systems processing phase is a more sophisticated data management structure in which there are multiassignments of data, reprocessing of data, data compression, and extensive sorting of data before they are assigned to an array of files. There are also control and security measures in the systems processing phase because this construct is typically applicable only where there are confidential data being processed and stored.

The coordination phase relates to the planning phase. The coordination phase permits partial planning or partial assignment of resources during the control phase. In other words, management has options for making changes while the control phase is in process.

The monitoring and inquiring phase relates to both the planning phase and the control phase. This is the online capability for interacting with the computer-based network and determining the status of operations, projects, tasks, or activities. These latter capabilities are frequently made available to customers, clients, or consumers.

2. *Organizational Structure.* The matrix organizational structure that is associated with an information system is supplemented by a committee organizational structure in the agency, association, company, or institution possessing an advanced information system. The traditional, functional organizational structure identified with entities possessing an operating system ceases to be applicable in entities with advanced information systems.

3. *Identification of Decision Maker.* The decision maker directly associated with an advanced information system will have the title, at least, of vice president, and will be in charge of a wholly-owned company, a major division, or a significant part of the organization. As indicated by the title, this decision maker will have an important position in the organization. However, it is not necessary that the decision maker be in close proximity with the computer center. Access to a high speed remote terminal by the decision-maker's staff is essential for making effective use of the advanced information system. The decision maker needs access to a slow speed remote terminal, and this type of access is also essential for other members of management associated with this computer-based network.

4. *Nature of Activities Supported by Network.* The management control, planning efforts, and decision-making activities associated with an information system are strengthened by additional decision-making activities and the opportunity of considering some policy matters. In other words, the nature of the activities supported by an advanced information system are directly related to the title and authority of the principal decision maker.

5. *Degree of Interaction by Decision Maker with Computer-Based Network.* The introductory description of an advanced information system indicated that there were online communication facilities for remote terminal users in two or more departments. As discussed under identification of decision-maker, access to a high speed remote terminal is needed by the decision-maker's staff in performing special analyses and in modeling activities. The decision maker along with

other remote terminal users need access to slow speed remote terminals so they can interact with the computer-based network. An
advanced information system will typically contain several personalized data bases for individual remote terminal users.

6. *Time Cycle.* The time cycle of an advanced information
system tends to be longer than that for an information system. The
coordination phase permits change in selected variables during the
control phase; with this modification feature, management is willing
to operate with a longer control phase. The monitoring and inquiring phase also permits timely retrieval of data without waiting for
the outputs of the control phase. The nature of the activities supported by an advanced information system is such that a longer time
period is desired; this is especially true of the policy matters.

7. *Interface of Network with Other Networks.* It is usual for an
advanced information system not to be interfaced with other information systems and operating systems. As the volume of management-
oriented data increases as well as the expansion of the scope of activities in an advanced information system, there is a strong tendency to
interface these separate networks. It should be clearly pointed out
that this is only a partial interface; the management control dimensions of the network are not interfaced. Selected management-
oriented data are interfaced among related networks; at the same
time, there is no effort to develop a "total system" of all the
associated networks.

8. *Data Structure.* The advanced information system copes with
a more dynamic setting than that associated with an information
system. Therefore, the previous argument on the need for up-to-date
data as well as a retrieval mechanism for obtaining the latest data
during the planning phase is even more valid in the case of the
advanced information system than that described for the case of the
information system.

Summary

In this part we have examined selected, multifacets of the information systems function as related to computer-based networks at the
operating system level and beyond. After briefly discussing the concept of management by systems, attention was focused on eight
common dimensions of the administrative process and the organizational arrangements encompassed in the typical operating system,

information system, and advanced information system. In subsequent chapters, five discrete models of computer-based networks beyond the operating systems level will be presented in detail. The current discussion emphasized the variations in the eight common dimensions for purposes of providing an overall orientation to multifacets of the information systems function.

The last part of the chapter is a brief presentation of the administrative arrangements for supporting and sustaining the information systems function through various stages of growth and advancement of computer-based networks within the organization. Selected committee arrangements are the primary vehicle for accomplishing these administrative objectives.

ADMINISTRATIVE ARRANGEMENTS FOR PLANNING AND COORDINATING A SERIES OF COMPUTER-BASED NETWORKS

Members of management in many organizations have planned, designed, implemented, documented, maintained, and updated computer-based networks. In performing these activities, a series of four committee structures has been developed: (*a*) code structure identification and maintenance committee, (*b*) data management committee, (*c*) information systems coordinating committee, and (*d*) confidentiality of data committee. We will examine the role, function, and membership of these four committees.

Code Structure Identification and Maintenance Committee

In any type of advanced information system, there are common data files being used by more than one department, and this arrangement necessarily poses a significant problem in the management of these data files. Decision makers in one department may desire to change or expand some portion of a code structure. While their request may have merit, these individuals do not possess the vital overall perspective to determine intelligently if the proposed change is in the best interest of the total organization. Therefore, some type of interdepartmental committee is needed to resolve this issue.

There are two long-run responsibilities for the code structure identification and maintenance committee: (*a*) interdepartmental coordination of existing codes and (*b*) monitoring and administering changes to the coding systems. During the program design phase (which is discussed in detail in Chapter 6) , this committee will also have the responsibility for (a) determining areas to be included within each common data file and each common data base, (b) specifying the contents and general code structure for each common data base, and (c) monitoring the detail code structure definitions developed by the various study teams so that these definitions conform with the overall plans. In addition to these coordinating and management activities, this committee must have overall responsibility for and supervision of common data bases. This responsibility may be partially performed by the information systems department, and a staff member in the information systems department may serve as the secretary for this committee.

In addition to representatives from the information systems department on this committee, a representative is needed from each department in which use is made of the computer-based network and data base. The selected members of this committee not only represent the respective interest of their department, but they serve as a communication vehicle with other departmental members. They are aware of changes in the data base and can keep other users informed. Their departmental orientation permits these members to have an informed assessment of the impact of a change in code structure on other remote terminal users. Overall, the title of these various departmental representatives is an immediate indication of the degree of management's commitment to the maintenance of a quality data base.

Data Management Committee

In the previous part, the editing and filtering phase and the systems processing phase were discussed as models of the administrative process. The data management committee is responsible for all the data processing, data screening, multiassignments of data, reprocessing of data, data compression, data sorting, and control and security measures associated with these operations. As indicated by the scope of this responsibility, the data management committee is a very important committee to the total organization.

The director of the computer center is typically on ex officio member of this committee, and the director of the information systems department or a member of her or his staff is also a key member of the data management committee. The remaining membership of this committee tends to consist of operating personnel from the various departments that primarily benefit from the computer-based networks. The title of "supervisor" is a common label for many members of this committee.

In addition to the above tasks, the data management committee serves as an organization-wide advisory committee on data processing, software, communication facilities, and program packages. This committee also performs an internal control function of reviewing the documentation of various programs and applications.

Information Systems Coordinating Committee

As previously explained, management must participate in the planning and designing phase of an information system, or else an information system will not be created. This general rule pertains to all levels of management including the members of the management committee or the administrative committee. In this section brief attention is given to one organizational arrangement that facilitates participation by management at all levels.

Any proposed large-scale information systems study should be approved by the management committee. The proposal setting forth this planned study should be sufficiently specific that executives fully appreciate what they are being asked to approve. The preliminary study proposal should at least call for the establishment of an information systems coordinating committee, which has responsibility for handling all policy issues that arise in planning and coordinating an information system. Generally, each member of the management committee has a representative on the information systems coordinating committee. Since each member of the management committee selects his or her own representative from this coordinating committee, any recommendation by this coordinating committee would most likely be approved by the management committee, if necessary. The director, information systems department, generally serves as chairman of this coordinating committee.

Each representative on the information systems coordinating committee serves in a dual capacity. First, he or she is the designee of a member of the management committee. Second, he or she is the representative of an individual department that will be using the services of the proposed information system. This representative is his or her department's primary contact with the information systems study team, and he or she acts as a channel for all formal communication between the study team and his or her department's operating and functional personnel. This communication function encourages, at least, a minimum level of involvement and participation by each member of the information systems coordinating committee.

Each member of the information systems coordinating committee is not equally involved with a particular information systems project. Some user departments are directly affected by the study; other departments are only indirectly affected. Those departments that are directly involved are normally represented by a full-time systems analyst on the information systems study team. The other departments will have a part-time representative on the study team who will participate when the study team is exploring areas indirectly affecting their departments.

Study Team. Someone must have primary responsibility for pushing and directing the study team. It is typical for the study team coordinator to be a manager or staff specialist in the information systems department. For the duration of the project, the coordination of this study team and the successful completion of the undertaking are his or her primary responsibilities. However, if a user department's representative is selected as study team coordinator, the project frequently becomes sidetracked as more pressing departmental activities take precedence over the proposed study.

The full-time members of the information systems study team will consist of the study coordinator (from the information systems department) and the representatives from those user departments that are primarily affected by the study. In addition, technical and staff personnel may be assigned to the project, and these individuals are selected because of their areas of expertise, regardless of the department in which they are currently located.

The part-time members of the information systems study team should include a representative from the certified public accounting firm that annually audits the organization's information systems and reports. This representative may desire to establish within the proposed information system certain checks and balances as well as other types of internal control features. The monitoring role performed by this external accountant is discussed in a subsequent chapter.

External consultants are also part-time members of the information systems study team. The team almost always includes at least one consultant; however, special problems can develop if management depends entirely on external consultants to design an information system. As previously explained, members of management must participate in the planning and designing of a computer-based network if it is to meet their unique information requirements. Moreover, if members of management have participated in planning a new information system, each member will retain his or her understanding of how the system operates long after the consultants depart.

Coordinating Group. If more than one information system is being planned and designed, then the coordinating committee is elevated to an information systems coordinating group with separate information systems coordinating committees maintained for each network. The director of each information systems coordinating committee serves on the overall, information systems coordinating group. The other members of the coordinating group will be the same composition as that described above for the coordinating committee.

Where there is a coordinating group, the scope of the responsibility for this organization-wide group is significant, especially in the area of priority setting. The group will consider the issue of when to select an off-the-shelf program versus committing the organization to a major systems' effort in developing its own application program. In pursuing priority setting, the group must determine when to modify an existing large-scale application versus deferring the matter. This group operates in an environment in which there is an impossibility of achieving any total answer for a given issue, but, at the same time, pragmatically the group must make day-to-day decisions as opportunities and problems arise and situations occur. There are other issues confronting this coordinating group in advanced information systems, and these issues are discussed in a subsequent chapter.

Confidentiality of Data Committee

A data file or data base may be one of the organization's most valuable assets. As the level of the computer-based network progresses to the point that it approaches the status of being an advanced information system, then it is unusual for this network not to contain a valuable data file or more elaborate data base. In these cases it is imperative that a confidentiality of data committee should be established to provide control and security over these valuable assets. The tasks of this committee are emphasized in the next chapter.

For purposes of the current discussion, it is sufficient to indicate the need for this committee in organizations possessing an advanced information system. The membership of this committee should be interdepartmental and should consist of at least four members, as a safeguard for internal control. Since this committee is concerned with protecting valuable, organizational assets, each member of the confidentiality of data committee should have the title of "manager" as a minimum.

In summary these four committee structures are indicative of the administrative arrangement required for providing a "supportive" environment for advanced computer-based networks. Other facets of these committees are deferred to subsequent chapters where these issues are considered in detail.

TOPICS FOR CLASS DISCUSSION

1. There are organizational and administrative factors that constrain the evolving structure of computer-based networks. Specify these factors for operating systems, for information systems, and for advanced information systems.

2. A computer-based network beyond an operating system level is analogous to the medical transplant of a "foreign element" and there are environmental reactions to this situation. Specify administrative arrangements which can assist in creating a conducive environment in which the *new* network can grow and mature.

3. As part of a major systems effort at the Douglas Manufacturing Company, members of the management committee have agreed on the composition of a new committee—Information Systems Coordinating Committee—and on the names of the committee members. In planning this systems effort, four study teams are required, and an agreement has been reached on the membership of each team and on the names of the team members. The primary contact personnel in each organizational unit have been identified and accepted by the management committee.

Now, the initial announcements within Douglas Manufacturing Company must be made of the existence of an information systems coordinating committee, study teams, and primary contact personnel as well as to designate the employees assigned to each position. How should these announcements be handled to minimize negative feedback and to foster a supportive environment for the major systems effort? In your response, specify the number of announcements you will recommend, the title of the individual who will issue each announcement, the date (or timing) of each announcement, and the contents of each announcement. Briefly justify your overall position.

4. Explain how the formal education of a computer scientist is different from that of a systems analyst. In illustrating the differences in these two professionals, indicate the types of tasks within the information systems department that each professional might be assigned early in his or her professional career.

5. Explain the concept of management by systems. Incorporate within your explanation the relationship of the management by systems concept to the models of the administrative process. In your response, specifically relate the concept of management by systems to the planning phase and control phase in an operating system.

6. Much attention has been given in the first four chapters of this book to the *need for members of management to participate* in planning, designing, implementing, and evaluating computer-based networks. Explain management's role in these efforts and indicate how members of management are prepared for these assignments.

7. "The life of an organization is equal to the summation of the individual control phases." Explain this statement.

8. Explain the types of controls which are encompassed within the control phase of an information system.

9. Explain the difference between a matrix organizational structure, a traditional organizational structure, and a committee organizational structure. How does the organizational structure relate to the design of a computer-based network?

10. In a decision theory context, differentiate among policy makers, decision makers, and planners. Indicate the relationship of these three levels to an advanced information system and to the direct and indirect users of the system.

11. Currency of data and timeliness of data retrieval arrangements are two important factors in the overall data structure for an advanced information system. Explain the interaction between these two factors.

12. Within the same organization as the computer-based networks evolve, why does the time cycle of an advanced information system tend to be longer than that followed in an information system? Why does the time cycle of an operating system tend to be longer than that followed in an information system? Explain your position.

13. Explain the purpose of a personalized data base for a remote terminal user in an advanced information system.

14. Differentiate among the tasks performed by the following four committees: (*a*) code structure identification and maintenance committee, (*b*) data management committee, (*c*) information systems coordinating committee, and (*d*) confidentiality of data committee.

15. Explain the relation between the information systems coordinating committee and the management committee.

16. The information systems coordinating group must make recommendations on priorities and select between competing alternatives. Explain why many of these recommendations on priorities are hazy.

CASE 4–1.   AMOCO CHEMICALS CORPORATION

The manager—information services department at Amoco Chemicals Corporation is currently reviewing the recently completed planning study report for the overall corporation. This report, dated May 1, 1969, represents a company-wide study of information systems requirements by systems analysts and user department personnel. The coordinated planning study included eight study teams that examined the major activities within the company.

The management committee at Amoco Chemicals had initially approved the planning study project, and this committee appointed an information systems coordination group to handle interdepartmental problem areas and to make recommendations on policy issues. The 178-page planning study report reflects the overall summary of these coordinating efforts during the past 12 months. The report has just been approved by the information systems coordination group and has been forwarded to the management committee with a recommendation for approval.

At this point in time, the manager—information services department is reflecting upon the activities over the past 12 months. In his reflection, he recalls the creation of the information services department, the planning for the scoping study, and the coordination activities that were required during the scoping phase. While these events were occurring, the company (Amoco Chemicals) was growing at a rapid rate. This growth was partially attributed to internal activities and was partially attributed to the acquisition of 11 small- and medium-size corporations.

The Company

Amoco Chemicals Corporation is a wholly-owned subsidiary of Standard Oil Company (Indiana). The letters "AMOCO" are used under a license from The American Oil Company, which is also a subsidiary of Standard Oil Company (Indiana). Since Amoco Chemicals is a wholly-owned subsidiary, annual financial statements on Amoco Chemicals' activities are not made available to the general public. (For purposes of this case study, a stand alone company equalling Amoco's 1968 sales would rank in the lower half of the *Fortune* list of 500 U.S. corporations.) Some operations of AMOCO are conducted by subsidiary companies. To simplify this case study, references to AMOCO include its subsidiaries.

Between 1961 and 1968, Amoco Chemicals annual sales tripled. With the recent diversification into plastic fabricators and polypropylene, it is expected that the annual sales will be at least double the present level by 1972.

Until 1965 Standard Oil Company (Indiana) operated about 40 computers in 30 locations. That year the decision was made to modernize and consolidate computing capacity into two major centers which would serve all elements of the total company. These two centers are located in Chicago, Illinois, and Tulsa, Oklahoma. Each center has an IBM 360 Model 65 and an IBM 360 Model 75 as its major computers. The centers are linked by broad-band lines, and outlying facilities and terminal devices are tied into one center or the other through a communications network. Amoco Chemicals currently has an IBM 360 Model 20 that is located in Chicago, Illinois, and is online with the Chicago center. An IBM 360 Model 30 is scheduled to replace the Model 20 during the early 1970s.

Prior to 1962, Amoco Chemicals was engaged almost exclusively in the manufacture and marketing of intermediate chemicals. The organization chart for that period showed a vice president—manufacturing and a vice president—marketing reporting to the president. In recent years the company has expanded into other product lines such as plastics and fabricated plastic products. This has been accomplished through a program of acquisition and internal expansion. As a result, changes in the organizational structure have taken place. Exhibit A presents the organization chart as of April 1, 1969. It

EXHIBIT A
Organization Chart
(April 1, 1969)

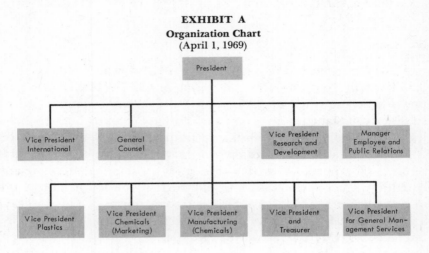

reflects one phase of the transition from a chemical company to a chemicals, plastics and plastics products company.

The position of vice president—plastics has primary responsibility for plastics, polymers (polypropylene, polystyrene and polyethylene) and fabricated products. As of April 1, 1969, the vice president—plastics had five members of management reporting to him:

President—Polymer Subsidiary
General manager—Fabricated Products
General manager—Commercial Development and Planning
Manager—Plastics Laboratory
Manager—Propellants Division

Information Services Department

The information services department at Amoco Chemicals was formed in October, 1967, by bringing together 22 individuals in Amoco's financial department, manufacturing department, and the parent company—Standard Oil Company (Indiana)—who had been working on computer applications of interest to Amoco. Additional staffing was accomplished by selective outside recruitment of experienced analysts and programmers. Exhibit B presents the organization

EXHIBIT B
Organization Chart
Information Services Department
(April 1, 1969)

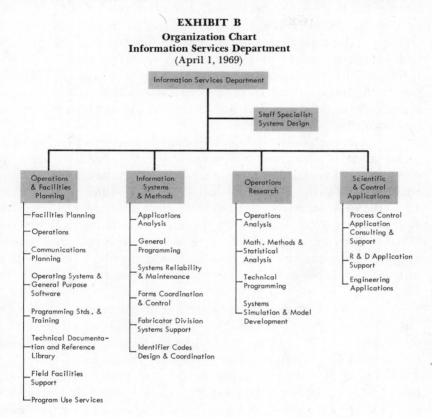

chart for the information services department. The manager—information services department reports to the vice president and treasurer.

Planning Study Project

On July 1, 1968, the Information Systems Planning Study was formally begun after being approved by Amoco's management committee. The resources requested by the information services department to cover the cost of the study were approved. Each major project recommended in the study was subsequently separately presented to the user department management for authorization of funds. In short, management is interested in and informed about the study, its objectives, risks, costs, and incentives.

The specific assignment of the study is to make a preliminary analysis of the operations and principal support, staff and administrative functions, and to draw initial conclusions concerning feasible information systems required to conduct these functions efficiently within the framework of corporate goals and policy. In addition, it is required that the study be fully coordinated and documented in final form on or before May 1, 1969.

The objective of the study is to provide for Amoco's management a statement of estimated incentives and costs associated with the development of computer-oriented information systems. Of necessity, these will be gross estimates because the time constraint does not allow the detailed study required to produce more refined estimates. Accuracy, per se, is not the critical issue in evaluating the estimates. What is needed is a measure of the ratio of incentives to costs, and an approximate measure of the resources which would have to be committed to information systems projects in order to achieve the benefits.

Management's immediate problem was one of determining how to allocate time and personnel so that Amoco maximized the likelihood that high-incentive applications will be found and confirmed during the study. This philosophy means allocating the major effort to those activities which directly impact profits and costs: sales, manufacturing, supply and transportation. In addition, there are activities in the "operating necessity" category—such as accounting—which inherently are focal points for the accumulation and dissemination of certain data. The study will include the information systems requirements of such activities.

The unique approach that Amoco took with this planning study reflects the realities and constraints associated with Amoco's rapid growth. Full-time participation in the study by user department key people was not feasible under existing conditions. On the other hand, the study would be worthless unless user department needs were properly identified and systems were designed which meet those needs. The way in which Amoco attempted to resolve this apparent conflict is explained in the following material.

Several organizations—e.g., international division; employee and public relations; legal department—were not specifically included in the planning study, although exploratory interviews were held with each organization. Information requirements of international division for its domestic offices will initially be covered by sales report extracts from chemicals marketing applications, and by other reports generated from the financial system. The foreign operations will be reviewed during the year ahead to determine what support and coordination of computing activities may be required. Employee and public relations needs are thought to be covered adequately for the present by the Standard Oil Employee Information System (EIS). No specific needs were identified in the legal department, although some interest was expressed in an information retrieval capability and a special-purpose simulation model. These leads will be pursued as time and user interest warrants.

As previously indicated, there are eight major study teams included in the overall planning study report. These study teams are (1) polymers, (2) chemicals, (3) financial, (4) supply and transportation, (5) fabricated products, (6) research and development and sales technical services, (7) economics, and (8) general engineering. Amoco's unique approach for handling the interface among these eight teams is explained in the following section.

Organizational Structure for the Study

Amoco's management committee established an Information Systems Coordination Group (ISCG) that would have overall responsibility for coordinating the company-wide study and for resolving problem areas. The ISCG was formed to represent user organization interests in the performance, progress and findings of the study. Each major department is represented on the ISCG by at least one member. Plastics division currently has three members; international has two. The manager—information services department serves as chairman, Information Systems Coordination Group.

ISCG members were the primary contacts in their respective organizations for study team analysts and assisted in steering analysts to key sources of information regarding detailed operations. They reviewed preliminary findings, evaluated the adequacy of proposed systems, and verified estimated benefits developed jointly by the study team and operating department personnel. For systems which cross departmental lines, ISCG representatives worked together to resolve questions affecting the departments involved. And finally, the ISCG members reviewed this report for accuracy, appropriateness and readability.

The general organizational structure within which the study was performed, coordinated and reviewed is shown in Exhibit C. Study

EXHIBIT C
Information Systems Planning Study
Study Team Structure

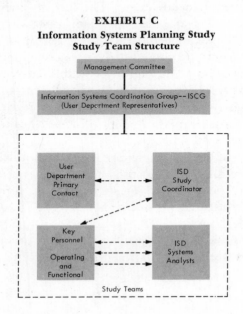

teams included people specifically assigned by user departments to contribute factual knowledge about their functions and to evaluate proposed alternative ways of supporting those functions via information flow. Systems analysts representing ISD were responsible for the fact-finding and initial analysis of information requirements leading to a preliminary body of documented systems proposals.

Composition of the study teams varied depending upon the functional area under investigation and the stage of the study. But in general, the skills represented within any given team included expertise in general business systems (order processing, finance and accounting), materials management (sales forecasting, inventory control, and production planning and scheduling), computer hardware facilities, and communications. User department personnel were chosen on the basis of their key positions within the operating and management structure of the respective organization.

The primary user groups provided the pertinent information to the ISD study team and developed information system requirements. They also determined if their requirements had been met in the conceptual design of the systems, and assisted the ISD study team in developing related economic justifications.

The ISD functions were to perform (with the assistance of the user group) a detailed analysis of the operations planning and decision-making functions at all levels of designated organizations, and to design systems which would support these functions and meet user group requirements.

Although the fact-finding begins in a given division or department, most systems of interest affect more than one department and must be defined in a way that recognizes the requirements of everyone concerned.

To avoid the confusion and duplication of effort that could arise if each study team covered every organization, a study team coordinator was assigned to each major organization.

The job of each coordinator was to keep the corresponding ISCG member informed regarding the status, progress and findings of the study team. He arranged initial briefings of the key departmental representatives, maintained liaison with other coordinators, arranged internal ISD reviews of interdepartmental systems developments and set up meetings with the ISCG representative and other user department personnel, and coordinated visits to outlying facilities.

Information Systems Principles

Like every company, Amoco Chemicals has an information system. It has served the company well. However, key operating department personnel are vocal in their demands for more timely, accurate information concerning the current status of orders, inventories, shipments and other aspects of the physical system. Likewise, management has requested improved systems for strategic planning, decision analysis and operations control, and a more efficient way to cope with the flood of data, paper work and internal coordination problems which accompany industrial growth.

As a matter of policy, information services department statements contain no reference to "total" or "integrated" management information systems. It is the view of the manager—ISD that such phrases tend to mislead the user groups and raise their expectations to unrealistic or impractical levels. As a result, the Planning Study Report does not consider or address the problem of building a *total* personnel-machine system encompassing every facet of Amoco's business. Rather, it is concerned with efficient manual and computer-oriented systems designed to support specific, profit-generating operations and essential control functions.

To emphasize the practical flavor of the study, the following working definition of an information system has been applied to each system proposed in the Planning Study Report: "An information system is any efficient arrangement of people, procedures, equipment and technology assembled for the purpose of providing the timely, reliable information required to manage an enterprise for profit."

Many factors influence the design and content of an information system which satisfies the above definition. Some of the more significant factors are:

Management's intermediate and long-range plans.

The organizational structure which the system must support.

Size and growth rate of the business.

Nature of the operations (integrated from raw materials through marketing; single phase; service only; etc.) .

Technical complexity of the business.

Geographic dispersion of the business.

Volume and size of transactions.

Time value of information flow.

Volume of information required to describe transactions, events or conditions.

These factors represent the major areas of investigation pursued by the ISD study team.

The Line of Profit Generation Concept

An adequately designed information system must distinguish between the changing organizational structure and the relatively stable operations mechanism inherent to the ongoing physical system of Amoco Chemicals Corporation. This underlying mechanism consists of many interlocking actions and events:

a. Products must be sold at a profit.

b. Raw materials must be purchased and transported to the plants.

    c. Manufactured products must be stored, packaged and shipped.

    d. Someone must administer inventories and costs, pay bills and invoice customers, pay the staff and the taxes.

This chain of logical events, beginning with a sale and ending with an invoice is, in the manager—information services department's terminology, *a Line of Profit Generation.*

This rather simple concept provides a rational starting point for system design and is fully consistent with the earlier definition of an information system. Once a Line of Profit Generation has been identified and analyzed, implementation can proceed by phases and produce subsystems which, upon completion, are immediately useful as stand alone components. Other system components can later be added under a priority sequence dictated by need without losing compatibility or system integrity.

Alternative Design Concepts

Alternatives to the Line of Profit Generation concept fall into two categories. One is the *nonsystem* or piecemeal application approach which limits the scope of work to generating a single report or set of reports. Such applications, viewed in perspective, tend to simulate exactly the procedures formerly carried out by clerks. Frequent manual intervention in the computer processing of such reports, with resulting vulnerability to error, is characteristic of this approach. And, finally, because user requirements and interests are seldom explored beyond the primary user level, such applications are subject to constant change in content and output and thus absorb excessive amounts of manpower for program modification and maintenance.

The second category contains information systems designed to support a single major department or division: for example, a manufacturing department information system. This approach is equivalent to the Line of Profit Generation concept *only* where the function of the department is self-contained. An example of a self-contained function is the engineering department. In day-to-day operations engineering is not affected by, nor does it directly affect, the processing of orders, product inventories, or shipments to customers.

This is not the case in activities such as sales, manufacturing, or supply and transportation. These are mainline operations, inter-locked in complex fashion. Any event, condition or transaction occurring in one mainline department creates a chain of interactions affecting operations in the other departments. As a result, efforts to define an information system for a single major department are usually self-defeating. The interactions among departments imply so many required in-and-out paths of information flow that it is impossible to know when the system is completely defined.

Exhibit D illustrates the Line of Profit Generation (LOPG)

EXHIBIT D

Information Systems Planning Study—Line of Profit Generation Concept

Product	Mainline Functions				Financial
	Sales	Manufacturing	Supply and Transportation	Other	
Polymers					P & L
					Tax
					Payroll
Chemicals					Invoicing
					Credit
Fabricated Products					Payables
					Property Accounting
Others					Control Budget
					General Ledger

concept in the context of information systems definition and development. Using polymers as an example, the analysis of information requirements to support management planning, control and evaluation of operations is accomplished by defining the sequence of events affecting polymers through all departments which have a direct impact on the physical system. In other words, the system requirements are defined in relation to the underlying mechanism which must operate as long as Amoco competes in the polymers business. As a result, LOPG systems reflect a corporate view of operations rather than a department view.

Note that information systems designed to support the physical system can readily provide reports and special studies using current operating data required to:

Analyze sales.
Manage inventories.
Schedule plants.
Trigger purchases of raw materials.
Operate the distribution system.
Forecast demands, production and material requirements.
Schedule preventive maintenance.
Gather data needed by the financial system and by other departments.

Systems designed under the Line of Profit Generation concept are capable of responding to the needs of operating departments for current information about the status of all sensitive phases of operation.

Designing the LOPG Information System

Accounting systems, being geared to month-end reports, are not designed to meet requirements for real-time information. Until quite recently, in fact, it was not possible to gather, edit, analyze and distribute operations data on a real-time basis. Consequently, large companies often pay the cost of maintaining two information systems. One is an accounting system which issues operations control reports describing the status of operations as of four to six weeks ago, and the other is a *sub rosa* manual system maintained within the individual operating departments in an effort to stay abreast of day-to-day events.

A prime characteristic of the LOPG concept is that the need for two systems is eliminated. Operating departments can capture and retrieve the information they need to schedule, flex and control current operations on whatever level of time response they can justify, and the financial people are relieved of the burden of clerical work to produce reports having nothing to do with their primary functional responsibility.

However, the financial department has a need for a certain accounting data which, while not of immediate interest to operations personnel, may easily be acquired in the plant or district sales office through an LOPG system. The systems design task is to recognize such requirements and satisfy them in the most efficient manner.

A fundamental principle of systems design is to develop a statement of requirements which is independent of the present means by which any requirement is met; and then proceed to examine all feasible alternative ways (including the existing way) by which each requirement *could* be met. This principle of uncoupling the statement of requirements from the means by which they are satisfied is applied in the design of LOPG systems and permits design alternatives to be subjected to cost/performance analysis.

To summarize, it is proposed to design and implement manual and computer-oriented systems which support specific product groups, or which meet the requirements of self-contained functions. Where desirable, appropriate linkage or interface capability between LOPG systems will be provided. LOPG systems lend themselves to implementation by phases so that useful system components can be installed without waiting for the entire system to be completed. These systems are complete within themselves, incorporating interfacing modules for data input, retrieval, analysis and output of operating data under whatever response-time requirement is justified.

REQUIRED:

1. From a conceptual standpoint, briefly indicate the advantages and disadvantages of the organizational approach that was followed for the planning study.
2. Compare and contrast the Line of Profit Generation (LOPG) concept with the information systems approach.
3. The organization chart (Exhibit A) indicates separate vice presidents of manufacturing and marketing for chemicals. There is one vice president—plastics who has five managers reporting to him. How may the conceptual arrangement of information flows be different between the chemicals and plastics divisions because of this organizational structure?
4. As indicated in the case, 11 companies have been acquired in the past three years. Several of these companies continue to operate with their former accounting and information systems; however,

they will soon begin to implement new systems as suggested by this planning study.

Most of these companies are under the vice president—plastics. All of the activities under the general manager—fabricated products are the results of these acquisitions. Some of the acquired companies are under the president—polymer subsidiary.

At the present time two large-scale planning and control *operating systems* are being planned, respectively, for fabricated products and polymers. After these planning and control operating systems become fully implemented, what types of informations systems developments do you envision for the plastics division?

CASE 4–2. NAUBERT-HAMBLIN CORPORATION

The management consulting firm with whom you are employed was engaged recently by Vance A. Williams, president of Naubert-Hamblin Corporation, to perform a high point review of the company's operations and to prepare a proposal for assisting the company in creating a management information system. The proposal shall set forth the specific steps that are required in planning, designing, and implementing this system, and the proposal shall be in sufficient detail so as to indicate the types of common data files that are encompassed in the supporting common data base.

The Company

The Naubert-Hamblin Corporation is a diversified manufacturing and distributing company with annual sales of $400 million. The 25 plants and operating divisions are clustered under three groups: (1) electronics, (2) high-quality tools, and (3) small electrical appliances. There are six manufacturing plants for the electronic components and assemblies group, eleven manufacturing plants for the high-quality tools group, and eight plants for the small electrical appliances group. Within the electronics and small electrical appliances group, there is little interaction among the divisions. Each of these operating divisions produced and marketed a line of products unrelated to those of the other divisions. However, within the high-quality tools group, there is considerable interaction among the divisions, and many of the scheduling and marketing decisions are made at the group headquarters.

The organizational structure for the Naubert-Hamblin Corporation has remained fairly constant over the past four years with the primary responsibility for managing the 25 divisions resting with the respective division presidents. The central corporate management has made the basic policy decisions, provided permanent capital for the divisions, determined salaries of division officers and approved capital expenditures and long-term financing.

Former Study of Control Budgeting and Reporting System

During your initial conference with Vance Williams, you are informed about an earlier study of the company's control budgeting and reporting operations which was conducted by the management services group with the certified public accounting firm that audits the Naubert-Hamblin Corporation. According to the consultant's final report, many changes were made in the detailed clerical, accounting, and data processing procedures required for the routine preparation of management reports. Some of the specific changes made are as follows:

1. Design of control reports that emphasize the controllability and behavior patterns of specific expenses
2. Establishment of a control reporting structure resembling a pyramid that provides detail information to lower levels of management while generating summary information for central corporate management
3. Inclusion of product price, volume, and programmed costs in the evaluation reports for the marketing organization
4. Development of predetermined product costs which are daily compared with actual product costs.

As you talk with management personnel at the division level, the earlier systems study is frequently criticized as a worthless effort from the division's perspective. It appears that many of the changes in the definition of "cost" were made by the management consultants for the benefit of the central corporate management. While the new system may provide relevant top management reports, most of the division managers were not satisfied with the information provided by this system. Moreover, most of the division managers stated that they were not asked to participate in the earlier systems study; they were told what changes they must make in their data accumulation system. The central corporate management issued a procedures manual that directed the specific changes to be made, and this set of changes was compatible with the consultant's report.

Upon closer examination you begin to discover that there is a small statistical group in each operating division which daily accumulates selected information for managing the day-to-day operations. This data accumulation system is not compatible with the information specifications for the centralized system.

Operating Systems

Computer-based systems are used throughout the company. Numerical control machines are employed in many of the plants within the electronics group and the high-quality tools group. Integrated inventory control and production control systems are now in existence at each of the twenty-five plants and operating divisions.

A large-scale, fourth generation computer system has recently been installed at the home office which was a replacement for a third generation system. Remote terminal facilities are rented from a national services group for some of the division managers. Other divisions have a small data processing room and transmit most of their jobs to the central computer center for processing. Other computer jobs are done at local service centers.

New Study

Vance Williams indicates that the company needs some assistance in more effectively using the computer-based systems which they already have and in expanding upon these systems. As previously indicated, you were specifically asked by Vance Williams to develop a *proposal* indicating how your firm can assist Naubert-Hamblin Corporation in planning, designing, and implementing a management information system including the supporting common data base.

REQUIRED:

1. How would you approach this assignment?
2. What are some of the key factors that you would consider in pursuing this engagement?
3. Explain in outline form the primary steps that you would follow in the *proposal*.

4. Briefly indicate some of the major information systems components that might be in operation within 36 months at the Naubert-Hamblin Corporation based on the facts in the case. Indicate the major constraints on the possible successful implementation of each of these components.

CHAPTER 5

Control, Security, and Management of Advanced Computer-Based Networks

FOUR COMMITTEE structures for planning and coordinating several computer-based networks in a large organization were discussed in the previous chapter, and this presentation emphasized management control procedures and administrative arrangements for effective operations. This examination followed an earlier analysis of the information systems function which included the physical control, technical control, and management control dimensions of the administrative process. While these administrative arrangements provide a supportive environment for planning and designing advanced computer-based networks, there are other internal control and security issues that must be addressed if these networks are to be maintained. These and other issues pertaining to the management of computer-based activities are considered in this chapter.

The current examination focuses on the multi-facets of control and security in advanced computer-based networks, and the discussion is presented in four parts. First, physical control as related to the computer center is discussed. Second, internal controls associated with personnel management are reviewed. Third, management control over computer-based activities is analyzed, and these activities include equipment controls, input and output controls, program controls, editing and screening system, and day file monitoring system. Fourth, security controls and confidential data arrangements are examined, and this latter analysis builds upon the detailed description of the four committee structures presented in Chapter 4.

141

PHYSICAL CONTROL OF COMPUTER CENTER

Members of management are responsible for the physical location of the computer center and should give ample attention to limiting those external factors that increase the risk of physical destruction to the center's facilities. Locating a computer center in the basement of a building can lead to innumerable problems. Besides the high risk of flood damage and the possibility of overflow sewage, the physical setting of the center makes it a likely target for temporary storage of items should a freak accident occur (such as a tanker springing a leak next to your building). In spite of the admonishments by consultants, members of management continue to locate computer centers in basements and continue to meet with disaster.

As an example, in 1972 a computer center was installed in the basement of the Playboy Building in Phoenix, Arizona, one of the dryer regions of the United States. An unexpected rainfall of less than two inches in a few hours brought a flood condition to major parts of Phoenix. The center of Phoenix is the low point of the valley, and this minimum amount of rain rushed toward the low point. Monitored by an agency of the United States government, the irrigation system had been close to the crest in order to provide an adequate supply of water for the dry valley and could not accept any of the rain water. In a few hours, the draining systems had removed all of the excess water from downtown Phoenix; however, in the interim the computer center was immersed.

Auxiliary equipment is frequently installed as a way of coping with such emergencies. However, location of a computer center in a basement continues to be like playing "Russian Roulette"; the auxiliary equipment adds more safety chambers to the weapon, but the "bullet of moisture" is always stored in one of the chambers.

There are many other instances of computer center destruction due to poor management planning. An organization with one of the larger time-sharing service facilities in the United States recently lost its computer center, which was located near the end of an airport runway. A jet aircraft crashed into the building and exploded; the resulting fire and water damage totally destroyed the computer center.

The computer center in another organization located near a metropolitan airport encountered "radar damage" to its magnetic files. In a third organization, the computer system would frequently cease operating and issue a diagnostic error message. The manufacturer's representative eventually discovered that a periodic extra pulse was being received from the municipal airport's radar system. Once the problem was identified, the solution was easy.

Large motors in a room adjacent to the computer center can create a magnetic field that will erase data stored on magnetic tapes. A central air conditioning and ventilation system can transfer smoke and hot gases from other parts of the building into the computer room; a computer center should always have its separate, auxiliary facilities for air conditioning and ventilation. While a check list is helpful, judgment applied to the specific case is required for optimal decision making.

Another dimension of physical control is the physical access to the computer room. Members of management must specify the rules for admission to the computer room, peripheral equipment rooms, and remote terminal areas; these critical decisions should not be delegated to subordinates. The military concept of "a need to know basis" should be rigorously applied to physical access to the computer center. Most employees do not have any reason, beyond idle curiosity, for being in the machine room. A monthly tour of the facilities can be arranged for purposes of employee morale; however, ample personnel should be on hand as protection against sabotage. Disgruntled employees have placed magnets in computer systems, poured liquids over electronic circuitry, and dropped materials into highly sensitive equipment. The loss from any one of these actions may be in the millions of dollars, and the disgruntled employee may be so emotionally disturbed as to be not legally responsible. The organization cannot afford not to have a "police state" in its computer room; strict compliance with management's rules of admission must be followed in the interest of protecting the organization's assets and resources.

A third dimension of physical control pertains to electrical engineering. There are variations in electrical current; there can be too few amperes or too many amperes. Special monitoring equipment is needed for protection against either of these extreme conditions which can damage or alter electronic circuitry. Where such monitoring equipment does not exist, a power variation may have destroyed online data, programs, and files without any notation being made of this event. It may be days before the problem is discovered. Another aspect of this dimension is a power failure. Some organizations have auxiliary equipment for use during such emergencies.

Other dimensions of physical control relate to management's plans for coping with crises. Fire, explosion, sabotage, bombings, floods, tornadoes, cyclones, earthquakes, and tidal waves have destroyed computer centers, and many of these crises are feasible events that might occur in a given organization. Therefore, members of management must plan how to respond to each of the feasible crises, and they should specify guidance for administering activities during the recovery and restart period. An important aspect of the recovery and restart program is the identification of back up facilities; the latter should be with several organizations including some which are not subject to the same, concurrent risk of natural disasters.

Participation by management in developing a plan for coping with a crisis is the critical issue. Once a problem area has been identified, the intellectual capabilities of individuals are such that appropriate strategies will generally be developed for safeguarding assets and minimizing losses. Getting a representative group of management to consider these situations is the major factor.

· INTERNAL CONTROLS IN PERSONNEL MANAGEMENT

The risk of loss in an organization with an advanced computer-based network has expanded proportionally with each step-increase in complexity. The risk, from employees, has not been fully appreciated, unfortunately, by members of management, probably because of the rate at which technological changes have occurred in the information systems area. If it were appreciated, then members of management would apply screening procedures to the hiring of personnel and would require the bonding of computer center personnel located in sensitive positions.

A cashier handles assets which have a high degree of liquidity. Because of the easy exchange nature of the assets, most cashiers are screened, investigated, and bonded. It is rare to have an organization in which an unbonded cashier handles a few thousand dollars in a day. The owner-manager serving as a cashier is about the only exception.

On the other hand, a computer center employee may have physical access to more organizational assets than does a cashier. Since the assets handled by the computer center employee typically require some effort to convert them into a liquid state, the organization's management places constraints over these conversion operations and frequently assumes the risk for such actions. Very few directors of computer centers are currently bonded. As of 1975, it is unusual to require that key employees in the computer center in sensitive positions should be bonded. In fact, security checks are frequently not run on prospective employees.

In many organizations a strong case can be made that the risk of loss from illegal activities by computer center employees is greater than that for cashiers. As the complexity of the computer-based network expands, the risk of loss is increased proportionally. While a cashier's bond in the tens-of-thousands to a few hundreds-of-thousands of dollars is an adequate range, the risk for computer center personnel is usually in the millions of dollars. Not only is a substantial bonding arrangement required, but, more importantly, a rigorous screening procedure should be followed for *all* prospective employees for the computer center.

We have some experience in working with a few organizations after they had a significant embezzlement. Generalizing from this experience, we believe that routine security checks of potential employees would have resulted in the rejection of many of these individuals before they had a chance to commit their crimes. In the subsequent legal prosecution of these individuals, it became apparent that in some cases the members of management in the hiring organization were about the only personnel recruiters in the geographical area who were not aware of the candidate's past and record. Some individuals had been fired from their previous position because of questionable practices. A few individuals had been employed by a series of organizations all within the previous twelve months without stable employment with any organization. If those employees with a record combined with those employees who had been fired because of questionable practices coupled with employees with unstable employment patterns had been eliminated from employment, then the set of employees who were legally guilty of embezzlment would not have been employed by those organizations. Of course, embezzlements might have then occurred by a different profile group.

An especially disturbing observation in a few organizations in which there had been an embezzlement was the strong loyalty of computer center employees to each other. From actual experience, this loyalty was stronger to each other than to the employer. Some computer center employees, for example, observed the theft of the employer's assets without expressing any comment or taking any action. It is hoped that the apparent value systems of these employees are a minority. If this is the case, then a rigorous interviewing, screening, and investigating procedure for personnel would probably have identified such attributes and characteristics before these individuals were employed.

It is important for members of management to remember that new employees in the computer center are exposed to many organization assets beginning with the first day of their employment. In many departments, a "wait and see" approach is taken with new employees as they perform their initial assignments; this approach is inappropriate with computer center personnel because of the risk involved.

Screening, investigating, and bonding are three parts of the internal controls in personnel management. Other controls include segregation of duties, rotation of duties, and mandatory vacations. Do not permit a programmer to also work as an operator, or an operator to also work as a programmer. The tasks assigned to each class of employees should be rotated among individuals within that class; this guards against excessive familiarization with a limited number of programs and operations. The act of rotation also introduces uncertainty as to who will be processing activities on a given day; it also exposes additional employees to detailed operations in the hopes that any unusual features will be called to the attention of management. The requirement of mandatory vacations provides an exposure period in which unusual features may emerge without selective employees being present to explain these operations.

Each shift of personnel in the computer center should include one bonded individual who understands the internal control system in operation and is responsible for all facets of security. The manager of operations for each shift should also be periodically rotated because of considerations of internal control. If we can generalize from the past experience, after 10:00 PM in the evening and the weekends are vulnerable periods during which unusual events are processed; of course, the next embezzlement may occur during the peak of the day shift when there is maximum exposure to the situation. Moreover, the manager of operations during the shift is not just responsible for security, but is also responsible for the equipment. If something goes wrong with the computer or with peripheral equipment, service representatives are immediately contacted. Any delay in contacting the service representative (such as has occurred in some large organizations over a weekend) may result in a multi-million dollar loss of assets as well as an opportunity loss because there will be no "free" computer time during the coming weeks for experimentation. The recovery and restart requirements for the system are such, in the latter case, that all unscheduled time is used in getting the system online and up-to-date.

The four committee structures were discussed in the previous chapter. One of these—the data management committee—is responsible for reviewing the internal operations of the computer center and the assignment of tasks among employees. There should be a periodic security review of all key computer center employees in sensitive positions, and this committee should examine this confidential report on these employees. The active participation by interdepartmental members on the data management committee is an important part of the program of internal control as related to personnel management; other aspects of this issue are briefly summarized in the last part of this chapter in the discussion of security controls and confidential data arrangements.

MANAGEMENT CONTROLS OVER COMPUTER-BASED ACTIVITIES

Physical control and technical control procedures are incorporated in hardware, software, firmware, and transmission and communication facilities. These control procedures encompass all types of reading, processing, calculating, assigning, sorting, reporting, and transmitting operations, and they serve as the base for an overall program of internal control. The procedures represented by this base can be classified as equipment controls, input and output controls, and program controls; standard arrangements for these three types of basic controls are discussed before examining higher levels of control procedures which require participation by members of management.

Basic Controls

Each manufacturer of computers, processing equipment, and transmitting facilities includes within the unit's internal logic a series of control procedures. These built-in procedures are highly operational in nature, and they monitor the data reading, data handling, data movement, and data storage operations. The most widely used of these procedures is the *parity check,* which is a built-in method of checking the validity of the binary representation of characters—numeric, alphabetic, and alphameric characters.

In a binary system, a binary indication can be either a "0 bit" or a "1 bit," and each alphameric character is represented by a different combination of bits. There is an automatic checking for parity as the equipment is processing a character of data, and this mehod examines the summation of the "1 bits" used to represent each character. Some equipment has the rule that an even number of 1 bits must always be used to represent each character; other equipment follows the specification of an odd number of 1 bits. In either case, the binary representation of typical alphameric characters includes both types. Therefore, a *check bit* must be included within each code so the desired state—either an even number or an odd number of 1 bits—can be rigorously followed.

It should be remembered that each time a character is read, processed, moved, or stored, the internal logic of the machine or equipment performs a parity check. For example, a particle of dust on a magnetic tape will be located through the diagnostic from the parity check. As more sophisticated equipment is used, there are dual heads in the unit so that the tape (for example) passes first over the write head and then over the read head; thus, all recorded data are checked for parity after they are written. These dual operations with each character of data increase the confidence in the data processing activities.

While the "write and read" dual heads are optional features of equipment, other types of dual activities are standard features. Input equipment has the reading of each character at two stations and a comparison is made of this; the control feature represented by this concurrent operation is called the *dual-reading validity check.* In a communication system when data are transmitted from one location to another, there is usually an *echo check;* the data received are returned to the point of input and compared with the original data.

Actually, the parity check on magnetic tape data is a two-dimensional comparison—a vertical check and a longitudinal check. The vertical check is made of each column of notations; the longitudinal record check is made of each track. (Seven-track records and nine-track records are the two popular arrangements of magnetic tape data for large-scale computer systems.) Concurrently with the performance of the longitudinal record check, the internal logic in the equipment is usually programmed to accumulate the number of records read. In some systems these latter totals are compared with control totals stored on magnetic tape trailer labels; other systems merely print these totals as an internal control procedure.

While equipment controls are standard, input and output controls and program controls are created in the systems design process; therefore, the latter two types of basic controls vary among installations. In a batch system, control totals are developed for each set of inputs, and these batch controls are compared with the respective totals for the data converted into machine-readable form and temporarily accepted into the system. The batch control procedures are also followed where the machine directly reads the source document (such as, magnetic-ink character recognition, mark sensing, and optical character recognition). In these cases the batch control totals may be developed by dual (or triple) preliminary reading of inputs, then comparing the respective control totals and obtaining agreement on each set before the data are moved into the formal processing stage.

Transaction counts, batch controls, and hash totals are the common types of control procedures over inputs. In a more sophisticated network these controls are supplemented by a rigorous editing and screening of inputs, and these filtering arrangements are examined subsequently in this chapter.

The electronic nature of computer equipment permits a high degree of operational reliability to be achieved through a variety of program controls that are stored online in the network. The first set of program controls is the edit routines used for further screening of input data to determine incomplete, unreasonable, or inaccurate data, and these edit screens include sequence checks, limit checks, historical comparisons, field checks, blank transmission tests, logical relationship comparisons, validity checks, and self-checking numbers.[1] Other sets of program controls focus on the operations of the machine room, and these online procedures detect equipment mal-

---

[1] A detailed description of each of these standard controls is presented in several introductory books on data processing; see, for example, C. Orville Elliott and Robert S. Wasley, *Business Information Processing Systems: An Introduction to Data Processing*, 4th ed. (Homewood, Illinois: Richard D. Irwin, Inc., 1975).

functions, operator errors, updating of master file controls, and output validity checks. These latter online procedures provide limits over the scope of the duties that can be performed by an individual, and the system automatically prepares an internal control message when a limit is exceeded or if a prescribed procedure is not followed.

The equipment controls discussed in the first part of this section are built-in procedures and dual arrangements that significantly increase the confidence in data processing operations over what can be achieved in a manual system. The input and output controls and program controls are designed at the installation; therefore, it is imperative that these procedures are described, documented, and subjected to an internal review by noncomputer center personnel. The latter review function should be performed initially by each interdepartmental study team that plans, designs, implements, and documents a computer-based application.

While these basic controls—equipment controls, input and output controls, and program controls—increase an individual's confidence in the data processing activities, these procedures are not designed to provide security. If management control is to be achieved, then members of management must participate in planning and designing the computer-based networks. Through this participation, members of management have the opportunity of incorporating in these networks appropriate controls for protecting assets and resources and for monitoring performance and utilization of resources in pursuit of organizational objectives. In this section we will examine two dimensions of these latter controls: (*a*) editing and screening system and (*b*) day file monitoring system.

Editing and Screening System

The editing and screening process is an important set of computer programs that filter all input data for a computer-based network, and as this set of programs expands in scope and increases in complexity, a higher level of integration is achieved in the editing system. We will examine both levels of filtering. Figure 5.1 presents a general model of the editing and screening process in a computer-based network. In this model we see that this filtering process contains two flows. Those inputs that are successful in passing through the "screen" are forwarded to a subsequent location where these data are reprocessed and sorted. Those data inputs that are rejected by the

FIGURE 5.1
Editing and Screening Process in a Computer-Based Network

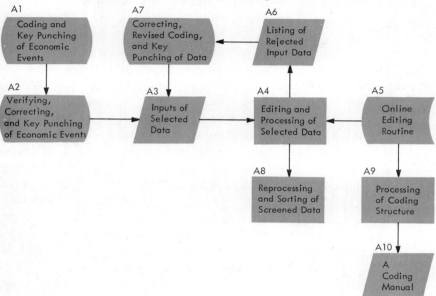

screen are returned to another station where they are corrected and recoded before being resubmitted as data inputs.

The mere existence of a filtering process or an edit routine indicates a high level of stability in the computer-based network. Specifically, the screen in the edit routine is based upon a prescribed coding of various combinations of data inputs to the system. Each document for a particular product, service, employee, account, or type of event will have a specified format for the descriptive data on that document, and the screen will test that the actual data are compatible with the specified format.

Symbol A4 represents the online screening which occurs for all data inputs; there is, of course, a set of online computer programs (symbol A5) that contains the detailed logic of the checks, comparisons, and relationships which are to be tested in the editing routine. This set of online computer programs (symbol A5) has the capability of being updated without significantly restricting the coding structure. A standard editing or sorting program can be used for reading (symbol A9) the online editing routine (symbol A5) and preparing a logical listing of the coding structure in the form of a manual (symbol A10). Some systems have the coding manual (symbol A10) stored online in the network, and this arrangement permits a remote terminal user to inquire of the system as to the current coding structure for a specific type of document or event. Regardless of whether the manual is stored online or must be printed, these arrangements permit the overall coding structure and edit routine to respond to a dynamic setting.

In one company the edit routine contains 45 digits of data, exclusive of dollar amounts. The specified format of these 45 digits of data varies not only by document—such as sales invoice versus a purchase order—but also by the product or service that is being purchased or sold. In other words, the unique characteristics of each type of product are encompassed in the prescribed 45 digits used in coding this event. The design of this edit routine required more than three man-years of effort; currently, there are monthly meetings of the code structure identification and maintenance committee that is responsible for updating and administering this structure.

From these comments, we can see that the edit routine cannot be established until after the team of systems analysts has completed its study of the types of documents, types of transactions, levels of organizational specification, measures of performance, and types of accounting records which are to be handled by the network. After this study has been completed, then the proposed screen can be programmed. The general ledger chart of accounts and the organizational chart of positions tend to be the backbones of the edit routine or the code structure.

The editing and screening process depicted by Figure 5.1 is a batch processing operation; within this model there were no interactive capabilities shown for remote terminal users. There are time delays between each step in the editing and screening process: coding, verifying, inputting, editing, listing of rejects, and correcting of input data. The network does not contain any "learning features" for users, such as an immediate identification that a certain type of key punching error or coding error has occurred and a requirement for corrective action.

Figure 5.2 is a model of the editing and screening system in an advanced computer-based network, and this model incorporates both interactive capabilities and learning features. The three remote

FIGURE 5.2
Editing and Screening System in an Advanced Computer-Based Network

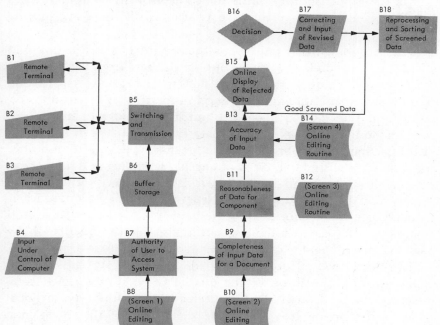

terminals (symbols B1, B2 and B3) are supported by auxiliary equipment for switching and transmission (symbol B5) which has buffer storage (symbol B6). When a remote terminal through the auxiliary equipment is online with the computer, the first screen of online editing (symbol B8) is applied to the checking of the remote terminal operator's authority to access the system (symbol B7). A key punching error or coding error will result in rejected data from the first screen, and the diagnostic response will follow the reverse arrows and flow from symbol B7 to a remote terminal (symbol B1, B2 or B3). This timely response to the remote terminal operator informs the individual of the error, and the overall network provides the opportunity for additional input of data and a learning experience.

In Figure 5.2 the first three screens (symbols B7, B9 and B11) all show a dual flow of data; thus, any key punching error or coding error that is identified by the first three sets of online editing

routines is interactive with the remote terminal operator. The operator of the input facilities under the control of the computer (symbol B4) is also in an interactive relation with the three editing
screens.

The processing of the online programs in the first screen (symbols
B7 and B8) attempts to keep unauthorized users from having access
to the system. There is frequently a dual specification—identification
of user and organizational designation of location. The second processing and filtering (symbols B9 and B10) represent an overall
comparison for the block of input data for a given type of document
or transaction with an online pattern for that type. This second filter
contains three distinctive types of checks: field checks, blank transmission checks, and sign checks. Input data that successfully pass the
second filter have the appropriate types of alphabetic, numeric, or
alphameric characters in each of the fields required for that overall
document; the second filter says nothing about the quality of the
data within each field.

The third level of filtering (symbols B11 and B12) attempts to
cope with one dimension of the quality of data issue. Each component of input data within the specified block (the type of document or transaction may determine the length of the block in a
variable field length system) is subjected to limit checks, validity
checks (for example, the appropriate general ledger and subsidiary
ledger accounts are used for the type of transaction contained on the
document), and logical relationship comparisons. As an internal
control procedure, there is usually an error listing made of all limit
rejects, and these limit check rejects are reviewed daily.

The validity checks incorporated in this third filter require an
exhaustive classification of all types of transactions, events, products,
services, employees, organizational positions, operations, functions,
and activities. The development of this multi-dimensional classification system is a major time-consuming effort; many organizations
have devoted two to five work-years of effort in merely planning and
designing this thorough classification system.

The fourth level of filters operates in a much more sophisticated
framework than that present in the first three levels, and the diagnostics from the fourth filter are intentionally not interactive with
the remote terminal operator. Instead, there is a controller for the
network (symbol B16) who monitors rejects from the fourth screen
(symbol B15) and who may take corrective action (symbol B17) so

the transaction progresses to the reprocessing and sorting stage in the computer network.

This more sophisticated level of editing is accomplished by having a refined set of programmed rules that perform a validity check in which there are also *decision criteria that can be modified.* This refined screen is used for internal control purposes and for testing for accuracy of input data. Typically, the fourth filter is not equally applicable to all types of transactions; instead, the filter will frequently relate to disbursement and regular revenue transactions.

In one organization the fourth filter is restricted to disbursement transactions and a controller monitors all disbursements over $4,949. The limit check (in the third filter) on a disbursement in this organization is $20,000. The controller performs a review function of the displayed disbursements (symbol B15) and administers the timing of payments from the standpoint of cash management. Depending on the economic situation, the criteria employed by the controller (such as disbursements of more than $4,949) can be quickly adjusted in the online programmed decision rules without stopping the online operations.

The four filters in Figure 5.2 (symbols B7, B9, B11, and B13) are depicted as being online within the computer system. Recent advancements in input equipment and switching and transmission facilities permit these screens and filters to be performed on auxiliary equipment; therefore, where this equipment has been installed there is instantaneous interaction between the operators and the filters.

In subsequent chapters we will examine a series of advanced computer-based networks, and the models for each of these networks will contain an *editing and screening phase.* The operation of this latter phase in the model will be identical with the four filters depicted by Figure 5.2. In some models of advanced information systems, a team of analysts interact with the fourth filter and monitor exceptional data on the environment.

Day File Monitoring System

The central processor in a third generation large-scale computing system or in a fourth generation large-scale computing system operates at extremely fast speeds in a microscopic part of a second. Computer access to memory has shifted from being expressed in microseconds to nanoseconds, and further reductions in time required for access is anticipated. For example, one machine manufacturer's research laboratory has an electronic switch which can operate at a speed of about ten-trillionths of a second.

Even before the central processor's access was expressed in nanoseconds, computer scientists realized that the central processor can operate faster if it randomly selects among operations at each queue rather than follows a set of programmed instructions. In other words, if there were two programs in the queue, the computer can randomly process both programs (assuming that neither program will require several minutes of central processing time) in less time than it can rigorously apply priority status to only one program. Because of this feature or characteristic of a central processor, where there is a priority system that is rigorously followed, the usual procedure is to abort all programs in the queue except the one having priority, and then to randomly process that computer program in minimum time.

The concept that the computer can *randomly process* faster than it can effectively *process by a set of programmed rules* brought about the need for a record of what the computer had accomplished. To compute under a time-sharing arrangement and switching of core with an array of software and peripherals being used, a mapping of operations was required. For almost a decade, it has been common practice for the computer in a large-scale system to take a "picture" of its internal core and operations every one-hundredth of a second. A printout of these status pictures is helpful in reestablishing the system whenever there is a failure.

There are usually three stages to this picture-taking process. First, a copy of the current status of computer operations at the specified point in time is made in the online core. Second, the data in the online core are transferred to storage on magnetic tape or magnetic drum. Third, a printout occurs daily of these data on status. This overall three stage process is usually referred to as a *day file.*

Copies of each of these three stages are maintained for several periods, depending on the stage and the storage location. Every few hours, the old data in the online core are deleted. Status data for each one-hundredth of a second (per the second stage) are usually maintained for a period of 8 to 10 days on magnetic tape. Printouts of the third stage are usually maintained for a period of 12 to 15 months.

The third stage is usually more informative than merely status pictures. Summaries are prepared while the data are in machine-readable form, and these may include hourly and daily recapitulations of computer program charges by identification number or computer charge number.

The day file monitoring system can be used by members of management in providing levels of security to the online operations. All computer access to confidential data can be summarizd and included in the hourly and daily recapitulations in the day file. For example, some confidential data are in a restricted online status that permits *selected* individuals to have access to *only read* these data. If desired, job card and identification codes for each program which has read these data can be included in a special hourly and daily summary location that is part of an expanded day file.

Where a higher level of security is desired, the day file can reproduce the complete set of operations for each computer program which reads confidential data. This latter task is a simple routine while the data are in machine-readable form (within the 8 to 10 days that the data are maintained on magnetic tape). It is a sorting of data and a retrieving of only those snap shots of programs which use selected confidential data.

Since the day file is a computer-generated record that is internal to the equipment and is not subjected to even machine-operator intervention, this file has special appeal in a court of law. Day files have been used to prosecute computer center employees who were unaware that their illegal activities were being monitored. We have used day files to "refresh the memories" of managers in other legal cases with surprising results; thus far each individual has changed his or her plea to "guilty." While these results are interesting, the main point is legal preference for using a day file in prosecution proceedings.

SECURITY CONTROLS AND CONFIDENTIAL DATA ARRANGEMENTS

In the previous parts of this chapter, we have examined many control procedures associated with computer operations and computer-based networks. Our confidence in the data processing activities was increased because of the built-in equipment controls, input and output controls, and program controls that are typically designed into the applications. We saw that the filters in the editing and screening systems can be used in restricting access to the computer system and that the day file monitoring system can be used for levels of control over access and use of confidential data. We also examined issues in personnel management and physical control of the computer center which could be resolved by other control procedures.

But, throughout the previous discussion, two issues repeatedly came to the surface: (*a*) the need for members of management to actively participate in planning, designing, implementing, and maintaining control procedures and (*b*) the need for an overall program of internal control that incorporates individual procedures into a complete plan. Alternatively, we can state that a standing committee on security is required with interdepartmental representation.

In organizations with advanced computer-based networks, this standing committee on security will be divided into two units, as discussed in Chapter 4: the data management committee and the confidentiality of data committee. The exact separation of duties between these two committees in the area of security varies somewhat by the personalities of the respective committee members; however, in general, there is a higher level of management represented on the confidentiality of data committee than on the data management committee. Higher level security issues are usually assigned to the confidentiality of data committee, and the subsequent discussion of duties performed by each of these committees is presented from the perspective of the "typical case."

The data management committee really serves as a permanent internal review committee that examines the organizational structure of the computer center, the staffing of personnel, the separation of responsibilities, the assignment of duties, the rotation of personnel, vacation practices, the documentation of applications and packages, the disaster plan, the back up arrangements, the maintenance of grandfather, father, and son data tapes for reestablishing the system, and other internal control procedures. Where the review of activities indicates a problem area, the committee will take approprite corrective action.

The confidentiality of data committee monitors a program of security in which change is efficiently introduced into the system at irregular intervals, and this program represents a blending together of a series of control procedures. Physical access to the computer room is monitored through using special identification cards. Computer access is limited by requiring user identification numbers. A librarian maintains a log of the details on each item issued, and the librarian requires an identification card and signature of the individual requesting a magnetic tape reel or a disk pack before issuing the item. Passwords are used to restrict access to online data files and to larger, online data banks, and this same type of security is achieved with data stored on magnetic tapes by using label control procedures that follow the header label. The security features of the day file monitoring system are reviewed and monitored by members of the confidentiality of data committee.

The most important control feature in this overall program of security is having members of management serve on the confidentiality of data committee and actively participate in internal reviews. These individuals not only bring their organizational status to the committee, but also their insights and their abilities to resolve complex issues. The speed at which this group of management can operate in the area of implementation of security is overwhelming.

TOPICS FOR CLASS DISCUSSION

1. The irregular introduction of change into a computer-based network is essential for a high level of security; however, the dissemination of the change is a problem. Because of security considerations, a written notification of a change in passwords or identification numbers should never be followed. The members of the confidentiality of data committee have the responsibility of planning an efficient network for this verbal notification. Drawing upon the organization theory literature, indicate administrative techniques that can be used in this verbal notification process.

2. The manager of the computer center at the Edgar Manufacturing Company purchased and installed an accounts receivable and invoicing package. Fifteen months later, there has been a tremendous build up in the balance of accounts receivable, and this change is the subject of a special study by the external professional accountants.

Many customers indicated on their confirmation forms for accounts receivable balances which had been sent to them by the external auditors that the Edgar Manufacturing Company's balance did not reflect certain adjustments and partial payments. Further examination by the external auditors revealed that the particular package installed has a special feature of only carrying forward the revised balance of the account. The package does not maintain in the online system any data on individual invoices, partial payments, or returned shipments.

In reflecting on this series of events, could an individual have predicted that the installation of this package would have resulted in a significant build up in the accounts receivable balance? Is there any organization (outside of a governmental agency) that can force other organizations to pay a bill without giving all the details of charges, adjustments, returns, and payments? What effect does this billing procedure have on the environment and the relations with customers? What committee within Edgar Manufacturing Company should be responsible for reviewing all packages before they are acquired? Explain the review process that the latter committee should have performed.

3. Any time a control procedure is programmed into the logic of an application, package, or process, there is the implicit assumption that members of management desire any deviation revealed by this control procedure to be investigated; otherwise, there is no logical reason for including the procedure. It is inevitable that a power reduction, equipment malfunction, or some other unusual event will occur that will cause a significant variance between some accumulated measure and a standard. Individuals assigned to the investigation of these variances become frustrated when the repeated cause of the deviation is attributed to a nonhuman origin. In some of the latter situations, the overriding problem is one of imbalance between the precision of the control procedure and the level of the activity. For example, electronic equipment will measure a power reduction of a one-thousandth of a second duration, and while this statistic may be important in the operation of the computer, it is not important in the operation of a remote terminal.

The data management committee has the responsibility for reviewing and approving each control procedure. In considering a proposed procedure, attention has to be given to the level and the time cycle in which it is to operate. Prepare a statement for the data management committee that indicates relevant time cycles for control procedures in the following areas: (*a*) computer operations, (*b*) program operations, (*c*) peripheral equipment operations, and (*d*) remote terminal operations.

4. The data management committee has the usual responsibility of priority setting, and in this role the committee must consider

many alternatives in which there are gray areas. What are the relevant criteria for determining when to schedule a major update of an application? If there is an announced change in technology, should an application using current procedures and scheduled for update be deferred until the new technology is operational and available? When should an application be purchased instead of being developed by the information systems department? Each of these questions has led some individuals to the conclusion that there are no absolute answers on priority setting for the data management committee. Do you agree? Explain your position.

5. In managing data processing operations, there are many issues related to standardization of symbols, notations, options, and features. At some point the considerations of standardization overlap with the responsibilities of the data management committee. In your opinion, where is this overlap? Explain your position.

6. Explain how the activities of the code structure identification and maintenance committee are directly related to the online editing routines. In your answer use the symbols in Figure 5.2 as a point of reference.

7. Indicate procedures that can be followed to minimize the loss of organizational assets from fire and sabotage. In your answer give particular attention to back-up considerations, restart arrangements, and procedures for reestablishing the system.

8. What is the argument for bonding computer center employees who have sensitive positions? Indicate the criteria you would follow in determining which employees should be bonded.

9. The data management committee has the responsibility of performing a confidential review of computer center employees in sensitive positions. To what extent can this confidential review be performed without being an invasion of privacy of the individuals involved? Explain the issues involved.

10. Indicate typical equipment controls and explain how each control procedure operates.

11. Explain the operation of the day file monitoring system.

CASE 5–1. UNIVERSITY HOSPITAL

University Hospital was selected as one of the twelve demonstration sites for evaluating physician's reactions to the use of online medical diagnostic computer programs. University Hospital is a 650-bed general medical hospital located in a metropolitan area of five million population. There are several other general medical hospitals, specialized hospitals, clinics, and nursing homes which provide health care for this population area.

The set of medical diagnostic computer programs was developed in several research laboratories with significant financial support from the U.S. Department of Public Health. These computer programs include multiphasic screening, hypercalcemia, electrolyte, and acid-base applications.

A total service contract was established with Metropolian Computing Service to provide computer services, time-sharing capabilities, remote terminals, and data communication networks as well as support services. As part of this contract, remote terminals were placed in selected physicians' offices, the physicians' lounge at University Hospital, specific locations in the hospital wards, and selected consultation rooms.

A U.S. Department of Public Health grant was awarded to University Hospital for purposes of establishing, demonstrating, and evaluating physician's reactions to the use of online medical diagnostic computer programs. The grant included funds for the contract with Metropolitan Computing Service to provide the total services outlined above. University Hospital was also to establish an evaluation team that would perform an in-depth analysis of the demonstration activities.

The evaluation team developed a research design that included the accumulation of utilization statistics by computer program, by day of week, and by time of day. Each utilization episode was stored as a unique event in the computer-based system. The details of each medical evaluation were not stored in the computer-based system; instead, cathode ray tube displayed the results, and there were four of these printers at University Hospital located in four convenient areas. The absence of any stored patient medical data eliminated most of the confidentiality of data problems from this overall installation. A minimum security was established using two passwords. After these two passwords had been entered at any remote terminal, then the set of diagnostic programs was in an online position for immediate use. It was hoped that this simple arrangement would facilitate the use of these computer programs by physicians.

During the first three months of this project, all remote terminals were installed, educational seminars were conducted, and over 120 physicians began to interact with the set of diagnostic programs in an online mode. In the fourth and fifth months, other physicians (primarily participating in medical training programs at University Hospital) began also to utilize these remote terminal capabilities. As the number of remote terminal users increased, there was a respective increase in the response time for each computer instruction. *It was anticipated that each physician would experience a rather sharp learning curve with each computer program;* as the physician gained experience in using a computer program, the computer-time required would decrease sharply.

By the seventh and eighth months of the project, some of the novelty aspects of the online computer programs were gone. At this point, the physicians utilized the terminals on an as-required basis. Some physicians did not utilize the programs on a regular basis; other physicians made extensive use of the remote terminal facilities. Some of the latter physicians began complaining to the administrator of University Hospital about the slow response time. As the response time increased, some physicians ceased using the online computer programs.

The administrator of University Hospital asked the project evaluation team to analyze the complaints and problems reported by the physicians in using these time-sharing facilities. As part of this assignment, the evaluation team began to analyze each episode of experience with each computer program. From the experience data accumulated, it appeared as though the "learning curve" approach was not applicable.

As previously indicated, a minimum security was established over access to the system since medical patient-data were not stored online. There were two passwords (which were periodically changed) which had to be entered within thirty seconds in order to secure access to the system. The remote terminal user did not have to use her name or physician number.

The overall objective was to have a very simple system with two passwords and, beyond that, an online tutorial was available to lead the user in accessing any computer program. The tutorial was optional at various points in the computer routines. This arrangement was so complete that it could lead a physician through each step of a routine medical analysis. Some of the computer programs contained ranges within which input data on a patient must fall. If the patient's data were outside the acceptable norms, the computer program would question the input data (as to error in input or decimal point) . For example, one of the questions asked the physician when the patient's data were beyond four standard deviations from "normal" was: "Is the patient alive?"

The absence of any job card by physician meant that the utilization experience stored in the computer system was not subject to any "learning curve" analysis by physician. Therefore, the evaluation team shifted its approach to online monitoring of the actual experience of a physician with a program. A remote terminal was installed in the evaluation team's office, and a special control arrangement was established at the Metropolitan Computing Service which permitted this special remote terminal to have the capability of monitoring other remote terminals. The evaluation team began to monitor the online use of the computer programs.

Each of the medical diagnostic programs has four parts. In the first part, a series of questions assist the remote terminal user in specifying the medical diagnostic program and options that are to be used in the current diagnostic. In the second part, pertinent patient profile information and other patient history data are inputted by the remote terminal user. Special data for the medical diagnostic application are systematically requested in the third part of the program; these data include laboratory and medical recordings of the patient. The fourth part contains evaluation types of responses to an overall series of individual diagnostics encompassed in the third part of the program.

Deep within the third part of the program, the most critical patient recordings also require the entering of the three initials of the individual performing the analysis. Typically, these three initials would be those of the physician who is also operating as the remote terminal user. This feature of recording three initials was incorporated in this general-purpose medical-diagnostic program by the research laboratory developing this application for control purposes within the laboratory setting.

The online monitoring of the set of medical diagnostic programs revealed the inclusion of these physician's initials within these applications. University Hospital's evaluation team developed a small computer program that accumulated utilization experience by each set of physician initials. As the utilization experience by physician was accumulated, this was cross-referenced to the complete name and number of the physician at University Hospital.

The cross-referencing of initials to physician name and number resulted in several unidentified sets of initials. Further study indicated that these initials pertained to physicians at other hospitals in the metropolitan area. Subsequently, it was determined that a sales manager for Metropolitan Computing Service had entered into a private, unauthorized arrangement with physicians at another hospital to permit them to utilize this same set of medical diagnostic programs. This latter set of physicians was experiencing their "learning curve" during the seventh, eighth and ninth months of the project, and the computer demands of this group were responsible for the lack of improvement in response time by remote terminal users at University Hospital.

The level of services provided by Metropolitan Computing Service to University Hospital during this period when the services were being shared by unauthorized users was within the legal terms of the contract. Therefore, the unauthorized use of the computer services was a matter between Metropolitan Computing Service and its sales manager.

Metropolitan Computing Service entered into a formal agreement with physicians at the other hospital to provide them with these online services. Additional computer facilities were assigned to the other hospital so that University Hospital physicians had the exclusive use of their purchased services. Metropolitan Computing Service also terminated the sales manager responsible for the series of unauthorized activities.

REQUIRED:

1. Was the two password approach to security too simple? What would you recommend and explain the reasons for your recommendation.
2. What effect will the security arrangement you propose have on the utilization experience of physicians?
3. Explain the "learning curve" approach to utilization experience.
4. From this experience with University Hospital, what internal control questions would you raise with Metropolitan Computing Service if you were considering purchasing additional computer services from them?

CASE 5–2.   FARLEY ENTERPRISES, INC.*

Roger Green, president of Farley Enterprises, Inc., engaged the management consulting firm with which you are employed to review the controls over confidential data and, where appropriate, to design and incorporate procedures to improve internal control. You have been assigned to this engagement.

The Company

This diversified Chicago-based corporation with annual sales of $350 million has seven divisions: mining, steel foundry, fabricating, chemicals, plastics, recreational, and educational. A series of common data files has been established by division for customers, suppliers, products, raw materials, and employees. Each of the files contains confidential data, and access to these files is closely monitored. Moreover, rigorous control is maintained over the computer center as well as over access to magnetic tapes and the online files.

Organizationally, there is a corporate vice president who directs each division, except the fabricating division which is headed by an executive vice president. In addition, the corporate staff consists of a president, senior executive vice president, vice president—administration, vice president—planning, vice president—marketing, vice president—finance, and executive vice president—corporate development. The Assistant Vice President—Information Systems is on the staff of the Vice President—Administration, and the Director, Facilities Operations reports to the Assistant Vice President—Information Systems.

The Situation

Roger Green indicated that he had reason to believe that there may have been some violation of the confidentiality of data procedures, especially in the customers file for the educational division. Many of the products in the educational division are sold on a direct-

---

* The name of this corporation and the location of the violation in confidential data procedures have been disguised; however, in all other respects, the descriptive setting of the computer-based operations is identical with the "real" organization.

mail basis, and customers with selected profiles (characteristics determined from credit application, procurement, and payment behavior) are given the opportunity to purchase life insurance by direct mail. (Farley Enterprises has a wholly-owned insurance company which sells only by direct mail using customer names obtained from the educational division.)

The insurance company's manager has developed a series of computer programs for selecting prospective customers from the educational division's data base and for classifying selected names among a set of marketing plans. Sampling procedures are used in testing a defined marketing plan with a stratified file of selected names before the time and expense of a complete mailing is incurred for a file (there are typically 10,000 names in each file of names that are selected periodically from the educational division's customers file for use by the insurance company).

A recent test performed by the insurance company's manager produced almost a zero response for procurement of insurance by direct mail. This was so unusual from the standpoint of experience and statistical analysis that a second sample was drawn from the same data base, and this second test mailing generated the same discouraging results. Since there are numerous names even in a test mailing, the physical size of the data files causes a highly impersonal approach toward marketing. However, a follow-up questionnaire was sent to those individuals included in the second test mailing for the purpose of gaining an improved understanding of the discouraging response.

As these questionnaires were completed and returned, a recurring response was that the prospective customer had recently purchased insurance from another company. Roger Green said the overall response was so unusual from a statistical standpoint that he felt the confidentiality of data procedures for the customers data file in the educational division must have been violated. This is why Mr. Green had asked for this review of internal control, and because of the nature of the problem, you were instructed to report directly to Mr. Green.

Management Review

You performed a high point examination of the internal control procedures over *physical access* to the computer processing room and the magnetic tape library as well as to *computer access* to processing capabilities and to retrieval of confidential data. You observed, flow-charted, compared, and analyzed each step in both areas of access.

In performing your review you noted that aborted printouts of confidential data were discarded in the nearest wastepaper basket. You intentionally retrieved printouts from these baskets over the next few days, and by this process you were able to identify several computer programs for processing confidential data from various aborted printouts (the stub of each printout indicates the major steps performed by the computer as well as the names of any library routines or functions used with a given job) .

A set of control procedures was employed over computer charge numbers and identification codes; the computer system was programmed so neither the computer charge number nor the identification code appeared on a printout. However, you were able to retrieve an array of job cards from the wastepaper baskets containing charge numbers and identification codes. These charge numbers and codes were then used with the data on the stubs of selected, aborted printouts in an effort to get computer access to confidential data stored online. Additional passwords were required to get access to the confidential data files (there is no computer generated record of these passwords even during the input phase) .

You made repeated attempts to get access to confidential data during the next five minutes, and with each attempt, an input of a different combination of words was made. You not only were unsuccessful, but you were notified on the cathode ray tube (which you were using to input your program) that your job had been aborted, that your computer access was being terminated, and that you were asked to telephone the computer center at once and to identify yourself.

Further inquiry revealed the existence of a computer program that monitored the *call statements* for confidential data including passwords. This program is designed to abort the program after the input of a specified number of erroneous passwords within a fixed period of time and, if appropriate, the program will also terminate the computer access or online status of the remote terminal used in processing.

To complete your review of internal control, you attempted to obtain magnetic tapes from the library, but you were denied access because you lacked the appropriate identification. From your review, it appeared that an unauthorized person could use the computer processing capabilities of the computer center through obtaining data from discarded job cards and aborted printouts. However, additional passwords were required to get computer access to confidential data files, and special identification was required to get physical access to data stored in the magnetic tape library. Based on these findings, your analysis shifted to a review of control procedures over those individuals who have been given the passwords and have permission to perform various levels of operations with confidential data.

Review of Access to Confidential Data

As previously indicated, computer charge numbers and identification on a job card are screened at the point of input by an online program. There is also a similar type of computer program that monitors the *call statements* (including passwords) for online, computer access to confidential data files. Selected data from both of these programs are stored in a three-stage *day file* and a three-stage *accounting charge file.*

The scope of the data included in the day file is fairly standard and represents a snapshot of the operations of the computer for each one-hundredth of a second. The online data in the first stage are maintained for six hours (if there is a machine failure, systems failure, communications problem, or mistake in online computer programs, these online data files are used in reestablishing operations and the data base). Data on these snapshots of operations are stored on magnetic tape for 10 days (the second stage). A printout of the day file is made with summary data included on an hourly basis and with an overall 24 hour recapitulation of job numbers identified with each charge number.

The three-stage accounting charge file contains the minimum data to document a charge to an account. The specifics of access time, central processing time, peripheral equipment time, words or blocks read and written, cards punched, and pages of printout are summarized in a record for each job which is cross-referenced to an accounting charge number and to identification data per the job card. The time cycles and data processing procedures for the three stages are identical with those described above for the day file.

At this point in your review, you began to integrate your findings and to draw some conclusions about the possible break in confidentiality of data procedures. Since the set of people who were given access to confidential data files was the same set of corporate officials who knew your management consulting firm was reviewing the internal control procedures within the company, you doubted that any violation of security would be discovered in the 10 days of data on the day file which were stored on magnetic tape. You looked at the boxes and boxes of printouts both for the day file and the accounting charge file, and you thought that there may have been some violation described in these one-hundredth of a second snapshots, but there was no convenient way of determining *if* and *when* a violation occurred. The overall study began to resemble searching for a "needle in a haystack" when there was no evidence that a needle had been lost.

A gratuitous event changed your study. The management consulting firm assigned a computer programmer to assist you at this point in your study. You give the assistant the task of reviewing the actual operations and control over confidential data that occur in the evening and early morning shifts (you have previously made this analysis for the day shift). As luck would have it, your assistant recently attended a computer conference that was attended by the night manager of the computer room. The night manager in a confidential discussion with your assistant said that she did not want to get anyone in trouble, but that one evening, about 8 weeks earlier, a corporate vice president (who had access to confidential data) had come to the computer room and had duplicated some tapes of confidential data. The manager indicated that the vice president was a competent programmer who had done some special analytical work a couple of years previously; however, the vice president had not been at the computing center since then, except for this special evening.

As the manager pursued the discussion, she stated that the vice president had to sign a release for the new magnetic tapes which he had created. These signed releases were in the locked files in the computer center's office.

With this new information, you and your assistant reviewed the locked file of tape releases and got the date of the alleged violation. From a review of the day file printouts for that day, you were able to reconstruct a series of 14 computer jobs processed by this vice president in which confidential data were used, summarized, and copied (both in lengthy printouts and on magnetic tapes). From the one-hundredth of a second snapshots per the day file, you were able to reconstruct the control cards and operations performed in each of the 14 jobs. From studying the matching data in the accounting charge file for these jobs, you were able to retrieve statistical data on blocks written and read, pages printed, and tapes used. The statistical data on blocks written were then traced through the day file to the establishment of those data within the online system (same number of blocks).

After you had documented the contents of the confidential data files which were duplicated, you prepared a summary statement of your findings with appropriate exhibits (such as copies of the day file and the signed release for taking magnetic tapes out of the computing center). You presented these materials to Mr. Green.

Mr. Green and the corporate legal department handled the matter from there. However, the vice president did sign a confession, returned the stolen tapes, and his resignation was asked for and accepted. Concurrently with the actions taken by Mr. Green and the legal department, you were asked if you could provide any evidence that would trace the data files to the competing insurance company.

Professionally, you really did not desire to pursue the latter request since you are not a private investigator, but you agreed to study the matter and to concurrently notify the management consulting firm with which you are engaged of the delicate nature of the request. You made an external, high-point review of the competing insurance company and you determined that their computer system was not compatible with the computer system at Farley Enterprises. One system used seven-track tape; the other used nine-track tape, and there were differences in the specification of a unit in each system. Therefore, a conversion process would be required to go from one system to the other.

You began to speculate on where the vice president might have gone to have the tapes converted, and you prepared a list of computer processing centers near both organizations. Your assistant worked on this task, and from some "tips" he was able to locate the computer processing center where the conversion occurred. An informal statement by the director of the computer processing center indicated that additional tapes were duplicated at the same time that the vice president asked for the magnetic tapes to be converted.

Since the signed confession by the vice president along with the returned tapes did not include any of these *other* duplicate magnetic tapes, you gave this new information to Mr. Green and Farley Enterprises' corporate legal department. At this point, you were advised by your management consulting firm's management to remove yourself from these legal issues and to prepare a summary statement on control procedures that should be installed at Farley Enterprises to monitor access to confidential data.

REQUIRED:

1. Review the existing computer programs relating to the job cards, computer charge numbers, identification, and passwords (for access to confidential data) . Suggest a set of criteria for inclusion in these programs.
2. Indicate what types of monitoring procedures might be included in the day file as related to access to confidential data files.
3. Assume that some type of confidentiality of data committee is going to be established to periodically review snapshots of programs related to processing of confidentiality of data (the details of this are based on your response to the previous requirement) , indicate which corporate officials should be on this committee. Justify or explain your selection.

CHAPTER 6

Formal Program for Planning and Implementing an Information System

OPERATING SYSTEMS may evolve through the integration of functional computer programs; however, it is not always possible to apply a step-by-step, building block, or modular approach toward the design of information systems. The application of additional systems efforts to an operating system does not necessarily move the computer-based network to a higher level of computer application.

In Chapter 3 we examined six reasons that may serve as constraints upon the advancement of a computer-based network beyond the level of an operating system. Eight common dimensions of the administrative process and the organizational arrangements encompassed in advanced computer-based networks were presented in Chapter 4, and comparisons were made of these eight dimensions for operating systems versus information systems versus advanced information systems. An alternative perspective for viewing the latter comparisons is to focus upon the multidimensional changes which must occur before the network can be classified at a higher level of computer application.

There is a lengthy planning phase in the *formal* program for any information system, and members of management must actively participate in *each part* of this formal program if it is to achieve its objective. Neither a "bottom-up" nor a "top-down" approach to planning an information system will suffice; instead, an information systems coordinating committee must be established by the management committee with the appropriate full-time and part-time repre-

173

sentatives as discussed in Chapter 4. The current examination of a formal program for an information system will be based upon the study teams that were described in the earlier chapter.

INTRODUCTION

To the systems analyst, the idea of creating her or his own plans for an information system is more attractive than the idea of following a formal program. However, a contemporary systems philosophy (which is compatible with the capabilities of existing computer equipment and transmission facilities) has been applied to planning, designing, and implementing information systems in various types of business corporations, health care institutions, governmental agencies, educational institutions, and other organizations. While there are always unique organizational arrangements and different sets of plans for achieving similar objectives, there is an overall process or formal program that must be followed.

This formal program does not commence until executive management has approved the systems analyst's or management consultant's preliminary report recommending that such a system study be undertaken. In other words, the high-point review or quick study of the existing operations suggests that there are substantial tangible benefits from an information system or from an increased utilization of computer systems in a particular business or organization. Moreover, these tangible benefits are great enough to justify the expenditure of funds and the utilization of management's time in carrying out an information systems study.

In a given organization, executive management frequently will ask one or two management consulting firms, as well as the organization's information systems department, to perform a high-point review or quick study of selected existing operations in order to identify profitable areas for increased computer utilization. After these preliminary reports are submitted, executive management must perform a resource allocation and capital expenditure analysis including ranking of projects and determining the extent to which outside consultants should be used.

As previously indicated, the formal program for planning and implementing an information system begins with executive management's approval of the preliminary report recommending such a study. This formal program encompasses all of the operations from this beginning through to the full implementation of the information systems designed as part of this study. However, this formal program may not be followed to that phase; instead it may be terminated at an intermediate position where another cost-benefit analysis is performed. This intermediate evaluation is emphasized in the subsequent discussion of the formal program for planning and implementing an information system.

We have found the following five phases to be a useful compartmentalization of the formal program to plan and implement an information system: (1) planning, including commitment and orientation by executive management; (2) organization review and administrative study; (3) conceptual systems design; (4) equipment selection and program design; and (5) implementation.

Management consultants and systems analysts frequently do not separately recognize the first three phases in this formal program. Instead, some parts of the planning phase, the organization review and administrative study phase, and the conceptual systems design phase are integrated into one overall process called a "scoping study" phase. In these cases the conceptual systems design activities (Phase 3 above) are generally not as thorough and complete as they are when these activities are pursued as a separate phase. Therefore, when we have a scoping study phase, the equipment selection and program design phase (Phase 4 above) usually includes more conceptual systems design activities than is the case in the framework used here.

The five phases in this formal program are separately examined in the following sections of this chapter. Since the equipment selection and program design phase and the implementation phase are highly procedural, only brief attention is given to these two phases. The major focus of this discussion is on the conceptual dimensions of this formal program embodied in the first three phases.

PLANNING PHASE

The executive commitment part of phase one has received considerable attention. The monetary and personnel commitment for an information systems project are extensive undertakings and should be evaluated like any other long-term capital expenditure. As indicated earlier, the formal program for planning and implementing an information system does not begin until executive management approves the preliminary report recommending such a systems study.

Obviously then, a preliminary monetary and personnel commitment evaluation in reference to this proposed system has already been performed. A more extensive and rigorous analysis is now performed to indicate more clearly the range of benefits and costs for this project.

While the executive commitment part of the planning phase has been frequently examined in the professional literature, the orientation part of phase one has not received the attention it warrants. This brief discussion will, therefore, focus on this orientation part.

If management, particularly executive management, does not appreciate the "management by systems" concept and have some feel for what the company or organization might do with an advanced computer system, then there is really no reason to begin a management information systems study. Management is a key element in an information system. The network provides relevant and timely data to management for decision-making purposes, and the network also contains the appropriate mechanism for responding to these decision-making activities. Members of management, therefore, must be oriented to the concept "management by systems," and they must have a feel for the types of decision-making activities which they may engage in after the information system has been implemented.

Sometimes individuals are more concerned with solving current problems than with planning for future settings where today's problems will be handled by new techniques. Frequently, members of management must be given a formal orientation program before they are willing to accept the fact that the proposed information system will process most of today's problems by a series of programmed decision rules.

When a series of large-scale systems studies are being initiated, it is common for the company or organization to sponsor a 4- to 10-day orientation program for key executives. This formal education program usually covers the "management by systems" concept, the information systems approach, orientation to computer equipment and communication equipment, management controls over computer operations, and the impact of information systems on organizational structure. Typically, the latter topic is not overemphasized because of the possible adverse repercussions that might result. In addition to these topics, considerable attention is given to discussing the business or organization as a system, and the sponsoring company is used as the example for these analyses.

After this orientation program is held for key executives, specialized training sessions are conducted for other management and supervisory personnel. Some of the latter sessions will be scheduled to coincide with the implementation phase of the information systems study.

ORGANIZATION REVIEW AND ADMINISTRATIVE STUDY PHASE

In a previous discussion it was explained *why* the team of systems analysts must obtain a basic feel for the nature of the company's business and for the types of major decision-making activities involved if the team is going to design an information system. The organization review or the rethinking phase is where this type of understanding is obtained.

After the basic understanding has been obtained, the team must perform detailed analyses of the major decision-making activities. From these thorough studies, the information requirements for the major decision-making activities can be ascertained. These information requirements will be matched with information sources in the process of establishing information flows, and these information flows will be integrated into information systems.

From these statements we can see that the desired output from the organization review phase is *a specification of information requirements for the major decision-making activities throughout the business organization.*[1] The attainment of this desired output does require that some degree of structure be superimposed upon the team of systems analysts' work. We have found it useful to classify this "structure" into three steps, which are separately explained in the following discussion.

Understanding the Business Process. The first step in the organization review and administrative study phase is to gain an understanding of the business process for the business organization under study. This requires a familiarization with the unique industry

---

[1] The following material in this section on "Organization Review and Administrative Study Phase" initially appeared as part of Chapter 11, "Information Systems for Planning and Control," in *Management Science in Planning and Control* (New York: Technical Association of the Pulp and Paper Industry, 1969), pp. 243–59. Permission of the Technical Association of the Pulp and Paper Industry was given to use this material in the current chapter.

characteristics and practices as well as an appreciation of the general environment in which the business organization is located. This appreciation will include a general insight into how the business organization reacts to its environment.

This first step in the organization review process requires that the study team obtain a basic feel for the nature of the company's business by seeking a general understanding of the following items:

1. What are the products and the product groups?
2. Who are the customers for each group of products?
3. What is the competitive situation with respect to each product group?
4. What is the demand forecast for the current products in each group?
    (It is surprising how many elaborate computer-based operating systems have been installed at about the same time that demand for the major product group was significantly reduced, and, in some cases, shortly discontinued.)
5. What is the nature of the company's products from the perspective of the customers?
    (What is the customer actually buying? Is the consumer's concept of the product compatible with management's concept?)
6. What is the environmental situation?
    (For instance, does some recent action by a governmental agency affect the future of some product line?)

Now, focusing more directly on the company:

7. What tangible and intangible resources does the company possess?
8. How are these resources being used?
9. How could they be used?
10. Are the resources being allocated in the most efficient manner?
    (The answering of this latter question will involve obtaining some rough marginal contributions by product groups, demand forecasts, and capacity requirements to produce a given product for a lot size.)

After the above types of questions are resolved, the study team begins to obtain a feel for the nature of the company's business—step one in the organization review process. The questions that are posed in this first step are common, basic business questions, and because the questions are of this type, study teams all too often merely give lip service to this type of organization review. "We have worked for the company for fifteen to twenty years; we know all aspects of this business." The facts are, of course, that management and even executive management may be too deeply involved in the day-to-day operations of the company to have an objective perspective of the company's business.

The following case study presents a situation where an organization review should have revealed some serious management problems. A family-owned industrial machine manufacturer with annual sales in excess of $25 million was recently sold because the president did not want to invest any more of the family funds in expanding the productive capacity of the 60-year-old company.

A representative of this machine manufacturing company approached an officer of a New York City-based investment group, and this investment group became interested in possibly purchasing the machine manufacturing company. A management consulting firm was engaged to perform a quick, high-point administrative review of the machine manufacturing company.

Three management consultants spent a week primarily performing an organization review of this reputable, industrial machine manufacturer. Incidentally, two of the consultants spent over half of their time at places other than the office or plant of the industrial machine manufacturer. They talked with old and new customers; they talked with the company's leading competitors; they went to a private business library and studied the economic forecast for this industry.

Based on the report of the three management consultants (which was supplemented by the investment group's staff studies), the industrial machine manufacturer was immediately purchased. Why? As part of the organization review, the consultants had attempted to answer the question: "Are the resources being allocated in the most efficient manner?" The engineering times required to produce the different types of machines were multiplied by the respective sales volumes for the different types of machines. This determined that there was not a shortage of capacity, but that there was a significant excess capacity. Obviously, there must be some scheduling problems. The talks with customers and with competitors had also suggested that there were some organization problems in production scheduling, plant operations, and marketing.

This case study does not end here or it would not have been cited as an information systems case. The investment group employed this same management consulting firm to design and implement a computer-based information system at this industrial machine manufacturing company. The consulting group already had some feel for the real nature of the industrial machine manufacturer's business, and these consultants worked with the new management group in planning this information system. Two years later this industrial machine manufacturing company was making the highest profits in the company's history and using the identified excess capacity to produce new products.

In summary, the first step in the organization review process is to perform an organization type of administrative review of the company and to gain a basic understanding of the nature of the company's business. The formal recognition of this first step is not the author's original idea. Peter Drucker devoted the sixth chapter of a book[2] he wrote in 1954 to this first step; the chapter was entitled, "What Is Our Business—and What Should It Be?" Drucker[3, 4] and Watson[5] have continued to focus on the first step from an administrative position. Johnson, Kast, and Rosenzwieg[6] and Ackoff[7] have examined this step from a systems point of view.

Develop Conceptual Model of Major Decision-Making Activities. The second step in the organization review and administrative study phase includes the thorough examination of the major decision-making activities in the company and the construction of an all-encompassing conceptual model that will contain these major decision-making activities. While this detailed analysis is being made, the

---

[2] Peter F. Drucker, *The Practice of Management* (New York: Harper & Row, Inc., 1954).

[3] Peter F. Drucker, "Managing for Business Effectiveness," *Harvard Business Review*, vol. 41 (May–June 1963), pp. 53–60.

[4] Peter F. Drucker, "The Effective Decision," *Harvard Business Review*, vol. 45 (January–February 1967), pp. 92–98.

[5] Edward T. P. Watson, "Diagnosis of Management Problems," *Harvard Business Review*, vol. 36 (January–February, 1958).

[6] Richard A. Johnson, Fremont E. Kast, and James E. Rosenzwieg, "Systems Theory and Management," *Management Science*, vol. 10 (1964), pp. 367–84.

[7] Russell L. Ackoff, "Management Misinformation Systems," *Management Science*, vol. 14 (1967), pp. B-147 to B-156.

study team is comparing its findings with the descriptive overview of the company's business process and environment that was developed as the final part of step one. Where the findings and the descriptive summary are not compatible, then further study is given to the activities involved.

The accomplishment of the second step in the organization review process requires that:

1. The major decision-making activities in the business must be identified.
2. The identified decision-making activities in the business must be matched against the previous overview of the business process to see if they appear to be reasonable and in harmony.
3. Each major decision-making activity is thoroughly examined with consideration given to such items as:
    A. What is the nature of the decision-making activity?
    B. What appears to be the company's policies or ground rules that relate to this decision-making activity?
4. The findings for each major decision-making activity are compared with the descriptive overview of the company's business process and where appropriate, further study is given to any items not in harmony.
5. Some type of model is developed for integrating all of these major decision-making activities into a large network with the interrelationships among major decision-making activities being clearly shown.

Another part of this second step in the organization review and administrative study phase is to examine the operating systems. For purposes of this discussion, let us assume that either the business organization has a series of operating systems or that a subgroup of this study team is designing such operating systems. These operating systems will handle most of the day-to-day transactions involved with a given set of major decision-making activities.

In summary, the second step in the organization review process is fairly easy to comprehend in terms of scope. It is logical that if we are going to plan an information system, then we have to examine the major decision-making activities that are to be serviced by this proposed information system. If we are going to have one system, the creation of a model to represent all of these major decision-making activities and the relationships among activities is a reasonable requirement. What is not so readily appreciated is the *time required* (1) to perform a thorough and comprehensive study of the decision-making activities, (2) to compare the findings of this study with the overview of the company's business, and (3) to examine the details surrounding the inconsistencies revealed by these comparisons.

Determine the Specific Information Requirements for System. The third step in the organization review and administrative study phase is to determine the specific information requirements for the proposed information system. This task is simplified by having a series of operating systems, such as integrated inventory control and production control system. These operating systems are closed data flows in a given time frame which match information requirements and information sources. Thus, in the existing set of operating systems, the day-to-day, repetitive types of requirements have already been identified and matched with information sources.

Therefore, the specific information requirements that are determined by this third step will typically be one of four types:

1.   The so-called "exceptional items" that are not handled by the series of operating systems.
2.   Management activities that have previously been accomplished by a "seat of pants" type of information or by some informal information flow that is now being formally recognized.
3.   Old decision-making activities that were part of the business process, in "name only." That is, these activities were recognized as being important, but management was often too busy with other activities to consider these matters. Now, with the new computer-based information system, all decision-making activities that are part of the business process will be serviced.
4.   New decision-making activities that were identified by comparing the overall understanding of the business and its environment (based on the organization type of review) with the business organization's present way of doing business. The latter would be revealed by studying the existing major decision-making activities within the business organization.

The specific information requirements that are determined by this third step may be classified into two groupings: "tentative information requirements" and "information requirements." The organization type of review of the company and the study of the decision-making activities may reveal certain types of decisions that could be made. Data for these proposed types of decision-making activities may be cited as "tentative information requirements" for the purpose of evaluating if it is economically feasible to provide for that specific, tentative information requirement.

This evaluation is based on a comparison of the direct benefit obtained from using the "satisfied" tentative information requirement in a decision-making activity versus the cost of creating the data to be used in "satisfying" this requirement. Items that do not pass this test are excluded from the "information requirements" grouping.

In summary, the third and final step in the organization review and administrative study phase is to determine which of the specific information requirements for the proposed information system are not satisfied by the existing set of operating systems. From this examination of the three steps in the organization review phase, we have a better understanding of the objectives and operations of this administrative process.

The organization review and administrative study phase in an information systems program represents a formal effort to incorporate into the proposed system a feel for the business and the major decision-making activities to be serviced by the proposed system. Where this process is not applied, an *operating* system will be implemented rather than an *information* system.

CONCEPTUAL SYSTEMS DESIGN PHASE

As previously stated, many management consultants do not separately recognize the third phase in planning and implementing an information system. Instead, their "scoping study" phase will encompass most of the conceptual aspects of the first three phases. Other management consultants may follow a five-phase program, but they will use a different compartmentalization of the steps included in the second and third phases.

In the latter case, the second phase will only consist of a high-point organization review. The second and third steps in the organization review and administrative study phase—the development of a conceptual model of major decision-making activities and the determination of specific information requirements for the system—are encompassed in the conceptual systems design phase. When these steps are included in the third phase, of course, the conceptual systems design phase becomes the major time-consuming activity in planning and designing an information system.

If *our* above framework is followed and the organization review and administrative study phase is fully accomplished, then the conceptual systems design phase represents a period of intent deliberation over possible alternative networks for handling the information requirements identified in step three of the second phase. The team of systems analysts will spend considerable time in questioning, examining, dissecting, pondering, and grasping the information dimensions of the organizational unit under scrutiny.

From this period of detail analysis and intent thinking, many proposed conceptual arrangements of information flows will be discarded, and the study team will envision a network of information flows that satisfies the information requirements identified in the second phase of this formal program. The overall objective in the third phase is for the study team to reach a consensus of the best conceptual arrangement of the information dimensions of the organizational unit under scrutiny. Once in agreement, the study team will begin to explore in the fourth phase to see if any technological constraints limit the immediate implementation of the proposed system.

In fact, a gap between the conceptual arrangement proposed in the third phase and the computer and systems programs designed in the fourth phase is so common that if an advanced information system is being planned, the *absence* of a gap between the third and fourth phases of the formal program would bring into question the quality of the systems planning effort. Further attention is given to this point and to the technological constraints in the subsequent section of this chapter.

The study team may use the following approach in performing the conceptual systems design phase. Using the specific information requirements for the major decision-making activities throughout the business organization as a beginning point, the study team begins to develop different arrangements of information networks which encompass these information requirements. In these proposed arrangements, the study team is not restricted to existing technology, such as the capabilities of current computer systems and transmission equipment. Instead, the team's focus is on the development of logical arrangements for carrying out the organization's activities and for servicing these identified information requirements.

In focusing on these logical arrangements of information flows, the study team is really examining the information dimensions of the decision-making activities within the organizational unit under scrutiny. Since all "information dimensions" must relate to "decision-making activities," we can specify this operation as follows: the study team is really examining the information dimensions of the organizational unit and is proposing new arrangements for these dimensions.

Study teams frequently use various management science techniques in performing this analysis. Systems flowcharts, program flowcharts, lattice networks, matrix models, and communication charts are some of the typical techniques used for analyzing these information dimensions. Various types of coding and classification models have also been employed, and cluster analysis is currently being experimented with as another technique for assisting the study team.

At the completion of the conceptual systems design phase, the study team will have reached a consensus as to the best, logical arrangement of the information dimensions in the organizational unit under scrutiny. Before this agreement can be obtained, the proposed arrangement must be fully described and thoroughly documented. Therefore, at the completion of the third phase, the study team will have produced a comprehensive report which summarizes the team's analysis and clearly presents the proposed arrangement of information flows. Descriptive models, diagrams, and flowcharts are integral parts of this documented report.

EQUIPMENT SELECTION AND PROGRAM DESIGN PHASE

This fourth phase in planning and implementing an information system is a subject that has been extensively covered in the professional literature over the past decade. What is most important about the fourth phase is that *the equipment selection and program design phase should not begin until after a preliminary attempt has been made to complete the third phase.* Frequently, a study team's analysis is in the domain of the fourth phase when, in fact, the study team should be concentrating on the latter steps in the second phase.

In the fourth phase, the study team has to consider carefully the various technological constraints in computer systems, transmission equipment, "software packages," and other supporting facilities. In addition, some recent equipment capabilities may not be currently available at a reasonable price. For instance, one type of proposed arrangement that is frequently not economically feasible is online transmission of volumes of raw data from many remote locations into large computer systems coupled with a return transmission of relevant information in response to specific inquiries. Periodically, new transmission developments permit some companies to install such arrangements, and we anticipate that this type of proposed arrangement may be economically feasible for many other organizations in the near future.

We believe that there should be a significant gap between the proposed arrangement of information flows in the third phase and what can be operationally and economically planned for in the fourth phase. The existence of such a gap tends to indicate the extent to which the study team in the third phase was really focusing upon proposed conceptual arrangements without thinking about technological constraints.

The major thrust of this argument can be viewed from another perspective. Specifically, what criteria are used in selecting members for the study team? We believe that the majority of the team members should not be too deeply aware of the "state of art" in regard to computer systems, transmission equipment, and other supporting facilities. Instead, the team members should be predominantly management-types with a strong orientation to the organization and its environment. If the study team consists of six individuals, then one member might be the director or manager of the computer center. The other five members should be from other departments, and their actual departmental designation will vary depending upon the organizational units encompassed in the information systems study.

In performing the fourth phase of this formal program, the study team will typically make extensive use of consultants. There are consultants who specialize in specific parts of the overall equipment selection and program design phase. This degree of specialization by consultants is an additional reason why the study team needs a comprehensive report representing the team's thinking at the end of the third phase. The detailed planning of an information system must be completed by the study team itself and must not be inhibited by the technological consultants. Otherwise, the study team may select the group of specialists and may participate in the detailed planning of an information system with a different set of characteristics than would have been the case if another group of specialists were the consultants.

There are several companies that sell general computer programs, and frequently these computer programs are fairly advanced. For example a computer program may contain a few subroutines that through experience have proven to be useful processors of data for a special class of decisions. While these decisions may not be important or critical enough to be planned for (in the sense of the special computer programming effort required for processing these data), the marginal cost of obtaining such general programs from a computer services company may be low when it is part of a "package."

In summary, the study team in performing the fourth phase in planning and implementing an information system primarily serves in a coordinating capacity. Specialists and computer systems personnel are assigned many of the tasks, and outside consultants and computer services companies are used in performing other tasks. The study team coordinates these efforts and questions the interface opportunities between assignments. In many companies the membership of the active study team may change during the fourth phase with only one or two members being retained who have participated in the first three phases of the formal program.

IMPLEMENTATION PHASE

The scope of activities encompassed in the fifth phase of a formal program to plan and implement an information system is rather obvious. The project manager for the systems study must coordinate, administer, and supervise the full implementation of the planned system. Priorities must be established so that the appropriate sequence of activities is followed. The project manager must give special attention to those related subsystems that have common information flows; otherwise, noncompatible information flows may be established.

The fifth phase is an extremely important part of the formal program for planning and implementing an information system. There are many techniques and procedures that project managers successfully employ in carrying out this function. However, because of the orientation of this book, attention is not given in this text to these techniques and procedures.

SUMMARY

The need for management to participate in planning for an information system is the overriding theme of this chapter. Management cannot participate in planning for a system unless management appreciates how the proposed system is going to be used. Thus, the "management by systems" concept is a perspective that management must possess before members of management can intelligently discuss how a proposed system might be used.

If an information system rather than an operating system is going to be established, then the systems analysts must examine management's decision-making activities so that selected responses to critical decisions can be anticipated and planned for in the design of computer programs. These anticipated responses are identified as change factors, and they are represented in the designed computer programs as parameters and variables.

The five phases in a formal program for planning and implementing an information system were examined in this chapter. These five phases are (1) planning, including commitment and orientation by executive management, (2) organization review and administrative study, (3) conceptual systems design, (4) equipment selection and program design, and (5) implementation. Because of the overall orientation of this book, only brief attention was given to the fourth and fifth phases of the formal program.

TOPICS FOR CLASS DISCUSSION

1. In a systems engagement at a commercial bank, the study team will frequently establish a simulation model to represent the proposed new system. Because customers of a commercial bank expect a new system to operate with a minimum number of delays and errors, the commercial bank's management is willing to pay for the design of a special simulation model that represents the proposed system.

In this systems study, where does the simulation model fit in? Is it part of the third phase? The fourth phase? The fifth phase? Explain your answer.

2. As a management consultant you are confronted with the following situation: You have undertaken an information systems

study in an organization, and you now discover that members of executive management are not willing to spend time in the organizational review and conceptual study phase of the study. Explain the philosophical problem confronting you.

3. "The successful application of the management-by-systems concept requires that members of management work under the assumption that the computer-based network has certain programmed decision-rules which aid in the location and compilation of data sources as well as in the implementation of changes made by management. The human decision maker is then free to concentrate on problems of wider scope."

Explain this statement and its relationship to the five phases in a formal program for planning and implementing an information system.

4. Explain the relationship of the information systems coordinating committee to the formal program for planning and implementing an information system. Indicate the primary focus of the relationship in each phase of the formal program.

5. Explain the relationship of the data management committee to the formal program for planning and implementing an information system.

6. Explain the relationship of the code structure identification and maintenance committee to the formal program for planning and implementing an information system.

7. Management of the Franklin Company has approved a preliminary report recommending a formal program for planning and implementing an information system. It is anticipated that the five phases in this formal program can be completed within 30 months and that two consultants will be retained for this period. A representative from the public accounting firm auditing the Franklin Company will also be requested to participate in monitoring these planning and implementing activities.

While two consultants will be retained for the 30-month study, it is expected that the individuals assigned by the management consulting firm will vary over the period. Specifically, different type of knowledge and experience is required in each of the five phases. Indicate the consulting service that will be requested in each of the five phases.

CASE 6–1. BROOKFIELD LABORATORIES, INC.

Mr. Bruce Whitman is vice president, manufacturing, at Brookfield Laboratories, Inc. He has requested the management consulting firm with which you are employed to perform a high-point review of Brookfield's manufacturing operations and to recommend a specific program for improving the existing computer-based information system.

This is not the first time that Mr. Whitman has engaged the services of your management consulting firm. Recently a management science team from this firm completed the design and implementation of a special computer program that concurrently assigns (1) products to vats and equipment, (2) employees to vats and equipment, and (3) employees to products. Mr. Whitman is especially interested in proposed extensions to this special program and in developing for the manufacturing operations an information system utilizing the new capabilities provided by this computer program.

The Company

Brookfield Laboratories, a subsidiary of a large, diversified corporation, is a drug and chemical manufacturing company with annual sales of $150,000,000. Brookfield is more indicative of a company in the pharmaceutical industry than one in the chemical industry. For example, Brookfield's return on invested capital last year was over 23 percent, and this return is comparable with that of companies in the pharmaceutical industry.

Brookfield is organized along traditional lines. In addition to the president and the executive vice president, the management committee consists of the following individuals: vice president, marketing; vice president, manufacturing; treasurer and financial manager; vice president, research and development; vice president, employee and public relations; and secretary and general counsel.

Computer equipment was installed at Brookfield in 1955, and this equipment has been updated when major technological developments have occurred. Currently a large-scale, computing system is being used. While the computing system is located at Brookfield, some of the computer applications are for other companies owned by the parent corporation. However, a large segment of the computer time and storage capacity on the computing system is devoted to Brookfield's research and development activities, and these computer applications include intensive testing of new products. The other major computer applications are financial accounting, payroll, invoicing, product and territory reports for marketing, and cost and performance reports.

The Manufacturing Division

Bruce Whitman, as vice president, manufacturing, has responsibility for the following daily decision-making activities. He must daily assign employees to products; some employees cannot produce all products. In fact, most employees can only create a limited number of products, and each of these are produced at varying degrees of efficiency. Second, he must assign vats and equipment to products; different products can be manufactured by different combinations of vats and machinery. The cost of production varies by the combination of vats and machinery actually used in the creation of the product. Third, he must assign employees to vats and equipment. Most employees have varying degrees of efficiency with some vats and equipment, regardless of what product is being manufactured in that vat.

Bruce Whitman is an extremely conscientious executive and has tried to stay abreast of developments in management science that relate to his operations. For the past several years he has used linear programming daily in making a two-way assignment of products to vats and equipment, and he has combined this assignment with business experience in assigning employees to products. Because of the procedure used, 7 to 8 percent of Brookfield's employees will be unassigned for a given shift. In other words, the unassigned vats and equipment cannot be used by the unassigned employees to produce additional products.

Management Science Technique

Based on the potential savings from more efficient use of the unassigned employees, a management science team was engaged to develop some type of mathematical technique for handling this task. The team's initial approach was to use the classical assignment model illustrated by Exhibit A. The cost data for the products to men

EXHIBIT A
Assignment of Products to Men to Vats
(for illustration purposes only)

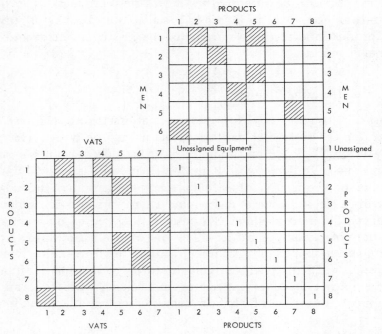

matter are based on the varying efficiencies that employees have in creating different products, regardless of which equipment is used in the manufacturing process. The cost data for the products to vats matrix represent the out-of-pocket cost for creating a product, exclusive of the varying efficiencies that employees have in manufacturing different products. The unused equipment row is necessary for this model so that the columns for vats and products equal the rows for men, products, and unassigned equipment.

The assignment model as presented in Exhibit A contains three matrices. The products to products matrix serves as a connection between the products to men matrix and the products to vats matrix. For illustration purposes, eight products are related to eight products with a series of "ones" shown in the diagonal cells. With the assignment algorithm, the total assignment for any row must equal one, and the total assignment for any column must equal one. The shaded areas in the products to men matrix and in the products to vats matrix indicate that certain assignments cannot occur. All vats cannot be used to produce all products; all workers cannot create all products.

Continuing with the illustration, assume that the best performance of products to vats is when Product 4 is assigned to Vat 6. In the assignment algorithm, the one in the Product 4 to Product 4 diagonal cell is replaced by a zero and a one is assigned to the cell for Product 4, Vat 6. After this assignment, the Product 4 row totals one; however, Product 4 column equals zero. Therefore, an assignment in the Product 4 column must occur. Assume that the highest efficiency in creating Product 4 is achieved by Man 2; therefore, a one is assigned to the cell for Product 4, Man 2. In solving Exhibit A by an assignment algorithm, we would require a dual assignment. In other words, whenever there is a product to man assignment, the same product must be concurrently assigned to a vat. By these concurrent assignments, the rows and columns will always, individually, total one.

The assignment model as illustrated by Exhibit A is not complete. Products are not manufactured in vats according to a one-to-one assignment; instead, certain products may require more than one vat for their creation. Moreover, selected products can be manufactured by different combinations of vats. In addition to these refinements of the problem, some employees have varying efficiencies with using selected equipment and vats, regardless of which products are being manufactured. These other dimensions of the problem cannot be adequately handled by the assignment model containing three matrices.

The management science team had to develop another algorithm for coping with the broader dimensions of this concurrent assignment problem. Using Alex Orden's transshipment problem (see *Management Science,* vol. 2, 1956, pp. 276–85) as a guide, the management science team developed an algorithm that linked a series of assignment models. A rough illustration of this approach is presented in Exhibit B; a more precise description of the algorithm is not possible because of the proprietary nature of the model.

The illustration depicted by Exhibit B is identical with the data shown in Exhibit A; however, Exhibit B, unlike Exhibit A, contains a men to vats matrix which reflects the men to vats efficiencies without regard to which products are being manufactured. The assign-

EXHIBIT B

Concurrent Assignment of Products to Men to Vats
(for illustration purposes only)

ment algorithm for Exhibit B requires four concurrent assignments. Using the same example as described for Exhibit A, a one is assigned to the cell for Product 4, Man 2; a zero is assigned to the cell for Product 4, Product 4; and a one is assigned to the cell for Product 4, Vat 6. Unlike Exhibit A, a zero is assigned to the cell for Vat 6, Vat 6; a one is assigned to the cell for Vat 6, Man 2; a zero is assigned to the cell for Man 2, Man 2; a one is assigned to the cell for Man 2, Product 4; and a zero is assigned to the cell for Product 4, Product 4. In summary, these concurrent assignments are as follows:

Cells Set Equal to One	*Cells Set Equal to Zero*
Product 4, Man 2	Product 4, Product 4
Product 4, Vat 6	Vat 6, Vat 6
Vat 6, Man 2	Man 2, Man 2
Man 2, Product 4	Product 4, Product 4

In Exhibit B, the products to products matrix, the vats to vats matrix, and the men to men matrix provide the linking capability. These matrices serve as the intermediate location in the transshipment. Beyond these similarities to the standard transshipment model, the actual algorithm developed was different for it had to cope with a combination of assignments of vats to a given product.

For purposes of this discussion, assume that a computer program was developed which would produce an optimum three-way assignment along the general lines suggested by Exhibit B. This computer program requires less than two minutes of computer time to determine the assignment of 150 products, 110 employees, and 130 vats. In this assignment, not all products are manufactured during any shift. In addition, there are constraints on the current assignment of vats to products, depending on which drugs and chemicals were produced in each particular vat during the previous shift. However, these variables and constraints are easily handled in the special computer program that was designed by the management science team.

Current Situation

Bruce Whitman initially had reservations about the management science team's proposed model. Eventually he was convinced that this three-way assignment model was acceptable and should be used at

Brookfield. After a period of time, Bruce Whitman was able to accept the fact that the new computer program, in less than two minutes, could perform a three-way assignment, a task which previously had taken all of his time. Moreover, the computer assignment was an optimum solution, while Whitman's manually derived assignment had been only a satisfactory approach to the problem.

Since *you* have been assigned to this engagement, you should begin to ponder how to plan an information system around this special computer program. Since all of Bruce Whitman's decision-making experience over the past 20 years has related to the three-way assignment, you cannot ask him to tell you his information requirements.

REQUIRED:

Indicate step-by-step how you will approach this consulting assignment. Be specific!

CASE 6–2. BARKER AUTOMATIC TRANSMISSION SERVICE

Ralph Barker, president of Barker Automatic Transmission Service, is confronting a situation that is typical of many small business firms. His firm's sales have increased at a rapid rate during the past six years, while the profit margin per dollar of sales has not only decreased, but the actual total dollar profit for the current year's increased volume of sales was less than the total dollar profit for a much smaller volume of sales in a former year. Furthermore, during the same period of time, Barker had expanded his operations from a one-location business to one main shop with three other outlets.

As a result of these developments and the keen competition that he is encountering, Ralph Barker has engaged the management consulting firm with which you are associated to perform a review of his operations. Your objective is to determine the type of information system that would best meet his requirements. Following are some of the data you ascertained in your review.

The Company

The Barker Automatic Transmission Service's operations are conducted through a main shop and three branch outlets in the metropolitan area of a large midwestern city. As indicated by the name, the principal activities of the firm are rebuilding and installing automatic transmissions in automobiles. In addition, general automotive repairs are performed during slack periods.

At the main shop, there are three different work areas. The automatic transmission rebuilding section maintains the inventory of parts and the inventory of rebuilt automatic transmissions. The supervisor, two mechanics, and a laborer work full time rebuilding automatic transmissions for inventory and for current installation requirements. The automatic transmission installation and general repairs section is the dominant work area. The shop manager and seven mechanics rotate between installing rebuilt automatic transmissions and performing general automotive repairs, depending on the hour-by-hour requirements. The third section is the central office for the company. In addition to Ralph Barker, there is a sales manager, a purchasing agent, and a combination cashier-bookkeeper-secretary. There is also a laborer at the main shop who makes deliveries to the outlets.

The first outlet (Outlet A) has a shop manager and three mechanics; the second outlet (Outlet B) has a shop manager and two mechanics; and the third outlet (Outlet C) has a shop manager. Outlet B and Outlet C receive all of their rebuilt automatic transmissions from the main shop. Whenever a customer comes to Outlet B or Outlet C for replacement of an automatic transmission in an automobile, if the appropriate type of automatic transmission is not on hand in inventory at the location, the shop manager will telephone the main shop. The desired automatic transmission is delivered by truck to the outlet. When there is a slack period at Outlet B or Outlet C, the mechanics and shop managers will perform general automotive repairs.

Previously, Outlet A operated on the same basis as the other two outlets. However, the shop manager at Outlet A recently received permission from Ralph Barker for the Outlet A mechanics to rebuild automatic transmissions during slack periods. This change occurred because of recent complaints over the performance of the automatic transmissions that were rebuilt at the main shop. Eventually, Ralph Barker fired the individual responsible for the poorly rebuilt transmissions and hired a qualified machinist. (The latter individual is the supervisor of the automatic transmission rebuilding section.) During this period, the manager of Outlet A felt that her volume of business had declined because of this poor performance and, therefore, she desired to have her own mechanics perform the rebuilding function.

The mechanics at Outlet A rebuild transmissions only during slack periods. If the volume of business is high and the type of automatic transmission required for installation is not in inventory, the manager of Outlet A will secure the desired automatic transmission from the main shop by the same procedure as was followed by the managers of Outlets B and C. Because Outlet A mechanics do rebuild transmissions, the shop manager must maintain an inventory of parts for use in rebuilding.

This discussion of "the company" would not be complete without some consideration being given to the president. Ralph Barker is a self-educated, aggressive entrepreneur, who through his own efforts has created a growing business enterprise. His office desk always contains several library books on business, which Barker reads at night. From books, periodicals, and discussions with bank officials and other business leaders, Barker gains ideas regarding new business procedures. For example, last year he decided to install an incentive system for shop supervisors. But shortly after the incentive system was established, it was terminated because Barker Automatic Transmission Service was paying large incentives to shop supervisors in the same months in which the bookkeeper reported that the firm had incurred some of its largest losses.

Periodically, Barker has tried other new procedures, but eventually has discontinued each new procedure because of other competing requirements for his time and energy. During rush periods, Barker will assist the shop supervisor. When business slacks off, Barker will assist the sales manager or will review the financial report for the previous month.

Accounting Records and Reports

All journals and the general ledger are maintained on a cash basis. The bookkeeper at the main shop maintains all records. The shop managers of the other three outlets send daily reports to the bookkeeper of their cash transactions and their ending cash positions. The shop managers are permitted to make small cash purchases as required by operations, and at the end of the day the shop manager will make a night deposit in the bank of all cash on hand, except a small reserve for cash purchases during the next day.

Previously, perpetual inventory records were maintained of parts in inventory and rebuilt transmissions. However, because of the cost involved, these records were discontinued several years ago. At present, no inventory records are maintained on a regular basis, and cost data on rebuilt automatic transmissions are not accumulated. An annual physical inventory count is performed, and an external accountant prepares the income tax return and the appropriate annual financial statements.

Ralph Barker complained to his bookkeeper that he needed timely information for controlling expenditures and managing operations. In response, the bookkeeper started preparing an accrual type of monthly operating report (see Exhibit A). From your analysis, you determine that the 12 monthly reports do not compare with the data reported on the annual report after adjusting for the difference between the cash and the accrual bases of accounting.

Competitive Situation

Ralph Barker informs you that his three primary competitors finance their own accounts receivable. He is wondering how much profit his competitors are making from financial charges. For example, one competitor advertised in a daily newspaper that he would install a rebuilt automatic transmission in a specified group (make and year) of automobiles for $56 and that the prospective customer did not have to make any down payment.

Since unit cost data are not maintained on a regular basis, Ralph Barker designed a record for accumulating the number of automatic transmissions rebuilt during February and the labor and parts costs associated with this production. During the month of February, 145 automatic transmissions were rebuilt. At this level of operation, the average direct labor cost for rebuilding a transmission was $17, and the average parts cost was $16. In addition to these two costs, there is the labor cost of installing the rebuilt transmission and the overhead cost; however, special data were not accumulated on these latter two elements of cost.

At present, Barker has a working relation with a small loan firm where the latter firm will finance most of Barker Automatic Transmission Service's prospective customers. Barker directs his efforts toward getting a prospective customer to telephone or visit one of his four locations. If the prospective customer does not have sufficient

EXHIBIT A Operating Statement for Month of February

	Total	Main Shop	Outlet A	Outlet B	Outlet C
Gross sales:					
Cash	$20,120	$4,990	$6,430	$6,100	$2,600
Charge	1,840	820	620	400	—
Transfers to outlets	4,600	4,600	—	—	—
	$26,560	$10,410	$7,050	$6,500	$2,600
Cost of sales:					
Purchases	$ 4,040	$3,110	$ 820	$ 60	$ 50
Transfers from main shop	4,600	—	1,400	2,400	800
Labor	10,200	6,350	1,950	1,400	500
Subcontractor	430	250	80	60	40
Supplies	80	35	15	10	20
Sales refund	200	200	—	—	—
	19,550	9,945	4,265	3,930	1,410
Gross profit	$ 7,010	$ 465	$2,785	$2,570	$1,190
Expenses:					
Accounting*	$ —	$ —	$ —	$ —	$ —
Advertising*	1,540	770	385	231	154
Auto and truck†	90	50	30	10	—
Commission†	30	30	—	—	—
Depreciation†	325	150	75	60	40
Donations*	15	7	4	2	2
Dues and subscriptions*	—	—	—	—	—
Insurance—fire*	460	230	115	69	46
Interest expense*	180	90	45	27	18
Laundry*	140	70	35	21	14
Maintenance and repair†	882	400	198	265	19
Miscellaneous†	10	10	—	—	—
Postage†	5	5	—	—	—
Rent†	1,520	970	300	150	100
Supplies—office†	20	20	—	—	—
Taxes—general†	18	18	—	—	—
Taxes—payroll‡	382	244	73	50	15
Tools†	20	6	12	—	2
Utilities†	540	230	135	130	45
Wages*	400	200	100	60	40
Welfare—employees‡	240	154	46	31	9
	6,817	3,654	1,553	1,106	504
Net profit	$ 193	(−$3,189)	$1,232	$1,464	$ 686

* Prorated between locations on a 50, 25, 15, 10 basis, respectively, for the main shop and Outlets A, B, and C.

funds (and the typical customer having an automatic transmission replaced in an automobile does not have said funds) , then one of Barker's employees will have the prospective customer prepare an application for credit statement. This latter information is telephoned to the manager of the local small loan firm, and a credit investigation is performed. This investigation is performed the same day the prospective customer applies for credit. If the loan is approved, the prospective customer is telephoned and asked to bring his or her automobile in for service. Sometimes on nonapproved loans (especially during slack periods) , Ralph Barker will agree to carry these accounts, if the customer has some down payment.

Barker asks you if he should start financing his own accounts receivable. He says that for less than $2 per application, a metropolitan credit screening service will perform the credit investigation and will provide quick service. Within three hours after the agency is contacted, the results of the credit investigation will have been telephoned to Barker Automatic Transmission Service. Furthermore, Barker says that he can borrow sufficient funds at 6 percent from a commercial bank to finance the accounts receivable.

The automatic transmission business experiences seasonal fluctuations. Snow and ice as well as vacation trips significantly influence the volume of business. Barker is wondering if he should not try to level off his volume of operations by entering into long-term contracts with two or three of the major automotive repair shops in the metropolitan area. Barker felt that he could secure enough business from two or three major automotive repair shops to finance a base of operations. In other words, these contracted sales would approximate the cost of operating the automatic transmission rebuilding section. Thus, there would only be variable cost associated with the rebuilt automatic transmissions for the regular customers of the Barker Automatic Transmission Service.

Ralph Barker also discussed with you the matter of slack time. Should Outlet A be permitted to rebuild automatic transmissions or should all transmissions be centrally rebuilt? What is a reasonable transfer cost for the centrally rebuilt automatic transmissions? What type of incentive system could be established so that Barker Automatic Transmission Service would actually experience an increase in profit when the employees receive an incentive payment? Should the Barker Automatic Transmission Service only rebuild and install automatic transmissions and not perform general automotive repairs?

If so, during the slack periods the mechanics might work on rebuilding old automobiles. When some customer comes in with an old automobile needing a rebuilt automatic transmission, then a salesperson might sell the customer another old automobile in excellent mechanical condition instead of selling the customer on reworking the present automobile.

REQUIRED:

1. Following the information systems approach, analyze the present operations.
2. Present in outline form the steps you would take in designing and installing a modified information system. Be specific.

PART II
TRADITIONAL INFORMATION SYSTEMS

CHAPTER 7

Responsibility Accounting Systems

PART I presented an overview of the information systems approach with special emphasis on the systems analyst's perspective or observing the information dimensions of the decision-making activities and further emphasis on how these various identified information flows are grouped into information systems. An analysis was made of the organizational and administrative arrangements that support the establishment of a conducive environment in which advanced computer-based networks can grow and mature. Attention was also given to the role of management both in (*a*) designing and monitoring security and control features in advanced networks and in (*b*) planning, designing, implementing, documenting, and maintaining an advanced computer-based network.

In the next four parts of this book, five discrete models of information systems are presented that build upon the definition of terms and explanation of concepts contained in the previous part. Within each of these general models, the eight common dimensions of the administrative process and the organizational arrangements encompassed in advanced computer-based networks are emphasized; in addition, these specified multifacets assist in clarifying distinctions and emphasizing the degree of variation and flexibility within each of these general models.

Part II on traditional information systems contains chapters on responsibility accounting systems, profitability accounting systems, and critical path planning and scheduling systems. While the systems described in these three chapters are based on the general model of a traditional information system, there are variations in the eight common dimensions among these systems, and these changes are emphasized in the discussion.

INTRODUCTION

An elementary information system was described in Chapter 3 as a computer-based network containing two or more operating systems that provide relevant data to management for decision-making purposes and possesses the necessary mechanism for implementing changes or responses made by management. Brief attention was given to the need for restructuring the data within a network from "input oriented" to "output oriented" before this change mechanism can be implemented.

A model of an information system at this elementary level was followed in the previous description of organizational and administrative arrangements that support these networks. This same level of sophistication in networks is followed in the model of a traditional information system presented in Chapter 7.

This chapter reexamines the general model for a traditional information system and reiterates the approach that the systems analyst follows in grouping information flows into larger information networks. Next, the general model for a responsibility accounting system is differentiated from the general model for a traditional information system. Then, attention is given to explaining how a responsibility accounting system is used in matching information requirements with information sources throughout the organization. This matching operation is dependent upon a reprocessing procedure using a predetermined coding pattern for initially coding all inputs to the responsibility accounting system. This reprocessing procedure and the coding pattern are examined and illustrated in the later sections of this chapter.

THE GENERAL MODEL

The general model of a traditional information system is a *closed* network encompassing all of the major information flows within an organization and serving as a vehicle for connecting that organization's information requirements with its information sources. The network supporting this closed system contains both vertical and horizontal flows. While the general model specifies *all* major information flows, there are numerous applications of the model in which the network encompasses only *certain types* of major information flows. In the latter situation, the traditional information system may be used in conjunction with another traditional information system (such as a responsibility accounting system used in conjunction with a profitability accounting system) , a production and operation information system, or a marketing information system.

When a systems analyst has progressed to the point of being able to state that a given organization's major information flows are indicative of a traditional information system, then the analyst has almost completed the initial phases of the analysis of that organization. As stated in the discussion of a formal program for planning and implementing an information system, in this initial phase the systems analyst is concerned with the nature of the environment in which the organization operates and the characteristics of the management process.

In following the information systems approach, the systems analyst begins by specifying the major information requirements of decision makers throughout the organization. Next, the analyst groups these major information requirements into more inclusive units using perhaps three criteria: (*a*) the general economic activity to which an information flow relates, (*b*) the general nature or characteristic of the information being processed and transmitted, and (*c*) the time frame of the information flow.

However, the systems analyst hopefully need not follow this step-by-step approach of identifying all major information flows and then laboriously grouping all these flows into larger and larger units of analysis until, finally, the traditional information system is developed. Instead, the systems analyst builds upon personal experience and employs some shortcuts.

The analyst still begins by specifying the major information requirements of decision makers throughout the organization. Next, the analyst examines the general nature of the management process in this organization. Using some minimum time frame (such as a day, a week, or other time unit) as an arbitrary point of departure, the analyst makes simplifying assumptions and attempts to force the time dimension of the specified information requirements for the various decision-making processes into his arbitrary time frame.

Specifically, the analyst looks for some minimum duration for which the general model of a traditional information system is applicable. This means that within this minimum time frame, all phases of the planning process must be completed before any of the activity commences in the time period covered by the plan. There may be numerous information inputs to decision makers collectively engaged in the planning process; however, all of the action by these decision makers must occur before the time period covered by the plan starts.

These decision makers must complete the following steps: (1) identifying the tasks to be performed within the time frame of the plan, (2) coordinating these identified tasks to be sure that there are no conflicts, (3) specifying the extent to which each task is to be performed (expressed in some unit of measure), (4) assigning personnel to tasks, and (5) allocating the resources and materials for the accomplishment of each task.

After all the assignment and coordinating activities have occurred, then action commences on the work toward the achievement of each task. As this work is performed, it is monitored by the control process, which seeks conformance or adherence to plans. Within the time frame of the cycle contained in the traditional information system, management does not plan on either responding or reacting to changes in the demand for services, the raw materials market, the finished goods market, or actions by competitors. This latter remark, of course, is a generalization; within the time frame of the cycle, management may be forced to change its procurement plans or its marketing plans (including the volume of services or the price of finished goods). However, what is important is that the overall system does not react or respond to these external changes. (In the production and operation information system this overall system response does occur.)

From the previous statements we can perceive the specific characteristics for a general model of a traditional information system. This general model is becoming more widely used, and it is now possible to present a flowchart representing this model which has some degree of acceptance in organizations. Although the above-defined set of characteristics for a traditional information system are beginning to become generally accepted, some systems analysts prefer not to have the word "traditional" as the primary descriptive adjective for such a system. Because of the negative connotations of the word "traditional," we will not label our general model with this descriptive adjective.

TYPE 1 INFORMATION SYSTEM

Figure 7.1 presents a generalized model of a TYPE 1 information system which will be our label for a traditional information system. The separation of the planning phase from the control phase is clearly indicated in this model; all inputs for the network are filtered, screened, and edited by an editing and screening phase. The decision-making group concludes the planning phase by specifying changes in the parameters and variables. The closed sets of online computer programs (symbols A18, A21, and A24) in the three operating systems are designed so that they can respond to these specified changes in parameters and variables (represented by symbol A27).

The editing and screening phase in Figure 7.1 (symbols A1 to A10) filters all input data through four online screens. The first three screens (symbols A6 and A7) are part of an interactive network in which the remote terminal user (symbol A1 or A2) or operator (symbol A5) is notified immediately of any rejects. The three screens are online editing routines that filter for (*a*) authority of user to access system, (*b*) completeness of input data for a document, and (*c*) reasonableness of data for component; other aspects of these three screens were discussed in the explanation of Figure 5.2.[1] The fourth screen (symbol A8 depicts the rejects from this processing operation) is a set of online control procedures and checks that attempts to determine the accuracy of input data, and the rejects from this filter go to the system controller (symbol A9) for review and correction (symbol A10). As explained in Chapter 5, management-oriented criteria can be included in this fourth filter.[2]

Selected relevant information from the control phase (symbols A19, A22, and A25) as well as special planning data including files (symbol A14), other selected data (symbol A13), and tapes from other networks (symbol A12) are filtered through this same set of

---

[1] *Supra,* p. 153.

[2] *Supra,* p. 154.

FIGURE 7.1
A Generalized Model of a TYPE 1 Information System

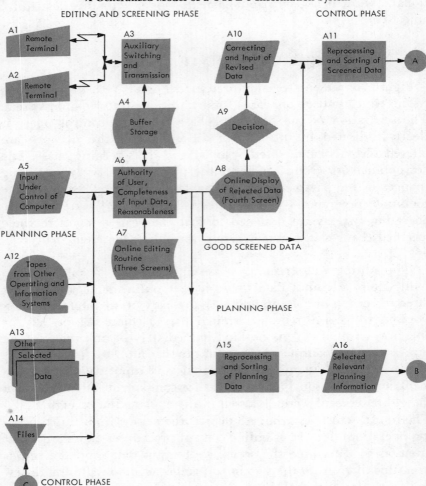

online screens. These planning data are assumed to be generated by a computer system and approaching the status of "screened data" even at the point of input to the screening process (symbol A6). Because of this assumption, the arrow from symbols A12 to A14 indicates a single direction for data flow. Where there are "raw" planning data, the interactive arrangements for rejects and handling input errors will also be followed with these data; in such cases, the data flow

FIGURE 7.1 (*Continued*)

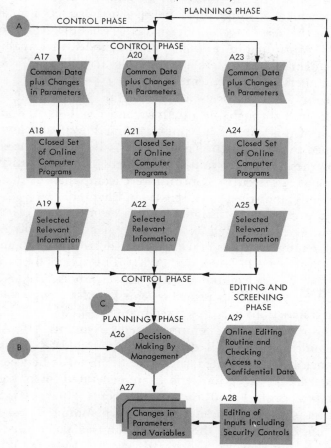

between symbols A12, A13, and A14 with symbol A6 will be in two directions.

The special feature in an information system for implementing the results of management decision-making process (symbol A26 in Figure 7.1) was discussed in the explanation of Figure 3.4.[3] As previously explained, selected elements in the online models are unspecified by design, and these elements require the assignment of values before each respective model is operational. This assignment of values is conveniently accomplished through an expanded "CALL

---

[3] *Supra,* pp. 64–67.

STATEMENT" (in the context of a computer programming statement) in which a value must be specified for each unassigned element in the respective online model. Thus, through processing the *control cards* used in *calling* an online model, the capability for online changes in parameters and variables (symbol A27) is available to members of management.

The set of control cards used in calling an online model (symbol A27) is filtered through the usual screens (symbols A28 and A29 contain all of the features in symbols A6 and A7), and any rejects are returned to management (symbol A26). Because of the sensitive nature of these assigned values of elements to the results of the online operations, security controls are encompassed in these filtering operations along the lines discussed in Chapter 5.[4]

After the changes in assigned values (symbol A27) have progressed through the editing and screening phase (symbols A28 and A29), these filtered inputs move into the control phase to an online location (symbols A17, A20, and A23). The specified changes are made in the online computer programs (symbols A18, A21, and A24), and each of the operating systems handles a high volume of recurring transactions in a prescribed manner.

The outputs from the operating systems (symbols A19, A22, and A25) include both control data and planning data. Measures of performance are accumulated, comparisons are made between actual and standard, and exception reports are generated for physical control, technical control, and management control purposes. Selected information is also accumulated for use in planning. These selected data are not only used in the current planning phase for the next control cycle, but they are also stored (symbol A14) for use in the planning phases in subsequent periods. Note that the planning phase is not restricted to reports and documents generated from the control phase (symbols A12 and A13); instead, the generalized model includes tapes from other operating and information systems as well as selected data from other information sources. Thus, the decision-making group in the TYPE 1 information system is not restricted to a *closed* system for providing data for use during the *planning phase;* a TYPE 1 information system is a closed system only with respect to the *control phase.*

---

[4] *Supra,* pp. 150–59.

THE EIGHT COMMON DIMENSIONS

The eight dimensions of the administrative process and the organizational arrangements encompassed in a TYPE 1 information system are briefly examined for purposes of facilitating comparisons among the five discrete models of information systems. The various combinations of these eight dimensions in networks that are extensions from these five discrete models are not discussed in the interest of time; there are a large number of feasible networks composed of various combinations of these eight dimensions.

First, the models of the administrative process in a TYPE 1 information system include three phases: (*a*) planning phase, (*b*) control phase, and (*c*) editing and screening phase. The organization's management is willing to operate as a closed network for the duration of the control phase; in other words, the time cycle of the control phase is a minimum period in which members of management are willing to forego the right of changing the assignment of organizational resources or assets in carrying out prescribed objectives. Second, the organizational structure of an agency, association, company, or institution possessing a TYPE 1 information system can be a traditional, functional arrangement. However, most organizations with a TYPE 1 information system will have some members of management with dual responsibilities that do not coincide with the standard organization chart. While there are some of these dual or matrix organizational arrangements in a TYPE 1 information system, these arrangements do not dominate the setting as is the case in TYPE 2 information systems.

Third, the decision maker directly associated with a TYPE 1 information system will typically be a major department head, a division head, or the vice president in charge of a functional area. Fourth, the nature of the activity supported by the TYPE 1 information system usually encompasses both vertical and horizontal flows associated with the overall set of activities under the jurisdiction of the decision maker (as specified by the third dimension). Fifth, the only interaction of the decision maker with the computer-based network is in the area of editing and screening; as previously indicated, there is no interaction during the control phase as far as the ability to make online changes in computer programs.

Sixth, the time cycle of the control phase in a TYPE 1 information system tends to be of limited duration. Since the control cycle is a *closed network* to online changes in computer programs, members of management located in changing environmental settings are not willing to forego the right of making a change for more than a day. If the organization operates on an 8-hour shift, an 8-hour interval is a customary time cycle for the network. However, some TYPE 1 information systems operating in organizations with 8-hour shifts have time cycles of less than eight hours, such as, a 4-hour cycle, a 2-hour cycle, or a 1-hour cycle.

Seventh, the interface of the TYPE 1 information system with other networks is represented in Figure 7.1 by Symbol A12. Within the control phase (even though it is not depicted in Figure 7.1), there may be activity and functional programs that assist in the performance of physical control, technical control, and management controls, and these latter types of programs may be included in any of the five discrete models of information systems.

Eighth, the data structure in a TYPE 1 information system includes consideration of both currency of data and timeliness of data. The absence of any online interaction by the decision maker with the online computer programs in the control phase minimizes the pressure for any immediate data retrieval capabilities. Complete, up-to-date data are required prior to the start of each control cycle, and this is the minimum period for feedback.

A given computer-based network may be a TYPE 1 information system with these exact characteristics of the eight dimensions of the administrative process and the organizational arrangements. As previously indicated, there are numerous degrees of variation from a given discrete model. We will examine only three major prototypes of variations from a TYPE 1 information system. This chapter presents the special characteristics of the responsibility accounting system; Chapter 8 presents the special characteristics of the profitability accounting system. Extensions from these two prototypes of TYPE 1 information systems are presented in Chapter 9 as the critical path planning and scheduling information system.

SPECIAL CHARACTERISTICS OF THE RESPONSIBILITY ACCOUNTING SYSTEM

The general model for a responsibility accounting system contains two refinements over the general model for a TYPE 1 information system. First, in a responsibility accounting system the information within all the major information flows can be precisely expressed as either accounting *financial* data or as accounting *statistical* data (such as performance data). Second, there is a hierarchy of decision makers compatible with the organization chart, and the activities of decision makers at one level of the organization structure are monitored by decision makers at the next level above.

If the general model contains these two refinements, then several generalizations can be made. First, all information used in the planning phase and in the control phase (the monitoring of activities during the period covered by the "plan") can be adequately expressed either as accounting financial data or as accounting statistical data. This generalization is applicable to three different conditions: (*a*) all information *requirements,* (*b*) all information *sources,* and (*c*) all information *uses* can be adequately expressed as either accounting financial data or as accounting statistical data.

Second, the financial and cost accounting system must serve as the framework for *all* information flows within a responsibity accounting model. In other words, the financial and cost accounting procedures used must be modified so that they are compatible with the information requirements of the various decision makers within the organization.

Third, the time frame of each cycle is the minimum time span within which there is a requirement for accounting information. Thus, an accounting reporting period that corresponds with the time frame of each cycle will meet the time dimensions of all information requirements of the various decision makers within the organization.

Fourth, the organization under scrutiny contains a clearly defined organization chart with well established lines of authority. Following these lines of authority, supervisory and administrative functions must be delegated to the various supervisory personnel. Concurrently with this delegation of responsibility, there is an accountability requirement which flows in the reverse order. This requires that the individual who has delegated the responsibility must be informed by his or her supervisory management what *was* and *was not* accomplished. In other words, there is feedback from supervisory management to department management. Figure 7.2 reflects this feedback relationship.

This delegation of responsibility loop exists also between departmental management and the chief executive officer of the organiza-

FIGURE 7.2
The Loop Relation

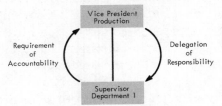

tion, with an accounting requirement incumbent upon the recipient. The chief executive officer of a company, for example, has been delegated authority from the stockholders, the board of directors, governmental bodies and agencies, and the general public (social society as a whole). Likewise, there is a reporting requirement incumbent upon this chief executive officer of accountability. This external loop relation of the chief executive officer with (*a*) board of directors, (*b*) stockholders, (*c*) governmental bodies and agencies, and (*d*) the general public would differ from Figure 7.2 only in terms of the titles of individuals, number of loops, and the substitution of the word "authority" for "delegation of responsibility."

Continuing with this example, this feedback relationship between the chief executive officer and individuals external to the organization can be viewed from another perspective that is more compatible with the information systems approach. These individuals external to the organization can be described as decision makers outside the organization who impose requirements for information upon the organization's accounting system. These external requirements for information are specified by legal institution and by custom and tradition; and these external decision makers include stockholders, governmental tax authorities, Security and Exchange Commission personnel, members of governmental regulatory agencies, and the general public.

For purposes of comparison, several distinctions can be made between the information requirements of internal and external decision makers. First, the time dimensions of the information flow for the typical internal decision maker is substantially different from that of the typical external decision maker. Internal decision makers desire information weekly, daily, or more frequently; external decision makers normally require information on either a quarter or an annual basis.

Second, the specific information requirements of various external decision makers are normally presented in a number of formal, written documents, and there is a high degree of homogeneity in their specified information requirements. On the other hand, the specific information requirements of the various internal decision makers have typically not been completely reduced to writing, and there is a high degree of heterogeneity in their specified information requirements.

Finally, the character of the information within the information flows is significantly different for the external decision maker versus the internal decision maker. Information transmitted to an external decision maker must be objectively measured by a financial accountant according to some prescribed set of procedures and rules. Frequently this measurement process must be attested by a certified public accountant. On the other hand, information transmitted to internal decision makers may be based on several different levels of measurement or scales of measurement.

In summary, the internal information requirements are quite demanding in terms of time dimension, range of requirements, scope, and measurement characteristic, and the typical external information requirements are normally completely contained within these more exacting internal requirements. Based on this latter fact, the systems analyst can design an internal information system for coping with the information requirements of internal decision makers while simultaneously satisfying all the information requirements of external decision makers. Since the time frame of the network of information flows for external decision makers is substantially longer than that for internal flows, the systems analyst will design an information system so that it is initially compatible with the internal requirements.

Consideration is now focused upon the development of a coding pattern that permits the responsibility accounting system to satisfy fully all internal and external requirements for information. For clarity, the internal and external reports generated by the application of this coding pattern to a given organization are illustrated and described before the coding pattern is discussed.

RESPONSIBILITY ACCOUNTING REPORTS

This section presents the responsibility accounting reports for the United Manufacturing Company. Since the organization structure is the backbone of a responsibility accounting reporting system, Figure 7.3 presents the organization chart for the United Manufacturing Company.

FIGURE 7.3
Responsibility System for Internal Reports*

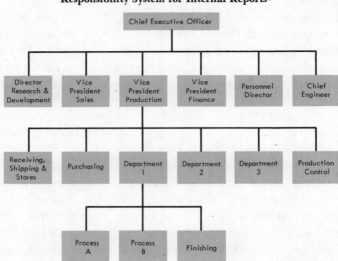

* Only selected segments of the organization chart are included, and between each segment of the organization chart it is assumed that the internal loop relation of delegation of responsibility with a requirement of accountability exists as illustrated in Figure 7.2.

The time dimensions or time frame of each cycle in the United Manufacturing Company's responsibility accounting system is one month. The responsibility reports covering the July cycle of the current year for Process A (see Figure 7.4), Department 1 (see Figure 7.5), vice president—production (see Figure 7.6) and chief executive officer (see Figure 7.7) are illustrated on the following pages. The reader should trace the cost data from one report to the next and note that a responsibility accounting system is like a group of building blocks or steps with each higher level indicating the

FIGURE 7.4
Process A Costs (Foreman) for the Month of July

	Current Month		Year to Date	
	Actual	(Over) Under Budget	Actual	(Over) Under Budget
Direct materials	$24,800	$(600)	$176,400	$(3,500)
Direct labor	3,850	(25)	27,000	(150)
Factory overhead—foreman's responsibility:				
Supplies	200	—	1,500	(100)
Power and utilities	100	—	700	—
Maintenance and repairs	200	(100)	1,500	(200)
Salaries—staff	700	—	4,900	—
Depreciation—equipment	700	—	4,900	—
Total foreman's responsibility	$30,550	$(725)	$216,900	$(3,950)
Factory overhead—others' responsibilities:				
Depreciation—plant	300	—	2,100	—
Insurance	100	—	700	—
Taxes—real estate and personal property	200	—	1,400	—
Payroll taxes and employee benefit programs	500	—	3,500	—
Total Process A costs	$31,650	$(725)	$224,600	$(3,950)

FIGURE 7.5
Department 1 Costs (Supervisor) for the Month of July

	Current Month		Year to Date	
	Actual	(Over) Under Budget	Actual	(Over) Under Budget
Supervisor's office	$ 1,800	$ (100)	$ 12,200	$ (300)
Process A foreman's cost	30,550	(725)	216,900	(3,950)
Process B foreman's cost	6,375	(115)	44,725	(800)
Finishing foreman's cost	3,875	(75)	26,150	(550)
Total supervisor's responsibility	$42,600	$(1,015)	$299,975	$(5,600)
Factory overhead—others' responsibilities:				
Depreciation—plant	900	—	6,300	—
Insurance	300	—	2,100	—
Taxes—real estate and personal property	600	—	4,200	—
Payroll taxes and employee benefit programs	1,100	—	7,700	—
Total Department 1 costs	$45,500	$(1,015)	$320,275	$(5,600)

FIGURE 7.6
Factory Cost Summary (Vice President of Production) for the Month of July

	Current Month		Year to Date	
	Actual	(Over) Under Budget	Actual	(Over) Under Budget
Vice president's office*	$ 10,400	$ 200	$ 74,500	$ 1,200
Dept. 1 supervisor's cost	42,600	(1,015)	299,975	(5,600)
Dept. 2 supervisor's cost	35,600	(1,275)	245,625	(5,350)
Dept. 3 supervisor's cost	38,100	(825)	264,700	(3,775)
Production control manager's cost . .	1,800	(100)	12,200	(300)
Purchasing manager's cost†	2,500	(800)	13,900	(2,000)
Receiving, shipping, and stores manager's cost	1,600	400	13,000	1,000
Total vice president's responsibility	$132,600	$(3,415)	$923,900	$(14,825)
Factory overhead—others' responsibilities:				
Depreciation—plant	3,100	—	21,700	—
Insurance	800	—	5,600	—
Taxes—real estate and personal property	1,900	—	13,300	—
Total factory cost summary . .	$138,400	$(3,415)	$964,500	$(14,825)
Other items:				
Materials purchased at standard (material records are maintained at standard)	$ 63,400	$ —	$484,100	$ —
Material price variance	800	(800)	1,900	(1,900)

° Payroll taxes and employee benefit programs for all factory-related employees are considered to be under the responsibility of the vice president of production. Since the charges vary significantly depending on the length of service by each worker, management at United Manufacturing Company feels that it would be inappropriate to hold foremen or supervisors responsible for such charges. (Note: it is acknowledged that some accountants would argue that it is not proper to hold the vice president of production accountable for such costs, but that the management labor relations committee should be held accountable for the cost of employee benefit programs. If a standard cost system for direct labor were employed, the costs of payroll taxes and employee benefit programs would be part of the standard cost hourly rate and thus would be included in the costs chargeable to the lowest level of accountability. Thus, the payroll taxes and employee benefit programs are special items demanding consideration at the United Manufacturing Company because direct labor is not charged at standard.)

† The purchasing manager's cost includes the material price variance.

source of data. At the United Manufacturing Company, the head of each responsibility unit participates in the planning of the budget for that responsibility unit and subsequently is held accountable for the expenditures charged to that unit. The budget columns in these reports present accounting data on a management-by-exception basis which are expressed in terms of standard cost data (in other words, only variations from standard are printed).

After the responsibility reports have been prepared, it is necessary to re-sort the data to prepare the traditional reports. This re-sorting

FIGURE 7.7
Departmental Cost Summary (Chief Executive Officer) for the Month of July

	Current Month		Year to Date	
	Actual	(Over) Under Budget	Actual	(Over) Under Budget
Chief executive officer's office (for purposes of emphasis, certain items charged to this office are identified as follows):				
Depreciation–plant	$ 4,000	$ –	$ 28,000	$ –
Insurance	1,100	–	7,700	–
Taxes–real estate and personal property	2,400	–	16,800	–
All other items	9,600	(100)	66,700	(200)
Total chief executive officer's office	$ 17,100	(100)	$ 119,200	$ (200)
Vice president production's cost	132,600	(3,415)	923,900	(14,825)
Director of R & D's cost	3,400	100	24,200	300
Personnel director's cost	4,200	–	29,800	(200)
Vice president–sales' cost	37,200	(400)	267,600	(900)
Vice president–finance's cost	15,600	(100)	108,000	500
Chief engineer's cost	8,200	–	57,200	200
Total chief executive officer's responsibility	$218,300	$(3,915)	$1,529,900	$(15,125)
Other items:				
Materials purchased at standard	$ 63,400	$ –	$ 484,100	$ –
Material price variance	800	(800)	1,900	(1,900)
Sales, net	274,200	100*	1,910,200	(1,200)†
Other income less other expense	9,100	(200)†	64,800	(300)†

* Indicates favorable variance, actual revenue higher than budgeted revenue.
† Indicates unfavorable variance, actual revenue less than budgeted revenue.

process can be performed in as much detail as desired by members of management. The extreme position would be to re-sort all the data until each type of cost is ascertained, such as determining the aggregate cost for supplies by totaling the supply cost by department or other responsible unit. At the other end of the gamut, no attempt would be made to specify the detailed cost below the vice president level. In this case, a detailed re-sorting of cost data would occur only when special cost studies were undertaken.

Figure 7.8 presents United Manufacturing Company's re-sorting of departmental costs to product costs. For purposes of illustration, the extreme right-hand column of this exhibit indicates the source of data by line.

Now that the data have been re-sorted according to product costs,

FIGURE 7.8

Re-Sorting of Departmental Costs to Product Costs for the Month of July

	Current Month		Year to Date		
	Actual	*(Over) Under Budget*	*Actual*	*(Over) Under Budget*	
Total chief executive officer's responsibility	$218,000	$(3,915)	$1,529,900	$(15,125)	
Other items:					
Materials purchased at standard	63,400	–	484,100	–	
Material price variance	800	(800)	1,900	(1,900)	
Sales, net	274,200	100	1,910,200	(1,200)	
Other income less other expense	9,100	(200)	64,800	(300)	
	The Re-Sorting Process				
Net sales	$274,200	$ 100	$1,910,200	$ (1,200)	Figure 7.7
Cost of production:					
Direct materials at standard					
Dept. 1:					
Process A	$ 24,800	$ (600)	$ 176,400	$ (3,500)	Figure 7.4
Process B	1,800	(100)	12,700	(700)	not shown
Total Dept. 1	$ 26,600	$ (700)	$ 189,100	$ (4,200)	
Dept. 2 (details omitted) . . .	23,800	(1,100)	163,200	(4,300)	not shown
Dept. 3 (details omitted) . . .	24,800	(700)	171,700	(3,000)	not shown
Total direct materials at standard cost	$ 75,200	$(2,500)	$ 524,000	$(11,500)	
Direct labor					
Dept. 1:					
Process A	$ 3,850	$ (25)	$ 27,000	$ (150)	Figure 7.4
Process B	3,375	(15)	23,625	(100)	not shown
Finishing unit	2,075	25	14,750	(50)	not shown
Total Dept. 1	$ 9,300	$ (15)	$ 65,375	$ (300)	
Dept. 2 (details omitted) . . .	7,800	(75)	54,425	(350)	not shown
Dept. 3 (details omitted) . . .	9,100	(25)	63,600	(75)	not shown
Total direct labor	$ 26,200	$ (115)	$ 183,400	$ (725)	
Factory overhead*					
Aggregate value included in vice president—production's factory cost summary†	$ 30,400	$ –	$ 214,600	$ (700)	not shown
Chief engineer's cost	8,200	–	57,200	200	Figure 7.7
Expenses not charged to department	8,200	–	57,400	–	not shown
Transfers	(700)	–	(4,900)	–	not shown
Total factory overhead . .	$ 46,100	$ –	$ 324,300	$ (500)	
Total cost of production with materials at standard	$147,500	$(2,615)	$1,031,700	$(12,725)	
Material price variance†	800	(800)	1,900	(1,900)	Figure 7.6
Total actual cost of production	$148,300	$(3,415)	$1,033,600	$(14,625)	

FIGURE 7.8 (*Continued*)

	Current Month		Year to Date		
	Actual	(Over) Under Budget	Actual	(Over) Under Budget	
Cost of goods sold:					
Total actual cost of production	$148,300	$(3,415)	$1,033,600	$(14,625)	
Change in finished goods inventory (increase)	(4,300)	–	18,000	–	not shown
Total cost of goods sold	$144,000	$(3,415)	$1,051,600	$(14,625)	
Operating expenses:					
Director of R & D's cost	$ 3,400	$ 100	$ 24,200	$ 300	Figure 7.7
Personnel Director's cost	4,200	–	29,800	(200)	Figure 7.7
Vice president—sales' cost . . .	37,200	(400)	267,600	(900)	Figure 7.7
Vice president—financ's cost . .	15,600	(100)	108,000	500	Figure 7.7
Chief executive officer's office cost	17,100	(100)	119,200	(200)	Figure 7.7
Expenses not charged to department	700	–	4,900	–	not shown
Transfers	(8,200)	–	(57,400)	–	not shown
Total operating expenses	$ 70,000	$ (500)	$ 496,300	$ (500)	
Other income less other expense	$ 9,100	$ (200)	$ 64,800	$ (300)	Figure 7.7

° Each element of factory overhead can be shown and each instance of the element reported as indicated for direct materials and direct labor; however, for purposes of illustration, only aggregate values are presented.

† The material price variance which was originally charged to the purchasing manager is not included in the computed value under "factory overhead," but (as indicated) is presented on a separate line.

‡ For purposes of illustration, only aggregate values are presented.

it is possible to prepare a traditional income statement (see Figure 7.9).

CODING PATTERN

The responsibility accounting reports for the United Manufacturing Company were illustrated in the previous section, and special attention was given to the re-sorting process. This re-sorting process is based upon a coding pattern. When financial accounting and cost accounting data are initially recognized as inputs to the responsibility accounting system, these sources of accounting data must be coded so that they can be easily processed and transmitted in the

FIGURE 7.9
Income Statement for the Month of July

	Current Month		Year to Date	
	Actual	*(Over) Under Budget*	*Actual*	*(Over) Under Budget*
Net sales*	$274,200	$ 100	$1,910,200	$ (1,200)
Cost of sales at budget†	140,585	–	1,036,975	–
Gross profit at budget	$133,615	$ 100	$ 873,225	$ (1,200)
Manufacturing variances:				
Material price variance	$ 800	$ (800)	$ 1,900	$ (1,900)
Material usage variance	2,500	(2,500)	11,500	(11,500)
Labor time variance.........	115	(115)	725	(725)
Overhead variance	–	–	500	(500)
Total manufacturing variance . .	$ 3,415	$(3,415)	$ 14,625	$(14,625)
Gross profit	$130,200	$ 3,515	$ 858,600	$ 13,425
Operating expenses	70,000	(500)	496,300	(500)
Profit from operation.........	$ 60,200	$ 4,015	$ 362,300	$ 13,925
Other income less other expense. . .	9,100	(200)	64,800	(300)
Earnings before taxes	$ 69,300	$ 3,815	$ 427,100	$ 13,625
Provision for income taxes	34,600	1,900	213,000	6,800
Net income for period	$ 34,700	$ 1,915	$ 214,100	$ 6,825

° Competitive conditions forced a reduction in the sales price per unit during the first quarter of the year; however, normal prices were reestablished during the second quarter. Extremely severe winter storms of ice and snow forced the production plants to be closed for 10 working days. When operations were resumed, management decided against working overtime to restore the inventory to its previous level.
† The data for "cost of sales at budget" and for each of the variances are presented in Figure 7.8. The former values are computed as follows:

	Current Month	Year to Date
Total cost of goods sold (actual)	$144,000	$1,051,600
Less unfavorable variance	3,415	14,625
Cost of goods sold at budget	$140,585	$1,036,975

appropriate format to the many decision makers that require information.

This coding pattern draws heavily upon the two refinements that the general model for a responsibility accounting system has over other TYPE 1 information systems. Specifically, the general ledger chart of accounts and the organization chart are used as the two sides of a large matrix in which the coding pattern is developed for a given business organization.

Figure 7.10 illustrates a segment of the matrix used by the United Manufacturing Company in the development of a coding pattern. Based upon this exhibit, it would appear that a seven-digit code would satisfy all requirements for information. These seven digits are illustrated as follows:

FIGURE 7.10
Coding Pattern Matrix

	Foreman Process A	Foreman Process B	Foreman Finishing	Supervisor, Department 1	Manager, Receiving, Shipping and Stores	Manager, Purchasing	Supervisor, Department 2	Supervisor, Department 3	Manager, Production and Control	Vice President—Production	Director, Research and Development	Vice President—Sales	Vice President—Finance	Personnel Director	Chief Engineer	Chief Executive Officer
CODE	431	432	433	430	410	420	440	450	460	400	200	300	500	600	700	100
Direct materials 631	1	1	1	5			5	5	5	5						5
Direct labor 641	1	1	1	5			5	5	5	5						5
Factory supplies 651	1	1	1	1,5	1	1	1,5	1,5	1	1,5						5
Factory power and utilities 652	1	1	1	1,5	1	1	1,5	1,5	1	1,5						5
Factory maintenance and repairs 653	1	1	1	5			5	5	5	5						5
Factory salaries— staff 654	1	1	1	1,5	1	1	1,5	1,5	1	1,5						5

Key:
1 = Cost for which decision maker is responsible for incurring expenditure.
2 = Amortization charges for which decision maker was initially responsible for incurring expenditure.
3 = Cost that benefit decision maker's activities but for which other decision makers currently have responsibility for incurring expenditure.
4 = Amortization charges that benefit decision maker's activities but for which other decision makers were initially responsible for incurring expenditure.
5 = Summary information on cost and amortization charges for which decision maker has an administrative responsibility for monitoring the activities of subordinates.

1234567	Seven-digit code.
123xxxx	The first three digits would designate the general ledger account number.
xxx456x	Digits four, five, and six would designate the organization unit to which an expenditure relates or the organization unit that benefits from the expenditure or the organization unit to which an amortization charge relates or benefits.
xxxxxx7	The seventh digit would designate the characteristic of the cost or amortization charge per the key presented in Figure 7.10.

Example:
6414311   Direct Labor (#641xxxx) that relates to or benefits Process A in Department 1 (#xxx431x) and for which the Foreman of Process A was responsible for incurring said expenditure (#xxxxxx1).

Illustration:

Assume that a payroll voucher was processed for the exact amount of direct labor for the month of July per Figure 7.8. The total direct labor voucher of $26,200 would be coded as follows:

code 6414311 for $3,850	Direct Labor, Department 1, Process A, Foreman of Process A responsible for incurring expenditure.
code 6414321 for $3,375	Direct Labor, Department 1, Process B, Foreman of Process B responsible for incurring expenditure.
code 6414331 for $2,075	Direct Labor, Department 1, Finishing, Foreman of Finishing responsible for incurring expenditure.
$9,300	The total direct labor for Department 1 is *not coded* 6414305; in fact, at the United Manufacturing Company it is not necessary to code this amount.
$7,800	The total direct labor for Department 2 is not coded 6414405; instead, the sections (which are not shown) within the Department are coded in the same way as that followed for Department 1.
$9,100	The total direct labor for Department 3 is likewise not coded 6414505.

At the United Manufacturing Company the lines of authority have been clearly specified and are compatible with the organization chart. Therefore, it is not necessary to use the code xxx4305, for this specified code can always be determined by adding the xxx43xx's for that general ledger account.

In other business organizations, the specified lines of authority may not be completely compatible with the organization chart. For example, the supervisor of the finishing section in Department 1 may report to the Superintendent of Department 1 except for matters relating to marketing, in which case she or he reports to the marketing manager. Furthermore, the supervisor of this finishing section in Department 1 may have the responsibility for initially incurring certain types of expenditures that relate to marketing.

Whenever the specified lines of authority are not completely compatible with the organization chart, the coding pattern will have to contain extra digits to provide for these additional information requirements. When this situation does occur, it represents a variation in the general model for a responsibility accounting system. (It is suggested that the reader re-examine the first paragraph under the heading "Special Characteristics of the Responsibility Accounting System" which was presented earlier in this chapter.)

ACCOUNTING STATISTICAL DATA

The first refinement that a responsibility accounting system contains over a TYPE 1 information system is that the information within all of the major information flows included in this analysis is such that the information can be precisely expressed as either accounting financial data or as accounting statistical data (such as performance data).

Attention thus far in this chapter has focused exclusively upon accounting *financial* data. However, the previous discussions, including the development of a coding pattern, are equally applicable to accounting *statistical* data.

When the various decision makers throughout the organization are collectively engaged in the planning phase of the information systems cycle, they may express the plan in more than dollar objectives. As previously stated, the general model for a responsibility accounting system will accept certain nonfinancial accounting data.

All of the significant information used in developing the formal plan may be included as yardsticks or criteria for measuring performance. This means that the responsibility accounting system must provide for recording, accumulating, and reporting the progress toward each of these criteria for measuring performance. Following are some typical yardsticks:

1. Units of material.
2. Hours of labor.
3. Amount of spoilage.
4. Number of purchase order processed.
5. Number of invoices processed.
6. Line items on invoices.
7. Letters written.
8. Customers called on.
9. Miles traveled by salespeople.
10. Day's subsistence paid to salespeople.
11. Sales orders received.

There are almost an unlimited number of yardsticks that may be used, and each possible yardstick must be evaluated in terms of the anticipated benefit derived from the accumulation of these data. Although, sometimes these data can be used in special management studies performed perhaps a year later, the cost of accumulating such information cannot be justified on the basis of its *possible* future use in studies yet unplanned. Rather, the systems analyst determines after evaluating the current computer-based network that additional information should be accumulated for use by decision makers in a study already planned to commence in the near future.

From another perspective, data in the TYPE 1 information system have been filtered, screened, edited, and reprocessed. At nominal additional cost, an array of statistical data can be accumulated, compared with standard, and subjected to exception reporting procedures. However, these reports are worthless unless the decision makers can and will use them. The systems analyst who adheres to the information systems approach does not worry about management not using a report. Members of management have participated in each of the five phases in a formal program for planning and implementing an information system. Members of management have participated in professional development and reorientation programs and have assisted in the analysis of their own information uses and in the specification of their information requirements. Therefore, after the information requirements and information sources are matched and encompassed in a network for a TYPE 1 information system, the resulting reports merely contain data previously requested and specified by members of management.

REPORTING GUIDELINES

The primary guidelines followed in designing effective internal reports in a responsibility accounting system must comply with the needs of the users of the reports (the decision makers) as to format, content, and frequently. Monetary factors regarding the cost of preparing such accountability reports are secondary considerations especially when the organization has a TYPE 1 information system and has the online capability of quickly reprocessing data in accordance with the unique requirements of a single user.

While these primary and secondary considerations may appear to be simple, difficulties are encountered in the practical implementation of an effective internal reporting system. First, many decision makers are unfamiliar with alternative reporting systems and are capable of requesting only those types of information presentations with which they are familiar. Second, though some decision makers are conversant with alternative reporting arrangements, they resist any change from traditional procedures (regardless of the monetary considerations) because of the organization aspects of any change.

Sometimes, in those situations where a decision maker is familiar with other reporting systems but adheres to traditional procedures because of organization factors and other considerations, a member of management may periodically request special information from an individual to whom responsibility has been delegated. These latter information data requests are as much a part of the reporting system as the prescribed traditional reports.

SUMMARY

This chapter examined the general model for a TYPE 1 information system and considered the practical steps that the systems analyst employs in grouping information flows and forming information systems. Next, the special characteristics of the general model for a responsibility accounting system were examined, and responsibility accounting reports were illustrated in detail for the purpose of emphasizing the re-sorting process that occurs at each step of the way in the responsibility accounting system. After seeing the application of the reprocessing of coded data, attention was given to the development of a coding pattern for accomplishing this re-sorting process.

TOPICS FOR CLASS DISCUSSION

1. Assume that you are a member of the confidentiality of data committee for an organization having a TYPE 1 information system. Indicate the types of security controls and monitoring procedures that you would suggest for a computer-based network similar to Figure 7.1. Explain your recommendations.

2. A TYPE 1 information system is described as a "closed network." How can it be a closed network while members of management engaged in the planning process can use any data they desire in the planning phase? Explain this apparent inconsistency of being an open network for planning but closed for other operations. Are there logical reasons for this position? Explain.

3. After completing her study, a systems analyst describes a given business organization's information network as a "typical responsibility accounting system in which the information cycle is one week." Based on this study, what would you expect to be the nature and general condition of the environment in which this business organization is located? What would you expect to be the nature of the administrative process in this business organization? Be specific and explain the above generalization in detail.

4. A TYPE 1 information system contains a special capability for online implementation of changes in parameters and variables as determined by members of management. Explain the operation of this capability including the nature of the task performed under each of the three phases: (*a*) planning phase, (*b*) editing and screening phase, and (*c*) control phase.

5. Explain the two refinements of a responsibility accounting system over the general model for a TYPE 1 information system.

6. Cost accounting reporting procedures as followed by many accountants in numerous business organizations are designed to provide historical cost data encompassing several kinds of information: (1) the results of operation, (2) unit costs for pricing inven-

tory, (3) cost accumulation to be used in pricing products for sales, and (4) cost data to be used for evaluating alternatives in capital expenditure decisions. While the typical accounting system may provide historical cost data for these information requirements, the system does not provide cost data in a manner that is most effective for cost control. In order to be effective in the area of cost control, the accounting and reporting system should permit control of expenditures by directly relating the reports of expenditures to the individuals within the business enterprise who are responsible for their control.

Do you agree with this statement? Evaluate this statement from the perspective of the information systems approach. Be specific.

7. Why is the time frame of each cycle in a responsibility accounting system so important to the systems analyst? Explain the impact that the time dimensions have upon design of a responsibility accounting system.

8. "In a very small business organization, a formal responsibility accounting system may not be necessary. Frequently, most of the benefits that would be derived from such a system can be achieved by establishing a monthly cost reporting system that features planned versus actual contribution to margin for each product. In addition, a system of control over direct labor and materials will satisfy most of the other benefits that would be derived from a responsibility accounting system." From the standpoint of a systems analyst, evaluate the above statement.

CASE 7–1. CENTRAL NATURAL GAS COMPANY

The Central Natural Gas Company serves 484,000 gas customers in five states. Organizationally, each state's operations are under the management of a general superintendent. In four of the five states, the area is divided into two divisions. The remaining state is not divided; thus, the Central Natural Gas Company has a total of nine divisions. Each division is headed by a division manager.

Each division is partitioned into three districts, and each district is headed by a district manager. The town is the next organizational unit below the district level, and each town's operations are under the direction of a supervisor. In summary, the Central Natural Gas Company has 5 general superintendents, 9 division managers, 27 district managers, and 353 town supervisors, and this organizational structure for the Central Natural Gas Company is depicted in Exhibit A.

The public accounting firm with which you are associated has been engaged by the management of Central Natural Gas Company to develop a responsibility accounting system. In addition to responsibility statements for the various responsibility units within the company and an annual detailed operating statement for the Federal Power Commission, the Central Natural Gas Company's controller requested detailed operating statements by town, by district, by division, and by state. These detailed operating statements will be based on full-absorption costing, and *a given general ledger account may contain elements of both direct and amortization charges.*

You are assigned to this engagement and begin to review the company's operations. You note that the 353 town supervisors are not all of equal status. In fact, some of the supervisors might more appropriately be called "foremen," since the supervisor in a given town may be over the supervisors in two or three of the surrounding towns.

After further study of the organization chart and the administrative process, you conclude that there are 286 area heads for responsibility accounting purposes. The controller also clarified what he meant by "responsibility accounting reports." The contents of a "responsibility accounting report" should be restricted to those costs for which the manager of a given responsibility unit has responsibility for incurring the related expenditure. Furthermore, company-wide responsibility for the procurement of certain items of supply and material has been assigned as an additional task to be performed by selected responsibility area heads.

You are asked by a manager from the public accounting firm to design a coding pattern which will produce operating statements on a responsibility basis and will consolidate into one top management report and, at the same time, will contain the appropriate designation of expenditures for preparing detailed operating statements on a full-absorption cost basis for the various geographical and political units: by town, by district, by division, and by state. The attached appendix presents the *Uniform System of Accounts* as prescribed by the Federal Power Commission for natural gas companies subject to the provisions of the Natural Gas Act. The Central Natural Gas Company is subject to these regulations.

EXHIBIT A
Central Natural Gas Company
(organizational structure)

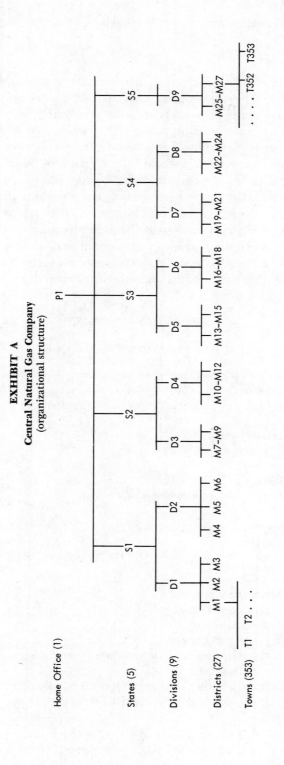

Home Office (1)

States (5)

Divisions (9)

Districts (27)

Towns (353)

REQUIRED:

1. Specify the broad types of information requirements, organizational arrangements, and administrative processes that must be satisfied by the proposed computer-based network.
2. Design a single coding pattern that will incorporate all the factors specified in item 1 above and that will be used in a TYPE 1 information system. Indicate the relation of your coding pattern to the filters in the editing and screening phase.
3. After the data have been coded, entered into the network, filtered, screened, edited, and processed, you are to design a computer-generated reprocessing and data compression arrangement that will represent multi-dimensional data in a minimum number of digits. Indicate your suggested coding pattern for this online state and explain the purpose of each digit.

APPENDIX TO CASE 7–1

UNIFORM SYSTEM OF ACCOUNTS

Prescribed for Natural Gas Companies (Class A and Class B)
Subject to the Provisions of the Natural Gas Act
Federal Power Commission

Balance Sheet Accounts
Omitted for purposes of this case study

Gas Plant Accounts
Omitted for purposes of this case study

Income Accounts

1. Utility Operating Income

400	Operating revenues.

Operating Expenses.

401	Operation expense.
402	Maintenance expense.
403	Depreciation expense.
404.1	Amortization and depletion of producing natural gas land and land rights.
404.2	Amortization of underground storage land and land rights.
404.3	Amortization of other limited-term gas plant.

405   Amortization of other gas plant.
406   Amortization of glas plant acquisition adjustments.
407.1   Amortization of property losses.
407.2   Amortization of conversion expenses.
408   Taxes other than income taxes.
409   Income taxes.
410   Provision for deferred income taxes.
411   Income taxes deferred in prior years—Cr.
               Total Operating Expenses

           Operating income.
412–413 Income from gas plant leased to others.
414   Other utility operating income.
               Total Operating Income

2. Other Income

415–416 Income from merchandising, jobbing, and contract work.
417   Income from nonutility operations.
418   Nonoperating rental income.
419   Interest and dividend income.
421   Miscellaneous nonoperating income.

3. Miscellaneous Income Deductions

425   Miscellaneous amortization.
426   Other income deductions.
               Total income deductions.
               Income before Interest Charges

4. Interest Charges

427   Interest on long-term debt.
428   Amortization of debt discount and expense.
429   Amortization of premium on debt—Cr.
430   Interest on debt to associated companies.
431   Other interest expense.
432   Interest charged to construction—Cr.
               Total interest charges.
               Net Income

5. Earned Surplus

216   Unappropriated earned surplus (at beginning of period) .
433   Balance transferred from income.
434   Miscellaneous credits to surplus.
435   Miscellaneous debits to surplus.
436   Appropriations of surplus.

           Net Addition to Earned Surplus
437   Dividends declared—preferred stock.

438   Dividends declared—common stock.
216   Unappropriated earned surplus (at end of period) .

Operating Revenue Accounts

1. Sales of Gas

480   Residential sales.
481   Commercial and industrial sales.
482   Other sales to public authorities.
483   Sales for resale.
484   Interdepartmental sales.

2. Other Operating Revenues

487   Forfeited discounts.
488   Miscellaneous service revenues.
489   Revenues from transportation of gas of others.
490   Sales of products extracted from natural gas.
491   Revenues from natural gas processed by others.
492   Incidental gasoline and oil sales.
493   Rent from gas property.
494   Interdepartmental rents.
495   Other gas revenues.

Operation and Maintenance Expense Accounts

1. Production Expenses

A. Manufactured Gas Production Expenses
        Omitted for purposes of this case study
B. Natural Gas Production Expenses
        Omitted for purposes of this case study
C. Exploration and Development Expenses
        Omitted for purposes of this case study
D. Other Gas Supply Expenses
        Operation
800   Natural gas well head purchases.
801   Natural gas field line purchases.
802   Natural gas gasoline plant outlet purchases.
803   Natural gas transmission line purchases.
804   Natural gas city gate purchases.
805   Other gas purchases.
806   Exchange gas.
807   Purchased gas expense.
808   Gas withdrawn from underground storage—Cr.
809   Gas delivered to underground storage—Cr.
810   Gas used for compressor station fuel—Cr.

811	Gas used for products extraction—Cr.
812	Gas used for other utility operations—Cr.
813	Other gas supply expenses.

2. Underground Storage Expenses

Operation

814	Operation supervision and engineering.
815	Maps and records.
816	Wells expenses.
817	Lines expenses.
818	Compressor station expenses.
819	Compressor station fuel and power.
820	Measuring and regulating station expenses.
821	Purification expenses.
822	Exploration and development.
823	Gas losses.
824	Other expenses.
825	Storage well royalties.
826	Rents.

Maintenance

830	Maintenance supervision and engineering.
831	Maintenance of structures and improvements.
832	Maintenance of wells.
833	Maintenance of lines.
834	Maintenance of compressor station equipment.
835	Maintenance of measuring and regulating station equipment.
836	Maintenance of purification equipment.
837	Maintenance of other equipment.

3. Local Storage Expenses

Operation

840	Operation supervision and engineering.
841	Operation labor and expenses.
842	Rents.

Maintenance

843	Maintenance supervision and engineering.
844	Maintenance of structures and improvements.
845	Maintenance of gas holders.
846	Maintenance of other equipment.

4. Transmission Expenses

Operation

850	Operation supervision and engineering.
851	System control and load dispatching.
852	Communication system expenses.

853   Compressor station labor expenses.
854   Gas for compressor station fuel.
855   Other fuel and power for compressor stations.
856   Mains expenses.
857   Measuring and regulating station expenses.
858   Transmission and compression of gas by others.
859   Other expenses.
860   Rents.
        Maintenance
861   Maintenance supervision and engineering.
862   Maintenance of structures and improvements.
863   Maintenance of mains.
864   Maintenance of compressor station equipment.
865   Maintenance of measuring and regulating station equipment.
866   Maintenance of communication equipment.
867   Maintenance of other equipment.

5. Distribution Expenses

Operation
870   Operation supervision and engineering.
871   Distribution load dispatching.
872   Compressor station labor and expenses.
873   Compressor station fuel and power.
874   Mains and services expenses.
875   Measuring and regulating station expenses—general.
876   Measuring and regulating station expenses—industrial.
877   Measuring and regulating station expenses—city gate check stations.
878   Meter and house regulator expenses.
879   Customer installations expenses.
880   Other expenses.
881   Rents.
        Maintenance
885   Maintenance supervision and engineering.
886   Maintenance of structures and improvements.
887   Maintenance of mains.
888   Maintenance of compressor station equipment.
889   Maintenance of measuring and regulating station equipment—general.
890   Maintenance of measuring and regulating station equipment—industrial.
891   Maintenance of measuring and regulating station equipment—city gate check stations.
892   Maintenance of services.

893	Maintenance of meters and house regulators.
894	Maintenance of other equipment.

6. Customer Accounts Expenses

Operation

901	Supervision.
902	Meter reading expenses.
903	Customer records and collection expenses.
904	Uncollectible accounts.
905	Miscellaneous customer accounts expenses.

7. Sales Expenses

Operation

911	Supervision.
912	Demonstrating and selling expenses.
913	Advertising expenses.
914	Revenues from merchandising, jobbing, and contract work.
915	Costs and expenses of merchandising, jobbing, and contract work.
916	Miscellaneous sales expenses.

8. Administrative and General Expenses

Operation

920	Administrative and general salaries.
921	Office supplies and expenses.
922	Administrative expenses transferred—Cr.
923	Outside services employed.
924	Property insurance.
925	Injuries and damages.
926	Employee pensions and benefits.
927	Franchise requirements.
928	Regulatory commission expenses.
929	Duplicate charges—Cr.
930	Miscellaneous general expenses.
931	Rents.

Maintenance

932	Maintenance of general plants.

Source: As indicated by the title of this appendix, the above data are reproduced verbatim from a Federal Power Commission's manual entitled *Uniform System of Accounts Prescribed for Natural Gas Companies (Class A and Class B) Subject to the Provisions of the Natural Gas Act: FPC A–12* (Washington, D.C.: U.S. Government Printing Office, n.d.) .

CHAPTER **8**

Profitability Accounting Systems

THE GENERAL model for a TYPE 1 information system was presented in the previous chapter along with the special extensions and features based on the TYPE 1 network that are incorporated in a responsibility accounting system. Computer-based networks classified as a TYPE 1 information system contain a series of capabilities including the following four general features. First, members of management are willing to apply a management by systems approach to administering and monitoring performance. Second, the existence of an editing and screening phase for filtering input data is evidence of a "managed" environmental setting in which most, if not all, *types* of economic activity can be anticipated, at least, as far as the general nature of the transactions.

Third, the establishment of a mechanism for members of management to make online changes in the parameters and variables in online computer programs indicates a predictable environmental setting that has been subjected to rigorous systems analysis. Fourth, there is a minimum time cycle (the length of the control phase) in which members of management are willing to forego the right of revising assignments of organizational resources or assets in pursuit of specific objectives. Each TYPE 1 information system will possess these four characteristics; in addition, if it is a responsibility accounting system, the network contains two other features pertaining to types of data and the organizational structure.

In this chapter we will examine the other extensions to the TYPE 1 information system that are possessed by a network classified as a profitability accounting system. This network does not necessarily possess the two special features in a responsibility accounting system.

BASIC CONCEPT

The words "profitability accounting" were initially used in the context of a business organization where members of marketing management are coping with a changing environment and desire special marginal and incremental data to assist them in these decision-making activities. While the concept originated in the institutional setting of a business organization, there is nothing in the concept which precludes it from being applied to other institutional settings, such as a governmental unit, a governmental agency, a health care institution, or a public administration group.

The "profitability-orientation" really means that marginal analyses are performed by members of management within a short-time cycle, such as a day or a week, and they make a complete response (a requirement of a TYPE 1 information system) to the marginal opportunities. This profitability-orientation requires incremental data for cost-benefit analysis and an organizational structure in which members of management can make a complete response to an opportunity within a limited time period. For purposes of this latter statement, performance data in a planning, programming, and budgeting (PPBS) context can represent the "cost portion" of the data in these cost-benefit analyses.

From the standpoint of managerial accounting, the concept of profitability accounting is a third-generation integrated, management accounting technique, and this historical origin is depicted by the following three simplifications. The first generation consisted of the integration of standard cost data with financial accounting data in the single accounting system. During the second generation, the idea of re-sorting data was introduced into the integrated standard cost and financial accounting system; specifically, the responsibility accounting concept was applied to relate expenditures to the individual who has responsibility for their occurrence. This identification of an individual with those expenditures for which the individual is accountable assisted all echelons of management in the control of expenditures.[1]

---

[1] Cf. John A. Higgins, "Responsibility Accounting," *The Arthur Andersen Chronicle,* vol. 12 (April 1952), p. 17: "Responsibility accounting does not involve a drastic change in accounting theory or principles. It is for the most part a change in emphasis from product cost to the cost control aspects of accounting

Subsequently, there was a change in emphasis in the administrative process with management planning and control assuming an increasingly more important position. Management planning was an integral part of the responsibility accounting system because the "plan" provided the criteria or yardsticks against which to "control." But this responsibility accounting system did not provide the marginal-analysis types of planning data as an essential part of the accounting network. In response to the increasing emphasis on management planning, an accounting technique was incorporated in the integrated standard cost, financial accounting, and responsibility accounting network that re-sorted selected incremental data for purposes of marginal analyses. These networks also contained the capability of measuring performance, comparing actual with standard, and preparing exception reports when corrective action was suggested by the deviations between actual and planned.

This latter development of profitability accounting technique was accompanied by other changes in the business environment, including the wide-scale use of computers and communication equipment in the processing and transmission of business data. Of course, these environmental changes permitted more extensive use of mathematical tools and techniques in all phases of the management process. The online editing, screening, processing, sorting, and reprocessing capabilities of a TYPE 1 information system permit all of these accounting techniques to be applied at nominal clerical costs.

The general model of a profitability accounting system presented in the next part of this chapter is a more complete network than might be suggested by professional accountants' use of the words, "profitability accounting." The profitability accounting system must include all of the eight common dimensions of the administrative process and the organizational arrangements that were described in the general model of a TYPE 1 information system. Therefore, the profitability accounting system must include all facets of the management planning and control process.

---

wherein the statements to management emphasize the control of costs by reporting and summarizing them on the basis of 'who did it' before they are adjusted and blended for product cost purposes to obtain the conventional financial statements. To say it another way, it is a system which emphasizes the information that is useful to operating management and de-emphasizes the accounting and bookkeeping aspects that clutter up so many of our financial statements today." [This paper by Higgins is one of the earliest papers on the subject of "responsibility accounting."]

THE GENERAL MODEL

A generalized model of a profitability accounting system is depicted by Figure 8.1, and this model is an extension to a TYPE 1

FIGURE 8.1
A Generalized Model of a Profitability Accounting System

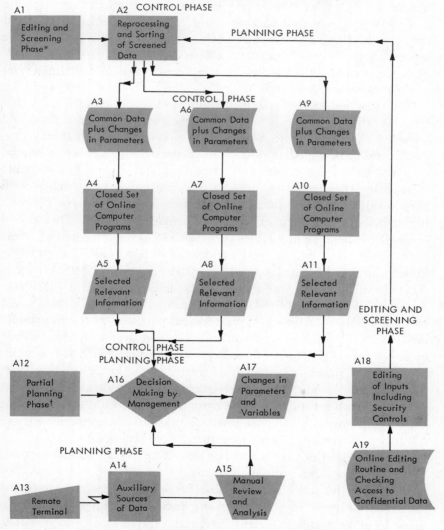

* The editing and screening phase is depicted by symbols A1 to A10 in Figure 7.1.
† The partial planning phase is depicted by symbols A12 to A16 in Figure 7.1.

information system. Note that the filtering operations in the profitability accounting system contain the identical features (symbols A1, A18, and A19 in Figure 8.1) as the editing and screening phase in a TYPE 1 information system. The planning phase and the control phase contain several extensions to the discrete level of these phases in the TYPE 1 network.

The three operating systems in the control phase contain three different time cycles. Note that the data flows from the reprocessing and sorting of screened data (symbol A2) to the online storage of data for the three operating systems (symbols A3, A6, and A9) are separate lines. These distinct data flows permit feedback to the start of the operating system without being constrained by the time cycles of the other two sets of flows.

The first operating system (symbols A3, A4, and A5) is the shortest duration—a day is a typical time cycle for this set of flows and a week is the upper limit. When the time cycle is shorter than a day, there tend to be other modifications in the system (such as a partial response rather than a complete response and a capability for online monitoring of selected changes in the external environment) with the overall result being that the network is classified as a TYPE 2 information system or a TYPE 3 information system. The second operating system (symbols A6, A7, and A8) is an intermediate time cycle—a week is a typical cycle for this set of flows and 15 days is the upper limit. The third operating system (symbols A9, A10, and A11) is the longest time cycle, which may be up to a month in duration. There is a definite relationship among the three time cycles. The shortest time cycle is a logical partition of the intermediate time cycle (such as a day in a week), and the intermediate time cycle is a logical partition of the longest time cycle (such as a week in a four-week "standard" month). Because of the latter relationships, there are no *partial* time cycles required in the multiple completion of the first and second operating systems during the duration of the third operating system. (The latter situation is present in a more advanced network discussed subsequently in this book.)

The three distinct flows and the time-dimension variances among the three operating systems are only two facets of the items that differentiate the three systems. The first operating system with the shortest time cycle provides relevant data for members of management to make cost-benefit and marginal analyses based on monitoring and sensory activities externally directed to the organization's environmental setting (symbols A13, A14, and A15 represent these activities). The online set of computer programs in these flows (symbols A4) accumulates selected performance data, operating statistics, and assignment information so members of management have the appropriate short-term planning data on internal activities that may be changed for the next cycle (symbols A16 and A17 represent these decision-making and change actions). The monitoring and sensory activities of the environment (symbols A13, A14, and A15) are manually reviewed and analyzed by members of management. Computer-generated decision tables and screens have been prepared for use in these manual reviews; however, these cost-benefit and marginal analyses do not become part of the online data flows. After the manual review (symbol A15), members of management engage in decision-making activities (make a *complete response* to the situation) and may initiate changes in parameters and variables (symbol A17) for the next cycle. Thus, it is only the decision-making *results* from the manual review of cost-benefit and marginal analyses that become part of the online network; the "raw" data do not become part of the network (which is the case in more advanced information systems subsequently discussed).

From these comments, we see that the first operating system focuses on management planning for a short-time cycle using cost-benefit, marginal, and environmental data. The other two operating systems handle the regular data (nonmarginal data) for management planning, management control, physical control, and technical control purposes. The third operating cycle with the longest time interval has incorporated within the online programs (symbol A10) data accumulation, data comparison, and data exception reporting routines for physical control and technical control purposes.

COMPARISON WITH OTHER MODELS

The generalized model of a profitability accounting system is a TYPE 1 information system in which the three operating systems contain three distinct time periods and there is a monitoring, sensory examination, and analysis of the environment. In both the TYPE 1 information system and the profitability accounting system, members of management make a complete response to the situation. In actual practice, we will probably find a group of individuals who represent the decision-making by management (symbol A16 in Figure 8.1) and the dominant individual in the group may vary among the three distinct flows. Furthermore, the organizational structure as related to the decision-making activities tends to vary among the three distinct flows.

For example, we might expect the vice president of marketing to be the decision-maker for the first operating system and that this individual is located in a *matrix* organizational structure in which he or she has organization-wide authority for making an immediate and complete response to the situation. Other members of management will establish policy guidelines within which this decision maker has organization-wide authority for reviewing and responding to marginal opportunities. These decision-making activities will require data on the environment, actions by competitors (if applicable), shifts in demand, and other physical movements.

Continuing with the example, the second and third operating systems are in marked contrast with the first. The members of management engaged in the management planning and management control activities associated with these two sets of flows are frequently the vice presidents in charge of the various functional areas, and the scope of the authority in which these individuals operate for purposes of these activities tends to be a *traditional* organizational structure.

Because of this matrix organizational structure of the decision maker associated with the marginal-planning activities, the general model of a profitability accounting system is not compatible with the general model of a responsibility accounting system. However, all of the features in a responsibility accounting network can be incorporated in the third operating system within a profitability accounting network. In fact, it is very common for an organization with a profitability accounting system to also have integrated within the online network a responsibility accounting system that operates in a monthly time cycle.

SYSTEMS ANALYST'S PERSPECTIVE

While the general models for responsibility accounting systems and for profitability accounting systems have been described and contrasted, the objective here is not to emphasize the differences between these two general models. Instead, the objective in studying these two prototypes of a TYPE 1 information system has been to emphasize that (*a*) organizational considerations can be recognized in the design and operation of successful management information systems, (*b*) the powerful technique of re-sorting information permits a single data accumulation process to be successfully used in diverse information-reporting situations, and (*c*) management needs critical information in the day-to-day administrative process. The nature of the critical information will vary to some extent with the personal preferences of each manager along with the restraint imposed by the cost of such special information.

Since these three points are the underlying emphasis of this discussion, the systems analyst should ponder the implications of these issues. For example, the technique of re-sorting information as used under responsibility accounting systems is a powerful device which has become even more potent by the widespread use and availability of computer facilities. This powerful technique has almost unlimited applications when it is coupled with an information system where information is processed into the computer network at almost the point of inception. The systems analyst must stretch his or her imagination and ask what other re-sorts of information will be meaningful to management. The thorough consideration of this question will include the measurement of the cost versus the estimated benefit derived from the new information created by the re-sorting process.

Frequently, the systems analyst will study the overall administrative process and the organization's environment and conclude that the major information flows appear to represent the general model of a TYPE 1 information system. However, as the analyst attempts to group information flows into larger information networks, some problems may be encountered in selecting the period of time for the information cycle.

After further study, the systems analyst finally perceives two general time frames with some overlapping of information flows. The shorter time frame will probably indicate a profitability accounting system while the longer time frame will indicate a responsibility accounting system. The information accumulated for marginal analysis (the profitability accounting system) is re-sorted and used in the historical cost reports (the responsibility accounting system). There is usually a planning cycle operating in the same time-frame as the responsibility accounting system that provides critical control guidelines for the short-term decision-making activities in the profitability accounting system.

CODING PATTERN

The coding pattern for input data in a computer-based network might be described as the "heart" of the system that provides the online capability for pumping selected data through an array of assigned data flows to decision makers. This coding pattern for each type of document and class of transaction is the structure around which the filters in the editing and screening phase are developed. After the data have been filtered and edited, these screened data are processed, re-sorted, assigned to various online data files, and then reprocessed; the elements within the coding pattern are used as a basis for these online specifications within a series of computer programs that perform these assignments and operations.

As indicated, the set of programmed instructions within the editing and screening phase is based on the elements within the coding pattern. These data within these online screens can be retrieved, processed, re-sorted, and presented in a special report as a coding manual. A miscellaneous report generator (the name of a typical online computer program which facilitates the preparation of special reports) is frequently used in preparing this coding manual. In addition, organizations with a TYPE 1 information system will frequently have the coding manual stored online so as to facilitate immediate access (at the document level) to selected areas within this overall coding structure.

In subsequent chapters we will progress through the five discrete models of information systems; as each new level of advancement is examined, we will observe that the coding pattern becomes increasingly complex. When we advance to a TYPE 3 information system, formal consideration will be given within the generalized model of the coding pattern as part of the systems processing phase. The relation of the coding pattern to common data files and common data banks is examined in Chapter 16 along with a consideration of alternative methods of coding.

In the context of the profitability accounting system, the coding pattern provides the specification around which marginal cost, direct cost, and historical cost can be derived from the same source document. The coding pattern also serves as the basis for the online assignment of data among the various operating systems to specific online data files. We will now examine these features of a coding pattern by looking at the application of the coding pattern to the Hardy Company.

There is a separate coding pattern for each type of document and class of transaction at the Hardy Company. For example, the sales invoice for this company with three divisions consists of 63 digits, and the elements within this pattern are as follows:

1234xxxxxxxxxxxx...	The first four digits designate the general ledger account.
xxxx567xxxxxxxxx...	Fifth, sixth, and seventh digits designate subaccounts based on organizational and responsibility accounting factors.
xxxxxxx8xxxxxxxx...	Eighth digit designates the division of this diversified corporation.
xxxxxxxx90123xxx...	These five digits 9th to the 13th digits) specify the customer number.
.....456789xxxxx...	These six digits (14th to the 19th digits) specify the product number.
.....xxxxxx012xx...	These three digits (20th to the 22nd digits) designate the date.
.....3456xxxxxxxx...	These four digits (23rd to the 26th digits) designate the invoice number.
.....xxxx7890xxx...	These four digits (27th to the 30th digits) specify the location code and the cost center.
.....1234xxxxxxxx...	These four digits (31st to the 34th digits) specify shipping instructions, such as, ship from and shipped to.
.....xxxx5xxxxxxx...	This digit (35th digit) indicates the packaging code.
.....xxxxx6789xx...	These four digits (36th to the 39th digits) specify sales channel and territory codes.
.....012345678xx...	These nine digits (40th to the 48th digits) specify the quantity.
.....xxxxxxxxx9x...	This digit (49th digit) indicates the unit of measure for quantity.

.....xxx0123456789.. These 10 digits (50th to the 59th digits) specify the price.

.......xxxxxxxx0123 These four digits (60th to the 63rd digits) specify the salesperson identification number.

The Hardy Company has a profitability accounting system in which there are three operating systems with the following respective time cycles: a day, a week, and four-weeks. The four-week operating system accumulates relevant planning information for specifying criteria and guidelines for the day-to-day activities, and this system also contains the special features of a responsibility accounting system. For illustration purposes, these latter two types of information accumulation activities are separately shown.

Each element within the Hardy Company's 63-digit coding pattern for a sales invoice is not essential for each of the operating systems. We will now examine each element and determine which digits are assigned to each of the operating systems. As previously suggested, the four-week operating cycle for responsibility accounting and the four-week operating cycle for planning criteria are separately presented.

Digits and Description	One-Day Marginal Analysis and Profitability Accounting	One-Week Management Planning and Management Control	Four-Week Responsibility Accounting	Four-Week Planning Criteria and Guidelines
1-4 General ledger account	no	no	yes	yes
5-7 Subaccount	no	no	yes	yes
8 Division	yes	yes	yes	yes
9-13 Customer code	yes	yes	no	yes
14-19 Product code	yes	yes	no	yes
20-22 Date	yes	no	no	yes
23-26 Invoice number	yes	no	no	yes
27-30 Location code and cost center	no	yes	yes	yes
31-34 Shipped to and shipped from	no	no	no	yes
35 Packaging code	yes	no	no	yes
36-39 Sales channel and territory code	yes	yes	no	yes
40-48 Quantity	yes	yes	yes	yes
49 Unit of measure	no	yes	no	yes
50-59 Price	yes	yes	yes	yes
60-63 Salesperson code	no	yes	yes	yes

Actually the above specification of the assignment of elements within the 63-digit coding pattern for a Hardy Company sales invoice to the four sets of activities is only the first step. It merely indicates that an element within the coding structure is to be assigned to a given operating cycle; this first step did not indicate what other processing, summarizing, re-sorting, and storage operations were to be applied to these same elements. For example, the storage and reprocessing of assigned data varies by data element within a given set of activities. Some data are stored at the document level; others are summarized and stored at the aggregate level. Most data for a given document or transaction progresses through a series of different kinds and types of access and storage arrangements. These run the gamut *from* detailed, complete data on an online basis with immediate access *to* summary, partial data stored on magnetic tapes which can be processed and summarized in a special report on a 24-hour basis.

Figure 8.2 highlights these online activities for assigning, re-sorting, and reprocessing of screened data in a generalized model of a profitability accounting system. As previously indicated, these online activities are built upon the foundation provided by the coding pattern. Symbol B3 depicts the online assignment of data elements in the coding pattern, and this overall process can be viewed as a cross-reference table that is online and focuses upon each element within the coding pattern.

The screened data are assigned to their respective online locations (symbols B4, B8, B11, and B14) as well as to back-up files for use in systems control, security, and internal review activities (symbol B17). As stated, there are multi-assignments of many data elements. For example, in the case of the Hardy Company, the general ledger account, subaccount, division, and cost center code are used in re-sorting and reprocessing financial data on a given document so they can be used for full absorption costing, direct costing, and responsibility accounting purposes.

One of the easier tasks confronting the systems analyst is the re-sorting of cost data for different purposes. After the three dominant accounting techniques have been applied to the situation, the analyst may begin to feel confident that the most difficult task has been solved. However, this is "false confidence" because there are other dimensions to each issue for which there are no simple answers. These other dimensions include levels of aggregation, extent of

FIGURE 8.2
Assigning, Re-Sorting, and Reprocessing of Screened Data
in a Generalized Model of a Profitability Accounting System

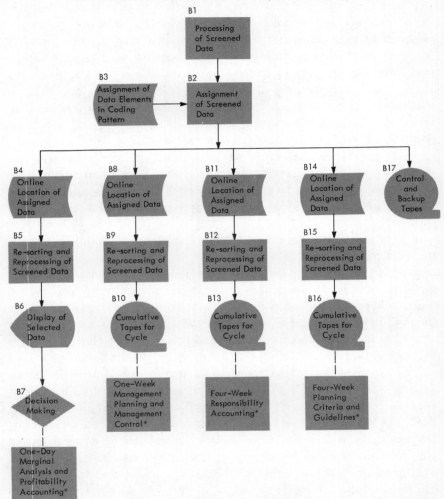

° For illustration purposes, this shows the time cycles included in the example described previously in this chapter.

supporting details for a given transaction, and retention program for online and offline data. These latter issues are not highlighted by Figure 8.2. The purpose of this network is to show in general how the assigning, re-sorting, and reprocessing of screened data occurs in a generalized model of a profitability accounting system.

SUMMARY

The systems analyst is concerned with the identification of the major information flows within an organization and with the systematic and orderly grouping of these major information flows into larger information networks. Chapters 7 and 8 have emphasized two general types of information networks that the systems analyst may elect to use. Both of these are TYPE 1 information systems, which means that the systems analyst envisions the management process occurring so that at some point in time all steps of the planning operation are completed before activity for the period covered by the plan commences.

Within the category of a TYPE 1 information system, the systems analyst has ample room for developing an information network that best meets the unique information requirements (in the areas of timing, type of information, and the degree of relevance of information) of the decision-making processes throughout the organization under scrutiny. The systems analyst may install a type of responsibility accounting system, a type of profitability accounting system, or may concurrently install both types of information networks under an integrated arrangement in the given organization. In more complex organizations, responsibility accounting systems and profitability accounting systems may be used in conjunction with production and operation information systems and marketing information systems.

TOPICS FOR CLASS DISCUSSION

1. In a profitability accounting system there is a *complete response* to marketing management issues and opportunities in a given area within a minimum time period. Explain how the network might be different if there were only a *partial response*.

2. Explain the eight common dimensions of the administrative process and the organizational arrangements that are incorporated in the general model for a profitability accounting system.

3. Explain the differences between a responsibility accounting system and a profitability accounting system.

4. To what extent are sensory data on the organization's environ-

ment included in the online network? Refer to Figure 8.1 in explaining your answer.

5. Explain why the coding pattern is the *heart* of a TYPE 1 information system.

6. The Murphy Engineering Company is the manufacturer of precision parts which are sold exclusively to two of the large automotive companies. Currently, the Murphy Engineering Company is producing 27 different parts for these two consumers per the terms of 30 different contracts (three parts are purchased by both automotive companies). These contracts specify the minimum volume of parts that the automotive company will purchase during the annual production season at a fixed price; the contract also includes a clause that the Murphy Engineering Company may be asked to supply a higher volume of parts at this same fixed price, depending on the production volume experienced by the respective automotive company. You, as a systems analyst, are asked by Richard Murphy, the president of Murphy Engineering Company, to evaluate the company's operations and to design a profitability accounting system. Mr. Murphy states that he wants an information system that permits him and his associates to respond daily to changes in the company's operations.

REQUIRED:

Explain the type of information system that you would probably design and install at the Murphy Engineering Company. Be specific.

A NOTE ON THE INDUSTRIAL CHEMICAL INDUSTRY

Prof. Jules Backman introduces a monograph on *Chemicals in the National Economy* with this comment: "*Test tube* competition has been the vital stimulating and driving force in the industrial chemical industry. Such competition is so intensive and so widespread that it has become indispensable to competitive success. The industry is constantly obsoleting its own products and processes. It is marked by intensive struggles for product leadership."[2]

The industrial chemical industry is a major investor in research and development. Many large chemical companies take pride in

---

[2] Jules Backman, *Chemicals in the National Economy* (Washington, D.C.: Manufacturing Chemists' Association, Inc., 1964), p. 1.

emphasizing that the majority of the products that they currently sell were unknown five years ago.

The Vogt Chemical Company, Inc., is not representative of a large industrial chemical company. For example, it is not included among the 100 largest chemical companies in the United States. Instead, the Vogt Chemical Company is a small company that manufactures four industrial chemicals which it sells in this highly competitive environment.

The raw materials that Vogt uses are subject to day-to-day major fluctuations in price. The various crushed ores and the basic chemicals that are raw materials to Vogt contain many short-run imperfections in price. In fact, a given required raw material may be obtained in several different ways, each from basic materials with different degrees of concentration of the desired substance. Therefore, the purchasing manager must frequently redetermine which raw materials in what form will be purchased from whom.

Since Vogt Chemical Company sells its products to other industrial companies including chemical companies, the demand and supply for Vogt's four products fluctuates on a day-to-day basis in the same manner as the day-to-day fluctuations in the raw materials to Vogt Chemical Company. In other words, Vogt's four products are raw materials to other chemical companies and are subject to the same short-run fluctuations in price that characterizes Vogt's raw materials.

Vogt Chemical Company sells some of its products to nonchemical companies, and these sales are on a regular order basis. These nonchemical company sales provide a certain amount of stability to Vogt's price system and volume of operations.

The physical plant of a chemical company is unique. Since some type of chemical is being manufactured (in either a solid, liquid, or gas state) under a set of prescribed conditions (such as temperature, humidity, and time), some type of physical network is typically required for controlling, processing, and transmitting the substance during the various phases of the manufacturing process.

This physical network is an enormous web of pipes connecting the storage containers of raw materials with the finished goods supply area. Often this series of pipes is a closed system from the raw materials point to the finished goods point. At various intervals within the pipes and conveyor system, there are pumps, control and regulatory equipment, processing equipment, storage tanks for chemicals being used in the manufacturing process, retrieval tanks for capturing these chemicals as they are used, purifying equipment for converting the used chemicals into their former state so that these chemicals can be used again in the next cycle of the manufacturing process, and transmission equipment.

In summary, each manufacturing plant in a typical chemical company (such as the Vogt Chemical Company, Inc.) will have the physical appearance of a single pipeline of connected vats, pots, processing equipment, transmission equipment, and control and regulatory equipment which spans the distance from the raw materials receiving point to the finished goods shipping point.

CASE 8–1. VOGT CHEMICAL COMPANY, INC.

Frederick Vogt, president of Vogt Chemical Company, Inc., has contacted the certified public accounting firm with which you are associated and asked for assistance in the area of administrative services. You are the manager assigned to perform this high-point review of the present system. The stated purpose of this general accounting and financial review is to determine (1) the nature of financial accounting information that would be useful to management and (2) the accounting procedures required to obtain this information.

In performing this task you discover the following information about the client.

The Company

George Vogt came to the United States from Europe immediately prior to World War I and was employed by a relative of the family in a family-owned chemical company. Within several years George Vogt discovered a new process for extracting the industrial chemicals. When his relatives would not use the new process, he left the company, moved to Pennsylvania, and started his own chemical company—the Vogt Chemical Company, Inc.

Later, Ernest Vogt came to the United States from Europe and joined his brother George in the management of the new company. Both men were well-educated in the sciences; George with a Ph.D. in chemistry and Ernest with a Ph.D. in physics. With the two brothers occupying the top positions in the firm, the history of the firm is a story of extensive scientific research and development with only minor considerations of financial management. As a result of this emphasis on scientific research, the firm had unique processes and employed specially constructed equipment which gave the company a significant competitive advantage over other firms. Some of its former competitors shifted to the manufacture of other chemical products, and Vogt Chemical Company, Inc., became one of the few producers in the United States of four different industrial chemicals. These four products have a current annual sales of approximately $4,500,000.

The company's major product has a wide variety of uses in several industries. Recently, this product was offered on the market for use in the metal fabricating industry as the "ideal wash solution." Scientists at Vogt Chemical Company, Inc., had been aware for some time that the company's major product was the ideal solution for the metal fabricating industry's problems. However, in the past it was not financially feasible to manufacture the chemical for this purpose. Recent inventions of new equipment and the discovery of a new manufacturing process by scientists at Vogt Chemical have permitted this chemical to be sold in the competitive market. Thus, in this sense, it is a new product on the market for sale in the metal fabricating industry.

At present, the market outlook for Vogt Chemical Company, Inc., is extremely favorable. Frederick Vogt, George Vogt's son, is the current president of the company, and he recently stated that the company was on the verge of expanding its annual sales of $4,500,000 to $9 or $10 million. With this expansion in mind, Frederick Vogt and his associates desired a general review to determine the type of information which would be useful in making management decisions, controlling costs, and obtaining outside financing.

Frederick Vogt stated that the present accounting system was useful primarily in generating historical data for income tax purposes, but the system provided very little financial information for the company's management to use in making operating decisions. Frederick Vogt had heard his friends in other manufacturing firms speak of the managerial information their controllers periodically provided them, and Frederick Vogt had frequently brought this matter up with his own controller. Each time the subject was discussed, the controller of Vogt Chemical Company, Inc. (who was employed 20 years ago as a bookkeeper immediately following graduation from high school) would comment about the unique aspects of company operations. The controller had stated that because of this unique condition, the accounting system for Vogt Chemical Company, Inc., could not provide the type of information which Frederick Vogt had heard friends speak of obtaining from their accounting systems. Furthermore, the controller stated that he was already using 24-column paper to accumulate detailed cost data, and there were not any more columns for additional breakdowns of cost data. The controller's typical comment was, "If any additional data are needed, it will be necessary to have a complete system's review."

Frederick Vogt had accepted the situation of not having timely financial information for managerial decisions, particularly since the firm was currently making a substantial profit. Like his father and uncle, he was more concerned with scientific research than with financial management. However, as he envisioned a doubling of the sales volume within a matter of months, he thought that now was the appropriate time to have the company's accounting system examined.

At a social gathering in a friend's home, Frederick Vogt mentioned his predicament regarding his lack of information for current managerial purposes. His friends advised him to obtain the services of a particular public accounting firm. One of the individuals making this recommendation stated that this public accounting firm had recently performed some administrative service work for his company.

The next day Frederick Vogt went to a city bank and talked with a bank officer regarding a possible loan to finance the anticipated increased volume of sales. After Frederick Vogt had explained his problem, the banker advised him to seek the administrative service assistance of a particular public accounting firm (which happened to be the same firm his friends had advised him to consult the previous night).

This background information explains why you are currently engaged in performing a general review of operations. Following is a summary of your findings regarding the current reporting system.

The Current Situation

In performing your general review you find the following statements have been prepared for the current period:

1. Balance sheet (annually)
2. Income statement (annually)
3. Cost of goods manufactured (annually)
4. Departmental profit and loss statement (annually)
5. Departmental profit and loss statement (for the fourth quarter)
6. Departmental cost of goods sold statement (annually)
7. Departmental cost of goods sold statement (for the fourth quarter)
8. Analysis statement reflecting unit cost data (annually)
9. Analysis statement reflecting unit cost data (for the fourth quarter)
10. Source and application of funds statement (annually)

As indicated, with the exception of the fourth quarter reports, all reports are prepared on an annual basis. Furthermore, your general review of operations and procedures suggests that the small certified public accounting firm which has performed the annual audit in the past did a thorough job of examining and testing financial procedures.

From an examination of these reports, you prepare a complete chart of accounts (see Exhibit A).

After preparing the chart of accounts, you make a detailed examination of the manufacturing process employed in the production of each of the four chemicals. Because of considerations of time and space, a detailed discussion is not included on the manufacturing processes involved in the production of the four products. However, it should be noted that Vogt Chemical Company, Inc. has three separate physical plants. Product A is manufactured in Plant 1; Product B is manufactured in Plant 2; and Product C and Product D are manufactured in Plant 3.

Some of the initial costs incurred with Product C and Product D are joint cost; however, the major portion of the processing cost is individual cost. Because of frequent measurements taken by the technicians working in the processing operations, reliable statistics are available for distribution of joint cost. Furthermore, the sales volume of Product C is four to five times as large as that experienced for Product D, and the profit margin per unit of Product C is also greater than that achieved for Product D. (Incidentally, Product D is

ASSETS

CURRENT ASSETS

Cash
Accounts receivable—trade
Accounts receivable—other
Inventories:
  Raw materials
  Materials in process
  Finished goods
  Shipping containers
Accrued interest on tax-exempt bonds
Accrued interest on XYZ Company notes
Prepaid insurance premiums
Unused factory supplies

INVESTMENTS

Stocks—First National Bank in Metropolis
Bonds—Tax exempt (at amortized cost)

LOANS

Notes receivable—XYZ Company
Notes receivable—officers and employees
Executive life insurance (cash value)

FIXED ASSETS

Land
Buildings
Allowance for depreciation—buildings
Machinery and equipment
Allowance for depreciation—machinery and equipment
Equipment under construction
Motor truck and locomotives
Allowance for depreciation—motor truck and locomotives
Office equipment
Allowance for depreciation—office equipment
Miscellaneous equipment
Allowance for depreciation—miscellaneous equipment

LIABILITIES

CURRENT LIABILITIES

Accounts payable—trade
Accrued payroll
Accrued taxes:
  State and local
  Social Security and unemployment
  Federal withholding
  Federal income tax

STOCKHOLDERS' EQUITY

CAPITAL STOCK

Capital stock (authorized and issued 2,000 shares, par value $100)

RETAINED EARNINGS

Retained earnings
Profit and loss summary

SALES*

Sales
Freight allowances
Dealers' discounts

COST OF GOODS SOLD*

COST OF GOODS MANUFACTURED

Purchases—raw materials
Purchases—shipping containers
Direct labor
Factory overhead:
  Repairs to equipment
  Repairs to buildings
  Depreciation—machinery and equipment
  Depreciation—motor truck and locomotives
  Depreciation—buildings
  Depreciation—miscellaneous equipment
  Insurance
  Taxes
  Indirect labor
  Indirect supplies and miscellaneous expenses
  Coal, fuel oil, and gas
  Purchased electric power
  Purchased steam

SELLING, ADMINISTRATIVE, and GENERAL EXPENSE

Officer's salaries
Office salaries
Office expenses
Professional fees—legal, audit, and surveys
Depreciation—office equipment
Publications, photostats, etc.
Taxes—sales, use, and franchise
Bad debts
Dues and miscellaneous expenses
Contributions
Traveling expense
Employee's pensions
Advertising
Sales commissions

EXHIBIT A (*Concluded*)

NONOPERATING INCOME

Dividends received
Interest received—tax exempt
Interest received
Discounts earned
Miscellaneous income

NONOPERATING EXPENSE

Expense of real estate held for future use
Discounts allowed
Executive life insurance premium
Cost of junking equipment
Experimental expense—current
Pilot plant expense
End use research (marketing research)

FEDERAL TAXES

Federal taxes on income

° The departmental profit and loss statement and the departmental cost of goods sold statement have five column headings: Total, Product A, Product B, Product C, and Product D. However, separate general ledger accounts are not maintained for the departmental breakdown of information, but this information is obtained from the detailed data reflected on the 24-column paper. Moreover, the departmental reports reflect detailed data only for the "sales" and "costs of goods sold" groupings of accounts; "selling, administration, and general expense" are allocated in total between the four departments. In other words, the departmental report would reflect, in *one amount*, the total "selling, administrative, and general expense" for the period, and this departmental report would not contain any individual extensions by item.

---

manufactured out of what was formerly waste created in the manufacture of Product C.)

Each plant contains a network of specially designed equipment (on which the Vogt brothers have patents) that is used throughout the manufacturing process. Since this manufacturing process is highly mechanized, the employees are technicians, and the direct labor cost tends toward being a fixed cost. Of course, with a significant change in volume, the direct labor cost is increased because of overtime work. However, for small changes in volume, the direct labor cost is constant. On the other hand, raw materials and containers are variable manufacturing costs. Within certain limits, the factory overhead cost tends toward being a fixed cost (see chart of accounts for suggestions of items that might vary with a change in volume).

Suggestions for New System

After you have carefully examined the current reports, chart of accounts, and manufacturing processes, Frederick Vogt says that he would like to have current financial information on the following areas:

1. Company management (the total company)
2. Engineering*
3. Process*
4. Accounting
5. Marketing
6. Process research and control
7. Administration

Furthermore, Frederick Vogt says that the following individuals are responsible for the various sections within the firm:

1. Company management	Frederick Vogt and Edward Vogt
2. Engineering	Edward Vogt
a. Maintenance	Irving Howard
b. Pilot plant	Henry Day
c. Engineering services	Edward Vogt
3. Process	John Snyder
a. Product A (Plant 1)	John Snyder
b. Product B (Plant 2)	George Rickard
c. Product C (Plant 3)	Charles Simon
d. Product D (Plant 3)	Charles Simon
4. Accounting	Robert Jones
5. Marketing and Sales	Bruce Williams
a. End use research (marketing research)	Maurice Weber
6. Process research and control	Arthur Bell
7. Administration	Frederick Vogt

---

* Manufacturing cost would include both engineering and process items. The separation between the two areas would be based on the nature of the work, that is, some direct labor costs for technicians would be classified as "engineering" and other similar cost as "process." However, the majority of the "engineering" cost is overhead cost.

REQUIRED:

Prepare a report reflecting the findings and recommendations gained from your high-point review of the present system. Incorporate in your recommendations the suggestions made by Frederick Vogt regarding areas of responsibility and type of information desired: ". . . information which would be useful in making management decisions, controlling costs, and obtaining outside financing."

CHAPTER 9

Critical Path Planning and Scheduling Information Systems

DURING THE past decade, there has been a significant change in the fundamental nature of organizations in all institutional settings—business, health care, and public administration. In addition to expansion and diversification, many organizations have had an important segment of their resources applied to activities which have varying or uncertain life-spans. These activities are called "projects." Management has exerted considerable time and effort toward developing adequate management tools for these projects.

In addition to research and development activities which are classified as "projects," many organizations have participated in space, defense, public health, and urban affairs contracts which are also of this project classification. Management in other organizations has found that the "project" perspective is appropriate for dealing with recent changes in management techniques and tools (such as operations research). In this case, management has applied the "project" approach to the various segments of the organization, even where the activities would not normally be classified as permanent activities of the organization.

There has also been a change in the management environment regarding the speed and quality of performance expected from a project leader. Today, the manager of a project must be able and willing to answer questions concerning progress, changes, deliveries, costs, and revenues. These questions must be answered more quickly and with much greater accuracy than ever before. The stakes are high, and corporate management, public management, and health care management cannot afford to allow project managers to rely on opinion and subjective guidance. Instead, an arsenal of tools and techniques is available for the modern professional manager to use in planning and scheduling activities, in selecting among various alternatives, and in controlling and monitoring activities according to the plan.

Two basic methods have emerged as the most powerful management techniques for planning, scheduling, and controlling larger projects. This chapter examines these two methods from the perspective of the information systems approach. Since both methods require the planning phase to occur before the activity for the period covered by the plan commences, these management processes are analogous to TYPE 1 information systems. We have found it meaningful to approach major segments of the organization or major "projects" as though they were TYPE 1 information systems.

BENEFITS FROM THIS APPROACH

The previous study of TYPE 1 information systems has emphasized that (1) organization considerations can be recognized in the design and operation of successful management information systems, (2) the powerful technique of re-sorting information permits a single information accumulation process to be successfully used in diverse information-reporting situations, and (3) management needs critical information in the day-to-day administrative process.

These three insights can be directly applied to those business processes that are classified as "projects." First, while the responsibility accounting system paralleled the organization structure, the *critical path planning and scheduling information system* will parallel the time sequence of jobs or activities to be performed. Second, the jobs or activities in the arrow or network diagrams of the critical path planning and scheduling information system are analogous to the responsibility units in a typical integrated standard cost and responsibility accounting system. Third, like the responsibility accounting system, the critical path planning and scheduling information system can serve as the backbone for such tools and techniques as cost determination, cost control, cash flow analysis, return on investment, and make or buy analysis. As is the case with all "information systems," the systems analyst will match the information requirements with the information sources. If the decision maker needs marginal analysis within a given time frame, then this is what will be provided.

Now that the perspective for viewing these "projects" has been established, attention is focused on different aspects of these two basic methods for planning, scheduling, and controlling larger projects. The remaining discussion consists of seven parts: (1) the history of these two methods: the *Critical Path Method* (CPM) and *Program Evaluation and Review Technique* (PERT), (2) a comparison of the two methods, (3) a list of the basic terminology for the CPM method, (4) illustrations of the CPM method applied to two situations, (5) advantages of both methods, (6) other considerations, and (7) examination of the two methods from the perspective of the systems analyst.

History

The critical path method (CPM) had its inception in January, 1957, on a job that the Remington Rand Division of the Sperry Rand Corporation performed for E. I. du Pont de Nemours & Company. The basic development was accomplished by Morgan R. Walker, who was with the Engineering Service Division of Du Pont, and James E. Kelly, who was with Remington Rand–UNIVAC.

While the CPM technique was being developed, a parallel development was in progress at the Special Projects Office of the United States Navy's Bureau of Ordnance. Members of the management consulting firm of Booz, Allen, and Hamilton were developing this new system for the United States Navy. The system was christened PERT—Program Evaluation and Review Technique—and was initially used in scheduling the numerous contractors engaged in the Polaris Missile Project.

Comparison

There are significant differences between these two methods of planning, scheduling, and controlling large projects. While PERT has been used almost exclusively on military projects, the CPM method has been applied to projects where enterprise survival is based more strongly on profit making. This points out one of the original differences between the two methods: namely, that as a planning tool, CPM includes consideration of dollar resources while PERT does not. PERT, being developed for military requirements, is primarily concerned with *time;* cost information does not enter into the analysis. Once the PERT network has been constructed, cost considerations are given to questions such as: "Should more dollars be applied to a given activity so that it will be completed on a 'crash basis' in order that the total time for the project is reduced?" "What is the minimum dollar cost required to complete the total project within a specified number of days?"

In contrast, management in organizations uses the CPM method in the initial steps of the decision project regarding whether or not a particular project should be undertaken. Thus, CPM networks are prepared for many proposed projects which are eventually rejected on grounds of insufficient return on investment or insufficient return for the risk involved.

The matter of time estimates is another significant difference between the CPM method and the PERT technique. Because of the difference in the manner in which the time estimates are specified, there is an important difference in the underlying mathematical support for the CPM and PERT methods. The CPM method has much stronger mathematical support.

PERT technique uses three time estimates for each activity—optimistic, most likely, and pessimistic. The "expected time" required to complete the activity is determined from these three estimates based on an assumed probability distribution. Following are the typical symbols used for these three time estimates:

$$a = \text{optimistic time}$$
$$m = \text{most likely time}$$
$$b = \text{pessimistic time}$$

The PERT formula for computing the expected time (t_e) is as follows:

$$t_e = \frac{a + 4m + b}{6}$$

While an individual may question the assumed probability distribution associated with these three time estimates, at least the PERT approach suggests that there may be some illusion regarding expected time required to perform some activity where the activity involved has no precedent. From a planning standpoint, it is easier to obtain three estimates of time from individuals responsible for a particular activity than to obtain only one time estimate. However, where the activities have been performed previously, a "standard time" may be used and reports prepared on a management-by-exception basis for major deviations from standard.

Because of the assumed probability distribution for PERT networks, it is possible to make inferences based upon the mathematical laws of probability regarding the expected completion date. For example, an individual might state that there is a 50 percent probability that the project will be completed within a specified number of days; there is a 60 percent probability of completion within a longer number of days; and so forth. On the other hand, the CPM technique uses only one time estimate and is completely deterministic.

Since CPM method (1957) and PERT technique (1958) were separate developments, each method has its own notations as indicated by the following chart:

CPM and PERT Notations Compared

CPM	*PERT*
Arrow diagram	Network
Node	Event
Job	Activity
Duration	Scheduled time
Total float	Slack (primary)
Free float	Slack (secondary)
Earliest start	T_E
Latest start	T_L

For purposes of this discussion, the CPM notations are discussed with the PERT notations (where appropriate) indicated in parentheses.

CPM Terminology

The basic terminology for the CPM method is presented in the list below, which is followed by an explanation of each term: *arrow diagram, activity, activity-oriented network, node, event-oriented network, critical path, dummy activity, duration, earliest start, earliest finish, latest finish, latest start, total float, free float, independent float, normal cost, normal time, crash time, crash cost,* and *cost slope.*

The *arrow diagram* (network) is a model or pictorial description of how a project is planned including an identification of the interrelationships between all required activities.

An *activity* is a time-consuming element of a network which has a definite beginning and end. Each activity is represented by an arrow; the tail is the start and the head is the finish. The length of the arrow means nothing. An activity cannot start until all preceding activities have been completed; no following activity can start until this activity is completed.

The *activity-oriented network* uses the activity as the basic building block. The activity arrow is titled with the name of the job or task, and this system is representative of the CPM approach.

A *node* (event) marks the beginning and end of each activity. The node occurs at a specific point in time; *it cannot consume time.*

The *event-oriented network* uses the event as the basic building block of the network in lieu of an activity. The event-oriented network originates from the PERT method. "Milestone" events in the project are the focal point of the PERT network, and "milestone" dates may be set before the network is developed.

The *critical path* is that particular sequence of activities, connecting the starting event with the ending (objective) event, which requires the greatest elapsed time to complete. A network will have one or more critical paths all equal to the project duration.

A *dummy activity* is used to maintain proper relationships between functional activities. The dummy activity requires no time and involves no direct cost. The dummy activity is usually shown as a broken-line arrow.

Duration is the time required by a job (activity) or project.

Earliest start (T_E) is the earliest time a given event takes place represented by the longest path between the project start (beginning event) and the given event. The earliest start for an activity is the latest, earliest finish of all preceding activities, or the earliest occurrence of all activities leading to the given event.

Earliest finish is the earliest time an activity can finish as determined by the earliest start (T_E) plus the estimated activity elapsed time.

Latest finish is the latest time an activity can finish without affecting completion of the project or terminal event.

Latest start is the latest time an activity can start without affecting completion of the project (terminal event). The latest start is determined by subtracting the estimated activity elapsed time from the latest finish.

Total float (primary slack) is the maximum time that can be made available for an activity minus the time required for the activity. The total float is the difference between latest finish and earliest finish; thus, it is the amount of flexibility an activity can have without affecting the critical path. (Computer programs have been designed to allocate float based upon a priority rating assigned by the planning engineer.)

Free float (secondary slack) is the float available to an activity if all activities are started as early as possible.

Independent float is the float available to an activity when all preceding activities are started as late as possible and all following activities are started as early as possible.

Normal cost is the cost associated with each activity if it is carried out in the *normal time*.

Crash time is the minimum possible time in which an activity can be carried out. *Crash cost* is the minimum cost to complete an activity in crash time.

Cost slope is the increase in cost units for each decrease in time unit of an activity: (crash cost minus normal cost) divided by (normal time minus crash time). Figure 9.1 illustrates this relationship.

In Figure 9.1, point D,C_1 is assumed to be, or is in the region of, the minimum cost at which this job can be performed. This would be considered as the *normal time* in which to accomplish this job. Point d,C_2 is, or is in the region of, the maximum cost at which this job can be accomplished under *crash conditions*. Furthermore, linearity is assumed between point d,C_2 and point D,C_1. The slope of this line is negative, since there is a decrease in cost for each increase in time unit. The slope of the line is indicated as follows:

$$m = \frac{C_2 - C_1}{d - D} \qquad m = \frac{\text{crash cost} - \text{normal cost}}{\text{crash time} - \text{normal time}}$$

Since an inverse relationship exists between the crash point and the normal point and a positive answer is desired from the formula, the signs of the denominator are reversed and the revised formula (which is the *cost slope formula*) is as follows:

$$\text{cost slope} = \frac{C_2 - C_1}{D - d} \qquad \text{cost slope} = \frac{\text{crash cost} - \text{normal cost}}{\text{normal time} - \text{crash time}}$$

FIGURE 9.1
The Cost Slope

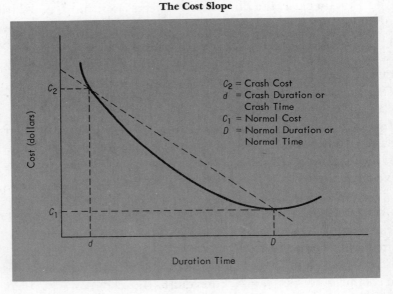

C_2 = Crash Cost
d = Crash Duration or Crash Time
C_1 = Normal Cost
D = Normal Duration or Normal Time

Illustrative Examples of CPM Technique

Figure 9.2 is an arrow diagram (network) of a project.

FIGURE 9.2
The Arrow Diagram of Project One

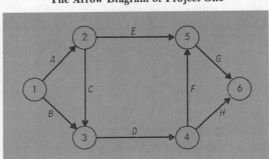

FIGURE 9.2 (*Continued*)

Activity	Normal		Crash		Cost Slope
	Time	Cost	Time	Cost	
A (1,2)	6 days	$140	3 days	$500	$120
B (1,3)	3	90	3	90	—*
C (2,3)	4	160	2	360	100
D (3,4)	5	110	3	410	150
E (2,5)	2	80	1	120	40
F (4,5)	4	100	2	260	80
G (5,6)	3	130	1	410	140
H (4,6)	5	120	2	390	90
		$930		$2,540	

* This activity cannot be expedited.

First, it is necessary to identify all the paths within the arrow diagram. Each path is identified by the combined letters that indicate the activities interrelated to form the path. Following are the paths within the previous arrow diagram:

Path	Normal Time
A,E,G	$6 + 2 + 3 = 11$
A,C,D,F,G	$6 + 4 + 5 + 4 + 3 = 22$
A,C,D,H	$6 + 4 + 5 + 5 = 20$
B,D,F,G	$3 + 5 + 4 + 3 = 15$
B,D,H	$3 + 5 + 5 = 13$

Path *A,C,D,F,G* is the critical path under normal conditions, and for a cost of $930 the project can be completed within 22 days. If the project is to be completed in less than 22 days, activity along this critical path must be expedited under crash conditions. However, if the project is to be completed within 21 days, which of the five activities along the critical path should be reduced? The cost slope provides the answer to this question. Activity *F* (4,5) has a $80 cost slope; thus, for an additional penalty of $80 (total of $930 + $80 = $1,010) the project can be completed in 21 days (22 days normal less 1 day saved by crash procedures) .

If the duration of the project is 20 days, path *A,C,D,F,G* must be reduced one day. Activity *F* (4,5) can be reduced one additional day by using crash procedures at a cost of $80. Thus, the total project can be completed in 20 days for a cost of $1,090 (total of $930 normal cost + $80 + $80 = $1,090) .

Following is a summary of all paths when activity F (4,5) has been completed on a crash basis:

Path	Time
A,E,G	$6 + 2 + 3 = 11$
A,C,D,F^*,G	$6 + 4 + 5 + 2^* + 3 = 20$†
A,C,D,H	$6 + 4 + 5 + 5 = 20$†
B,D,F^*,G	$3 + 5 + 2^* + 3 = 13$
B,D,H	$3 + 5 + 5 = 13$

* Indicates that activities are reduced to their limits by being completed on a crash basis.
† Indicates a critical path.

Path A,C,D,F^*,G and path A,C,D,H are critical paths. On path A,C,D,F^*,G the cost slope for activity C (2,3) is the minimum ($\$100$ per day) ; the duration time of the project can be reduced by two days (20 days $- 2 = 18$) if activity C is completed on a crash basis for an additional cost of $\$200$ (total of $\$930$ normal cost $+ \$80 + \$80 + \$100 + \$100 = \$1,290$). Since activity C is also on the critical path A,C^*,D,H, this path is likewise reduced to 18 days.

Note in the above example that if path A,C,D,H was considered before path A,C,D,F^*,G, the cost slope for activity H (4,6) would be the minimum. However, if activity H is completed on a crash basis, it is still necessary to complete activity C of path A,C,D,F^*,G on a crash basis if the total project time is to be reduced below 20 days. Since activity C is an activity common to both paths, the total cost is minimized by reducing the time element only on activity C and leaving the time element for activity H at normal. This type of consideration is possible where a simple arrow diagram is manually computed and where there are only a limited number of activities and events. With an increase in the number of activities and events, it would be a time-consuming process to check common activities to various critical paths and to determine which common activities would minimize total cost. Therefore, a simple rule has been established: *Reduce that activity along the critical path that has the lowest cost slope.* The above example will be modified according to this rule; thus, two days are saved at an additional cost of $\$180$ by completing activity H on a near-crash basis. The total cost for the project being completed within 18 days would be increased from $\$1,290$ to $\$1,470$ ($\$1,290 + \$180 = \$1,470$). The revised paths are indicated as follows:

Path	Time
A,E,G	$6 + 2 + 3 = 11$
A,C*,D,F*,G	$6 + 2* + 5 + 2* + 3 = 18†$
A,C*,D,H‡	$6 + 2* + 5 + 3‡ = 16$
B,D,F*,G	$3 + 5 + 2* + 3 = 13$
B,D,H‡	$3 + 5 + 3‡ = 11$

* Indicates that activities are reduced to their limits by being completed on a crash basis.
  † Indicates a critical path.
  ‡ Indicates some expediting is being performed but activity has not been performed on an all-crash basis.

The next objective is to reduce the total time to 15 days. Path $A,C*,D,F*,G$ and path $A,C*,D,H$ are over 15 days and must be reduced. Activity A (1,2) has the lowest remaining cost slope on the first path (\$120), and the time can be reduced by three days if the activity is completed on a crash basis (total additional cost $3 \times \$120 = \$360$). A three-day reduction in time on path $A,C*,D,F*,G$ would mean the project would be completed in 15 days (18 days $-\ 3 = 15$). Activity H on path $A,C*,D,H‡$ can be completed on an all-crash basis and the total time reduced by one day, which would mean the project would be completed within 15 days. Additional cost for activity H would be \$90 (total cost would be \$930 normal cost $+$ \$80 $+$ \$80 for activity F $+$ \$100 $+$ \$100 for activity C $+$ \$90 $+$ \$90 $+$ \$90 for activity H $+$ \$120 $+$ \$120 $+$ \$120 for activity $A =$ \$1,920). Following are the revised paths:

Path	Time
A*,E,G	$3* + 2 + 3 = 8$
A*,C*,D,F*,G	$3* + 2* + 5 + 2* + 3 = 15†$
A*,C*,D,H*	$3* + 2* + 5 + 2* = 12$
B,D,F*,G	$3 + 5 + 2* + 3 = 13$
B,D,H*	$3 + 5 + 2* = 10$

* Indicates that activities are reduced to their limits by being completed on a crash basis.
  † Indicates a critical path.

Note that path $A*,C*,D,H*$ was reduced by an additional three days because activity A was common to both paths (paths $A*,C*,D, F*,G$ and path $A*,C*,D,H*$); however, the rule of applying the lowest cost slope to each critical path was applied—any path having over 15 days is a critical path if 15 days is the desired goal.

This procedure of completing activities on a crash basis can be continued until the project is completed within 11 days for a cost of $2,500. This amount is $40 less than the maximum cost; the reason is that no time is saved by completing activity E on a crash basis. The final listing of paths is as follows:

Path	Time
A^*,E,G^*	$3^* + 2 + 1^* = 6$
A^*,C^*,D^*,F^*,G^*	$3^* + 2^* + 3^* + 2^* + 1^* = 11\dagger$
A^*,C^*,D^*,H^*	$3^* + 2^* + 3^* + 2^* = 10$
B^*,D^*,F^*,G^*	$3^* + 3^* + 2^* + 1^* = 9$
B^*,D^*,H^*	$3^* + 3^* + 2^* = 8$

* Indicates that activities are reduced to their limits by being completed on a crash basis.
† Indicates a critical path.

The previous example of an arrow diagram for a project presented the simplest type of situation. Another example is cited in Figure 9.3 for purposes of illustrating some other important considerations.

Activity G, activity K, and activity L are dummy activities; although they do not require any time for being completed, they are essential coordinating activities that must be recognized in the accomplishment of the overall project. For example, path A,D,G and

FIGURE 9.3
The Arrow Diagram of Project Two

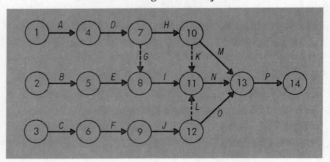

Activity	Normal Time	Activity	Normal Time
A (1,4)	10 days	I (8,11)	5 days
B (2,5)	3	J (9,12)	7
C (3,6)	2	K (10,11)	0 (dummy)
D (4,7)	4	L (12,11)	0 (dummy)
E (5,8)	6	M (10,13)	7
F (6,9)	3	N (11,13)	7
G (7,8)	0 (dummy)	O (12,13)	6
H (7,10)	3	P (13,14)	4

path *B,E* must both be completed before activity *I* (8,11) can be started.

The systems analyst approaches an arrow diagram for a project in much the same manner as he approaches a network diagram of the major information flows for a given business organization. These various major information flows must be grouped into larger units of analysis in order to get a "handle" on the mass of information. Likewise, all activities in an arrow diagram must be carefully examined and all separate paths of activities indicated. Each path of activities is a *unique* ordering of events to be performed through time; therefore, each possible path must be ascertained and separately considered if the overall project is to be managed. Following are the paths within the previous arrow diagram:

Path	Normal Time
A,D,H,M,P	$10 + 4 + 3 + 7 + 4 = 28$ days
A,D,G,I,N,P	$10 + 4 + 0 + 5 + 7 + 4 = 30$ days
A,D,H,K,N,P	$10 + 4 + 3 + 0 + 7 + 4 = 28$ days
B,E,I,N,P	$3 + 6 + 5 + 7 + 4 = 25$ days
C,F,J,O,P	$2 + 3 + 7 + 6 + 4 = 22$ days
C,F,J,L,N,P	$2 + 3 + 7 + 0 + 7 + 4 = 23$ days

Close scrutiny of the arrow diagram shows there are only six paths, and path *A,D,G,I,N,P* is the critical path under normal conditions. In this situation, management could delay activity *C* (3,6) for 7 days (not 8 days; note that activity *C* is a part of two paths and both paths must be considered) and still complete the overall project in the same number of days—specifically, 30 days under normal conditions.

Advantages of the Method

The previous illustrations of the CPM method have emphasized the mechanical and procedural aspects of the method without giving proper attention to other aspects of this method. These nonmechanical aspects are briefly mentioned in the following discussion of advantages gained by employing the CPM method.

First, a Foundation for Other Analyses. In order to prepare a CPM or PERT network, the systems analyst must identify in detail all the essential steps required for the accomplishment of a given operation. After these steps are listed, then time and cost estimates are made for each step. These time and cost estimates may include the appropriate information for (1) cost sensitivity analysis, (2) cost control, (3) direct costing type of analysis, (4) contribution to margin analysis, (5) cash flow analysis, and (6) other analyses. Thus, the CPM or PERT method serves as a foundation from which the arsenal of management tools and techniques may be employed.

Second, Effect on Management. The power of the critical path method is not simply the identification of those items that determine the minimum time period within which the total project can be accomplished (the critical path), but is the effect or influence that the application of this method has on management's thinking. The controller of a large corporation listed on the New York Stock Exchange recently spoke of the impact on his associates that a company training program on CPM method had made:

> It is surprising what effect this program has had on management's behavior. They are requiring their subordinates to submit CPM networks in support of any new project. It is not as if we did not plan before, for we did. We were just never so specific in relating both the steps to be accomplished and the time required for the attainment of each step.[1]

Third, Statement of Problem. The CPM method is a practical example of the application of the principles of the scientific method. The most difficult and the most important task confronting the management scientist is "the determination of the problem." Once the problem has been identified and precisely stated, the management scientist has an easier task selecting, from the available alternatives, the particular procedure that will be employed in either the minimization or elimination of the identified problem. Likewise, the CPM method includes the identification and specification of the problem area—the critical path which encompasses these activities . . . with a cost of . . . and a time of. . . .

Fourth, Stimulation for New Alternative. Once the critical activities have been ascertained, then management's attention is focused on the most important activities. Not only are these "critical" activities *identified* by the application of the CPM method, but the approach also expresses the *degree of criticalness* and the *sensitivity* in terms of time and cost measures. As a result, management has often formulated a new alternative for the accomplishment of a critical activity. For example, the plans may be modified to substitute, at

---

[1] From notes of private interview by Thomas R. Prince with the controller whose name is withheld at his request.

an overall savings, more expensive equipment or construction for existing proposed equipment or construction. In one company several thousand dollars was saved by having a furnace shipped in sections and assembled on the construction site. The additional cost of assembly was more than offset by erecting the steel beams and pouring the concrete for the main floor before the furnace was installed, thus making it possible to complete the construction project three months earlier.

Other Considerations

Many critical paths are manually solved, but there are practical restrictions regarding the size of any network that can be manually solved in a reasonable length of time. On the other hand, the procedural aspects of the critical path method make it an ideal application for the computer. The combination of a large storage capacity and a tremendous speed for processing information enables an enormous critical path schedule to be solved in a matter of minutes.

Strange as it may seem, there are many major construction projects where the combination of activities and events exceeds the capacity of existing CPM computer program packages. It is not financially feasible to prepare a special CPM computer program to be used only once. Therefore, different approaches are used to cope with this situation.

One approach is to reduce the CPM network to a size that can be handled by existing CPM computer program packages. This is accomplished by taking groups of activities and expressing them as a single activity. Of course, under such conditions, the computer's solution will probably not be optimum, especially if there were significant differences in the time requirements of the various activities that had been handled as a single activity.

Another approach in coping with this problem of the "oversize" CPM network is to divide the total network into segments which can be handled on the computer. The computer outputs for each of the segments are the inputs for another computer program which determines a practical (in all situations it may not be optimal) solution to the total CPM network.

Regardless of whether the CPM schedule is going to be solved manually or by the computer, it is not always desirable to prepare the CPM schedule at the activity level. For example, it may not be economically feasible to identify the activities at the lowest level or to determine the time and cost estimates for each activity. Instead, groups of activities may be scheduled as though they were one activity.

At this point, a warning is appropriate. The CPM method cannot provide any better answer than the quality of the input information. It is well to remember that any improvement in the CPM program depends more on the quality of input information than on the preparation of CPM schedules at a lower level.

From a practical standpoint, it may be desirable to sketch cost curves for each of the critical activities under both normal and over-time conditions before deciding which crash procedures will be employed. In other words, the suggested solution by the CPM method may be analogous to the suggested solution of alternative financial investments measured by "return on investment" formula. The real advantage of both the CPM method and the return on investment formula is not in solving a problem, but in focusing attention on the problem area which management should evaluate.

But even more important than the *selection* of the area or activity to be evaluated is the *elimination* of areas and activities that need not be evaluated.

As far as applications are concerned, the CPM or PERT method may be used to cope with any scheduling assignment. For example, a certified public accounting firm can use the method to determine the staffing requirements of employees by grade or to assign jobs to existing personnel. The CPM method has frequently been used to expedite the preparation of the end-of-the-month statement or to plan and supervise the audit program for a large organization. The CPM method can also solve a maintenance problem for a multi-plant operation by identifying the significant factors (such as the idle and travel time of mechanics, the lost time of machine operators, production delays, the size of the maintenance parts inventory, and the location of the inventory).

THE METHOD FROM THE PERSPECTIVE OF THE SYSTEMS ANALYST

The systems analyst views the critical path method as a combination of elements from two accounting systems. It is an extension of the *control features* of responsibility accounting systems (each activity is a "responsibility unit") combined with the *short-term planning features* of profitability accounting (the time and cost estimates for each planned activity are core ingredients in the CPM system, and this information is accumulated in such a manner as to permit marginal analyses). For example, as time passes and activities are performed, the CPM network can be reused, with actual information substituted for planned data; thus, the periodic application of this method to the same project will provide management with revised, up-to-date, critical information.

The systems analyst also sees this extension of traditional information systems as a practical example of the implementation of the scientific method, particularly from the standpoint of the emphasis given to the identification and statement of the problem.

SUMMARY

The CPM method is a powerful tool which can be employed in diverse situations, limited only by the imagination of the systems analyst. The systems analyst sees the method as a technique to be used in conjunction with other management tools and techniques. Furthermore, the analyst recognizes that the method is a connecting network that permits the matching of data sources with the information requirements of all decision makers associated with a given project.

If it were not for the *information dimensions* associated with the critical path method, this chapter would not have been included in this book. These information flows must be considered in the same manner as the evaluation made by the systems analyst in the previous TYPE 1 information systems. The system analyst must measure and evaluate the expected benefit derived from the application of the CPM method versus the cost of implementing the method. In addition, there are practical restrictions from the standpoint of available computer capacity and from the standpoint of the level at which the CPM network should be prepared.

TOPICS FOR CLASS DISCUSSION

1. Why are critical path planning and scheduling information systems presented as an extension of TYPE 1 information systems? Explain.

2. Explain the similarities between a responsibility accounting system and a critical path planning and scheduling information system. Be specific.

CASE 9–1. JAEGER MANUFACTURING COMPANY

CPM Exercise

The Jaeger Manufacturing Company is a small tool and die company which operates strictly on a job order basis. Currently, Carl Jaeger, who is president of the company, is evaluating a customer's request regarding the construction of a proposed project.

This project (which is a job order type of special item) is normally completed within 17 days at a selling price of $1,350. The customer stated that she urgently needs this particular item and will pay a premium of $150 a day for the completion of the project by an earlier time (for example, $1,350 + $150 = $1,500 is the selling price if the project is completed in 16 days; the price for 15 days is $1,350 + $150 + $150 = $1,650; and so forth).

Although this offer of a premium for "crash" construction sounds inviting, Carl Jaeger is concerned with the efficient employment of all of the resources of the company during the current "busy" season. In evaluating the customer's offer, an arrow diagram (see Exhibit A) was prepared to show the sequence of activities, and a cost table (see Exhibit B) was developed showing the normal and crash time and cost for each activity.

EXHIBIT A
Arrow Diagram

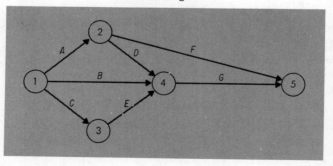

EXHIBIT B
Cost Table

Activity	Normal Time	Normal Cost	Crash Time	Crash Cost	Cost Slope
A (1,2)	4 days	$100	2 days	$ 200	$ 50
B (1,4)	7	160	5	300	70
C (1,3)	3	50	1	110	30
D (2,4)	7	120	2	620	100
E (3,4)	3	90	3	90	—*
F (2,5)	8	130	4	210	20
G (4,5)	5	120	2	360	80
		$770		$1,890	

* This activity cannot be expedited.

REQUIRED:

1. Assuming that Carl Jaeger desires to maximize income by having the *highest return per dollar of cost incurred,* determine which schedule of operations should be followed if the project is undertaken. Include quantitative computations in support of your answer.
2. What assumption is made regarding the nature of the cost slope in the above question?
3. Using the additional information revealed by Exhibit C, redetermine the schedule of operations that should be undertaken.

EXHIBIT C
Cost Data

Activity	Basis	Material	Labor	Other Expense	Total Cost
A (1,2)	Normal	$ 20	$ 70	$10	$100
	Crash	150*	40	10	200
B (1,4)	Normal	20	130	10	160
	Crash	190*	100	10	300
C (1,3)	Normal	10	35	5	50
	Crash	10	95	5	110
D (2,4)	Normal	10	100	10	120
	Crash	10	600	10	620
E (3,4)	Normal	5	80	5	90
F (2,5)	Normal	10	115	5	130
	Crash	10	195	5	210
G (4,5)	Normal	10	100	10	120
	Crash	10	340	10	360

* The material cost includes a purchased part which is partially finished, and this "partially finished part" can only be purchased in this given state. (There are two such partially finished parts: one for activity A and another for activity B.)

4. With the following additional information, prepare a daily cash forecast for the schedule of operations that was selected to be undertaken in the above step (3) :

   a. Assume that all purchases are for cash. Except for activities *A, B,* and *C,* all material for each activity must be purchased the *day before* work on that activity begins. In the case of activities *A, B, and* C, assume that the materials are purchased in the morning of the first scheduled work day for each activity.

   b. Assume that each activity's labor and other expenses are incurred on a proportional basis and must be paid for on a daily basis.

CASE 9–2.   WOODRUFF GROCERY COMPANY

CPM EXERCISE

The management consulting firm with which you are associated was engaged by the Woodruff Grocery Company, a regional wholesaler for frozen foods, to (1) perform an overall review of the data processing operations for inventory control, sales management, and accounts receivable collection procedures and to (2) design an improved integrated information system for these operations.

You have accompanied your immediate superior, a manager, on a high-point review of the above specified data processing operations at the Woodruff Grocery Company. After you completed your preliminary examination of the company's operations, your manager decided that:

1. A scientific inventory system should be established in place of the existing inventory system which uses last period's sales as the minimum inventory level for the current period.

2. Unit cost data should be available for each line item on a sales invoice, and gross margin type of reports should be prepared for each line item and each invoice and on a monthly basis for each customer and each salesperson.

3. The accounts receivable collection procedures should be modified to include an information system for monitoring cumulative balances in customer accounts versus approved credit limits.

Your manager outlined the work to be performed (see Exhibit A) and indicated the estimated number of work-hours that members of the management consulting firm (Information Systems Specialists, Inc.) would spend in accomplishing each step.

**Description of Work to Be Performed in Developing an
Integrated Information System for Inventory Control, Sales
Management, and Accounts Receivable Collection Procedures**

Step No.	Description	Assigned to	Estimated Time
1.	Inventory Control System:		
1.1	Obtain copies of monthly stock status report for the past 36 months	Woodruff Grocery Co.	
1.2	Obtain copy of current month's monthly stock status report in punched-card form	Woodruff Grocery Co.	
1.3	Develop projected sales quantities for each item by month for the next twelve months, which would include identifying seasonal demand patterns for certain items	Information Systems Specialists, Inc.	50 work-hours
1.4	Review projected sales quantities developed in previous step with sales manager	Information Systems Specialists, Inc.	7 work-hours (7 consecutive hours, only)
1.5	Develop reorder quantities for each item, which would include giving consideration to sources of supply, shipping time, price breaks, storage and handling costs, and total storage capacity (Step 1.5 cannot begin until after Step 1.4 is completed)	Information Systems Specialists, Inc.	120 work-hours
1.6	Review reorder quantities developed in previous step with Inventory Manager and Purchasing Manager	Information Systems Specialists, Inc.	7 work-hours (7 consecutive hours, only)
1.7	Develop reorder points for each item (Step 1.7 cannot begin until after Step 1.6 is completed)	Information Systems Specialists, Inc.	50 work-hours
1.8	Review reorder points developed in previous step with sales manager, inventory manager, and purchasing manager (a comparative report of monthly forecasted sales, reorder quantity, and reorder point by item)	Information Systems Specialists, Inc.	5 work-hours (5 consecutive hours, only)
1.9	Assist in designing a computer program so that when the existing perpetual inventory system indicates that the balance of a given item has reached the reorder point, a purchase request for the reorder quantity of the desired item is initiated (Step 1.9 cannot begin until after Step 1.8 is completed)	Information Systems Specialists, Inc.	30 work-hours (minimum of 14 consecutive hours)
1.10	Monitor the installation. testing, and operation of designed system, including the monitoring of input cards (punched cards) for transmitting the computed reorder points and reorder quantities onto magnetic tape (the perpetual inventory system is maintained on magnetic tape) (Step 1.10 may be partially performed concurrently with Step 1.9; however, 10 work-hours and a minimum of 7 consecutive hours must be performed *after* Step 1.9 is completed)	Information Systems Specialists, Inc.	45 work-hours (minimum of 14 consecutive hours)

EXHIBIT A (*Continued*)

Step No.	Description	Assigned to	Estimated Time
2.	Sales Management System:		
2.1	Obtain copy of the current month's monthly stock status report	Woodruff Grocery Co.	
2.2	Obtain a list of the per unit cost data for each item included in the monthly stock status report	Woodruff Grocery Co.	
2.3	Assist in the design of computer program for sales management system which would include: 2.31 Master tape file of cost data for each item of inventory 2.32 Program routine and report format for comparing and extending cost data against item sales data per sales invoice 2.33 Program routine and report format for computing monthly gross margin by invoice for each customer 2.34 Program routine and report format for computing monthly gross margin by customer for each salesperson	Information Systems Specialists, Inc.	80 work-hours (minimum of 21 consecutive hours)
2.4	Monitor the installation, testing, and operation of the designed sales management system (Step 2.4 cannot begin until after Step 2.3 has been completed)	Information Systems Specialists, Inc.	24 work-hours (minimum of 14 consecutive hours)
3.	Accounts receivable collection procedures:		
3.1	Obtain a printout from the master tape file of the identification code, name, and address of each customer	Woodruff Grocery Co.	
3.2	Obtain a list of approved credit limit per order and in total for each customer	Woodruff Grocery Co.	
3.3	Assist in the design of a computer program for exceptional reporting, where each salesperson will receive weekly a list of his or her customers whose current accounts receivable balance *plus* the approved credit limit per order will exceed the maximum approved credit limit for that customer	Information Systems Specialists, Inc.	40 work-hours (minimum of 20 consecutive hours)
3.4	Monitor the installation, testing, and operation of designed system (Step 3.4 cannot begin until after Step 3.3 is completed)	Information Systems Specialists, Inc.	10 work-hours (10 consecutive hours, only)
3.5	Assist in the design of computer program routine and report format for an exceptional reporting system to the credit manager of all overdue accounts. This report will be prepared on the first and the fifteenth days of each month, or at any other time bared on request.	Information Systems Specialists, Inc.	14 work-hours (minimum of 7 consecutive hours)
3.6	Monitor the installation, testing, and operation of designed system (Step 3.6 cannot begin until after Step 3.5 is completed)	Information Systems Specialists, Inc.	7 work-hours (7 consecutive hours, only)

REQUIRED:

1. Prepare a critical path schedule of the steps to be performed.
2. The Woodruff Grocery Company is an out-of-town client, and the manager is wondering if there should be *three* or *four* people assigned to this job. Because of high transportation cost, the minimum assignment of a worker to the job is on a weekly basis (35 work-hours, consisting of five 7-work-hour days). Quantitatively determine the number of workers *by week* that should be assigned to this project.
3. If six workers were assigned to this project on a full-time basis, how many days would be required to complete the project? Determine the number of idle work-hours under this assignment of six workers.

CASE 9–3. WEBSTER CONSTRUCTION COMPANY, INC.

The construction firm with which you are associated, the Webster Construction Company, Inc., has a contract to erect a $10 million educational complex at a leading midwestern university. Because of labor difficulties climaxing in an eight-week strike, the construction project is two to three months behind the contract completion date, according to the project manager.

The contract provides for $500-a-day liquidating damages for noncompletion of the project by the specified date.

You were just transferred by the home office management of the Webster Construction Company from a Massachusetts construction project (which was ahead of schedule) to this critical construction project at the midwestern university.

Ralph Worthington, the project manager, was desperate for some way to expedite the construction operations and agreed to your suggestion of using the critical path method. Worthington stated that he had seen articles in trade publications on the CPM method but that he had never actually supervised a project where the CPM method was employed. Worthington also said that most of his associates were in the same predicament as himself regarding CPM. However, Worthington said he was sure the various supervisors would cooperate with you.

You devoted the next several days to reading blueprints, scheduling the operations, and preparing network diagrams. Considerable time was spent with different supervisors asking for "estimated time" to complete the different jobs (activities or operations) and also in verifying that the sequence of activities per the network diagrams was correct.

Eventually, the CPM network was completed and reviewed with Ralph Worthington. According to the network, there was a 110-day period between the contract completion date and the earliest actual completion time, which, at $500 per day, totaled $55,000 penalty.

Worthington said that he would discuss the jobs along the critical path with the various supervisors to see if they were not too pessimistic in stating their "estimated time."

These talks resulted in several revised critical path schedules, which eventually reflected a shift in the critical path and a 90-day delay (rather than a 110-day delay). The forecasted penalty was $45,000. However, the delay would probably mean that the Webster Construction Company would not be selected for another proposed construction project which this midwestern university was currently seeking to finance.

Worthington summarized his predicament:

I have 210 days remaining before the contract completion date and your CPM schedule tells me that it will really be 90 days beyond the contract completion date before we finish the project. Of the more than 1,500 activities that I have to supervise, the CPM network tells me where to focus my attention. However, there are still too many activities on the critical path involving too many dollars for me to efficiently and economically manage by mere observation. Frankly, this CPM approach has been overrated; it just tells the project manager "how bad off we really are."

REQUIRED:

Design an information control system that will assist Worthington in his management activities and yet not upset the normal accounting routines. In accomplishing this task, you review the current accounting routines:

1. The Webster Construction Company's management requires that a bill of materials (units and prices) and a schedule of labor (hours and average wage per hour for groups of workers) be prepared as a basis for determining the *bid price*. Then, on all projects, actual material and labor costs are compared with the estimated costs.

2. Ralph Worthington has a manager of materials and supplies who is responsible for seeing that required items are on hand. Furthermore, the manager is responsible for maintaining a record of the actual materials and supplies used.

3. As a control device, each supervisor maintains the payroll records for her or his employees and submits a weekly report to the accounting payroll clerk.

4. In addition to these procedures for materials, supplies, and labor costs, a special bank account is established for each construction project. All expenditures, including general and administrative overhead, are charged against this special bank account.

CASE 9–4. LEVI CONSTRUCTION COMPANY, INC.

The management consulting firm with which you are associated has been engaged by the Levi Construction Company, Inc., to assist management in the construction of a $2,000,000 public school building. George Bradford has been assigned by the Levi Construction Company as the project manager for this school building.

Based on the architectural drawings and the General Superintendent's narrative of the major steps in construction of the school, you prepare an arrow diagram consisting of approximately 300 events and 550 activities. When the proper dependencies among activities are recorded, time estimates are assigned to each activity, and the earliest possible completion times are calculated. Next, the activities are placed on a time scale and the dependencies are appropriately identified. In addition to the scale drawing, a working day calendar and delivery schedule for major outside purchased equipment are prepared.

Bradford, in reviewing your drawings with you, makes the following comment:

Although the specifications on the contract indicate a delivery date of the school building by September 1, we would like to avoid incurring heating and maintenance costs during January–September. Is it possible that the school building can be completed by December? If it can be completed by the earlier date, we are sure that the school board will accept the building and use the facilities during the second semester of the school year.

Your critical path diagrams for the planned project indicate a normal completion date on June 10. Therefore, you tell Bradford that you will reexamine the plans to see if some alternative types of construction might be followed to shorten the construction period.

The delivery time for the boiler was previously believed to be the governing factor in the completion time for the basement of one of the wings. As a result of your reexamination and thorough analysis of the boiler's specifications, it is revealed that the boiler can be delivered in sections and lowered through the stairwells at a later date. Your reexamination also indicates other alternative procedures including a different plan for excavation and different sources for selective purchase items, thereby enabling the planned project to be completed by December 30.

After preparing revised arrow diagrams, working day calendars, and a schedule for major outside purchased equipment, Bradford discusses with you his other requirements:

Since the project has not begun, I would like to have a suggested information system that would not only aid me in completing the school building by December 30, but would also assist me in (1) controlling costs and (2) forecasting cash requirements. As the construction proceeds and unexpected events occur, this suggested information system must permit the easy re-scheduling and re-computation of (1) the earliest completion date for each step in the project, (2) the planned and actual costs, and (3) the cash requirements.

REQUIRED:

1. Reply to Bradford's request.
2. As a systems analyst, what are some of the practical problems involved in the design of such an information system? (Your comments should include such considerations as data restrictions, time restrictions, and the out-of-pocket costs in designing and monitoring such a system versus the estimated benefit to be derived from the system.)

PART **III**

PRODUCTION AND OPERATION
INFORMATION SYSTEMS

CHAPTER 10

Operations Management Information Systems

In our examination of the five discrete models of advanced computer-based networks, the focus is on the eight common dimensions of the administrative process and the organizational arrangements associated with each model. While the five discrete models are presented as multidimensional levels of advancement, there is *no underlying assumption that a higher level is preferred to a lower level.* The five levels are neutral with respect to preference.

The systems analyst does not aspire to any particular level of advancement for a specific organization; instead, the analyst is concerned with assisting members of management in determining which level of advancement meets the unique requirements of that organization, including the eight common dimensions. The five phases in the formal program for planning and implementing an information system (Chapter 6) must be rigorously followed with active participation by members of management at all organizational levels if a given balanced, level of advancement is to be achieved in a specific organization.

THE GENERAL MODEL

The second of the five discrete models of advanced computer-based networks is an operations management information system. The general model for this multidimensional level of advancement is a *partially open* system that (*a*) permits online interaction by members of management with a predetermined segment of the organization's environment and (*b*) has the online capacity for making changes in parameters and variables during the *control phase*. The decision makers associated with this network make a *partial response* to selected types of events while activities specified by the current cycle's "plan" are occurring.

The general model of the operations management information systems encompasses all types of major information flows within the organization. In other words, this means that all the flows in a TYPE 1 information system, a responsibility accounting information system, and a profitability accounting information system *may* be part of this integrated model. Thus, we are concerned with those facets of the eight common dimensions which are different from the previously described models and extensions.

The environment surrounding the typical organization in which an operations management information system is employed is flexible enough to permit a quick response to certain types of events within the information network. Management needs an information network that (*a*) not only informs them of a significant change in certain economic events, (*b*) but also contains a necessary direct communication link which allows them to respond quickly to that change by modifying the network's operating criteria.

In this environment, the nature of the administrative process cannot be separated into (*a*) the editing and screening phase, (*b*) the planning phase, and (*c*) the control phase as described for the TYPE 1 information system. Within the time frame of an "information cycle," management must be able to respond to the actions of competitors, to indications of a possible change in customer preferences, to changing levels of customer demand, to shifts in demand for services, and to special requirements of certain customers, clients, and constituents. The latter may include priority services or rush sales orders that must be expedited in all aspects of the production and distribution functions.

Therefore, in the general model of an operations management information system, a fourth phase has been added to the three phases in the TYPE 1 information system. This new phase—the *coordination phase*—is, of course, the most distinctive characteristic in the operations management information system.

The coordination phase of the administrative process permits inputs to the information network at any time. These inputs may ask that certain tasks be performed requiring the use of personnel, machines, raw materials, and resources already assigned to previously scheduled tasks. The information system must be able to handle these conflicting requirements.

The crux of the coordination phase is the establishment of a set of criteria and the assignment of priorities to be followed in coping with future events. Thus, the predetermined responses are used to manage conflicts in assignment of personnel, machines, raw materials, inventories, services, or resources. The predetermined response may span the gamut from "no action" (in which case there is no modification in the specified set of assignments for the online operations being monitored by the control phase) to a total response (in which case there might be a complete reassignment of tasks to be performed within a given time period using the specified personnel, equipment, inventories, services, and resources). While it is conceivable that a complete reassignment of all tasks covered in the master "plan" for this control cycle can occur on a sequential basis in the coordination phase, this would be a rare situation. It is more likely that the coordination phase in a dynamic organization might affect 15 per cent to 25 per cent of the planned activities; thus, the majority of the activities is not influenced by the coordination phase. (This 15 to 25 per cent range is a generalization based on experience with the network in several organizations and it is valid only when there is a short time cycle for the control phase.)

In accomplishing these objectives through the coordination phase, there are really three facets of the administrative process that are concurrently evaluated. First, there is the monitoring and sensory function which focuses on selected variables in the external environment. Second, there is the online awareness of (a) the status of existing resources, equipment, inventories, supplies, personnel, and services, and (b) the current assignment of these in pursuit of organization's objectives. Third, there is the online capability of (a) performing "weighted," sensitivity analyses of selected variables, (b) determining if a revised assignment is required for the remainder the control phase, and (c) making a revised, online assignment as suggested from the analyses.

From these three facets, we see a generalizable concept of the administrative process that may be applicable to changing environmental settings in any type of institutional location. This generalization, combined with the previously described inclusive-nature of the organization's major information flows that are integrated into the operations management information system, suggests that the

words "operations management" are too restricted for the broad
scope of this network. While the operations management function
dominates many of these networks, there are many cases where the
marketing function and the distribution function are the dominant
activities. In some organizations other types of activities may dominate the management of change as related to this network. Because of
these multiinterests in this type of network, we will not continue to
use the label "operations management information system" in referring to this network. Instead, we will call this network a TYPE 2
information system.

TYPE 2 INFORMATION SYSTEM

Figure 10.1 presents a generalized model of a TYPE 2 information
system containing four phases— (*a*) editing and screening phase, (*b*)
planning phase, (*c*) control phase, and (*d*) coordination phase. The
editing and screening phase contains the identical features incorporated in the TYPE 1 information system (symbols A1, A31, and
A32) ; in addition, there is a special screen (symbols A6 and A7) for
use in filtering the selected environmental data within the coordination phase.

The planning phase is very similar to previous networks; the
partial planning phase (symbol A27) is identical with these features
in the TYPE 1 information system. The general relations of the
other features in the planning phase (symbols A28, A29, and A30)
are comparable to those in Figure 8.1 for the profitability accounting
system. It is important to note that the establishment of a coordination phase with online monitoring of selected environmental data
does not eliminate the need for a manual review and analysis of environmental activities (symbol A29). If the organization's environment is changing significantly so as to justify a TYPE 2 network with
a coordination phase, there are normally many other environmental
activities that should be monitored and evaluated. This latter point
is expanded into a major separate phase in the TYPE 4 information
system.

The control phase in the TYPE 2 information system contains
similar features with those presented in Figure 8.1 for the profitability accounting system. Each of the online reprocessing operations
(symbols A18, A22, and A25) uses a closed set of online computer

programs (symbol A19) ; however, in the interest of a simple flow-chart these online symbols for these computer programs have not been shown. Symbol A19 is specifically shown in Figure 10.1 because the online coordination phase pages this online program in the control phase to see if proposed changes in parameters and variables (symbol A14) were properly processessed, sorted, and assigned (symbol A15). The solution matrix of the current assignment (symbol A16) is also updated by the same changes (symbol A14), and this online storage information is in convenient form for further analysis. The latter is in marked contrast with the minimum data that can be retrieved from the online computer programs (symbol A19), even though both sets of online data pertain to the same set of assignments.

The coordination phase focuses on selected changes in the external environment, and this cluster of activities monitors, filters, analyzes, evaluates, and re-computes (when appropriate) a partial set of resource assignments in the current period's control cycle. This is accomplished by first having special remote terminals (symbols A2 and A3) for monitoring selected changes in the external environment; there is a minimum filter of the input data in an interactive environment (symbols A4 and A5) with the remote terminal operators being informed of rejected data. After the data have passed this minimum filter, they are subjected to the regular editing and screening operations (symbols A6 and A7). The screened input data are then analyzed by a sensitivity test (symbol A8) which is based on a set of online computer programs that have assigned values and critical ranges for each element. If these selected data are found to be critical, they are reprocessed, weighted, and tested in existing online computer programs (symbols A10, A11, and A12). A computer analysis is made of the new computations to determine if a change in the current assignment is required. If so, changes in parameters and variables (symbol A14) are made in the closed set of computer programs contained within the operating systems.

The time factor used in weighting these selected data is the critical element in the overall process. For example, the price of raw material no. 1874 is defined as critical (symbol A8) if it is less than $21.18 per unit, or if it is more than $22.37. Assume that an input of new data is accepted into the system that specifies the price as $22.41 per unit. Since $22.41 is more than $22.37, this price change is

FIGURE 10.1
A Generalized Model of a TYPE 2 Information System

* The editing and screening phase is depicted by symbols A1 to A10 in Figure 7.1.

determined to be sensitive. If the overall operating cycle is eight hours and these new data on price of raw material no. 1874 occur during the first hour of the cycle, then it is highly likely that a revised assignment will occur for the remaining seven-plus hours in the cycle. On the other hand, if the new data on raw material price

FIGURE 10.1 (*Continued*)

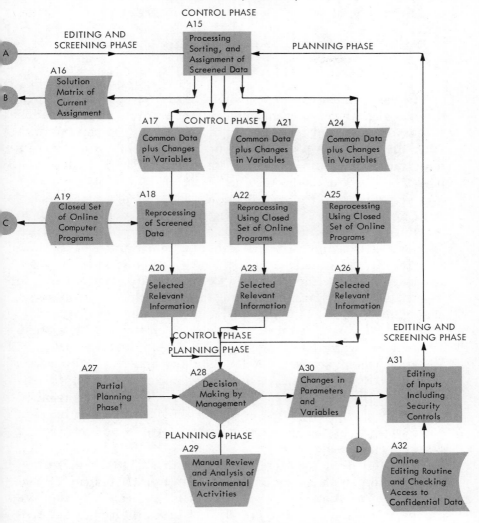

* The partial planning phase is depicted by symbols A12 to A16 in Figure 7.1.

occur late in the sixth hour of the cycle, then it is highly unlikely that a revised assignment will occur.

The flowchart of the coordination phase shows a series of online activities that are supported by closed sets of online computer programs. Therefore, the time factor used in weighting the critical data (symbol A10) must be computed within the system. The online solution matrix of current assignment (symbol A16) will also include the time at which the control phase began for the current cycle.

THE EIGHT COMMON DIMENSIONS

The eight dimensions of the administrative process and the organizational arrangements encompassed in a TYPE 2 information system are examined for purposes of facilitating comparisons with other discrete levels of advancement. First, the models of the administrative process in a TYPE 2 information system include four phases: (*a*) editing and screening phase, (*b*) planning phase, (*c*) control phase, and (*d*) coordination phase. Members of management are willing to follow a management by systems approach to monitoring of performance, comparing of actual with planned performance, and taking corrective action on an exception basis. However, the environmental setting is such that some members of management must have the capability for making a partial response to selected changes in the environment, and this means changing the set of assignments derived from the previous cycle's planning phase.

Second, the organizational structure of an agency, association, company, or institution possessing a TYPE 2 information system is, at least, a matrix arrangement for those decision makers associated with the coordination phase. The decision makers associated with the planning phase in a TYPE 2 network are frequently organized around dual responsibilities, especially those members of management engaged in the monitoring and manual review of selected environmental change elements.

Third, the decision makers associated with a TYPE 2 information system are usually members of management from *two* organizational units. The coordination phase is frequently directed by the vice president of marketing, vice president of manufacturing, vice president of distribution, or group vice president of customer services. Concurrently, the planning phase is directed by one of the other listed individuals. Fourth, the nature of the activity supported by a TYPE 2 information system includes all major flows—both vertical and horizontal—within the organization under the jurisdiction of the two decision makers (as specified by the third dimension).

Fifth, there is online interaction between users of the TYPE 2 network and the computer-based system at three places: (*a*) in the area of editing and screening, (b) in the coordination phase where raw data are filtered, processed, sorted, tested for sensitivity, reprocessed, and evaluated for partial change in assignment, and (c) in the online implementation of partial change in assignment while the control cycle is in process. Sixth, the time cycle of the control phase in a TYPE 2 information system is usually much longer than is the case in a TYPE 1 system. It is also common for the three operating systems to be three distinct flows with the same internal characteristics as the three operating systems in the profitability accounting system (see Figure 8.1). However, the shortest cycle in a TYPE 2 system tends to be for two or three days (this is in marked contrast with the 8-hour shift in the TYPE 1 system).

Seventh, a responsibility accounting system and a profitability accounting system are frequently incorporated within a TYPE 2 information system, and this network interfaces the online common data files from other organizational systems, such as, a personnel management subsystem, inventory planning and control subsystem, and financial management subsystem. The TYPE 2 system is, of course, interfaced with policy and objective data provided by the long-range planning activities of executive management. In addition, there are activity and functional programs interfaced with the TYPE 2 network that measure performance and assist in physical control, technical control, and management control.

Eighth, the data structure of a TYPE 2 information system requires consideration of currency of data and timeliness of data viewed in an interactive environment. The monitoring of the environment in the coordination phase which is interfaced with the overall assignment models in the planning phase and online schedules in the control phase places increased emphasis on data structure in a TYPE 2 system over that in a TYPE 1 network. The online change of parameters and variables in the control phase requires not only a sophisticated series of online computer programs, but also an online retrieval system that communicates with the decision maker in the coordination phase as to the revised online assignment model.

Members of management desire up-to-date information on each of the group of activities being performed in the control phase. Since there is no "time gap" between the end of this period's control phase and the start of the next period's control phase, the planning decisions must be made based on some *forecasted* data regarding the current period's actual performance. Members of management prefer to have the capability for immediate retrieval of data as they occur within the control phase, and through this arrangement, members of management hope to have a minimum period of control-phase activities that are based on projected data. Thus, the pressure is there for online retrieval of performance data as they occur for use in planning for the next period's control cycle.

CODING PATTERNS AND PROGRAMS FOR THE COORDINATION PHASE

A *partial response* in a TYPE 2 system in contrast with a *complete response* in a TYPE 1 system significantly expands the scope and complexity of the online computer programs that handle large volumes of recurring transactions. Numerous combinations of partial responses must be anticipated, and computer programs must be redesigned to handle marginal data.

If the online assignment model is the result of the 43d iteration of calculations, a computer capability is needed that will *start* at the 43d iteration (as a variable element in the computer program that is specified each time the program is called) and will begin performing sensitivity analysis as to whether a 44th iteration is an economic improvement. Alternatively, each of the online computer programs that may be responsive to a partial assignment must be redesigned so the program can be loaded at its previous assignment level or iteration; this is easily accomplished through incorporating this variable in the *call statement* for the online computer program. Once the online computer program is activated at a given iteration, then all marginal values of substitution and changes in assignments can be determined from the residual data identified with the given iteration which was loaded. Thus, a major systems investment is required for redesign of online computer programs before they can be loaded at a given level to handle a specific partial response.

The interactive relation of the decision maker in the coordination phase with the online computer programs in the control phase requires a timely, communication network among the parties. As soon as a partial response is made in the form of changes in parameters and variables in the online computer programs, the tests for sensitivity analysis that are online in the coordination phase must be updated with the revised ranges. Otherwise, the sensory measures of environmental data that are being monitored may continuously show the "need for a partial response" when, in fact, the proposed partial response is already in an operational mode.

An online, interactive environmental setting in which monitoring and sensory activities are processed online within the integrated network requires a high level of attention being given to data structure, format, coding, editing, screening, and filtering. Any reasonably competent practitioner can design a data processing system which will efficiently handle 90 percent of all transactions. However, it is the remaining 10 percent of the transactions that are the most difficult to anticipate and when they do occur, they may require management's time in exceptional processing arrangements.

The above statement of 90 percent is a generalization based on organizational experience. In some organizations we have studied, 92 to 95 percent of the transactions have been easily predictable; only 5 to 8 percent of the transactions were not anticipated. The filters in the editing and screening phase and the predetermined decision rules in the online computer programs draw heavily upon this 90 percent plus ability to anticipate in detail coming events and transactions.

The online monitoring and sensory activities within the coordination phase only pertain to a portion of the predictable transactions. Thus, the scope, nature, and combination of events associated with these monitored activities can be completely programmed. The monitoring and sensory activities do not capture any raw data that have not been anticipated; thus, all captured data which pass the initial input filter are predictable and can be fully processed without any participation by members of management.

ILLUSTRATION OF COORDINATION PHASE

Jackson Laboratories, Inc. operates on a three-shift a day basis, and this company is always able to sell its products at some price. There are significant variations in the return per product, and members of management desire to produce and distribute the maximum number of products with high marginal returns while producing and distributing the minimum number of products with relatively low marginal returns.

Jackson Laboratories' products are bulky, and because of the volume and weight of these products, all scheduled manufacturing is for immediate shipment to specific customers. There are constraints both as to which products can be manufactured on which equipment and as to which employees can manufacture which products regardless of the availability of equipment. There are also limitations on which products can be manufactured *after* specific products have been processed by the same equipment. Thus, the current set of products being manufactured constrains the set of feasible products that might be manufactured subsequently.

The company is a union shop; however, the leaders of organized labor support the concept of changing the scheduled production within an 8-hour shift *if* labor is given a portion of the extra profits from the change. A change in scheduled production will increase the organization's profits for the 8-hour shift, but the workers have to apply extra efforts in adjusting to these changes. The labor-management agreement provides that a bonus is paid to employees who are required to adjust or change their scheduled production (the agreement calls for a specified payment per change) and that a maximum of two changes per machine or vat can be made within an 8-hour shift.

The computer-based network for Jackson Laboratories is a TYPE 2 information system in which salespeople, field representatives, and marketing personnel are periodically transmitting to the home office the sales orders by customers as well as proposed, special sales orders. Figure 10.2 presents a model of the coordination phase at Jackson Laboratories. Most sales orders are for delivery in approximately 10 days; however, each sales order is very explicit as to delivery date. Because of the bulky nature of the product, early delivery is not desired; most customers prefer delivery on the specified date. This means that most processed sales orders flow through the editing and screening phase (symbols B1 or B2 to B7) where they are placed in online storage (symbol B8) and are held for three or four days (depending on estimated distribution time) before being scheduled for production.

If all of Jackson Laboratories' sales orders were for delivery in approximately 10 days, then these operations could easily be handled by a TYPE 1 system with an 8-hour control cycle. But, there are unusual sales orders and proposed sales orders (which are frequently for products on which there are relatively high returns) that must be processed by the coordination phase in a TYPE 2 system. A salesperson at remote terminal (symbol B1 or B2) uses the coordination phase in an interactive mode for determining if a proposed, special sales order can be manufactured and distributed within a

FIGURE 10.2
Model of Coordination Phase for Jackson Laboratories, Inc.

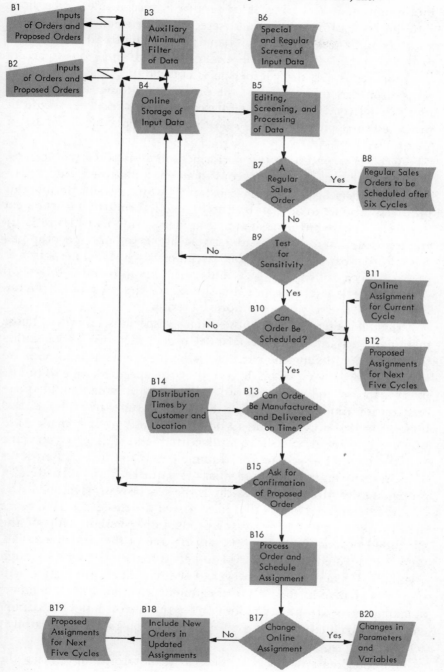

minimum amount of time. This proposed, special sales order flows through the online editing and screening operations (symbols B4 and B5) and a test for sensitivity analysis is made based on marginal analyses (symbol B9). If it is not marginally advantageous to accept the proposed order, the salesperson is notified of this situation. The salesperson may then try to get the proposed customer to change the terms or delivery schedule; in either case, a new sales order would be processed through each of the steps in the flowchart (symbol B1 or B2 to B9).

There is a second-stage test performed on a proposed sales orders. It may be marginally advantageous to accept a proposed order; however, there may be scheduling constraints which do not permit this proposed product to be manufactured during the current or the next five cycles. These online assignment models (symbols B11 and B12) are accessed, and a test is made as to whether or not the proposed special order can be accomplished (symbol B10). The salesperson is immediately notified of this second-stage response, and a follow-up can be made with the proposed customer for the purpose of obtaining a revised delivery date or improved terms.

A third-level test is made of the proposed special sales order. Those marginally advantageous special sales orders that can be scheduled for production during the current cycle plus the next five cycles are tested to see if they can be delivered at the specified time. The delivery date on the proposed order may not provide for adequate distribution time. Therefore, the distribution times by customer and by location are stored online (symbol B14) and a test is made as to whether the order can be manufactured and delivered on time (symbol B13). The salesperson is immediately notified of the results of the test and an immediate feedback is required for confirmation of proposed sales orders that pass the three sets of tests (symbol B15).

The filtered sales orders that have passed the three sets of tests are then processed and scheduled for production (symbol B16). If the scheduled production is to occur during one of the next five cycles, then the proposed assignment is handled automatically by the system (symbols B18 and B19). However, if the scheduled production will require a change in the online assignment (symbol B17), members of management are asked to monitor the proposed changes in parameters and variables (symbol B20) before the on-going production is actually changed.

The coordination phase at Jackson Laboratories interfaces the other phases in the TYPE 2 system in the same manner as the general model presented in Figure 10.1. As soon as there is a change in the online computer programs or in the assignment of products to equipment, the online assignment models accessed in the coordination phase are immediately updated.

SYSTEMS ANALYST'S PERSPECTIVE OF COORDINATION PHASE

As previously indicated, the sets of activities from the environment which are to be monitored and evaluated in an online, interactive mode must be items whose nature and scope are highly predictable. Otherwise, an exceptional response to the environmental variable may stop the online operations.

It is important that the systems analyst fully applies the first three phases in the formal program for planning and implementing an information system before selecting the environmental variables to be monitored in the coordination phase. The planning, organization review and administrative study, and conceptual systems design phases encompass a rigorous approach for analyzing, studying, and evaluating the organizational setting. The systems analyst working with members of management can then identify environmental, change variables whose anticipated nature can be evaluated and subjected to online, computer programs containing tests for sensitivity.

There are also significant systems maintenance costs associated with the coordination phase. Periodically, the systems analyst must reassess the online screens and reconfirm the economic feasibility and relevance of the specified, change variables. It is not unusual for these variables to shift in relative importance every few months in a changing environment, and often other items should then be subjected to the monitoring and sensory activities within the coordination phase.

LEVEL OF SERVICE

The general model of a TYPE 2 information system includes two decision makers—one decision maker directly associated with the coordination phase and another decision maker identified with the planning phase. A high degree of cooperation is needed between these two decision makers as well as with the other members of management who are indirectly associated with the TYPE 2 network.

The *level of service* to a client, customer, or constituent is really a *measure of the internal cooperation* among members of management. Specifically, the level of service is a rough statistic as to the percent of goods and services which are delivered on the promised date to the client, customer, or constituent. This particular measure is not weighted by the "degree of lateness"; instead, it is a very simple ratio of *orders delivered on time* expressed to *total orders*. But, from this rough measure, the systems analyst can quickly obtain an overall assessment of the degree of cooperation among members of management in different departments within the organization.

When the level of service is not favorable to the organization, the systems analyst encounters the problem of not knowing whom to blame for lack of cooperation. For example, in a manufacturing company with a goal of 95 percent level of customer service that is currently approaching a 75 percent level, what corrective action can be taken? It may be that the initial promised date is not compatible with the physical plant and operating cycle, and either more facilities are required or a longer time period is needed in which the fluctuations in demand can be averaged and the overall demand can be satisfied. Alternatively, it may be that the criteria followed by the manufacturing department in scheduling production are not compatible with the delivery schedule being used and quoted by marketing personnel. There are, of course, cases where a few people in marketing may make unauthorized promises in hopes of obtaining a sale or where selected individuals in the manufacturing department may follow their own set of criteria rather than use the organization's stated criteria in scheduling production and deliveries.

The customer, constituent, or client does not really care about the explanation; he or she is merely assessing the odds on whether or not the goods or services will be delivered on time. In many organizations, the proven *level of service* on deliveries is frequently a more important factor than *price* in determining to which competing organization the purchase order will be given.

Again, cooperation among members of management is an inherent feature of a TYPE 2 information system. The level of service is an important, rough measure that the systems analyst should apply in the initial high point review which precedes the formal program for planning and implementing an information system.

SUMMARY

The general model of a TYPE 2 information system was examined with special attention given to the online capabilities for monitoring selected environmental factors, performing sensitivity analyses, and making partial changes in the online operations. We saw that a partial change in assignments was much more involved and complicated than a complete change in assignments incorporated in a TYPE 1 system.

The eight common dimensions of the administrative process and the organizational arrangements encompassed in this second discrete model of advanced computer-based networks were described for purposes of facilitating comparisons among models. The four parts of the administrative process— (a) the editing and screening phase, (b) the planning phase, (c) the control phase, and (d) the coordination phase—imposed new requirements for interactive capabilities, redesign of computer programs, and specification of coding patterns. The latter three features were highlighted in an examination and illustration of the coordination phase.

TOPICS FOR CLASS DISCUSSION

1. The general model for a TYPE 2 information system is a *partially* open network in which members of management can make a *partial* change in assignment during the control phase. Explain these *partial* features.

2. Explain the function performed by the coordination phase in a TYPE 2 information system.

3. The online sequence of operations encompassed within the coordination phase frequently includes using a time factor as a weight in reassessing current assignments. Explain the extent to which this weighting is self-contained within the online programs.

4. Explain why a matrix organizational structure is at least partially applicable to an agency, association, company, or institution possessing a TYPE 2 information system.

5. The Jasper Chemical Company manufactures three products—Product A, Product B, and Product C—and there are three chemicals required in the manufacture of each product. Each of these chemicals is available in alternative states and compositions; thus, there is an array of feasible raw materials for each chemical.

For illustration purposes *using only Product A,* prepare a model of the coordination phase for the Jasper Chemical Company in which there is online monitoring of the external changes in raw material prices for alternative sources of chemicals. In your model, refer to the three chemicals in Product A as Chemical 1, Chemical 2, and Chemical 3, and specify the alternative raw materials for each chemical as follows:

Chemical	*Alternative Raw Materials*
Chemical 1	Item 111, Item 112, Item 113, and Item 114
Chemical 2	Item 115, Item 116, Item 117, and Item 118
Chemical 3	Item 119, Item 120, Item 121, and Item 122

In your illustrated model, select the initial assignment of a raw material for each of the three chemicals, and specify the dollar ranges to be used in testing sensitivity for the excluded raw materials that are to be monitored.

6. Continuing with Topic 5, explain how the online guidelines for testing sensitivity are updated after there is an online, revised assignment of raw materials. Be very explicit in showing how the ranges for the new partial assignment are determined for use in the online monitoring.

7. Explain how a *call statement* can be used in specifying the iteration level for an online assignment model.

8. Inherent within a TYPE 2 information system is the need for cooperation among members of management in more than one department. Explain this feature and the rough measure, level of service.

CASE 10–1. McCLURE PRESS, INC.

The management consulting firm with which you are employed has been engaged by the vice president of finance of the parent corporation owning McClure Press, Inc. The purpose of this engagement is to examine the overall inventory and procurement system for

McClure Press with the objective of minimizing the loss from excess inventory and establishing a management control system so as to prevent the recurrence of the present situation. You were assigned as the junior on this engagement and have been asked to perform a preliminary high point review.

The Company

McClure Press, Inc. is the wholly-owned subsidiary of a major corporation, and McClure Press's annual sales of $6,000,000 (which represents less than 3.5 percent of the parent corporation's total annual revenue) are indicative of the typical, small-to-medium size commercial press. Currently, McClure Press has 1,130 titles that encompass a diverse line of fields and interests, and the books are sold through book stores and retail outlets as well as by direct mail to individuals, libraries, companies, and organizations. Some titles are for a restricted, specialized reader, and these represent one of the basic references for that professional group. However, most titles are of a more general nature and appeal to a wide variety of readers. The marketing and promotion activities appropriately accommodate these diverse types of readers.

There are some differences in the monthly sales experience of books in a given area. Fortunately, the peaks and valleys of these monthly patterns do not coincide among different areas. McClure Press has books in many areas with diverse sales patterns that tend to offset each other. Therefore, in aggregate, a given month's sales does not vary more than 18 percent from the average monthly sales value.

There are variable and fixed components of cost in publishing a book. The setup cost is identical between a 5,000 print run and a 2,000 print run; paper, labor, and machine time are the variable components. On the other hand, bindery costs tend to be constant on a per unit basis regardless of the print size. As a result, the typical strategy is to print more books than are bound, at the same time; the unbound copies are stored at the bindery (for which there is a minimum storage charge) until they are needed. For example, a 5,000 print run may be used for production while only 2,000 copies are initially bound. The remaining 3,000 are stored at the bindery, and these may be subsequently bound in lots of 1,500, depending on forecasted demand.

The Situation

Recently, the ending inventory of books increased from $2,910,816 to $4,154,094 in the ten months since the last audit by a certified public accounting firm. This 42.71 percent increase in inventory caused the vice president of finance for the parent corporation to engage your management consulting firm to perform this study.

As you begin your scrutiny, you determine that management of McClure Press has operated fairly autonomously. The parent corporation's time-sharing computer system is used for invoicing, billing, accounts receivable, accounts payable, inventory, and status of new titles. The inventory record for each of the 1,619 titles includes the following data:

Identification number
Book title
Author
Price per book
Cost per book
Special discount terms
Quantity on hand
Quantity sold, year-to-date
Quantity returned, year-to-date
Examination copies, year-to-date
Complimentary copies, year-to-date
Dollar sales, year-to-date
Dollar sales returns, year-to-date
Month, net quantity sold
Month, net quantity returned
Month, net examination copies
Month, net complimentary copies
Date of publication
Date of last print run
Net quantity sold last year
Net dollar sales last year
Cumulative net quantity sold since current edition was published
Cumulative net dollar sales since current edition was published
Specification of edition of book
Specification of number of print runs for this edition of book

You develop a simple computer program to use on the parent corporation's time-sharing computing system which will read the 1,619 inventory records and will develop three cumulative values:

Cumulative physical quantity of inventory
Cumulative assigned dollar cost of inventory
Cumulative net dollar sales, year-to-date

Your simple computer program permits you to select among the 1,619 inventory titles based on various criteria (per the inventory record), and those titles that satisfy the set of criteria are placed in an array in either ascending or descending order. The cumulative values are developed only for those items selected for inclusion in each array.

One of the first analyses you perform is to array the titles with assigned cost by net dollar volume of sales, year-to-date. There were 744 titles with assigned cost of $4,154,094 that had $4,069,766 of net sales for the ten month period. The detailed data by title were summarized for the ten layers with each layer containing 74 or 75 titles. Exhibit A presents this information by layer for the cumulative

EXHIBIT A
McClure Press, Inc.
(analysis of inventory with assigned cost as of June 30)

	Number of Items	Physical Quantity of Inventory	Assigned Cost of Inventory	Net Dollar Sales Year to Date
Regular Books	744	1,729,350	$4,154,094	$4,069,766
Items 1-75	75	158,360	457,571	67,364
Items 76-149.	74	153,280	446,447	70,911
Items 150-224	75	147,360	430,815	75,450
Items 225-298	74	130,530	388,427	88,076
Items 299-372	74	172,980	477,750	210,953
Items 373-446	74	159,588	384,132	227,409
Items 447-521	75	129,822	309,606	308,448
Items 522-595	74	198,138	347,112	365,381
Items 596-670	75	175,758	443,292	846,056
Items 671-744	74	303,534	468,942	1,809,718

physical quantity of inventory, assigned dollar cost of inventory, and net dollar sales for year to date (ten months).

Your second analysis of the 744 titles with assigned cost is to develop an array of net selling prices by title. Summary data for 7 ranges were accumulated, and this information is presented in Exhibit B. All books in the $2.00 to $4.99 range are paperback; a few

EXHIBIT B

McClure Press, Inc.

(distribution of sales for inventory with assigned cost)

Range of Selling Price	Net Dollar Sales Year to Date
$ 2.00 to $ 4.99	$ 945,924
5.00 to 9.99	479,766
10.00 to 14.99	1,082,321
15.00 to 19.99	1,264,918
20.00 to 29.99	241,512
30.00 to 49.99	34,576
50.00 to 67.00	20,749
	$4,069,766

paperback books have selling prices from $5.00 to $6.50. All books with selling prices over $6.50 are hard-bound. The books with selling prices of $30.00 to $67.00 are leather-covered and represent reference volumes to specialized readers.

Your third analysis is to examine the inventory and sales data for all titles, regardless of the assigned cost. You find that there are 386 titles of McClure Press's books where the assigned cost of inventory has been written off. McClure Press follows a 4.5 year life for each title, and the assigned cost of inventory is written off when the annual sales after 4.5 years is less than 100 books.

In addition to the 386 titles with zero assigned cost, your analysis reveals that there are 489 titles in inventory which are held on consignment. These titles owned by other presses and sold by McClure Press on a commission basis permit some specialized readers to obtain most of their references from a single source. Exhibit C presents the summary data for the three categories of books: 386 regular books with zero assigned cost, 744 regular books with assigned cost, and 489 commission books.

After performing these three studies, you are asked by the senior from the management consulting firm to perform other analyses of the inventory, to outline a management control system you will recommend for monitoring and administering the achievement of specific objectives, and to develop the outline of a marketing program to dispose of excess books.

EXHIBIT C
McClure Press, Inc.
(analysis of inventory)

	Number of Items	Physical Quantity of Inventory	Assigned Cost of Inventory	Net Dollar Sales Year to Date
Regular books with zero assigned cost	386	368,802		$ 572,407
Regular books with assigned cost	744	1,729,350	$4,154,094	4,069,766
Commission books	489	183,239		319,689
Total	1,619	2,281,391	$4,154,094	$4,961,862

REQUIRED:

1. Specify the separate analyses and comparisons you will perform of the 1,619 titles in inventory. For purposes of these analyses, assume that sales in July and August by title are indicative of the average sales experience, year-to-date.
2. Specify the objective of your proposed management control system for inventory and indicate the special features of the system.
3. Specify the general strategy you will incorporate in your marketing program and indicate the criteria you will employ in stratifying the inventory for the marketing program.
4. Indicate any management information system changes you will explore in an effort to improve the earnings and management control and to minimize the inventory investment.

CASE 10–2. WALKER MILL COMPANY

The Walker Mill Company manufactures sash, doors, windows, trim, molding, and custom cabinets. The company is located in a large mid-western city and provides delivery service within a 100-mile radius of the plant. Sales are made through representatives to general contractors, industrial contractors, lumber companies, and selected retail stores.

Company management is concerned with recent complaints regarding customer service. A 90 percent level of customer service has been the goal, and the president of the company asks you to investigate the situation and to see if the company's goal is being achieved.

You spend the next two days reviewing the operations of the plant

EXHIBIT A
Data on 68 Selected Orders

Order Date	Promise Date	Shipment Date	Order Date	Promise Date	Shipment Date
2/5	2/26	3/1	2/16	3/2	3/11
2/8	3/1	3/1	2/9	3/2	3/11
2/8	2/24	3/1	2/8	3/1	3/11
2/3	2/22	3/1	2/15	3/2	3/11
2/2	2/19	3/1	2/15	3/3	3/11
2/5	2/24	3/1	2/16	3/2	3/12
2/8	2/26	3/2	2/9	3/2	3/12
2/10	3/3	3/2	2/15	3/8	3/12
2/4	2/25	3/2	2/15	3/8	3/12
2/2	2/23	3/2	2/16	3/9	3/12
2/1	2/22	3/2	3/5	3/12	3/12
2/4	2/25	3/3	2/16	3/9	3/15
2/3	2/24	3/3	2/17	3/10	3/15
2/5	2/26	3/3	2/18	3/11	3/15
2/8	3/1	3/4	2/18	3/4	3/16
2/9	3/2	3/4	2/19	3/12	3/16
2/9	3/2	3/4	2/18	3/11	3/16
2/25	3/5	3/4	2/17	3/10	3/16
2/10	2/26	3/5	2/22	3/11	3/16
2/5	2/26	3/5	2/19	3/12	3/17
2/11	3/4	3/5	2/22	3/15	3/17
2/12	3/5	3/8	2/23	3/16	3/17
2/12	3/1	3/8	2/22	3/15	3/17
2/9	3/1	3/8	2/19	3/12	3/17
3/3	3/9	3/8	2/18	3/11	3/18
2/11	3/4	3/9	2/17	3/10	3/18
2/12	3/5	3/9	2/22	3/15	3/18
2/11	3/3	3/9	2/24	3/10	3/18
2/8	3/1	3/9	2/23	3/5	3/19
2/12	3/3	3/9	2/25	3/18	3/19
2/11	3/3	3/10	2/24	3/17	3/19
2/15	3/8	3/10	3/11	3/18	3/19
2/9	3/1	3/10	2/23	3/9	3/19
2/8	3/1	3/10	2/25	3/18	3/19

and talking with superintendents, supervisors, managers, administrative personnel, and the plant superintendent. From the latter individual you are told that the company tries to provide three-day delivery service on all stocked items and three-week delivery service on all custom-built cabinets and millwork. Furthermore, you are told that all rush orders must be personally approved by the plant superintendent and that these orders are expedited as fast as possible.

Sales orders are prepared by the various representatives whose salaries are primarily on a commission basis. Many of these representatives are part-time employees in the sense that they are also representatives of several different manufacturers, concurrently.

As part of your study, you have selected 68 delivery orders for custom-built cabinets and millwork which were completed during the first three weeks in March. Exhibit A presents the order date, promise date, and delivery date for these selected sales orders.

REQUIRED:

1. Specify the appropriate assumptions under which the selected 68 items may be used in further statistical analyses.
2. Compute the level of customer service that appears to be currently provided by the Walker Mill Company based upon this sample.
3. Prepare a letter to the president of the company containing any insights that you have gained from your study.

CHAPTER 11

Inventory Management Information Systems

WITHIN THE computer-based networks identified as TYPE 2 information systems, the most common model is an inventory management information system. The online computer programs contain predetermined decision rules which monitor the status of inventory items (such as raw materials, component parts, manufactured units, work in process, and finished goods) and take prescribed actions when available quantities are below a specified level.

The procedural aspects of the programmed decision rules incorporated within an inventory management information system are well established in the professional literature, and these procedures have been applied to numerous organizations in diverse environmental settings. But, all too often, the management science teams designing and implementing these programmed decision rules have begun at the fourth phase of the formal program for planning and implementing an information system—equipment selection and program design phase.[1] In many of these cases there is an absence of participation by members of management in the planning phase, the organization review and administrative study phase, and the conceptual systems design phase. Since members of management have not participated in the planning and designing activities for the computer-based network containing these programmed decision rules, the resulting systems approach the classification of an operating system.[2]

In this chapter we are concerned with the full application of the

---

[1] *Supra*, p. 185.

[2] *Ibid.*, p. 60.

formal program for planning and implementing an information system as described in Chapter 6 to those organizations having dominant activities in the inventory management area. The computer-based networks for the latter organizations must include all of the features in a TYPE 2 information system as described in Chapter 10.

Rather than reexamining the common dimensions of a TYPE 2 system associated with inventory management, we are especially interested in those inventory-related issues that are resolved as the computer-based network progresses from the functional program to an operating system and then moves on to an information system. Therefore, the topics discussed in this chapter include a brief consideration of the diverse objectives served by inventory activities and an examination of mechanical and processing issues presented as four separate areas: (*a*) identification system for inventory items, (*b*) reorder quantity, (*c*) reorder point, and (*d*) safety stock and cushion. These issues are integrated in the concluding discussion of a program for improving the quality of data in computer-based inventory models.

DIVERSE OBJECTIVES

An effective inventory management information system is a network designed to provide the maximum inventory "service" to all inventory users at the minimum cost. The establishment of such a system within a large, complex organization is difficult because of the conflicting objectives of the use of inventory stock. For example, production management desires inventory stock to absorb the short-term demand variations and resultant fluctuations in production requirements. Such inventory stocks permit economical production runs and production balancing which will result in the least number of line changeovers consistent with effective leveling of the labor force.

Marketing management desires inventory stock at a level which will minimize the chance of a stockout condition. In the case of stocked items, marketing management may argue for a level of inventory that will almost eliminate the risk of having insufficient stock for immediate delivery on customer orders. On the other hand, financial management is concerned with reducing the dollar investment in inventory in order to release funds for use in other operations and opportunities.

Without elaborating any further, it is obvious that an effective inventory management information system must be compatible with the long-term policies of the organization. This requires that management policy in various areas must have been previously specified so that the inventory management information system can operate within the boundaries established by that policy. Following are some of the critical areas that the organization's inventory policy must encompass:

1. Customer service
2. Back orders
3. Model and engineering changes
4. Facilities
5. Personnel policy (including labor leveling)
6. Crash programs

These critical areas within the organization's inventory policy can be collectively expressed as the relation between the following two costs: (*a*) the cost of carrying inventory versus (*b*) the cost of not carrying inventory. The latter is also called the cost of a stockout.

The Cost of Carrying Inventory

Many of the costs associated with carrying inventory are obvious; others are less apparent. These costs include interest on investment, storage and handling, obsolescence, deterioration, pilferage, personal property tax, and insurance. As long as the focus is on *all* inventory versus *no* inventory, it is easy to identify and measure in dollars the cost of carrying inventory. Unfortunately, this is not the normal situation but there are many marginal and partial decisions that must be made.

Typically, we assume that each inventory item has been selected because the anticipated benefit of having the item in stock exceeds the cost of not having the item in stock. Thus, in analyzing inventory, the systems analyst is not speaking of *all* inventory, but only of the stock on hand for a given item.

The inventory analysis, therefore, becomes much more difficult. Which of the total inventory related costs are relevant or applicable to a given item of inventory? A standard must be developed for coping with this question which will include consideration of the time and extent of change as well as an assumption regarding the independence of each item in inventory. In other words, costs that vary only with changes in *two or more* inventory items are not considered in the analysis. Instead, a marginal approach is followed where relevant costs are identified only in relation to changes in a *single*, selected item of inventory out of the total mass of inventory.

Most of the relevant costs associated with carrying inventory are available or easily determined from the formal accounting records. However, one significant item is not available from these data sources: the investment cost of carrying inventory. This component may be as large as the aggregate value of the remaining components of the total cost of carrying inventory. Another significant area of cost is associated with the risk elements of inventory, such as the risk of obsolescence, the risk of deterioration, and the risk of pilferage. Some analysts concurrently examine the risk elements of inventory along with the investment cost of carrying inventory; however, we prefer to separately quantify each element including the marginal rate of interest for the organization under scrutiny.

Actually, more often than not, the critical cost is the "negative stockout cost." In other words, members of management feel that the organization cannot afford to fail to carry the item in inventory. Thus, in the choice between carrying and not carrying an item of inventory, the marginal rate of interest is believed to be an appropriate item for use in the analysis *provided* that the risks of obsolescence, deterioration, and pilferage are separately considered along with the relevant cost of storing and handling the inventory item.

In the matter of determining whether the organization should invest in inventory or in other aspects of the organization's operations (such as investment in plant expansion, new products, or research and development), it might be more appropriate to use the long-run average cost of capital in these analyses. However, as previously suggested, we believe that even in this general class of study, the negative stockout cost is probably the most appropriate measure to use in decisions regarding investment in inventory. After the decision has been made that a given inventory item is to be stocked, then another order of question arises: How much to purchase? When to purchase? In thse subsequent discussion of these questions, the matter of interest on investment will be reexamined.

The Cost of Not Carrying Inventory

There are different aspects of this measurement. Is there sufficient demand for a given inventory item to justify carrying it? In those situations where the answer to this question is negative, then are there other factors which will suggest that the item should be stocked anyway? For example, customers and clients may expect your organization to have a full stock of inventory, including slow-moving items. If the organization does not have a full line, then the organization might be expected to lose some customers.

The systems analyst would like to quantify this belief. How many customers will be lost if slow-moving items were not stocked but were sold on an "order basis"? What are the expected, average annual sales for each of these customers? With answers to these two questions, the systems analyst has the appropriate information with which to begin a study of the situation.

Frequently, where members of management have faced these inventory questions, they have reached their own conclusions before even responding to the systems analyst's second question. In other words, after an estimate is made of the number of customers that will be lost from a change in inventory policy, members of management make their decision without regard to the size of these customer's accounts. This decision may be to eliminate the given inventory item from the list of regular stocked items. However, there are shortcomings to these quick decisions. Members of management should delay making a decision on the matter until after the systems analyst has completed a study, which encompasses all dimensions of the problem.

In many organizations, members of management view the organization's sales and services activities and customer relations in a mystic manner and will not permit even a management scientist to question customers in order to understand what it is that presently attracts customers. Members of management are afraid that in the process of resolving this question or other related questions on the matter of customer services, some customers may be offended and, therefore, terminate their relation with the organization.

In some of the previously described organizations, there may be a subsequent change in management personnel or else current members of management may have to cope unexpectedly with a tight monetary situation. In either of these cases, members of management may, for the first time, systematically examine the organization's inventory policy. When this has occurred, a substantial change in all facets of inventory management has usually resulted. Some items are eliminated from inventory; faster service is provided for other items; special expediting procedures are designed for those critical situations; price reductions are announced because of economies from the new inventory policy; and so forth.

In summary, the relevant items included in the computation of the cost of not carrying inventory is a matter that varies not only by organization, but by division and department within an organization. While there are many items, some within and some outside the formal accounting records, we believe that the estimated loss of customers from the stockout condition is the dominant factor in most situations. Furthermore, the contribution to margin from these estimated lost customer sales is probably the best practical measure of the stockout cost.

IDENTIFICATION SYSTEM FOR INVENTORY ITEMS

Each inventory item must be uniquely specified for identification purposes. A code structure can be developed in which product groups, similar physical characteristics, appearance, size, and special attributes can be used as the basis for the coding pattern. These criteria can be expressed in a coding pattern by an array of alternative methods. At one extreme position is a compressed, numerical coding pattern which minimizes the number of digits required for identification, such as the following eight-digit coding structure.

12xxxxxx   The first two digits designate the product group.

xx34xxxx   The third and fourth digits indicate subgroups with special characteristics. For example, in the case of chemical inventory items, a number *10* in these digits might represent a perishable, flammable item which must be stored in a given type of controlled environment; a number *20*, a perishable, nonflammable item which must be stored in a given type of controlled environment; a number *30*, a nonperishable, flammable item which must be stored in a given type of controlled environment; and so forth.

xxxx5678   The fifth, sixth, seventh, and eighth digits specify the unique inventory items with the same classification for product group and subgroups.

This traditional coding arrangement has the advantage of being a compressed specification with the risk of a relatively high rate of input errors because of the absence of any descriptive features within the digits. However, internal control features can be established around the input process so there is interaction between the remote terminal user and an online set of programmed decision rules supported by a data base. The latter will serve both in a screening and editing function and in a questioning function. For example, after an eight-digit identification number is specified as an input, the online, interactive system prints the stored description of the item associated with the specified, eight-digit input, and the remote terminal user is questioned as to whether this description is valid for the given inventory item.

At the other extreme, the coding pattern can be expanded with alphanumeric characters that tend to convey a description of the inventory item. While additional time is required in the input of identification data, there is a relatively low rate of input errors. In the latter case, the remote terminal user can make a direct association between the identification input and the inventory item.

The coding pattern for inventory items can also have incorporated within the structure provision for specifying different types of control procedures; this is illustrated in Chapter 12. Sensitivity analysis can be applied to the inventory items and included within an expanded structure, and these analyses may highlight inventory items by profit contribution, turnover rate, distribution procedures, marketing strategies, and degree of "criticalness" of items as perceived by the customer to the latter organization's operations. Coding patterns featuring sensitivity analysis for inventory items in an organization with advanced computer-based systems are examined in Chapter 13.

Regardless of the format of the coding pattern, each inventory item must be uniquely identified, and a data record must be established within the computer-based system for description purposes and accumulation of usage experience. After this has been accomplished, there are statistical techniques for improving the quality of the data in computer-based inventory models, and an overall program for improving the quality of data is presented subsequently in this chapter.

REORDER QUANTITY

Within an inventory management information system, one of the basic decisions for each specified inventory item is how much to order from suppliers or from the production department. Economic order quantity (EOQ) formulas are used in coping with this decision. The reorder quantity (the economic order quantity, standard order quantity, or economic lot size) is that quantity which produces a balance between the cost of ordering and setup on the one hand, and the cost of holding and storing inventory on the other hand.

Following is a simple EOQ formula.

$$Q = \sqrt{\frac{2AS}{UI}}$$

where

Q = Economic order quantity, the amount to order for least total annual cost

A = Annual quantity used in units

S = Setup cost for production or the cost of placing an order from suppliers

U = Unit cost

I = Inventory carrying charges expressed as a percent of cost

Given the terms Q, A, S, U, and I as specified, the above formula is derived as follows:

$\dfrac{A}{Q}$ = Number of orders placed annually

$\dfrac{AS}{Q}$ = Annual setup costs for production or the annual cost of placing orders with suppliers

$\dfrac{Q}{2}$ = Average number of units in inventory at any given point in time

$\dfrac{UIQ}{2}$ = Annual inventory carrying cost

$\dfrac{AS}{Q} + \dfrac{UIQ}{2}$ = Total annual cost of inventory which is designated by C

This latter equation is solved as follows:

$$(1) \quad C = \frac{AS}{Q} + \frac{UIQ}{2}$$

$$(4) \quad \frac{UI}{2} = \frac{AS}{Q^2}$$

$$(2) \quad \frac{dC}{dQ} = \frac{-AS}{Q^2} + \frac{UI}{2}$$

$$(5) \quad Q^2UI = 2AS$$

$$(3) \quad \text{Set } \frac{dC}{dQ} = 0; \quad \frac{-AS}{Q^2} + \frac{UI}{2} = 0$$

$$(6) \quad Q = \sqrt{\frac{2AS}{UI}}$$

The above EOQ formula is used at the Kruse Company in determining orders from suppliers. For example, an inventory item with annual requirements of 400,000 units, cost of ordering of $15, unit cost of $20, and investment carrying charge of 19 percent has an economic order quantity of 1,777.047 units. The substitution of these values in the formula and calculations are as follows:

$$Q = \sqrt{\frac{2AS}{UI}} \qquad\qquad Q = \sqrt{\frac{2\,(400,000) \quad (\$15)}{\$20 \quad (19\%)}}$$

$$Q = \sqrt{3,157,895} \qquad\qquad Q = 1,777.047 \text{ units}$$

As indicated by the above inventory item at the Kruse Company, it is easy to determine the reorder quantity if the relevant cost and statistical information are known. However, this task of determining and collecting relevant cost information for the EOQ formulas is difficult. In performing this task, there are two conflicting objectives. On the one hand, the task should be given enough scrutiny so that all relevant costs are considered and properly measured. On the other hand, the task of determining and collecting relevant information does not have to become a cost accounting study.

The EOQ formulas are used as management techniques and tools for planning and control, and these formulas are not considered rigorous and inflexible methods. Furthermore, some of the relevant information possesses the unusual characteristic that it must be considered for any valid measure of the economic order quantity, even though it is the type of information where precise measurement is not required. In other words, some of this latter relevant information may be approximate value (for example, plus and minus 15 to 20 percent) without significantly changing the value derived by the EOQ formula.

Thus, the systems analyst views the collection of data for the EOQ formulas in much the same way as the process of determining which measures of performance will be employed in a given standard cost system. The anticipated benefit from using the new information should at least equal (if not exceed) the expenditures required for collecting and processing the information. Although this matter of measuring the anticipated benefit from using the new information is not emphasized in the subsequent discussions, the reader must maintain this questioning perspective, particularly when applying this approach to a real situation.

In the search of relevant data for the EOQ formulas, sensitivity analyses are used to identify which costs are influenced by changes in the reorder quantity or in the number of orders processed. When the inventory is provided by an outside supplier, the following questions are asked: Which costs increase (or vary) with changes in the number of orders placed? Which costs increase (or vary) with changes in the size of the reorder quantity?

The response to the first question is included in the S factor in the illustrated EOQ formula and includes such items as clerical costs, data processing costs, paper and stationery costs, postage, and telephone. The response to the second question is included in the I factor in this formula and includes such items as investment cost, storage and handling cost, obsolescence, deterioration, pilferage, insurance, and personal property taxes.

When the inventory is not being provided by outside suppliers but is being provided by the production department, a different set of basic questions is asked: Which costs increase (or vary) with changes in the number of lots of a part manufactured? Which costs increase (or vary) with changes in the average lot size used in the production process? The responses to these questions are included in the S and I factors, respectively, in the given EOQ formula.

Costs Varying with the Number of Lots Processed

The S factor is expressed in terms of *dollars per order* and encompasses the following items:[3]

---

[3] This list of costs varying with the number of lots processed draws heavily from a paper used by the staff at Arthur Andersen & Co. in a production control training course. Used by permission.

1. Machine setup costs
   a. Setup personnel hours
   b. Maintenance or materials used with each machine setup
   c. Raw material "preparation labor costs" for an order
2. Paperwork costs
   a. Setup documents
   b. Dispatching documents
   c. Shop order documents
   d. Payroll documents
   e. Inspection and quality control documents
   f. Purchase order and records
3. Indirect order preparation costs
   a. Production time lost per lot if not used
   b. Production control costs per order processed (Of the total production control costs, which costs vary with the number of orders processed? From a practical standpoint, an average cost per order will generally suffice.)
   c. Inspection or quality control time varying with the number of lots processed
   d. Tabulating and data processing costs associated with the volume of orders processed (Generally, an average of variable costs is appropriate for this component.)
   e. Accounting and related processing costs generated as a result of handling production orders or lots (For example, pricing, scrap recording)
   f. Material handling costs that vary with the number of orders processed (In many cases, material handling activities—outside of the storeroom—are somewhat independent of the order quantity or lot size and are more dependent on the overall level of activity of the plant.)
   g. Purchasing effort resulting from the ordering of an item as a part

Costs Varying with the Size of an Order Quantity

The *I* factor is expressed as a *percent of unit cost* and includes the following items:[4]

---

[4] This list of cost varying with the size of an order quantity draws heavily from a paper used by the staff at Arthur Andersen & Co. in a production control training course. Used by permission.

1. Cost of investment
    a. The cost of funds invested in inventory (This is a subject that is frequently discussed in the professional literature, and a subject for which there is no single conclusion. Each position on the subject varies depending on the company's management and situation. Many approach the subject and immediately say that the current cost of funds for working capital should be used. The prime loan rate, therefore, is frequently used. Generally, management should make this decision based upon company policy, company conditions, and the general economic conditions.)
    b. Insurance cost of inventory (Many companies have insurance costs based upon a percent of the investment in inventory or other assets. Normally, this cost is not large and may be less than 1 percent of the unit cost for the items included in inventory.)
    c. Tax cost of inventory (Local, state, or national taxes may be based upon a percent of the investment in inventory.
    d. Storage costs (The first consideration in determining storage costs is to identify the *variable costs*. Heating, depreciation, maintenance, supplies, and so forth are generally variable as more or less space is used. However, the cost of storage space may not be variable if there is no alternative use for this space. If the storage space has an alternative use, then the costs associated with maintaining or providing the work space-storage space are variable with the inventory size. This cost can generally be expressed as a percent of inventory invested in stores. The second consideration in determining storage costs is to ascertain the relevant stores administration and operating costs which vary with the size of an order quantity. This is a difficult task because stores administration and operating costs tend to follow the total investment in inventory and the total inventory stock level. It is unusual for the stores administration and operating costs to vary significantly based on a change for a single item of inventory. Instead, stores administration and operating costs tend to vary based on changes for groups of items. In this case, these costs may vary with the number of orders processed as well as with the size of the inventory. When this situation does exist,

these two costs should be measured separately; costs varying with the orders processed should be included in that category and costs varying with inventory size should be accumulated and expressed as a percent of inventory in stock.)

2. Other costs
   a. The risk of obsolescence (When there are many different items that are sold to only a few customers, the imputed cost for obsolescence may be high and may be the dominant factor in determining the size of the order quantity. Case 11–1, Precision Screw Company, at the end of this chapter illustrates this situation.)
   b. Deterioration, pilferage, and other similar types of cost.

Note that in many industries the cost of inventory and investment (the *I* factor) is in the range of 15 to 20 percent of cost.

REORDER POINT

The second basic decision in an inventory management information system is when to order the EOQ determined quantity. If the items to be included in inventory have previously been decided upon based on a systematic examination of each inventory item as suggested by the first step or based on the organization's inventory policy which is taken as a given, then the question of when to order each selected item can be resolved as follows:

1. What is the annual forecasted demand for the selected inventory item?
2. Is there an expected seasonal variation in this forecasted demand?
3. What degree of confidence does executive management desire with respect to the nonoccurrence of a stockout condition?
4. How much lead time is required for initiating and placing an order, shipping the items ordered, and receiving and storing the items ordered?
5. How much minimum stock of inventory is required for use during this reorder period?

Each of these questions is examined in the following discussion.

Forecasting Demand

Estimating the demand for each inventory item is a critical step in any inventory planning and control operation and is a prerequisite for determining both the reorder quantity and the reorder point. The forecasted demand is a significant factor in each of these computations, and this discussion will focus on the general statistical approaches followed for forecasting demand.

Under the "pure," traditional statistical approach, the systems analyst will thoroughly consider the past demand pattern of an inventory item in conjunction with a study of the general economic forces. Based on the insights gained from these studies, the annual forecasted demand is determined using three variances: trend, cyclical, and random. After the annual forecasted demand is determined, then the seasonal variation is considered in estimating the demand within the year.

If there are many inventory items where each item has its own unique demand pattern, then the pure, traditional statistical approach will require the services of several professional statisticians. Thus, this approach is not generally followed in most organizations. Instead, some practical technique is used as a substitute for the professional statistician's insight. The "least squares" technique or the "moving average" method can easily be programmed for the computer so that the estimated demand trend for each inventory item is quickly determined. The computer program can include adjusting this estimated demand trend by some adjustment factor to compensate for the cyclical and random forces. Finally, the computer program can contain an adjustment factor for the seasonal variation which is applied to the previously adjusted demand in determining the forecasted actual demand for a given quarter.

An alternative procedure for coping with trend, cyclical, and random variation is to apply the "12-month centered moving average" method. Seasonal indexes can be used in adjusting the 12-month centered moving average to the actual forecast for a given period. This alternative procedure is widely used in inventory forecasting because of its simplicity, which permits the complete procedure to be encompassed in a simple computer program.

Another alternative procedure that is used by several organizations is "exponential smoothing." This particular procedure is especially suitable for the organization with a highly fluctuating short-term demand pattern that is not attributable to seasonal forces. From a practical standpoint, the exponential smoothing technique is frequently used in the initial establishment of a systematic inventory management information system by those organizations that do not have readily and easily retrievable historical data on demand for each inventory item.[5]

Each of the above procedures is a variation of the traditional, statistical forecasting technique for time series analysis wherein the actual activity for an item is the result of the interaction of four forces: trend, seasonal, cyclical, and residual. There is another statistical approach toward forecasting that is based on probability models. Estimates are assigned for each of the possible levels of activity for an inventory item, and an expected value is computed. This probability approach is especially useful when dealing with a new product for which there is neither historical experience nor any other product whose experience might be comparable.

After the actual demand has been forecast by some statistical technique, then the systems analyst's attention focuses on the question: What degree of confidence does executive management desire with respect to the nonoccurrence of a stockout condition? This question can be rephrased in a positive manner: What level of service does executive management desire for the inventory item in question?

In coping with these questions, the statistical formula, "the standard error of the arithmetic mean," can be used in certain circumstances to indicate the probability of the occurrence of a stockout condition for a given inventory item under consideration. However, these "certain circumstances" under which the formula may be used do not often exist in inventory management information systems. The reason for this is basic. The traditional statistical approaches for time series analyses are most frequently employed by organizations. Unfortunately, the assumptions regarding the distribution of data upon which these traditional forecasting techniques are based do not coincide with the assumptions associated with the use of the formula, the standard error of the arithmetic mean.

On the other hand, the forecasting approach based on probability models is compatible with these latter assumptions. Thus, in those

---

[5] It is assumed that the reader is familiar with these statistical techniques, and no attention is given in this book to explaining in detail these techniques. A basic reference in statistics should be consulted for such descriptive material.

organizations where probability models are used in forecasting demand, estimates can be made regarding the likelihood of a stockout condition, and the amount of the shortage for different average levels of inventory stock can be ascertained.

Since the traditional forecasting approach is based on assumptions that are not compatible with the previously-mentioned statistical formula, alternative techniques based on other data must be employed to quantify the level of customer service. One such alternative procedure is to compute an index of customer service based on the promised date of delivery compared to the actual shipment date. This particular index is frequently used in job order shops and in those companies where special items are manufactured on a "per customer request" basis. The appropriate information for computing the index is available on the sales order document and the shipping report.

In other organizations, present and former customers have been interviewed by professional statisticians in an effort to quantify the level of customer service that has been provided. In other extreme cases, statisticians have interviewed the competitors of the organization in an effort to quantify the level of customer service.

In summary, the procedures employed in attempting to quantify the level of customer service vary not only by organization, but also by division and department within an organization and also by the product lines within a department. Each item in a product line may have its own unique demand pattern which is not compatible with any of the well-known distributions: the binominal distribution, the normal curve distribution, and the Poisson distribution. Therefore, the statisticians will have to select some *ad hoc* set of procedures for measuring customer service in this situation, even though this set of procedures may not be completely applicable to all products.

Lead-Time Demand

This is the average demand for the lead-time period, which is the time required for replenishment of the stock. This will be the summation of the time required to order an item (the reorder quantity), to receive delivery, to handle and store the order (place the inventory on the shelves, in the bins, and so forth), plus the period of time that elapses between the actual reduction of the physical inventory stock to the reorder point and the time at which this event is known by the reorder clerk.

Under a real-time computer system, the occurrence of a reorder condition and knowledge of such a condition are simultaneous events. Under a perpetual inventory system that is daily processed by the computer or that is daily processed manually by a clerk, the maximum time delay between the occurrence of a reorder condition and knowledge of such a condition is one day, with one-half day being the average time delay. Under a nonperpetual inventory control system where each item in inventory is checked once a month, for example, the maximum time delay between the occurrence of a reorder condition and knowledge of such a condition is one month, with one-half month being the average time delay.

The lead-time demand represents a required investment in inventory which must be controlled if management is to maximize the use of the organization's resources. The primary method for controlling the size of this investment is to reduce the lead-time period by installing a perpetual inventory system. Another approach is to try to reduce the administrative time required for processing orders. For example, a prepunched data processing card containing the identification and description of the item under question along with the reorder quantity and the supplier's identification number might be the input document to the computer which has in storage the name and address of the supplier by identification number. Thus, the computer program can match the supplier's identification number, retrieve the name and address of the supplier, and process the complete purchase order. In a more advanced computer system, the input document is not necessary; the perpetual inventory system is maintained by the computer, and the computer program can encompass all phases of the reorder process.

In summary, the lead-time demand is an estimate of the number of units required during a reorder period so there is not a stockout. Because of unusual events, there can be a significant variation between estimated lead-time demand and actual lead-time demand. Techniques for coping with this variation are presented in the next part of this discussion.

SAFETY STOCK AND CUSHION

Regardless of the statistical procedures employed in forecasting demand, there will be a variance between the actual and forecasted demand. The safety stock is supposed to provide for these unplanned variances between actual and forecasted demand.

One of the major variances is associated with the lead-time demand. The lead-time demand is an *average* and is subject to the limitations of any statistical average. The *actual* demand during the lead-time period will probably not exactly equal the *average* demand. Instead, a frequency distribution can be constructed of the actual demands during the lead-time period for several years, and this frequency distribution will probably represent a normal curve where the average demand is the arithmetic mean of the frequency distribution. Thus, the safety stock should provide for this predictable variance between actual and average demand during the lead time.

Some inventory management systems employ a moving average technique where the lead-time demand is not an "average" demand (measured in terms of past experience) but is the forecasted actual demand based on an analysis of the time series data. Even in these situations, the forecasted demand will differ from the actual demand, and this variance must be provided for if a nonstockout condition is desired. On the other hand, the amount of this variance is statistically predictable for various levels of confidence, and these statistical tools should be employed in controlling the size of the safety stock.

If the safety stock is restricted to the variance between actual and forecasted demand under conditions of certainty, then the remaining variance because of conditions of uncertainty can be called the cushion. Specifically, the cushion provides the allowance for this latter type of variance.

Some writers differentiate between safety stock and cushion in another manner. The safety stock is designed to provide for that predictable variance that occurs between actual and forecasted demand because of unusual action (or behavior) on the part of customers. The cushion is designed to provide for the unusual action on the part of management and personnel of the company in question. For example, the cushion is supposed to provide for a clerk temporarily misplacing a purchase order.

Another approach toward differentiating between safety stock and cushion is to define safety stock as that value determined by a statistical formula containing two factors: (1) degree of customer service desired and (2) the standard deviation of the lead-time demand. Of course, these latter two factors must be expressed in terms of units of the product in question. All variances not associated with this formula are assumed to be represented by the cushion.

PROGRAM FOR IMPROVING THE QUALITY OF STATISTICAL DATA

A large, complex organization that is initially establishing a computer-based system for inventory management has significant constraints in directly implementing the processing procedures previously described. Historical data on utilization and delivery experience of suppliers are not available in machine-readable form. In fact, the organization may not even have a well established coding pattern for identifying inventory items. When members of management are confronted with this almost impossible situation, the following program can be followed in establishing the network and in slowly improving the statistical quality of the data stored online for use in the computer programs.

The first step in the program is to quickly establish an online set of computer operations that will assist in administering the inventory items. Many organizations have confronted this same predicament, and management consultants have developed a statistical formula for handling this situation. This formula is as follows:

$$\text{Reorder point} = \overline{LTD} + K \sqrt{\overline{LTD}\,(\overline{AD} + 1)}$$

where

$$K = \text{Number of standard deviations of lead-time demand}$$
$$\overline{LTD} = \text{Average lead-time demand}$$
$$\overline{AD} = \text{Average demand}$$
$$\sqrt{\overline{LTD}\,(\overline{AD} + 1)} = \text{Estimate of ``standard deviation'' of lead-time demand}$$

The management consultants typically make two simplifying assumptions. First, a K factor of 2 is used for purposes of providing about 95 percent level of customer service. Second, it is assumed that there are common suppliers for all products; thus, there is a stable relationship between the average lead-time demand $(\overline{LTD})$ and the average demand $\overline{(AD)}$ which can be specified and stored online in the system.

In an organization in which these two assumptions are valid, it is possible to quickly establish a computer-based set of operations for inventory management with only a minimum amount of statistical data. There are only two unique inputs for each inventory item: (a) identification code and (b) average demand. The online computer program will use the specified K factor and the specified $\overline{AD}$ multiple for $\overline{LTD}$ in calculating the reorder point.

By studying an example of using this formula in the Kerr Company, we can see that the only limitation is a tendency toward excess inventory. But, in general the formula will give the desired level of customer service with only these rough statistics, and the tendency toward excess inventory is an acceptable cost for the other benefits.

The Kerr Company has four products—Product A, Product B, Product C, and Product D. The estimated average weekly demand for these four products are, respectively, 250 units, 245 units, 230 units, and 255 units. Furthermore, it is estimated that the average lead-time demand is four weeks. Using the above formula with a K factor of 2, the reorder points for the four products are as follows:

Product	$\overline{LTD}$	$+$	$K \sqrt{\overline{LTD} \ (\overline{AD} \ + 1)}$		
A	1,000	$+$	$2\sqrt{1,000 \ (250 \ + 1)}$	$= 1,000 \ + \ 2(501)$	or 2,002
B	980	$+$	$2\sqrt{980 \ (245 \ + 1)}$	$= \ 980 \ + \ 2(491)$	or 1,962
C	920	$+$	$2\sqrt{920 \ (230 \ + 1)}$	$= \ 920 \ + \ 2(461)$	or 1,842
D	1,020	$+$	$2\sqrt{1,020 \ (255 \ + 1)}$	$= 1,020 \ + \ 2(511)$	or 2,042

The online computer operations will immediately calculate these four reorder points, these values will be stored online, and the inventory management programs will become operational. With a slight increase in computer-processing time, the network could handle 125,000 inventory items with the same simple procedure as that followed for the four products. Another essential part of this first step in the program for improving the quality of statistical data used in the inventory management operations is to store online the actual average demand experience.

After eight weeks of operations, the Kerr Company has the following experience with calculations being made of actual average demand and standard deviation:

	Product A	Product B	Product C	Product D
Estimated average demand	250	245	230	255
Actual experience:				
Week 1	248	270	195	260
Week 2	225	240	265	263
Week 3	264	230	230	259
Week 4	253	255	235	275
Week 5	249	240	240	265
Week 6	252	235	230	260
Week 7	245	260	210	257
Week 8	252	243	255	270
Actual average demand	250	240	234	272
Standard deviation	13.58	17.13	23.20	15.64

If we were to generalize from the Kerr Company's experience of eight weeks, we might conclude that there is considerable excess inventory. Members of management desire 95 percent level of customer service. In computing this level of service, we are only concerned with the right side of the normal distribution curve. Therefore, plus 1.64 standard deviations will include 45 percent of the activity under the normal curve, which will all appear on the right side. All of the activity on the left side will also be included (50 percent of the area under the normal curve is represented by the left side) ; thus, the 95 percent level of customer service is encompassed by these two amounts. If the average lead-time demand is exactly four weeks, then the following values for reorder point will represent 95 percent level of customer service based on the revised demand data:

	Product A	Product B	Product C	Product D
Standard deviation	13.58	17.13	23.20	15.64
Times 1.64 sigmas	22.27	28.09	38.05	22.65
Actual average weekly demand . .	250.	240.	234.	272.
Total per week	272.27	268.09	272.05	294.65
Times four weeks	1,089.08	1,072.36	1,088.20	1,178.60

Comparing the above figures with the values computed by the previous formula, it appears as if the Kerr Company has about seven weeks of inventory for each of the products instead of four weeks, while maintaining a 95 percent level of customer service.

Thus, at first it would appear that a significant reduction can be made in the inventory levels at the Kerr Company; however, this may not be a valid conclusion. There are only two months of data for the Kerr Company. Will the third month have a similar experience to the first two months? What about seasonal fluctuations? We will need at least 52 weeks of data before any detailed study can even begin to be made, and 104 to 156 weeks of data are required before much confidence can be ascribed to the issues of seasonal fluctuations.

Statistically, it is unusual for lead-time demand to be exactly four-weeks; a more ordinary occurrence is a distribution around the four-weeks with the right-hand tail extending at least to eight-weeks. The latter extreme point represents the case of the supplier who loses the order and does nothing until Kerr Company's management inquires as to why a product was not delivered on time. In the extreme case, the supplier may repeat this process one or more times.

The reason for the above discussion is that when there have not been any previous reports there is a tendency for inexperienced members of management to overreact to the first set of organizational performance measures. Often, the limited time period represented by the performance data means that no conclusions can be made now. In general, this is the case of the first step in the program—start the online operations, accumulate performance data, and continue to use the initial rough estimates.

The second step in the program for improving the quality of statistical data in the inventory management computer-based applications is to begin to apply slightly more sophisticated formulas in determining the reorder quantity and the reorder point. In this second step, these improvements are based on insights gained from studying historical data of utilization experience by inventory item. As more historical data are accumulated, processed, and evaluated, the following statistical techniques may be successively applied: (*a*) moving average method, (*b*) least squares techniques, (*c*) 12-month centered moving average method, and (*d*) exponential smoothing method.

The third step in the program for improving the quality of statistical data is a significant shift in perspective. In the first two steps, the reorder quantity and the reorder point are based on statistical techniques applied to historical experience. In the third step, there is a shift from responding to the past to planning for the future; thus, forecasting methods are applied to specifying demand by inventory item.

The final step in the program consists of periodic refinement of the forecasted demand by inventory item based on more sophisticated analyses of experience, economic projections, and short-term plans by the organization. The advanced information systems featuring marketing operations that are discussed in Chapter 13 are based on the existence of inventory management information systems operating at this fourth step in this overall program for improving the quality of statistical data.

In summary, pragmatic approaches are available that facilitate the establishment of a computer-based inventory system where there are only limited data. Because of the crude nature of the initial inventory models, it is assumed that there are excessive amounts of inventory on hand as a guard against the "unknown." As historical data are accumulated, processed, and evaluated, more sophisticated statistical techniques can be applied and the aggregate investment in inventory can be reduced without incurring any additional risk. The zenith is reached when sophisticated forecasting techniques have been repeatedly applied to the management of inventory in accordance with other strategic plans and marketing activities. In the latter case, members of management have an informed opinion of the inventory level by item and are confident that each of these levels is compatible with the marketing and distribution plans.

SUMMARY

The inventory management information system is more than just a perpetual inventory system that has been modified to include reorder quantities and reorder points for each item in inventory where the network automatically handles the purchasing process. Systems analysts must first understand the nature of the organizational activity represented by this system before they can design and evaluate an information system for this activity.

For example, from a procedural standpoint, the reorder point is a predetermined value which signals that another reorder quantity should be requested. From the standpoint of the organization, the reorder point represents the minimum inventory stock for an item that is required to provide a specified level of customer service during the reorder period.

Therefore, the purpose of this chapter has been to focus on some of the underlying assumptions and conflicts encountered in inventory management operations and to point out some of the systematic inventory operations. Through this type of understanding, the systems analyst is able to design an effective inventory management information system that appropriately copes with the real organizational activity handled by this network.

TOPICS FOR CLASS DISCUSSION

1. Some members of management say that in inventory control they are attempting to match the cost of ordering versus the cost of maintaining inventory. What is the basic question for which this statement is the answer? Where in the sequence of general inventory questions does this question fall? If applicable, cite other general inventory questions that both precede and follow this question.

2. The controller of Guyton Chemical Corporation is currently examining the inventory carrying costs for EOQ formula. She is using 17.5 percent of inventory cost with the following parts:

Cost of invested capital	4.95%
Estimated costs for taxes, insurance, building, tanks, bins, utilities, supplies, labor, and supervision	5.60
Obsolescence, deterioration, pilferage, and shrinkage	6.95
Total inventory carrying costs	17.50

An officer of a local bank suggested to the controller that Guyton Chemical Corporation should not use the cost of working capital (4.95 percent) in the EOQ formula but should be based on the long-run average cost of capital (which at Guyton Chemical Corporation has ranged from 22 to 26 percent). Do you agree? Submit a report to the controller in which you clarify the various issues raised regarding the determination of carrying costs of inventory.

3. Explain the relationship between the lead-time demand and the need for safety stock and cushion for an inventory item.

4. Explain the critical areas encompassed within an organization's inventory policy. Include within your discussion a statement as to the objective of each area.

5. Within an organization, individuals at several levels of management may be given the task of determining the *negative stockout*

cost for a specific inventory item. Explain at what level you feel this decision should be made and justify your position.

6. In an organization where reorder quantities and reorder points are in the process of being initially established concurrently with an identification system for the inventory items, the systems analyst may skip the first step of measuring the cost of carrying inventory versus the stockout cost. Instead, the analyst takes as given the organization's inventory policy and devotes total attention to getting the inventory network in an operational state. Explain the strengths and weaknesses of this approach.

CASE 11–1. PRECISION SCREW COMPANY

Obsolete inventory has been an annual problem confronting the management of the Precision Screw Company. The amount of obsolete inventory has decreased during the past five years, and last year's amount was reduced by a greater amount than any previous year because automobile screws were daily monitored toward the end of the automobile production period. However, as management reviews the operations for the past year,[6] the perennial question remains, "How can we further reduce the annual loss from obsolete inventory without jeopardizing customer relations or restricting our expanded volume of sales within the framework of an integrated inventory control and production control system?"

Historical Development

Thirteen years ago the management of the Precision Screw Company, a midwest manufacturing firm, partially changed to automatic data processing equipment as a means of coping with problem areas in the timely flow of information. The transition to ADPS (Automatic Data Processing System) was started with punched card equipment and has gradually been developed with the eventual goal of a total computer system. The processing of factory orders for shipment

---

[6] Following are pertinent data on the operations for the past year. Inventories (at cost on the last-in, first-out basis) represent 35 percent of the assets of the firm (total assets $5,250,000), and cost of goods sold represents 75 percent of net sales (net sales $8,500,000). Raw materials are a minor element of cost; labor and machine time being the primary elements. For example, setup cost for the production of a screw averages $20 to $25.

to customers was the first item programmed for the ADPS unit. Next, billing operations were programmed which, on a re-sorting basis, provide statistical sales data.[7] Inventory control and production control were the third and fourth areas to be programmed.

Today the assistant controller, who is the director of the data processing operations, envisions a total information system using the present computer system. This system would encompass the other accounting operations—specifically, cost accounting data for internal information requirements, payroll processing, accounts receivable collection and other cash receipts, voucher processing and cash payments, and financial statement preparation. The assistant controller plans to program these other operations in the order cited because of the interrelations between steps.[8] This ordering of phases or steps has been determined on a priority system of trying to maximize the benefit derived from each additional hour employing the computer facilities.

Integrated System

The integrated inventory control and production control system has been in full operation for over a year and is automatically administered by the computer. For each of the 8,000 items of finished goods inventory,[9] a 200-character record is continuously maintained giving the following information: (1) description of the

---

[7] Statistical sales data, by groups of items, are continuously accumulated by the computer and stored in the IBM 1405 disk storage unit. These data are reported in four ways: today, week to date, period to date, and year to date. In addition to the statistical sales data stored in the computer, by-product cards are prepared when orders and shipments are processed, and these by-product cards are fed into the IBM 1401 system whenever detailed statistical sales data are desired.

[8] For example, cost data can be applied to the present integrated inventory control and production control system, and from this extension, standard cost data can be obtained. With the addition of the payroll records being programmed, actual cost data will be available in the computer system. Phase two of the proposed total information system commences with the total programming of payroll operations, which, for example, would include the maintenance and reporting of all payroll tax data. In other words, each proposed phase is an extension of the data requirements achieved in the previous phase plus the addition of the minimum of new data.

[9] Thirteen years ago there were over 12,000 items, but close inventory supervision has reduced the number of different items to 8,000. The long-range goal is 6,000 items.

item, (2) stock on hand, (3) unshipped sales, (4) reorder point (minimum level of inventory), (5) reorder quantity, (6) items in process (that is, items being manufactured in the production department), and (7) identification of the week of the year in which the last sales order was processed. Again, this 200-character record is maintained on a perpetual basis, which means that it is up-to-date; however, the 200-character record does not contain the historical details of how the present position was achieved. This latter information can be obtained in detail from the by-product cards or on a group basis from the data stored in other sectors of the computer.

As stated, 200-character records are maintained by the computer for each of the items of finished goods inventory. For this purpose, an IBM 1405 disk storage unit is used which contains 25 disks (Model 1). The total capacity of the 25 disks is 50,000 200-character sectors.[10] An indelible 7-digit record address precedes each 200-character sector. Daily, punched cards are processed by the IBM 1401 data processing system, and simultaneously with the preparation of the billing or production orders, the 200-character inventory records are updated.[11]

The integrated aspects of inventory control are as follows: when a given item of finished goods inventory reaches the reorder point, the computer is programmed in such a manner that a production request

---

[10] Each 200-character record is called a "track sector," and each track of a disk contains 10 track sectors. Furthermore, each disk has 200 concentric tracks on which information is recorded. Thus, the capacity of each disk is 2,000 track sectors or 2,000 200-character records. Since Model 1 contains 25 disks, the capacity of this unit is 50,000 200-character records.

[11] In this particular industry it is highly advantageous to know continuously the position of the finished goods inventory. The 200-character records provide this type of data. For example, it is an industrial practice to provide a weekly list of finished goods inventory for which there is an overstockage, and such lists are supplied to various users of screws. It is not management's objective to have items included on the overstockage list; however, if overstockage exists, then it is desirable that this information be made available to individuals needing such finished goods. (This is one of the reasons that in the initial phases of ADPS the programmers at Precision Screw Company concentrated on perpetual inventory data and statistical sales data rather than upon the usual payroll processing and cost data accumulation programs.) Another example of the use of the 200-character records is as follows: during the closeout phase of automobile production, daily records (if desired) can be provided on the status of the special screws that are used only by the automobile industry. This permits close monitoring of both production and inventory so as to meet the demands of the automobile industry and at the same time minimize the amount of obsolete inventory.

is initiated. The appropriate raw materials are ordered, a production order is processed, and the particular machines that will be used in the production process are identified. (This system permits the manual initiation of a production order whenever desired; this may be for a new item or a rush order of an existing item or when seasonal sales demands are relatively low and it is necessary to manufacture some items for stock that would not be ordered on an automatic basis.) Thus, when the finished goods inventory reaches the critical level, the computer takes the initial action required for the production of a new reorder quantity. As previously mentioned, the 200-character inventory record reflects that the production order is in process for a new reorder quantity (unless some other quantity is manually requested). This information is recorded on the disk simultaneously with the preparation of the production order.

The integrated inventory control and production control system may appear to be a logical, ideal system; however, in spite of this automatic system, one major problem remains: obsolescence of finished goods inventory. This problem is compounded by several factors. First, approximately 60 percent of the finished goods inventory is special items which may be sold to *only one customer.*[12] A large volume of a given item may be sold to a particular customer over an extended period of time, and then, abruptly, the customer does not make any additional orders. The remaining quantity of specially engineered screws becomes obsolete.

Second, 15 to 20 percent of the 8,000 items of finished goods inventory (approximately 1,400 items) are special items for the same collective customer: the automobile industry. Usually every three years this major group of items is completely changed by the new automobile designs. Since the automobile replacement parts market frequently uses different types of screws than used on the original equipment, any remaining finished goods inventory at the time of the automobile style change becomes obsolete inventory.

Third, management's policy is for increased emphasis on special screws rather than upon general screws. Wood screws sold in hardware stores are prime examples of standard or general screws. Since they are standard, price is the major factor. There is little room for

---

[12] In fact, the common situation for *special screws* is to have one salesperson selling to one customer or to two customers. If there are several customers, the item will be classified as a "regular stock item" instead of a "special sales stock item."

product differentiation. In fact, if there is an imperfect screw, the customer does not usually bother to complain to the hardware store manager. On the other hand, engineered screws for production lines in manufacturing and assembling plants must be "perfect." This is particularly true where workers are paid on a "production basis" and where automatic equipment is employed. In the latter instances, a uniform, "perfect," durable screw is desired rather than a less "perfect" screw at a substantially lower price. As previously stated, 60 percent of the 8,000 items of finished goods are special items, and management desires to increase this percentage.[13]

Fourth, this factor is really the summation of the previous factors: how do you establish the reorder point on a special screw that is sold *only to one customer?* (This reorder point is the critical factor that permits the inventory control and production control systems to be integrated.) Management established a task group to study the various quantitative models for determining economic lot size measures. After a thorough study, the mathematical-formula approach was abandoned because none of the formulas applied to the unique situation of Precision Screw Company, since they had only one customer for a special screw.

Sales Stock Committee

Recognizing that the establishment of the reorder point (the point at which a new reorder quantity is requested from the production department) is the critical element in the automatic system, management decided that the primary point of control would be the initial level of evaluating negotiations over a proposed contract for the production of a new screw. A standing committee, called "sales

---

[13] Management's preference for special screws rather than general screws can be viewed from another standpoint. The tool cost for a new screw may range from $10 to $500 depending on the mix of standard versus new, specially engineered tools. Any competitor will have to incur these same tool costs if the competitor successfully obtains a contract for the production of any screw Precision Screw Company is currently manufacturing. Since the screw market is highly competitive, there is a slight advantage to the company that is presently manufacturing a special screw because the latter firm has already absorbed the initial expenditures. (Some competitors follow the "average cost" basis rather than "direct costing." These individuals average tool cost over the total volume of all types of production rather than charge such cost to the particular screw to which it is related. Competitors following this "average cost" practice may outbid a firm for the continuation of an existing order.)

stock committee," was established with seven representatives: (1) sales manager, (2) controller, (3) production control manager, (4) tool manager, (5) inventory control manager, (6) assistant controller, and (7) "junk manager" (the individual who has responsibility for disposal of obsolete inventory and scrap).

This committee operates as follows: a salesperson must formally request that a special item be manufactured and stocked. The salesperson's request is evaluated by the Sales Stock Committee, and there may be formal and informal transmissions of information between the committee and the salesperson. For example, the salesperson may be requested to negotiate for a larger order at a lower price (the salesperson initially had rough guidelines to follow in quoting prices for different size orders). At the conclusion of the action by the sales stock committee, the reorder point and the reorder quantity are established for the new item of inventory, and a 200-character record is opened in the IBM 1405 disk storage unit.

This system may sound as if it would be a simple system to administer; however, there are unusual industrial practices that aggravate the situation. For example, Precision Screw Company officials may negotiate to provide 15 units of a given type of screw for each automobile manufactured by a given firm. It is an open-end contract, and the automobile firm does not desire to maintain an inventory of screws at the assembly plants. Thus, Precision Screw Company officials must always have the items in finished goods inventory, available for immediate shipment whenever the automobile firm decides to manufacture more automobiles.[14]

Even though the previous examples highlighted the automobile industry, the same problem exists in other industries. For example, a television, radio, or electrical appliance manufacturer might order six screws of a given type for each unit the firm manufactures over a stated period of time, with a minimum commitment for 100,000

---

[14] The dilemma that faces Precision Screw Company officials is to calculate the moment at which the automobile manufacturer will stop production. Usually, because of shipping time, there is a three-week supply of screws in the "pipeline." As an illustration, assume that 25 screws of a given type may be used in the same automobile. Multiply the expected production of automobiles during a three-week period times 25 in order to determine the obsolete inventory at the end of the year for this particular screw if the closeout date is not "properly" estimated. Now to get the total magnitude of the situation, multiply the previous answer by 1,400. There are 1,400 special items of inventory for the automobile industry.

screws. Furthermore, the screws must always be available with the possibility of a penalty clause covering shortages. To complicate the situation even more, the special customer (for example, an automobile manufacturer or electrical appliance manufacturer) under an open-end contract will not provide a monthly projected production report which could be used to administer the required volume of screws for the coming period. The Precision Screw Company officials must estimate the customer's production which, in turn, establishes the estimated volume of special screws that will be required.

Sales Stock Report

The obsolescence problem has continued to plague management; therefore, it was decided to establish an additional control feature: a "Sales Stock Report." (See the appendix for an illustration and detailed description of the report.) Each month a salesperson was notified regarding any special items of inventory that that person had requested to be manufactured. The report for each item contained a listing of the data in the 200-character perpetual inventory record, and for each sales stock item (special screws) there was a report of the total sales in units for each of the accounting periods (see appendix to this case study for discussion of this) .

The salesperson that requested the production of a special screw is held responsible for the continuous stock of that type of screw, and can be relieved of this responsibility in one of two ways. First, the salesperson can cancel a special request and complete the sale of the present stock. (Another variation of this same approach would be the situation where the salesperson requested that 50,000 screws be manufactured on a one-shot basis with the total production being sold to one customer; after this is sold, the salesperson is relieved of responsibility.) Second, the salesperson can cancel the order and state that he or she cannot finish selling all the screws on hand. In the latter case, the "junk manager" is asked to try to find some alternative market for the screws, with authority to lower the price. If the junk manager is successful, then the salesperson is notified by the computer on the next sales stock report that the responsibility has been satisfied. If the junk manager cannot sell the screws under adjusted price conditions, then the salesperson must wait until the obsolete stock committee formally declares the screws obsolete. In the latter case, the junk manager is asked to sell the obsolete screws for scrap.

In addition to notifying each salesperson of the particular items (special screws) personally requested to be manufactured, a summary containing a detailed listing of all salespeople's reports is also prepared with copies for the (1) production control manager, (2) inventory control manager, (3) sales manager, and (4) assistant sales managers. This latter group receives three copies of the report.

With these facts in mind, management seeks additional ways of reducing the annual loss from obsolete inventory.

APPENDIX TO CASE 11–1

PRECISION SCREW COMPANY SALES STOCK REPORT

Following is a detailed explanation of the sales stock report (Exhibit A) which is illustrated on a subsequent page. The description is in the same order as the block captions on the report.

YEAR: Fiscal year is July 1 to June 30.

DATE 1,   The fiscal year is divided into twelve periods, consist-
DATE 2,   ing of 10 four-week periods and 2 six-week periods.
ETC.:   The periods found in boxes captioned "Date 2" through "Date 11" are the ending dates of the 10 four-week periods. During the latter part of June and the first part of July there is a two-week vacation, and most of the vacation usually occurs during the first period, which in effect reduces the first period to a four-week period. The 12th period is the longest period, encompassing all the time remaining in the fiscal year.

SS NO.:   Sales stock number. This number is assigned to the salesperson's request for the manufacture of a special screw. Production and control keeps the log of numbers.

Example: SS No. 950070

                    9   refers to the year: 1969
              .50... refers to the 50th week in the year of 1969
           ...070 refers to the sequential requisition number within the 50th week

Sales Stock Report

SS# (1969)	GROSS (YEAR 1970)	Code	MAN	DATE 1 8-1	DATE 2 8-29	DATE 3 9-26	DATE 4 10-24	DATE 5 11-21	DATE 6 12-19	DATE 7 1-16	DATE 8 2-13	DATE 9 3-13	DATE 10 4-10	DATE 11 5-8	DATE 12 6-30
					DESCRIPTION		CUSTOMER	PART NO.		ON HAND	UNSHIP	IN PROC	REOR PT	RE QUAN	LAST WK#
950070	2500	C / C	15	1	QMT – 916A / 2	3	General Motors / 4	1945723 / 5	6	184 / 7	/ 8	/ 9	142 / 10	426 / 11	022 / 12
940083	1821	C / C	15	1	POMI – 1041A / 2	3	Ford / 4	9763441 / 5	6	263 / 7	/ 8	/ 9	134 / 10	397 / 11	021 / 12
002017	2083	C	15	1	5/16 X 16/32 / 2	3	FLAT IMS / 4	United Co. / 5	6	627 / 7	45 / 8	/ 9	50 / 10	300 / 11	021 / 12
001046	14044	C	15	1	1 3/4 X 10 PH / 2	3	FLT WD New England Sales / 4	/ 5	6	481 / 7	/ 8	694 / 9	347 / 10	694 / 11	020 / 12
		SS		1 / 374	2 / 347	3 / 359	4 / 1459	5 / 694	6 / 35	7	8 / 3100	9	10 / 21	11 / 366	12 / 406
049018	1642	C	16	1	X1–4314–C / 2	3	Auto Repl / 4	/ 5	6	247 / 7	51 / 8	/ 9	114 / 10	342 / 11	022 / 12
003094	900	C	16	1	DI–1116–A / 2	3	Western Electric / 4	/ 5	6	350 / 7	/ 8	/ 9	50 / 10	350 / 11	022 / 12
002040	2300	C / X	16	1	POMI–1038–A / 2	3	Chrysler / 4	8429362 / 5	6	372 / 7	/ 8	/ 9	120 / 10	365 / 11	008 / 12
024013	2500	C / O	16	1	HSP 65 2X8 / 2	3	R1W RCA / 4	/ 5	6	130 / 7	/ 8	520 / 9	200 / 10	450 / 11	12
951014	1300	C	16	1	X1–4217–B / 2	3	Auto Repl / 4	/ 5	6	375 / 7	/ 8	/ 9	60 / 10	340 / 11	021 / 12
001024	1471	C / C	16	1	PX1–82–A / 2	3	Western Electric / 4	/ 5	6	50 / 7	/ 8	750 / 9	10 / 10	11 / 11	024 / 12
024036	800	G	16	1	PMS–1832–A / 2	3	Frigidaire / 4	/ 5	6	7	8	9	10	11	12

GROSS:

All gross amounts are expressed in terms of 144 pieces. For example, GROSS 2083 means (2083) (144 pieces) = 299,952 pieces. The numerical amount that appears under "Gross" indicates the salesperson's cumulative sales for the specified sales stock number.

> Example: GROSS 2083 means that 299,952 pieces of this item are expected to be sold over the life of this sales order number to the customer indicated.

C:

Code. Normally this block is blank. Following are some letters that may appear in this block:

C This indicates that the salesperson requesting this item has *canceled* the request for the item; however, the quantity on hand must still be disposed of before the salesperson's responsibility is terminated.

R The salesperson requesting this special item now feels that conditions have changed and the reorder point and reorder quantity must be *reduced*. An "R" will appear in this block of the report until the stock level comes down to the new desired level.

X This means that the salesperson requesting the item reports inability to sell it. The "junk manager" attempts to find alternative markets in which to sell the items. The "X" will appear until either (1) the junk manager sells all the inventory or (2) the obsolete stock committee declares the items obsolete, and they are dropped from the inventory.

O This indicates that the customer has telephoned us that the paperwork is on the way but asks that we begin production. The "O" is removed when the written contract arrives. With some customers it is common to have a two-week delay between the telephone call and the receipt of the written order.

SALES:

This refers to the salesperson's payroll number. It is a way of identifying the salesperson who requested the particular screw to be manufactured.

DESCRIPTION,
CUSTOMER,
PART NO.: The description refers to our identification of the item. The name of the customer and the customer's part number are included in the remainder of this block. (The customer's part number is for the benefit of our salespeople; they can keep up with their customers' catalogs for parts.)

ON HAND: Stock on hand. This amount (like all other figures in this report) is expressed in terms of 144 pieces (gross). The stock on hand includes the items sold but unshipped.

UNSHIP: Unshipped. This refers to items sold but unshipped.

IN PROC: In process. This refers to items that are currently being manufactured in the production department.

REOR PT: Reorder point. This is the minimum level of inventory. When this minimum level is reached, the computer will initiate the action for the production of the reorder quantity.

RE QUAN: Reorder quantity. This amount and the reorder point are established by the sales stock committee.

LAST WK NO.: Last week number. This refers to the last week in which a sales order for the particular item was processed.

Example: LAST WK NO. 022

0.. refers to the year 1970

.22 refers to the 22nd week in 1970

The second line of the two-line report is filled in only for sales stock items (symbol "SS") which are sold on a continuous basis. If the second line is blank, it means one of two things: (1) either it is a special order for a specific amount with no inventory or (2) it is a regular stock item for which there is an abnormal, large request that is superimposed upon the normal reorder level. In the latter situation, there might be a large order of a normal, standard item. For example, in the past we have used a reorder point of 50 and a reorder quantity of 300. The special order requires a reorder point of 500 and a reorder quantity of 1500; therefore, the new reorder point for this item is 550 and the reorder quantity is 1800 (300 + 1500 = 1800).

The remainder of line two of the report is used to present the sales in gross during each of the 12 accounting periods. By-product cards are fed in the computer to provide the data for this line of the report. Again, the second line is filled in only for sales stock items, that is, special, engineered screws. Open-end contracts with an automobile, television, radio, appliance, or small electrical appliance manufacturer are prime examples of sales stock items.

When a salesperson has completed responsibility with regard to a particular screw, the computer prints a small rectangular box □ in the column headed "Last Wk#." Of course, this would be the last time this item is reported on the sales stock report.

CASE 11–2. TAYLOR MANUFACTURING COMPANY

The Taylor Manufacturing Company, a subsidiary of a diversified corporation, is one of the country's major manufacturers and distributors of high-quality kitchen utensils and appliances with annual sales of approximately $25,000,000. The company does not engage in retail sales but sells exclusively to selected retail outlets. Furthermore, the company has approximately 1,700 items in its product line.

The company's manufacturing plant is centrally located in Ohio and the plant employs about 1,000 people. In addition to the main warehouse that is located near the manufacturing plant in Cleveland, Ohio, the company also maintains 20 branch warehouses plus a sales force of 70 people throughout the country.

Recently, the company's executive management decided to install a medium-size computer system for inventory control and sales analysis, even though this will probably increase Taylor Manufacturing Company's current operating costs. Executive management felt that the increases in reporting effectiveness in both the sales and inventory functions, plus the anticipated benefits from future applications, justified the added expense. The future applications included production control and payroll accounting.

Each of the 20 branches does its own billing; however, the accounts receivable and inventory functions are centralized in Ohio. Branch inventories are replenished automatically from the Cleveland warehouse stocks based upon computer-generated orders.

Former System

Prior to conversion, inventory replenishment was handled on a manual decentralized basis. Monthly, each branch manager would take a physical inventory and would then place orders equal to 30-day usage (the branch's reorder quantity) for any item in inventory falling below a predetermined level. This predetermined level or order point was based upon each branch manager's own estimate of sales for the next 90-day period. With this 90-day base figure for each item, the branch manager would place a new order if *quantity on hand plus quantity on order but not received is less than the next 90-day sales*. Under this procedure, the Taylor Manufacturing Company was consistently carrying a 45- to 60-day inventory of finished goods.

New System

Under the new system, the inventory control function has been centralized at the main office and converted to computer processing. All branch inventory transactions are analyzed weekly by the computer system. Any items requiring replenishment as well as the quantities needed are determined automatically by the computer system.

The formula used by the computer program for inventory replenishment is basically the same method used by the branch managers under the previous system. However, because the inventory levels are being reviewed weekly instead of monthly, the reorder point has been lowered to 75-day usage (from the original 90-day level), and the reorder quantity has been reduced to a 15-day supply for many of the items in the product line (from the original 30-day level). Using this new system, company management feels that inventory levels have been reduced from 15 to 20 percent.

Management decided against adopting any of the "sophisticated" inventory control formulas for determining reorder points and for forecasting future sales initially because (1) there was a lack of sales history data upon which to base such forecasts and (2) management felt that a new purchasing concept would aggravate any centralization problems which might arise during the conversion of the branch inventory functions. A master file, however, has been established in the computer system to record the high month's sales and the low month's sales quantity in addition to total sales and number of months included in total sales. These statistics can be used in the future to determine average sales and deviations. With these latter data plus seasonal trends, management plans on developing more sophisticated formulas in the near future.

With the conversion to automatic data processing, management now obtains more effective and timely sales analysis reports as well as information which will permit reductions in inventory investment without increasing the number of stockout conditions. Now that the sales analysis and branch inventory functions have been converted to electronic equipment, management is proceeding into the production control application. Following this, the plans are to program the complete payroll function and to integrate this system with the other computer programming systems.

REQUIRED:

1. Evaluate the centralized inventory control and sales analysis system.

2. Your brief study of the Taylor Manufacturing Company's operations indicates that the company is extremely profitable. From your review of the new centralized inventory control and sales analysis system, what would you expect to be the general nature of the company's environment? What type of cost-selling price relation would you expect to exist?

3. Do you agree with company management's movement toward a "total computer system" (integrated inventory control and sales analysis system; next, integrated inventory control, production control and sales analysis system; then, mechanized payroll operations with integrated inventory control . . .) ? Be specific and include illustrations and examples in support of your comments.

4. Assume that company management is reconsidering the question of maintaining the reorder point at 75 days and the reorder quantity at 15 days. Indicate the format of a report that you might prepare for management which would provide guidelines for making a decision on this question. Even though the format of the report may be sketchy, please be specific as to *where* and *how* the information on the report would be *obtained* and *processed*.

CHAPTER 12

Inventory Control Information Systems

THE GENERAL model for a TYPE 2 information system was described in Chapter 10, and the most common application of this TYPE 2 model was presented in Chapter 11 as an inventory management information system. After a determination was made as to which items should be stocked in inventory, this latter model contained a perpetual inventory control system which was modified to include reorder quantities and reorder points for each item in inventory. From the program for improving the quality of data in computer-based inventory models (which was described in Chapter 11), members of management can periodically reduce the overall financial investment in inventory while having increased assurance that a stockout will not occur.

Inventory management and inventory control systems like most other computer-based networks will contain a series of monitoring and exception reporting features that assist personnel in carrying out their responsibilities. For example, these features incorporated in the inventory management information system monitored the inventory status and determined when various types of expediting actions should be taken so as to avoid a stockout. The inventory control networks described in this chapter contain additional monitoring and control features for operating control and management control purposes.

This chapter presents the general model for a more advanced

inventory control information system which fully encompasses the inventory management information system plus other control features. This advanced inventory control network builds upon (*a*) a thorough knowledge of the economic environment in which the organization under scrutiny is located, (*b*) a comprehension of the administrative process in said organization and of the role of inventory in this administrative process, and (*c*) an understanding of the heterogeneity among the various items in inventory.

CONTROL PROCEDURES

What is the most efficient and economic method of controlling inventory in a given situation? This demanding question calls for the systems analyst to exercise a different type of ability and understanding than that used to specify the requirements and processing procedures for inventory management information systems. Specifying the requirements and processing procedures involves several matters that cannot be precisely determined but which are based on the systems analyst's study and understanding of the situation. Thus, the topics of requirements and processing procedures might be classified as "scientific inventory management," while the topic of control procedures in advanced inventory systems might be classified as "systematic inventory control administration."

The practical task of evaluating and designing systematic inventory control procedures is predicated on two assumptions. First, there is a high degree of heterogeneity in the inventory. The systems analyst, therefore, begins by examining the characteristics of the inventory in order to identify the major differentiating attributes possessed by the various items in inventory. Whatever common attributes the analyst discovers will serve as a basis for classifying the inventory into groups.

Second, there is the belief that what is good control for one group of items in inventory may be poor control for another group. The general practice of establishing one control system for all items is good for the *average* item, but it usually leaves many others either with too little or too much control. Although most of the criticism is associated with those items for which there is insufficient control, the systems analyst is equally concerned with the elimination of excessive control procedures. It is not unusual for substantial financial savings to result from a change in the inventory control procedures without any significant change in the degree of control over inventory.

SELECTIVE ANALYSIS AND INVENTORY CONTROL

This practical method for evaluating and designing systematic inventory control procedures is referred to as "selective analysis and inventory control" or simply as "selective inventory control." The object of selective inventory control is to establish the best possible control at the least possible cost for each item or group of items in the inventory.

As previously stated, generally there is a high degree of heterogeneity in the inventory. In fact, the items in inventory can be sorted and re-sorted in numerous ways based on various criteria that point out some of this heterogeneity. The three most prevalent classification systems are as follows:

A. Dollar selectivity
    Criteria: unit cost and usage value in dollars for specified period of time (annual, quarter, month, and so forth)
B. Commodity selectivity
    Criteria: type of item, product on which item is used, and characteristics of item
C. Usage selectivity
    Criteria: activity of item to determine obsolescence and slow moving items

No single classification system is best for all organizations, but, as is the case with other matters, the systems analyst will select that coding pattern which most appropriately meets the unique requirements of the economic situation. While this classification system is being examined from the standpoint of inventory control, the systems analyst's overall perspective will suggest that a coding pattern can be developed for classifying the inventory items so these groupings can be used not only in inventory control and inventory management, but also in marketing management. In a subsequent part of this chapter, a suggested classification scheme is presented for purposes of stimulating the systems analyst (*a*) to examine closely this heterogeneity in the inventory and (*b*) to determine the inventory information requirements of different decision-making groups within the organization.

Typically, the systems analyst is not developing an inventory classification code that will meet the information requirements of the overall organization; rather, the analyst is coping with a given problem in an economic situation where there is an existing identification system for inventory items. In many cases there is a financial problem of relating the degree of inventory control to the relative dollar importance of the inventory items. The inventory control information system which is based on *dollar selectivity* is especially suitable for coping with this general type of problem. In fact, the dollar selectivity method has been used so often that the terms "dollar selectivity" and "selective inventory control" are used synonymously by some practitioners. Since dollar selectivity is used so frequently, this method is examined in detail in the following discussion.

DOLLAR SELECTIVITY

Under the dollar selectivity method, the systems analyst follows a two-step approach establishing the best possible control at the least possible cost for each item or group of items in the inventory. First, the inventory items are classified based on a composite evaluation of two criteria: unit cost and usage value in dollars. Second, the most efficient and economic control system is chosen for each class of inventory items. In implementing this latter step, the systems analyst reviews each inventory item which has been selected for *a change* in operating and management control procedures to determine if other factors (that is, factors other than unit cost and usage value in dollars) might suggest that the control procedures for the inventory item in question should not be changed.

Classifying the Inventory

Simple statistical procedures are used in sorting the items in inventory by the stated criteria: unit cost and usage value in dollars. First, the inventory items are sorted based on their unit cost. For example, assume that there are 3,000 different inventory items (not *unit* of stock on hand, but *items* in inventory) and that the cost per unit of these items ranges from one cent to $100. These 3,000 items are sorted as follows:

Item Identification Number	Unit Cost	Number of Item
2896	$100.00	1
1021	98.00	2
1874	97.00	3
2472	50.00	297
2361	49.95	298
3487	49.95	299
3942	10.00	930
4072	9.98	931
3824	9.97	932
3358	1.00	2730
1431	.99	2731
1214	.98	2732
2986	.02	2999
1878	.01	3000

The above list of items is summarized as follows:

Range	Number of Items	Percent of Total	Cumulative, More than Lower Limit	
			Number	Percent
$50.00 to $100.00	297	9.9	297	9.9
$10.00 to $ 49.99	633	21.1	930	31.0
$ 1.00 to $ 9.99	1,800	60.0	2,730	91.0
$ 0.01 to $ 0.99	270	9.0	3,000	100.0
	3,000	100.0		

Figure 12.1 presents this same relation on a cumulative basis. This cumulative graph suggests that a small number of inventory items have a relatively high unit cost (in dollars) , but that a large majority of the items have a very low unit cost. This same relation depicted by the previous graph (Figure 12.1) has been charted for the inventory items for numerous organizations. Unless there are policy issues that exclude the distributions at the extremes, in each of these organizations there are a few items with a relative high unit cost, while the vast majority of the items have a relative low unit cost.

Second, the inventory items are re-sorted by usage value in dollars.

FIGURE 12.1
**Cumulative Inventory Items Presented
in Descending Order by Unit Cost**

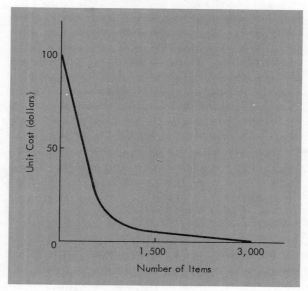

The expression, "usage value," of course, means the forecasted demand for the inventory item during a specified period (such as a year, quarter, or month), and the computation of this forecasted demand was discussed in the previous chapter.

Continuing with the same example of 3,000 inventory items, the list of re-sorted items will appear as follows:

Item Identification Number	Per Unit Cost	Forecasted Annual Usage Requirements	
		In Units	*In Dollars*
4116	$96.00	10,000	$960,000
1951	$85.00	11,000	$935,000
1874	$97.00	9,500	$921,500
1727	$95.00	9,500	$902,500
1534	$ .02	100,000	$ 2,000
1878	$ .01	100,000	$ 1,000
1460	$ .02	25,000	$ 500

This list of items is summarized as follows:

Range	Number of Items	Percent of Total	Cumulative, More than Lower Limit Number	Cumulative, More than Lower Limit Percent
$500,000 to $960,000	420	14.0	420	14.0
$ 90,000 to $499,999	597	19.9	1,017	33.9
$ 20,000 to $ 89,999	1,683	56.1	2,700	90.0
$ 500 to $ 19,999	300	10.0	3,000	100.0
	3,000	100.0		

Figure 12.2 presents this same relation on a cumulative basis. The graphic representation in Figure 12.2 is indicative of the inventory position in many organizations that we have studied. It is common for 10 percent of the inventory items to represent 65 percent of the total annual usage dollars, for 25 percent of the inventory items to represent 25 percent of the total annual usage dollars, and for 65 percent of the inventory items to represent 10 percent of the total annual usage dollars.

These three natural groupings of the inventory items based on

FIGURE 12.2
Cumulative Inventory Items Presented
in Descending Order by Dollar Value

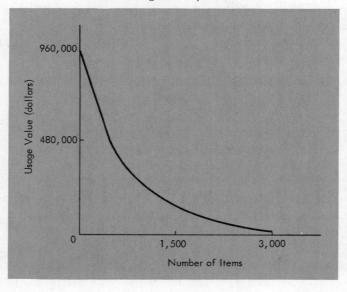

annual usage dollars are labeled "Class A," "Class B," and "Class C," respectively. These natural groupings with these respective labels have been used so often that the dollar selectivity method of inventory control is frequently called the "ABC Method." The Class A item always refers to that small group of inventory items which represents the majority of the total annual usage dollars, while the Class C item always designates that large group of items which represents a relatively minor part of the total annual usage dollars. Actually, there is another characteristic that varies by class which was presented in the previous graph: the range of unit cost for each class of inventory items.

The simultaneous consideration of both criteria—unit cost and usage value in dollars—is the third step in the process of classifying the inventory items according to the dollar selectivity method. Supplementing what was previously stated, the Class A grouping refers to that small group of high-unit-cost items which represents the majority of the total annual usage dollars The Class B grouping refers to a larger group of medium-unit-cost items which represents a proportional share of the total annual usage dollars. The Class C grouping refers to that major group of low unit cost items which represents a relatively small share of the total annual usage dollars.

Continuing with the example, the following criteria are established for each class:

Class A
Unit cost: $50 to $100 (approximately 10 percent of items)
Annual usage value: $600,000 to $960,000 (approximately 11 percent of items)
Class B
Unit cost: $10 to $49.99 (approximately 21 percent of items)
Annual usage value: $99,000 to $599,999 (approximately 23 percent of items)
Class C
Unit cost: $0.01 to $9.99 (approximately 69 percent of items)
Annual usage value: $500 to $89,000 (approximately 66 percent of items)

Those inventory items which meet only one of the two requirements for a class must be individually studied, and they are so examined in the following discussion of selecting control procedures for each class of inventory.

Selecting Control Procedures

High unit cost and high usage dollar items (Class A inventory items) deserve perpetual control and close record control and follow-up. On the other hand, low unit cost and low usage dollar items (Class C inventory items) may be appropriately managed by physical control without record control. In other words, the high-cost items should be watched almost constantly, while letting the low-cost items "take care of themselves."

Before examining the selection of control procedures for each class of items, it might be appropriate to review the alternatives available. *Perpetual control* means there is a continuous control over the physical units of inventory. Generally, there are inventory records that are kept up-to-date with an entry being made each time an item is issued or is received from a supplier. These daily records may be (*a*) manually recorded, (*b*) processed by EAM equipment on punched cards, or (*c*) processed by a computer for disk, paper tape, or magnetic tape storage. In summary, there are four common features of a perpetual control system: (*a*) an inventory clerk (who might also be a key punch operator under an online perpetual control system), (*b*) daily records, (*c*) material issue and receiving slips, and (*d*) a guarded or locked storeroom.

Physical control is the opposite of perpetual control. Records are not maintained of the day-to-day changes in inventory stock, and the units of inventory are withdrawn by any worker on an open or "free" access basis. In other words, the inventory stock is available for any worker to use on a first-come basis. Generally, there is some type of physical indication that the stock level for a given item has reached the reorder point. Five common examples of this are as follows. First, the lead-time stock and the safety stock are stored in a locked storeroom. When all of the "free access units" in open stock are consumed, the supervisor must secure the additional units from the locked storeroom. When the supervisor does this, he or she is required to initiate a repeat requisition to replenish the stock.

Second, the lead-time stock and safety stock are tied in a bundle or bag, and a repeat requisition form is attached to the bundle or bag. When all of the units in the open stock have been used except those in the bundle or bag, the "bank is broken," the bag is opened or the bundle is untied. Concurrently, the repeat requisition form is processed.

Third, a "two-bin" procedure is followed. One bin is on an open stock basis, and the second bin triggers the repeat requisition form in the same manner as breaking the bank did in the previous example.

Fourth, a line is painted inside the storage bin or barrel. When the inventory stock reaches the painted mark, a repeat requisition is started into process by the worker who withdrew the units from stock at this critical point.

Fifth, the lead-time stock is controlled by any of the previously cited physical control procedures including attaching a repeat requisition. However, the safety stock is separately controlled, and the attached repeat requisition form is stamped EXPEDITE. This fifth type of physical control procedure is especially suitable for production operations where a shortage of any single item would stop the assembly line.

The task of selecting the control procedures for a given class of items is not an independent act, instead, there is a close relation between the inventory class of an item and the procedures followed in administering the reorder quantity and the reorder point. Furthermore, the amount of safety stock directly varies by the inventory class of an item. There is a natural relation, of course, between the high unit cost, high annual usage dollar items (Class A) and the frequency of ordering per EOQ formula.

Because of this interrelationship, practitioners do not begin the study of inventory with processing procedures and then subsequently study control procedures. Instead, the practitioner classifies items of inventory according to Class A, Class B, and Class C. (This grouping of items by class does require that the forecasted annual usage in dollars must be determined for each item in inventory; thus, this act overlaps the previously discussed processing procedures for forecasting demand.) If the practitioner labels an item of inventory as Class A, then this will limit the possible range of choice of processing procedures.

In other words, the practitioner establishes classes of inventory, and each class contains specified ranges in which the other variables must appear. Conversely, the degree of control applied to a class of items may be varied (*a*) by changing the frequency of ordering, (*b*) by varying the quantity of safety stock, and (*c*) by shifting from either a perpetual or physical record control to the other method. Thus, in selecting the control procedures for a given class of inventory items, it is necessary to specify what these other variables are. These other variables are cited in the following description of each of the groupings.

Class A items

Criteria: high unit cost, high annual usage value in dollars.

Frequency: low; generally, approximately 10 percent of the total items in inventory.

Reorder: frequently per EOQ formula, usually ranging from ordering on a weekly basis to ordering on a monthly basis.

Safety stock: none.

Type of control: perpetual records with weekly review. The item may be so critical (not only in terms of high unit cost and high annual usage dollars but also in terms of the production process) that two sets of records will be maintained, one set in the stockroom and one set in production control. Since no safety stock is going to be maintained, the Class A items require very close attention to avoid running out of stock and perhaps stopping a production line. Again, the Class A items represent only about 10 percent of the total number of items so that this close control is being given to only a small portion of the total number of items in inventory.

The reader may be surprised by the statement that no safety stock is maintained for Class A items while a double set of records is frequently recommended for controlling these Class A items. Using the EOQ formulas, the analyst can quickly determine the approximate break-even point between maintaining a safety stock of these high unit cost, high annual usage dollar items versus eliminating the safety stock and replacing this control measure with a duplicate set of records.

Class B items

Criteria: medium unit cost, medium annual usage value in dollars.

Frequency: more often than Class A items; typically, approximately 25 percent of the total items in inventory.

Reorder: less often than Class A items; per EOQ formula, usually ranging from ordering on a monthly to ordering on a quarterly basis.

Safety stock: small amount such as one to two weeks' supply.

Type of control; perpetual control with periodic review. The use of the EOQ formulas will result in Class B items having a higher average inventory stock level than Class A items. In addition the carrying of safety stock will further increase the average stock level. However, there is less usage value and less dollar investment for the Class B items than for Class A, and the maintenance of safety stock decreases the necessity for close attention to the changes in stock level.

Class C items

Criteria: low unit cost, annual usage value in dollars.

Frequency: high; generally, approximately 65 percent of the total items in inventory.

Reorder: seldom, usually ranging from ordering on a semiannual basis to ordering on an annual basis.

Safety stock: two weeks to a month's supply.

Type of control: physical control. Ordering on a semiannual or annual basis will mean larger quantities in inventory, but being low-cost, low-usage-value items, the dollar investment in inventory is relatively small.

In addition to the above-cited variables, there are other factors which are considered in classifying the inventory items. These other factors include the consistency of rate of usage, lead time and procurement peculiarities, shelf life, likelihood of theft by employees, obsolescence risk, and the physical size of the bulk stock.

As is true of any classification system, there are those unusual items which tend to fall between class intervals. It goes without saying that the analyst must exercise considerable judgment in classifying all the inventory items. The analyst may make mistakes in both directions: too much control as well as too little control. The little publicized condition of too much control may be of more financial importance to the organization than the publicized condition of too little control.

It is difficult to offer any positive method for identifying those items where there is too much control, aside from suggesting that a competent analyst should thoroughly examine each inventory item for purposes of making this evaluation. On the other hand, there are several practical ways of identifying a too little control situation. For instance, the most critical type of mistake will be to classify an inventory item as Class C and to employ *physical* control procedures when a different control system is really needed.

To prevent against this, a general procedure followed in installing an ABC inventory control system is to prepare a schedule of all inventory items identified as Class C. The schedule will list each Class C item and will give the following data for each item: per-unit cost, forecasted annual usage value in dollars, reorder quantity, reorder point, and safety stock. This schedule will be distributed to different members of management for their close review and comment. As a result of this procedure, inventory items originally labeled Class C may be redesigned Class B and subjected to Class B control and management procedures. Following are some of the reasons for not classifying an item for Class C control and management: (*a*) difficult procurement problem (such as long or erratic lead time), (*b*) susceptible to theft, (*c*) difficult forecasting problem (occasional usage in varying quantities), (*d*) shelf life too short for Class C control, and (*e*) too large a storage space requirement for bulk inventory under the Class C control procedures.

In summary, the overall selection of the appropriate control procedures for a given organization's inventory is a complex decision involving many factors and with implications for various activities throughout the organization. In addition to these organizational considerations, this selection process is even more complicated by the existence of numerous dissimilar inventory items. The analyst sorts the inventory items into arbitrary classes for purposes of establishing uniform control procedures for similar items. The analyst attempts to determine for each class the most efficient and economical method of controlling the inventory in the given situation.

In this discussion, the different available methods of inventory control were cited. However, most of the attention was given to only one method—the dollar selectivity method of inventory control—which is the method that is most frequently used.

The emphasis now shifts from the selection of inventory control procedures to the systems analyst's evaluation of existing systems and to suggestions of how to proceed in designing new systems. Before moving to this topic, however, a ten-digit coding pattern is suggested for identifying the inventory items. This pattern encompasses a coding system that permits the retrieval of pertinent data regarding the inventory for the various decision-making groups throughout the organization.

The eight-digit coding structure presented in Chapter 11 is encompassed verbatim as the first eight-digits in this ten-digit coding pattern.

12xxxxxxxx   The first two digits designate the product group.

xx34xxxxxx   The third and fourth digits indicate subgroups with special characteristics. For example, in the case of chemical inventory items, a number *10* in these digits might represent a perishable, flammable item which must be stored in a given type of controlled environment; a number *20,* a perishable, nonflammable item which must be stored in a given type of controlled environment; a number *30,* a nonperishable, flammable item which must be stored in a given type of controlled environment; and so forth.

xxxx5678xx   The fifth, sixth, seventh, and eighth digits specify the unique inventory items with the same classification for product group and subgroups.

xxxxxxxx9x   The ninth digit designates a composite rating of two classification schemes: (*a*) price and degree of importance and (*b*) turnover frequency. The first classification scheme might include three alternatives:

   A—high unit cost
   B—critical item to the particular firm (excludes Group A)
   C—bulk items (which would represent the majority of the items in inventory for most business firms)

The second classification scheme might include three alternatives:

   F—fast-moving
   N—normal
   S—slow-moving

The composite rating would include nine possibilities, and the appropriate number to designate the composite rating would appear as the ninth digit in this inventory classification code. These nine possibilities are as follows:

   AF—high unit price, fast-moving
   AN—high unit price, normal

AS—high unit price, slow-moving

BF—critical item (non-high unit price), fast-moving

BN—critical item, normal

BS—critical item, slow-moving

CF—bulk item, fast-moving

CN—bulk item, normal

CS—bulk item, slow-moving

This latter composite rating as expressed by the ninth digit in the inventory classification code might be an index based on different weights assigned to several classification schemes rather than just the two schemes cited.

xxxxxxxxx0   The tenth digit designates special data for marketing purposes. For example, a marketing composite rating might be developed based on two classification schemes: (*a*) average margin per dollar of sales and (*b*) approved marketing strategies for the item. Each of these classification schemes might have three alternatives with a composite rating determined in the same manner as stated for the ninth digit in this classification code.

Again, the above inventory classification code is presented only for purposes of encouraging the analyst to examine seriously the requirements for data regarding inventory by various decision-making groups throughout the organization and by inventory managers responsible for physical control and management control *before* the analyst specifies the inventory classification code. A given inventory identification coding pattern can be a composite of the requirements of various control and decision-making groups. The richer the coding pattern is in meeting these diverse requirements, the higher is the quality of service provided to different users of inventory data, for an individual can subsequently retrieve only what was previously coded to be retrieved.

SYSTEMS ANALYST'S PERSPECTIVE

Following the information systems approach, the systems analyst examines the production and operation activities and begins to specify the information requirements and data sources. In determining the information requirements, the systems analyst follows a three-step procedure. First, the analyst must understand the administrative process of the organization in question and have an appreciation of those unique characteristics of this organization. Second, the analyst must determine the goals and objectives of the production and operation activities at each level within the organization. This second step, of course, draws heavily upon organization theory and might be described as a high-point organization review. Third, the systems analyst must specify which information requirements are incumbent upon the production and control information system in order to satisfy the previously determined goals and objectives.

After the systems analyst has specified the information requirements, the analyst begins to ascertain the data sources. Next, comes the practical task of matching information requirements with data sources. In the process of performing this matching process, the systems analyst will select from those tools and techniques available (reorder point, reorder quantity, EOQ formulas, safety stock, cushion, perpetual control, physical control, repeat requisitions, and so forth), those which seem appropriate for the economic situation in question.

In the process of bridging the gap between the information requirements and the data sources, the systems analyst is governed by the practical guidelines of desire for simplicity, speed, economy, and accuracy. The management control system must function *through people;* therefore, it must be simple if it is to be effective, to provide accurate information, and to be processed in the minimum time. The management control system must be capable of coping with the exceptional item or event. While all regular items can be handled on a predetermined or automatic basis, the system must be capable of coping with the exceptional item without upsetting normal operations. There should be sufficient flexibility in the system to permit growth and expansion or internal change without upsetting the network. Furthermore, the network should be capable of being integrated with other information systems, possibly serving as the building block for the integrated inventory control, production control, and marketing information system.

Other types of problems are encountered in the installation process. First, as problems arise in the operation of an inventory management information system (such as described in the previous chapter), it becomes apparent that some of the statements previously made by executive management regarding the organization's inventory policy were incorrect. In addition, it is discovered that some of these statements regarding inventory policy are in conflict. The experienced systems analyst can reduce the frequency of these situations by more thoroughly questioning management when the requirements are being originally specified. For example, the executive vice president of a manufacturing company stated that it was the organization's policy to provide a 95 percent level of customer service. But after learning how much buildup in inventory must occur before the company can offer this level of customer service, he admitted that this was only an "advertised goal." Eventually, after considerable study, the uniform level of customer service idea was abandoned; instead, each of the Class A items in inventory (high unit cost and high annual usage value in dollars) was individually examined, and a management group decided what level of customer service should be provided for that inventory item.

Second, after the decision has been made to install an inventory management information system, it may be a long time before the computer-based, information system is in operation. For example, the production control manager for a large manufacturing company commented that her division has been in the process of implementing reorder quantities and reorder points for over 12 months. This company's executive vice president will not approve the uneven production schedule which would be required if the company rapidly installed the suggested inventory management information system.

Furthermore, in order to establish the company's banks of inventory above the reorder level so that the inventory management information system can have a fresh start, production employees would have to work overtime in the short run. Later, after the inventory banks are established and during the initial phase of operating under the planned inventory system, production workers will have idle time until enough activity has occurred to activate the reorder quantity (in other words, until the reorder point was reached).

Faced with this situation, the production control manager weekly schedules a new group of inventory items for conversion to the new inventory management information system. The production manager believes that within a few months all of the inventory items will be under the new system.

Third, case after case can be cited where the workers and some of the supervisors have opposed the installation of an inventory management information system. This opposition eventually resulted in a poor operating system that was subsequently discarded. This organizational problem is not unique with the installation of production and operation information systems, but is analogous to situations encountered in installing a budgetary control and standard cost system in other organizations.

SUMMARY

TYPE 2 information systems encompassing inventory management and inventory control features represent a blending of (*a*) physical control, (b) management control, and (*c*) management planning activities in a sophisticated computer-based environment. The systems analyst expects to observe a high degree of heterogeneity among the inventory items within the system and to find a combination of physical and perpetual control procedures employed.

A computer-based network containing inventory management and inventory control features is capable of being periodically upgraded. As the program for improving the quality of data in computer-based inventory models is applied, there are shifts in the EOQ models from focusing on historical experience toward focusing on forecasted settings. As the overall network approaches the TYPE 2 level of sophistication, these EOQ models with a forecasting focus are operating at a high level of confidence.

In this type of setting, the systems analyst is concerned with the quality of the decision-making activities that are supported by this sophisticated computer-based network. An important indicator of this process is the extent to which the coding pattern for identifying the inventory items is used in retrieving special data for decision-making purposes. Statistical data on retrieval request per month by each member of executive management can be used as a rough surrogate of these decision-making activities.

The systems analyst will expect that *after* members of management have experienced a six to nine month learning curve with using a TYPE 2 information system for inventory control and inventory management, there should be a significant increase in the number of inquiries by remote terminal users. The absence of such an increase might suggest the need for a professional development and educational program for new members of management. Otherwise, the systems analyst might review the original justification for designing this network; it may be that this sophisticated network is no longer required to support the revised organizational setting.

When a systems analyst (serving as an outside consultant) makes an initial review of an ongoing, computer-based network for inventory management, the analyst expects to find an ABC distribution of inventory items by some composite criteria. If the inventory items are not distributed by the ABC groupings, then the analyst looks for policy statements or environmental constraints that preclude the expected distribution. In other words, the analyst expects heterogeneity among the inventory items and is concerned when this type of distribution does not exist. The nature of these distributions has been examined in many diverse organizations with a high degree of similarity among these ABC groupings. If the analyst discovers a situation where these distributions are not valid, the analyst is immediately in search for an explanation for these variations.

In conclusion, the information flows in production and operation activities are much more extensive than what was cited in this discussion. For example, complete textbooks and several university courses are concerned exclusively with this general problem area. The information flows cited in this discussion were selected based on their general application to numerous organizations.

TOPICS FOR CLASS DISCUSSION

1. A TYPE 2 information system for inventory management contains a coordination phase that permits an online monitoring of selected changes in inventory items. As this general model is expanded to encompass inventory control procedures, the resulting integrated network increases in complexity. One dimension of this complexity is the number of diverse decision-makers within the organization whose information requirements can be partially accommodated by an expanded inventory identification coding pattern.

Describe this latter dimension including citing examples of decision makers whose information requirements can be part of this data matching process.

2. From a data processing perspective, there are always choices between re-sorting data coded for one purpose so they can be used in another decision-making setting versus including an expanded coding pattern in the initial data specification structure. These choices are not relevant as the overall computer-based network approaches a TYPE 2 information system level of sophistication. The dominant focus becomes one of increasing the interactive support that the computer-based network provides each decision maker.

In this TYPE 2 information systems setting, an expansion in the number of identification patterns which are built upon an array of decision-oriented, item characteristics permits the remote terminal user to apply selected criteria in a management-by-exception retrieval of those items that are pertinent to the situation. As members of management become experienced in interacting with this type of computer-based capability, the analyst may expect an increase in the frequency of these data retrievals.

Explain the major factors that influence the scope and frequency of these information retrieval requests.

3. The ABC groupings of inventory items are based on the analysis of inventory positions in numerous organizations, and the range of these distributions for each group among these organizations is relatively narrow. For example, the systems analyst will expect approximately 10 percent of the inventory items to be in group A, 25 percent in Group B, and 65 percent in group C.

In those organizations where these expected groupings of inventory items do not occur, explain the types of investigations that you would make. Be specific and indicate the reasons for your inquiries.

4. There is a significant amount of computer-based support in a TYPE 2 information system featuring inventory management and inventory control capabilities. In this setting, why would a systems analyst use *physical* control procedures rather than online *perpetual* control procedures? Explain your position.

5. An analyst at the Bixby Company estimated the annual sales dollar volume for each inventory item based on an examination of sales invoices for selected periods. After entering this information on each perpetual inventory card, these cards were arranged in a long box in the relative order of sales volume. Next, the analyst measured the length of the box. The group of items whose perpetual inventory

cards covered the initial one-fifth of the box's length was classified as Group A. The group of items representing the next 20 percent of the box's length was classified as Group B. The remaining group, consisting of 60 percent of the box's length, was classified as Group C. After each perpetual inventory card contained the appropriate group designation, these cards were re-sorted into their traditional sequence and filed. The card classification system was now used to make production scheduling decisions.

In evaluating this arrangement in the Bixby Company, explain how this process is different from the ABC selective inventory management control system. Are these differences important?

6. In your further study of the Bixby Company (per topic #5), you determine that the company is in a highly competitive industry where the per-unit cost and cost-selling price relation are significantly different for each item in inventory. In this environmental setting, indicate the types of management decisions in which the company's ABC grouping of data will provide useful information. In what types of management decisions might this ABC grouping of data tend to mislead members of management? Be specific.

CASE 12–1.   WALLACE TOOL INDUSTRIES, INC.

James Brock recently became the controller of Wallace Tool Industries, Inc., following the unexpected death of the former controller. Brock has been employed by a certified public accounting firm for the past five years, and he terminated his employment with this firm last month to accept the controller position. The president of Wallace Tool Industries, Inc., stated that Brock's diversified background and experience should bring needed, increased competence for coping with the firm's problems.

The president of the firm discussed with Brock the findings of the recent annual audit. Specifically, the audit manager of the certified public accounting firm performing the audit expressed concern over the increase in size of finished goods inventory. The president said that he had discussed this problem with the previous controller, who had worked a few days in analyzing the inventory position based on a sample. The president said that he was sure Brock's secretary (employed by the former controller) knew where the working papers were for the inventory study.

The president asked Brock to complete the inventory study and to take into consideration the question: "Would a reduction in inventory result in a reduction in customer services and extend delivery dates?"

The Company

Brock was already familiar with the history of the Wallace Tool Industries, Inc.—how the firm had grown from its small two-man shop to its present size of almost $3 million sales in a period of less than 15 years. It seemed to be the consensus of opinion of Wallace's top management that the company had almost reached its "fair share of the market" in terms of new customers, and some of the key officers stated that emphasis should be shifted from the new customer area to trying to expand the volume of services to existing customers. Furthermore, recent changes in the financial market necessitated that accounts receivable and inventory levels be reduced to a minimum.

Wallace Tool Industries, Inc., designs, develops, manufactures, and sells industrial tools. Currently, there are 2,647 different stock items which on December 31, 1974, had a cost of $1,042,137. About 80 percent of the inventory is stored at the home office warehouse in Chicago, with the remainder of the inventory located in five regional warehouses: Boston, Cincinnati, Dallas, Denver, and San Francisco. Annual sales are $2,850,000.

Perpetual inventory records, including the identification of place of storage, are maintained on a manual basis for each finished goods inventory item. Another set of records is manually maintained in production and control to provide the appropriate information, including production scheduling, for manufacturing operations.

Previous Study

Brock's secretary located the former controller's working papers for the inventory study. These papers contained:

1. An analysis of finished goods inventory turnover for stocked tools (Exhibit A).

2. An analysis of finished goods inventory for stocked tools based on the working papers for December 31, 1974, physical inventory count with cost extensions (Exhibit B).

3. A random sample of finished goods inventory with an identification of the number of units on hand at each of the six warehouses

EXHIBIT A
Wallace Tool Industries, Inc.
(finished goods inventory turnover for stocked tools for 1974)

Annual sales for stocked tools	$2,850,000
Cost of sales (40 percent)	× .40
	$1,140,000

Average finished goods inventory	
Beginning	$ 826,715
Ending	1,042,137
	$1,868,852

Average	$ 934,426

$$\frac{\text{Cost of Sales}}{\text{Average Inventory}} = \frac{\$1,140,000}{\$934,426} = 1.22$$

Note: The tool industry surveys indicate that the finished goods inventory turnover ranges from 2.0 to 5.0, with 3.4 being an average of these surveys.

EXHIBIT B
Wallace Tool Industries, Inc.
(an analysis of finished goods inventory for stocked tools for 1974)

Number of Items	Percent of Total	Percent of Total Inventory Value
662	25%	76%
397	15	15
1,588	60	9
2,647	100%	100%

Number of Items	Percent of Total	Unit Cost
318	12%	Over $.50
873	33	$.50-$.25
1,456	55	Under $.25
2,647	100%	

° Exhibit B is based on the working papers for December 31, 1974 physical inventory count with cost extensions.

as of December 31, 1974, and an identification of the number of units sold from each warehouse during the past six months (Exhibit C).

4. An analysis of the above random sample including the cost, sales, gross profit, and carrying cost for finished goods inventory (Exhibit D).

5. A analysis of 697 orders shipped from the home office directly to customers for the period November 1–10, 1974. This exhibit

EXHIBIT C

Wallace Tool Industries, Inc.

(inventory and sales information for a random sample of units)

Number	Cost	Chicago Inventory 12/31/74	Chicago Sales for 6 Mo.	Cincinnati Inventory 12/31/74	Cincinnati Sales for 6 Mo.	Denver Inventory 12/31/74	Denver Sales for 6 Mo.	San Francisco Inventory 12/31/74	San Francisco Sales for 6 Mo.	Dallas Inventory 12/31/74	Dallas Sales for 6 Mo.	Boston Inventory 12/31/74	Boston Sales for 6 Mo.
WTI-													
421610	24¢	120	65	140	—	210	—	—	—	—	—	—	—
622612	72	704	71	—	—	—	—	11	3	70	28	47	—
532621	38	320	460	198	—	40	—	65	—	48	—	54	—
422636	10	1,450	225	114	—	102	—	—	—	—	—	—	—
621621	24	6,520	12	510	62	230	—	104	—	65	—	100	—
846614	46	4,210	1,236	—	310	—	—	—	—	—	—	—	—
231617	46	2,620	4,172	450	24	250	—	120	—	96	23	47	—
423632	8	3,605	—	140	278	52	—	89	—	—	—	75	—
174612	98	1,850	1,630	350	—	131	—	100	—	75	—	—	—
842624	20	2,210	265	503	—	140	545	25	—	48	—	—	—
622642	16	93	62	110	—	195	—	—	—	—	—	—	—
533512	26	578	—	50	—	—	—	800	600	—	—	650	—
422721	30	1,742	78	259	—	—	—	52	—	25	—	55	—
544721	24	1,247	122	30	—	300	110	25	—	75	15	—	—
832738	20	806	218	—	—	—	—	74	25	—	—	—	—

EXHIBIT D

Wallace Tool Industries, Inc.

(analysis of inventory and sales information for a random sample of units)

Number	Cost	Chicago Inventory 12/31/74	Chicago Sales for 6 Mo.	Cincinnati Inventory 12/31/74	Cincinnati Sales for 6 Mo.	Denver Inventory 12/31/74	Denver Sales for 6 Mo.	San Francisco Inventory 12/31/74	San Francisco Sales for 6 Mo.	Dallas Inventory 12/31/74	Dallas Sales for 6 Mo.	Boston Inventory 12/31/74	Boston Sales for 6 Mo.
WTI-													
421610	24¢	120	65	140	—	210	—	—	—	—	—	—	—
		a 28.80 d	d 39.00	a 33.60	—	a 50.40	—						
		b 1.44 e	e 23.40	b 1.68	—	b 2.52	—						
		c 2.88		c 3.36	—	c 5.04	—						
622612	72¢	704	71	—	—	—	—	11	3	70	28	47	—
		a 506.88 d	d 127.80	—	—	—	—	a 7.92 d	d 5.40	a 50.40	d 50.40	a 33.84	—
		b 25.34 e	e 76.68	—	—	—	—	b .40 e	e 3.24	b 2.52	e 30.24	b 1.69	—
		c 50.69		—	—	—	—	c .79		c 5.04		c 3.38	—
532621	38¢	320	460	198	—	40	—	65	—	48	—	54	—
		a 121.60 d	d 437.00	a 75.24	—	a 15.20	—	a 24.70	—	a 18.24	—	a 20.52	—
		b 6.08 e	e 262.20	b 3.76	—	b .76	—	b 1.24	—	b .91	—	b 1.03	—
		c 12.16		c 7.52	—	c 1.52	—	c 2.47	—	c 1.82	—	c 2.05	—
422636	10¢	1,450	225	114	—	102	—	—	—	—	—	—	—
		a 145.00 d	d 56.25	a 11.40	—	a 10.20	—	—	—	—	—	—	—
		b 7.25 e	e 33.75	b .57	—	b .51	—	—	—	—	—	—	—
		c 14.50		c 1.14	—	c 1.02	—	—	—	—	—	—	—
621621	24¢	6,520	12	510	62	230	—	104	—	65	—	100	—
		a 1,564.80 d	d 7.20	a 122.40 d	d 37.20	a 55.20	—	a 24.96	—	a 15.60	—	a 24.00	—
		b 78.24 e	e 4.32	b 6.12 e	e 22.32	b 2.76	—	b 1.25	—	b .78	—	b 1.20	—
		c 156.48		c 12.24		c 5.52	—	c 2.50	—	c 1.56	—	c 2.40	—
846614	46¢	4,210	1,236	—	—	—	—	—	—	—	—	—	—

ID	Rate	Block 1 (a/b/c)	Block 1 (d/e)	Col 2 (a/b/c)	Col 3 (d/e)	Col 4 (a/b/c)	Col 5 (d/e)	Col 6 (a/b/c)	Col 7 (d/e)	Col 8 (a/b/c)	Col 9 (d/e)	Col 10 (a/b/c)
		a 1,936.60 / b 96.83 / c 193.66	d 1,421.40 / e 852.84	—	—	—	—	—	—	—	—	—
231617	46¢	2,620 · a 1,205.20 / b 60.26 / c 120.52	4,172 · d 4,797.80 / e 2,878.68	450 · a 207.00 / b 10.35 / c 20.70	310 · d 356.50 / e 213.90	250 · a 115.00 / b 5.75 / c 11.50	—	120 · a 55.20 / b 2.76 / c 5.52	—	96 · a 44.16 / b 2.21 / c 4.42	23 · d 26.45 / e 15.87	47 · a 21.62 / b 1.08 / c 2.16
423632	8¢	3,605 · a 288.40 / b 14.42 / c 28.84	—	140 · a 11.20 / b .56 / c 1.12	24 · d 4.80 / e 2.88	52 · a 4.16 / b .21 / c .42	—	89 · a 7.12 / b .36 / c .71	—	—	—	75 · a 6.00 / b .30 / c .60
174612	98¢	1,850 · a 1,813.00 / b 90.65 / c 181.30	1,630 · d 3,993.50 / e 2,396.10	350 · a 343.00 / b 17.15 / c 34.30	278 · d 681.10 / e 408.66	131 · a 128.38 / b 6.42 / c 12.84	—	100 · a 98.00 / b 4.90 / c 9.80	—	75 · a 73.50 / b 3.68 / c 7.35	—	—
842624	20¢	2,210 · a 442.00 / b 22.10 / c 44.20	265 · d 132.50 / e 79.50	503 · a 100.60 / b 5.03 / c 10.06	—	140 · a 28.00 / b 1.40 / c 2.80	545 · d 272.50 / e 163.50	25 · a 5.00 / b .25 / c .50	—	48 · a 9.60 / b .48 / c .96	—	—
622642	16¢	93 · a 14.88 / b .74 / c 1.49	62 · d 24.80 / e 14.88	110 · a 17.60 / b .88 / c 1.76	—	195 · a 31.20 / b 1.56 / c 3.12	—	—	—	—	—	—
533512	26¢	578 · a 150.28 / b 7.51 / c 15.03	—	50 · a 13.00 / b .65 / c 1.30	—	—	—	800 · a 208.00 / b 10.40 / c 20.80	600 · d 390.00 / e 234.00	—	—	—
422721	30¢	1,742 · a 522.60 / b 26.13 / c 52.26	78 · d 58.50 / e 35.10	259 · a 77.70 / b 3.89 / c 7.77	—	—	—	52 · a 15.60 / b .78 / c 1.56	—	25 · a 7.50 / b .38 / c .75	—	—

EXHIBIT D *(Continued)*

Number	Cost	Chicago Inventory 12/31/74	Chicago Sales for 6 Mo.	Cincinnati Inventory 12/31/74	Cincinnati Sales for 6 Mo.	Denver Inventory 12/31/74	Denver Sales for 6 Mo.	San Francisco Inventory 12/31/74	San Francisco Sales for 6 Mo.	Dallas Inventory 12/31/74	Dallas Sales for 6 Mo.	Boston Inventory 12/31/74	Boston Sales for 6 Mo.
544721	24¢	1,247 a 299.28 b 14.96 c 29.93	122 d 73.20 e 43.92	30 a 7.20 b .36 c .72	—	300 a 72.00 b 3.60 c 7.20	110 d 66.00 e 39.60	25 a 6.00 b .30 c .60	—	75 a 18.00 b .90 c 1.80	15 d 9.00 e 5.40	—	—
832738	20¢	806 a 161.20 b 8.06 c 16.12	218 d 109.00 e 65.40	—	—	—	—	74 a 14.80 b .74 c 1.48	25 d 12.50 e 7.50	—	—	—	—

Symbol *a* represents the cost of inventory (unit cost × number of units on hand).

Symbol *b* is an estimate of the carrying cost of inventory based on an estimated annual cost of 10 percent of cost (since this information is for six months, 5 percent of cost is used).

Symbol *c* is also an estimate of the carrying cost of inventory based on an estimated annual cost of 20 percent.

Symbol *d* represents sales (sales price × number of units sold) which was based on the assumption that cost of stocked tools was 40 percent of selling price.

Symbol *e* is the gross profit on sales.

Recap of Exhibit D

	Total Inventory Cost of Sample	Total Sales of Sample for 6 Mo.	Gross Profit on Sales of Sample for 6 Mo.	6-Mo. Carrying Cost of Inventory Based on Annual Estimate of Cost	
				10%	20%
Chicago	$ 9,200.52	$11,277.95	$6,766.77	$460.01	$ 920.06
Cincinnati . . .	1,019.94	1,079.60	647.76	51.00	101.99
Denver	509.74	338.50	203.10	25.49	50.98
San Francisco . .	467.30	407.90	244.74	23.38	46.73
Dallas	237.00	85.85	51.51	11.86	23.70
Boston	291.48	–	–	14.58	29.14
	$11,725.98	$13,189.80	$7,913.88	$586.32	$1,172.60

compares the cumulative percent of the number of items promised for delivery within varying number of days with the cumulative percent of deliveries on time (Exhibit E).

EXHIBIT E
Wallace Tool Industries, Inc.
(customer service—promise dates)

Number of Days from Order Day That Shipping Date Is Promised	Cumulative Percent of Orders Promised for Shipment within Specified Days	Cumulative Percent of Orders Shipped on Time
1	30	19
2	36	24
3	55	36
4	60	40
5	62	41
6	64	42
7	69	46
8	72	48
9	74	49
10	80	54
11	82	55
12	84	56
13	86	57
14	100	69

Exhibit E is based on an analysis of 697 orders shipped from the home office directly to customers for the period November 1–10, 1974; at Wallace Tool Industries, the salesperson has the authority of specifying the shipping date on an order.

6. An analysis of the above orders indicating the number of days elapsing between the promised delivery date and the actual delivery date (Exhibit F).

EXHIBIT F

Wallace Tool Industries, Inc.

(customer service—lateness of orders)

Number of Days after Promised Shipping Time	Cumulative Percent of Orders Shipped within Specified Days from Promised Time
0	69
1	75
2	82
3	85
4	88
5	90
6	92
7	94
8	95
9	96
10	97
11	98
12	99
Over 12	100

Exhibit F is based on an analysis of 697 orders shipped from the home office directly to customers for the period November 1–10, 1974.

EXHIBIT G

Wallace Tool Industries, Inc.

(customer service—lead-time analysis)

Lead Time—Days from Order Date to Shipment Date	Cumulative Percent of Total Orders That Were Shipped within Specified Days from Order Day
1	28
2	33
3	51
4	58
5	60
6	62
7	67
8	70
9	73
10	78
11	80
12	83
13	85
14	95
Over 14	100

Exhibit G is based on an analysis of 697 orders shipped from the home office directly to customers for the period November 1–10, 1974; at Wallace Tool Industries, the salesperson has the authority of specifying the shipping date on an order. The manager of the production department has the responsibility of determining when shipments from the home office warehouse will occur.

7. An indication of the lead time on the above orders, in other words, the actual number of days from order day to delivery date (Exhibit G).

Brock's Insights

Organizationally, there are five departments at the Wallace Tool Industries, Inc.: administration department, inventory control department, production department, sales department, and research and development department. However, from Brock's inquiries during the past month and from his observations, he was aware that the separation by department was more "in name" than "in fact." From his analysis, he felt that the organization structure was extremely informal with most of the top members of management having been employed by the firm for at least 10 years. In other words, management had collectively participated in most of the dynamic growth that Wallace Tool Industries, Inc., had experienced during its 15-year history.

REQUIRED:

1. Analyze, compare, and interpret the exhibits and the descriptive material presented in this case.
2. Prepare a concise report highlighting your findings from the previous step with *specific* recommendations regarding your approach to the solution of the problem confronting Brock.

MARKETING INFORMATION SYSTEMS

CHAPTER 13

Marketing Management Information Systems

PART III presented the general model of a TYPE 2 information system and described the major features of the two most dominant networks so classified: inventory management information systems and inventory control information systems. The unique sensory and monitoring capabilities of the coordination phase in these partially open networks were emphasized. Alternative uses of economic data for management planning, management control, and technical control were also examined.

The focus is shifted in Part IV to marketing management information systems in which the underlying network is even more multidimensional and complex than that of a TYPE 2 information system. As previously indicated, this more sophisticated level of integration within the organization and online interaction with the environment is not necessarily a reasonable goal for organizations possessing computer-based networks, even for those organizations with a TYPE 2 information system. The organization's environmental setting must contain economic opportunities which require the multitime frames, multidata flows, alternate levels of aggregation, and multigeographical locations of remote terminal users who may have key interactive roles within the computer-based network. Unless there are major changes in the exogenous factors comprising the external environment, we do not expect a significant increase in the annual rate at which organizations are implementing marketing management information systems.

THE GENERAL MODEL

The third of the five discrete models of advanced computer-based networks is a marketing management information system. The general model for this overall level of advancement is an *open* system encompassing certain types of major information flows within an organization and between an organization and its environment. While many organizations in complex settings may have a series of operating systems with varying time cycles and with dissimilar data flows, the general model for a marketing management information system includes within a single, complex network all of this diversity and these various multidimensions.

The information within the marketing management information system may be expressed by four measurement methods: (*a*) complete enumeration, (*b*) sample, (*c*) management by exception based on complete enumeration, and (*d*) management by exception based on sample. From another standpoint, the individual information flows within this general model contain a wide variety of time dimensions. At one extreme, information may be required continuously, as it is happening on a real-time basis (or instantaneously, as is the case in airline reservations and in selected commercial banking operations). At the other extreme, information may be required periodically, such as monthly statistical data on the Consumer Price Index, quarterly forecasts on general economic conditions, or annual statistical data on the gross national product. Information required periodically also includes weekly, daily, hourly, and other time frames. For example, when a stereo record is released by a commercial recording studio, the response by the general public to the record in selected localities during the first twenty-four hours after the record has been released is used to make the decision on how many copies will be initially cut and distributed.

The multidimensions of this general model are not limited to the selection of measurement methods applied to the information and to the specification of time dimensions for various data flows. In addition to these two facets, there are at least four other levels of reference for drawing distinctions about the general model for a marketing management information system. These other dimensions are (*a*) sources of information, (*b*) types of information, (*c*) location of the decision maker requiring such information, and (*d*) use of the information by the decision maker.

The above six levels of reference for the general model do not really get at the heart of the issue of complexity. The implicit role of management in this general model is one of conflict; on the one hand, members of management are controlling operations, monitoring performance, revising plans and short-term objectives, and planning for the next periods based on evaluations of the organization's experience; on the other hand, members of management are trying to change the organization's external environment. These latter efforts may be the result of advertising, promotional, developmental, or other management by change endeavors.

Several large organizations are in the process of planning, designing, and implementing a multidimensional, open system that will approach the composite ranking of a marketing management information system. Where we find such advanced systems being designed, there is usually a series of information systems studies which include an upgrading of the operations management information system, the sales analysis operating system, the marketing media and advertising operating system, and the cost and performance reporting system. These latter identified systems are only some of the networks that are typically used to support a large-scale, marketing management information system.

In the complex, multidimensional environment of a marketing management information system, the nature of the administrative process cannot be separated into (*a*) the editing and screening phase, (*b*) the planning phase, (*c*) the control phase, and (*d*) the coordination phase as described for the TYPE 2 information system. In addition to these four phases, the intensity of online interaction with remote terminal users and the diversity of inquiries requires the establishment of a monitoring and inquiring phase. The integration of the diverse time cycles, data flows, types of data, levels of aggregation, geographical location of remote terminal users, and measurement methods requires a significant upgrading of the features within the control phase. The data processing, data assignment, sorting, and information retrieval capabilities associated with both the monitoring and inquiring phase and the upgraded control phase require the establishment of a systems processing phase.

In this type of setting, a new level of management is formally recognized in the general model of an information system. "Executive management" is a term used to refer to policy makers, and the policy makers are individuals who can specify the parameters in a decision model. Individuals who can specify the variables within these models are called "decision makers." Thus far in our flowcharts of information networks, we have used the symbol of a diamond to represent the decision-making process by management, and we have indicated that this group can specify changes in parameters and variables.

In the marketing management information system's control phase, management personnel immediately below the decision-making level serve as an integral part of each modified operating system. Technically, we can think of management personnel at this organizational level as *"planners,"* for they are able to select among alternatives that are available within the guidelines described by the parameters and variables. These planners are represented in our generalized model by the symbol for manual operations that is labeled *"Human" Activities.*

These planners provide the necessary flexibility in the overall structure so that unique time cycles and unique data flows can be easily handled by the system. The manual operations performed by these individuals provide the mechanism for permitting multidata flows and multitime cycles within a single, overall network.

The general model for a marketing management information system is based on an evolutionary process that encompasses within the single network all the features of a TYPE 1 information system and a TYPE 2 information system. The management control aspects of a responsibility accounting system or a profitability accounting system are usually an essential element within a more sophisticated network. As previously stated, after these management control models are fully implemented, then members of management begin to have time for *planning.* Moreover, an environment is established in which there is the capability of monitoring performance and implementing the results of the planning activities.

A prerequisite of an environment that requires the intensity of online interactions represented by a marketing management information system is the monitoring and interface features of the coordination phase in a TYPE 2 information system. While the TYPE 2 network monitors selected changes in variables within a limited set, the marketing management information system has an expanded set of sensory requirements. In addition to the online monitoring of change in selected variables, various remote terminal users which are supported by this advanced computer-based network have different types of information requirements. levels of aggregation, and response intervals. Many of the remote terminal users may have personalized operating systems that assist them in carrying out their functions, and these users serve as "human" connectors of these operating systems with the marketing management information system. The monitoring and inquiring phase of this general model must contain an array of software, computer programs, and reporting routines to support these diverse, interactive requirements.

TYPE 3 INFORMATION SYSTEM

Figure 13.1 presents a generalized model of a TYPE 3 information system containing six phases— (*a*) editing and screening phase, (*b*) planning phase, (*c*) control phase, (*d*) coordination phase, (*e*) monitoring and inquiring phase, and (*f*) systems processing phase. The editing and screening phase, planning phase, and coordination phase have the identical features in this generalized model as those incorporated in the TYPE 2 information system; therefore, our attention is focused on the other three phases.

Control Phase

Each of the operating systems within a TYPE 3 information system may have a unique time cycle and a unique data flow arrangement. The latter arrangement is further complicated by varying geographical locations of major remote terminal users, data sources, measurement methods, levels of aggregation, and types of information.

The integration of these multitime cycles, multidata flows, and complex arrangements into a common network requires considerable professional experience in detailed coordination and design. Symbols A26, A31, and A36 in Figure 13.1 are labeled *"human" activities,* and, as previously explained, these human processing symbols in the control phase indicate the location of *planners,* who provide both the flexibility for coping with diverse situations and the capability for interfacing multidimensions.

The planners in the control phase are among the principal users of

FIGURE 13.1
A Generalized Model of a TYPE 3 Information System

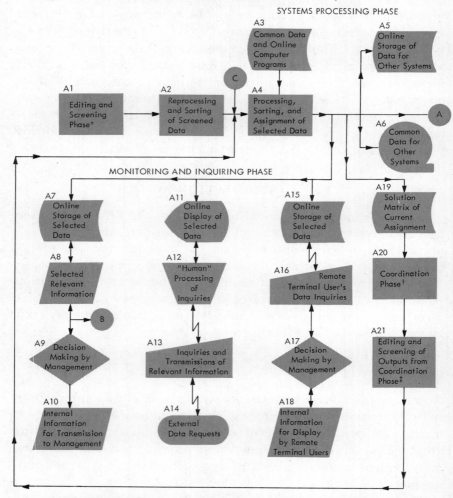

° The editing and screening phase is depicted by symbols A1 to A10 in Figure 7.1.
† The coordination phase is depicted by symbols A2 to A5 and A8 to A14 in Figure 10.1.
‡ The editing and screening of outputs from the coordination phase is depicted by symbols A6 to A7 in Figure 10.1.

the online, interactive capabilities of the monitoring and inquiring phase. In Figure 13.1 we see a connecting link (B) from symbol A8 ("selected relevant information") to symbols A26, A31, and A36, which formally presents this interactive relationship between plan-

FIGURE 13.1 (*Continued*)

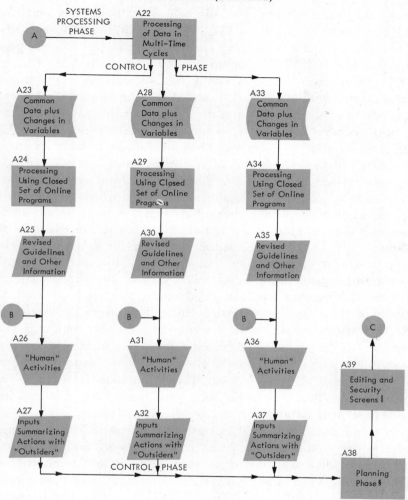

§ The planning phase is depicted by symbols A12 to A16 in Figure 7.1 and by symbols A28 to A30 in Figure 10.1.

|| The editing and security screens are represented by symbols A31 and A32 in Figure 10.1.

ners and the monitoring and inquiring capabilities of the computer-based network. Other dimensions of this link are examined subsequently in the discussion of the monitoring and inquiring phase.

The role of planners in the control phase can be viewed from an alternative perspective. These manual activities (symbols A26, A31, and A36) which provide the mechanism for permitting multidata flows and multitime cycles within one overall network and these input capabilities (symbols A27, A32, and A37) can be viewed as extensions of regular operating systems. That is, the typical operating system contains an input unit (such as symbols A23, A28, and A33), a processing unit (symbols A24, A29, and A34), and an output unit (symbols A25, A30, and A35). These extended operating systems as presented in Figure 13.1 contain two additional units.

In the context of this flowchart, each planner (symbols A26, A31, and A36) receives guidelines and other information from an output unit (symbols A25, A30, and A35) within that planner's expanded operating system. The information provided by these reports gives the planner a modified set of alternatives from which to select. The planner's response to these alternatives typically includes an interaction with the organization's external environment. For example, the planner's response or revised actions may be in the form of new prices for products, new distribution arrangements, "special deals" for the short-term, adjusted advertising programs, and so forth.

After the planner has responded to the revised guidelines, the results of these human activities (including interactions with the external environment) must be entered into the computer-based network so members of management can be informed of these accomplishments. In Figure 13.1 these input notations (symbols A27, A32, and A37) are labeled "inputs summarizing actions with 'outsiders.'" These actions may be in the form of sales orders, advertising agreements, transfer of salespeople, and so forth.

In summary, the manual operations performed by the planners serve as the vital connecting link in our network and provide the mechanism for a high degree of interaction with the external environment. If it were not for this conceptual arrangement, our model could not handle the multidimensions of a TYPE 3 information system—specifically, the multidata flows and multitime cycles encompassed within one structure.

Another perspective for examining the control phase is to focus on the three operating systems within a TYPE 3 information system. The operating system in Figure 13.1 represented by symbols A23 to A27 might consist of a one-hour time cycle; the operating system represented by symbols A28 to A32 might consist of a one-day time cycle; and the operating system represented by symbols A33 to A37 might consist of a one-week time cycle. The one-day time cycle, in this illustrative case, will have a multiple set of data flows fully encompassed within this time cycle from the first operating system (either eight, sixteen, or twenty-four data flows depending on the number of shifts represented by a one-day period). Continuing with this case, the third operating system will complete one time cycle in the same period that seven time cycles are completed for the second operating system.

The varying time cycles is one of the simpler features of the multidimensions incorporated within a TYPE 3 information system. For instance, the operating system represented by symbols A23 to A27 might be a summary network of all the manufacturing operations and integrated distribution activities that are interfaced, online with the coordination phase (this TYPE 3 information system may have a complete TYPE 2 information system for integrated operations management and distribution which is encompassed within this network). The other two operating systems (symbols A28 to A32 and A33 to A37) might depict, respectively, the sales management activities and the marketing program efforts.

Monitoring and Inquiring Phase

The online interaction between users and the computer-based system is significantly strengthened by the software, retrieval programs, processing capabilities, and inquiry facilities contained within this monitoring and inquiring phase. These overall capabilities permit an intensity of online interaction with remote terminal users beyond that available in a TYPE 2 information system.

Advancements in telephone and communication equipment have significantly extended the geographical location of remote terminal users who are adequately serviced by an organization's monitoring and inquiring phase. In addition to the policy-making and decision-making activities, individuals throughout the organization who are labeled as "planners" (symbols A26, A31, and A36 in Figure 13.1) are also serviced by this phase. External to the organization, major customers, clients, or constituents may be given special instructions so they can directly access this monitoring and inquiring phase. Telephone inquiries from other external parties who do not have direct access to the capability are handled by the *"human" processing of inquiries* (symbol A12). As the latter transmissions are received (symbol A13) over the communication equipment, the "human activities" (symbol A12) serves as the connector between the external data request (symbol A14) and the internal network for responding to information retrieval request (symbol A11).

The monitoring and inquiring phase contains two other integrated sets of operations (symbols A7 to A10 and A15 to A18): online storage, input and output, decision making, and interactive capabilities with other internal networks, data bases, and users. The intensity of online interactions and diversity of activities supported by these computer-based capabilities are indicated by the following types of uses:

a.   Status of a production order.
b.   Status of a sales order (integrated manufacturing and distribution).
c.   Scheduling of product distribution.
d.   Profitability report by salesperson, by territory and by customer.
e.   Marketing report by product.
f.   Computer-support assistance in selecting media for marketing program.
g.   Briefing to management on new products.
h.   Briefing to management on national economic developments.
i.   Briefing to management on major environmental issues.
j.   Briefing to decision makers and planners on status of pending legal, financial, and other issues pertaining to organization.

As suggested by the above descriptions, typically, in this phase policy makers, decision makers, planners, and other remote terminal users are receiving periodic information rather than continuous information.

As previously discussed and specified by the connecting line from symbol A8 to symbols A26, A31, and A36, the planners in the control phase are among the principal users of the online, interactive capabilities of the monitoring and inquiring phase. This line also represents those cases where data from the common data banks are merged with data created within the given operating network, and these combined data are incorporated in the control and planning reports. For example, a planner with product and territory responsibility might desire a salesperson's profitability report, a salesperson's performance report (which includes a comparative report of budget versus actual sales volume by major customers), and the sales potential report for the area where salesperson is assigned.

Systems Processing Phase

A series of processing, sorting, reprocessing, and assignment operations which provide the necessary computer support for a TYPE 3 information system is called the "systems processing phase." These sophisticated computer operations serve as the backbone for the monitoring and inquiring phase and the control phase, and they are located at the intersection of (a) the editing and screening phase, (b) control phase, (c) monitoring and inquiring phase, and (d) planning phase. There are data flows, of course, from the systems processing phase to the coordination phase; however, most of the complex data issues in the systems processing phase do not pertain to the coordination phase.

In Figure 13.1, symbols A2 to A4 and A22 depict this series of processing, sorting, reprocessing, and assignment operations which service the diverse data requirements of policy makers, decision makers, and planners throughout the organization. The information requirements for these diverse members of management may not even be in the same time frame, much less at the same precise moment that these data flow through the channel. Therefore, a typical feature of the systems processing phase is for these common data to be stored in a series of banks, files, and disks, and some of these storage locations are represented in this flowchart by symbols A5, A6, A7, A11, A15, A23, A28, and A33. The same set of data may be concurrently stored in more than one location, depending on the overall information requirements for these data.

There is a high degree of similarity in how the systems processing phase has been employed in various organizations. After the editing and screening phase has been fully implemented, then attention is focused on the reprocessing, sorting, and assignment of screened data. Frequently, the latter operations are initially applied to the handling of all financial accounting and cost accounting activities. These sets of transactions will include order entry, invoicing, shipment, accounts receivable, purchase order, receiving reports, issue slips, accounts payable, selling expenses, administrative expenses, general expenses, and others.

While the arrows in Figure 13.1 depict the movement of filtered data from the editing and screening phase (symbol A1) to the systems processing phase (symbols A2 to A6 and A22), there are periodic improvements and refinements in the filtering operations based on insights gained from processing, sorting, reprocessing and assignment of screened data. The reliability and proper coding of inputs become extremely crucial factors in this setting where members of management in two or more departments may be using common data. Erroneously coded data in these cases may trigger a series of responses in different information subsystems, and such occurrences can have severe economic consequences.

This close relationship between the editing and screening phase and the systems processing phase can be examined from an economic perspective. Sophisticated filtering routines were included in the editing and screening phase for a TYPE 1 information system. As multidimensional advancements occur in the network using these online, filtered data, further refinements in such screening routines can be economically justified. Because of these refinements and improvements, there is a high *quality* of data structure and data specification incorporated in each of the advanced computer-based networks, such as a TYPE 3 information system.

In summary, the systems processing phase in a TYPE 3 information system provides the essential processing, sorting, reprocessing, and assignment operations for filtered data in a controlled setting so the other features of a TYPE 3 network can function at a level of high quality. The attainment of such a state is not a random occurrence, but is the result of a significant financial investment in systems analyses over an extended period of time as refinements and advancements occur in the computer-based network.

THE EIGHT COMMON DIMENSIONS

An examination of the eight dimensions of the administrative process and the organizational arrangements encompassed in a TYPE 3 information system assists the reader in comparing this general model with other discrete levels of advancement. First, the models of the administrative process in a TYPE 3 information system include six phases: (*a*) editing and screening phase, (*b*) planning phase, (*c*) control phase, (*d*) coordination phase, (*e*) monitoring and inquiring phase, and (*f*) systems processing phase. In this network, there is an increased effort on the part of members of management to follow a management-by-systems approach to monitoring of performance, comparing of actual with planned performance, and taking corrective action on an exception basis. There is also an increased intensity of monitoring and coordinating activities which may cross departmental lines, functional areas, and geographical locations. The planning and coordination phases in the TYPE 2 information system emphasized interactions and online monitoring of selected segments of the external environment; this focus on the external environment is expanded in the TYPE 3 information system with formal recognition of these administrative activities in both the control phase and the monitoring and inquiring phase. The computer capabilities incorporated within the systems processing phase permit these multidimensional, quality data flows to occur in this sophisticated setting.

Second, the organizational structure of an agency, association, company, or institution possessing a TYPE 3 information system is a matrix arrangement for those decision makers associated with the coordination phase and, at least, for the planners in the control phase. These planners (who operate within the guidelines specified by the parameters of policy makers and the variables of decision makers) represent a third level of management and frequently possess dual responsibilities related to environmental change factors. As increases occur in the number of dual responsibilities for a given member of management, there is a gradual introduction of selected committees into this complex set of organizational arrangements. The traditional organizational structure is primarily used for technical control and management control purposes.

Third, three levels of management—policy makers, decision makers, and planners—from throughout the organization may be associated with a TYPE 3 information system. Many members of management are only directly related to the monitoring and inquiring phase where they receive through remote terminal facilities, computer-based support, including information, analyses, and exception reports of monitored activities. Members of management directly associated with the coordination phase and the planning phase in a TYPE 3 information system will consist of at least two vice-president level personnel from different organizational units. A frequent arrangement for the TYPE 3 network is to have both the vice president of marketing and the vice president of manufacturing directly associated with the system; any or all of the following personnel may also be directly associated with the network: vice president of planning, vice president of distribution, and group vice president of customer services.

Fourth, the nature of the activity supported by a TYPE 3 information system includes all major information flows—both vertical and horizontal within the organization that are directly associated with the primary decision makers. The contents of the activity related to the monitoring and inquiring phase may include any information flow within the organization in any area.

Fifth, the degree of online interaction between remote terminal users and the computer-based system is a relevant factor for differentiating a TYPE 2 system from a TYPE 3 information system. The intensity of this interaction, as previously indicated, is one of the reasons for establishing the monitoring and inquiring phase, and the diverse set of users of these online, interactive capabilities was specified in the above discussion of the control phase. In addition to the monitoring and inquiring phase, the three types of interactive areas explained in the TYPE 2 network—editing and screening area, coordination area, and partial changes within the control area—are also present in the TYPE 3 information system. The systems processing phase provides the quality data flows, reporting and retrieval capabilities, and prompt response times for the online, interactive features of this fifth dimension.

Sixth, the concept of time cycle is implemented differently in a TYPE 3 information system than that in a TYPE 2 network. A prerequisite of a TYPE 3 network is the integration of multitime cycles within a common control phase, and the manual interface activities of planners are methods of interrelating these multiple time periods. The overall time period of the control phase (using the longest time cycle) tends to be at least five days, and frequently is seven to ten days. Other aspects of these multitime cycles were discussed previously in the explanation of the control phase.

Seventh, an organization with a TYPE 3 information system usually has a series of common data bases, activity programs, functional programs, and operating systems which are interfaced with the TYPE 3 network, and this series significantly expands the computer-based support provided to remote terminal users. These interfaced, data-supporting capabilities may include sales management, media selection, advertising effectiveness, credit management, personnel administration, economic modeling, and financial management. In addition to these interfaced, computer-based services, the TYPE 3 information system frequently encompasses within this advanced network responsibility accounting system, profitability accounting system, inventory management information system, and inventory control information system; in other words, subsystems within the TYPE 3 network can be labeled TYPE 1 information system and TYPE 2 information system.

Eighth, the data structure in a TYPE 3 information system is multidimensional. The data structure issues of currency and timeliness have been expanded by the intensity of the concern with the external environment, including sophisticated sensory and monitoring capabilities. Alternative measurement methods, varying types of data, and differing levels of aggregation have further increased the complexity of the data structure in this multidimensional setting. Because of this complexity, the systems processing phase in a TYPE 3 information system contains sophisticated computer programs for indexing, sorting, classifying, and retrieving information. Otherwise, the richness of these multidimensional data files will not be available to the various remote terminal users affiliated with this advanced network.

APPLICATION OF THE INFORMATION SYSTEMS APPROACH

The systems analyst attempts to specify the information requirements, to determine the data sources, and to match the information requirements with the appropriate data sources by employing some of the current management science tools and techniques. In applying this approach, the systems analyst encounters numerous problems because of the inherent nature of the multidimensional marketing management information system. Some of these problems are examined in the following discussion.

Information Requirements

Specifying the information requirements is the last step in a three-step sequence. The first step is to understand the administrative process for the organization under study. This requires a familiarization with the unique industry characteristics and practices as well as an appreciation of the general environment in which the organization is located. This includes a general insight into how the organization reacts to this environment.

In the second step, the systems analyst deepens her or his understanding of the administrative process in this particular segment of the organization's operations which has been selected for detailed study. This second step is completed when the systems analyst is able to determine that segment's exact missions (goals or objectives). In the case of marketing activities, it is difficult to accomplish this second step because of the complexity of the situation.

Although this task can be accomplished if the systems analyst uses "general statements," the results may not be precise for completely representing the complex organizational setting by mathematical statements. In this situation, simplifying assumptions are made in order to develop a mathematical model of a "reasonable" size.

For example, do members of executive management view themselves as limited by the environment, able only to *react* (as quickly as possible) to changes in the environment? Or, do they see themselves as capable of modifying the present environment through the stimulation of demand for the organization's products, goods, and services? To what extent do managements' perspectives change between points in time? The systems analyst must make some assumptions in order to cope with this complex situation in order to proceed to the third step—specifying the exact information requirements that are needed for achieving the determined missions.

Members of management (policy makers, decision makers, and planners) may be unwilling to accept forecasted demand for each product, good, or service as a basis for scheduling hour-to-hour, day-to-day, or week-to-week production and operation activities. Managements' views on *reacting rather than planning* are based to a large extent on their individual familiarization with the data within the network. A program for improving the quality of statistical data as presented in Chapter 11 represents one approach for coping with this situation, which must be supplemented by orientation and educational efforts.

Today, most of the computerized marketing information networks are really just integrated sales analysis, inventory control, and production control information systems where the computer equipment and communication facilities are used for quick *reaction* to hour-to-hour, day-to-day, or week-to-week changes in inventory stock or estimated sales. There are very few computer-based marketing networks in which forecasted inventory and sales data at a high level of statistical confidence are used in online, programmed decision environments. But, as organizations pursue a program for improving the quality of statistical data within such networks, an increased number of organizations will achieve this sophisticated level of handling the administrative process.

Within a TYPE 3 information system, the information requirements can be classified by several factors other than environmental versus internal orientation. These other dimensions include time cycle, level of aggregation, currency of data, types of data, and measurement methods.

Data Sources

Arbitrarily, we can group the data sources for marketing management information systems into three categories. First, from the cost accounting and financial accounting records, the systems analyst obtains the following types of information: marginal cost, contribution to margin, and contribution from each salesperson or each territory. Second, from the sales invoices, accounts receivable file, and the financial accounting records, the systems analyst obtains information on customer characteristics. Third, there are many special sources of information that can be used in satisfying information requirements of marketing activities.

These special sources include market surveys, market research, research and development activities, and secondary sources. The published input-output analysis for the United States has been widely used for external criteria to evaluate a given business organization's sales potential for a group of products. Industry reports, governmental reports and studies, private research studies, and the professional literature are some of the major groupings of secondary sources which are frequently used as data sources for marketing management information systems.

Matching Process

Frequently, the data that are needed by decision makers and planners in marketing-related activities are available in the accounting records and accounting documents. However, all of these data may not be readily available for retrieval. In other cases, these data are accumulated according to a classification system which is different from what is needed for marketing decisions. The editing and screening phase combined with the systems processing phase in a TYPE 3 information system contain the appropriate filtering, processing, sorting, reprocessing, and assignment capabilities for handling all of these matching requirements. While the computer capabilities are there, the systems analyst must plan for each of the multi-assignments of common data in the various files and tapes.

Transmission and Coding Patterns

Recent developments in communication equipment have permitted many organizations' decentralized operations to be integrated into a single network. Production facilities, warehouse and storage facilities, and regional marketing offices are integrated into a single management information system.

In such situations, the systems analyst is primarily concerned with the determination of the variable information that must be transmitted. For example, a large group of independent grocery stores throughout the state of Illinois uses a common coding pattern for transmitting purchase orders to a large, central wholesaler. this wholesale grocery company makes deliveries the following morning for all orders received daily from grocery stores located as far as 250 miles away.

A six-digit identification code has been established for each stock item in the wholesale grocer's inventory. A two-digit identification code has been assigned to each of the independent grocery stores. The remaining 2 digits in a 10-digit group of information are used for specifying the quantities requested by the identified independent grocery store. Thus, each 10-digit group of information represents a complete purchase order.

In another case, a large, diversified corporation has its major computer facilities in Chicago. Daily, each of the subsidiary corporations will transmit to Chicago the variable data on each sales invoice, including the identification of the customer's name. A predetermined coding pattern is used for transmitting this information in the minimum amount of digits. The major computer facilities in Chicago contain programs that accumulate and process information for all requirements throughout the diversified corporation and its subsidiaries (for example, the perpetual inventory records and accounts receivable files for each of the subsidiary corporations are centrally maintained in the Chicago computer facilities) .

In summary, there are many major information requirements of decision makers in marketing-related activities that the systems analyst can satisfy by the establishment of the appropriate predetermined coding pattern. From another perspective, whenever inventory identification codes, customer identification codes, cost accounting identification codes, and financial accounting identification codes are being designed or revised, the systems analyst should give special consideration to the marketing information possibilities of each of these codes.

SUMMARY

The marketing management information system is a complex, multidimensional network of computer-based data flows that permits an organization to interact with its dynamic environment. The organization's internal response to the external environment usually includes activities in two or more functions, departments, organizational levels, and geographical locations.

The processing, sorting, reprocessing, and assignment of screened data in the systems processing phase provided the required computer capabilities for supporting the intensity of the online interactive demands in the monitoring and inquiring phase and the complexity of the multidimensional data flows in the control phase. Implicit within this level of online processing and assignment operations is a significant financial investment in systems analyses with the participation by members of management over an extended period of time.

TOPICS FOR CLASS DISCUSSION

1. A TYPE 3 information system contains multidata flows and multitime cycles within a single integrated network. Explain from a conceptual standpoint how these multidimensions can be accommodated in the structure of a TYPE 3 system.

2. There are six phases in the generalized model of a TYPE 3 information system—editing and screening phase, systems processing phase, monitoring and inquiring phase, coordination phase, planning phase, and control phase. Explain the interfaces and interrelations between and among these phases.

3. A TYPE 2 information system contained online interaction between the users of the network and the computer-based system at three places, and in a TYPE 3 information system there is an increase in the number of places and in the intensity of the online interaction. Explain the nature of this online interaction in a TYPE 3 information system and indicate the locations of these activities.

4. Differentiate between policy makers, decision makers, and planners.

5. The generalized model of a TYPE 3 information system contained a connecting line between monitoring and inquiring phase's input and output capabilities and the planners in the control phase. Explain the purpose of this construct.

6. Assume that the Martz Corporation has $150,000,000 in annual sales from the manufacture and distribution of consumer goods in three major product areas. If a team of systems analysts appropriately designed and implemented a TYPE 3 information system over a twenty-month period, what would you expect to be the nature of the environment in which Martz Corporation is located? Briefly describe what you would expect the management and administrative processes of this company to be like.

7. Differentiate between the following: (*a*) responsibility accounting system, (*b*) profitability accounting system, (*c*) inventory control information system, and (*d*) marketing management information system.

8. From the standpoint of the business organizations's internal marketing information network, explain the importance of establishing a coding pattern for each of the following items: (*a*) inventory identification codes, (*b*) customer identification codes, (*c*) cost accounting identification codes, and (*d*) financial accounting identification codes.

CASE 13–1. BEDFORD PUBLISHING COMPANY

A CODING PATTERN EXERCISE

The Bedford Publishing Company, a division of a large, diversified corporation, is a major publisher and distributor of books for the adult education market. Many of these basic books are "programmed texts" in mathematics, statistics, quantitative methods, critical path method, data processing, computer programming, English, and bookkeeping. A second group of Bedford books are regular adult education books for the general market and include such topics as American history, English literature, business letter writing, principles of speech, composition, introduction to sociology, introduction to economics, introduction to psychology, introduction to anthropology, and the classics in philosophy and religion. The third group of Bedford books are designed for the trade market at the supervisor level, and these books are applied descriptions with a "how to do it" slant.

Currently, the assistant controller is coordinating the establishment of a marketing information system which would encompass the sales analysis and accounts receivable activities. This marketing information system will be programmed and integrated with other computer programs in the Bedford Publishing Company's large-scale computer system.

The current focal point of the assistant controller's work is on the development of a coding pattern for customer identification numbers. Based on the number of customers and the forecasted growth pattern by customer category, the assistant controller determines that an 11-digit identification code will be required.

Bedford's marketing manager would like to direct sales and marketing efforts by selective cities throughout the United States. Therefore, the assistant controller has agreed to assign the first five digits in the 11-digit customer account designation number of the zip code for the state and city.

Thus, the assistant controller is wondering how to assign customer identification numbers within each city using the remaining six digits in the overall 11-digit code. Finally, the assistant controller begins the long process of assigning the six-digit identification number to each customer. Numbers are arbitrarily assigned on a sequential basis.

The management consulting firm with which you are associated is asked to review the proposed marketing information network at the Bedford Publishing Company. You are assigned to this job.

You quickly determine that there are three major groups of customers within each city: (*a*) educational institutions and public libraries, (*b*) governmental agencies and industrial companies (including both training programs and private libraries), and (*c*) individuals.

You also determine that although there are 999,999 digits available within each zip code specification for customer designation purposes, the total number of customers in a given zip code area is less 90,000. Thus, the six digits contain sufficient space for expansion, which will be especially applicable for individual customers.

REQUIRED:

1. Evaluate the present proposed marketing information network.
2. Design an 11-digit customer identification code for the Bedford Publishing Company. (Suggestion: review secondary sources of information on the publishing industry for purposes of obtaining a better understanding of how a typical publishing company does business.)

CASE 13–2.   WICKER MANUFACTURING COMPANY

A CODING PATTERN EXERCISE

The systems analyst has completed the first part of a study, including (a) studying the administrative process and the environment of the organization in question and (b) specifying the information requirements for the major decision activities. At the Wicker Manufacturing Company, the analyst believes that the financial accounting, cost accounting, and statistical information now being accumulated will be adequate data sources for all information requirements. The analyst wants to establish a coding pattern to assist in matching data sources with information requirements. While pursuing this task, the systems analyst reviews the notes of the company and its operations.

The Company

The Wicker Manufacturing Company is a producer and distributor of industrial supplies and consumer goods, with a total annual sales volume of $22,000,000. Organizationally, the company has three major product lines, with a product marketing manager being assigned to each line. The company has extensive marketing activities throughout North America and has a sales force of 240 people.

The business environment is characterized by highly fluctuating prices. Marketing management does not have sufficient information with which to set short-term prices. Therefore, management has delegated this responsibility to the salesperson. Each salesperson has the authority of negotiating the selling price with a certain group of industrial purchasers. The salesperson may reduce the selling price by as much as 10 percent of the established selling price without seeking prior approval from the product marketing manager.

Prices tend to fluctuate on a regional basis. Thus, on a given day the Wicker Manufacturing Company may have 20 sales orders for a given item of industrial supply, and each sales order will be at a slightly different per-unit sales price.

In addition, marketing management does not have the appropriate information with which to supervise the marketing and sales effort. Monthly statistical sales reports are prepared that indicate the dollar volume of sales by customer, salesperson, territory, and product. Monthly responsibility accounting reports show cumulative expenditures by individuals.

Thus, the total salesperson's salaries and commissions, travel and per diem expenses, delivery cost, sales supplies cost and advertising charge, for example, are known. However, the accounting reports do not relate the above monthly expenses to the product line.

Existing Information Reports

Monthly, a company income statement and balance sheet are prepared. In addition, 74 responsibility accounting reports are issued. These latter reports are representative of the strict responsibility accounting variety, and they do not contain any overhead and administrative items being allocated to other responsibility centers. The monthly sales statistical reports have been previously cited.

Major Concerns

There are significant differences in the contribution to margin of different products. While everyone is aware of this situation, marketing management feels that they need a better understanding on a more timely basis of the current market price and cost relationship. For example, frequently they are surprised that a lower company profit results from a higher dollar volume of sales.

Marketing management would like an information system to provide them with daily or weekly guidelines for reacting to sales price fluctuations. This proposed information network might really consist of two information systems that are interfaced. First, there might be a monthly information flow (a responsibility accounting type of traditional information system) encompassing a planning phase in which marketing management will establish pertinent criteria for monitoring short-term changes in sales price of raw materials and finished goods. Second, there might be a daily or weekly information flow (a profitability accounting type of traditional information system) containing the critical information to which marketing management can react.

Marketing management would also like an information system that will assist them in supervising, monitoring, and controlling the marketing and sales efforts. The lack of gross margin and product line information has been previously discussed. One complicating factor in this issue is the problem that some expenditures chargeable to a distribution expense account cannot be easily identified with an individual sales effort for a particular product. For example, in the case of advertising expense, there are "programmed advertising expenditures" that are more closely related to a "period of time" than to the stimulation of demand for any product. On the other hand, major portions of the total advertising expenditures *can* be so identified with the stimulation of demand for a particular item of finished goods inventory.

REQUIRED:

1. Design a coding pattern for coping with the above situation.
2. Illustrate the application of your coding pattern by sketching major information flows in the Wicker Manufacturing Company's operations. Indicate the separate nature of the information in each flow and show how your coding pattern provides this information. Also, indicate the time frame of each information flow and the location of the decision makers.

CASE 13–3. SCHNEIDER FROZEN FOODS, INC.

Recently, all the capital stock of Schneider Frozen Foods, Inc., was acquired by RBD Diversified Enterprises, Inc., which has corporate offices in New York City. The parent corporation (RBD Diversified Enterprises, Inc.) has a data processing center to service all of its enterprises, and this center contains a large-scale computer system with extensive time-sharing capabilities. A large communications network has been established so that all subsidiaries are connected to this center.

Members of the executive management of the parent corporation are wondering which of the following two actions should be taken with respect to Schneider Frozen Foods: (*a*) keep its present data processing equipment and acquire a slow-speed remote terminal for access to the parent corporation's computer center or (*b*) sell its present data processing equipment and acquire a high-speed remote terminal for access to the parent corporation's computing center.

The management consulting firm with which you are associated was asked by the parent corporation's executive management to make a high-point review of Schneider Frozen Foods' operations and to recommend which of the above two courses of action should be taken. In addition, the management consulting firm was asked (*a*) to examine the present inventory control activities and sales analysis reporting procedures and (*b*) to design a new information system that will more effectively cope with these aspects of Schneider Frozen Foods' operations.

You were assigned to this engagement and have made the following notes on the company and its operations.

The Company

Schneider Frozen Foods, Inc., is a general wholesaler for frozen foods in the midsouth area and has an annual sales volume of approximately $14,000,000. The company's assets include major warehouse storage facilities, controlled zero temperature storage rooms, air-cooled storage rooms, and refrigerated trucks (at present, there are 20 such trucks). The company has 12 salespeople and employs 150 other personnel.

The inventory turnover rate at Schneider Frozen Foods has averaged 10 times a year, while the frozen food industry information would suggest that the inventory turnover rate should be between 13 and 23 times a year. According to the frozen food industry information, a given frozen food wholesaler's inventory turnover rate would vary between 13 and 23 times a year, based upon the institutional relationship of the given wholesalers' customers. If most of the customers are classified as "retail," then a high inventory turnover would be expected. On the other hand, if there are many customers classified as "institutional," then a lower inventory turnover would be expected.

As suggested by the previous comments, a frozen food wholesaler has two types of customers. The retail grouping includes the independent grocery store as well as the chain grocery store. The retail grouping at Schneider Frozen Foods is the dominant grouping of customers and will generally include from 60 to 90 percent of the customers. The institutional grouping includes governmental agencies, military institutions, public and private schools, universities, hospitals, hotels, motels, restaurants, company cafeterias, and airline food operations.

Inventory Activities

Schneider Frozen Foods handles 940 different items. The reason for such a large number of line items is that the company has to maintain, for all practical purposes, two inventories. The 10-, 12-, and 16-ounce packages of vegetables are for the retail customer, while the 2-, 2.5-, and 3-pound packages of vegetables are for the institutional customer. This same situation exists for other items in inventory; the institutional customer always prefers the large, economy package with a plain wrapper. The retail customer prefers the small package with a highly decorative wrapper.

At Schneider Frozen Foods, the inventories for the two groups are physically separated in the respective storage facilities. In addition, the perpetual inventory records are separately maintained.

The company has a small-scale computer system with additional storage facilities. The perpetual inventory records for both the retail and the institutional items are maintained in this data processing system. Quarterly, a physical inventory count is performed for all items in inventory. The results are compared with the perpetual inventory records, and significant deviations are rechecked. When necessary, the perpetual inventory records are adjusted to reflect the actual number of items on hand.

The data processing system provides a daily inventory stock status report for all retail items and a weekly inventory stock status report for all institutional items. In both cases, the inventory stock status report shows (a) identification code of inventory item, (b) description of item, (c) number of units on hand, (d) number of units on order, and (*e*) the "minimum" inventory level. This latter amount is computed monthly and represents the previous month's sales.

The purchasing manager uses the inventory stock status report as a guide in determining what items should be purchased. The resulting purchase orders are not prepared by the data processing system but are manually typed by a clerk in the purchasing office.

From statistical information, you observe that there are significant differences in (*a*) the per-unit selling price of items in inventory, varying from a few cents per unit to $25 per unit, (*b*) the dollar volume of sales per unit, (*c*) the frequency with which certain items are sold, and (*d*) the selling price-cost relationship. There are two aspects of this latter observation. First, the selling price-cost relationship varies not only among major groups of items in inventory, but also among the individual items within a group. (The frozen food wholesale operations are highly competitive, and the marketing strategy is to have loss leaders as well as to have varying markups on items within the same product group.) Second, in the case of institutional sales, the selling price for each item is at a negotiated price. Therefore, on a given day the actual sales price of an institutional item in inventory may differ greatly with each customer.

Sales Activities

Ninety-five percent of all sales orders are telephoned by a salesperson or customer to the home office of Schneider Frozen Foods. In the remaining cases the salesperson brings the orders to the home office. The procedures followed in processing a sales order are different, depending on whether it is for a retail customer or an institutional customer.

If the order is for a retail customer, a master preprinted form is used for recording the details of the sale. This form is immediately sent to data processing where a punched card is prepared for each item ordered by the customer. All customers and stock items have been previously assigned identification numbers. All inventory details are stored on magnetic disks in the small-scale computer system. Thus, after the punched card has been prepared for each item ordered, the cards are processed through the computer system, and the inventory is reduced by the quantity of each ordered item.

The customers' names and addresses are also permanently carried on magnetic disks within the small-scale computer system. In the case of retail customers, the selling price for each item is predetermined; thus, the magnetic disks also contain the product identification number and selling price for each item. With this combined information available, the computer system can prepare the complete sales invoice.

A day's retail sales orders are filled that night and are shipped to the customer the following day. Therefore, while the data processing group is handling the daily retail sales orders, it is also accumulating the total number of each line item that is needed for filling that day's sales orders. At the appropriate cutoff point, a print out of these inventory items is prepared by the computer system, and copies of this report are sent to the order-filling department and to the control desk.

Schneider Frozen Foods' warehouse facilities are multistory, and different items in inventory must be maintained in different controlled-temperature rooms. During the early evening, workers will transfer the number of items requested by the above report to the order filling area. Here, each sales order is filled, and the designated items are loaded onto a specified refrigerated truck.

To complete the physical flow cycle, during the day, workers will unload the new shipments of stock and will place these units in the appropriate, predetermined storage locations.

As indicated previously, one copy of the sales invoice is used by the order-filling group. Other copies go to the control and shipping desk. Two copies of the sales invoice are given to the truck driver: one copy is to be signed by the customer as confirmation of delivery and returned to the home office, and the second copy is given to the customer for use as a receiving report. Another copy is used by the control group to notify a clerk in the data processing room that the sales invoice can be mailed to the retail customer. Some retail customers may purchase on a cash basis only; thus, the truck driver collects from these customers at the time of delivery.

If the sales order is for an institutional customer, a special sales order form is used which contains the necessary carbons for preparing five copes. Different copies of this handwritten sales order are used by the order-filling group, by the control desk, by the truck driver (two copies used in the same manner as specified for retail customers) , and by the data processing group.

Frequently, there are substitutions of items on institutional sales.

Therefore, the original handwritten sales order is marked up by the order-filling group. Subsequently, the other copies are also changed. The control group will send a corrected copy of the sales order to data processing. Here, a punched card is prepared for each item on the sales order.

Before the keypunch operator is given the marked-up copy of the sales order, a control manager writes on the document the appropriate price per unit *for this customer.*

Once this appropriate information has been processed into the computer system, sales invoices are prepared by the computer, and the accounts receivable balances are updated to reflect these new sales orders.

Reports

Separate reports are prepared for the retail customers and the institutional customers. The following three reports are prepared daily for both groups. First, the daily balance run is prepared as a control procedure which indicates each item per sales order. Second, the daily sales register shows, as a single line, the total information for each sales order. Third, the daily sales register recap lists, as a single line, the cumulative information for a given salesperson. This information would be a summary of all the sales invoices identified with a given salesperson. Since each salesperson has an assigned territory, these two classifications (salesperson and territory) are identical. This third report, the daily sales register recap, contains totals for each sales district. The information included in these three reports are strictly sales statistics.

Twice a month, the credit manager is given a report of the overdue accounts receivable. The report presents an aging of such delinquent accounts.

The data processing system also provides inventory stock status reports, which have been previously discussed.

REQUIRED:

1. Evaluate the present information systems. Be specific in your comments.
2. Should Schneider Frozen Foods acquire a slow-speed remote terminal or a high-speed remote terminal? Indicate your overall

recommendation on this point to the parent corporation's management.

3.   Based on the information in this case, sketch a new information system that might be used at Schneider Frozen Foods. Explain in detail your proposed information system.

CHAPTER 14

Credit Control Management and Marketing Information Systems

THE GENERAL MODEL of the marketing management information system presented in Chapter 13 was a multidimensional network of diverse data flows which supported decision makers and planners in two or more departments within the organization, and this network was an open system with respct to the interface between the organization and its environment. The administrative process and organizational arrangements were represented by six phases within this general model.

Some of the essential features in this model were (a) extensive monitoring of the organization's external environment with online response capabilities within the system, (b) interfacing of diverse, multidimensional data flows in multitime cycles within a single, integrated network, (c) active participation by decision makers and planners in a common network, (d) a high intensity of online interaction between remote terminal users and the computer-based system, (e) special computer programs and software for processing, sorting, reprocessing, assigning, retrieving, and reporting information in an interactive mode, and (f) a series of online files and data bases to support an interactive environment.

After this TYPE 3 information system has become operational and fully implemented within an organization, a series of management actions may occur. This chapter emphasizes a set of these actions in the sales analysis and credit control area, and the computer-based support for this set of actions can be incorporated as an extension to a TYPE 3 network. This latter extension is "hidden" in the sense that no new phase is being added to the general model of marketing management information system. Instead, the modifications and improvements are in the scope and function of the common data bases.

Inherent within these changes is the concept of a program for improving the quality of the data over a specified period of time. In a typical organization where detailed, historical experience in relevant areas was not captured in machine-readable form, such data must be captured, accumulated, and stored for several months *before* this program for improvement can even begin. The reasons for these time requirements are explained in the subsequent discussion.

DATA BASES FOR SALES ANALYSIS

In the marketing management information system, the systems processing phase and the monitoring and inquiring phase provided the online capabilities for processing, sorting, reprocessing, assigning, storing, retrieving, and reporting data for multipurposes. The team of systems analysts viewed each data specification from the standpoint of maximizing the utilization by various remote terminal users, and these data specifications include customer identification numbers, product identification numbers, supplier identification numbers, personnel identification numbers, organizational designation numbers, management accounting classification arrangements, and external financial reporting frameworks. These multipurpose data were edited, screened, processed, and stored in common data files to facilitate online access.

As members of management begin to interact with these online data, logical comparisons are made across several dimensions—cost, expense, revenue, performance, customer response to alternative media and advertising arrangements, and sales management efforts. An informed analysis can be made in a composite manner of a given salesperson's efforts with a specific product group for major customers in a given territory or of a marketing program for selected products within a given territory.

Figure 14.1 presents a marketing application to the systems processing phase and the monitoring and inquiring phase. Symbols A1 to A4 indicate that marketing management and planners are among these remote terminal users who participate in online interaction with these data files and data bases which emphasize sales analysis data. Symbols A5 to A8 specify the data movement and data process-

FIGURE 14.1

**A Marketing Application to the Systems Processing
Phase and the Monitoring and Inquiring Phase**

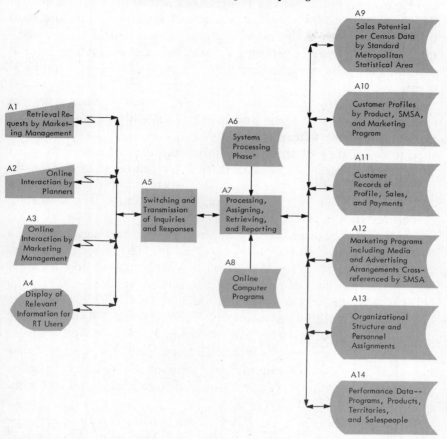

* The processing, sorting, reprocessing, and assignment operations in the systems processing phase are depicted by symbols A2 to A6 and A22 in Figure 13.1.

ing operations that are required to support this interactive environment in which members of management make composite analyses based upon these related data. Symbols A9 to A14 depict the online, common data files which represent the multipurposes that are initially, separately pursued by remote terminal users *before* the composite types of analyses are performed.

The sales potential file (symbol A9) was mentioned in the previous chapter,[1] and the data in this file are based on United States Census Data which are accumulated and reported by the Bureau of the Census, an agency of the Department of Commerce. Population data are available for various geographical areas including the total number of people, their age, education, employment, income, marital status, race, and sex. Housing information and selected household consumption data are also available for each of these geographical areas.

The Bureau of Census's computer-based system contains a unique collection of socioeconomic and demographic information for each geographical area within each state, and a census tract number is used to designate that area. The public can purchase computer tapes containing selected census information by census tract. When an organization's marketing efforts are directed toward small areas within a metropolitan area, then separate information by census tract is required for integrated analyses.

Symbols A9, A10, and A12 in Figure 14.1 indicated aggregate data by *S*tandard *M*etropolitan *S*tatistical *A*rea (SMSA), which is an integrated economic and social unit with a large population nucleus. The definition of a SMSA unit was changed on April 27, 1973 by the Office of Management and Budget, and as of July 1, 1973, there were 273 SMSA's (including 4 in Puerto Rico).[2] These SMSA units are used in the annual reporting by government officials of vital statistics (such as birth, marriage, divorce, sickness, and death) and other statistical data (such as hospital beds, number of physicians, number of dentists, governmental expenditures, money income, and number of families).

An organization with a TYPE 3 information system uses the SMSA data as one of several sources of information. Members of

---

[1] *Supra,* p. 399.

[2] U.S Bureau of the Census, *Statistical Abstract of the United States: 1973* 94th ed., Washington, D.C., 1973, p. 849: "Each SMSA contains at least:

   a. One central city with 50,000 inhabitants or more, or

   b. A city having a population of contiguous places (incorporated and unincorporated) having a population density of at least 1,000 persons per square mile, constitutes for general economic and social purposes a single community with a combined population of at least 50,000; provided that the county (or counties) in which the city and contiguous places are located has a total population of at least 75,000. (In New England, the cities and towns qualifying for inclusion in an SMSA must have a combined population of at least 75,000.) "

management are concerned with the response by the organization's customers within each SMSA location (symbol A10 in Figure 14.1) to various aspects of the marketing program. Similar population profiles in different geographical locations may have opposite reactions to the same marketing program, and knowledge about these unique response patterns is essential information for marketing management. Symbol A12 in Figure 14.1 depicts the online storage of detailed data on the marketing programs, including the media and advertising arrangements which are cross-referenced by SMSA location. Comparative analyses can be performed by retrieving performance data (symbol A14) for a given organizational unit (symbol A13) with the marketing program used (symbol A12) and for the area's sales potential (symbol A9).

As the organization's unique data base of customer experience is developed, then informed analyses can be made below the SMSA level. The zip code specification in customer's address can be used in establishing statistically significant groupings between the census tract level and the SMSA level. The organization's data base of customer experience can be supplemented with survey data acquired from various marketing research companies. (In the TYPE 4 information system discussed in the next chapter major attention is given to the need for continuous accumulating of marketing and environmental data by survey personnel and research teams.)

There is a movement by members of management in an organization with a TYPE 3 information system away from *reacting* to changes in the environment toward *creating* changes. Specifically, the marketing program will be designed toward stimulating demand for a product in a given area with a positive residual effect. The organization's objective may be to sell replacement units to the same customer over a period of time or to sell a series of products to the customer as the customer's requirements change. In either case, detailed data on the customer's profile, procurement patterns, and payment behavior are stored online (symbol A11 in Figure 14.1) for subsequent analysis in planning and evaluating the subsequent period's marketing activities.

As the organization's data base of historical experience is expanded, members of management can develop new marketing strategies for coping with shifts in sociodemographic profiles and changes in population movements. In addition, monitoring capabilities can be established within the TYPE 3 information system that will even signal the need for a reconsideration of the marketing program. The latter may be based upon recent customer experience or new secondary data sources which have been received and processed.

As members of management interact with these computer-based capabilities over an extended period of time, there is an increase in the level of specificity employed. The programs and routines for data retrieval and comparative-reporting must be capable of responding to this level of specificity. For example, marketing expenditure decisions are made at a very detailed level based upon the insights gained from comparative analyses of the organization's historical experience. Therefore, it is imperative that the data accumulation efforts as represented by the online storage locations in Figure 14.1 must be maintained over an extended period of time if a high degree of statistical confidence is to be placed upon these analyses.

In addition to these changes related to increased awareness and understanding by members of management, there have been several movements and shifts in the external environment during the past decade. Three of these changes in exogenous factors are briefly discussed in the last section of this chapter; however, another exogenous factor which has changed during this period has had a dominant impact on marketing operations. Specifically, a significant change in consumer consumption patterns has occurred, and there has been a tremendous growth in consumer installment credit. Because of the importance of this latter change, it is highlighted in the next section of this chapter.

For example, since World War II, the total outstanding consumer credit grew from $5.1 billion as of December 31, 1944, to $180.8 billion as of December 31, 1973. This dynamic growth in consumer credit occurred in all types of operations, as indicated by the schedule of selected data from the U.S. Department of Commerce, Office of Business Economics publications which is presented in Figure 14.2.

For comparison purposes, the gross national product for 1944 was $211.4 billion, while the gross national product for 1973 was $1,289.1 billion.[3] If the total outstanding consumer credit had changed in the same proportion as the change in the gross national product, the 1973 consumer credit total would have been approximately $30.6 billion instead of $180.8 billion. Part of this increase in consumer credit is attributable to the increase in population, but, of

---

[3] *Business Statistics 1963 Edition* (a supplement to the *Survey of Current Business*), p. 3, and *Survey of Current Business*, vol. 54 (May 1974), S–1.

FIGURE 14.2

Selected Data on Consumer Credit

Consumer Credit	*End of Year (millions of dollars)* 1944	1950	1960	1964	1970	1972	1973
Total outstanding	5,111	21,471	56,141	80,268	126,802	157,564	180,846
Total installment credit	2,176	14,703	42,968	62,692	101,161	127,332	147,437
Automobile paper	397	6,074	17,658	24,934	35,490	44,129	51,130
Other consumer goods paper	791	4,799	11,545	16,333	29,949	40,080	47,530
Repair and modernization loans	119	1,016	3,148	3,577	4,110	6,201	7,352
Personal loans	869	2,814	10,617	17,848	31,612	36,922	41,425
Total noninstallment credit	2,935	6,768	13,173	17,576	25,641	30,232	33,049
Single-payment loans	624	1,821	4,507	5,874	9,484	12,256	13,241
Charge accounts	1,517	3,367	5,329	6,195	8,850	9,002	9,829
Service credit	794	1,580	3,337	4,507	7,307	8,974	9,979

Sources: *Business Statistics, 1963 Edition* (a supplement to the *Survey of Current Business*), pp. 91–92; *Business Statistics, 1971 Edition* (a supplement to the *Survey of Current Business*), pp. 92–93; and *Survey of Current Business*, vol. 54 (April 1974), S–18.

course, we believe the primary increase represents a change in consumer buying habits.

The extension of consumer credit is one marketing technique that some business organizations have only recently begun to employ. This marketing technique is now so widely used that the extension of consumer credit is a major function of business, even of those organizations not traditionally engaged in the "finance business."

For example, a small manufacturer of consumer goods was experiencing a declining net profit rate on a substantially increasing volume of sales. Currently, the manufacturing company was operating at about 80 percent of capacity. After studying the market situation and the cost picture, the president of this manufacturing company decided to operate at full capacity (thus spreading the fixed costs over more units of output) and to sell these additional consumer goods by increased advertising efforts and by installment credit sales.

The president decided that her company would sell to any purchaser who could make the down payment (which amounted to approximately 20 percent of the selling price), since this down payment almost equaled the total direct material and direct labor costs embodied in the finished goods. A year later, the president commented that her company has made a substantial profit from consumer sales, even though the noncollectible accounts have been approximately 10 percent of the total installment sales. The president continues: "To some extent, we have changed the nature of our business. Much of our profit has been made from consumer credit. It is almost as though the manufacturing facilities existed so that we could produce a product that we could sell on credit."

The above example is not an isolated case. Many small manufacturing companies with unused capacity are discovering that consumer installment sales can be a profitable method of expanding sales volume. The contribution to margin is high on these additional units, and the carrying charges will typically more than offset the normal loss from noncollectible accounts.

While the extension of consumer credit has only recently become a major function of business in numerous business organizations, it has always been a major function of business in a select group of large corporations. Furthermore, from recent studies of business operations, it would appear that credit management will be an increasingly important function in the future.

CREDIT MANAGEMENT AND CONTROL*

Credit managers are generally aware of the nature of high-risk applicants. They have either analyzed or observed significant differences in lifestyle between "good" and "bad" risks. Differences in such characteristics as marital status, home ownership, automobile ownership, age, occupation, and so forth may be more or less prevalent in the two basic classes of credit risk. One analysis of a sample of good and bad accounts revealed the magnitude of these differences, as indicated by Figure 14.3.

FIGURE 14.3
Profiles of Good and Bad Risks*

	Percent		
Characteristics of Applicant	Good	Bad	Difference
1. Married	91.2	87.0	4.2
2. Owns automobile	81.8	69.2	12.6
3. Owns home	81.6	43.8	37.8
4. Less than 4 children	85.1	80.2	4.9
5. Age 35 or over	96.9	89.4	7.5
6. At present address 3 years or more	91.9	71.2	20.7
7. Employed with present company 3 years or more	74.3	58.6	15.7
8. Has bank reference	93.7	70.5	23.2
9. Has telephone	97.6	92.1	5.5
10. Has a business address	62.5	39.6	22.9

° These values are for illustration purposes only.

As indicated by Figure 14.3, there is a significant difference between the occurrence of each characteristic in the good and bad credit risk categories. It is certainly reasonable to expect that the poorer risks would tend to possess each of these characteristics less frequently. However, experience has shown that the relative importance of each of these characteristics cannot be predicted accurately from this type of analysis.

Some characteristics tend to occur together or have a high degree

---

* We are indebted to William P. Boggess for many of the ideas presented in this section. Mr. Boggess did extensive basic research on the topic of scientific sales analysis and credit control, and he discussed his findings with the author. Mr. Boggess is currently an independent management consultant and was formerly a manager in administrative services at the Chicago office of Arthur Andersen & Co.

of correlation, in which case these correlated characteristics should have the same relative importance. Also, there are certain combinations of characteristics forming a unique set which is highly correlated with bad risks. If it were possible to evaluate all possible combinations of the above ten characteristics, it might be possible to select those combinations which have the greatest accuracy in predicting poor risks.

Unfortunately, the statistical work required to test all potential combinations of these ten characteristics (depicted in Figure 14.3) is substantial. Actually, there are many more than these ten characteristics to be considered, and the number of combinations of characteristics will grow accordingly. Determining which of a hundred or so traits are the most significant and which combinations are best for predicting credit risks is a staggering task, if each potental combination of customer characteristics were tested separately.

If the above approach were followed, eventually all combinations of characteristics will be identified, and each combination will be assigned a value to indicate its relative position on a continuum between the two extreme positions: bad risk and good risk. With a hundred characteristics, the number of combinations will be unwieldy from the standpoint of a clerk who must compare the combination of a given prospective customer with this tremendous list of combinations in order to classify the applicant.

Because of the unwieldy nature of the "combination approach," another statistical technique is followed for coping with the hundred or so characteristics. Stepwise multiple regression or, more specifically, stepwise discriminant analysis is used. The computer program covering this latter technique is designed so that the most important characteristics are selected in the order of their statistical significance, and the relative weight of each factor is determined by this computer program.

Multiple Regression Analysis

The concepts of multiple regression analysis are explained in several basic references, including any standard statistical reference. This statistical technique has received notable use in many scientific and practical endeavors.

In the simplest application, multiple regression analysis is a method for developing a linear (first degree) equation relating a single dependent variable to two or more independent variables. The following example illustrates a "regression equation" for the ten characteristics presented in Figure 14.3.

$$Y = a + b_1X_1 + b_2X_2 + b_3X_3 + b_4X_4 \ldots + b_{10}X_{10}$$

where

$X_1 =$ Married or not (use "1" for "yes"; use "0" for "no")

$X_2 =$ Owns automobile or not (use "1" for "yes"; use "0" for for "no")

. . .

$X_{10} =$ Has a business address or not (use "1" for "yes"; use "0" for "no")

$b_1 =$ Coefficient or multiplier for the first independent variable

$b_2 =$ Coefficient or multiplier for the second independent variable

. . .

$b_{10} =$ Coefficient or multiplier for the tenth independent variable

In the above example, the coefficients are the unknowns. The stepwise multiple regression program for the computer must determine the appropriate degree of emphasis that each independent variable should possess. This determination is accomplished by entering into the computer system numerous regression equations, where each equation represents the "yes" and "no" answers of a given customer or applicant to the ten characteristics. The computer program evaluates these numerous regression equations and determines the coefficients that can be assigned to the general regression equation.

Discriminant Analysis

A special type of multiple regression analysis is called "discriminant analysis." In the simplest case, the objective of discriminant analysis is to compute weights as before (that is, to determine the coefficients) but only for purposes of distinguishing between the two types of accounts (or any finite number of classes of accounts), instead of predicting an individual general regression equation. This latter equation theoretically assumes an infinite number of values.

The discriminant analysis technique is useful because it is not always possible to have a very detailed breakdown by grades of actual credit ratings. Therefore, a "good" and "bad" breakdown is a simplification, although in theory it could be expanded to include more categories, such as "good," "fairly good," "medium," "fairly bad," and "bad." (Some business organizations using this technique for credit control have found it beneficial to use four to seven categories, rather than the simple "good" and "bad" groups.) However, for purposes of illustration, only the two classes are considered.

In summary, discriminant analysis is used not only for determining the most significant customer characteristics, but also for establishing the relative weight for each customer characteristic. The sum of the weights or the scores assigned to each prospective customer's application form (on the basis of the applicant's characteristics) determines the credit rating for the applicant. The higher the score, the higher the credit rating, and the better is the risk.

Shifts in Weights of Characteristics

The coefficients assigned to each characteristic change by time period. For example, Figure 14.4 shows the shifting emphasis on coefficients that exist among the ten characteristics presented in

FIGURE 14.4
Monitoring the Change in Profiles

	Credit Rating Points Allowed				
Characteristics of Applicant	*19x1*	*19x2*	*19x3*	*19x4*	*19x5*
1. Married	6	7	7	9	?
2. Owns automobile	6	5	5	7	?
3. Owns home	19	21	18	20	?
4. Less than 4 children	11	9	10	9	?
5. Age 35 or over	8	8	9	8	?
6. At present address 3 years of more. .	12	14	13	14	?
7. Employed with present company 3 years or more	7	6	8	5	?
8. Has bank reference . . . . . . : . .	26	24	25	23	?
9. Has telephone	5	6	5	5	?
10. Has a business address	16*	15*	16*	17*	?*
Total	100	100	100	100	100

* Bonus points, thus the maximum number of points equals 100 plus the points assigned for characteristic No. 10.

Figure 14.3. Because of these changing tendencies, it is necessary to periodically test and evaluate the credit rating system to see if a thorough study is required. In other words, should a large sample of applicants be subjected to stepwise discriminant analysis?

Selection of Relevant Characteristics

The previous discussion has omitted an important consideration. A prospective customer's application form may contain a hundred or so separate characteristics. However, many of these characteristics do not have any statistical significance in terms of predicting "good" and "bad" credit risk. In addition, there are many groupings of characteristics that have the same statistical significance, and these correlated characteristics can be indicated by a single factor.

Therefore, the stepwise discriminant analysis is really being used to select from the hundred or so characteristics that small group of characteristics (for example, a dozen) which will statistically differentiate between "good" and "bad" credit risks. Not only do the relative weights of these differentiating characteristics shift through time (as illustrated by Figure 14.4), but the characteristics selected based on their statistical significance also change through time.

Illustration of Credit Rating Procedures

The above technique is applied to the Oregon Company, a manufacturer and distributor of consumer goods which are primarily sold by advertisements in newspapers and magazines and by direct sales efforts through the mail. Members of the Oregon Company's management have conducted sufficient studies to give a high degree of reliance to the credit rating system, and a credit rating has been established for each applicant in a sample of 34,650 applicants. Figure 14.5 presents a schedule of the number of good and bad risks by each credit rating.

For purposes of illustration, assume that the profit from each of Oregon Company's goods is $150 and the loss for "bad risk" is $100. There are, of course, accounting issues involved in the precise measurement of the profit from a good risk or the loss from a bad risk, and these issues must be carefully considered in an actual situation. But, continuing with the illustration, Figure 14.6 com-

FIGURE 14.5

Oregon Company

(good and bad risks by credit rating)

Credit Rating (Midpoint of Class)	Good Risk Applicants		Bad Risk Applicants	
	Number	Cumulative	Number	Cumulative
10	0	0	1,250	1,250
20	0	0	2,500	3,750
30	700	700	3,000	6,750
40	1,700	2,400	2,900	9,650
50	4,300	6,700	1,800	11,450
60	6,000	12,700	700	12,150
70	5,800	18,500	0	12,150
80	3,100	21,600	0	12,150
90	900	22,500	0	12,150
100	0	22,500	0	12,150

FIGURE 14.6

Oregon Company

(cumulative profit by minimum credit rating)

Credit Rating (Midpoint of Class)	Good Risk Profit*	Bad Risk Loss†	Net Return	Cumulative Return if Minimum Credit Rating Is Lower Limit of Class‡
10	0	$125,000	($125,000)	$2,160,000
20	0	250,000	(250,000)	2,285,000
30	$105,000	300,000	(195,000)	2,535,000
40	255,000	290,000	(35,000)	2,730,000
50	645,000	180,000	465,000	2,765,000
60	900,000	70,000	830,000	2,300,000
70	870,000	0	870,000	1,470,000
80	465,000	0	465,000	600,000
90	135,000	0	135,000	135,000
100	0	0	0	0
	$3,375,000	$1,215,000	$2,160,000	

° $150 multiplied by the number of applicants in each class per Figure 14.5. The total of $3,375,000 equals 22,500 "good" applicants multiplied by $150 profit per applicant.

† $100 multiplied by the number of applicants in each class per Figure 14.5. The total of $1,215,000 equals 12,150 "bad" applicants multiplied by $100 loss per applicant.

‡ If the 34,650 applicants were accepted, the net return would be $2,160,000 ($3,375,000 profit less the $1,215,000 loss). If the minimum credit rating is set so that all applicants in Class 10 are eliminated, then the cumulative return would be increased by the amount of the net loss from Class 10 (2,160,000 cumulative return plus $125,000 loss for Class 10 equals $2,285,000 cumulative return for Class 20). By repeating this procedure, the data for this column are determined.

pares the profit and loss from accepting all applicants within each credit rating class range. This exhibit indicates that the class range for which 50 is the midpoint (the interval from 45.0 to 54.9) has the highest cumulative return, if the minimum credit rating is the lower limit of this class. However, if this were a real situation, an analysis would be made of all items in Class 40 and Class 50 for the purpose of determining the slope of these lines. Since the "good risk" line is rising rapidly while the "bad risk" line is falling slowly, and since the profit is $150 per good risk while the loss is $100 per bad risk, the overall effect is that a minimum credit rating of approximately 43 will generate the highest return of $2,800,000.

The Credit Management and Control Screen

The previous discussion has explained the procedures involved in establishing a credit rating system. Once the credit rating points have been specified for a given time period and the minimum "acceptable" point has been determined, then the overall credit management and control procedure becomes a clerical task. As credit applications are received, each application is scored on the basis of the statistical point system. Next, each application score is examined, and if the score is above the minimum acceptable point, the application is accepted. If the score is below the minimum acceptable point, the application is rejected.

This process of scoring each credit application and comparing each application score with the minimum acceptable point is referred to as the "credit management and control screen." In other words, this is the practical application of knowledge regarding customer characteristics to the task of selecting and rejecting credit applications.

Basic Concept

As previously indicated, the tremendous increase in consumer credit has created the need for the administrative function of *credit management and control*. This function can be described as a systems concept designed to assist credit management in achieving maximum profits. Credit management and control is composed of four sequential and related management action phases: (*a*) monitor and report, (*b*) analyze and test, (*c*) determine policies, and (*d*) implement policy changes. Figure 14.7 illustrates these four phases in the credit management and control cycle.

The credit management and control concept is similar to the "process control cycle" of a closed loop computer-controlled manufacturing process. For example, through special electronic, mechanical, and other measuring devices, the credit management and control

FIGURE 14.7
Credit Management and Control Cycle

process is monitored by the computer. The set of computer programs "senses" the data inflow and "records" pertinent data for other uses and maintains a log of the process. Through predetermined logic and mathematical formulations, the computer system "analyzes" the data it has monitored, then "calculates" the necessary changes or improvements in the different parts of the process.[4] After calculation, the computer automatically "sets controls" to effect the improvements, and the credit management and control cycle repeats.

Obviously, this is a grossly oversimplified description, but it does serve to demonstrate the interrelated control concepts in the credit management and control cycle. The principal difference between the process control cycle and the credit management and control cycle is that the latter process is not automatic but employs management judgment to execute each major phase of the cycle. However, the credit management and control cycle is very similar to the closed loop control system in that it employs measures of the credit process in order to determine the need for action.

Extensions from Basic Model

The credit management and control process is similar to inventory control procedures in that emphasis is given to the heterogeneity of

---

[4] Typical "monitoring" indices are "average credit ratings accepted," "percent refused business," "percent accounts 90 days + overdue," "percent collected of amount due current," and so forth. Collection indices are the key to the effectiveness of credit policies, and very frequently these early indications can be used to forecast profits. Review and analysis of these indices plus good credit management should provide the foundation for control. Furthermore, this system permits the credit manager to experiment with various collection techniques.

the mass. But instead of specifying control procedures and reorder points for each class of inventory (the ABC Method), the credit management and control system sorts and re-sorts credit applications into several groups for administration purposes. For example, Figure 14.8 shows the relation of the dunning procedures to credit reference.

FIGURE 14.8
Relation of Dunning Method to Credit Rating

Credit Rating of Customer	Dunning Procedure
High, Group A	Eliminate all Group A accounts from the automatic dunning procedures; handle on an exception basis
Good, Group B	Group B accounts are dunned after missing two payments; handled automatically by the computer
Medium, Group C	Group C accounts are dunned when the account becomes 45 days overdue; handled automatically by the computer
Low, Group D	Group D accounts are dunned when the account becomes 30 days overdue; handled automatically by the computer

Not only will the initial dunning procedures vary by the credit rating of the customer, but the follow-up procedures will also vary by this rating. For example, a Group D account might be dunned on a monthly basis, and if the account becomes six months past due, the account might be transferred to a collection agency. On the other hand, a Group A or Group B account would probably never be transferred to a collection agency; instead, the company would attempt to collect all Group A and Group B delinquent accounts itself.

SALES ANALYSIS AND CREDIT CONTROL MANAGEMENT

As indicated by the data flows of marketing information in Figure 14.1, sales invoices, credit application forms, payment records, and customer-related documents contain a substantial amount of multipurpose data that are stored in online locations to facilitate interaction by remote terminal users. After several months of these multipurpose data have been captured, accumulated, and stored, then informed, comparative analyses can be made. Sales effectiveness analyses can be made by territory, by salesperson, by product, and by major customer. Marketing studies can focus on channels, packaging, media, advertising, premiums, and pricing. Beyond these analyses and studies, there are supporting data files which permit a decision maker or planner to gain an insight into concurrent or parallel occurrences.

Figure 14.9 highlights the interactive use of data for sales analysis and credit screen management. Symbols B1 to B9 reflect the filtering, editing, screening, and processing of a sales application in an online system. If the application is rejected by the online credit control screen (symbol B8), then the returned application (symbol B10) is reviewed by a credit manager. While Figure 14.9 does not indicate this action, the credit manager might ask the salesperson to inquire if the proposed customer will increase the suggested down payment (a set of online computer programs that focus on the customer's credit profile will initiate a unique series of printed statements based on the relative profile; therefore, the credit manager's actions are suggested by these printouts). In other cases, the proposed customer is notified that the application has been rejected.

Applications that are accepted by the credit control screen are subjected to further processing, sorting, and assigning operations, as depicted by symbol B11. The data files and data bases to which the multipurpose data are assigned (symbols B12 to B16) are maintained in an online state so as to facilitate interaction by remote terminal users. Symbols B17 to B20 indicate a general type of online interaction. Since these data are stored online, other remote terminal users in the TYPE 3 information system may also retrieve and analyze these multipurpose data.

Symbol B12 represents the online data for the credit screen control data base. A line could be drawn from B12 to B8 to indicate the maintenance activities for updating the online credit control screen. The initial analysis of customer profile data for the credit screen is based on the data stored in the sample data base, as depicted by symbol B13. After an informed study has been made of the sample data base, then attempts are made to replicate the analysis with the control data base (symbol B12). If the latter analysis is valid, then the online computer programs stored in symbol B8 are revised.

The master file of accounts receivable data for each customer is stored online, as depicted by symbol B14. Selected data on marketing programs and performance are stored in symbols B15 and B16. The latter three online files and data bases (symbols B14 to B16)

FIGURE 14.9
Sales Analysis and Credit Screen Management

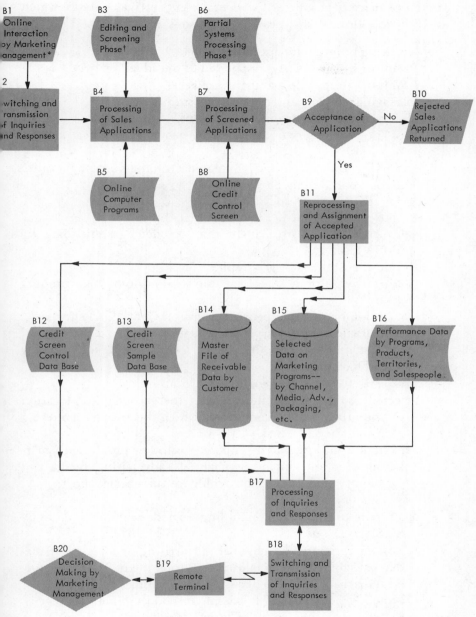

* Other types of online interaction by planners and decision makers within the monitoring and inquiring phase are depicted by symbols A1 to A4 in Figure 14.1.

† The editing and screening phase is depicted by symbols A1 to A10 and A28 to A29 in Figure 7.1.

‡ The processing, sorting, reprocessing, and assignment operations in the systems processing phase are depicted by symbols A2 to A6 and A22 in Figure 13.1.

are the primary data sources for several comparative analyses, which are listed as follows with types of comparisons indicated:

Advertising program for specific product.
>Profile of customers who responded to the advertisement.
>Profile of salespeople making the sales.
>Packaging, pricing, and distribution studies.

Cash forecasting for customer collections.
>Profile of customers by product, by geographical area, and by date of sale.
>Experience of sample file of related customers and generalize to total population.

Regular assignment of salespeople.
>Profile of salespeople per personnel data base.
>Sales potential of area including sociodemographic data by SMSA locations.
>Profile of customers by geographical location.
>Comparative profiles of salespeople with customers by product group.

Special assignment of salespeople for unusual marketing effort.
>Profile of salespeople per personnel data base.
>Sales potential of area including sociodemographic data by SMSA locations.
>Profile of customers by geographical location.
>Selected profile of customers within the geographical location or potential customers in area to which this special marketing effort will be addressed.
>Selection of an integrated proposed customer profile with marketing program (including channels, advertising, media and packaging) and salesperson profile for this special effort.

New product opportunities.
>Sales potential of area including sociodemographic data by SMSA locations.
>Customer responses by channel, advertising arrangement, media, packaging, pricing, and distribution methods.
>Special marketing studies of customer demand.
>Customer's perspective of existing products—what is the customer purchasing from the latter's standpoint.

Decision makers and planners in the marketing area will be interacting over the remote terminal facilities (symbols B19 and B20 in

Figure 14.9) with the online data bases and reporting capabilities for purposes of making the above types of comparisons. As members of management gain experience in making these types of comparisons, there is also a concurrent improvement in the quality of the data used in these studies. (The latter is primarily because more historical experience is available in machine-readable form under a controlled setting, which will generally result in improved statistical results from a given analysis.) From both of these improvements, the overall level at which the administrative process is performed is elevated. In addition, functional and departmental boundaries associated with traditional analyses are dissolved in the sales analysis and credit screen management. The organizational aspects of this latter extension are examined in the next chapter in the discussion of the TYPE 4 information system.

In summary, the data flows in Figure 14.9 have emphasized how multipurpose marketing data are used in an online, interactive environment by several decision makers and planners. With more historical data combined with gains in management experience in making comparative analyses, there are substantial improvements in the level at which the administrative process is performed. One final note as a word of caution—the multipurpose data as presented in this chapter only reflect *associations,* and do not reflect *causality.* In other words, there tends to be an association between sets of customer traits and performance; however, if a customer were to possess this set of traits, this does not cause this performance. Since these relations only reflect associations and not causes, there is a continuous need for monitoring, sampling, and testing in order to determine when there appears to be a shift in these associations.

OTHER EXOGENOUS FACTORS

In addition to the expansion of installment credit sales and the four movements cited in the first chapter of this book—advancements in behavioral science, developments in electronic computers and communication equipment, developments in mathematical tools and techniques, and the application of scientific method to the study of economic activity—three other significant changes have occurred in the environment during recent years which have a direct influence on marketing operations. First, increases in productivity and technological changes have created an environment in which production costs represent a minor portion of the sales dollar, while distribution cost represents the dominant portion of the sales dollar. This change has not been static, but annually the distribution costs have assumed an increasingly important position. Members of management in many diverse organizations have begun to recognize this change, and new types of marketing techniques have been developed for maximum employment of distribution cost dollars.

Second, the United States Congress passed Public Law 91–508 in October, 1970, which is otherwise known as the Fair Credit Reporting Act. This law, which became effective in 1971, partially restricted the operations of credit reporting agencies, such as giving a consumer the right to an oral summary of the information stored on him or her. The law also provides a way of correcting errors and noting differences of opinion concerning facts. These latter facets were clarified as well as the specification of additional safeguards for an individual against an invasion of personal privacy by Public Law 93–579 which was passed by the United States Congress on December 31, 1974 and is cited as the "Privacy Act of 1974."

While Public Law 91–508 and Public Law 93–579 have given the consumer certain rights to knowledge about information stored in credit reporting systems, other governmental agencies have imposed stronger legal pressures upon large organizations who make extensive use of consumer profile data. There are two dimensions of this pressure. First, an organization can be forced to prove that credit was not withheld from an individual because of race, religion, or sex. Second, an organization with a sophisticated data base of consumer profiles is almost prohibited from selling this information to another organization. Thus far, governmental agencies have not brought legal suits against small marketing research groups (with annual billings in the hundreds of thousands of dollars), which may sell a mailing list of selected profile data. On the other hand, a large organization (with annual sales in millions of dollars) is threatened with legal action by governmental officials even when members of management begin to negotiate such a sale. (In this latter case, the governmental officials may accuse the organization of accumulating discriminatory data on consumers, and the burden of proof is on the organization to present the evidence to the contrary.)

The legal constraints and governmental pressures encompassed in this second exogenous factor have stimulated the management of organizations to create new divisions and companies (which are wholly owned) whose only asset may be this large data base of consumer profiles. Book clubs, travel groups, insurance companies, and consumer product companies are typical types of subsidiaries that are created to legally use these profile data. Frequently, the profits on these wholly-owned companies are substantial, since there may only be limited amounts of fixed assets and other investments in these ventures.

Third, the *rights of citizens* to information on interest rates, service charges, insurance fees, and other charges have been strengthened by new public laws. In additon, governmental agencies have recently been established to examine complaints where citizens feel their rights have been violated. On the other hand, many citizens are not aware of their legal rights; and bar associations, public television, and news media have employed a variety of dissemination methods to inform such individuals of their rights in typical business transactions.

TOPICS FOR CLASS DISCUSSION

1. Members of marketing management who interact with an expanded TYPE 3 information system over a period of time will gradually increase their level of specificity for data retrieval and comparative reporting. This movement may impose new demands on the computer-based network. Explain the nature of the increase in specificity and the impact on the system.

2. After examining the profiles of good credit risks versus bad credit risks with stepwise discriminant analysis, the credit manager has a schedule of credit rating points by significant characteristic. There are frequent movements in the *precise,* relative importance of differentiating characteristics during a period of only a few months. Therefore, sample files and control files for monitoring, testing, and evaluating possible shifts in differentiating characteristics are an integral part of this system.

Is the credit rating screen too precise for the data or is this type of reassessment inherent within this overall method for managing consumer credit? Explain.

3. If the data sources for the sample file and control file are exclusively the accounts receivable records and supporting documents,

then the resulting credit management and control screen will tend to have an upward bias. Furthermore, the actual application of the resulting credit screen to "live" applications for credit may be operating with only a reasonable level of statistical confidence.

Explain the statistical problems in developing a credit control screen from the organization's accounts receivable data.

4. The management of a major corporation engaged in consumer finance operations desired to establish a credit management and control screen without going through the time-consuming process of accumulating "good" and "bad" risk experience. Instead of using the stepwise discriminant analysis approach, corporate management held a conference of its 20 "best" credit managers. Each credit manager was asked to draw upon experience and to select from a list of customer characteristics those which that credit manager felt were the most significant. Next, each credit manager was asked to assign weights to the characteristics which he or she had selected, so that the combined total equaled 100 points. Finally, a composite was made of the 20 credit managers' separate reports, and a tentative credit rating point system was established. A test was made of this tentative credit rating point system, and an 80 percent degree of confidence was assigned to the tentative credit rating point system. Corporate management desires a 95 percent degree of confidence before it will use the credit rating point system.

Explain the different approaches that corporate management might use in achieving this desired degree of confidence, and evaluate each approach you suggest in terms of time, effort, and expense.

5. One SMSA location is labeled "Davenport-Rock Island-Moline, Iowa-Illinois." Using this specification as a point of departure, explain the difference in the size of the geographical area included in the following three codes:

    a. Standard Metropolitan Statistical Area (SMSA) location.
    b. Zip code.
    c. Census tract number.

6. There are problems in that the boundaries of a zip code and a group of census tract numbers do not exactly coincide. In building the organization's historical data file, which data retrieval requests will favor using each of these as the basic unit of analysis? Explain how the data specification is used.

CASE 14–1. MIRREX COMPANY*

Members of Mirrex Company's management have had several years use from the company's specially designed customer experience retrieval system. The system has provided basic customer profile and collection information which has been useful for both marketing and collection purposes. A major question currently facing members of management is: what other relevant information can be developed from the computer-based system to aid in directing sales effort or in controlling other aspects of the company's operations?

Specifically, Mirrex Company's retrieval system is presently being used for:

a.   Basic management statistics on the quality of business.
b.   Identification of potentially fruitful areas for further investigation for improved credit and collection strategies.
c.   Testing suggested changes in policies or in credit and collection measures.
d.   Information on field sales performance in order to assist in keeping the quality of sales high.
e.   Forecasting, to the extent possible, probable cash flow measuring the cumulative effect of longer contracts and changes in collection performance.

Even though the list of current uses of the retrieval system may seem impressive, the management team is convinced that Mirrex is only beginning to realize the benefits of the retieval system. Members of management feel that after more insights have been gained through the analysis of computer-based information regarding customer experience, it may be possible to state in a precise manner the differentiating characteristics of various types of customers.

The relative weight of each of the differentiating characteristics could then be determined. When this is achieved, a computer program can be developed which would classify each customer by interpreting the customer's answers to certain questions. In other words, the computer would classify each customer by interpreting

---

* The name and products of this business organization have been disguised; however, in all other respects, the information system and the descriptive setting surrounding this system are the same as those of the "real" company.

the responses on the application form which each customer must prepare before the sale is completed.

Moreover, because of the speed of the computer, it will be possible to check periodically the customer experience to see if the previously determined classification labels are still valid. For example, are the special geographical and regional considerations still appropriate?

Or, from a different perspective, is it possible through an analysis of customer experience to identify exceptionally profitable geographical areas for a particular product? The full realization of this goal will include consideration of customer characteristics (regarding type of item desired and payment behavior) and salesperson characteristics (pertaining to type of customer and type of item sold). What other potential applications of the retrieval system might be employed?

Members of management continue to examine the current retrieval system for customer experience to see what specific new applications can be adopted on a financially feasible basis. In making this determination, management reexamines the characteristics and operations of the firm.

The Company

Mirrex Company, Inc., a wholly owned subsidiary of a major corporation, designs, manufactures, and sells a wide variety of consumer goods with particular appeal to young, single women and to brides. These consumer goods include all types of kitchen utensils and silver. The Mirrex Company is one of the largest companies in this field of business, with both domestic and international operations,

Except for special arrangements with a few selected firms, all of the Mirrex Company's products are sold door-to-door (which management calls "direct selling"). There are 30,000 representatives in the United States and Canada selling Mirrex Company's products on either a full-time or a part-time basis. Current sales volume is $125,000,000, and management expects this volume to increase.

The average sale is somewhat over $200, and 90 percent of Mirrex Company's sales are time payment accounts. Therefore, the Mirrex Company uses a rather substantial amount of effort to manage its accounts receivable accounts. In fact, the company has 650,000 open accounts, on the average, which must be balanced twice each month, billed once each month, and if they are delinquent, dunned once each month. On a correspondingly large scale is the task of writing commission checks to any one of the 30,000 representatives whenever they make a sale.

In addition to these considerations of sheer volume, there is the added aspect of growth. Over the past decade, the company and industry have enjoyed a dynamic expansion of sales. As a result of such growth, management has become even more keenly interested in effective ways of managing this rapidly increasing business.

The Integrated Management Information System

In coping with the firm's dynamic growth over the past decade, a unique integrated management information system has been developed which employs a large computer with several extra magnetic tape units. Order processing, commission accounting, and accounts receivable applications were the initial procedures to be programmed for the computer system. Later, dunning procedures were also mechanized. Recently, the statistical sampling system was established, and this system made extensive use of the computer facilities. This latter application is the unique element of the total system and is the area which appears to have the greatest potential for the future.

The following discussion explains the unique aspects of this statistical sampling system, and the explanation consists of three parts: (*a*) statistical sampling method (including sample size, data accumulated, and processing procedures), (*b*) reporting, and (*c*) graphs.

Statistical Sampling Method

The total installment accounts receivable consists of 650,000 active accounts. For each account (or customer) there is a two-page application form which is prepared by the prospective customer at the time of the sale (see Exhibit A for the format of this application form). In addition to this sales contract (after the application has been approved by the company officials, it becomes a sales contract), there is the transaction experience for each customer (payment activity and so forth). Originally, a customer's history record was manually maintained to reflect the transaction experience. Now, an accounts receivable record is maintained in the magnetic tape unit

EXHIBIT A
Customer Application Form

INFORMATION ON PURCHASER - PLEASE PRINT - ORDER WILL BE RETURNED UNLESS INFORMATION IS GIVEN IN FULL

Order Signed by
Mr/Mrs/Miss _____

Present
Address _____

Number and Street

_____
City   State   Code

Give Previous Address if Less Than One Year at Present
Address _____

Age ____ ☐ Married   ☐ Single   ☐ Widowed   ☐ Divorced
Number of Years   Telephone
at Present Address _____ Number _____
☐ Owns   ☐ Rents   ☐ Other
☐ Home   ☐ Explain

Ages of   Boys _____   Owns ☐ Yes
Children   Girls _____   Auto ☐ No

HUSBAND'S
First Name _____
Employed By _____
Business Address _____
No. of Years with Company _____ Job Title _____

WIFE'S
First Name _____
Employed by _____
Business Address _____
No. of Years with Company _____ Job Title _____

BANK REFERENCE
Name of Bank _____
Address _____
_____
_____

☐ Checking Account
☐ Saving Account
☐ Loan

NEAREST RELATIVE
Name _____ Relationship _____
Address _____
_____
_____

BUSINESS REFERENCE
Name of Company _____
Address _____

☐ 30-Day Charge
☐ Time Payment

Name of Insured for Credit Name _____
Life if Other Than Person Address _____
Signing Contract   Relationship _____
Age _____

Additional
Information _____
or Remarks _____

Additional
Information _____
or Remarks _____

I Hereby Certify That This Contract Sets Forth the Entire Agreement between
the Purchaser and Me and That the Purchaser's Signature Is Genuine

_____
Sales Representative's Signature

STATISTICAL DATA

HOME OFFICE USE ONLY

ACCOUNT NUMBER

THIS SPACE FOR HOME OFFICE USE ONLY

SHIP TO: Mr.
            Mrs.
            Miss. _____
            _____
            _____

Special Instructions for Shipping or Terms:
_____
_____

This Order Is for the Following Products:
_____
_____
_____
_____

MIRREX COMPANY, INC.

Date of Order	Rec. with Order	Pay Monthly	First Payment Due Approximately
	$	$	☐ 30 Days ☐ 45 Days
			From Date of Order

Identification Number: $ _____

(Contract Terms)

Tax (if any)
Total $ _____
Less Down Payment
Balance to Pay $ _____

(Notice to Buyer)

Signature _____
Mailing Address _____
Number and Street

_____
City   State   Code   County

Representative: _____ Representative's Number: _____
Please Print Name

for each customer. Thus, the transaction data regarding payment action are available for retrieval by the computer.

While management used the customer transaction data (which was retrieved, processed, and summarized by the computer), they also recognized the desirability of having other statistical data to compare and correlate with the monetary data. Assisted by the administrative service staff of a certified public accounting firm, management developed a statistical sampling system which made available for retrieval not only all the data on the sales contract (see Exhibit A) and transaction experience but also certain correlation analyses determined by comparing all the data available for a given customer.

Sample Size and Sample Selection.   Each of the 650,000 active accounts has an account number. A program was developed for the computer to generate random numbers, and this program was designed to achieve nearly automatic sample selection with a small probability of bias. These features were necessary to select large numbers of accounts at a low cost while avoiding faulty samples. This system of generating random numbers was used to select the sample accounts from the 650,000 file of accounts, and this sample (which was taken at the time the sampling program was initiated) represented all the outstanding accounts.

This same computer program is used daily to select samples from the *new* orders commissioned. The computer daily selects two samples from the new accounts: (*a*) a control sample and (*b*) a special sample. The special sample is used for special tests of alternative collection actions.

Data Accumulated for Sample Accounts.   A 600-character sample file record, including forty characters available for new information, was designed for use on magnetic tape. Following are some of the data included in this 600-character record:

a.   Identification number and data regarding location of record on tape unit.
b.   Initial payment and sales information (date of sale, due date for first payment, monthly payment, total dollar contract, down payment, transportation, taxes, commission, and bonus).
c.   Type of purchase (product identification and marketing ar-

rangement—package purchase involving several products, etc.) .

d. Sales organization (sales representative's identification number, division, region, district, state, county, and so forth) .

e. Descriptive data regarding sales representative (representative's cumulative sales for specified period of time, pay, and so forth) .

f. Customer characteristics (an exhaustive accumulation of the data contained on the application form as well as a report of the credit review) .[5]

g. Transaction history (an exhaustive report of the payment behavior of the customer) .[5]

h. Collection action (several "characters" of space are reserved for full coverage of this action if and when it occurs) .

i. Attorney action (the 600-character record has several spaces reserved for attorney information and attorney collection activity) .

As indicated, this 600-character sample file record contains an exhaustive accumulation of the data on the sales contract and the data regarding the transaction experience for the customer. In addition, a special coding form was designed for the accumulation of interpretative data (statistical classification data) gained through an analysis of all of the customer experience data.

Processing Procedures. Daily the computer selects from the new order accounts a sample, and a list is prepared of the new order accounts so elected. (This list is subsequently used in reconciliation and verification procedures.) Later, *as time permits,* the sales contract for each new order account (which has been selected) is pulled, and these data are keypunched for inclusion in the 600-character sample file record. As previously stated, a coding form has been prepared for use in the conversion of the data from the sales contract and other documents to the sample file maintained on magnetic tape.

The aggregate daily accounts included in the new order sample during any month are called the "monthly sample" accounts. These selected accounts are supposed to be representative of the new accounts for that month. A sample account file is opened on the

---

[5] A special coding form has been developed for extensive classification of customer characteristics and business transaction data.

magnetic tape for each selected account, and the customer experience with this account is periodically processed on tape for storage purposes. Once an account has been selected for inclusion in the sample, the account becomes part of the "monthly sample," and the data for this account (along with the other new accounts selected during that particular month) are monthly reported over the life of the sales contract.

From another perspective, there are 650,000 active customer accounts. Since each sales contract is for approximately 30 months, there are, on any given day, 30 different groups of monthly sample accounts which collectively are supposed to be representative of the total (650,000 accounts). In other words, all the accounts receivable accounts are identified by month and year of sale. The sample accounts are also handled in this manner. This month and year identification is specified on all sample account reports, and a separate series of reports is prepared for each of the 30 groups. Thus, on any reporting date, there are 30 detailed reports (one for each group) and a summary report to reflect the accounts included in all samples. As will be explained later in the discussion of reports, a statistical inference is made from the characteristics of the sample to the total mass that each sample represents, and each report contains columns for the sample and for the total group represented by the sample. The computer is programmed to make this statistical inference from the sample to the total mass for each item on each report.

At the end of the month, the aggregate accounts receivable information for that month for each sample customer in all 30 monthly groups is processed in detail to the 600-character sample file records on magnetic tape. The detailed accounts receivable information is already on tape; thus, the computer can process the transaction experience from the accounts receivable records to the sample file records. Some information regarding attorney action and collection activity is processed by clerks and subsequently keypunched for entry on magnetic tape.

In terms of time restraints, the daily selection of new accounts is the only critical item. The pulling of the sales contract for the account, the keypunching of these data, the opening of a 600-character sample file record, and the processing of data to this record can be performed on any day during the month—as time permits. Likewise, the monthly retrieval of detailed data regarding customer experience (transaction experience) from the accounts receivable files can be processed on a flexible basis.

Reports

Seven monthly reports are prepared to provide management with useful information on a regular basis, to assist in decisions on policy matters, and to provide guides in the administration of credit and collection actions. These seven reports make maximum utilization of the regular monthly computer runs (as it becomes apparent that additional information and analyses are required beyond these reports, special computer programs and other processing methods will have to be designed and initiated; however, the current reports are a by-product of the regular monthly computer runs) .

Report 1—New Order Sample File Detail Listing. This report lists each sampled account for the month and a print out of the coded data in the record. This report is intended to aid in checking sample information input and in reviewing account characteristics at a later date.

Report 2—Analysis of Current Status of Receivables. This monthly report breaks down sales contracts and receivables in a variety of summaries by product and in total, for each sample month to date. It is a comprehensive report on the condition of sales contracts outstanding and includes statistics on write-offs attorney transfers, paid-in-full, paid ahead, paying on time, one to three months late, and so forth. The report contains a projection from the sample to the total for all contracts sold in a month. A report summarizing this information is issued to management monthly, and shows current and past month's condition by product and for all products.

Report 3—Projection of Collections by Month. The expected monthly cash revenue generated by new orders is projected in this monthly report. These projections facilitate comparison of actual collections per month to the collections required by terms for each product and in total. Similarly, net cash flow (collections minus variable costs) for each month can be estimated statistically.

Report 4—Summary of Collection Status by 90-Day Pattern and Section. This analysis is designed to help find the most effective tool to predict an account's collectivity from its early pattern of payment. Eight payment patterns are possible during the first 90 days of transaction history. If *P* means paid and *M* means missed payment, these 90-day patterns are as follows:

0. *PPP*	4. *MPP*
1. *PPM*	5. *MPM*
2. *PMP*	6. *MMP*
3. *PMM*	7. *MMM*

Management hopes that through this type of analysis it will be able to determine whether the 90-day report, for example, can be improved upon by earlier reports of a similar type. The report contains analyses on a geographic and ethnic basis in the hope that some significant differences in collectibility by these characteristics will become apparent from a continuous examination of these data.

Report 5—Analysis from Statistical Sample. This monthly report summarizes product and total sales by geographic section (not restricted to sales area) and according to terms sold under, for example, "cash sales," "balance payable," and "terms." This information is primarily useful in the statistics department. It is an indicator of sample coverage and has potential as a barometer of future collections based on terms granted and where sold. The report includes information on sample size and percent of total, projected term sales, down payments, and statistical variance of all projections. All of these data are essential for projecting sample data to all accounts.

Report 6—Miscellaneous Totals and Analysis of Attorney Accounts. This monthly report provides statistical information for projecting and making special calculations. It includes information required to calculate variable product costs. A special calculation is made of the month's sample pay code and its statistical variance. The "pay code" is a sensitive indicator of performance and is essentially the ratio of the amount due to the amount actually paid to date. Study of this code should aid in forecasting collection experience.

The attorney analysis is intended to assist in evaluating ways to improve the net return from attorneys, such as improved timing of action. The report relates attorney collections to age of account when transferred, balance transferred, and company collection experience.

Report 7—Summary of New Account Characteristics. Since the ultimate desire is to relate customer characteristics to account performance, this summary of contract and other data is included. The information is used later to develop improved credit review and collection methods. In other words, this report summarizes current activity in the hope of providing historical data for analysis and correlation purposes which might eventually be used in some type of "scientific" credit review and collection method.

Graphs

The integrated management information system currently contains four graphs which highlight significant relationships of different aspects of customer experience.

Graph 1—Collectibility.   Of key importance is the actual month-to-month and year-to-year relative collection experience. Current month collection percent data may directly indicate that the business situation has changed and that the firm's profits will eventually be affected, or the percent data may indicate changes in economic conditions that may require tighter credit and collection action. On the other hand, longer term collection trends are necessary as a base for judgment and policy decisions. For short-term history, a more sensitive collectibility statistic has been developed which considers only the current three months' collections against the terms of these same three months. This more sensitive collectibility measure is then augmented by year-to-date percent collected data, and these two groups of data are broken down into product and total collection data.

Graph 2—Cash Collections.   Although percent collectibility data are useful for decision-making purposes, management should also be cognizant of the dollar value of the collectibility performance. For this purpose, a special graph of monthly projected cash collections has been prepared. These projections consider the sales volume, mix of products, and terms under which the products are sold. Based upon reasonable sales projections, this cash collection line on the graph can be extended beyond current experience. The incremental dollar significance of current collection performance will be determined by plotting actual dollars collected versus expected collections.

Graph 3—Net Cash Flow.   Changes in product mix and sales levels have a significant effect on month-to-month cash position. For this reason, it is important to know net cash income and its fluctuations. As a by-product of reporting new order samples and collection experience, the basic data are available within the computer system for the preparation each month of the forecasted net cash flow. This forecast considers the directly variable costs as being the most important, and these costs include such items as product costs, average commissions, taxes, transportation, and accessory expenditures.

Graph 4—Sales Volume and Forecast. This graph compares actual sales with forecasted sales on a month-by-month basis. The comparison is in terms of units of sales rather than in terms of dollar volume.

REQUIRED:

Submit a brief report to management which outlines in detail the possible additional uses that might be made of the computer retrieval system for customer experience.

PART V

MOVEMENT TOWARD A TOTAL INFORMATION SYSTEM

CHAPTER **15**

Interactive Planning and Management Control Information Systems

THE MOVEMENT from a computer-based operating system to a TYPE 3 information system has been described in the previous parts of this book at three discrete levels of multidimensional improvement in the nature and scope of the information content of data flows. At the first level, the editing and screening phase was added to the planning phase and the control phase. At the next level, the monitoring and sensory capabilities of the coordination phase were interfaced with the other three phases. At the third level, the data flows within the control phase were expanded and were designed to accommodate multitime cycles, and these improvements were accompanied by a monitoring and inquiring phase and a systems processing phase which collectively, supported a high intensity of interactive inquiry by members of management in an online mode.

As progress is made beyond a TYPE 3 information system, the administrative process, organizational arrangements, and data dimensions of the network assume new levels of complexity. For example, security and confidentiality of data assume a dominant role at this level of sophistication. Specification of data and demands for access, software and personalized storage tend to increase exponentially at each step beyond the TYPE 3 network.

The code structure identification and maintenance committee, the data management committee, the information systems coordinating committee, and the confidentiality of data committee were discussed

457

in Chapter 4. The functions of these committees in data specification, software selection, retrieval capabilities, data flow design, and data security were *indirectly* examined in each of the discrete levels of advancement from an operating system to a TYPE 3 information system. However, beyond the TYPE 3 information system, it is imperative that close attention is *directly* given to the operations of these four committees.

The latter issue can be examined from an alternative perspective. In the three discrete movements thus far, partial implementation of the four committees may have resulted in a satisfactory design, implementation, and maintenance of an integrated, computer-based information system. Beyond this level, coordination, quality control, and security must be closely analyzed and monitored if continued advancement is to occur.

In addition to the issues of security, coordination, access, and special retrieval capabilities, the organization is confronted with a new class of problem as the computer-based network reaches the position that it is classified as being beyond a TYPE 3 information system. Specifically, there is a serious issue with the perspective of members of management, and this problem is especially prevalent among those members of management who have participated in the three discrete levels of advancement in the computer-based network.

In this movement, members of management are consistently applying the same general type of synthesizing techniques and making simplifying assumptions in order to reduce the attention given to exceptional items and activities. There is almost a syndrome associated with members of management who have participated in the advancement to a TYPE 3 information system. Those traits and characteristics which were most helpful in the advancement to date, tend to be inconsistent and contrary to further improvement. New points of view are required as well as a questioning of existing relationships.

Since the evaluation of performance is somewhat restricted by the availability of machine-readable data that are appropriately coded, in retrieving such data and making analyses, some members of management may attach an aura of closure to their evaluation which are not supported by the facts. In the absence of data on exceptional activities, some members of management may become insensitive to their occurrence. This latter problem along with the issues of security, coordination, and access are examined in this chapter.

THE GENERAL MODEL

The fourth of the five discrete models of advanced computer-based networks is an interactive planning and management control information system. The high intensity of online, interaction between remote terminal users and the computer-based network that was achieved in the TYPE 3 information system is an integral part of this model. This includes the required capabilities for data processing, sorting, reprocessing, assigning, retrieving, and reporting which were encompassed in the combined systems processing phase and the monitoring and inquiring phase of a TYPE 3 network.

In this extension, selected members of management are assigned unique segments of online storage for their respective individual use. Appropriate security and control procedures are in force so there is confidential inquiry and use of the information stored in each of these online locations. Each individual's items are stored in a separate location and are referred to as a *personalized data base.* These items may include data, computer programs, computer routines, a series of data files that can be separately accessed, or any combination of data, programs, routines, and files.

A personalized data base is essential for interactive planning by members of management. While a given analysis may use selected common data which are online within the network, the interactive planner will not take the time to input all the special data (including weights assigned to factors) that are required for this special study. Instead, the interactive planner establishes in advance a unique, personalized data base which provides the online storage for most of the data, programs, routines, and files that are frequently used by this planner. Therefore, in a given interactive episode, the planner can quickly access and apply these online capabilities to a specific, complex study, and all of these interactions may occur with only four or five data inputs by the planner. Special computer software facilities are available which assist the planner in indexing, data specification, cross-referencing, accessing, and using a personalized data base in an interactive mode.

The monitoring and sensory capabilities encompassed in the coordination phase of a TYPE 2 network are strengthened in the general model of an interactive planning and management control information system. The selected environmental change data are not only edited, processed, tested for sensitivity, weighted, and used in recomputing the online assignment solution, but these data are filtered and assigned to common data bases for planning.

The *open* system represented by the TYPE 3 network is extended in this general model with a special focus on data gathering of environmental activities and the identification and selection of data from secondary sources. The teams which are assigned to these data gathering, classifying, and storage operations really have two distinct purposes. First, the accumulation of additional environmental change data serves to strengthen and expand the content and timeliness of the common data bases. Second, management briefings using these online environmental data tend to sensitize members of management to exceptional environmental activities that may relate to informed analyses of organizational performance. The latter briefings are partially directed toward breaking the syndrome that some members of management may experience from their previous efforts to simplify, synthesize, consolidate, and integrate data requirements.

In the complex, multidimensional environment of an interactive planning and management control information system, the nature of the administrative process cannot be separated into (*a*) the editing and screening phase, (*b*) the planning phase, (*c*) the control phase, (*d*) the coordination phase, (*e*) the monitoring and inquiring phase, and (*f*) the systems processing phase. A second set of processing, sorting, and assigning operations are added to the systems processing phase, and many of the existing capabilities are also expanded. Therefore, a new label, "advanced systems processing phase," is used to refer to these features.

Two other changes in the administrative process were previously discussed. First, the special efforts by data gathering teams that focus on environmental change factors are presented as a separate administrative and organizational phase which interfaces with the regular editing and screening phase. Second, the personalized data bases and online processing features of the interactive planner were explained.

TYPE 4 INFORMATION SYSTEM

Figure 15.1 presents a generalized model of a TYPE 4 information system containing eight phases— (*a*) editing and screening phase, (*b*) planning phase, (c) control phase, (d) coordination phase, (e) monitoring and inquiring phase, (f) advanced systems processing phase, (g) information gathering, classifying, and storage phase, and (h) interactive planning phase. The editing and screening phase, planning phase, control phase, and monitoring and inquiring phase have the identical features in this generalized model as those incorporated in the TYPE 3 information system; therefore, our attention is focused on the other four phases.

Information Gathering, Classifying, and Storage Phase

This new phase in a TYPE 4 network is necessary to satisfy the continuous requirement for revised intelligence on the external environment. These continuous information requirements include data on consumer behavior, customer product acceptance, actions by competitors, actions by governmental officials, and changes in international markets.

Symbols A1 to A3 in Figure 15.1 represent the data gathering activities by study teams and library resource personnel. The "human processing" symbol depicts the nature and speed of these monitoring and screening operations. Symbols A4 to A7 indicate that the raw data captured by these study teams and library resource personnel are transformed into machine-readable form and entered into the computer system; however, these data are in *raw form* (pre-edit) and can only be read, displayed (per symbol A6), copied, and assigned to storage (symbols A8 to A11 represent the copying and assignment operations). Those raw data which are selected for retention (per symbol A7) and online use within the primary network (per symbol A11) are entered into the detailed filtering processes of the editing and screening phase (symbol A23 in Figure 15.1 which really refers to symbols A1 to A10 in Figure 7.1).

The processing, classifying, and storing of data captured by this phase are the least significant aspects of the operations. The most important aspect is the formal recognition by executive management of the need for these operations, including the assignment of personnel and financial resources required for accomplishing the function. A major benefit from these new operations is the information dissemination to members of management on selected changes in the environment as well as status information on critical environmental

FIGURE 15.1
A Generalized Model of a TYPE 4 Information System

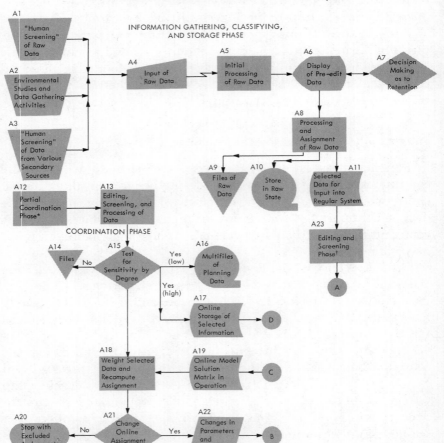

° The partial coordination phase is depicted by symbols A2 to A5 in Figure 10.1.
† The editing and screening phase is depicted by symbols A1 to A10 in Figure 7.1.

factors. The latter information dissemination role is not specifically presented in Figure 15.1, but is part of the raw data that are processed by the editing and screening phase (symbol A23), then are further processed, sorted, reprocessed, assigned, and retrieved in the advanced systems processing phase (symbols A24 to A30), and are placed in online storage for planning (symbol A44). Overall, this new function highlights the need for "human screening" of the

FIGURE 15.1 (*Continued*)

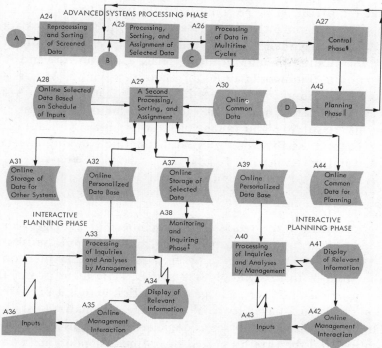

† The monitoring and inquiring phase is depicted by symbols A7 to A18 in Figure 13.1.
§ The relevant control phase is depicted by symbols A23 to A37 in Figure 13.1.
‖ The regular planning phase is depicted by symbols A12 to A16 in Figure 7.1 and by symbols A28 to A30 in Figure 10.1.

environment, including secondary sources of data, and dissemination of this intelligence to members of management.

Advanced Systems Processing Phase

The computer programs, data routines, data sorting and retrieval capabilities, and software required for a high intensity of online use by decision makers and planners were presented as the systems processing phase in a TYPE 3 information system. Symbols A24 to A26 represent the systems processing phase associated with the monitoring and inquiring phase, the control phase, and the planning phase for a TYPE 3 network.

Each of these computer-support facilities is expanded in a TYPE 4 information system, and a new set of processing, sorting, and assignment operations (symbols A28 to A30) is added to provide for the special requirements of personalized data bases (symbols A32 and A39). The assignment of edited data to online storage of data for other systems (symbol A31), to online storage of selected data for use in the monitoring and inquiring phase (symbols A37 and A38), and to online common data files for planning (symbol A44) is similar to these assignment activities in a TYPE 3 information system. However, primarily because of the operations of the information gathering, classifying, and storage phase, there is a significant change in the content, quality, currency, and timeliness of the data being assigned and retrieved.

Interactive Planning Phase

As previously indicated, selected members of management are assigned online computer storage space, and these unique locations may contain data, computer programs, routines, data files, or any combination of these. Symbols A32 and A39 represent two of these online locations; however, a large organization with a TYPE 4 information system may have fifty to sixty of these personalized data bases.

The personalized data bases as depicted by symbols A32 and A39 are online, and they are supported by online, secondary data screening and selection facilities (as depicted by symbol A28). Because of the degree of online support for each personalized data base, the organization's data management committee must initially approve the establishment of each personalized data base. Moreover, the computer center will provide staff assistance in specifying data codes, in designing routines, programs, and file layouts, in using sorting and retrieval software, and in interacting with the network under a user determined confidentiality of data setting.

The online storage, processing, retrieving, display, interaction, and input capabilities associated with the use of a personalized data base in an interactive planning phase are depicted by symbols A32 to A36 and A39 to A43 in Figure 15.1. The second processing, sorting, and assignment operations in the advanced systems processing phase (symbols A28 to A30) partially provide the computer-based support for this interaction; not illustrated in Figure 15.1 is the staff assistance that is given to each interactive planner in both the design and maintenance of these online, interactive capabilities. For example, many of the online computer programs are maintained in a modular arrangement to facilitate quick alteration of major components.

Another dimension of the interactive planning phase that is not depicted in Figure 15.1 is the learning process of the interactive planner and the time required for a minimum level of performance. We have examined the learning process of various interactive planners in different types of organizations. There tends to be a five to nine month lag between the point at which the personalized data base is established and the point at which these interactive capabilities are operated with a high level of efficiency. In those organizations where members of management had prior experience using the online inquiring capabilities of a monitoring and inquiring phase, they were able to efficiently use these interactive capabilities of a personalized data base in the minimum time.

Coordination Phase

In general, the operations performed in this phase are similar to those performed by their counterparts in the TYPE 3 information system. Symbols A12 and A14 to A22 indicate these similarities; however, symbols A16 and A17 are not included in the TYPE 3 network. There are really three aspects of these new features.

First, the set of data that are monitored and screened in a TYPE 4 network is more encompassing than the set used in a TYPE 3 network. These additional environmental factors are primarily associated with the residual benefit of the efforts of study teams in the information gathering, classifying, and storage phase.

Second, a finer scale is used for testing sensitivity (symbols A14 to A17). This improvement in the refinement of the measurement process is primarily attributable to the overall program for improvement in the quality of data used in the models.

Third, as the finer scale is employed, selected data are immediately placed in an online state for use in the planning phase (symbols A17 and A45 depict this relation). Other data with a low degree of sensitivity are stored offline in multibanks of planning data (symbol A16 depicts this situation). Even nonsensitive data on environmental factors are tentatively retained in offline files (symbol A14 represents this type of rejection) for possible use in planning for the next cycle.

THE EIGHT COMMON DIMENSIONS

An examination of the eight dimensions of the administrative process and the organizational arrangements encompassed in a TYPE 4 information system assists the reader in comparing this general model with other discrete levels of advancement. First, the models of the administrative process in a TYPE 4 information system include eight phases: (*a*) editing and screening phase, (*b*) planning phase, (*c*) control phase, (*d*) coordination phase, (*e*) monitoring and inquiring phase, (*f*) advanced systems processing phase, (*g*) information gathering, classifying, and storage phase, and (*h*) interactive planning phase. Members of management who are interacting with a TYPE 4 network are experienced in following a management-by-systems approach to monitoring of performance, comparing actual with planned performance, and taking corrective action. The latter may be in an interactive mode in a TYPE 4 network. The monitoring, coordinating, and planning activities associated with this sophisticated network typically encompass the dominant data flows throughout the organization. The latter means that all organizational, departmental, functional, and geographical boundaries may be permeated by this series of data flows included within a TYPE 4 information system.

Second, the organizational structure of an agency, association, company, or institution possessing a TYPE 4 information system is shifting toward a committee arrangement and away from a matrix arrangement. The planners associated with the control phase in a TYPE 3 information system are also included in the TYPE 4 network. While the committee arrangement tends to replace the matrix arrangement in short-term decision making, the traditional organizational structure continues to serve as the primary arrangement for technical control and management control purposes. But as extensions are made to the TYPE 4 network, considerable use is made of the committee arrangement for management control purposes.

Third, policy makers, decision makers, and planners from various parts of the organization may be directly associated with a TYPE 4 information system. Some members of management also participate in the new information gathering, classifying, and storage phase. Selected members of executive management and key decision makers may participate with personalized data bases in the interactive planning phase. Members of management who are not involved with the interactive planning phase tend to be direct participants in the monitoring and inquiring phase. In other words, a TYPE 4 information system is of sufficient scope that most members of management from throughout the organization tend to be directly involved in some role with the network.

Fourth, the nature of the activity supported by a TYPE 4 information system includes all major information flows—both vertical and horizontal—within the organization that are directly associated with members of management. The scope of these information flows in this network tends to be significantly more encompassing than those included in a TYPE 3 information system, and, as previously indicated, the TYPE 4 network tends to penetrate all organizational units.

Fifth, the degree of online interaction in the monitoring and inquiring phase tended to differentiate the TYPE 3 information system from earlier networks. The personalized data bases and online interaction of selected members of management participating in the interactive planning phase clearly differentiate the TYPE 4 network from the TYPE 3 system. The advanced systems processing phase provides the necessary computer-support capabilities to permit the expanded intensity of this online interaction in the TYPE 4 network.

Sixth, the concept of the time cycle in a TYPE 4 network is very similar to that in a TYPE 3 system. Extensions to the multidimensional control phase encompassed in a TYPE 3 system will frequently include more discrete time cycles; however, there is nothing conceptually different with the time aspects of these constructs.

Seventh, an organization with a TYPE 4 information system usually has computer-based operations for all major activities within the organization. Most, if not all, of the major activities are integrated into the TYPE 4 network, and the other activities are usually supported by activity programs and functional programs. Most of these other computer-based operations are formally interfaced with the TYPE 4 information system.

Eighth, the data structure in a TYPE 4 information system is even more complex and multidimensional than that in a TYPE 3 network. The advanced systems processing phase contains special indexing, sorting, classifying, retrieving, and assignment operations that assist in coping with this complex data structure.

ADMINISTRATIVE SUPPORT OF THE TYPE 4 NETWORK

The administrative arrangements for planning and coordinating a series of computer-based networks were discussed in Chapter 4. This previous examination included the role, function, and membership of the four typical committees used in planning, designing, implementing, documenting, maintaining, and updating computer-based networks. The existence of these administrative arrangements is a prerequisite to the implementation of a TYPE 4 information system; therefore, attention is given to reviewing the activities of each of these committees in this type of sophisticated network.

Code Structure Identification and Maintenance Committee

The design of the code structure for common data files is a continuing requirement in all facets of a TYPE 4 information system. The remote terminal users who are accessing the monitoring and inquiring phase of the TYPE 4 network include policy makers, decision makers, and planners from all organizational units throughout the organization. In addition selected members of management are participating in an interactive mode with personalized data bases. Because of the diversity of users from all organizational units, departments, functions, and geographical locations, any changes in the code structure will probably have to be disseminated through the online communication facilities of the TYPE 4 network.

The retrieval of online data from a common data base is only one part of the work of the code structure identification and maintenance committee. Data specification and data classifying are essential requirements before inputs can be accepted by the editing and screening phase in a TYPE 4 information system. The diverse members of the code structure identification and maintenance committee are concerned that their respective interests and points of view are reflected in the specified code structure. However, it is not necessary that the input coding arrangement be maintained for retrieving data. In fact, the processing, sorting, assigning, and storing operations in the advanced systems processing phase are predicated upon using alternative coding arrangements. Other aspects of these coding capabilities are examined in detail in Chapter 16.

In summary, the code structure identification and maintenance committee in a TYPE 4 information system really serves in an overall communication role with the total organization containing this network. Each major information flow in the organization must be specified so that it can be transmitted, edited, processed, sorted, assigned, and retrieved by diverse members of management. A significant portion of this communication is in an online, interactive mode.

Data Management Committee

The 50 to 60 members of management who have been selected for interactive planning with personalized data bases will place individual, specific requirements on the data management committee for various types of staff assistance, special programming assistance, and software capabilities. These demands are normal and are anticipated. The absence of such demands will suggest that the interactive planning phase is not being used; therefore, if the data management committee is not coping with these demands after a few months, then there is probably an imbalance between the information requirements and the computer-based support provided by the TYPE 4 information system.

The data processing, data screening, multiassignments of data, data compression, data sorting, and reprocessing of data are some of the detailed activities that must be coordinated by the data management committee. Regardless of the size of the computer-based system, there are practical limits on the services that can be provided to users. Because of the number of remote terminal users in the monitoring and inquiring phase, the control phase, and the interactive planning phase, a considerable amount of computer processing capabilities are assigned to online interaction. In addition, the environmental setting surrounding an organization with a TYPE 4 information system is supportive toward encouraging individual growth and increased utilization of these interactive capabilities.

The latter point can be examined from another perspective. As a rough guideline, we will expect a utilization crisis to occur in about the seventh to eighth month after a TYPE 4 information system has

been implemented. This utilization crisis is positive in that it indicates that the network is being used; however, it must be managed in
an economic and efficient manner. The data management committee
has the responsibility of coping with these complex issues.

Information Systems Coordinating Committee

The role of the information systems coordinating committee
varies based on the status of the computer-based network. For purposes of this discussion we assume that a TYPE 4 information system
has been implemented and is in operation. Almost concurrently with
the implementation of the network new sets of demands are considered which may require extensions of the TYPE 4 network. If
major subsystems are involved, the coordinating efforts can probably
not be politically and organizationally handled by the data management committee. Thus, there is almost a continuous need for an
information systems coordinating committee. The representative
from a department who attends a committee meeting will vary based
on the issue and the time period; an individual with the title of vice
president will represent a given department at key meeting; otherwise, an assistant vice president or manager will attend the meeting.
However, the department will always be represented by one of these
three individuals, and there is a close communication among these
individuals.

Regardless of the nature of the subsystem or extension that is
being considered, the information systems coordinating committee
has several inherent problems associated with any efforts to design a
subsystem which will interface the TYPE 4 information system.
First, the overall extension or subsystem that is envisioned for the
next twenty to twenty-four months must be segmented into smaller
parts if the program design phase is to be completed within a reasonable time period. Second, there is frequently a relatively high turnover of systems analysts who are capable of handling major segments
of the program design phase; therefore, it is imperative that interim
reports are prepared. In those exceptional situations where there is
no turnover of personnel on a large-scale project, then the preparation of interim reports will not always be an optimal use of time.

Third, as soon as the overall extension or project is segmented, we
run the risk of nonuniform and noncompatible subunits. Fourth,
there may be duplication of efforts when different study teams inde-

pendently solve the same problem. Fifth, changes in the environment or in the organizational structure may force one study team to redefine the set of information flows while another study team continues to work on extensions from the original set of information flows. This situation results, of course, in a series of mismatched subsystems or units.

Accepting the premise that the overall extension or project *must* be segmented during the program design phase, the information systems coordinating committee is concerned with how to overcome these problems. The answer is simple! We must establish some type of continuous dialogue among the study team directors so that through the communication process these pitfalls are avoided. Regularly scheduled weekly meetings of study team directors, frequent interim reports, and monthly meetings of all study team members are three approaches used to provide the necessary continuous dialogue. The information systems coordinating committee must monitor these information systems activities to be sure the organizational interests are protected.

Confidentiality of Data Committee

An organization with a TYPE 4 information system necessarily has a significant amount of valuable data in its computer-based network which must be maintained on a confidential basis. Figure 5.2 presented some of the online control features that can be included in the editing and screening system in an advanced computer-based network, which is certainly the classification of a TYPE 4 system. The four filters discussed and examined in Figure 5.2 were included in the editing and screening phase incorporated within the TYPE 4 information system. The day file monitoring capabilities were also discussed in Chapter 5, and some attention was given in the last section of that chapter to security controls and confidential data arrangements.

A confidentiality of data committee with four or five members with the rank of vice president is a minimum response to the key security issues in a TYPE 4 information system. The tremendous processing, retrieving, and copying capabilities of the advanced systems processing phase, the monitoring and inquiring phase, and the interactive planning phase can be illegally used for the detriment of the organization. As the number of interactive users expands and as members of management become more familiar with the capabilities of the TYPE 4 information system, there is an increase in the risk of a security violation. The confidentiality of data committee has the key task of monitoring security controls and confidential data arrangements in a TYPE 4 information system, and the committee cannot delegate this responsibility. It is also recommended that there should be no alternates for the committee members; it is not a task to be handled by a subordinate.

TOPICS FOR CLASS DISCUSSION

1. Some members of management who have participated in the movement of the computer-based network from the level of an operating system to the level of a TYPE 3 information system may encounter problems in assisting the systems design activities required for a TYPE 4 information system. Explain the syndrome that confronts some of these members of management. Indicate in a positive manner how these problems can be overcome.

2. Explain the function of the information gathering, classifying, and storage phase in a TYPE 4 information system.

3. Explain how an advanced systems processing phase differs from the systems processing phase in a TYPE 3 information system.

4. Can an interactive planning phase exist with a personalized data base for each selected planner and supported by a systems processing phase? Explain your answer, including the justification for your position.

5. Explain how the coordination phase of a TYPE 4 information system differs from the coordination phase of a TYPE 2 information system.

6. Why is there an increased risk of security violation in a TYPE 4 information system over that in previous networks? Explain your position.

7. Briefly summarize the role of the following four committees in planning, designing, implementing, documenting, maintaining, and updating a TYPE 4 information system:

   a. Code structure identification and maintenance committee
   b. Data management committee
   c. Information systems coordinating committee
   d. Confidentiality of data committee

CASE 15–1.   THE MEAD CORPORATION

The Mead Corporation is reported by various management consultants to have the most advanced information system in the paper industry and to have one of the most advanced computerized information systems in any major industrial firm. This present position is the result of many years of planning and effort on the part of system analysts, programmers, operation researchers, management consultants, and representatives from manufacturers of electronic computer equipment coupled with strong administrative support from Mead executive management.

The director—information systems is considering insights gained from a recent study of regional sales offices where an online information retrieval system appeared desirable to obtain customer order status and inventory status. In the past, the systems philosophy of providing information only on an exception basis has been closely followed; thus, a management reporting system, for example, reports only summary customer information and provides for additional supporting detail on demand.

Stimulated by this suggestion, the director—information systems paused and reviewed the progress that Mead has made in the design and implementation of a total information planning and control system for the paper and related group. As part of this review, he reflected upon the company, history of current total information system project, overview of total system, organization changes, current status of paper and related system, and current concerns.

The Company

The Mead Corporation is one of the larger companies in the paper industry with annual sales in 1965 of $548 million. This volume of sales is equally divided among Mead Corporation's three major divisions: (1) paper and related operations, (2) paperboard and related converting facilities, and (3) merchant sales—the wholesaling of paper and paper supplies.

The division for paper and related operations encompasses the manufacturing and distribution of bleached and unbleached chemical wood pulp, white paper mills that produce the world's broadest line of fine printing papers, and the creation, production, and distribution of 'industrial and technical papers. The division for paper-board and related converting facilities includes multiple packaging, packaging machinery and systems, folding cartons, speciality pack-ages, point-of-purchase marketing aids, multiduty corrugated con-tainers, paperboards and technical fiberboards in a wide range of trims, calipers, treatments, laminations, and combinations, and the international sales of excess board. The merchant sales division consists of seven wholesalers who offer a full line of papers, including both Mead and competitive brands.

The company's annual sales has increased $380 million over the past nine years—from $168 million in 1956 to $548 million in 1965. The rapid expansion of domestic and overseas packaging operations is a significant factor in the growth of sales during the past two years; these operations accounted for over $100 million in sales during 1965.

History of Current Project

In 1960, executive management of the Mead Corporation, assisted by the management consultants from an international certified pub-lic accounting firm, embarked on a comprehensive study of Mead's data processing activities. The major objectives of this study were to:

1. Develop a long-range plan for data processing that would take full advantage of commercially available data processing and communication equipment and which would provide for an efficient management information and control system.
2. Review short-term planning in data processing to determine whether it is consistent with the long-range plan.
3. Make recommendations to Mead management as to organiza-tion, systems, equipment, and such other points necessary for the implementation of the long-range plan.

This study group's reviews revealed certain basic weaknesses in the flow of management information. For example, data processing was basically a decentralized function guided by loosely defined proce-dures and methods, particularly with respect to organizations ac-quired over the last six to eight years. The present management information system for internal happenings had delays, inaccuracies, multiplicity of sources, and a lack of timely decision information.

The system for external purposes had an apparent deficiency of data with which to supply the paper and related group customers with timely paper availability information, order status, and answers to other types of inquiries.

Based on these and other findings, the study group concluded that the recommended data processing system would have to include the solution to customer service and related production planning problems. Since the order cycles in the paper and related group and board mills were basically parallel, the study group believed that the solution to the more complicated problem—paper and related group —would, with appropriate modifications, solve the problem of the other. Using this premise the study group concentrated its detailed efforts in the paper and related order cycle with attention being given to board mills insofar as its cycle differed. The order cycles of containers and packaging required additional study to determine the feasibility of a board and related cycle including the converters.

In addition to the study group's detailed plans for the paper and related activities, the study group recommended the establishment of a central information service center, reporting to the director-information systems. The director—information systems would be provided with (1) corporate-wide *functional* (activity) control of all information systems development including systems personnel and (2) corporate-wide administrative and functional control of all data processing equipment and data processing operating personnel. The group proposed that an additional study of data processing requirements in board and related operations should be performed after the system for paper and related activities had been established.

Management of the Mead Corporation accepted the above *Report on Electronic Data Processing* and began to implement many of the recommendations. This action by Mead management in 1961 was not unusual for them, while the same action by management in most other companies in the paper industry would have been revolutionary. For example, one member of executive management could foresee in the mid-1950's that the computer had significant promise for improving operations of a paper company. This executive along with other members of management had given continuous support to Mead's studies and activities in electronic data processing. This environmental setting is an important element to understanding the progress in total information system at Mead.

During the remaining part of 1961 and 1962, most of the recommendations in the *Report on Electronic Data Processing* were implemented, and a group of competent information systems personnel was organized. The director—information systems was recruited from a management consulting firm, and other specialists in systems design and data processing activities were employed. The corporate information systems department also received personnel from within Mead Corporation; individuals with a diversity of background and experience in operations of the paper and related activities were among those transferred to the corporate information systems department.

The information systems department made significant progress in developing the details of the proposed plan for the paper and related activities and in implementing these programs. While the director—information systems was supervising these activities, he was also concerned with the advancements that were occurring in both electronic data processing and communication equipment. He desired to update the master plan for a total system.

In September, 1963, the Mead Corporation entered into an agreement with a major manufacturer of electronic equipment to develop the detailed systems concepts and plan the implementation of the recommendations set forth in the *Report on Electronic Data Processing,* issued in June, 1961, and subsequently approved by Mead management. The overall objective of both the original recommendations and the current study was to design a total information planning and control system which would encompass all of the activities of each other. Thus, information created as a result of an action in one activity would result in a chain of related actions through the other activities on an automated basis. The system envisioned was to utilize complete computer files of dynamically maintained data relating to the current status of the company, and each of its activities. These files would be updated either continuously or on a periodic basis depending on the requirement within the system for up-to-date information.

A study group was formed consisting of 12 members—6 representatives from Mead information systems department, 1 member of Mead internal audit department, 3 representatives from the major manufacturer of electronic equipment, and 2 management consultants from the international certified public accounting firm that participated in the 1960–61 systems study.

The thorough and detailed report of this study group was completed in March, 1964; the general system description from this report is presented in the next section.

Overview of Total Information Planning and Control System for the Paper and Related Group

Introduction. The proposed total information system, according to research performed by the study group, is the most advanced data handling system planned in the paper industry today. It incorporates the latest techniques of data collection by having information on orders and production status flow directly into a computer located in the corporate computer center. It embodies all the features of a completely integrated data handling system for maintaining all necessary records with the single entry of a particular unit of information. It operates on a preplanned control scheme which measures deviations and reports these deviations on an exception basis.

Exhibit A is a pictorial representation of this total system. The left-hand portion of the chart illustrates how management and operating personnel interact with the automated part of the total system. Corporate management determines the direction of the corporation by establishing plans and goals. Operating management converts the plans and goals into actual schedules and specific objectives. The operating personnel then strive to meet the schedule and attain the specific objectives. This, then, is the oversimplified theory of management and of the system. Under such a system, management must constantly have answers to the question "How are we doing?" because the plan is rarely executed precisely.

To find out "How we are doing," management must first determine what it is trying to do by establishing goals. Examples of such goals might be:

1. Maintain or improve profit for paper and related activities
2. Provide stable employment for all workers
3. Operate paper machines at full capacity
4. Reduce stock inventory to the lowest possible level
5. Provide maximum service to customers from stock inventory

These goals would then form the basis for the planning, reporting, and control techniques to be provided in the total information system. For management to determine if it is attaining the first goal, a sales analysis report would need to be provided that would show the

EXHIBIT A
Total Information Planning and Control System

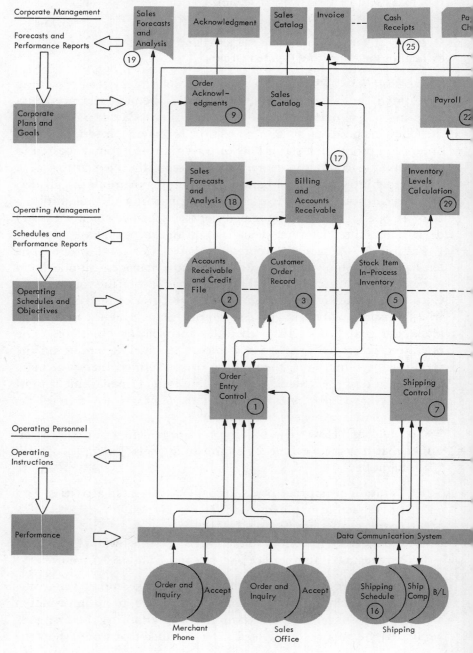

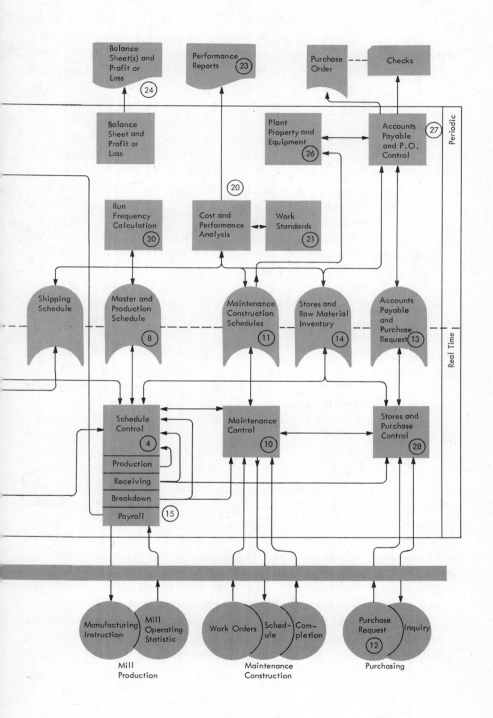

profit for Mead paper and related activities and the detailed information used to arrive at this profit, such as gross profit by grade, distribution costs, and warehousing costs. This report would then allow management to review the profit in relation to goals and take action on the items which are causing profit to deviate from the goal. The provision of stable employment and operation of paper machines at capacity are compatible goals since both imply operation at capacity. Stability of employment at less than full capacity may be provided through good scheduling techniques which balance work loads over the periods of less than capacity requirements. However, the goal to reduce inventory clashes somewhat with the concept of providing maximum service. How, then, can these conflicting goals be achieved? Compromise is the answer just as it is the answer to problems in a noncomputer-oriented system. However, in the computer-oriented system, these compromises must be translated into mathematical models which will always produce the optimum solution based on all the goals and resources involved. These goals or objectives then form the underlying foundation for computation of inventory levels and run frequencies and create the basis for developing sound scheduling techniques.

The corporate computer center will be able to assist operating management in arriving at a sound sales forecast and production schedule. The system will then be constantly monitoring operations and aiding operating management in its attempts to meet the schedule or plan as it was assigned. The plan, however, is constantly changing because orders, order changes, quality, and equipment failures must be incorporated into an actual operating schedule. Since the scheduling system will be able to quickly respond to change by examining the interrelationships of various elements in the manufacturing process in order to determine a new optimum schedule.

Operating management will thus be relieved of the many detailed and minor decisions currently required because of the necessity for schedule changes. This will enable operating management to insure that schedules are effected properly and to devote more time to the creative tasks of improving the actual production processes.

Operating personnel are the sensors in the system because they are constantly reporting back on job progress and completed tasks. The feedback of operating status will cause the system to update necessary records, while simultaneously examining the records for any deviations from preestablished schedules and standards. Deviations found will then immediately be reported back to operating management for necessary action.

The chart then depicts how the overall system reacts with its environment of management objectives, outside influences, and internal reporting systems. The various lines on the chart attempt to show which system will provide the necessary data flow between other systems to bring about the desired results.

Information Flow and Interaction.   A narrative linked to Exhibit A now follows which presents in summary form the information flow and interactions of the total system, as conceived by the study group. It is suggested that the reader give close consideration to Exhibit A while reading the following description, since the reference numbers in the following description refer to numbers presented in Exhibit A.

Orders, order changes, and inquiries form the triggers to put the system in motion. As these orders flow into the system, they enter the order entry control (1) system. Here the order is checked for completeness. A credit check is also performed using data stored in the accounts receivable (2) files. The order, having passed these initial tests, is checked against the stock item record (5), if it is a stock item, or entered into the schedule control (4), if it is a making item. The stock item record provides complete information about the ordered item. If in stock, the item is scheduled for shipping through shipping control (7). The planned shipping date is returned through the order entry control system back to the original entry terminal. In attempting to fill the stock order, and out-of-stock condition might be discovered in which case the system immediately checks the manufacturing schedule (8), or in-process inventories (5) to see if the item can be supplied from either of these. In this event, the item would be handled in a manner similar to a making item.

Making items are immediately referred to the schedule control (4) where they are fitted into the master and production schedule using information available as to run schedules and in-process inventory. When the appropriate manufacturing date is determined, the date is sent to shipping control (7) where the shipping date is determined and returned to the order entry terminal or customer. After the order is returned to the entry terminal and accepted by the customer, the order data are transferred to the acknowledgment system (9) which prepares the necessary customer acknowledgments on a daily basis.

All of the above steps occur in a few seconds, and the customer receives immediate response to his order requirements.

Maintenance and construction (10) also effect the schedule. As work orders requesting maintenance enter the system, they are entered into a maintenance schedule (11). Maintenance information on production equipment is automatically relayed to schedule control (4) where the maintenance is fitted into the master schedules.

Maintenance or repairs frequently require replacement parts. By entering a stores stock number and the quantity required with the work order, the stores records are examined (14) and the parts reserved until they are actually required on the job. A materials delivery schedule is prepared daily for use in delivering stores items to the facility. Any deficiency in the balance on hand for a particular item automatically triggers off a purchase request (12) which enters the purchase request file (13) for consolidation with other requests.

Other purchase requests are initiated by appropriate supervisory personnel or automatically created when demands are made against stores or raw materials inventory (14).

Schedule control (4) is constantly updating and monitoring the schedule so that within the system there is always an up-to-date schedule. When the appropriate time arrives, schedule control (4) issues the necessary manufacturing instructions to the mill which include operating instructions as well as raw material requirements. As the mill operations occur, the data describing the completed operations are returned to the computer where they are distributed (15) to the appropriate system. Any of the subsystems detecting an imbalance condition automatically provides management with an exception report describing the imbalance situation.

Daily shipping schedules (16) based on customer requirements are supplied to the warehouses. Completed shipping information is transmitted back to the corporate computer center where it will trigger the preparation of bills of lading. In addition, information will be transmitted to the billing (17) system where the invoice will be prepared and the necessary information for the sales analysis system (18) and accounts receivable system (2) will automatically be created.

Certain files and subsystems are of a more static nature where the information still must be altered or manipulated, but on a periodic, rather than a real-time basis. Earlier attention was given to the establishment of corporate goals. To enable management to establish realistic goals or modify them, provision of information, such as sales analysis, sales forecasts, and economic data must be made. This information (19) is provided for by the sales forecast and analysis (18) system. In addition to providing the data on past and future sales conditions, sound information on production performance must be provided. The cost analysis (20) system in conjunction with the work standard file (21), payroll data (22), storage usage (14), and production status (8) provide the basis for performance reports (23). Management is also provided with the conventional financial reports, such as balance sheets and profit or loss statements (24). Many levels of management are involved in the reporting system, and it will not be until the implementation phase is begun that the study group can determine the exact format, method of submission, level of detail, and frequency required for these management reports.

Other systems of a more static nature are those required to provide the backup information for the balance sheet and profit or loss statement. Cash receipts (25) and billing (17) information will be used to maintain the accounts receivable files (2). The property, plant, and equipment records (26) are maintained by information supplied by the accounts payable (27) and maintenance and construction (11) systems. Accounts payable (27) receives information from the purchasing control system (28) which monitors all requisitioning and purchase order writing operations.

The three most vital subsystems are the inventory levels calculation (29), run frequency calculation (30), and work standards determination (21). These three systems determine the predictive and control power of the schedule control system (4). The inventory levels calculation determines the response the Mead Corporation will be able to give the customer requirements for stock items. These inventory calculations also provide data for the run frequency calculations.

The run frequency calculations provide overall production requirements, and the results form the basis for the master schedule. The production standards will provide the scheduling control system (4) with all the necessary data to determine how long it will take a particular work center or piece of equipment to produce a given amount of paper.

Much historical data will be required to maintain these standards, but while the data will be gathered on a real-time basis, the actual calculations will only be required on a periodic basis to adjust any standards which are out of line. The frequency of calculation will be determined as progress is made into the implementation phase.

The report, *Total Information Planning and Control System for the Paper and Related Group,* was issued in March, 1964, and was endorsed by corporate management. Members of the information systems department had continued to work during the study phase on implementing selected limited-scale information system projects. As a result of this overall study, a revised order of priorities for proposed systems projects was determined, and systems analysts continued to work on the implementation phase of the new master plan.

Organization Changes

To recognize the growing importance of Mead's developing computer technology and, also, to recognize merit and accomplishment, the director—information systems was elected vice president of administration in April, 1964. As a means of providing closer coordination of related corporate headquarters functions, the vice president of administration was given responsibility over three departments in addition to the information systems department: purchasing, traffic, and distribution.

The executive who was in charge of Mead's 1963–64 study group was promoted to the position of director—information systems.

During 1965 several organization changes have occurred. Each of the three major divisions, that were previously discussed, is now organized under a group vice president who is responsible for coordinating production and sales and for producing a predetermined rate of return on the capital employed in his division. The group vice president for paper and related products directs Mead Papers, central planning, customer services, white papers, affiliated pulp companies, Gilbert Paper Co., and industrial and technical papers. The group vice president for paperboard and related products supervises Mead Packaging, Mead Containers, board development, Mead Board Sales (overseas), new board products, and central planning. The other group vice president is in charge of Mead Merchants—the seven wholesalers.

The vice president of finance has retired, and the three individuals who previously reported to him—the treasurer, the administrative vice president, and the financial accounts director and controller— now report to the executive vice president. The executive vice president previously administered marketing services; recently a director of marketing services was announced.

Exhibit B presents the Mead Corporation plan of organization as of December, 1965.

During 1966 the administrative vice president's area of responsibility was increased. He has staff responsibility over the personnel department and has direct responsibility over the following seven administrators: director of traffic, director of distribution, director of purchasing, director of information systems, manager of operations research, manager of Mead Management Services Division (sells excess computer time and provides other administrative service to small business firms), and manager of the Cincinnati computer center (handles all the data processing for the board group). Exhibit C presents the plan of organization for the administrative vice president as of June, 1966.

Current Status of Paper and Related System

Exhibit D presents the projected status of the paper and related system at the end of 1966. The reader should make frequent use of this chart while reading the following description of the current system.

Sales Orders. Each regional sales office has data speed transmitters and data speed receivers for communicating with the corporate computer center. All sales orders are processed by data speed transmitters on paper tape; this means that even sales orders in the Dayton sales office must be processed through these data speed transmitters. The sales order system makes maximum use of constant information, which is contained on various strips of punched paper tape in a storage file adjacent to each data speed transmitter.

At the corporate computer center, the sales orders on paper tape are converted to magnetic tape, and on a batch basis, these sales orders are processed through the computer center. This action en-

EXHIBIT B
Plan of Organization
(December, 1965)

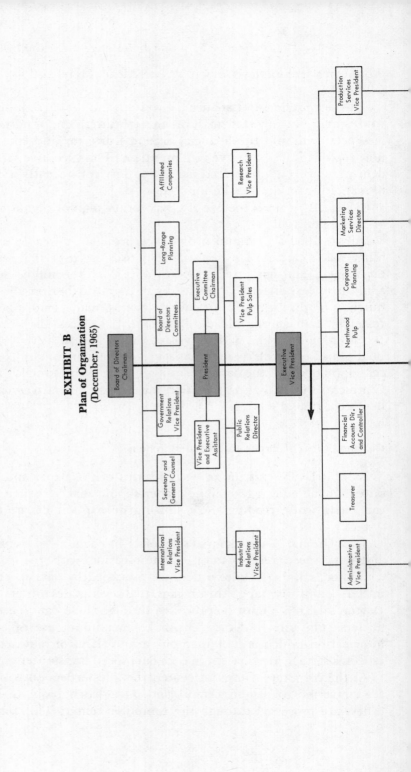

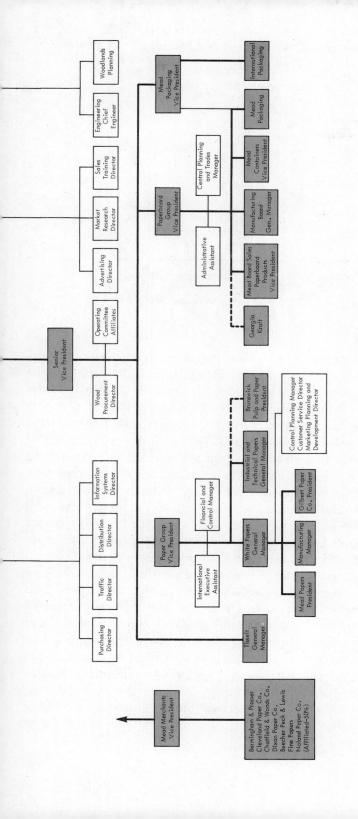

EXHIBIT C
Administrative Vice President
Plan of Organization
(June, 1966)

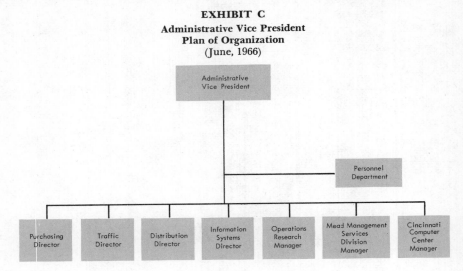

compasses (1) sending order acknowledgment to customer, (2) updating the inventory status of stocked items, and (3) entering the sales order in a customer open order file. Exhibit D also indicates that appropriate information is transmitted to a shipment planning file; this system has not been fully implemented, and the current position of the system is explained at a later point.

Each customer is mailed a sales order acknowledgment containing such information as sales class, terms, freight, office entering sale, status, how to ship, routing, product codes, grade, grade description, finish, item information, and type of packaging. The inventory status system is self-evident. The customer open order file is used by paper and related group's central planning department to schedule manufacturing orders, and this operation is subsequently discussed.

Planning and Scheduling. The central planning department for the paper and related group will schedule each sales order. This scheduling operation is consistent with the monthly assignment of products to machines and with the planned run frequency and sequencing of products by paper machine. In this planning and assignment process, central planning uses four types of planning and scheduling operations: forecasting, long-range planning, master scheduling, and production scheduling.

Forecasting is for a 12-month period. The exponential smoothing

EXHIBIT D
Projected Status—Paper and Related System, End of 1966

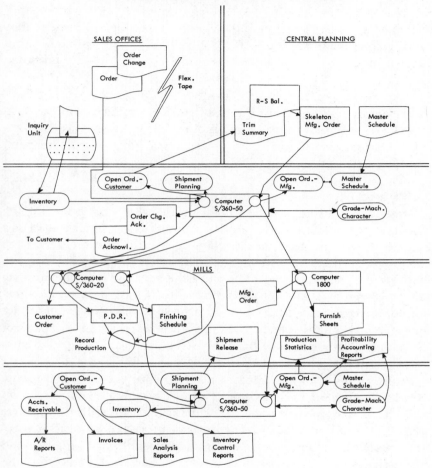

technique is applied to the data for the past two years using one of four equations average, trend, seasonal, and a combination of trend and seasonal. The major paper and related forecasting model is a linear program (LP) consisting of a 700 by a 5,000 matrix. Mead has 190 white paper products. If different product sizes are considered, then there are over 4,000 items. The LP model can only encompass the 190 products, 441 destinations, and 3 group regions (a weighted distribution is computed for each region for each product, including the freight) . An LP model is also used for forecasting the assignment of production by machine. At present, Mead has 22 white paper machines (a paper machine and related processing equipment may range in cost from $20 million to $30 million) . The LP model uses 24 machines; the two extra machines are used in evaluating proposed plant sites.

Long-range planning is periodically performed on a regular basis in five areas: capital expenditures, plant site, product mix (the estimated maximum and minimum amounts for each product) , allocation of production among paper mills for a quarter, and financial planning for next quarter. The production and operation aspects of long-range planning are primarily concerned with which machines will be assigned to which products in which months.

Master scheduling involves determining the exact schedule by machine for the first month and the planned schedule for the second and third months. The master schedule by machine includes both run frequency and sequencing. In operation of paper machines, the learning curve is very important, and the variable cost of manufacturing is higher than transportation cost. Thus, in a short time-period, it is normally more economical to have all units of a product manufactured on one paper machine and shipped to various parts of the country, rather than to have the demand satisfied by production on a decentralized basis.

Production scheduling is performed daily for the next three days. Mead management believes that a three-day exact schedule is typically the minimum time period in which the paper mills can operate efficiently. When a sales order is initially processed by central planning, a scheduler will review the master schedule of frequency and run assignment of products to machines and will determine the planned "available date" for shipment by line item on each order. A copy of the sales order is then sent to the appropriate mill.

A manufacturing order is prepared for a group of sales orders and stock replenishment for like grades of paper, and the information on each sales order is stored in the computer system. Each manufacturing order is transmitted to the appropriate mill by card to card communication equipment.

Central planning uses the corporate computer center to process programs that incorporate the details of each manufacturing order into master production schedules. This exact schedule is also communicated via data speed transmitters to the appropriate mill, and this schedule includes the special operating instructions for the paper machine, cutter, trimmer, rewinder, calendar, coater, and so forth.

Production and Operation. The production process of three paper machines is currently controlled by a process control computer system, and other paper machines will be controlled by such a computerized system in the near future. The Mead Corporation is recognized as being the leader in the paper industry in process control computers (see *Pulp and Paper,* January 31, 1966, or "Total System in the Mill," *Business Automation,* July, 1965). Early in 1962 Mead management began a program to install an IBM 1710 process control computer system on No. 4 paper machine at its Chillicothe Paper Company Division, Chillicothe, Ohio. This process control system has been in full operation since January, 1963, and subsequently, the process control system was expanded to include the adjacent No. 3 paper machine.

Recently, a process control computer system was installed with a new No. 5 paper machine at Kingsport, Tenn. Mead is scheduled to receive an IBM 1800 process control computer at the Central Research Laboratories in Chillicothe, Ohio, during July, 1966. A second IBM 1800 computer system is scheduled to replace the IBM 1710 process control computer system on No. 4 and No. 3 machines in Chillicothe during the fall of 1966.

Management has made many changes and improvements as a result of its experience with process control computer system. The papermaking process has been stabilized; new instruments have been added for measuring and controlling the flow of operations. Manufacturing standards for operation of the various processes have been established, and an alarm program covering important variables has been developed. Mathematical procedure for material balance was established, and computerized process control extended until it encompassed all operations. Currently, management is working on the integration of this computerized process control system with management information systems.

During the production process, on a 36-second cycle the computer records the measurements of the various instruments and gauges, and every 7 minutes an average is computed for each measurement. A detailed production performance report is prepared daily consisting of base yield data, department, cost, chargeable hours by department, average speed, percent of excess trim, percent of down time, grade code, and other information. This production reporting system coupled with good engineering standards for most operations provides the basic data for a wide range of production management activities.

Profitability Accounting.   The information systems department assisted by consultants from a certified public accounting firm is installing a profitability accounting system in white paper mills. This system will provide profit contribution by item, by sales area, by customer, by producing mill, and by individual paper machine.

Shipment Planning.   The annual volume of traffic is $50 million; thus, close supervision is given to the determination of optimum routes and rates. Shipment planning also involves the relating of customer order status file with the projected date for delivery on shipping dock at the destination. The shipment release operations for each sales area is administered by a separate clerk; thus, each sales office will call this latter individual whenever there is a question regarding the release of a shipment.

Monthly Reports.   The accounts receivable reports and inventory control reports are self-explanatory. Marketing management uses the customer open order file as a basis for analysis. An order received analysis is performed by sales office, and a margin is computed by customer. External data are used in marketing potential studies.

Current Concerns

A member of the information systems department visited each regional sales office, and talked with sales personnel about how the information processing and transmitting system could be improved. Regional sales personnel unanimously assigned a first priority to a proposed perpetual inventory information system. Salespeople felt that major customers should have the opportunity of inquiring of this perpetual inventory information system to see if a given item is in the warehouse. The salespeople desired the proposed system to give "no negative answers." If an item was out of stock, appropriate information would be obtained from the customer so that a representative of the regional sales office could contact the customer within an hour. Of course, this information would be obtained before the customer's inquiry is accepted by the information system, and the customer would be notified by the system that a salesperson will contact the customer within an hour about the inquiry.

These interviews indicated that the second priority should be assigned to the development of a different system for acknowledging customer orders. Many orders are less than a carload size; thus, the order must wait for other orders from customers in the same geographical location. Sales personnel would like a system that would give a definite commitment for delivery price (regardless of size of order) and delivery date. The present system quotes prices f.o.b. mill and indicates the day the order will be completed at the mill.

EXHIBIT E
Information Systems Department
Organization Chart—February 1, 1966

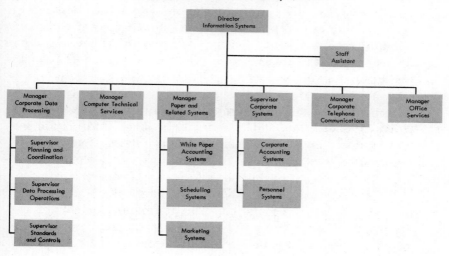

The interviews revealed that the third priority should be assigned to the development of an order status information system. At present, on an exception basis, customers are notified when goods will not be available on promised dates. Salespeople feel that there would be a significant competitive advantage from offering the customer the ability to inquire into the total information system as to the status of an order.

REQUIRED:

1.   Study the approach Mead management followed in the design implementation of a total management planning and control information system for the paper and related group. What are the advantages and disadvantages of this approach? Indicate other approaches that might have been followed, and explain how these suggested approaches would have differed from the approach actually followed.

2.   Evaluate the total information system for the paper and related group. Indicate how different information requirements are satisfied by different information sources. As part of your analysis, indicate information requirements that you have imputed for the current environmental setting in the paper industry which are not matched with information sources.

3.   As the installed advanced information system becomes one of housekeeping aspects and attention is shifted toward corporate planning considerations, what types of new information systems do you foresee as being required for this environment? Explain the reasons for your selections.

4.   The financial accounting director and controller has responsibility for financial analysis, corporate accounting, internal audit, federal and state tax, and external audit. Each information system produces journal vouchers as a final report; thus, accounting is one of the areas the director-information systems services. The current operations of the information systems department as of February 1, 1966, is indicated by Exhibit E. *After* the total management planning and control information system for the paper and related group and an appropriate total information system for the board paper group have been designed and implemented, what types of organization changes do you envision for these two departments? Explain the support for your observations.

5.   The director—information systems has followed the procedure of taking major undertakings and dividing these major undertakings into small projects. For example, there are many information systems projects that require two or three people for two or three weeks. At the present time, there are 35 planned projects for the current year. What are the advantages and disadvantages from dividing these major undertakings into small projects? In-

dicate other methods the director—information systems might follow in administering these activities.

CASE 15–2. GARSIDE CORPORATION
(A Review Case)

The Garside Corporation is a major manufacturer and distributor of chemicals and fertilizer products. The company has 15 manufacturing plants located in five cities in the eastern part of the United States. The distribution facilities are located throughout the United States and consist of both regional sales offices and warehouses. The home office is located in a major metropolitan city, and the company's common stock is listed on the New York Stock Exchange.

Four years ago, the president and chairman of the board of Garside Corporation became interested in computers and business technological developments. He attended several seminars on computers, quantitative methods, and information systems. Later, the mayor of the metropolitan city in which the home office is located appointed the president and chairman of the board of Garside Corporation to a new, special advisory committee on business.

Three years ago, the metropolitan newspapers contained several statements by the president of Garside Corporation regarding computers and business technological developments. At this point, the executive vice president and other members of the executive management met to discuss what action the Garside Corporation would take in the area of computers and business technological developments.

Organization

The president and chairman of the board of Garside Corporation is not actively involved in the day-to-day management activities of the company. The executive management group handles all the day-to-day activities, and this group consists of 10 individuals. First is the executive vice president and the six individuals reporting directly to him: (*a*) vice president of marketing, (*b*) vice president of administration, (*c*) controller, (*d*) treasurer, (*e*) director of research and development, and (*f*) senior vice president of manufacturing. The latter individual has three assistant vice presidents reporting directly to him: (*a*) assistant vice president for chemical products, (*b*) assistant vice president for fertilizer products, and (c) assistant vice president for engineering maintenance and services.

The executive management group decided that a management consulting firm should be engaged to design and implement an advanced information system at Garside Corporation. A few days later the executive management group reconsidered this matter. The executive vice president suggested that Garside Corporation should have its own management services group, and that this group should have the responsibility for implementing the advanced information system designed by the management consulting firm.

Furthermore, the executive vice president suggested to the other members of executive management that the director of management services group should temporarily report directly to him. This new management services group would not appear on the organization chart on the same level with the vice presidents, but would temporarily appear in a special position to the right of the executive vice president's box, with a line connecting the two boxes. The executive vice president's suggestions were approved by the executive committee, and the board of directors authorized these temporary arrangements.

Proposed Advanced System

A management consulting firm was engaged to design an advanced information system. The management consultants completed a thorough study of the company's operations, and eventually, they prepared a written report. The management consultants' report recommended that a "total system" should be developed. The report specified that all manufacturing and distribution facilities should be connected to a centralized computer center at the home office. A special communication network should be established to provide this continuous communication channel. Under this proposed system, all information processing would be performed by the centralized computer center, and the communication network would serve to transmit inquiries and information from or to the various decision makers throughout the organization.

Under the proposed system, production planning and scheduling activities would be based on the forecasted sales for each product. A special subsystem would be established that would continuously provide these forecasts. Certain data from day-to-day transactions would be stored in a special information retrieval subsystem, and this library would provide most of the raw data for the projected sales forecasts. The remaining data would come from governmental publications and industry sources.

While the production planning and scheduling activities would operate based on forecasted sales, a production control system would be established to monitor those activities based on reaction to actual sales. This latter system, providing actual sales data, is really an integrated inventory control, production management and control, and sales analysis system. Thus, on a management by exception basis, production management would administer the production activities for those products where the forecasted activity was significantly different from actual.

When the management consultants' report was prepared, existing transmission and communication equipment did not contain the required capacity and speed for coping with the estimated information requirements of this suggested total system. This limitaton of existing equipment was equally applicable to both the management of manufacturing facilities and to the management of distribution facilities. The management consultants' report indicated that equipment was being developed which would satisfy these requirements, and that this equipment was scheduled to be on the market in the near future. In the meantime, the production facilities in each of the five cities should have their own data processing capabilities, and summary reports should be mailed to the home office. The consultants' report suggested, however, that most of the information processing for the distribution centers' activities should be performed on a centralized basis at the home office.

Management Services Group

The management services group was established at Garside Corporation, and action was begun on the implementation of the "master plan." Members of the management services group quickly discovered that the management consultants' report was general and did not contain the necessary details for achieving the total information system. Thus, the director of the management services group undertook the task of completing the design phase.

In completing the details of the design phase, agreement had to be reached among various management groups on different matters. In one of these areas, a conflict arose between the director of the management services group and the assistant vice-president for chemical products. Finally, the assistant vice president for chemical products decided to retire under a special retirement program that had just been approved by the board of directors. A professor of engineering at the state university was employed as the new assistant vice president for chemical products.

The director of the management services group continued to work toward the completion of the elaborate computer programs and coding systems required by the master plan. This work continued throughout the fifteen month period ended with March of last year.

The executive vice president suggested in March of last year that executive management reconsider the responsibilities of the management services group and reach a permanent decision on the organizational location of this group. After many discussions over the following few weeks, the executive management group recommended to the board of directors (*a*) that the management services group should be discontinued and (*b*) that a new "management science and information systems group" should be established. This new group would be directly under the assistant vice president for engineering maintenance and services. After the board of directors approved this recommendation, the director of the former management services group resigned.

Management Science and Information Systems Group

By June of last year, the manager for the management science and information systems group had been appointed, and had immediately begun to recruit new members for the group. Many of the former members of the management services group had resigned from the Garside Corporation during May and June. After employing a few individuals, the manager accepted the task of completing the design phase of the master plan.

Subsequently, a point arose in the design phase where agreement was required from the assistant vice president for chemical products, the assistant vice president for fertilizer products, and the controller. The manager sought assistance from his superior, the assistant vice president for maintenance and services, in resolving this conflict. Agreement was not reached, and a stalemate occurred.

A few days later, the executive vice president suggested that a moratorium be placed upon the total information system project. Instead, the management science and informations system group was asked to perform a feasibility study regarding the purchase of a large-scale computer for the home office's centralized computer center.

During the third and fourth quarters of last year, the management science and information systems group devoted all its attention to the feasibility study. Last December, the president and chairman of the board of Garside Corporation unexpectedly announced that a large-scale computer was being purchased by Garside Corporation. This public release also specified that this large-scale computer system will be installed and in full operation within a six-month period.

The manager of the management science and information systems group was immediately assigned the task of installing this new large-scale computer system. The manager developed a critical path schedule of the tasks to be performed if the computer system was to be installed in this "record time." Problems arose during the first quarter of this year, and the installation activities were behind schedule. However, the president restated that the new computer system will be in operation by the scheduled date. He also announced that the existing computer facilities had been sold and will be removed from the premises shortly after the scheduled completion date.

During the first and second quarters of this year, the manager of the management science and information systems group as well as his associates each worked twenty or more hours of overtime each week in order to achieve the president's announced objective. About thirty days prior to the announced "scheduled completion date," the majority of the experienced members of the management science and information systems group resigned from the Garside Corporation.

REQUIRED:

1. Evaluate the Garside Corporation's movement toward a total information system.
2. What is the probability of achieving this total information system? Include in your comments the primary constraints you see impeding the attainment of this objective.

CHAPTER **16**

Planning and Data Base Elements in Large-Scale Information Systems

THE GENERAL model for the interactive planning and management control information system contains numerous features and operations that support individual members of management in the accomplishment of their respective tasks. In Chapter 15 the eight common dimensions of the administrative process and organizational arrangements encompassed in the TYPE 4 information system were examined. Brief consideration was also given to the administrative support required in planning, designing, implementing, documenting, maintaining, and updating a TYPE 4 network.

In this chapter the planning, code structure, and common data base elements in the TYPE 4 information system are highlighted. In addition, attention is given to extensions to the general model for an interactive planning and management control information system. A construct representing a balanced advancement beyond the TYPE 4 network is presented in the last part of this chapter, and this construct is called a general model of a long-range planning and management control information system. It has the designation of a TYPE 7 information system, and the missing digits between a TYPE 4 and a TYPE 7 network represent other balanced levels of advancement not now anticipated.

PLANNING ACTIVITIES

Technical control and physical control are the dominant focuses of an activity program and a functional program. At the operating systems level, considerations of management control enter the pic-

500

ture and technical and physical control assume secondary, but important, roles. As the computer-based network is elevated from an operating system to a TYPE 4 information system, different dimensions of the planning process assume primary roles within the network. We will now examine these dominant planning activities in each of the eight phases in the general model of an interactive planning and management control information system.

In a TYPE 4 Network

In the editing and screening phase of a TYPE 4 information system, there is a monitoring of rejects for indications of changes internal to the organization and between the organization and its environment. This management analysis of rejects is very selective. As indicated in Figure 5.2 (a detailed model of the editing and screening system in an advanced computer-based network), there are online, programmed decision rules that perform logical tests as to (*a*) authority of user to access system, (*b*) completeness of input data, (*c*) reasonableness of data for component, and (*d*) accuracy of input data. The rejects that are of most concern for planning purposes are those for which there is not an applicable code specification.

In the information gathering, classifying, and storage phase, the data gathering teams and library resource personnel are performing a "human screening" of raw data and secondary sources of data for purpose of determining *planning intelligence* which should be disseminated to members of management. This planning intelligence includes (*a*) facts about the environment, (*b*) status of selected exogenous factors that are indicators of other changes, and (*c*) findings from market research, consumer interviews, governmental analyses, international developments, and environmental research efforts related to the organization's external surroundings. The dissemination of this planning intelligence is made through management briefings, summary statements of environmental assessments and exogenous conditions which are stored online for use by planners, and online common data in planning files which are entered into the network by these data gathering teams.

The coordination phase of a TYPE 4 network contains four separate planning activities. First, the ability to make online changes in the current assignment of the control phase, while these specified operations and activities are in progress is certainly a planning activity in the traditional sense of the term. Second, the number of factors which are subjected to online monitoring in a TYPE 4 network is expanded over that in a TYPE 3 network, and these data on change factors are used in the planning process. Third, a finer scale for measuring sensitivity is applied to these monitored data in improving the level of the online planning process associated with changing the current assignment. Fourth, this sensitivity scale is also used to classify these monitored data for planning activities. These assignments include (*a*) temporary offline storage, (*b*) regular offline storage in a multipurpose file, and (*c*) online storage for use in the planning process for the subsequent control cycle's operations.

In the control phase and the related planning phase for a TYPE 4 information system, multiple time cycles of multidimensional data are processed through this network, and selected data are provided to planners within the control phase in the format of guidelines. These planners operate within the constraints specified in these guidelines (policy level parameters and decision level variables), interact with the external environment, perform various tasks, and input summary results of these human operations. The latter inputs serve as new data for the control phase in evaluating performance and are used in planning for the next control cycle.

The monitoring and inquiring phase permits members of management from throughout the organization (various departments, units, functions, and geographical locations) to interact with the computer-based network, to determine the status of activities, and to request special computer-generated reports and comparisons. The advanced systems processing phase provides the necessary processing, sorting, reprocessing, assigning, and retrieving operations to support the data requirements of members of management using the monitoring and inquiring phase, the planning phase, and the interactive planning phase. The personalized data bases and related inquiry capabilities in the latter phase place special, secondary assignment and processing requirements upon the advanced systems processing phase.

In summary, there is online planning in the coordination phase of responding to selected environmental change factors. There is regular planning in the planning phase associated with specifying the detailed assignment for the operations in the next cycle's control phase. There is short-term planning in the monitoring and inquiring phase of responses to activities and performance which may extend beyond the time horizon of the next cycle's control phase. The decision-making activities in the interactive planning phase are part of the overall strategic planning process. Not shown as a separate element in the TYPE 4 network is the long-range planning activities performed by executive management which provides the policy constraints within which the interactive planning phase is performed.

In an Extended Network

50 to 60 members of management who are individually assigned a personalized data base represent the organization's overall population of strategic planners. Over a six- to nine-month time period, there is a significant improvement in the level at which this strategic planning process is performed. This overall improvement is related to four developments: (*a*) the gaining of experience by members of management in online interaction with personalized data bases, (*b*) the updating by members of management of the specialized programs and routines stored in their respective personalized data bases, (*c*) improvements in the quality of the special planning data used in their evaluations from increased awareness of various data sources and from individual data accumulation efforts, and (*d*) the broadening of the scope of the analysis as an improved, composite understanding is achieved by the individual members of management.

The above comments are based on our analysis of strategic planners using an interactive planning phase over a 24 month period in three organizations. We have not observed strategic planners in an organization with a TYPE 4 information system where extensions have been made beyond this 24 month period. Because of the magnitude of the complex organizational and political issues involved, we are not making any conjectures as to how the online strategic planning process may eventually interact with an online long-range planning process.

In this section, we have seen the technical control, physical control, and management control activities have assumed secondary roles to planning activities in advanced computer-based information systems. The implementation of these planning activities in a computer-based setting requires that the essence of the results of the planning process is captured as data. In the next section of this chapter, we will examine the assignment and translation operations that can exist between symbols and events, objects, or properties.

CODE STRUCTURE

Data represent the lifeblood of a computer-based network, and the code structure establishes, interprets, and maintains this lifeblood. Specifically, the code structure consists of an orderly collection of assigned symbols, usually numerals, to objects, events, or properties according to a set of rules. In a given application, the code structure serves both to capture the object, event or propery as assigned symbols and as a thesaurus to interpret the assigned symbols as meaningful data. This movement may occur from the assigned symbol through a thesaurus to a property or from a property through a thesaurus to an assigned symbol.

In a simple, computer-based operation, the individual knowledge of members of management may be of such depth that they will not erroneously respond to errors and mistakes reflected in the data. Or, from another perspective, their views of the activities associated with the computer-based operations may be more timely and complete than the feedback which is suggested by the computer-based network. In the latter case, members of management will respond to their understanding of the situation rather than to interpretations of specific data.

However, as the computer-based network increased in scope and complexity, the activities associated with the network were of such magnitude that individual members of management were not totally informed of the situation. In the more encompassing network, such as a TYPE 4 informaton system, many members of management from throughout the organization in various departments, organizational units, geographical locations, and functional areas have become *data dependent*. In fact, these data serve as the communication among members of management as to the current status of activities and operations, the measurement of performance, and the statement of objectives and plans for the coming periods.

The model of an interactive planning and management control information system contained eight phases which permeate the total organization and encompass all major information flows. In this type of complex, environmental setting, the organization's future is probably *more dependent on data as its lifeblood* than is even visualized by the most ardent supporter of computer-based systems.

This overall movement toward data dependency on the part of members of management in complex organizations with advanced computer-based networks also serves to underscore the need for key members of management to participate on the confidentiality of data committee. The function and purpose of this committee were briefly discussed in Chapter 4; the internal control and monitoring operations performed by the members of this committee were discussed in Chapter 5. A restatement of the need for the confidentiality of data committee was presented in Chapter 15.

Coding

The coding process is the assignment of symbols to objects, events, and properties by a set of rules. This set of rules is arbitrarily developed out of the classification process in which relations are expressed among a number of variables. While the overall set of rules is arbitrarily developed, there are many institutional constraints and legal considerations which influence the designing process. These latter factors may be either direct or indirect. For example, legal considerations can be accommodated by designing the set of rules so the desired data are directly provided by the coding system. Alternatively, these specified data may be obtained by further processing and sorting of data initially coded for another purpose. It is becoming increasingly common for institutional constraints and legal considerations to be handled on an indirect basis.

Conceptually, the coding process is based on classification and, as such, can be operationally applied at the lowest level of measurement. It can, of course, be applied at the higher levels of measurement; using Stevens' model, this includes the ordinal scale, the interval scale, and the ratio scale.[1]

Since the coding process is based on classification, it presupposes the existence of a classification system. The arbitrary set of rules used in the coding process is developed from the attributes and elements identified in the classification process. This set of rules will permit the conversion and transformation of data from one set of representation to another.

---

[1] S. S. Stevens, "On the Theory of Scales of Measurement," *Science,* vol. 103 (June 1946), pp. 677–80.

As information systems analysts, we are especially interested in the design of this set of rules. Where there is a choice of which attributes and elements will be incorporated in the set of rules, we believe that this decision should be monitored by the Code Structure Identification and Management Committee.

The latter recommendation is a reflection of the current "state of the art." The coding process has only recently become a major area of research. Some individuals are applying various management science techniques, including cluster analysis,[2] to the process of identifying relevant attributes and elements for inclusion in the set of rules.

The assigned symbols may be alphabetic, numeric, mnemonic, alphameric or word codes. There are varying efficiencies and error rates with each of these different types of symbols. A computer program can be developed so that the classification and the coding process are concurrently performed, and the resulting assigned symbols can be stored online in a code dictionary. There are many other choices in selecting assigned symbols, but for our purposes, we are especially interested in those *assigned symbols that are in machine readable form.*

Input-Oriented Coding Pattern.   In designing a coding pattern, there are two extreme positions: input-oriented and output-oriented. Where there are limited processing and storage facilities, the output-oriented coding pattern is the best strategy. In a manual operation the output-oriented coding pattern is probably the only feasible solution. Since, in most organizations we are not confronted with the problem of limited facilities, we can select between these two extreme positions primarily on the basis of how to reduce errors.

In most information systems, an input-oriented coding pattern is employed. Typically, the predetermined data on each source document are transformed into assigned symbols that are in machine-readable form. The raw data contained on the source document will usually be a combination of individual elements and groups. For example, on a sales invoice in a company with three divisions, a single digit may be used to designate which division is making the sale. Twenty digits may be assigned for use in describing the product

---

[2] Nancy Price and Samuel Schiminovich, "A Clustering Experiment: First Step towards a Computer-Generated Classification Scheme," *Information Storage and Retrieval,* August 1968, pp. 271–80.

that was sold, and eight digits may be used for designating the product identification number. Other groups of digits will be assigned for use in recording such data as quantity, per-unit selling price, total, freight, route, shipping instructions, customer name and address, billing instructions, credit terms, salesperson identification number, and so forth.

The objective of the input transformation process is to represent quickly in machine-readable units the raw data on a source document. This can be accomplished by coding clerks or by an optical scanner. The source documents can be eliminated and a remote input terminal can be used in directly recording within the computer system the initial transaction data.

A Second Processing

The advanced systems processing phase in the generalized model of a TYPE 4 information system contained the capability for a second processing, sorting, and assignment of data. This capability is depicted by symbols A28 to A30 in Figure 15.1.

The latter operation is really a second transformation process performed by a series of computer programs stored within the information system. This second transformation process can be described as an output-oriented coding pattern. There is another aspect of this second transformation process. The selected data must be sorted and assigned to various common data files, common data banks, and control files.

Obviously, these sorting and assignment processes are performed by a closed set of computer programs that are online in the system. The mere existence of this degree of online capability indicates that some analysis has been made of the information requirements of decision-making activities. Moreover, these information requirements have been clustered on some basis and related to common data files and common data banks.

Earlier in this chapter, the planning activities associated with each of the eight phases in a TYPE 4 information system were highlighted. Another perspective for examining these planning and decision-making activities is to emphasize the various distinct time cycles within the general model of an interactive planning and management control information system. Figure 16.1 presents this type of model which specifies six distinct time cycles in the second processing, sorting, and assignment of data within the advanced systems processing phase. These six cycles are as follows:

FIGURE 16.1
**Within the General Model of an Interactive Planning and
Management Control Information System***
(six distinct time cycles in the second processing, sorting, and assignment
of data within the advanced systems processing phase)

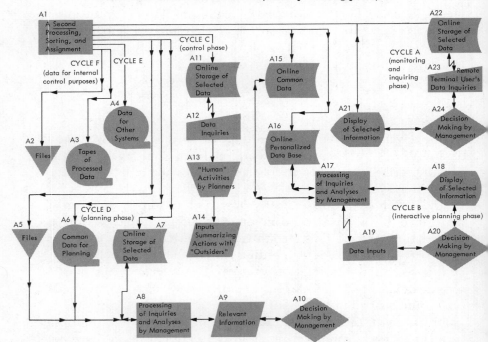

° See Figure 15.1 for the eight phases in the general model of a TYPE 4 information system.

    a. Monitoring and Inquiring Phase.
        Instantaneous information for status and inquiry purposes.
    b. Interactive Planning Phase.
        Immediate information for decision-making purposes.
    c. Control Phase.
        Guidance information for planners.
    d. Planning Phase.
        Regular information for planning the assignment for the next
        control cycle.

e. Part of the Advanced Systems Processing Phase.
    Selected data for use in other systems including long-range planning activities (which are not represented by a separate phase in the TYPE 4 information system).

f. Editing and Screening Phase.
    Data for systems maintenance and internal control purposes.

Cycle A, Cycle B, and Cycle C provide online information; however, there are significant differences in the content and processing capabilities between Cycle B versus the other two cycles. Cycle B contains a personalized data base that is unique with the decision maker and online processing capabilities; Cycle A and Cycle C do not contain either of these features.

The typical content of the information flows in Cycle A is an identification code or number combined with quantitative and statistical data. The prescribed coding pattern for identification purposes in Cycle A may also reflect many critical data that can be immediately used by decision makers. For example, a ten digit product code might contain the following sensitive information:

1234567890	There are 10 digits in the product identification code.
12xxxxxxxx	The first two digits designate the product group.
xx345xxxxx	Third, fourth and fifth digits designate the product subgroups. Since there are 1,000 possible assignments within these three digits, we would expect these subgroups to be narrowly defined and not to contain an excessive number of items within any one subgroup.
xxxxx6xxxx	Sixth digit designates special physical characteristics of an item, such as, perishable, nonperishable, flammable and nonflammable.
xxxxxx7xxx	Seventh digit designates a composite rating of three classification schemes: (1) distribution, (2) packaging, and (3) storage.
xxxxxxx8xx	Eighth digit designates a composite rating of two classification schemes: (1) price and degree of importance, and (2) turnover frequency.
xxxxxxxx9x	Ninth digit designates the organizational level at which the decision is made for pricing this specific

product. (In a different organization another type of marketing data might be reflected in this ninth digit.)

xxxxxxxxx0   Tenth digit is used to specify a particular product among a group of products which have the same assigned numbers in the first nine digits.

In Cycle A, the monitoring and inquiring function is performed by a manager located at a remote terminal. As previously indicated, the contents in Cycle A normally consist of identification codes combined with quantitative and statistical data. Thus, the manager can use the remote terminal to inquire about the status of a specific product, customer, contract, vendor or other object. In evaluating the online response from the system, the manager is provided (through the vehicle of the identification code) with a framework in which to make an informed analysis of a wide range of issues.

In Cycle B, the interactive data requirements of selected members of management with assigned personalized data bases containing, online data, computer programs, routines, and data files are supported in this online mode. The scope of the decision-making process tends to be toward strategic planning and away from day-to-day activities which would be identified with Cycle A, Cycle C, and Cycle D.

In Cycle C, online information is provided for the guidance of planners who operate within the policy parameters and decision variables specified by the top two levels of management. The contents of the information flows in the case of a business firm tend to contain marginal price, marginal cost, alternative distribution arrangements, and profit planning data. The contents will contain different types of data in a governmental agency: they will feature sensitive service and performance measures. The inquiries processed in Cycle C tend to be more complex than the inquiries processed in Cycle A. Because Cycle A frequently services a higher level of management, many data management systems are designed to provide faster response to Cycle A than is given to Cycle C.

In Cycle D, the information required for planning the next control cycle's detailed assignment is accumulated in both online and offline locations. The response time for the processing in Cycle D (symbol A8) tends to be relatively slow, especially when contrasted with the online processing (symbol A17) in Cycle B. However, members of management engaged in these decision-making activities have the full duration of the current control cycle before a new assignment must be specified for the next period's control cycle.

In Cycle E, selected information is accumulated for use in other systems, including long-range planning activities. As previously indicated, a long-range planning phase is not included in a TYPE 4 information system; however, this phase is included in the TYPE 7 network presented subsequently in this chapter.

In Cycle F, "father" and "grandfather" tapes are stored so that the online data files can be reestablished in case of machine or systems failure. Other data for internal control and internal review purposes are also stored in the files created in Cycle F. These and other aspects of security are examined previously in this book in Chapter 5.

From the above discussion, the online processing and interactive capabilities of selected members of management using personalized data bases in Cycle B can be easily differentiated from management's role in the other cycles. A finer distinction can be made among Cycle A, Cycle C, and Cycle D by using an example of a coding pattern. The 63-digit coding pattern for a sales invoice at the Hardy Company, which was illustrated and explained in Chapter 8, is repeated here as a point of reference.

1234xxxxxxxxxxxx...	The first four digits designate the general ledger account.
xxxx567xxxxxxxxx...	Fifth, sixth, and seventh digits designate subaccounts based on organizational and responsibility accounting factors.
xxxxxxx8xxxxxxxx...	Eighth digit designates the division of this diversified corporation.
xxxxxxxx90123xxx...	These five digits (9th to the 13th digits) specify the customer number.
.....456789xxxxx...	These six digits (14th to the 19th digits) specify the product number.
.....xxxxxx012xx...	These three digits (20th to the 22nd digits) designate the date.
.....3456xxxxxxx...	These four digits (23rd to the 26th digits) designate the invoice number.
.....xxxx7890xxx...	These four digits (27th to the 30th digits) specify the location code and the cost center.

.....1234xxxxxxx...   These four digits (31st to the 34th digits) specify shipping instructions, such as, ship from and shipped to.

.....xxxx5xxxxxx...   This digit (35th digit) indicates the packaging code.

.....xxxxx6789xx...   These four digits (36th to the 39th digits) specify sales channel and territory codes.

.....012345678xx...   These nine digits (40th to the 48th digits) specify the quantity.

.....xxxxxxxxx9x...   This digit (49th digit) indicates the unit of measure for quantity.

.....xx0123456789...   These 10 digits (50th to the 59th digits) specify the price.

...xxxxxxxxx0123   These four digits (60th to the 63rd digits) specify the salesperson identification number.

For purposes of the current discussion, we will assume that these 63 digits are manually coded. In the subsequent section on common data bases we will reconsider this sales invoice from a different perspective.

The monitoring and inquiring activities in Cycle A do not require all 63 digits. The contents of the information flows in Cycle A might include the following elements: customer number, product number, invoice number, date, quantity and price. Managers at various remote locations can request online information on any or all of these elements. It is assumed that these identification codes (like those for the 10-digit product code presented earlier in this chapter) are based on sensitive attributes of the element; thus, the manager obtains additional information from the assigned symbols in these identification codes.

The decision-making activities in Cycle C will include only those marginal and profit planning data which can be utilized by management. This set of data will vary considerably among companies because of the differences in information requirements of decision makers in different environmental settings. In a given environmental setting, the contents of the information flows in Cycle C might include customer number, product number, invoice number, date, packaging code, sales channel and territory codes, quantity and price. The decision makers in this setting might desire to alter price and packaging in selected territories where planned volume is not being achieved.

In Cycle D, all 63 digits are stored as a group; in addition, separate files are maintained of data on selected elements within the coding pattern. These files serve as a source for a machine-prepared billing of the customer. Weekly, marketing reports are prepared by sales channel, territory, and customer. Monthly, the first eight digits in this coding pattern combined with dollar amounts are used to prepare a series of responsibility accounting reports. The Hardy Company's financial statements are also prepared from files maintained by Cycle D

COMMON DATA BASES

The generalized models for advanced information systems contained references to online common data and common data files. However, thus far in the book, we have not explained what is meant by a common data file or a common data base. In this section we will define these terms, illustrate some of the properties of a common data base, and examine some of the problems encountered in designing and implementing a common data base.

Characteristics

The term "data base" indicates that a depository of information has been established which is independent of the remote terminal users. To qualify as a *data base,* the total set of data elements must be stored in machine-sensitive media and be accessible to policy makers, decision makers, planners, and other remote terminal users. According to this definition, the term data base includes both online and offline situations. Some of the data bases in a large information retrieval system are usually stored offline, and they are periodically brought online for the processing of inquiries and for updating purposes.

In an advanced information system, we typically use the term data base only in referring to online information. If we have an offline depository of information, we refer to it as a "library" or an "information retrieval system." While a data base is a depository of information that is independent of users, we expect this depository or *data bank* (the terms *data bank* and *data base* can be used interchangeably) to be actually used by more than one decision maker. When decision makers in more than one department or division of an organization make online use of the *same data base,* we may label this depository as a "common data base." Moreover, if the term *common data base* is used, we expect only online use of the common data bank.

In a diversified organization, each division may have a series of online depositories, and each of these series may be called "common data bases." Thus, in the overall, complex organization there may be sets of *common data bases.*

A *file* or *data file* is a collection of records treated as a unit within a data base or a data bank. For example, the information within a metropolitan telephone directory could be reduced to machine-readable form and sorted into a set of data files. The first file might list, in alphabetical order by name, the telephone number and address of each subscriber. A second file might be a list, in alphabetical order by name, containing the name and address of each business and governmental unit. A third file might be a list by street address of each subscriber with the name and telephone number indicated. A fourth file might be a computer-generated version of the "yellow pages" and might consist of an alphabetical list of services, facilities, and activities and under each item, there is a list, in alphabetical order by name, containing the name and address of each business and governmental unit that provides the specified service, facility, or activity. Collectively, the four data files in this example can be called a common data bank or a common data base.

Example

Figure 16.2 presents a generalized model of a common data base for financial, manufacturing, and marketing departments in a particular company. Since this figure is presented for illustration purposes, the online processing activities are shown for only one of the four subsystems: order entry subsystem. The other subsystems—marketing analysis and financial management subsystem, sales forecasting and production scheduling subsystem, and inventory planning and control subsystem—also contain online processing activities.

FIGURE 16.2

Common Data Base for Financial, Manufacturing, and Marketing Departments

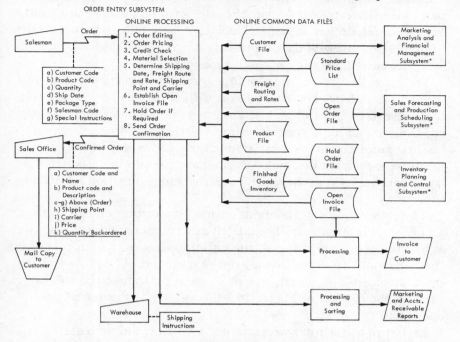

° The order entry subsystem is emphasized in this presentation; marketing analysis and financial management subsystem, sales forecasting and production scheduling subsystem, and inventory planning and control subsystem also have online processing activities and are online with the common data files.

This generalized model illustrates the information flow for old customers, but it does not show the other procedures required for a new customer. The latter is handled by a subroutine incorporated into the operating system to accomplish the online processing activities.

In our model we have two manual operations: processing inputs (orders) into system by salesman and mailing machine-prepared order confirmations to customers. All other coding, processing, sorting, and assigning is accomplished by the online operating systems. These systems clearly indicate that code structure identification and specification activities are prerequisites to the design of a common data base.

Note that the salesperson at the remote terminal is coding a minimum amount of data: customer code, product code, quantity, ship date, package type, salesperson code, and special instructions. As part of the protected file system, the salesperson must have previously identified his or her organizational unit and sales territory. This combined grouping of data represents the total *variable* information for order entry processing in this company.

We have illustrated eight online common data files within this common data base. For clarification we will briefly review the contents of two of these files. The customer file includes the customer code, name, address, special billing instructions, unusual product quality requirements, recent transactions, account balance, credit limits, year to date sales, and estimated annual sales by product. The latter data are used in the sale forecasting and production scheduling subsystem.

The open invoice file contains online information on the status of an order. It is automatically updated as changes occur in this status. When the goods are shipped, the online operating system processes these data and sends an invoice to the customer. The record in the open invoice file is closed, and these data are transferred to offline files (in the context of Figure 16.1 this is a Cycle F internal control operation).

Earlier in the chapter we examined a 63-digit coding pattern for a sales invoice. We will now examine each of the elements in this complete coding pattern based on Figure 16.2 and determine which digits are assigned manually and which ones are assigned by the computer system.

Digits	Description	Machine	Salesman
1-4	General ledger account	4	
5-7	Subaccount	3	
8	Division	1	
9-13	Customer code		5
14-19	Product code		6
20-22	Date	3	
23-26	Invoice number	4	
27-30	Location code and cost center		4
31-34	Shipped to and ship from	4	
35	Packaging code		1
36-39	Sales channel and territory codes		4
40-48	Quantity		9
49	Unit of measure	1	
50-59	Price	10	
60-63	Salesperson code		4
	Total digits	30	33

Thus, at least 30 of the 63 digits can be assigned by the computer system. This is possibly a conservative appraisal because we may be able to create a new set of groupings to encompass location code, cost center, sales channel, and territory code. If this is possible, then the computer system can be used to assign digits to part of this new set. In any case, using the computer system to assign digits in our coding pattern will significantly reduce the error rate.

An Approach to Designing a Common Data Base

When large-scale information systems are being planned, a significant function is determining a common data base. But we must determine the information requirements of decision makers that are to be serviced by a proposed common data base before we can even begin to consider how to design such a data base. In the context of our five phases for planning, designing, and implementing an information system (see Chapter 6) , a rough plan for a common data base might be created in phase three: conceptual systems design phase. This rough plan will be revised and modified however in the subsequent program design phase.

Hardware-software constraints or economic constraints may force us to abandon our plans for a common data base. The proposed common data base may be eliminated entirely by any one of the following factors: (*a*) location of decision makers; (*b*) time cycles of various decision-making activities; (*c*) stability of information requirements for various decision makers; (*d*) stability of environment in which decision-making activities are performed; (*e*) extent to which information requirements can be projected, classified, coded, and structured; (*f*) legal requirements; and (*g*) security requirements.

Assuming though that our rough plan created in the conceptual systems design phase is able to survive the preliminary analysis performed in the program design phase, then we are ready to determine a common data base. At this level the following five steps are necessary for determining a common data base:

a. Identify areas for each common data base.
b. Establish logical groupings of areas (such as hierarchy, functional, or activity) .
c. Integrate in cross-reference the logical groupings of areas.

d. Specify the contents and general code structure of each base.
e. Establish study teams for detailed code structure definition.

In performing these five steps, we are confronted with a tremendous monitoring and coordinating function. When we faced this same type of problem earlier (see Chapter 15), we recommended that a Code Structure Identification and Management Comittee should be established. This type of interdepartmental committee is needed to coordinate, monitor, and administer the common data base.

As the study teams work on specifying common codes and major codes, they must determine the *code element*. To analyze the major codes in the marketing area, we will focus on the customer, product, sales analysis, and invoice. The invoice codes, for instance, will include location, shipping instructions, billing instructions, special instructions, product and packaging. Each of these items might be called an *element,* in the sense of a "code element." To analyze the related codes in the financial management area, we will examine the accounts receivable record. The accounts receivable codes will include customer code, invoice number, and so forth. Therefore, one of the fundamental problems confronting these study teams is to determine at what level to define the coding units. For example, will we use the accounts receivable level or will we use the invoice location level? Obviously, code specification must occur at as low a level as is feasible.

A matrix is a useful device for determining at what level these coding elements will be specified. We might begin by cross-referencing the major coding documents in each department and placing X's for the intercepts where these same coding elements are being used in other departments. This initial matrix will be followed by a series of matrices which move progressively to more detailed levels of specification. Through this tedious process we can specify our common data base.

Organizational Considerations

One of the characteristics of a data base is that the depository is independent of information users. In a given company this will probably mean that some members of executive management will be asked to relinquish control over selected data files that they have directly monitored for many years. It is not unusual for this organizational consideration to negate the project completely.

There are two sides to most issues. There are some types of information requirements that executive management must control. Judgment in these areas cannot be relinquished to the manager of the common data base. For example, there are certain legal requirements and institutional considerations that preclude the treasurer and controller from permitting the manager of the common data base to handle all external reporting requirements. The corporate annual reports, statements for the Securities and Exchange Commission, and personnel reports are some of these reports that must be reviewed by the treasurer and controller prior to their distribution.

If we are to design a common data base, we must face this organizational problem. We can help solve this problem by reviewing with each major decision maker the list of information requirements that have been specified for his decision-making activities. It is assumed that we have previously met with this decision maker and that he concurs with the list of information requirements.

In jointly reviewing this list of requirements, we ask the decision maker to indicate the *extent to which* a common data base might perform certain functions related to each requirement. As an example of what can be accomplished by this approach, in reviewing the sales invoicing and accounts receivable management activities in a given company, it was determined that all 13 types of information files could be handled by a common data base. These 13 areas are as follows:

1. Customer files.
2. Product files.
3. Credit limits and terms.
4. Pricing.
5. Freight rate and routing.
6. Tax reports.
7. Systems control (order and shipment information).
8. Accounts receivable aging.
9. Credit management.
10. Sales returns and adjustments.
11. Sales analysis reports.
    a. Order analysis.
    b. Distribution analysis.
    c. Profit contribution by customer/product line/salesmen/ district.
    d. Budget and actual comparisons.

12.   Customer tax status.
13.   Legal constraints.
      a.   Pricing.
      b.   Freight payment.
      c.   Safety and physical.

In some organizations an alternative approach is recommended for solving this problem. In reviewing the list of information requirements with each decision maker and planner, we ask this individual to forecast the general nature of his or her function five years from now when a series of information systems and common data bases will exist. In this alternative approach the decision maker is not confronted with incremental changes in day-to-day activities, rather he has the opportunity to conceptualize about his future overall operations. Obviously, we must then assist the decision maker to move from the proposed state five years in the future back to the present.

In the last two sections of this chapter, we have seen how data are the lifeblood of the organization. The relationship between this lifeblood and the planning activities described in the first section of this chapter was depicted by the six time cycles within the advanced systems processing phase as shown in Figure 16.1. Attention is now shifted to a consideration of balanced extensions to this planning process in a more sophisticated computer-based network.

LONG-RANGE PLANNING AND MANAGEMENT CONTROL INFORMATION SYSTEMS

In the balanced, multidimensional extensions to a TYPE 4 information system, there is an increased emphasis on planning activities and the availability of multipurpose data to support these management efforts. For example, personnel related data files which were accumulated in various integrated subsystems are centralized and used for personnel planning and control purposes. Concurrent with these movements, there are shifts in the organizational arrangements which are supportive of these advanced networks.

The exact direction of these balanced advancements beyond a TYPE 4 information system can only be speculated, since this is beyond any existing systems. While several types of advancements can be anticipated (such as personnel planning and control, centralized files, organizational arrangements, and interactive planning) , it is highly likely that other developments will also occur. Therefore, we have skipped some digits to provide for these other developments and advancements, and we have used the digit "7" to designate our fifth discrete level of advancement. The general model for this fifth level of advancement is examined and is contrasted with the previously discussed discrete levels of advancement.

General Model

The fifth of the five discrete models of advanced computer-based networks is a long-range planning and management control information system. The interactive planning, online inquiry, and operational planning activities which were contained in the TYPE 4 network are also encompassed in this general model. The information gathering teams and library resource personnel are strengthened, since the overall network and the total organization become more "data dependent." For example, a team of professional research librarians are a part of the library resource personnel at this level.

The design of formal statistical and simulation models to represent significant segments of the organization's operations becomes an important part of the regular planning process. As these sophisticated models are designed, developed, and tested, management briefings are conducted to disseminate information on these new capabilities to other members of management, especially to the strategic planners participating in the interactive planning phase. These formal models may also be used for operational planning and long-range planning purposes.

A set of online, interactive activities for long-range planning is included in this general model. One important part of these long-range planning activities is the design, implementation, and application of supplementary editing, processing, and data transforming operations. These tasks are essential for converting operational planning data into strategic planning and long-range planning data. Close management supervision is required over these transformation processes because many of these data conversions may only be rough approximations of actual events. Therefore, considerable judgment must be exercised by members of management.

In addition to the statistical and simulation modeling phase and the long-range planning phase, personnel management has assumed a dominant position. A simple computer-based application for an organizational unit in which there are assigned employees must contain selected payroll, tax, benefit, and personnel data. As the size of the computer-based application is expanded to the position of a TYPE 4 information system, a series of payroll and personnel files is established. These personnel data files include (*a*) personnel record file, (*b*) payroll file, (*c*) wage, salary, and benefit file, (*d*) tax report file, (*e*) labor relations file, (*f*) skills inventory file, (*g*) job specification file, (*h*) current application file, (*i*) terminated personnel file, (*j*) historical application file, (*k*) recruiting file, and (*l*) safety analysis file.

In the general model of a long-range planning and management control information system, a series of four operating systems for personnel management are represented by online processing capabilities. These features include (*a*) the housekeeping functions of payroll; external reporting; wage, salary, and benefit administration; and internal reporting, (*b*) employment selection; wage, salary, and benefit planning; a job specification; and recruitment; (*c*) human resources operations and administration; and (*d*) allocation and utilization.[3] Personnel planning and management control decisions can be made utilizing the processing and analysis capabilities of these four operating systems as support.

As this general model is implemented, there is a shift in the organizational structure, and there is a tendency toward the formation of three permanent groups. The "housekeeping group" encompasses the day-to-day housekeeping, monitoring, status reporting, inquiring, and coordinating activitites. The "planning group" has a longer time horizon and includes the planning for the subsequent period's control cycle and the interactive, strategic planning activities. The "long-range planning group" focuses on policy level constraints and considers issues in a lengthy time horizon.

TYPE 7 Information System

Figure 16.3 presents a generalized model of a TYPE 7 information system containing eleven phases— (*a*) editing and screening phase, (*b*) planning phase, (*c*) control phase, (*d*) coordination phase, (*e*)

---

[3] For an expanded description of these and other personnel data files and functions, see: Ronald D. Picur, *A Framework for a Manpower Information System,* Unpublished Ph.D. dissertation, Northwestern University, 1973.

FIGURE 16.3

A Generalized Model of a TYPE 7 Information System

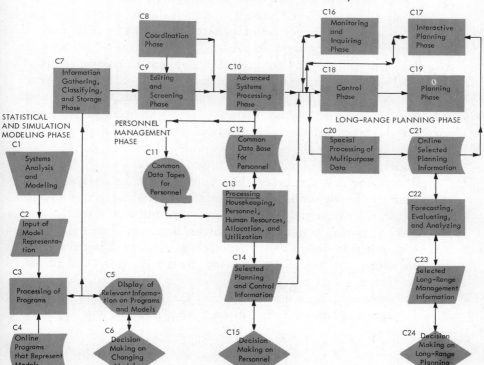

monitoring and inquiring phase, (f) advanced systems processing phase, (g) information gathering, classifying, and storage phase, (h) interactive planning phase, (i) statistical and simulation modeling phase, (j) personnel management phase, and (k) long-range planning phase. Since phases one through eight have the identical features in this generalized model as those incorporated in the TYPE 4 information system, our attention is focused on the last three phases: statistical and simulation modeling phase, personnel management phase, and long-range planning phase.

Symbols C1 to C6 in Figure 16.3 represent the statistical and simulation modeling phase. The members of management engaged in this full-time model building activities will brief other executives on the capabilities of these computer-based representations. An informal communication line, therefore, can be drawn from symbol

C6 to symbol C15 (regular planning operations), and symbol C24 (long-range planners).

Symbols C11 to C15 in Figure 16.3 depict the personnel management phase. The personnel data files described earlier in this section are grouped into a common data base (symbol C12 for the online data base and symbol C11 for the offline magnetic tapes), and the series of four operating systems is represented by online processing capabilities (symbol C13). With these online capabilities, personnel management decision makers (symbol C15) can interact with the system and retrieve selected planning and control information (symbol C14).

Symbols C20 to C24 depict the long-range planning phase. As indicated in the first section of this chapter, we have analyzed strategic planners participating in an interactive planning phase over a twenty-four month period. However, we have not examined online, long-range planning activities in an organization as sophisticated as that represented by this TYPE 7 information system. Therefore, the symbols within this phase are only for illustrative purposes. Please note that there is a formal connection between the special processing of multipurpose data (symbols C20 and C21) and the use of these data by strategic planners in the interactive planning phase (symbol C17).

The Eight Common Dimensions

Brief attention is given to the eight dimensions of the administrative process and the organizational arrangement encompassed in a TYPE 7 information system. First, the models of the administrative process in a TYPE 7 network include eleven phases; the three additional phases that are added to the TYPE 4 information system are (*a*) statistical and simulation modeling phase, (*b*) personnel management phase, and (*c*) long-range planning phase.

Second, the organizational structure of the company or institution possessing a TYPE 7 information system is shifting from a committee arrangement to a standing committee construct. A housekeeping group, a planning group, and a long-range planning group tend to be the three dominant clusters of management activities.

Third, policy makers, decision makers, and planners from the total organization tend to be directly associated with the TYPE 7 network.

Fourth, the nature of the activity supported by the TYPE 7 information system includes all major information flows within the total organization. Fifth, the degree of online interaction has been increased with policy makers participating in interactive, long-range planning activities. Sixth, the concept of the time cycle in a TYPE 7 network is similar to that in a TYPE 4 network.

Seventh, it is expected that all operations within an organization with a TYPE 7 network will, at least, be computer-based; the addition of the personnel management computer-based activities are examples of the benefits to be derived from these all inclusive data processing capabilities. Eight, the data structure in a TYPE 7 network is more complex than that in a TYPE 4 information system. As previously indicated, a special processing function (symbol C20 in Figure 16.3) was included in the long-range planning phase to handle the supplementary efforts to convert data from operational planning to strategic planning and long-range planning.

TOPICS FOR CLASS DISCUSSION

1. Explain the four planning activitites in the coordination phase of a TYPE 4 information system.

2. Present a comparative analysis of technical control, physical control, management control, and planning activities in each of the major computer-based models examined in this book: (*a*) operating system, (*b*) TYPE 1 information system, (*c*) TYPE 2 information system, (*d*) TYPE 3 information system, (*e*) TYPE 4 information system, and (*f*) TYPE 7 information system.

3. Present a comparative analysis of the models of the administrative process and organizational arrangements encompassed in the major computer-based models examined in this book.

4. Explain the relationship between the coding process and the classification process.

5. How do organizations with advanced computer-based networks become "data dependent?" Can this be prevented? Explain your position.

6. Explain the six distinct time cycles in the second processing, sorting, and assignment of data within the advanced system processing phase.

7. Differentiate between a data file and a common data base.

8. Differentiate among "housekeeping group," "planning group," and "long-range planning group."

CASE 16–1. STATE FOUNDATION FOR HEALTH CARE, INC.

The State Foundation for Health Care, Inc., a nonprofit professional association within your state, was established in 1974 under the auspices of the State Medical Association and with the endorsement of the State Hospital Association and the State Department of Public Health. State Foundation for Health Care, Inc. was formed to implement the Professional Standards Review Organization (PSRO) per Public Law 92–603.

The international certified public accounting firm with which you are employed has been engaged by the directors of State Foundation for Health Care to design and implement a data accumulation and reporting effort that supports the PSRO activities in the 158 short-stay general hospitals within the state. Specifically, local practicing physicians will perform a concurrent quality assurance review of the health care services provided to the patient while the patient is still in the hospital. This peer review will include a determination as to whether the services provided to a patient were medically necessary and consistent with professionally recognized standards of care. Another objective of the PSRO program is to encourage the use of less costly sites and modes of treatment where medically appropriate.

After being assigned as a staff member on this project, you examine Public Law 92–603 and the U.S. Department of Health, Education and Welfare (DHEW) publications pertaining to the implementation of PSRO activities. The following paragraph from the March 15, 1974 draft copy of DHEW's *P.S.R.O. Program Manual* (page 1, chapter 1 of the draft distributed by the Office of Professional Standards Review, 5600 Fishers Lane, Rockville, Maryland 20852) summarizes the purpose of this legislation:

The 1972 Amendments to the Social Security Act provide for the creation of Professional Standards Review Organizations (PSROs) designed to involve local practicing physicans in the ongoing review and evaluation of health care services covered under the Medicare, Medicaid and the Maternal and Child Health programs. The legislation is based on the concepts that health professionals are the most appropriate individuals to evaluate the quality of medical services and that effective peer review at the local level is the soundest method for assuring the appropriate use of health care resources and facilities. The PSRO is the means by which the legislation attempts to translate these concepts into practice.

As required under this legislation, the Secretary of DHEW has designated the geographical area within your state as representing a single PSRO activity. State Foundation for Health Care, Inc. has been approved by the Secretary of DHEW as the PSRO unit for your state. The State Foundation for Health Care has established an advisory group consisting of representatives of hospitals, health care practitioners (other than physicians), and other health care institutions. In addition, several committees have been formed to assist in the implementation and conduct of the PSRO program within the state.

Within each of the 158 hospitals, the peer review examination includes (*a*) admission certification concurrent with the patient's admission, (*b*) continued stay review, and (*c*) medical care evaluation studies. Profile data by patient, by disease entities, and by hospitals will be developed as part of the PSRO program. From an evaluation of these data and other information, the PSRO will develop criteria and standards that can be used as norms for each type of review conducted under the auspices of State Foundation for Health Care, Inc.

A partner with the international certified public accounting firm has suggested to the directors of State Foundation for Health Care that the uniform hospital abstract's minimum data set might be followed in this PSRO study. The partner specifically recommended the use of the following nineteen items and definitions as specified by the *Uniform Hospital Abstract: Minimum Basic Data Set, A Report of the United States National Committee on Vital and Health Statistics,* Hospital Research and Educational Trust, reprinted with permission of the National Center for Health Statistics from *Vital and Health Statistics,* series 4, no. 14, DHEW Publication No. (HSM) 73-1451 (Washington, D.C.: U.S. Government Printing Office, 1973).

1. Person identification
2. Date of birth
3. Sex
4. Race

5.   Residence (zip code)
6.   Hospital identification
7.   Admission date and hour (00–23)
8.   Discharge date
9.   Attending physician's identification number
10. Operating physician's identification number
11. Diagnoses
     a.   Principal diagnosis
     b.   Other diagnoses
12. Procedures and dates
     a.   Principal procedure and date
     b.   Additional procedures and dates
13. Disposition of patient
     a.   Discharged to home (routine discharge)
     b.   Left against medical advice
     c.   Discharged or transferred to another organization
     d.   Discharged or referred to another organized home care service
     e.   Died
14. Expected principal source of payment (select one)
     a.   Self-pay
     b.   Workmen's compensation
     c.   Medicare
     d.   Other government payments (including CHAMPUS, Medicaid)
     e.   Blue Cross
     f.   Insurance companies
     g.   No charge (free, charity, special research, or teaching)
     h.   Other
15. Source of patient
     a.   Routine admission
     b.   Admission from ambulatory service or outpatient department
     c.   Admission from emergency service
     d.   Transfer from affiliated institution
     e.   Transfer from another hospital
     f.   Admitted for special services (not transfer)
     g.   Readmission of patient previously receiving care for current problem
     h.   Newborn within hospital

16. Nature of admission
17. Service to which patient was admitted
18. Patient's address
19. Charges

The partner also reported to State Foundation for Health Care's directors that the staff had directly communicated with the medical records personnel and medical records librarians within each of the 158 hospitals included within this project. From these communications, the partner was pleased to report that all hospitals are using either the H-ICDA-2 or the ICDA-8 for diagnoses and procedures (items #11 and #12 in the above list) ; therefore, there should be no instances of a hospital using an unusual specification for a diagnosis.

The directors of the State Foundation for Health Care accepted the partner's recommendations and requested the development of a formal implementation program for the project. A document representing this detailed program should be submitted to the directors within thirty days.

REQUIRED:

1. You are asked to prepare a list of schedules and tables that can be developed from the uniform data set which will assist in the PSRO activities at the *hospital* level. Following are two examples of such items:

   a. A table of the average length of stay per discharged case classified by aggregate diagnostic ICDA code and by expected principal source of payment.

   b. A schedule of the number of discharged cases having *other* diagnoses (in addition to *principal* diagnosis) classified by aggregate diagnostic ICDA code.

2. Prepare a list of schedules and tables which can be developed from the uniform data set that will assist in the management of the PSRO activities at the *state* level.

3. Some consideration has been given to using socioeconomic and demographic data as reflected in the census tract information for comparative analyses of patients by disease categories and by average length of stay.

   The specification of a census tract number was not a part of the above uniform data set. Explain the statistical problems that can be encountered in relating the patient's address with census tract number when this cross-referencing is not performed on a house address basis.

4. Assume that a large-scale computer-based data system will be established containing the uniform data set for each patient discharged from one of the 158 short-stay general hospitals within the state. Briefly indicate how the availability of this data base can assist in overall state health care planning.

CASE 16–2. PHYFER CORPORATION

The Phyfer Corporation, an international conglomerate with headquarters in Chicago, Illinois, has annual sales of over $600,000,-000. The major divisions and companies within the Phyfer Corporation are in the consumer goods, food, metal, plastics, petroleum, and machine tool industries. Much of the parent corporation's growth occurred in the late 1960s, and many of these companies were acquired by cash purchase and by issuance of stock in the parent corporation, which is listed on a major exchange.

During the same period, various governmental agencies began requiring payroll information and other personnel data. Subsequently, skills and minority information were required when bidding for government contracts. In labor negotiations by industry, members of Phyfer Corporation's management were concerned with maintaining a competitive position within each industry; however, they were not certain as to the total cost if the proposed benefits in one industry were eventually to be given to all employees.

An information systems coordinating committee for personnel management was established at the Phyfer Corporation for the purpose of planning and designing common data files which can be used throughout the organization. This committee, whose members were at the corporate vice president level, had several working sessions with the code structure identification and maintenance committee and the data management committee. The reason for these working sessions was to gain an appreciation of the impact of changing the payroll file, tax report file, personnel file, wage-salary-and-benefit file, distribution reports, safety file, and labor relations file.

The housekeeping type of personnel records and files in many of the acquired companies was converted to Phyfer Corporation's computer system with only minor adjustments. In other cases, where Phyfer Corporation already had similar operations, the acquired company's personnel records were converted to the computer-based data files already existing in that area. In addition to the problems from acquisition of companies, until recently, personnel management was primarily performed on a decentralized basis. Because of this decentralized responsibility, the personnel specifications in one computer-based network may not be similar to those in another network within the Phyfer Corporation.

After many committee sessions supported by staff work throughout the organization, a proposed set of common data files for personnel management was developed. A time schedule was prepared as to when each of the existing computer-based networks within Phyfer Corporation will be fully operational with the new, centralized arrangement. The functions of (*a*) payroll, (*b*) external reporting, (*c*) wage, salary and benefit administration, and (*d*) internal reporting and analysis were centralized under the corporate vice president for personnel.

As each of these common data files for personnel management was implemented within a computer-based network, modifications and changes were required in various computer programs, data assignment routines, and data retrieval specifications. There were several work-years of systems effort required in implementing this uniform personnel program within each of the major computer-based networks.

Concurrently with the establishment of common data files that will support the centralized housekeeping type of operating system for personnel management, Phyfer Corporation's executive management commissioned a systems study of the personnel operations. Most of the personnel activities currently depended on manual records. This new systems study will establish computer-based data on applications, skills inventory, job specification, and recruitment. A series of computer programs was designed and implemented for the functions of (*a*) employment selection, (*b*) wage, salary and benefit planning, (*c*) job specification, (*d*) recruitment, and (*e*) analysis of employment activities. The corporate responsibility for these new, centralized operations was assigned to the vice president for employment administration.

In addition to the vice president for personnel and the vice president for employment administration, there is a separate corporate office for human resource management. This office, which originated as a special project to recruit and train minority workers, is concerned with the identification of underdeveloped management talent. Gradually, this office has assumed other responsibilities in training and educational administration. However, some training activities are conducted under the direction of the vice president for employment administration. Recently, the office for human resource management began to monitor and update individual employee career plans.

At this point, the vice president for personnel (who had corporate-wide responsibility for payroll, wage-salary-and-benefit administration, external reporting, and internal reporting) announced plans to make a career change and to accept a full-time position with a religious body. Upon the dissemination of this information, the director of the office for human resource management demanded to be appointed the vice president for personnel with the combined responsibilities of the two offices. Because of the nature of these demands, Phyfer Corporation's executive management accepted the latter director's resignation and engaged the management consulting firm with which you are employed to provide temporary administrative assistance.

After the departures of the vice president for personnel and the director of human resource management, some members of Phyfer Corporation's executive management began to wonder if it was not time to centralize personnel housekeeping activities with human resource management. A performance rating system has been proposed several times, and there have been attempts to use management science models in personnel allocation studies; however, neither the rating system nor the allocation models has become a permanent feature of Phyfer's personnel management.

In addition to providing temporary administrative assistance, the management consulting firm with which you are employed was asked to perform an overall review of personnel management and to propose a series of alternative arrangements for personnel planning, allocation, and utilization. Within these arrangements, performance rating systems and management science models for personnel allocation should be presented as possibilities.

As a junior staff member on this project, you perform selected clerical functions for the senior members on the team of systems analysts. From the insights gained from these team efforts, you prepared the following list of additional planning requirements:

a. Planning simulations of personnel requirements by division and major product group for the next five years
b. Forecasts of advancements, retirements, resignations, and terminations of personnel
c. Comparative analyses of the simulated personnel requirements for the next five years with the forecasts of available personnel
d. Simulation of unique features in recruitment programs and education and training programs during the next five years that will be required if projected activities in A, B, and C are valid
e. Identification of a "back up" administrator for each planner, manager, and decision maker within the organization in the event of an emergency
f. Identification and location of "blue collar" skills among salaried employees in the event of a strike

REQUIRED:

1. Under the four headings of (a) housekeeping, (b) employment, (c) human resources, and (d) allocation and utilization, prepare a list of the dominant personnel functions. After completing these identification activities, specify each item by its group heading and number, such as A1, A2, A3 and so forth.
2. Prepare a list of the common data files which are identified in the case or are implied by a given personnel management capability. After completing this list, assign the letter "T" followed by a number to each file for purposes of reference, such as T1, T2, T3 and so forth.
3. Prepare a list that cross references the common data files (requirement 2) with each of the functions within each of the four headings (requirement 1). Review this composite presentation and add additional files or personnel functions as suggested by your analysis.
4. Review the list of six additional planning requirements which was specified in the case. For each of these requirements, indicate the types of comparisons and common data files that can be used in performing these planning activities.
5. Continuing with these six planning requirements (requirement 4), indicate the confidentiality of data and security problems involved in computer-based analysis of *each* requirement. To what

extent, if any, will these considerations suggest a decentralized arrangement instead of a centralized arrangement. Explain your position on each planning requirement.

CASE 16–3.   MERCANTILE FINANCIAL CORPORATION AND SUBSIDIARIES

Preface to Case

This lengthy case study illustrates the organization chart, the responsibilities of different departments, the document flow by activity, and the reports prepared by each activity in a major financial corporation. With all of these detailed data, the case study serves as an excellent integrated device, where the information systems approach can be applied to a total organization in a described environment.

The case study can best be handled on a team basis, with five to six participants per team. Much of the benefit derived from the case study is based upon the detailed analyses, flowcharts, and team discussions of different segments of the company's operations. If a team approach is followed, then the requirements can be separated into four steps: (a) identify the existing data flows and prepare a flowchart that contains the major information flows, (b) define the purpose for which each major information flow is occurring, (c) evaluate the usefulness of the information that is received, and (d) recommend alternative information flows which are quantitatively justified. The first step is frequently assigned to individual team members along major organizational units, such as (a) commercial division, (b) automobile and motor operation, (c) furniture and appliance operation, and (d) small loan operation. After the flowcharts are completed, the other three steps are often accomplished on a group basis.

The Case Study

In the late 1950s the executive vice president of Mercantile Financial Corporation and Subsidiaries was of the opinion that the public accountants who annually audited the firm were more interested in assuring the creditors that their assets were safe, than they were in assisting the management of the firm being audited. Therefore, in 1959, the executive vice president initiated managerial accounting system studies. The studies established proper control patterns and specified the preparation of managerial reports by each location within the overall corporation. In addition, increased emphasis was given to internal auditing. The descriptive procedures of the firm's present operations, as indicated in this case, are highly influenced by these studies.

Currently, the executive vice president is considering the possibility of increased mechanization of the information systems. During the past 18 months, a data processing service center has been used to prepare two statistical reports and to maintain customer ledger cards for one of the firm's operations—small consumer loans. Should other operations be converted to data processing? When should the firm stop using a data processing service center and acquire its own capabilities in this area? These are some of the questions facing the executive vice president.

Frequently, management consultants and representatives of equipment manufacturers ask for interviews with the executive vice president for the purpose of trying to convince him that a particular type of systems review and feasibility study should be undertaken. Each of the different sales presentations emphasizes what some of the larger firms in the financial area are currently doing and that some of the smaller firms, according to reliable confidential sources, are reported to be moving in the same direction. Furthermore, the speaker discusses some of the unusual applications in other industries that might be implemented at Mercantile Financial Corporation, in which case a tremendous competitive advantage and savings might be gained from being the first firm in the industry to adopt these new techniques and procedures. Of course, in the conclusion of each of these interviews, the speaker tries to convince the executive vice president that the speaker is the best-qualified person to make such studies.

Thus far, the executive vice president has refused to have either a general systems review or a feasibility study conducted. However, members of executive management have begun to informally re-examine their operations and consider the cost of the present system.

For example, the executive vice president feels that the major information systems problem facing management is one of assembling data in known areas rather than a problem of not knowing what information it wants. These known areas include the ability to distinguish between desirable and undesirable dealers by source of business. Immediate information is also needed on changes in the volume of new loan applications and the reasons for such changes by type of business—accounts receivable loans, inventory loans, equipment loans, second mortgages, small consumer loans, consolidated loans, combined personal-business loans, furniture and appliance loans, and motor and automobile loans. In the commercial area, immediate information is needed regarding an unfavorable change in the financial status of a customer. The customer's financial status may appear adequate at the time the loan is made, but subsequently the customer changes to an undesirable classification.

The following discussion examines the different aspects of the corporation's overall operations and consists of four parts. First, a brief synopsis is presented on the history of the firm. Second, a highlight review is made of the organization structure, including top management and home office operations and the operations of each of the divisions. Third, a more extensive and thorough analysis is made of the data accumulation, processing and reporting activities of each section within the overall corporation. In this lengthy third part of the case study, consideration is given to (1) customer characteristics, (2) legal aspects of different types of loans, (3) procedures followed in processing data including the format of selected documents, (4) the format, content and uses made of selected reports, and (5) the administrative and internal control functions encompassed within these operations.

The fourth and final part of the case study presents other financial and statistical data including the formats of responsibility reports; historical financial data for the consolidated company from 1954 to 1963; a summary of the increase in net worth, by source, for the same 10-year period; and finally, selected cost and statistical data regarding data accumulation and processing activities.

The Company

This financial institution is engaged in commercial and consumer financing operations and on December 31, 1963, had outstanding accounts receivable and notes receivable from these two divisions totaling $65,000,000. The current level of operation is a substantial improvement over the previous year (which totaled $53,000,000), in spite of the fact that there was a reduction in the total volume of automobile loans because of the aggressive competition by commercial banks, who offered lower interest rates to consumers than the rates offered by consumer financial institutions. (This latter matter is discussed in detail subsequently in this case study.) All indications suggest that a significant rate of growth will be achieved at Mercantile Financial Corporation in each future year.

The original company began in 1917 as an automobile finance company, and in 1924 the commercial finance operations were added. The same management operated the firm from 1917 to 1954, at which time the founder of the firm died. The founder's son, who had a number of years' experience with the firm, began to direct operations, and he was committed to a policy of growth. In 1954 the operations of the then Mercantile Discount Corporation and Subsidiary Companies were restricted to the Midwest, and the firm was privately owned. During the next six years (1955–60), the total accounts receivable and notes receivable were increased four times ($8,000,000 to $33,000,000), and operations were expanded outside the Midwest area.

In September, 1960, the firm was changed to a public corporation by the issuance and registration of stock under the corporate name of Mercantile Discount Corporation and Subsidiary Companies. In 1962, the corporate name was changed to Mercantile Financial Corporation and Subsidiaries. The stock is sold over the counter, with The First National Bank of Chicago serving as transfer agent and Continental Illinois National Bank and Trust Company of Chicago serving as registrar.

Currently, the firm consists of 22 corporations which are engaged in all types of commercial and consumer financing operations and in insurance brokerage activities.[4] The commercial financing operations are directed from four regional offices: New York City, Atlanta, Chicago, and St. Louis. The consumer division operations consist of 10 consumer loan offices, a motor and automobile discount office, and a furniture and appliance discount office; all of the consumer division's offices are in Chicago. The motor and automobile office also

---

[4] For internal management purposes, some operations are considered as separate units, when in fact they are only responsibility units and not separate corporations. These different accounting units (there are 32 such accounting units) are discussed in a subsequent section of this case study under the heading of "Responsibility Reports." The large number of corporations is partly indicative of the manner in which the firm has grown (by acquisition of existing financial institutions) and is partly necessary because of legal reasons.

handles insurance transactions, and a given consumer loan office manager may serve as an agent for four different corporations, depending on the type and amount of the consumer loan.[5] Thus, most consumer financing division offices have activity associated with several corporations.

The services offered by the Mercantile Financial Corporation and Subsidiaries cannot be obtained by its customers from regular commercial banks. For example, a given commercial firm might desire to borrow more money on its accounts receivable, inventory, and equipment than can be obtained from a commercial bank; the commercial firm is willing to pay a higher rate of interest for the additional risk inherent in this type of loan. If the commercial firm desires a loan under the terms of a higher interest rate, obviously the commercial firm's management must believe that the investment opportunities are such that the firm will realize a substantial net gain from the employment of these additional funds, or else management would not desire such a loan under these conditions.

The executive vice president recently explained the activities of the Mercantile Financial Corporation and Subsidiaries in the following manner:

The relation of our loan officers to our customers is analogous to the doctor-patient relation of the pediatrician to the infant. The infant becomes too old for the pediatrician and is treated by other types of medical doctors, or else the infant dies. Likewise, a client becomes self-sufficient (including being able to borrow from commercial banks at a lower rate of interest) and no longer needs our services, or else the client becomes bankrupt.

Thus we, like the pediatrician, must constantly obtain new clients to replace our present clients. Unlike most other business firms, we cannot plan on our present customers as being a major group of our future customers. Annually, new customers must be obtained in order to maintain our present level of activity, and if an increase in volume is desired, then a larger volume of new customers is necessary.

---

[5] Each consumer loan office may make small loans up to $800 (one corporation), personal loans of $801 to $5,000 (another corporation), semibusiness loans up to $5,000, and nonlicensed (referring to the Illinois State Regulatory Authority) loans over $5,000 (both of these latter types of loans are activities of a third corporation); the office may also finance time-sale paper for the purpose of converting to direct consumer operations (a fourth corporation). A different corporation is used for loans over $800 that were made before the 1962 Illinois law was passed to regulate this type of loan, and consumer loan offices may collect funds due on these accounts.

Organization Chart

Exhibit A is the organization chart for the top level of management. Note that the vice presidents are at the operating level and actually participate in day-to-day operations.

EXHIBIT A
Organization Chart—Top Management

```
                    ┌──────────────────────┐
                    │  Chairman of the Board │
                    │    (Semiretired)       │
                    └──────────┬───────────┘
                               │
                    ┌──────────────────────┐
                    │  President and Vice    │
                    │  Chairman of the Board │
                    │ (Chief Executive Officer)│
                    └──────────┬───────────┘
                               │
                    ┌──────────────────────┐
                    │ Executive Vice President│
                    │     and Director       │
                    │ (Administrative Officer)│
                    └──────────┬───────────┘
      ┌────────────┬──────────┼──────────┬──────────────┐
┌───────────┐ ┌───────────┐ ┌───────────┐ ┌───────────┐
│Senior Vice│ │Senior Vice│ │ Secretary │ │ Treasurer │
│President   │ │President   │ │(Corporate │ │(Financial │
│Commercial │ │Consumer    │ │ Secretary │ │ and       │
│Division   │ │Division    │ │and Legal  │ │Accounting)│
└───────────┘ └───────────┘ │ Counsel)  │ └─────┬─────┘
                            └───────────┘       │
                                         ┌────────────────┐
                                         │Assistant Secretary &│
                                         │Assistant Treasurer │
                                         │(Chief Accounting   │
                                         │Officer and Controller)│
                                         └────────────────┘
```

Commercial Division

Exhibit B is the organization chart for the Commercial Division. The St. Louis branch office is semiautonomous, and the manager of the St. Louis branch office, a senior vice president, is independent as far as internal operating matters. The St. Louis Commercial Branch was opened last year after acquiring an existing corporation, and one of the stipulations of the purchase agreement was that extra shares of stock in the parent corporation would be distributed to former stockholders of the purchased company, depending on the extent to which the total earnings for the St. Louis branch were above a certain level for the first three years of operation as a subsidiary of Mercantile Financial Corporation and Subsidiaries.

The managers of the other three commercial branch offices are

EXHIBIT B
Organization Chart—Commercial Division

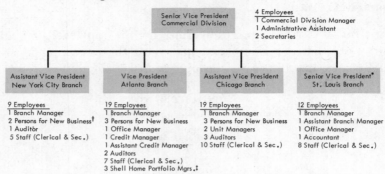

* The St. Louis branch was recently acquired under the stipulation that the current manager would be a senior vice president of Mercantile Financial Corporation and Subsidiaries and a member of the board of directors; of course, there were also other considerations in the pooling of interest agreement.

† New business persons are also called "solicitors."

‡ Shell home portfolio managers work out of the Atlanta office, calling on accounts in that area.

under the direct supervision of the Commercial Division manager, who is physically located at the home office. However, each branch office is a fully operating office. The accounting functions are decentralized, and each office must develop its own new business. Furthermore, each office is responsible for the audit of its clients; however, the auditors are alternated between the different Commercial Division branch offices for purposes of internal control.

This audit function regarding clients is extremely important for loans from the Commercial Division. Management needs to know if there has been a change in the financial status of the customer since the loan was made (the customer may appear desirable at the inception but subsequently change to an undesirable classification) and if all collections by the client, under certain types of loans, have been forwarded to the branch office. In addition to these areas, the other internal audit functions relate to verification of account balances and the physical location and use of equipment covered by a loan agreement, including both the verification of client's balances with the account balance per branch office's records and the verification of the pertinent account balances of the client's books with the client's customers.

As previously indicated, the St. Louis Commercial Branch Office was opened as a result of acquiring an existing corporation in 1963 under a pooling of interests arrangement. Likewise, expansion into the Atlanta and New York City areas was the result of purchasing existing corporations. In the Chicago area, a separate corporation was created for commercial operations in the state of Wisconsin because of legal considerations.

In total, there are eight separate corporations in the Commercial Division that, from an accounting standpoint, are treated as nine companies—some of the commercial operations in the Atlanta area are handled as if they were the complete operations of the parent corporation. The accounting entities for the Commercial Divisions are as follows: Atlanta area, three companies; New York City area, two companies; Chicago area, three companies; and St. Louis area, one company.

Since the activities of each company do not overlap into other branch office areas, the total operations for a given commerial office is equal to the summation of the company reports under that branch. Furthermore, the types of activities conducted by each company under a Commercial Division branch office do not overlap and are easily identified by type of transaction, which is based on legal considerations. Each transaction document indicates the corporation to which the transaction relates. Thus, the accounting records readily permit the preparation of company reports (which are required to be submitted to the Secretary of the State in which the corporation's charter is granted) and Commercial Division branch office reports.

CONSUMER DIVISION

When the first branch office was opened, it was organized into three sections: (1) automobile and motor operations, (2) furniture and appliance operations, and (3) small loan operations. There was a branch manager and a collection manager for each section. Each section within an office was considered to be a separate accounting entity. This type of organization for the Consumer Division branch office just did not work. Even though all three sections relate to consumer financing, different techniques and methods are required for activities associated with each section. The techniques used in the small loan operations are not equally applicable to the automobile and motor discount operations, and vice versa. Eventually, a different office was opened for each type of consumer financing operation.

EXHIBIT C
Organization Chart—Consumer Division

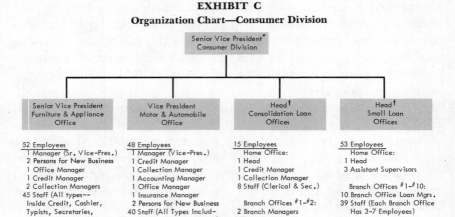

| Senior Vice President* Consumer Division |

| Senior Vice President Furniture & Appliance Office | Vice President Motor & Automobile Office | Head† Consolidation Loan Offices | Head† Small Loan Offices |

52 Employees
  1 Manager (Sr. Vice-Pres.)
  2 Persons for New Business
  1 Office Manager
  1 Credit Manager
  2 Collection Managers
45 Staff (All types--
  Inside Credit, Cashier,
  Typists, Secretaries,
  Clerks, and so forth)

48 Employees
  1 Manager (Vice-Pres.)
  1 Credit Manager
  1 Collection Manager
  1 Accounting Manager
  1 Office Manager
  1 Insurance Manager
  2 Persons for New Business
40 Staff (All Types Including the Insurance Dept.)

15 Employees
  Home Office:
  1 Head
  1 Credit Manager
  1 Collection Manager
  8 Staff (Clerical & Sec.)

  Branch Offices #1-#2:
  2 Branch Managers
  2 Secretaries

53 Employees
  Home Office:
  1 Head
  3 Assistant Supervisors

  Branch Offices #1-#10:
  10 Branch Office Loan Mgrs.
  39 Staff (Each Branch Office
  Has 3-7 Employees)

* The senior vice president of the Consumer Division is also head of the furniture and appliance office. A separate office is not maintained for the overall management of the Consumer Division. The channel between the senior vice president of the Consumer Division and the managers of the three sections is extremely loose. Each section head answers jointly to the division head and to the executive vice president of the corporation.

† The heads of the consolidation loan offices and small loan offices are not officers of the parent corporation; however, they are officers of various subsidiary corporations.

Exhibit C illustrates the current organization chart for the Consumer Division. While the chart shows the senior vice president as the manager of the Consumer Division, the relation between the Consumer Division manager and the heads of the various offices is loose. Each section manager reports jointly to the Consumer Division manager and to the executive vice president of the parent corporation. Furthermore, the Consumer Division manager also serves as head of the furniture and appliance office. A separate office is not maintained for the functions of Consumer Division manager.

Within the Consumer Division, there are many corporations, because of the following reasons: (1) some of the expansion occurred through the acquisition of existing corporations, (2) there are legal considerations which in some instances dictate that separate corporations must be established for the performance of certain types of activities, (3) there are important tax consequences of having several corporations instead of one corporation, (4) the decentralization of operations into separate companies is an advertising point employed by the firm, and (5) this separation into units provides better profit control and determination.

Specifically, there are 13 corporations within the Consumer Division, and they are dispersed by sections in the following manner: furniture and appliance office, one corporation; motor and automobile office, two corporations; consolidation loan offices, two corporations; and small loan offices, eight corporations. Each of the 10 small loan offices is handled as a separate accounting entity; however, 3 of the offices are really divisions of the same corporation. Likewise, one of the corporations in the consolidation loan area has 12 branch offices. All of the operations of the motor and automobile section are centered in one office, and, excluding some collection activities, all of the operations of the furniture and appliance section are centered in one office.

Home Office

Exhibit D presents the administrative staff for the home office operations. Selected members of the home office staff actively participate in the day-to-day supervision of all types of commercial and consumer financing operations. Even though the parent corporation

EXHIBIT D
Organization Chart—Top Management Staff

has exploded in size, most of the key members of management have grown up with the firm and have a "feel" for the data. For example, the treasurer looks at a report submitted by the controller and tells the latter individual, "That figure doesn't look right; recheck it." In many cases the controller discovers that the figure was wrong.

Therefore, when members of executive management review the financial and statistical reports for a branch office, they are reviewing an operation with which they are familiar. Because of this familiarity, they may be able to spot possible trouble areas that may not be apparent even to the manager of the particular branch office responsible for the report being reviewed.

Members of management also review various statistical and financial reports for the purpose of determining if previous management policy decisions should be reconsidered and possibly modified. For example, $400 to $500 is considered to be the ideal small loan in terms of balancing minimum handling cost with maximum return and with a minimum advertising exposure per loan. Do the current reports substantiate this policy? Do the reports of different branch offices vary in respect to the suggested answers to this question? If so, why?

While other loan companies have expanded into new geographical areas, the executive management of Mercantile Financial Corporation and Subsidiaries has decided to concentrate its efforts in small loan operations to the city of Chicago.[6] Expansion has come not only from opening new small loan offices within the city of Chicago, but also by concentrating the efforts by office. For example, offices may offer different types of loans, such as consolidated loans, loans over $800, and joint personal-business loans for over $5,000. In spite of the fact that a few small loan companies in Illinois are several times as large as Mercantile Financial Corporation (measured both in terms of assets and in terms of the number of branch offices), the consumer loan subsidiaries of the corporation collectively are one of

---

[6] While small loan operations have been restricted to the city of Chicago, frequently management has the opportunity of acquiring small loan corporations in other cities. Thus far, each of these opportunities has been declined. While each opportunity must be evaluated on its own merits, one management policy has influenced many of these decisions. One or two small loan offices in another city normally are prohibitive because of the administrative cost; ideally five or six small loan offices should be acquired in a given city if maximum return is to be realized from the administrative cost.

the leading consumer loan groups in the state of Illinois, based on the criteria of dollar volume of personal loans over $800.

The expansion has not been restricted to the Consumer Division area. As previously indicated, the operations of the Commercial Division have been extended into three other geographical areas, and the volume of transactions in each area has been increased. The magnitude of these changes is indicated by the comparative financial reports presented in a subsequent section of this case study.

Data Accumulation, Processing, and Reporting Activities

The responsibility for data accumulation, processing, and reporting activities is decentralized to each office manager. While there is uniformity between different offices as to procedures followed in processing transactions of comparable sections, there is substantial difference in the procedures followed by each section within an office. Therefore, the data accumulation, processing, and reporting activities are separately examined for each section of the overall corporation.

Commercial Division

Each of the four regional offices of the Commercial Division is similar in respect to data accumulation, processing, and reporting activities. The differences in the administration of activities relate to the type of commercial financing: accounts receivable loans, inventory loans, equipment loans, notes receivable loans, and rediscounting operations. Similar administrative activities are followed in each regional office in respect to each type of loan.

A National Cash Register (NCR model #3300) bookkeeping machine is used at most regional offices in the data accumulation process for all types of commercial loan operations, except equipment loans. While equipment loans aggregate a multimillion dollar volume, there are less than 200 separate equipment loans ranging on the average from $300,000 to $400,000 per loan.

Equipment Loans. Since the total number of equipment loans is less than 200, the administration of each loan can be maintained effectively and efficiently on a manual basis. The equipment loan contract will specify the amount of the monthly payments, and the home office management of the parent corporation administratively watches (through the reporting system) the payment behavior of these equipment loans.

If there is a serious problem in relation to a given equipment loan, the administrative management of the parent corporation must decide on what action is to be taken.[7] Since there are, typically, only three to four delinquent equipment loans each month, the administrative review of equipment loans is not time-consuming. If a customer is behind in payment of an equipment loan, management may telephone the customer and discuss the matter—remember the dollar value of each equipment loan.

Throughout the Commercial Division, management must follow a policy of "periodic administrative review" rather than any type of "automatic follow-up policy"; this periodic review is required because of the substantial amount of funds involved in each loan and the degree of uniqueness associated with each customer.

The collateral for an equipment loan—this term is used in the broad sense to include all types of machinery and equipment loans exclusive of real estate—includes a chattel mortgage on the equipment.

Accounts Receivable Loans. The accounts receivable loan is the most common type of commercial loan; on the average, there are two accounts receivable loans for every single inventory loan, which is the second most frequent type of commercial loan.

For each new accounts receivable loan, a check is written for the designated amount and recorded by the bookkeeper, through using the National Cash Register bookkeeping machine (model #3300), in the cash disbursements journal. The NCR bookkeeping machine is used to open a ledger card for the customer that summarizes much of the data regarding the loan transaction, as indicated by Exhibit E. Note that the running balance of both the loan and the accounts

---

[7] The board of directors of the Mercantile Financial Corporation and Subsidiaries has established an administrative committee that has responsibility for the management and operation of the firm, without removing any direct responsibility from individuals in their designated corporate capacities. The members of the administrative committee are (1) the chairman of the board, (2) the president, (3) the executive vice president, (4) the treasurer, (5) the secretary, (6) the Commercial Division senior vice president, and (7) the senior vice president of the St. Louis Commercial branch office. Except for the latter individual, all of the members of the administrative committee are located at the home office.

EXHIBIT E
Format of Customer Ledger Card for NCR System

Solicitor		Bond Premium		Line M	Customer's	Dun and Brad
First Payment_____ % Date of Contract		Expires_____ 19___		Class No._____ Rating		Other_____
Final Payment_____ %		Line of Business_____		Maximum Percentage Off-Rated_____ %		

Date	Schedule or Remittance Report No.	Acct. No.	ACCOUNTS RECEIVABLE					AMOUNT DUE M.F.C.			
			100% Accounts Purchased	100% Accounts Paid	Daily Balance	Cumulative Daily Balance	Cash Received	Check No.	Cash Paid	Daily Balance	Cumulative Daily Balance

Name _____
Address _____
Town and State _____

ADJUSTMENTS			FINAL PAYMENT			
Debit	Credit	Balance	Debit	Credit	Balance	Verification Factor

receivable which are collateral for the loan are separately recorded and balanced.

The NCR record system is designed in such a manner that selected data from the NCR ledger card are simultaneously printed by the NCR machine on another set of records, and the duplicate copy of the latter set of records serves as the monthly billing document to the customer.

Without going into detail, there are several legal documents that may be prepared to accompany the original transaction for a new loan. The most common documents include a schedule of accounts receivable and a security agreement. The supporting evidence for the transaction may include actual invoices and shipping documents. If shipping documents are not available, the customer prepares an affidavit regarding the terms, conditions, and locations of both properties and receivables. (Subsequently as part of the audit program, the individual accounts receivable will be confirmed.)

Accounts receivable loans are of two types: specific assignment and bulk assignment. Under specific assignment, the collateral for the loan is a specific group of customer accounts receivables which have been selected. The number of customer accounts involved in the specific assignment is usually small. Therefore, a manual ledger card may also be opened for each individual accounts receivable that is pledged by the commercial firm as collateral for the accounts receivable loan. If the commercial firm (which has been granted a specific assignment accounts receivable loan) issues a credit memorandum for returns or allowances, these data are circled on the ledger card for the pledged accounts receivable. While the credit memorandum does not affect the running balance of the accounts receivable loan, it does affect the collateral for the loan—both of these types of data are maintained on the customer's ledger card. A noncash voucher is used to process these data to the ledger card of the pledged account.

On specific accounts receivable loans, the customer must send to the Commercial Division branch office of Mercantile Financial Corporation and Subsidiaries the gross receipts on its collections. A check is prepared for the 20 percent excess (assuming the maximum rate, an accounts receivable loan will not exceed 80 percent of the collateral) and the check is mailed to the customer. This check is for the net amount owed to the customer, which is increased by overpayments (collections on invoices not assigned) and reduced by shortages (discounts and allowances granted by the loan customer to its receivables) . (For accounting purposes, a notation is made on the customer's ledger card to indicate which invoices have been paid.)

The specific accounts receivable loans are generally for 90 days or less. (There are exceptions that might be for five months.) Whenever an accounts receivable becomes 90 days delinquent, the customer must immediately repurchase the account. It is common for the repurchasing activity to occur even when the loan is for less than 90 days, since a given accounts receivable pledged as collateral may be 30 days or more delinquent at the time the loan is made. Monthly, a list is prepared from the cards (specific assignment type of accounts receivable loan) for the delinquent accounts, and the list is mailed to the customer indicating the accounts receivable which the customer must immediately repurchase.

The bulk assignment type of accounts receivable loan is more difficult to administer. The collateral for this type of loan includes all "qualified accounts receivable." Most accounts receivables are "qualified" under the bulk assignment; however, if a given account is a predetermined number of days delinquent on one transaction, this account is considered "nonqualified" on any and all other transactions. In addition, an accounts receivable may be nonqualified because it is a contra account, is specifically rejected by the loan officer for any number of reasons, and so forth. As part of the collateral for the bulk assignment type of accounts receivable loan, the customer is required to submit a schedule of accounts receivable. A determination is made of the maximum amount of loan that would be made to the customer on this collateral (which is based on *qualified* accounts receivables). A check is issued and mailed to the customer for either the maximum amount or the requested amount of the loan, whichever is smaller.

The bulk assignment type of accounts receivable loan is a continuing type of loan arrangement. The customer is required to submit all gross collections to Mercantile Financial Corporation; the 20 percent excess of the collateral over the loan is not automatically returned to the customer. Instead, this amount goes in the customer's reserve until it is requested.

The availability report (see Exhibit F) is a one-page transmittal document which the customer prepares each time in submitting a transaction to Mercantile Financial Corporation. The availability report provides a place for the customer to request a loan for a given amount (a new loan based on the running balance of the collateral)

EXHIBIT F
Availability Report

Number _____   Date _____   19 ___

Accounts Receivable Outstanding Assigned to MFC (Prev. Report) $ _____

Additions to Accounts Receivable:

    New Billings (Invoice #   to #   ) $ _____

    Less Credit Memos _____

                                                   $

Deductions to Accounts Receivable:

    Invoices paid per Collection Report Attached $ _____

    Miscellaneous _____

Accounts Receivable Outstanding Assigned to MFC $

Less:

    Delinquents $ _____

    Contras   _____

    Miscellaneous   _____ $ _____

Accounts Receivable Balance Available for Loans $ _____

Initial Purchase Price _____% $ _____

    Loan Balance Previous Report $ _____

    Less Cash Remitted Today $ _____

        Loan Balance (Before Borrowing) $ _____

    Additional Borrowing This Report $ _____

        Loan Balance Today $ _____

Excess Availability $ _____

For the purpose of inducing Mercantile Financial Corporation to grant loans to us, we hereby certify that the foregoing Statement of accounts receivable is true and correct as of this report and is acceptable collateral in accordance with the terms of the agreement dated _____ between _____ _____ and Mercantile Financial Corporation.

By: _____

or for the maximum amount. Normally, the customer will wait and borrow the additional funds on the day they are needed, since interest is computed on a daily basis. Thus, the customer will apply all cash collections on the existing loan and will withdraw additional cash from Mercantile Financial Corporation only when it is necessary to meet payroll requirements, on the due date of invoices, or for other needs.

Accounts receivable loans are risky, regardless of type. There can be a quick change in the quality of the collateral, and it is imperative that management is aware of this condition. This administrative function regarding both types of accounts receivable loans is partially achieved through a formal audit program. Periodically, an audit is made of the customer's accounts receivable transactions to verify that all cash receipts due Mercantile Financial Corporation have been properly forwarded and that no unauthorized adjustments (returns and allowances) have been made on customer's accounts. This audit program includes the confirmation of the customer's accounts receivable balances with the individual companies. At a minimum, the audit function is performed every 60 days (that is, all aspects of the audit program exclusive of the actual confirmation of the detailed accounts receivable balances, which is performed more often on a test basis). The customer knows before the loan is made that frequent audits will be made on the company's books and that the interest rate provides for this type of service.[8]

The auditors are on the staff of each regional commercial loan branch office, and the auditors may be provided with a summary of the loan customer's balances along with other selected documents, which they use to verify the customer's accounting records. These other documents include a list of all pledged accounts for specific accounts receivable loans, which is prepared from the manual cards maintained for each individual account. The auditors also have a list of delinquent accounts for both types of accounts receivable loans.

---

[8] Remember the customer did not secure a loan from a regular commercial bank; either more funds were requested on the collateral than would be granted by the commercial bank's management or else the application was refused; some commercial banks are hesitant about making loans on accounts receivable. Other commercial banks require a substantial amount of collateral for a very small loan. In some states, commercial banks are restricted by law from making loans on accounts receivable. Thus, the commercial financing operations of Mercantile Financial Corporation and other commercial loan companies provide a service to this type of customer which cannot be obtained anywhere else.

(In the case of bulk assignment, the auditors determine the delinquent accounts from reviewing a list submitted by the customer and from reviewing the accounts receivable records.)

Manual ledger cards are not maintained by Mercantile Financial Corporation for each individual customer's accounts receivable that are pledged under the bulk type of accounts receivable loan. If such manual ledger cards were maintained, it would mean duplicating the customer's complete accounts receivable subsidiary ledger and daily updating this ledger. Instead, attention is given under the bulk type of accounts receivable loan to verification that the customer's records are correct. Periodically, the customer is asked to prepare a schedule of accounts receivable and to age the accounts.[9] Personnel at the commercial loan branch office review the customer's list, exclude "nonqualified" accounts, compare this report with previous reports (including the daily availability report) and then prepare a formal list of delinquent accounts. The following paragraph appears in the heading of this latter report (which is only for specific assignment accounts) :

All the following delinquent accounts require your prompt attention. Please make a special effort to collect those accounts which are "more than 60 days past due." *All accounts over 60 days past due, or where goods have been returned, reconsigned, etc., and against customers who are in any financial trouble whatsoever must be repurchased by you at once. Accounts not repurchased by you will be deducted from schedules or your reserves.*[10]

This auditing function of the customer's activities (transactions) is more than a traditional verification of account balances and proof of cash. It also includes a managerial interpretation regarding the customer's business, such as an implicit forecast of what will probably happen in the next few weeks and how this might change the credit rating of the customer.

At each regional office of the Commercial Division, the collections for all types of accounts receivable are received by the cashier, and a daily report of collections is prepared by this latter individual. The posting to the customer's accounts receivable ledger card is daily

---

[9] Most payments on accounts receivable loans occur between the 10th and the 20th of each month. Therefore, the monthly report of delinquent accounts receivable is generally prepared around the 20th of the month.

[10] The formal list of delinquent accounts is submitted to the customer for immediate attention.

recorded by the NCR bookkeeping machine, which provides subtotal detailed data for several control groups. Therefore, the summation of the daily report of collections must equal the appropriate control totals, as determined from the NCR daily proof page.

All disbursements are recorded in the cash disbursements journal, and the aggregate daily disbursements applicable to accounts receivable loans are compared with the appropriate proof totals from the NCR proof page. The NCR separately accumulates daily totals by several categories which provide detailed group control totals. The latter totals are for groupings of ledger cards.

Many transactions are both disbursements and collections. For example, a customer sends in $1,000 as the gross collections on a bulk accounts receivable loan (the $1,000 is compared with the cashier's report and with the change in the customer's account maintained on NCR), the customer requests $100 payment from that company's reserve (a check is issued for this, compared with the check register and the NCR proof page), and $900 is applied on the account (this latter amount is proved and compared with the change in the accounting balances as indicated by the NCR proof page).

Inventory Loans. The inventory loan is not based on acquisition cost but is based on the appraised value of the inventory as determined by representatives of Mercantile Financial Corporation. The risk on inventory loans is generally higher than the risk on accounts receivable loans; therefore, the maximum inventory loan is generally 50 to 60 percent of the appraised value of selected items of inventory.

Inventory loans are made under three conditions: (1) where the goods are in a public warehouse, (2) where the goods are in a field warehouse on the customer's premises, and (3) where the goods are on the customer's premises but not in a warehouse. This latter condition is referred to as a "factor's lien." Under the first two conditions, the collateral for the inventory loan would include the warehouse receipt, and the customer will pay Mercantile Financial Corporation at the time the goods are released from the warehouse. Under some circumstances, a schedule of payments is specified for the inventory loan and the customer must make payments according to this schedule irrespective of the release of goods from the warehouse. Under the third condition (a factor's lien), the inventory loan agreement includes a repayment schedule which must be followed. The factor's lien agreement does not contain any release conditions, since the goods are not in a warehouse. (Thus, in this latter case, payments must be made according to the payment schedule regardless of whether the goods are sold.)

The inventory loans under all three conditions are accounted for in approximately the same manner as that followed for accounts receivable loans. Furthermore, a customer who has an inventory loan will generally also have an accounts receivable loan. Therefore, the administration of inventory loans is partly achieved through the auditing program; the audit of the inventory transactions occurs at the time the accounts receivable transactions are being examined.[11]

Other Types of Loans. Mercantile Financial Corporation also engages in rediscounting operations and may purchase notes receivable and second mortgages. Periodically, a small loan company or small finance company will have an excessive amount of investments in notes receivable and in second mortgages. Management of the small loan company or small finance company will arrange with management of Mercantile Financial Corporation to rediscount these second mortgages or other documents.

The accounting for the other types of loans is similar to that followed for accounts receivable loans.

Each Commercial Division branch office manually prepares a weekly report of its activities. This report includes a detailed list by name of each portfolio, the loan balance, and the volume generated during the week. This weekly report is three to four pages in length, is purely statistical data, and is sent directly to the executive vice president of the parent corporation and to the senior vice president in charge of the Commercial Division. A liquidation progress report is also prepared, when appropriate, by each Commercial Division branch office to cover the liquidation activities of its customers.

Consumer Division

The data accumulation, processing, and reporting activities are similar in both the consolidation loan offices and the small loan offices. Therefore, for purposes of this case study, attention is given only to the small loan offices. The furniture and appliance office and

---

[11] This generalization can also be applied to equipment loans. A customer who has an equipment loan will generally also have both an accounts receivable loan and an inventory loan. Thus, the auditing for all three types can be performed at the same time; however, there is not a large amount of audit work associated with equipment type of commercial loans.

the motor and automobile office have individually unique administrative procedures. Thus, the data accumulation, processing, and reporting activities for the Consumer Division are described in three sections: small loan offices, furniture and appliance office, and motor and automobile office.

Small Loan Offices. Each small loan office uses a McBee accounting set for both cash receipts and cash disbursements. This manual accounting system permits the simultaneous recording of entries on several forms by a single writing.

A prospective customer is asked to prepare a loan application form, which is presented in Exhibit G. Within a matter of hours, the references, employment and other data contained on the completed application form have been verified, and the prospective customer's loan request is acted upon. Assuming the decision is positive, the customer returns to the branch loan office to receive a check for the requested amount of the loan (or checks are issued to pay off obligations, depending on the situation) after completing some additional forms. The forms prepared vary by customer, depending on collateral, and might include (1) the note and chattel mortgage, (2) financial statement listing present indebtedness and liabilities, (3) application for corrected motor vehicle title, (4) wage assignment, and (5) State of Illinois, Uniform Commercial Code—Financing Statement—Form UCC-1.[12]

A clerk in the loan office types a loan set covering the new loan. Exhibit H presents the original copy of the loan set. The loan set contains an original and seven carbon copies, with each copy containing only selected data which are obtained by using special carbon paper. The different copies are for collateral purposes and include wage assignments, the formal loan note, security agreement, and so forth. The customer must sign various copies of the loan set before being permitted to leave with the loan check. Subsequently, one of the copies from the loan set will be mailed by the home office of Mercantile Financial Corporation (after the document has been processed) to the customer as a confirmation form.

The original copy of the loan set serves as the customer ledger card, which is maintained in the small loan branch office. The pay-

---

[12] The latter document is the official form for securing a lien against specified collateral. The document is prepared in an original and four copies, and one of the copies is acknowledged by the appropriate State of Illinois official and returned to the loan subsidiary of Mercantile Financial Corporation.

ment behavior of each loan customer is closely observed by the manager of the small loan branch office. If a customer becomes delinquent, five days after the due date, the customer receives a notice in the mail. If there is no payment, three days later the second notice is mailed. If there is no payment, then three days later the customer is contacted by telephone. Thus, 11 days after the actual due date of the payment, the manager of the small loan branch office is trying to contact the customer by telephone.

One of the carbon copies from the loan set is used in the small loan office for an alphabetical present-customer file. This particular copy of the loan set contains both the customer's account number and the due date of the monthly payments. The customer ledger card (original copy of loan set) is maintained in the small loan office by account number according to the due date of the payments. The alphabetical file is used whenever a customer comes to the loan office to make payment and does not know the account number and due date.

Daily, the manager of each small loan office reviews the customer ledger cards; a red flag is attached to any account that is past due; and the manager decides what action will be taken regarding interest and service charges for the delinquent accounts. When a small loan account becomes 10 days' overdue, the Illinois statute prescribes the amount of the penalty that can be charged the customer. If there is a 30-day delay in payment, an extension charge is made. At any time after an account becomes overdue, the manager of the small loan office has the option of converting the customer's original loan from "precomputed interest" to simple interest. The "precomputed interest" is rebated according to the 1278 method, where the interest is computed in advance and each payment is both for interest and principal per the predetermined schedule. By converting to simple interest, simple interest is computed on the daily running balance in the customer's account.[13]

---

[13] Strange as it may seem, the manager welcomes a small delay in payment. Of course, one consideration is the extra service charge that will be received from the same amount of principal. But another consideration is not so obvious. The manager wants to make the maximum amount of loans within restrictions of certain degrees of risk; thus, whenever a loan is paid off, the task now is to put those funds back out as a new loan. If there is a slight delay in payment, then additional funds which draw interest are outstanding for a longer period of time and, for example, there are no additional advertising costs connected with the revenue from this slight overdue period.

EXHIBIT G
Loan Application Form

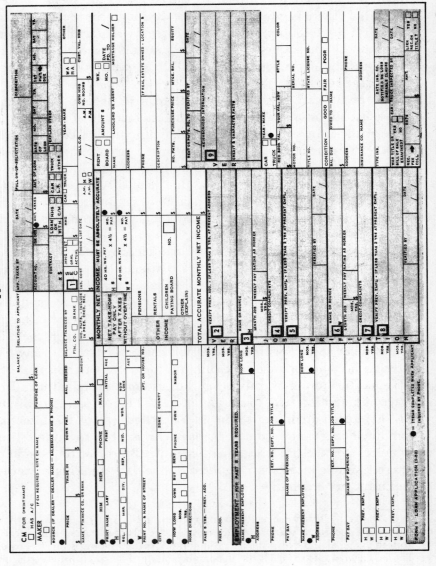

FORM 1 LOAN APPLICATION (1-60)   ● = ITEMS COMPLETED WHEN APPLICANT INQUIRES BY PHONE.

PRESENT & FORMER CREDITORS | PHONE NOS. | DATE OPENED | ORIG. DEBT | BALANCE APPLICANT | VERIFIED BAL. DUE | CONTRACT AND MO. PAYMENTS | SECURITY | SEC. | DATE LAST PMT. | HOW PAID & VERIFIED (SEE RECEIPTS IN OFFICE ON HOME) | VER. BY | CHECKS (EXACT AMT.)

PC ☐ FC ☐ CM ☐

10 LOAN CO. OR BANK

AUTO FINANCE CO. (PRESENT OR BUYING)

CREDIT UNION

IS CO-MAKER FOR

CAR DEALER

FURNITURE

FURNITURE

APPLIANCE

JEWELRY

DEPT. STORE

GROCERY

CLOTHING

CAR REPAIR

HOSPITAL & MEDICAL

OTHER

11

TOTAL AMT. CRD. ISSUED

HOME INTERVIEW & LISTING
YES / NO

CORR. POOR

CORR. HOME

HOME RENT

NEIGHBORHOOD INFORMATION

DOES WIFE APPROVE LOAN?

DOES WIFE FEEL LOAN CAN BE REPAID SAFELY

VERIFICATION IDENTITY

BADGE NO. | PAYROLL NO. | SOC. SEC. NO. | CREDIT CARDS

DRIVER'S LIC. NO. | STATE | IDENTIFYING PHYSICAL MARKS | GLASSES YES ☐ NO ☐ | BIRTH DATE / /

NO. CHILDREN | AGES CHILDREN | B

NO. DEP.

H

W

G

HT. | WT. | EYES | HAIR

TOTAL
12 ALL DEBT
SEC. DEBT
13 UNSEC. DEBT

TOT. MONTHLY NET INC.

LESS TOTAL MO. PMTS. TO BE PD. FROM LOAN

14 LOAN EXCHANGE VER. BY   DATE / /

CREDIT BUREAU VER. BY   DATE / /

MONTHLY EXPENSES

BAL. MO. PMTS. ON DEBTS

RENT OR HOUSE PMTS.

FOOD $30 PER ADULT — $15 PER CHILD

CLOTHING

LIGHT — GAS — PHONE

HEAT (COAL — OIL — GAS)

CAR EXP. (GAS - OIL - TIRES $30 MIN. PER CAR - TRUCK)

BUS TRANSPORTATION

FAMILY INSURANCE

CHILD CARE (IF WIFE WORKS)

CHILD SUPPORT — ALIMONY

OTHER

TOTAL ACCURATE MONTHLY EXPENSES

15 ACCURATE EXCESS INC. OVER EXPENSES

MANAGER DECISION

HOW ☐ ☐ ☐

FINANCE DEALER ☐ ☐

BY PHONE ☐   IN PERSON ☐

LOAN REJECTED FOR FOLLOWING REASONS

TO

AM'S RECOMMENDATION

COMPLETE BEFORE CHECK BY MANAGER. ALL RECEIPTS ON ALL DEBTS MUST BE SEEN AND VERIFIED IN PROPER PLACE. UNDER "PRESENT & FORMER CREDITORS" PRECAUTION FOR SAFETY OF LOAN

1. REJECT ☐ THIS AS "SAFE,
APPROVE ☐ GRADE A LOAN" IN AMOUNT OF
$_____ IN ACCORD WITH 5
RULES AND 3 FUNDAMENTALS.

A.M.'S INITIALS

EXHIBIT H
Master Loan Set

SOURCE OF LOAN

DIRECT MAIL
NEWSPAPER
RADIO
SIGNS
TELEPHONE
FORM REF
CUST REF
EMP REF
COMP REF
DEALER REF

DEALER 35 NAME
PRES. CUST
OLD CUST
N.W. RENEWAL

MONTH LOAN MADE
YEAR

PHONE NUMBER
SECURITY

TIME AT ADDRESS
SPOUSE
JOB
ADDRESS
PHONE
SALARY

HOW LONG
PAY DAYS

FULL PAID BY SOMEONE'S (T PLAN)
HOW PAID
DATE
AMOUNT
BALANCE DUE OR DATE PAID

BORROWER'S NAMES AND ADDRESSES

ACCOUNT NUMBER
OFFICE
DUE DATE
DATE MADE

BRING ADDRESS AND PHONE NUMBER TO BE TYPED IN BELOW

DATE FILED
DATE PAID

DATE	RATE OF INTEREST	TYPE OF COLLATERAL	COR.	NOTES REC.	NOTES REC.	NOTES REC.	UNEARNED	REBATES	RECORDING FEE	EX-CHECK	M.B.A.	LOAN BALANCE	B.O REC.	DUE DATE		
DATE	SIMPLE INTEREST	LATE FEE	DEFERRED FEE	AMOUNT OF MONEY REC	NOTES REC. SIMPLE	NOTES REC. PRECOMPUTED	UNEARNED INTEREST	ACC.	TOTAL	BANK	BANK	AMT. CHARGE	BALANCE	ACCT	AMOUNT	DR	NO.

1
2
3
4
5
6
7
8
9
10
11
12
13
14
15
16
17
18
19
20

USE SPECIAL CARBON WHILE TYPING NAME & ADDRESS ON MASTER BELOW

MAKE OF VEHICLE
YEAR
BODY
SERIAL NUMBER
MOTOR NUMBER
LICENSE NUMBER
WORK NUMBER
NO. NEW OR CTL 100

ONE
ONE

IF LOAN INCLUDES WAGE ASSIGNMENT, TYPE IN NAME OF EMPLOYER IN AREA TO RIGHT. IT WILL AUTOMATICALLY APPEAR ON WAGE ASSIGNMENT

NAME OF EMPLOYER

CASHIER SOLICITATION

CO-MAKER, LOAN NAME, ADDRESS AND PHONE NUMBER

JAN FEB MAR APR MAY JUNE
JULY AUG SEPT OCT NOV DEC

OUTSTANDING DEBTS

PURPOSE OF LOAN

BORROWER'S AGE   RACE   NO. IN FAMILY

REMARKS ENTER ALL NOTATIONS - BRIEFLY - LEGIBLY

On the 10th day of the month, the manager of the small loan office prepares a brief report from the customer ledger cards. A summary is made of all accounts 60 days or more past due, and these aggregate data are entered on a form containing four column headings: (1) number of accounts delinquent, (2) percentage of delinquent accounts to total accounts, (3) dollar amount of delinquent account, and (4) percentage of dollar amounts of delinquent accounts to the dollar amount of total accounts.

The loan register and disbursements journal (see Exhibit I) is prepared in duplicate, and the duplicate copy is daily submitted to the home office. This document is used for several purposes and will be discussed subsequently in this case study. Note the different types of data included in this daily report, such as volume by type of collateral, volume by type of borrower, and volume by source.

The cash receipts journal (see Exhibit J) is also prepared in duplicate, and the duplicate copy is daily submitted to the home office. The McBee accounting set permits the simultaneous recording of the data on (1) the customer's receipt form, (2) the cash receipts journal, and (3) the customer's ledger card. The duplicate copy of the cash receipts journal is also used for several purposes and represents a daily report of certain types of activities.

In addition to the above reports, the manager of each small loan office prepares a daily report, a monthly delinquent report entitled "2-Month and Over Past Dues," and a monthly statistical report entitled "Mercantile Loan Organization Report." The daily report is a one-page digest of selected data presented in three sections: bank balance, a recapitulation of daily transactions with customers, and different types of summary aggregate data. The "2-Month and Over Past Dues" report shows not only the detailed data by delinquent account but also shows the promises and results of action taken toward the collection of each account.

The mercantile loan organization report is a two-page report which presents a summarization of the monthly transactions with customers; statistical data, the precomputed interest, the late and extension charges for the month for different groups of delinquent accounts; number of employees and the average customer accounts per employee; dollar average of new loans made during month; dollar average of all loans; and a schedule of statistical data by source of loans. This latter schedule contains *rows* for the different types of advertising media, references from different organizational units

EXHIBIT I
Loan Register and Disbursements Journal

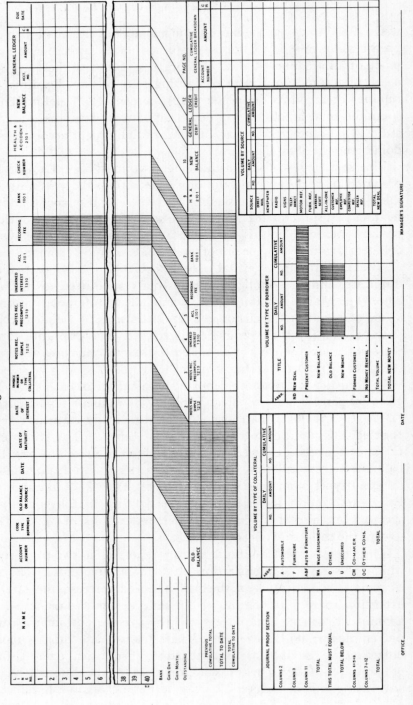

EXHIBIT J
Cash Receipts Journal

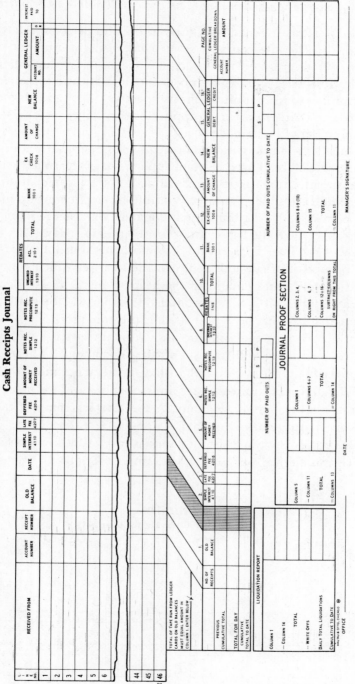

within Mercantile Financial Corporation, and personal references by type. The schedule contains seven *columns:* (1) number of loans made, (2) aggregate amount of new loans, (3) number of loan applications received, (4) number of loan applications turned down, (5) number of loan applications prospective customers turned down, (6) year to date, number of applications received, and (7) year to date, number of loans made.

Some of the administration of small loan operations is performed at the home office. Three assistant supervisors of the small loan offices (note organization chart per Exhibit C) are located at the home office, and each supervisor is responsible for a given group of branch loan offices. Daily, the branch office manager sends the home office a duplicate copy of the transactions for the previous day. This includes a copy of the loan register and disbursements journal, a copy of the cash receipts journal, and a copy of the loan set which contains the statistical and other data from the heading of the master loan set as indicated by Exhibit K. This latter document will be mailed to the customer after it has been processed by the home office.

For accounting, the assistant supervisor reviews the daily transaction reports along with the supporting documents. The next steps are to verify the footing of both cash disbursements and cash receipts, verify that check numbers are in sequence, and verify that cash receipts numbers are in sequence. A spot check is made of the extensions and recapitulations of data.

This review by the assistant supervisor is made for both administrative and clerical purposes. For example, periodically the assistant

EXHIBIT K
Fourth Copy of the Master Loan Set*

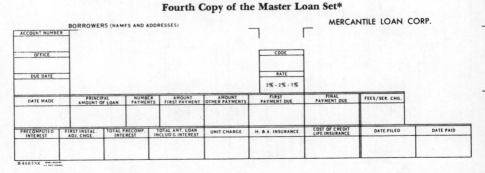

* Only the heading of this document is illustrated above. The remainder of the document is a form letter that is mailed to the new customer.

supervisor will go to the branch loan offices over which she or he is responsible and verify the cash balance and perform internal checks of customer ledger cards. (The internal control aspects of the assistant supervisor's operations overlap the functions of the internal auditor, who is a member of the treasurer's staff—note Exhibit D.)

After the assistant supervisor has approved the daily transaction reports and supporting documents from his or her branch offices, the duplicate copies of the loan register and disbursements journal, the cash receipts journal, and the loan set are forwarded to a data processing service center. Punched cards are processed for each customer, by branch loan office, and by type of loan. The outside—external to the corporation—data processing service center also maintains control summary cards for each type of loan by branch office, and these are compared with the balances indicated on the daily transaction reports. Weekly a report of mathematical errors by branch office is prepared by the data processing service center and forwarded to the assistant supervisor who is responsible for the accounting operations of that branch loan office.

The use of a data processing service center was only begun a year ago, and the transition was gradual. Each month one or two small loan branch offices were converted from the complete manual system to the limited data processing system. Data processing cards were punched for each customer of the branch office that is being added to the data processing system. Incidentally, a $6,000 error was discovered in the customer account balances when one branch office was brought under the control of the data processing system. (The bonding company repaid the $6,000.)

At the present time, the last small loan branch office has only recently been added to the data processing system which has been used for only a limited number of operations. The limited data processing activities include control over account balances of each branch office, computation and accumulation of unearned income, accumulation of historical data and preparation of the data for the Robert Morris Associates reports, and the preparation of a statistical report by type of loan for each branch loan office.

This latter report, the loan receivable report, includes the following column headings: (1) account number, (2) borrower, (3) present balance, (4) date purchased, (5) date loan made, (6) original charge, (7) remaining unearned portion of charge, (8) number of installments, (9) last payment, (10) total contractural amounts past due, (11) amount 30 days past due, (12) amount 60 days past due,

(13) amount 90 days past due and (14) amount over 90 days past due.

The data processing service center also prepares a list of new borrowers by name, address and telephone number. This list is used in advertising the various services offered by the overall corporation.

Furniture and Appliance Office. All furniture and appliance loans are made through dealers, and these operations can be described as a discounting of customer notes from participating dealers. There is considerable difference in the arrangement made with participating dealers. Some dealers guarantee all customer loans, and if a note is not paid according to contract, the dealer will repurchase the note. Other dealers operate through a reserve agreement, where a certain percent of the note is retained by the furniture and appliance subsidiary of Mercantile Financial Corporation until the customer has paid off the note. In the latter case, if the note is not paid, the dealer can lose only the amount of funds in the reserve. For some dealers, there is an arrangement where a certain portion of the discount rate is placed in a cushion (reserve) and is paid to the dealer only after the customer has paid off the note; in other words, the dealer participates in the revenue from the discount rate after the note has been paid off.

There are other differences in the arrangement with dealers regarding the relation of the customer to the furniture and appliance subsidiary of Mercantile Financial Corporation. Some dealers do not desire that their customers know that they are financing their furniture and appliance accounts through an outside financial institution. In these cases, the dealers will make all collections and forward them intact to the furniture and appliance subsidiary of Mercantile Financial Corporation. If a customer does default in payment and the dealer is not required by the arrangement to repurchase the note, then the furniture and appliance subsidiary of Mercantile Financial Corporation will enter the picture and will notify the delinquent customer that the account has recently been acquired by the furniture and appliance subsidiary of Mercantile Financial Corporation and that all future payments must be made to the latter firm.

Other dealers tell their customers at the time of the sale that their accounts will be financed by the furniture and appliance subsidiary of Mercantile Financial Corporation. In fact, under some financial arrangements the dealer may tell a customer that the proposed sale is dependent upon the acceptance by Mercantile Financial Corporation of the customer's note. In any case, under this second type of arrangement the customer makes payments directly to the furniture and appliance subsidiary of Mercantile Financial Corporation, and the dealer does not become involved again until the customer pays the account in full or there is a default in payment.

As is suggested by the above discussion, the document evidencing the arrangement with the dealer is the beginning point in the data accumulation, processing, and reporting activities for the furniture and appliance office. There are two solicitors for the Chicago area, and these solicitors work full-time at the task of entering into arrangements with dealers and then monitoring the arrangement. Each solicitor will closely watch the quality and terms of the installment paper submitted by personally acquired participating dealers. For example, an arrangement may be made with Dealer A, where that company's customer's notes will be discounted at a given rate. Subsequently, the company discovers that Dealer A has arrangements with several financial institutions and that Mercantile Financial Corporation is only receiving the low-quality paper. The solicitor will tell Dealer A to either send higher quality paper to Mercantile Financial Corporation, or the financial arrangement is terminated.

If a given dealer sends only short-term paper to Mercantile Financial Corporation and sends long-term paper to another financial institution, then this is bad for Mercantile Financial Corporation. There is not that much difference in the administrative cost for short-term paper versus long-term paper, and under the latter condition, there is a longer period of time over which to receive interest. Furthermore, when any paper is paid off, there is the problem of getting new loans to replace the paid-off accounts. Additional advertising cost may be required for the new account, along with the usual administrative cost.

In this type of business operation, management has the continuous problem of watching the dealers. A dealer can usually take "choice" customer notes to another financial institution and get the choice notes discounted at a lower rate of interest than the dealer would receive from Mercantile Financial Corporation. The discount rate that has been set by the solicitor for Mercantile Financial Corporation assumes that there will be an averaging out of the choice customer notes with the extremely poor customer notes. The earnings on the choice notes will hopefully more than offset the losses on the extremely poor customer notes.

While the solicitors work full-time in the administration of the financial arrangements with dealers, other members of the furniture and appliance office and selected members of the home office will periodically review the results of given dealer arrangements. In evaluating the dealer arrangements, consideration is given not only to the dealer statistical report (a monthly report of the total transactions by dealer, including the computations of yield by dealer, and this report is based on the statistical data available at the time the loan is made), but also to the repossessions by dealer. If there is a large group of delinquents occurring from a given dealer's customers, this is also considered.

After the document evidencing the financial arrangement with the dealer has been prepared, the "dealer card" is maintained by the credit manager. Each credit manager is responsible for a specified group of dealers, and the credit manager periodically checks Dun & Bradstreet's *Reference Book* and other credit services' publications for indications of unfavorable changes in the financial position of the dealer. The need for being aware of changes in the financial position of a dealer varies directly with the type and the conditions of the financial arrangement between the dealer and Mercantile Financial Corporation.

When a customer purchases furniture or a major appliance from a dealer, the dealer asks the customer to prepare a one-page credit questionnaire which intentionally does not have a heading on the form so that the questionnaire cannot be identified with Mercantile Financial Corporation in those situations where the dealer prefers to work on an indirect basis with Mercantile Financial Corporation.

A dealer calls the furniture and appliance office and notifies a clerk of a desire to have a given customer's note discounted, and the dealer may request that the credit investigation immediately begin on the customer. (In the latter case the clerk will secure appropriate data from the dealer so that the credit investigation can begin.) Instead of calling, the dealer may mail the customer's credit questionnaire to the furniture and appliance office. The questionnaire contains the complete details of the sales agreement, including description of article, cash price, taxes, trade deductions, cash deductions, insurance charges, finance charges, total contract, amount of monthly payments, and the starting date for payments.

Clerks in the furniture and appliance office immediately perform a credit investigation on the customer, and the results of the investigation are entered on a specially designed office form. The credit investigation report along with the customer's credit questionnaire (maybe the title "sales agreement" might be more appropriate for this document) are submitted to the supervisor who is responsible for transactions with that dealer. The credit manager, assuming he agrees to buy the "deal," attaches a one-page work sheet to the other two documents and assigns an account number to the deal. A major portion of the work sheet is designated for contract analysis and service charge analysis, and these computations are performed by a clerk as soon as the credit manager approves the deal.

The work sheet with the attached documents are given to a typist who prepares a master loan set. This loan set contains an original and six copies. The original serves as the detailed ledger card for the customer. The first copy is a dealer notification report and is mailed to the dealer. The second copy is mailed to the customer, unless there is an indirect arrangement with the dealer, in which case the customer does not receive this copy. The third copy is placed in the numerical file according to assigned account number for the customer. The fourth copy is currently submitted to a data processing service center where data processing cards are punched, and these punched cards are used monthly in the preparation of the dealer statistical report (see Exhibit L for the format at the dealer statisti-

EXHIBIT L

Dealer Statistical Copy* of Master Loan Set for Furniture and Appliance Office

				REFERENCE		ACCOUNT NUMBER	
PURCHASER		ACCOUNT NO.	DAY DUE			DATE DUE	
ADDRESS		HOME PHONE	AGE			FURNITURE	☐
CITY AND STATE		OCCUPATION		SELLING PRICE	OTHER ☐	APPLIANCES	☐
EMPLOYED BY	YRS. MOS.	BUSINESS PHONE		DOWN PAYMENT	%	FURN. & APPL.	☐
	DATE PURCH.	AMT. OF NOTE		UNPAID BALANCE	LOSS RESERVE	H.B. $	
	FINAL INSTALL.	DATE OF NOTE		SERVICE CHARGE	OVER–REBATE	D.P.L.R.	
NO. AND AMT. OF INSTALLMENT	WA'S DLR END GUAR. MOS. c			AMOUNT OF NOTE	CHECK OR DRAFT	NET S.C.	

* Normally, this form is 5½ × 4.

cal copy). The fifth copy is placed in the customer's file folder. The sixth and final copy is used for direct advertising purposes.

At the same time the master loan set is prepared, the typist prepares the insurance policy. The customer's account number is also the credit life insurance policy number.

Next, all of the documents are compared; the master loan set is proofed against the work sheet and other supporting documents. The mathematical extensions are recomputed and verified. The insurance policy is compared with the master loan set. The amount of the loan is compared with the check which was issued to the dealer. At the completion of this internal review step, the master set is separated, a customer file folder is opened, a perforated payment-coupon book is prepared for the customer, and all documents are processed to their appropriate locations.

The bookkeeper for the furniture and appliance office only maintains the detailed ledger for customers. Control pages are established for groups of accounts. Daily, the bookkeeper receives an adding machine tape of the total work sheets processed that day; this total is compared with a tape of the new customer ledger cards. If there is a difference, a tape is run on those approved customer loans (as evidenced by the work sheets) which are in process. A comparison is also made between the total checks issued and the new loans.

The accountant for the furniture and appliance office maintains the general ledger and the appropriate journals, which are recorded on a manual basis. The accountant also prepares the normal financial reports for the furniture and appliance office. As previously indicated, there is one report which is not prepared by the accountant but which is prepared by a data processing service center—the statistical report. This latter report shows yield by dealer based on the actual terms and conditions of the customer loans accepted from that dealer.

The volume of business in the furniture and appliance office fluctuates by the day of the week. Monday is the busy day; many sales are made over the weekend and the dealers are on the telephone on Monday asking that credit investigations begin on their customers. If everything is approved, the dealer should receive a check in the mail on Wednesday. Dealers expect this quick service and telephone the furniture and appliance office if their checks are not in the mail on Wednesday. In coping with this uneven work load, the furniture and appliance subsidiary of Mercantile Financial Corporation has three permanent, part-time clerks who work two or three days a week.

The extent of this uneven work load is indicated by the following statistics. On a Monday, 110–120 applications may be approved and 20 applications rejected. The monthly average of applications accepted ranges from 1,100 to 1,500. To complete the statistical data, some of the loans extend for more than a year, and the average volume of active accounts on a given day ranges from 18,000 to 20,000.

The collection procedures on the accounts vary depending on whether the customer will pay the furniture and appliance subsidiary of Mercantile Financial Corporation directly, or whether the customer will pay the dealer. Under either method the collections are posted to the detailed customer ledger cards maintained at the furniture and appliance office. For internal control purposes, there is a daily comparison of the total cash receipts (per the cashier's daily report) with the changes in the bookkeeper's control accounts for customer accounts.

The 18,000–20,000 accounts are separated into books, and seven collectors are responsible for the administration of the collection function. Each collector is personally responsible for a given group of accounts. Monthly, the first Friday of each month, all collectors plus other clerks review the 18,000–20,000 customer ledger cards and prepare a delinquent listing and aging of receivables by book–a specified group of ledger cards. The formal delinquent report is submitted to the supervisor of collections.

The collectors will immediately concentrate attention on the 90-day delinquents. Next, they will try to reduce the 60-day delinquents, and so forth. The collector who does a good job of reducing the short-term delinquents this month, will not have many long-term delinquents next month, that is, new long-term delinquents.

When an account becomes 90 days delinquent, if not before, the collector asks the customer to refinance the loan, which will mean additional financing charges and extension charges. When the loan is refinanced, subject to new credit approval, the account is taken off the delinquent listing. In other cases, the dealer may buy back any delinquent account or the customer may be referred to the small loan offices of Mercantile Financial Corporation, where the customer will take out a consolidated loan to pay off the furniture and appliance note. In either of these cases, the customer ceases to be a problem of the furniture and appliance office collectors.

In furniture and appliance operations, the gross yield and losses are not subject to the variation that exists in the motor and automobile operations. Usually, *new* furniture or appliances are involved, and the rate of interest is constant from one period to the next. Furthermore, the volume of business is fairly constant per participating dealer. There are exceptions to this latter generalization as previously indicated in the discussion of the solicitor's activities.

Motor and Automobile Office. An appreciation of characteristics and recent changes in motor and automobile loan operations is an essential prerequisite to a thorough understanding of the data accumulation, processing, and reporting activities of the motor and automobile office. Brief consideration is given to these characteristics and changes before an examination is made of the data accumulation procedures.

In contrast with furniture and appliance loans, the mix determines the gross yield. The collateral is not the same—all *new* furniture and equipment. Instead, there are *new* cars, cars *one year old, two years old,* and so forth. The age of the car is a big factor in determining the rate of interest that ideally should be charged. The older the car, the higher the rate of interest should be in order to compensate for the additional risk involved. However, administrative considerations preclude the establishment of completely flexible interest rates on automobile loans that vary directly with customer characteristics and the age of the car. In addition to these factors, consideration is given to the dealer's volume of business and to the quality of automobiles handled by the dealer (used automobiles vary considerably in condition for the same make and age of automobile, and from experience the quality of used automobiles handled by a given dealer can be estimated). Assumptions are made regarding these variable factors, and a given interest rate is established for use in discounting customer notes of a particular automobile dealer.

Mix can only be determined by an analysis of the historical transactions with each dealer. Monthly, a report is prepared by the data processing service center that indicates the mix of automobile loans and the yield per dealer. This first report is a statistical analysis of the available data at the time the automobile loan is made—a copy of the master loan set is furnished to the data processing service center for use in preparation of this statistical report.[14] A second report is prepared by the data processing service center that includes the repossessions by dealer; these latter data are obtained from the motor and automobile's accountant, who manually maintains a repossessions journal. This second report contains the number of repossessions by dealer, losses if any from repossessions, and other statistical data regarding the age of the car and the amount past due at the time of the repossession.

The administration of automobile loans not only requires knowledge of the forecasted yield per dealer, based on a copy of the original loan transaction and knowledge of repossessions by dealer, but also requires knowledge of unusual payment behavior by the customers of a given dealer including losses on uncollectible accounts. The type of recourse that the motor and automobile subsidiary of Mercantile Financial Corporation has with the automobile dealer is also important.

Legally, there are four forms of recourse or contingencies on automobile loans which are followed in the financial arrangements between the motor and automobile subsidiary of Mercantile Financial Corporation and the various automobile dealers: (1) repurchase arrangement, (2) recourse arrangement, (3) guarantee arrangement, and (4) holdback arrangement. Under a repurchase arrangement, it is necessary to actually have physical possession of the automobile *before* the automobile dealer is required to buy back the vehicle. Under a full recourse arrangement, the dealer is required to buy back the vehicle after a certain period of delinquency has occurred, even though the vehicle cannot be located. Under a guarantee arrangement, the dealer guarantees a specified amount of money for a given number of months. Under the holdback arrangement, part of the proceeds on the automobile loan are held by the motor and automobile subsidiary until the customer has made a specified number of payments. At the end of this time period, the dealer is paid the remainder of any balance due the dealership. In the latter case, the dealer is no longer responsible for losses that may result from a delinquent account or from repossession of that particular customer's automobile. The guarantee and holdback arrange-

---

[14] The monthly reports prepared by the data processing service center are filed in a cumulative ledger called "Dealer's Experience Book," and these reports are frequently used by management of the motor and automobile office in evaluation and administration of dealer transactions.

ments may both be incorporated in a contract with an automobile dealer. (The guarantee type of arrangement is frequently employed, and the dealer may be required to guarantee up to one third of the contract price.)

With some dealers, there is a reserve agreement (which is similar to the reserve agreement with furniture and appliance dealers) where the automobile dealer receives additional revenue when an automobile loan is paid in full. However, the reserve agreements are not as common today as they were two years ago. Commercial banks do not follow the reserve agreement procedure, and the motor and automobile office's management has begun to comply with competition.

The most significant change in automobile loan operations in recent years has been the strong entry by commercial banks into this type of operation. The interest rates charged by commercial banks are substantially lower than those charged by the automobile and motor subsidiary of Mercantile Financial Corporation or than those charged by other financial loan institutions. Surprisingly enough, managers of commercial banks in the Chicago area have followed the policy of making an automobile loan to almost anyone at competitively low interest rates. For example, some loan applicants who were refused an automobile loan by the credit managers of the motor and automobile subsidiary of Mercantile Financial Corporation have gone to commercial banks and immediately received an automobile loan.

The effort by commercial banks in the automobile loan area were not significant until two years ago. Furthermore, the board of directors of commercial banks were thought to have had a rather conservative policy regarding excessive investments in the automobile loan area. Then, the pendulum began to swing to the other extreme. The financial terms and time periods covered by various types of automobile loans were modified, and the commercial banks assumed an increasingly important position in terms of the national volume of automobile loans made.

Management of the motor and automobile office is of the opinion that commercial banks have heavy losses which are currently hidden by the high volume of transactions. There is a lag between the time an automobile loan is made and the time that the typical repossession occurs. This lag averages 9 to 16 months. Commercial banks have been deeply involved in automobile financing for less than two years under conditions of these modified financial terms and extended time periods. Therefore, from a purely statistical standpoint it is almost impossible for a given commercial bank to have had sufficient historical statistical experience upon which to base its rates that pertain to the results of following the bank's current automobile loan policy.

The dynamic increase in the volume of automobile loan operations by commercial banks has produced substantial short-term profits to the commercial banks, and the appropriate losses that should be matched against these short-term profits will not be known until another 9 to 16 months. If the dynamic growth rate continues, the profits 16 months hence from the then higher level of activity will dominate over the losses that might occur by then (these losses would be indicative of the lagged results of lower levels of volume).

Several competent financiers have expressed the opinion that if the volume of automobile loans financed by commercial banks were to achieve even a stable position during the next 18 months, then some boards of directors of commercial banks may revert to their former position regarding automobile loan operations. If this leveling off in volume occurs, some commercial banks who have gone all out in accepting automobile loan customers may have such a large loss from uncollectible accounts and repossessions that the boards of directors will demand that the former credit terms and rates be applied to future automobile loans.

Management of the motor and automobile office tends to agree with this latter position regarding the future and has not adopted a policy of meeting the commercial banks' rates. Instead, management has accepted the short-term forecast of a reduced volume of operations in the automobile loan area.

The following statistical data indicate the degree of impact that commercial banks have had upon the volume of business handled by Mercantile Financial Corporation's motor and automobile office. Two years ago, the monthly average of automobile loans made totaled 700; now, there are approximately 250 automobile loans made each month. Currently, there are 8,500 open accounts, but this level of volume is constantly decreasing at a slow rate. Old accounts which were at the 700 volume level are being paid off at the end of 30 months, and new accounts at the 250 volume level are being added. However, the time period over which new automobiles are financed has been extended beyond 30 months. This latter factor slows the pace at which the total volume of open accounts is decreasing. These 8,500 open accounts have an aggregate balance, on the average, of $11,000,000.

For the corporation as a whole, this substantial reduction in volume in the automobile loan area has been more than offset by substantial gains in the commercial division's operations and in consumer loans, particularly in the area of personal loans for more than $800 (which may be called all-in-one loans or consolidated loans) . Furthermore, the entry by commercial banks has permitted management of the motor and automobile office to be even more selective in the screening of customers, and this has resulted in an increase in the profitability of the average automobile loan during the past two years.

For example, a customer's loan application from an automobile dealer is not accepted, and subsequently this customer's loan application is accepted by a commercial bank. The automobile dealer may be upset because of the inconvenience caused by the nonapproval of the loan application but as long as the dealer can get the loan approved elsewhere and sell the automobile, the dealer is happy. A few dealers have expressed their dissatisfaction with the motor and automobile office's operations in disapproving their customer's notes; however, the manager of the motor and automobile office does not believe that the current series of events will damage or affect the long-term relation between the automobile dealers and his office staff. If and when commercial banks become more selective in screening applicants for automobile loans, the volume of transactions by the motor and automobile office will increase.

The positive side of this change of events can be explained as follows. When an automobile dealer has a prospective customer who desires to buy a two-year-old automobile and does not have very many funds for a down payment or desires to repay the loan over an extended period of time, the automobile dealer must get this type of loan accepted by a financial loan institution. Commercial banks will not make such a loan. For example, on a two-year-old automobile, a commercial bank may loan $1,350 to be repaid over 24 months; the motor and automobile subsidiary of the Mercantile Financial Corporation will loan slightly more to be repaid over a longer period. The risk is higher on this latter type of loan, and thus a higher interest rate is demanded. In the aggregate volume of automobile loans, a substantial percent is of the riskier, high interest rate type. This explains the increase in average earnings by the motor and automobile subsidiary on automobile loans during the past two years.

Because of the substantial reduction in volume during the past two years, the number of employees in the motor and automobile office has been reduced significantly. However, the data accumulation, processing, and reporting activities are approximately the same; there are just fewer transactions to process and administer.

An automobile dealer will ask a customer to prepare a purchaser's confidential statement, a one-page document containing both credit reference data and the appropriate descriptive data regarding the proposed automobile sale. This latter data would include all of the financial terms—cash selling price, trade-in, total down payment, and so forth. The automobile dealer will also initiate a bank draft for the net amount due under the arrangement with the motor and automobile subsidiary of Mercantile Financial Corporation. These bank draft forms are of the envelope type; the automobile dealer will complete the bank draft and enclose in the envelope the automobile sales contract. The automobile dealer takes the bank draft with the enclosed document to the bank.

Eventually, the bank draft arrives at the commercial bank representing the motor and automobile subsidiary of Mercantile Financial Corporation. The motor and automobile subsidiary's management has an agreement with the officers of the commercial bank, and according to this agreement, a bank officer will notify the manager of the motor and automobile office at 2:00 each afternoon of the names and amounts of drafts that have been received by the bank. The manager has 24 hours in which to accept or refuse each draft, and a complete notification procedure is followed. (Even when all drafts are accepted, the manager will notify the bank officer accordingly.)

At the same time the automobile dealer takes the bank draft to the bank, he or she also sends the purchaser's confidential statement directly to the motor and automobile office. A credit manager in the motor and automobile office will initially review the purchaser's confidential statement. A work sheet is prepared, which is a one-page cover document containing insurance analysis on one segment of the page and draft analysis and collateral details on the other segment of the page. Next, a credit investigation is made of the customer. After the credit references are checked, the work sheet and attached documents are returned to the credit manager, and the credit manager reaches a decision regarding the approval of the automobile loan.

(All of this action has occurred before the bank draft is processed through banking channels.)

When the bank officer calls the manager of the motor and automobile office regarding the acceptance of the automobile draft, the manager is ready to make a decision. However, the manager will go to the bank and secure the automobile sales contract for each draft, and during the 24-hour period that the motor and automobile office has to consider the drafts, the clerks in the motor and automobile office will closely scrutinize the terms and details of the actual contract against the application document. If there is any difference, the draft is refused for payment at the commercial bank. (From a statistical standpoint, the number of drafts accepted per day ranges from 10 to 20.)

If the bank draft is approved for payment at the commercial bank, a check is drawn for payment of each draft. A typist prepares a master loan set and a set of Galloway registration cards, which are used for registering the lien against the automobile. The master loan set is similar to the master loan set for furniture and appliance operations, with two exceptions. The fourth copy is also called the "Dealer Statistical Copy"; however, it is not sent to the data processing service center. Instead, the manager of the motor and automobile office uses this copy as the beginning point for accumulating various types of statistical data on automobile loan operations. Subsequently, the manager integrates reports of repossessions, losses, and delinquent account statistics with these data. Thus, confidential managerial statistics which reflect different types of risk are determined from this integrated statistical program, which is administered by the office manager. Exhibit M represents the dealer statistical copy of the master loan set for motor and automobile loan operations.

The sixth copy of the master loan set for motor and automobile loan operations is sent to the data processing service center, where data cards are prepared, processed, and used in the preparation of the monthly reports of mix and yield by automobile dealer.

After the master loan set and Galloway registration cards have been prepared, the insurance policy is typed. An internal review is made of the various documents in much the same manner as was followed in the furniture and appliance office. At the completion of this step, a perforated coupon payment book is prepared for the customer, and all documents are processed to their appropriate destinations.

EXHIBIT M

**Dealer Statistical Copy* of Master Loan Set
for Motor and Automobile Loan Office**

NAME OF CAR	SERIAL NUMBER		BODY CYLS.	YEAR	INSURANCE TERM	TYPE OF POLICY	ACCOUNT NUMBER
PURCHASER			ACCOUNT NO.	DAY DUE	NEW USED DLR INS. ☐ ☐		DATE DUE
ADDRESS			HOME PHONE	AGE	DEALER		
CITY AND STATE		·	OCCUPATION		SELLING PRICE	HOLD BACK	INSURANCE CHARGE
EMPLOYED BY		YRS. MOS.	BUSINESS PHONE		DOWN PAYMENT	%	1st YEAR COST
COMPANY NO.	PLAN	DATE PURCH.	DATE OF NOTE	AMT OF NOTE	UNPAID BALANCE	LOSS RESERVE	A C L
NO. AND AMT. OF INSTALL.		FINAL INSTALL		DEALER NO.	SERVICE CHARGE	OVER–REBATE	S C L
SPECIALS			WA'S REPUR. GUAR. MOS		AMOUNT OF NOTE	CHECK OR DRAFT	REPURCHASE NET S .C.

* Normally, this form is 8½ × 4.

Seven collectors and two supervisors are responsible for the 8,500 open accounts. As in the furniture and appliance operations, accounts are grouped in books, and a given collector is responsible for one or more books. A few dealers have such a volume of transactions with the motor and automobile subsidiary of Mercantile Financial Corporation that a separate book is established for each of them.

If a customer goes to the motor and automobile office to pay his monthly installment, the cashier will call the appropriate collector. The collector assigned to that customer will meet and talk with the customer while the cashier accepts the installment payment. If the customer is delinquent or there is any problem regarding his account, this collector-customer meeting provides the opportunity for a face-to-face discussion of the matter.

The nondealer books of customer accounts are designated a number according to the due date of the payment. Within the dealer books, the customer accounts are located in the appropriate order based on the due date of the payment. (The 15th, 16th, and 17th days of the month are the largest groupings of accounts, because they are the typical pay days.)

Monthly, a delinquent report is prepared by customer book, and the original copy of the delinquent report is given to the collection manager. The delinquent report is manually prepared by reviewing the payment column of each customer ledger card and observing the "key" designation. The bookkeeping machine records in the payment column the amount and date of the collection. Subsequently, clerks or collectors "key" each collection to indicate the appropriate monthly installment for which a particular payment is related and if there is any amount delinquent on that particular payment. For example, if a review is being made for the May delinquent account report and a given customer is keyed "3–$10," this would mean that the last payment was for the third month—March—and that the customer is $10 delinquent on the March installment; furthermore, the customer is delinquent on the April and May installments. Assuming the monthly installment is $65, the delinquent account list would appear as follows for May:

	Total Delinquent	1–30 Days	31–60 Days	61–90 Days	Over 90
NAME	$140	$65	$65	$10	–0–

The administration of the collection function is similar to that followed in the furniture and appliance office. The pressure is on the collector to reduce the number of delinquent accounts for which he or she is responsible. The action taken by the collector depends to a large extent upon the arrangement with the automobile dealer—a repurchase arrangement, a full recourse arrangement, a guarantee arrangement, or a holdback arrangement.

Periodically, an internal audit is made of the motor and automobile office's operations, and this includes an examination and confirmation of the balances in the customer accounts. The cash collection and cash payment procedures have internal control and internal check procedures similar to those followed in the furniture and appliance office.

Other Financial and Statistical Data

Consideration is given in this section to other data that are appropriate for a general understanding of the corporation's overall activities. The discussion will consist of three sections: responsibility reports, financial and statistical reports, and selected data regarding data processing activities.

Responsibility Reports

Monthly, a statement of income and expense (see Exhibit N and Exhibit O for the format of the report for all operations) and a

EXHIBIT N

Statement of Income and Expense

Period _____

	Budget	Current Year		Previous Year	
		Month	*YTD*	*Month*	*YTD*
Income					
Purchased accounts					
Equipment loans					
Inventory loans					
Shell home loans					
Rediscounts					
Purchased notes					
Retail motor loans					
Wholesale motor & direct loans					
Retail furniture & appliance loans					
Small loans					
Other consumer loans					
Late charges					
Bad debt recoveries					
Insurance commissions					
Miscellaneous income					
Total					
Operating Expenses					
Salaries					
Administrative travel expense					
Solicitors expense					
Telephone & telegraph					
Office supplies & expense					
Stationery, printing, & postage					
Repossession expense					
Rent					
Legal expense					
Legal expense, consumer					
Taxes, payroll, & misc.					
Credit reports					
Insurance					
Auditing					
Auditors expense					
Collectors expense					
Depreciation & amortization					
Advertising					
Entertainment					
Supervisory expense					
Commissions					
Pension plan					
Profit sharing					
Service car expense					
General expense					
Total Operating Expense					
Income before interest, BDP, S&A expense & FIT					
Interest expense					
Income before S&A expense, BDP & FIT					
Supervisory and administrative expense					

EXHIBIT N (*Continued*)

		Current Year		Previous Year	
	Budget	Month	YTD	Month	YTD
Bad debt provision					
Income before federal income tax					
Provision for federal income tax					
Net Income					
Branch or Subsidiary					

EXHIBIT O
Statement of Income and Expense
Period _____

		Current Year		Previous Year	
	Budget	Month	YTD	Month	YTD
Small Loan					
Precompute					
Simple					
Extensions					
Total					
Miscellaneous Income					
Dividends					
Regular loans					
Capital loans					
Other					
Total					
Salaries					
Administrative					
Accounting					
Advertising					
Auditors					
Collection/Credit					
Collectors					
Credit					
Service					
Solicitors					
Commercial supervision					
Legal, consumer					
Sales finance supervision					
Small loan supervision					
Total					
Stationery–Postage					
Stationery & printing					
Postage					
Total					

EXHIBIT O (*Continued*)

	Budget	Current Year Month	YTD	Previous Year Month	YTD
Repossession Expense					
Garage					
Repossessions					
Total					
Taxes					
Payroll					
Personal property					
State franchise					
Total					
Depreciation—Amortization					
Depreciation					
Leasehold improvements					
Noncomplete					
Total					
General Expense					
T/E Accounting					
T/E Credit					
Bank exchange					
Appraisal					
Donations					
Miscellaneous					
Total					
Branch or Subsidiary _____					

statement of financial position (see Exhibit P for the format of the 4-page report) are manually prepared for each of the 32 accounting units. From a legal standpoint, there are 22 corporations contained in the consolidated Mercantile Financial Corporation and Subsidiaries, and each subsidiary corporation is wholly owned by the parent corporation.

The difference between the 22 corporations and the 32 accounting units can be explained as follows. There are three branches of a particular small loan corporation, and each branch is handled as though it were a separate corporation; thus, these three branches would add two accounting units to the compilation (the small loan corporation is already included in the 22 corporations) —22 corporations + 2 extra small loan branch reports = 24 units. Certain types of commercial activities in Chicago and Atlanta are separately accounted for as though each were a separate corporation; the compilation is 24 units + 2 commercial division responsibility units = 26

CASH IN BANKS AND ON HAND
1001 Cash Regular
1002 Cash Payroll
1003 Cash Depository
1004 Cash Dividend
1005
1006 Cash Bank Lines
1007 Petty Cash
1008 Ex-Check
1009 U.S. Securities
1010 Bank Transfers
1011
1012

         Total Cash

NOTES AND ACCOUNTS RECEIVABLE
1101 Equipment Loans
1102 Inventory Loans
1103 Purchased A/R Net
1104 Purchased A/R Net
1105 Rediscounts—Net
1106 Rediscounts—Gross
1107 Purchased Notes
1108 Shell Home Loans
1109 Factored Accounts
1110
1112
1201 Retail Motor Loans
1202 Wholesale Motor Loans
1203 Retail Furniture Loans
1204 Wholesale Furniture Loans
1205
1206
1212 Simple Interest Small Loans
1213 Precomputed Interest S. Loans
1214 Simple Int. S. Loans (Acc. #2)
1215
1216 Other Consumer Loans
1217
1218
1219
1220 Regular Loans
1221 Capital Loans
1224 Employee's Accts. Rec.
1225 Insurance Accts. Rec.
1226 Burglary & Theft Loss
1229 Customer Service Charges
1230 Miscellaneous Accts. Rec.
1320 Dealer Holdbacks
      Sub Total
      Branch or Subsidiary _____

LESS
1121 Final Payment—Equipment Loans
1122 Final Payment—Inventory Loans
1123 Final Payment—Purchased Notes
1124 Final Payment—Shell Home Loans
1125 Final Payment—Factored Accounts
1126 Final Payment—Rediscounts
1301 Unearned Service Charge—Equip. Loans
1302 Unearned Ser. Ch.—Purchased Notes
1303 Unearned Ser. Ch.—Shell Homes
1304 Unearned Ser. Ch.—Purchased Accts.
1306 Unearned Ser. Ch.—Retail Motor Loans
1307 Unearned Ser. Ch.—Retail Furn. Loans
1310 Unearned Interest—Precomputed Loans
1312 Unearned Ser. Ch.—Other Cons. Loans
1315 Unearned Ser. Ch.—Regular Loans
1316 Unearned Ser. Ch.—Capital Loans
1320 Dealer Holdbacks
1321 Dealer Participating Loss Reserve
1322 S.C.L. Reserve
1323 Other Reserves
1324 Reserve Accounts—Subsidiaries
1325 Reserve for Doubtful Accounts
      Sub Total (Reserves)
      Net Receivables

FIXED ASSETS (NET)
1401 Furniture and Fixtures
1402 Service Cars
1403 Leasehold Improvements
      Total Fixed Assets

PREPAID OR DEFERRED EXPENSES
1501 Prepaid Expenses
1502 Prepaid Insurance
1503 Prepaid Interest
1601 Deferred Financial Services
1602 Deferred Insurance Expense
1603 Deferred Legal Expense
1604 Deferred Liquidation Expense
1605 Deferred Rebates—Repossessions
1610 Unamortized Debt Discount
1611 Unamortized Documentary Stamps
1612 Unamortized Noncompete Agreement
1701 Cash Surrender Value—Insurance
1702 Borrowed Premiums
1703 Deposit for Redemption—Class "A"
1704 Reserve for Redemption—Class "A"
1705
      Total Prepaid or Deferred Expenses
      Branch or Subsidiary_____

EXHIBIT P *(Continued)*

ADVANCES TO AND (FROM)
AFFILIATES
1801 Investments in Subsidiaries
1901 Current Account M.F.C.–
      Atlanta
1902 Current Account T.M.F.C.
1903 Current Account M.C.P.C.
1904 Current Account S.M.C.P.C.
1905 Current Account M.S.H.F.C.
1906 Current Account C.B.D.C.
1907 Current Account R.F.C.
1908 Current Account M.F.
1909
1921 Current Account M.M.D.C.
1922 Current Account M.I.B.
1923 Current Account S.M.F.C.
1924 Current Account M.C.F.C. (All)
1925 Current Account M.A.I.O.
1926 Current Account M.L.C. Corp.
1927
1928
1929
1930
1931 Current Account M.L.C. #1
1932 Current Account M.L.C. #2
1933 Current Account M.L.C. #3
1934 Current Account 4th M.L.C.
1935 Current Account 5th M.L.C.
1936 Current Account 6th M.L.C.
1937 Current Account M.C.L.C. (#7)
1938 Current Account 8th M.L.C.
1939 Current Account 9th M.L.C.
1940 Current Account 10th M.L.C.
1941
1942
1943
1950 Intracompany Insurance
      Total Advances
      TOTAL ASSETS

NOTES PAYABLE
2001 Notes Payable–Unsecured Bank
2002 Notes Payable–Commercial Paper
2003 Current Maturities on Long T.D.
2004
2005
      Total Notes Payable
      Branch or Subsidiary _____

ACCOUNTS PAYABLE AND
ACCRUED EXPENSES
2010 Dividends Payable
2015 Agency Obligations
2020 Collections Due Affiliates
2101 Accts. Payable–Insurance A.C.L.
2102 Accts. Payable–Insurance Auto
2103 Advanced Premiums

2104 Unclaimed Dividends
2105 Accounts Payable–Miscellaneous
2201 Rebates Due Dealers
2202 Suspense (Due Dealers)
2203 Suspense
2301 Accrued Contributions–E.R.P.
2302 Accrued Contributions–P/S
2303 Accrued C.R.I.
2304 Accrued Donations
2305 Accrued General Expense
2306 Accrued Interest Payable
2307 Accrued Legal Expense
2315 Accrued Taxes–Payroll, F.I.C.A.
2316 Accrued Taxes–Unemployment,
      Federal
2317 Accrued Taxes–Unemployment,
      State
2318 Accrued Taxes–Withholding,
      Federal
2319 Accrued Taxes–Withholding,
      State
2320 Accrued Payroll and Bonus
2325 Accrued Taxes–P.P. and R.E.
2326 Accrued Taxes–Franchise and
      Other
2327
2330 Estimated Federal Income Taxes
2331 Estimated State Income Taxes
      Total Accounts Payable &
      Accr. Exp.

LONG-TERM DEBT
2401 Unsecured Notes and Debentures
2402 Unsecured Subordinated Notes–
      Senior
2403 Unsecured Subordinated Notes–
      Junior
2404 Capital Indebtedness
      Total Long-Term Debt

STOCKHOLDERS EQUITY
3001 Preferred Stcok–First Series "A"
3002 Preferred Stock–First Series "B"
3003 Preferred Stock–First Series "C"
3004 Preferred Stock–Class "A"
3005 Preferred Stock–Second
3006 5½% Class "A" First Preferred
      Stock
3010 Common Stock
3015 Paid-in Surplus
3016 Contributed Surplus
3020 Income and Loss Summary
3025 Retained Earnings
1802 Parent Current Account
      Total Equity
      TOTAL LIABILITIES
      Branch or Subsidiary _____

EXHIBIT Q
Historical Financial Data
(thousands of dollars)

ASSETS:

Date	Total	Cash	Total Notes	Customers' Equity	Unearned Service Charges	Reserves for Losses	Rec. from Lending Inst.	Invent. of Reposs.	Prepaid Intr., Etc.	Fixed Assets (Net)	Deferred Charges
Dec. 31:											
1954	$ 7,885	$ 1,026	$ 7,905	$ (435)	$ (473)	$ (212)	$	$ 3	$ 35	$ 37	$
1955	9,274	1,117	9,671	(727)	(663)	(219)		7	53	37	
1956	10,845	1,195	11,474	(904)	(785)	(246)		5	63	43	
1957	12,661	1,409	13,164	(986)	(889)	(233)		11	140	44	
1958	16,250	2,233	16,901	(1,983)	(920)	(254)		21	150	81	21
1959	21,349	2,737	21,493	(2,271)	(1,095)	(541)	650	20	186	79	90
1960	29,335	2,679	32,565	(4,988)	(1,599)	(433)	750	23	152	106	78
1961	35,340	4,261	40,831	(7,912)	(1,769)	(471)		13	138	173	76
1962	45,966	4,475	52,572	(7,805)	(3,035)	(722)		10	133	217	120
1963	56,517	5,393	64,377	(8,740)	(4,128)	(1,509)		393	227	262	242

EXHIBIT Q (Continued)

LIABILITIES:

Date	Total	Notes Payable Short Term	Accounts Payable & Accrued Expenses	Federal Income Taxes	Dividends Payable	Long-Term Obligations			Stockholders' Equity		
						Current Maturities	Nonsubordinated	Subordinated	Capital Stock	Ret. Earnings and Capital in Excess of Par Value of Stock	Total
Dec. 31:											
1954	$ 7,885	$ 4,960	$ 116	$ 151	$	$ 203	$ 467	$ 525	$ 555	$ 907	$1,463
1955	9,274	5,280	111	182		255	1,050	770	555	1,070	1,626
1956	10,845	5,225	144	217	19	255	2,050	665	1,058	1,212	2,270
1957	12,661	6,253	174	230	19	355	2,440	704	1,138	1,348	2,486
1958	16,250	9,045	303	203	15	315	2,180	1,583	1,093	1,513	2,606
1959	21,349	10,398	259	221	15	318	4,030	2,801	1,563	1,744	3,307
1960	29,335	15,960	388	306		408	3,825	3,628	1,819	3,003	4,821
1961	35,340	16,820	499	279		853	5,800	5,267	2,577	3,245	5,822
1962	45,966	24,273	479	387		1,292	7,775	5,725	2,577	3,457	6,034
1963	56,517	28,593	812	465		1,243	11,000	6,858	3,209	4,337	7,546

units. The remaining six accounting units are consolidated accounting units (26 units + 6 consolidated accounting units = 32 accounting units).

The administrative cost of the home office's management is prorated among the other accounting units. In the distribution of this administrative cost, the basis is the cash employed in the accounting unit plus a direct allocation where applicable. Each accounting unit is charged 5 percent of the estimated average cash employed during the accounting period by that particular accounting unit for interest.

The monthly reports from the 32 accounting units serve dual purposes. They are used first for managerial evaluations and second for legal requirements of a separate report for each corporation. As had been discussed in another section of this case study, the activities of each subsidiary corporation do not overlap from an organization standpoint. For example, the monthly statements for the motor and automobile office are equal to the consolidation report for the two subsidiary corporations doing business in this area.

Financial and Statistical Reports

Exhibit Q presents historical financial data for the consolidated company from 1954 to 1963. These data have been restated to include a subsidiary corporation that was acquired during 1963 and accounted for as a pooling of interests. Exhibit R presents a summary of the increase in net worth, by source, for this same 10-year period.

As indicated by the exhibits, the earnings per share of common stock decreased for 1963 over 1962. Executive management believes that this decrease can be attributed to the increased capital and number of shares outstanding because of the recent acquisitions and expansions. The purpose of this increase in capital is to provide the necessary leverage for borrowing purposes. Furthermore, executive management feels that the firm is now in the relevant range or area where earnings can benefit from this growth pattern.

In the small loan operations, another type of report is prepared quarterly by each supervisor and assistant supervisor. This latter report is a thorough questionnaire type of report on all types of activities for which that supervisor or assistant supervisor is responsible. The questions cover human relation items as well as statistical data. This quarterly report is sent directly to the executive vice president of the parent corporation for his review and consideration.

EXHIBIT R

Sources of Increase in Net Worth

Year Ended	Net Proceeds of Stock Issuances	Consolidated Earnings	Less— Dividends Paid	Increase in Net Worth
December 31:				
1954	$	$159,080	$ 26,775	$ 132,305
1955		189,832	26,775	163,057
1956	502,240	233,480	91,499	644,221
1957	50,000	261,607	95,910	215,697
1958	(45,000)	262,973	97,712	120,261
1959	520,000	290,575	110,082	700,493
1960	1,307,200	363,038	155,380	1,514,858
1961	833,470	426,833	259,514	1,000,789
1962		514,597	303,014	211,583
1963	1,313,297	529,674	330,293	1,512,678

Selected Data Regarding Data Processing Activities

As previously indicated, three types of activities are currently performed by the data processing service center: (1) customer transactions for each of the small loan offices, (2) a monthly statistical report of yield data by dealer for the furniture and appliance office, and (3) a monthly statistical report of mix and yield data by dealer for the motor and automobile office.

The average monthly service charge for these activities is $1,385. In the small loan area, the charge is $92.50 per 1,000 transactions processed, and the monthly average charge for the small loan area is $1,100. Statistical computations for the furniture and appliance office are billed at the rate of $165 per 1,000 transactions, with the monthly bill for these statistical reports amounting to $185. The computations for the motor and automobile office's statistical reports are more involved, and the rate is $400 per 1,000 transactions, with the average monthly bill of $100 (there are 250 automobile loans per month).

Most of the recording and processing activities in the furniture and appliance office and in the motor and automobile office are performed on a manual basis. Following are the appropriate monthly, clerical costs—the amounts are based on payroll and do not include any fringe benefits—for these two offices at the current volume of operations:

	Furniture and Automobile Office (per month)	Motor and Appliance Office (per month)
Administration	$ 690	$2,423
Accounting	2,848	1,360
Maintenance services . . .	1,982	3,888

The above clerical-cost data include cashiers, bookkeepers, switchboard operators, and so forth. The clerical costs do not include supervisory personnel such as the branch manager. The term "maintenance services" encompasses the cost for the cashier and switchboard operator types of activities (clerical maintenance service). (Note the organization chart for each office as a basis for relating the clerical cost to the number of employees and to "titles.")

REQUIRED:

1. Should a complete systems review be performed? If you were the executive vice president, what action would you take? How much money would you allocate to each part of your action?
2. If you were employed by the executive vice president to perform a systems review, what questions would you ask? Why would you ask each question?
3. If you were employed to perform a general systems review, indicate in outline form the steps you would follow in performing this task.
4. How much of an increase in each type of activity—number of small loan offices and transactions, number of commercial loans, number of commercial regional offices, and so forth—would you desire *before* you would change your present recommendations?

CHAPTER 17

Simulation and Management
Information Systems

THE GENERAL model of a long-range planning and management control information system contained a statistical and simulation modeling phase which was *directly* interfaced with the other ten phases within this network. Some organizations that are located in highly competitive environments may have an expanded TYPE 2 information system in which a statistical and simulation modeling phase may be directly interfaced with the coordination phase, the control phase, and the planning phase. However, more often the case is an organization with a regular TYPE 2 or TYPE 3 information system in which there is a statistical and simulation modeling phase, but the latter is *not directly interfaced* with the advanced computer-based network.

In a few organizations which only have a computer-based operating system, we may find the existence of a statistical and simulation modeling phase. In these cases, the statistical and simulation modeling phase is being used as a surrogate for a regular planning phase.

An alternative perspective for examining this issue is to ask the question: Who are the principal users of time-sharing services? It is not an organization without any computer facilities; instead, the biggest users are large organizations with computer-based networks that do not have immediate access for members of management to engage in modeling on an interactive basis. If many members of management desire to participate in online, interactive modeling, then it may be economically justified for the organization's computer center to support these access capabilities with simulation packages.

Otherwise, the nominal cost of using time-sharing services for simulation modeling with a standard, interactive package makes this purchased service an attractive arrangement to the organization. The latter is even more appealing when you reflect on the immediate access features of time-sharing coupled with the minimum number of data input requirements for using a simulation package.

STATISTICAL AND SIMULATION MODELS

A model is a representation of the real world which is often expressed by exogenous factors, policy parameters, and decision variables that are related through a functional statement. In a statistical model, the internal richness of the specified relationship among variables, parameters, and factors is not of major importance; the statistical model is evaluated primarily based on the "reasonableness" of the output. The relationship among variables in a statistical model may be entirely by association or by some rough approximation. If the results suggested by the statistical model are intuitively appealing, then they are accepted. Otherwise, the variables, parameters, factors, and specified relationship are altered until the range of desired results is achieved.

As an example, the XYZ Corporation has a production and operation information system which reacts daily to changes in stock level. This system contains a computerized, integrated inventory control and production scheduling subsystem that maintains perpetual inventory control and triggers the reorder quantities which should be produced. Another segment of the information system relates, on a daily basis, the total group of items that should be produced with the existing plant capacity and restrictions of machines and personnel.

The XYZ Corporation is operating in a marketing environment where the sales for each item cannot be forecast with a high degree of confidence, and, at the same time, the plant is operating at, or near, full capacity. In this situation, how does the systems analyst forecast the monthly (or weekly) financial requirements that are necessary for the operation of the production department?

The traditional statistical technique of *expected value* can be used wherein ranges will be specified for each product and the daily demand for each product determined. After the daily demand for each product has been determined, the expected time at which the reorder point will be reached for each product can be computed. Next, the machinery, raw materials, and equipment requirements can be daily forecasted for the previously computed reorder quantities.

Although this statistical technique does generate a complete budget, the technique does not give any suggestion of the range of variation that is expected in the actual day-to-day behavior of the system. Furthermore, a statistical technique is needed which is not based on a single expected value for each variable but, instead, permits each variable to vary according to its assumed frequency distribution. These and other reasons are responsible for the development of the simulation technique.

In designing a simulation model, we are equally concerned with the internal logic of the relationship among the model elements as we are with evaluating the reasonableness of the outputs generated by the model. There are minimum time periods for which specific data must be accumulated *before* the quality of the internal logic could be of sufficient accuracy to suggest the assignment of the label "simulation model" to the overall construct. Otherwise, the model will be referred to as a statistical model.

When the first edition of this book was written in the mid-1960s, the theoretical distinction between a statistical model and a simulation model was not appreciated in professional practice. This is not the case in the mid-1970s, and this concern with the distinction between these two models focuses our attention on other unique attributes of a simulation model.

In a simulation model, the specified relationship among the elements has implicit within the construct the identifiable organizational structure associated with these activities. In addition, a well-planned simulation model is modular so that individual items or modules can be modified while holding other items constant. For example, the simulation model for an organization with 192 sales areas will have a unique, modular set of specifications for each of the 192 sales areas. The management scientist can alter any number of these modules, hold other modules constant, and then calculate the composite impact of the adjustments. This modular feature in a simulation model makes it an especially appealing technique to use in long-range planning where numerous alternatives are considered (such as dropping a division, introducing a new product line, or purchasing a company) .

A statistical model permits a quick response; however, it is not subject to internal scrutiny. It is entirely output oriented.

The quality of the data base, the internal richness of the specified relationship among the elements, and the modular arrangement of the model tend to indicate that a simulation model will represent a multiple of the cost of what is required for a statistical model. But, if there is an extended period of time in which it can be used, the unique features within a simulation model permit the management scientist to continue to improve the quality of the insights provided by this technique.

The common availability of time-sharing services in which one or more standard simulation packages can be accessed has encouraged members of management in many organizations to begin to utilize these facilities. Many of the time-sharing services have online tutors that will assist the novice in accessing and interacting with a given simulation package. Moreover, the online tutor permits the novice to work at his or her pace and provides a confidential relationship over any lack of knowledge or other possible embarrassments.

Simulation models for integrated financial management, planning and control are probably the most prevalent type of utilization. Production scheduling, marketing strategies for a new product, and personnel scheduling are also widely used. Many management consulting firms will offer special models to evaluate possible mergers or to build and operate a new plant (the simulation model includes these activities: plan, design, construct, recruit and train employees, install equipment, and commence operations).

This simulation technique may be applied to different organizational situations for various purposes, and the general character of the simulation model will vary with the purpose. This discussion considers two purposes: (*a*) short-term planning and (*b*) long-term planning.

The simulation technique is normally used where a computer program is available for processing the information. However, before the reader can intelligently interpret and evaluate the output from the simulation model, you need to gain an appreciation of the steps necessary to process the data through the simulation routine. Therefore, the following discussion presents the simulation models as though they were going to be manually processed. After the reader has a general understanding of the simulation process, then, computerized applications of the technique can be explored.

SHORT-TERM PLANNING

The general simulation models are modified as dictated by the economic situation. Because of these numerous modifications and adjustments, it is difficult to group simulation models. However, if these various simulation models were sorted in reference to their environment, the following two groupings might be the end points on a continuum. The first group can be labeled "simulation under certainty." In these simulation models, all of the alternatives are known, and members of management desire to determine the outcome under different combinations of alternatives.

The second group can be labeled "simulation under risk." In these simulation models, each alternative cannot be precisely specified, but instead only the frequency distribution of the range for each variable is known or can be estimated.

Simulation under Certainty

In a given project there may be 20 or more variables that members of corporate management can change at their discretion. A computer program can be used in coping with the project, and this program will express the mathematical relationship among these 20 variables. Each of the variables is modified in turn, and an outcome is determined for each possible combination of variables. By this process, members of management can select that group of choices which most nearly coincides with their objectives.

The use of simulation is similar to the technique of preparing a budget. The major difference is that the budget technique is applied over and over again, with different values being specified for the variables. This relation between budgeting and simulation is emphasized in the following illustration.

The Alpha Company has four regular products. A consultant has just completed the computation of the reorder quantity and the reorder point for each of the four regular products. These four products are similar and are equivalent units for production scheduling purposes. At present, there are 620 units of inventory in stock. The plant capacity for any eight-hour shift is 370 units if no setup is required; 355 units if one setup is required; and 340 units if two setups are required. It is against company policy to have more than two setups per eight-hour shift. The average daily sales for the four products equals 315 units.

Members of management want to employ the reorder quantities and the reorder points in the daily scheduling of production. Therefore, since the production capacity is greater than average daily sales, there will be a gradual increase in the balance of inventory stock. Alpha Company's management seeks to have an average balance of 1,100 units in inventory. Whenever, the average daily balance reaches 1,200 units or more, the next day a 100-lot-size quantity of the marginal product (a fifth product) is scheduled for production, and this lot-size quantity is sold the following day to a local manufacturer.

Using the following rules, Alpha Company's management wants to simulate the production cycle for purposes of determining (a) how soon the 1,100 unit balance will be reached and (b) how frequently the fifth product will be manufactured once this average balance (1,100 units) is reached:

1. Less than lot-size quantities may only be scheduled during the first three cycles. It is recognized that this predicament may occur in the initial conversion to the reorder quantity and reorder point procedure.

2. If at the completion of production for the regular reorder quantity for a given product, no other product's inventory level is at the reorder point, then the remaining capacity for that cycle may be scheduled as a "special" quantity for the product currently being manufactured. However, a test will be made during the next four cycles, and if a negative value is forecasted for any product, then the special quantity for the former product will not be scheduled. Instead, after the regular economic lot-size quantity is manufactured, the computer program will determine which product is forecasted to reach the reorder point first, and this product will be scheduled for production.

Simulations for the first 17 cycles are shown in Figure 17.1. Note from the data in this exhibit that the average balance of 1,100 units in inventory is not achieved until the 13th cycle.

The rules cited in the previous example can easily be incorporated into a computer program. After this computer program has been written, members of management can quickly recompute the simula-

FIGURE 17.1

Alpha Company
(simulation of production cycle)

		A	B	C	D	E*	Total
				Products			
Reorder point		140	145	150	170		605
Reorder quantity		210	220	230	250		910
Beginning inventory		80	210	200	130	–	620
1st Cycle:	Production	210†			145		355
	Sales	70	75	80	90		315
	Balance	220	135	120	185		660
2nd Cycle:	Production		15	220‡	105		340
	Sales	70	75	80	90		315
	Balance	150	75	260	200		685
3rd Cycle:	Production		370§				370
	Sales	70	75	80	90		315
	Balance	80	370	180	110		740
4th Cycle:	Production	210			130		340
	Sales	70	75	80	90		315
	Balance	220	295	100	150		765
5th Cycle:	Production			235§	120		355
	Sales	70	75	80	90		315
	Balance	150	220	255	180		805
6th Cycle:	Production				355§		355
	Sales	70	75	80	90		315
	Balance	80	145	175	445		845
7th Cycle:	Production	210	130				340
	Sales	70	75	80	90		315
	Balance	220	200	95	355		870
8th Cycle:	Production		90	265§			355
	Sales	70	75	80	90		315
	Balance	150	215	280	265		910
9th Cycle:	Production			370§			370
	Sales	70	75	80	90		315
	Balance	80	140	570	175		965
10th Cycle:	Production	210	130				340
	Sales	70	75	80	90		315
	Balance	220	195	490	85		990
11th Cycle:	Production		90		265§		355
	Sales	70	75	80	90		315
	Balance	150	210	410	260		1,030
12th Cycle:	Production				370§		370
	Sales	70	75	80	90		315
	Balance	80	135	330	540		1,085
13th Cycle:	Production	210	130				340
	Sales	70	75	80	90		315
	Balance	220	190	250	450		1,110
14th Cycle:	Production		370§				370
	Sales	70	75	80	90		315
	Balance	150	485	170	360		1,165
15th Cycle:	Production	355§					355
	Sales	70	75	80	90		315
	Balance	435	410	90	270		1,205
16th Cycle:	Production			240§		100	340
	Sales	70	75	80	90		315
	Balance	365	355	250	180	100	1,230
17th Cycle:	Production			370§			370
	Sales	70	75	80	90	100	415
	Balance	295	260	540	90	–	1,185

* A 100-lot size quantity of the marginal product (Product E) is manufactured in the following cycles: 19th, 21st, 24th, 27th, 29th, 32nd, and so forth.
† Machine setup for A. ‡ Less than lot size. § Special lot size.

tion under alternative conditions. For example, the daily sales for each product in the Alpha Company example were estimated, and these values can be changed, and a new simulation computed under revised estimates.

In other words, the computer program for simulation is viewed by the systems analyst as analogous to the computer program for a critical path planning and scheduling model. In both cases, the major cost is the establishment of the computer program. The second, third, and subsequent uses of this computer program have a relatively low marginal cost. Thus, members of management can use the simulation model of a project for coordinating, monitoring, and controlling the activities associated with the project while those activities are being accomplished. In achieving this objective, the computer program is rerun frequently using revised information.

In addition to scheduling of production, the technique of simulation under certainty is frequently used in evaluating and managing a special project. For example, a land development company might be formed to construct and sell commercial and residential properties on a given tract of land. The simulation technique can assist in determining (a) the best parceling of the land among different types of houses and buildings, (b) the extent to which a given plot should be filled and improved, (c) the best terms and conditions under which the properties should be sold, (d) the weekly cash flow for the duration of the project, and so forth.

Simulation under Risk

A project may have 20 or more variables, but the value that each variable will take may not be determined by members of management. The technique of simulation under risk permits members of management to specify a range and the nature of the frequency distribution for each variable. Values for each variable will be selected at random from that variable's estimated frequency distribution and used in computing a total value for the project. This procedure is repeated over and over again. This repetition is necessary so that the systems analyst can determine the range of the probable outcomes based on the interaction of all the variables. The following example illustrates this type of situation.

The Beta Company is considering the introduction of a new product for purposes of having a better product mix and using idle

FIGURE 17.2
Beta Company
(selected data on the two products)

	Product A	Product B
Selling price	$48	$32
Variable production cost	$16	$10
Variable marketing cost	12	8
Overhead expense	8	6
Total expenditures	$36	$24
Net profit per unit	$12	$ 8
Number of units (annually) . . .	10,000	15,000
Total net profit for product . . .	$120,000	$120,000

capacity. After a thorough study, members of management have found two new products—Product A and Product B—which meet these objectives and have the same estimated profit. See Figure 17.2 for a comparative presentation of selected data on the two products.

Members of management have decided to use the technique of simulation under risk in evaluating these two products. First, the range and frequency distribution for each variable are estimated by members of management. Next, random numbers are assigned to each class interval in proportion to that class's frequency distribution. Finally, random numbers are drawn or selected by some process, and each random number so drawn is compared with the previous grouping of random numbers to determine what number should be used for that variable in the first simulation cycle. This procedure is repeated as often as the systems analyst feels appropriate.

Figure 17.3 illustrates the assignment of random numbers to each of the variables for Product A and Product B. Figure 17.4 presents 25 simulations that, for purposes of illustration, show the same random number being used for all variables in a given simulation cycle. Statistically, it is preferable to have a random number separately selected for each variable, even though the assignment of random numbers for each class range has been systematically performed.

Based on the 25 simulations illustrated in Figure 17.4, the average profit for Product A is $125,200 and for Product B is $116,080. Product A has a net profit range of $90,000 to $168,000, a median of $120,000, and a mode of $99,000. Product B has a net profit range of $64,000 to $180,000, a median of $120,000, and a mode of $135,000. Thus management has more information on the interaction of the

FIGURE 17.3

Beta Company

(assignment of random numbers to each of the variables)

	Product A			Product B		
	Value	Fre-quency	Random Numbers	Value	Fre-quency	Random Numbers
Selling	$45	8%	790-869	$29	7%	112-181
Price	46	16	630-789	30	12	992-111
	47	22	050-269	31	18	562-741
	48	30	330-629	32	28	182-461
	49	18	870-049	33	19	802-991
	50	6	270-329	34	10	462-561
				35	6	742-801
Variable	$14	15%	516-665	$ 9	15%	285-434
Production	15	15	166-315	10	65	635-284
Cost	16	50	666-165	11	20	435-634
	17	20	316-515			
Variable	$10	5%	373-422	$ 7	15%	048-197
Marketing	11	16	023-182	8	70	198-897
Expense	12	60	423-022	9	15	898-047
	13	19	183-372			
Overhead	$ 6	5%	897-946	$ 5	15%	759-908
Expense	7	13	947-076	6	70	059-758
	8	65	247-896	7	15	909-058
	9	17	077-246			
Number of	8,000	5%	484-533	12,000	10%	751-850
Units	9,000	16	324-483	13,000	10	551-650
	10,000	50	824-323	14,000	15	101-250
	11,000	20	624-823	15,000	30	251-550
	12,000	9	534-623	16,000	15	951-100
				17,000	10	651-750
				18,000	10	851-950

variables which it can use in choosing between Product A and Product B.

As indicated by the previous example, the technique of simulation under conditions of risk is easy to apply. The difficult and critical part of this technique is the management task of specifying the range for each variable and the appropriate frequency distribution for each variable.

This risk simulation procedure is especially suitable for testing alternative marketing strategies. For example, in the Mirrex Company case study (Chapter 14), after the multiple regression technique has been applied to customer characteristics and payment behavior, to customer characteristics and products, and to customer characteristics and salespeople, then the simulation technique can be

FIGURE 17.4
Beta Company
(twenty-five simulations of operations)

Random Number:	601	167	814	519	976	444	735	228	353	820	791	542	941
Product A													
Selling price	$48	$47	$45	$48	$49	$48	$46	$47	$48	$45	$45	$48	$49
Variable production cost	$14	$15	$16	$14	$16	$17	$16	$15	$17	$16	$16	$14	$16
Variable marketing cost	12	11	12	8	12	12	12	13	13	12	12	12	12
Overhead expense	8	9	8	8	7	8	8	9	8	8	8	8	6
Net profit	$14	$12	$9	$14	$14	$11	$10	$10	$10	$9	$9	$14	$15
No. of units (000)	12	10	11	8	10	9	11	10	9	11	11	12	10
Net profit (000)	$168	$120	$99	$112	$140	$99	$110	$100	$90	$99	$99	$168	$150
Product B													
Selling price	$31	$29	$33	$34	$33	$32	$31	$32	$32	$33	$35	$34	$33
Variable production cost	$11	$10	$10	$11	$10	$11	$10	$10	$9	$10	$10	$11	$10
Variable marketing cost	8	7	8	8	8	8	8	8	8	8	8	8	9
Overhead expense	6	6	5	6	7	6	6	6	6	5	5	6	7
Net profit	$6	$6	$10	$9	$8	$7	$7	$8	$19	$10	$12	$9	$7
No. of units (000)	13	14	12	15	16	15	17	14	15	12	12	15	18
Net profit (000)	$78	$84	$120	$135	$128	$105	$119	$112	$135	$120	$144	$135	$126

FIGURE 17.4 (Continued)

Random Number:	382	058	437	116	925	310	662	706	278	875	023	589
Product A												
Selling price	$ 48	$ 47	$ 48	$ 47	$ 49	$ 50	$ 46	$ 46	$ 50	$ 49	$ 49	$ 48
Variable production cost	$ 17	$ 16	$ 17	$ 16	$ 16	$ 15	$ 14	$ 16	$ 15	$ 16	$ 16	$ 14
Variable marketing cost	10	11	12	11	12	13	12	12	13	12	11	12
Overhead expense	8	7	8	9	6	8	8	8	8	8	7	8
Net profit	$ 13	$ 13	$ 11	$ 11	$ 15	$ 14	$ 12	$ 10	$ 14	$ 13	$ 15	$ 14
No. of units (000)	9	10	9	10	10	10	11	11	10	10	10	12
Net profit (000)	$117	$130	$ 99	$110	$150	$140	$132	$110	$140	$130	$150	$168
Product B												
Selling price	$ 32	$ 30	$ 32	$ 29	$ 33	$ 32	$ 31	$ 31	$ 32	$ 33	$ 30	$ 31
Variable production cost	$ 9	$ 10	$ 11	$ 10	$ 10	$ 9	$ 10	$ 10	$ 10	$ 10	$ 10	$ 11
Variable marketing cost	8	7	8	7	9	8	8	8	8	8	9	8
Overhead expense	6	7	6	6	7	6	6	6	6	5	7	6
Net profit	$ 9	$ 6	$ 7	$ 6	$ 7	$ 9	$ 7	$ 7	$ 8	$ 10	$ 4	$ 6
No. of units (000)	15	16	15	14	18	15	17	17	15	18	16	13
Net profit (000)	$135	$ 96	$105	$ 84	$126	$135	$119	$119	$120	$180	$ 64	$ 78

used in estimating the reaction of prospective customers in a given geographical area to a given type of promotion program. The risk would be in estimating the characteristics of the customers receiving the promotion literature.

Summary

The general simulation models used in short-term planning are limited in scope and can be operated with a minimum amount of data base support. A novice guided by an online tutor for a standard program package may use simulation techniques in short-term planning. The outputs of a daily production and operation information system may be inputs to a management simulation model used for financial planning or for marketing administration.

LONG-TERM PLANNING

As previously stated, the use of simulation models in long-term planning is at the other end of the continuum from their use in short-term planning. It is a team effort in place of an individual effort. There is a significant amount of processing capability and special programming assistance required to maintain and support simulation models for long-term planning. There is a significant personnel and financial resource investment in the design of a simulation model for long-term planning. While short-term models may use a machine oriented language or an assembly level language (such as FORTRAN), a general purpose simulation language, such as SIMSCRIPT, GASP, or GPSS, is used in long-term planning models.[1]

Large-scale computer-based modeling in the context of high level analysis for long-term planning must possess the characteristics of flexibility and adaptability. The simulation language used must contain (*a*) list processing functions, (*b*) dynamic storage allocation, (*c*) memory word packing, and (*d*) a number of computational processes and standard utility routines. All of these hardware and software requirements indicate a large-scale computer-based system, possibly with an extended core and other special processing features.

---

[1] For a description of the characteristics of SIMSCRIPT, GASP, or GPSS, see a standard systems reference, such as, Claude McMillan, and Richard F. Gonzalez, *Systems Analysis: A Computer Approach to Decision Models*, 3d ed. (Homewood, Illinois: Richard D. Irwin, Inc., 1973).

As to the choice of simulation language, we favor the greater flexibility and unstructured computational power of the SIM-SCRIPT language over the predefined macro processing, effective debugging diagnostics, and widely available documentation and systems-support features in the GPSS language.[2] The reasons for this selection in computer-based models for long-term planning are similar with those expressed by Professor James Thies:

> However, in the context of an advanced management environment where highly diverse and complex systems relationships are being examined, where sophisticated systems support resources are available and where continuing heuristic evolution of the computer-based model is an important aspect of the analysis process, SIMSCRIPT appears to constitute a more effective formal modeling medium.[3]

Regardless of the simulation language used, members of management must participate in the analysis, refinement, and updating of the computer-based model. The systems analysts cannot perform these tasks alone, especially for long-term planning. This team approach toward the design of a computer-based simulation model is comparable to the argument made earlier in this book of the need for management's participation in the design of an information system.

In a long-term planning model, we desire a well designed, planned, and implemented simulation model which utilizes a general purpose simulation language in which the key organizational structure and operational processes are incorporated and that is supported by a quality data base as well as by computer-based facilities. There are several organizations which have spent 18 to 24 months capturing such detail data and organizational specification for inclusion in large-scale simulation models. Subsequently, members of management used these computer-based models for considering alternative organizational arrangements, for monitoring programmed changes within the organization, and for examining systems interdependencies.

---

[2] For a lengthy description of the criteria used in selecting a general purpose simulation language for high level analysis, see James B. Thies, *Computer-Based Modeling and Simulation as a Methodological Base for High-Level Information Systems Analysis,* Unpublished Ph.D. dissertation, Northwestern University, 1972 (especially, pp. 129–133).

[3] *Ibid.,* p. 132.

This complex, flexible, and adaptive simulation model has many useful features. It permits members of management to improve their previous specifications as experience is gained in using the model. It is composed of modules which can be quickly manipulated and used in recomputing the impact of complex relationships. The internal logic of the simulation model represents such a close approximation of the actual organizational structure and operational processes that it facilitates the transference of insights provided by the simulation model to the real world. It also provides an iterative, heuristic process that can respond to improved understanding as well as to new data.

The inclusion of the statistical and simulation modeling phase as an essential feature in the TYPE 7 information systems is an indication of the importance which we attach to using simulation models in long-term planning. The formal consideration of alternative constructs, organizational structures, and operational processes can only be accomplished in a thorough manner through large-scale computer-based modeling and simulation.

CONCLUSION

As the systems analyst begins to cope with complex economic environments, the need to use the different types of simulation techniques becomes increasingly important. For example, in the case of production and operation information systems, the systems analyst wants to design an information system which can be successfully maintained in operation because (*a*) capacity restrictions prohibit the establishment of the initial stock levels required prior to the conversion to the new system (in other words, "we cannot get to the new position from where we are today") and (*b*) short-term monetary constraints are incompatible with the probable range of financial requirements that the unrestricted production and operation information system might need. Both types of short-term simulation models can be used in trying to eliminate this type of situation.

At present, the systems analyst sees the long-term simulation models as a means of testing the effect of different executive policies as well as a means of evaluating the effect of alternative strategies on products, advertising, personnel, and so forth. The interactive, adaptative, and modular features of this heuristic process also contain a continuing educational dimension for members of management.

TOPICS FOR CLASS DISCUSSION

1. A simulation model permits management's experience and insights to be brought to bear upon a problem. Explain how this is achieved.

2. Differentiate between a statistical model and a simulation model.

3. Explain how a simulation model for short-term planning under conditions of risk is different from a financial budgeting model.

4. Executive management of a major corporation recently applied the simulation technique to each step of a new plant construction project. Simulation models were used for (*a*) site selection, (*b*) architectural planning of buildings and facilities on the new site, (*c*) coordinating construction of buildings and facilities, (*d*) installation of machinery, (*e*) training of personnel, and (*f*) overall financial management of the project. Explain some of the benefits that management might have obtained from using the simulation technique in each of these six cases.

5. There are many similarities between the construction of a critical path schedule and the development of a simulation model for short-term planning. Explain how a critical path network is different from each type of simulation model for short-term planning.

CASE 17–1. SIMULATION PROBLEM

Members of Beta Company's management still have some questions regarding which new product should be introduced—Product A or Product B (please review Figure 17.2 and the related facts in situation). Figure 17.4 contained only 25 simulations of operations, and some members of management desire more simulations before they will accept the insights gained from this technique.

Therefore, a computer program in FORTRAN IV was prepared for this case, and this computer program contains a subprogram for a random number generator. Ten random numbers are generated for each combined simulation run for Product A and Product B. The computer program calls for 1,000 simulations or an array of 1,000 values for Product A and Product B.

This computer program was run 10 times, each time beginning

the random number generator library program at a different point. The results of these 10 runs are as follows:

	Product A	Product B
Run 1	$ 121,112	$ 119,223
2	119,917	117,930
3	120,421	116,164
4	121,047	119,128
5	120,286	118,214
6	121,279	116,895
7	120,795	119,104
8	121,040	117,569
9	119,318	119,359
10	120,410	118,476
Total	$1,205,625	$1,182,062
Average . . .	$120,562	$118,206

While the average for Product A was larger than the average for Product B, some members of management were concerned with the distribution of values for each product. The computer program was expanded to include a subroutine for computing the frequency distribution by class interval.

Exhibit A presents this modified computer program. Exhibit B presents the frequency distribution for 35,000 simulations of Product A and Product B; this latter exhibit shows the results obtained by running the computer program 35 times.

REQUIRED:

1. Which product would you select? Quantitatively support your answer.
2. Why do the frequency distributions in Exhibit B not approximate a normal curve? Explain the statistical reasons for the existing distributions.
3. *Possible extensions:* (*a*) Reproduce the computer program. Change the degree of expected occurrence for certain costs (without changing the overall range of values), and run the computer program to see how sensitive the results are to this change. (*b*) Repeat this procedure, but eliminate some current extreme point, or extend the range of other extreme points. In other words, through the simulation process you are attempting to see how sensitive the overall results are to changes in one or more factors in the model.

EXHIBIT A
Beta Company
Computer Program

```
      PROGRAM BETASIM(INPUT,OUTPUT,TAPE60,TAPE61=OUTPUT)
      DIMENSION PA(1000),PB(1000),C(1000),D(25,4),E(25)
      COMMON/1/C
      COMMON/2/E
      READ 89,N,NR
   89 FORMAT(I5,1X,I1)
      READ 90,R
   90 FORMAT(F5.4)
      CALL RANSET(R)
   91 IF(N.GT.1000)92,93
   92 ATIMES=N
      BTIMES=ATIMES/1000.
      BTIMES=BTIMES+.9999
      NTIMES=BTIMES
      GO TO 94
   93 NTIMES = 1
   94 DO 980 M=1,NTIMES
      DO 95 J=1,1000
      PA(J)=0000.0
      PB(J)=0000.0
   95 C(J)= 0000.0
      DO 96 I=1,25
      DO 96 J=1,4
   96 D(I,J)= 0000.0
      DO 97 I=1,25
   97 E(I)=0C0.0
      PAT=000.0
      PBT=000.0
      AMEDIN =000.0
   98 IF(N.GT.1000)99,102
   99 IF(M.EQ.NTIMES)100,101
  100 JTIMES=N-((M-1)*1000)
      GO TO 103
  101 JTIMES=1000
      GO TO 103
  102 JTIMES=N
  103 CONTINUE
  104 DO 800 J=1,JTIMES
  110 X=RANF(1)
  111 IF(X-.0840)120,120,112
  112 IF(X-.2400)121,121,113
  113 IF(X-.4600)122,122,114
  114 IF(X-.7600)123,123,115
  115 IF(X-.9400)124,124,125
  120 SLPRC= 45.
      GO TO 200
  121 SLPRC= 46.
      GO TO 200
  122 SLPRC= 47.
      GO TO 200
  123 SLPRC= 48.
      GO TO 200
  124 SLPRC= 49.
      GO TO 200
  125 SLPRC= 50.
```

EXHIBIT A (*Continued*)

```
200 X = RANF(1)
201 IF(X-.15000)210,210,202
202 IF(X-.30000)211,211,203
203 IF(X-.80000)212,212,213
210 PRODC = 14.
    GO TO 300
211 PRODC = 15.
    GO TO 300
212 PRODC = 16.
    GO TO 300
213 PRODC = 17.
300 X = RANF(1)
301 IF(X-.05000)310,310,302
302 IF(X-.21000)311,311,303
303 IF(X-.81000)312,312,313
310 XMARC = 10.
    GO TO 400
311 XMARC = 11.
    GO TO 400
312 XMARC = 12.
    GO TO 400
313 XMARC = 13.
400 X = RANF(1)
401 IF(X-.05000)410,410,402
402 IF(X-.18000)411,411,403
403 IF(X-.83000)412,412,413
410 XCVEC = 6.
    GO TO 500
411 XCVEC = 7.
    GO TO 500
412 XCVEC = 8.
    GO TO 500
413 XCVEC = 9.
500 X = RANF(1)
501 IF(X-.05000)510,510,502
502 IF(X-.21000)511,511,503
503 IF(X-.71000)512,512,504
504 IF(X-.91000)513,513,514
510 UNITS =  8000.
    GO TO 600
511 UNITS =  9000.
    GO TO 600
512 UNITS = 10000.
    GO TO 600
513 UNITS = 11000.
    GO TO 600
514 UNITS = 12000.
600 PA(J) = (SLPRC -PRODC -XMARC -XCVEC)* UNITS
700 X = RANF(1)
701 IF(X-.07000)710,710,702
702 IF(X-.19000)711,711,703
703 IF(X-.37000)712,712,704
704 IF(X-.65000)713,713,705
705 IF(X-.84000)714,714,706
706 IF(X-.94000)715,715,716
```

```
710 SLPRC = 29.
    GO TO 720
711 SLPRC = 30.
    GO TO 720
712 SLPRC = 31.
    GO TO 720
713 SLPRC = 32.
    GO TO 720
714 SLPRC = 33.
    GO TO 720
715 SLPRC = 34.
    GO TO 720
716 SLPRC = 35.
720 X = RANF(1)
721 IF(X-.15000)730,730,722
722 IF(X-.80000)731,731,732
730 PRODC =  9.
    GO TO 740
731 PRODC = 10.
    GO TO 740
732 PRODC = 11.
740 X = RANF(1)
741 IF(X-.15000)750,750,742
742 IF(X-.85000)751,751,752
750 XMARC =  7.
    GO TO 760
751 XMARC =  8.
    GO TO 760
752 XMARC =  9.
760 X = RANF(1)
761 IF(X-.15000)770,770,762
762 IF(X-.85000)771,771,772
770 XCVEC =  5.
    GO TO 780
771 XCVEC =  6.
    GO TO 780
772 XCVEC =  7.
780 X = RANF(1)
781 IF(X-.10000)790,790,782
782 IF(X-.20000)791,791,783
783 IF(X-.35000)792,792,784
784 IF(X-.65000)793,793,785
785 IF(X-.80000)794,794,786
786 IF(X-.90000)795,795,796
790 UNITS = 12000.
    GO TO 800
791 UNITS = 13000.
    GO TO 800
792 UNITS = 14000.
    GO TO 800
793 UNITS = 15000.
    GO TO 800
794 UNITS = 16000.
    GO TO 800
795 UNITS = 17000.
```

EXHIBIT A (*Continued*)

```
      GO TO 800
 796  UNITS = 18000.
 800  PB(J) = (SLPRC - PRODC -XMARC -XCVEC)* UNITS
      DO 801 J=1,JTIMES
      PAT = PAT + PA(J)
 801  PBT = PBT + PB(J)
 802  IF(NR.EQ.2)803,806
 803  PRINT 804
 804  FORMAT(1H1,35X, 10HPRODUCT A , 31X, 10HPRODUCT B )
      PRINT 805,(PA(J),PB(J),J=1,JTIMES)
 805  FORMAT(36X,F8.0, 32X,F8.0)
 806  CONTINUE
      TIMES=JTIMES
      AVA=PAT/TIMES
      AVB=PBT/TIMES
      PRINT 1804,AVA,AVB
1804  FORMAT(1H1,//////,30X,16HAVERAGE FOR A = ,F8.0///30X,16HAVERAGE FOR
     1 B = ,F8.0)
      DO 1805 J=1,JTIMES
1805  C(J)=PA(J)
 807  CALL ARRAY(JTIMES)
 808  CALL MEDIAN(JTIMES,AMEDIN)
      PRINT 809,AMEDIN
 809  FORMAT(25X,19HPRODUCT A MEDIAN = , F10.0)
      DO 810 J=1,JTIMES
 810  C(J)=PB(J)
 811  CALL ARRAY(JTIMES)
 812  CALL MEDIAN(JTIMES,AMEDIN)
      PRINT 813,AMEDIN
 813  FORMAT(25X,19HPRODUCT B MEDIAN = , F10.0)
      DO 814 J=1,JTIMES
 814  C(J)=PA(J)
 815  CALL CLASS(JTIMES)
      DO 816 I=1,25
 816  D(I,3)=E(I)
      DO 817 I=1,25
 817  E(I)=0000.0
      DO 818 J=1,JTIMES
 818  C(J)=PB(J)
 819  CALL CLASS(JTIMES)
      DO 820 I=1,25
 820  D(I,4)=E(I)
      D(1,1)=0000.
      D(1,2)=9999.
      DO 821 I=2,25
      DO 821 J=1,2
 821  D(I,J)=D(I-1,J) + 10000.0
      PRINT 822
 822  FORMAT(1H1,32X, 12HCLASS LIMITS,9X,9HPRODUCT A,7X,9HPRODUCT B)
      PRINT 823,((D(I,J),J=1,4),I=1,25)
 823  FORMAT(29X,F8.0,2X,F8.0,6X,F8.0,8X,F8.0)
 980  CONTINUE
      STOP
      END
```

EXHIBIT A (*Concluded*)

```
      SUBROUTINE CLASS (JTIMES)
      DIMENSION C(1000), E(25)
      COMMON/1/C
      COMMON/2/E
30    DO 26 J=4,JTIMES
      AMT=(C(J)/10000.)+ 1.0001
      K=AMT
      IF(K.GT.25) GO TO 25
      GO TO(1,2,3,4,5,6,7,8,9,10,11,12,13,14,15,16,17,18,19,20,21,22,23,
     124,25)K
 1    E(1) = E(1) + 1.0
      GO TO 26
 2    E(2) = E(2) + 1.0
      GO TO 26
 3    E(3) = E(3) + 1.0
      GO TO 26
 4    E(4) = E(4) + 1.0
      GO TO 26
 5    E(5) = E(5) + 1.0
      GO TO 26
 6    E(6) = E(6) + 1.0
      GO TO 26
 7    E(7) = E(7) + 1.0
      GO TO 26
 8    E(8) = E(8) + 1.0
      GO TO 26
 9    E(9) = E(9) + 1.0
      GO TO 26
10    E(10) = E(10) + 1.0
      GO TO 26
11    E(11) = E(11) + 1.0
      GO TO 26
12    E(12) = E(12) + 1.0
      GO TO 26
13    E(13) = E(13) + 1.0
      GO TO 26
14    E(14) = E(14) + 1.0
      GO TO 26
15    E(15) = E(15) + 1.0
      GO TO 26
16    E(16) = E(16) + 1.0
      GO TO 26
17    E(17) = E(17) + 1.0
      GO TO 26
18    E(18) = E(18) + 1.0
      GO TO 26
19    E(19) = E(19) + 1.0
      GO TO 26
20    E(20) = E(20) + 1.0
      GO TO 26
21    E(21) = E(21) + 1.0
      GO TO 26
22    E(22) = E(22) + 1.0
      GO TO 26
23    E(23) = E(23) + 1.0
      GO TO 26
24    E(24) = E(24) + 1.0
      GO TO 26
25    E(25) = E(25) + 1.0
26    CONTINUE
      RETURN
      END

      SUBROUTINE ARRAY(JTIMES)
      DIMENSION C(1000)
      COMMON/1/C
      ICOUNT=1
1000  LTIMES=JTIMES-ICOUNT
      DO 1006 J=1,LTIMES
1002  IF(C(J+1).GE.C(J))1006,1003
1003  TRANSR=C(J+1)
      C(J+1)=C(J)
      C(J)=TRANSR
1006  CONTINUE
1007  ICOUNT=ICOUNT+1
1008  IF(ICOUNT.EQ.(JTIMES-1))1010,1009
1009  GO TO 1000
1010  CONTINUE
      RETURN
      END

      SUBROUTINE MEDIAN (JTIMES,AMEDIN)
      COMMON/1/C
      DIMENSION C(1000)
1100  IF(JTIMES-((JTIMES/2)*2))1108,1105,1101
1101  INUM=(JTIMES+1)/2
      J=INUM
      AMEDIN=C(J)
1104  GO TO 1108
1105  INUM=JTIMES/2
      J=INUM
      AMEDIN=(C(J)+C(J+1))/2.0
1108  CONTINUE
      RETURN
      END
```

Beta Company

(frequency distribution of simulated profits)

Range	Product A				Product B			
	Number	Cumulative	Percent	Cumulative	Number	Cumulative	Percent	Cumulative
20,000– 29,999	0	0	0	0	3	3	.01	.01
30,000– 39,999	0	0	0	0	38	41	.11	.12
40,000– 49,999	2	2	.01	.01	178	219	.51	.63
50,000– 59,999	21	23	.06	.07	234	453	.67	1.30
60,000– 69,999	93	116	.27	.34	1,023	1,476	2.92	4.22
70,000– 79,999	453	569	1.29	1.63	2,147	3,623	6.13	10.35
80,000– 89,999	1,586	2,155	4.53	6.16	1,994	5,617	5.70	16.05
90,000– 99,999	3,906	6,061	11.16	17.32	4,596	10,213	13.13	29.18
100,000–109,999	3,900	9,961	11.14	28.46	4,179	14,392	11.94	41.12
110,000–119,999	5,381	15,342	15.38	43.84	3,383	17,775	9.67	50.79
120,000–129,999	6,003	21,345	17.15	60.99	5,324	23,099	15.21	66.00
130,000–139,999	5,479	26,824	15.65	76.64	3,240	26,339	9.26	75.26
140,000–149,999	4,001	30,825	11.43	88.07	2,601	28,940	7.43	82.69
150,000–159,999	2,416	33,241	6.91	94.98	2,202	31,142	6.29	88.98
160,000–169,999	1,141	34,382	3.26	98.24	1,860	33,002	5.31	94.29
170,000–179,999	274	34,656	.78	99.02	706	33,708	2.02	96.31
180,000–189,999	236	34,892	.67	99.69	782	34,490	2.23	98.54
190,000–199,999	76	34,968	.22	99.91	347	34,837	.99	99.53
200,000–209,999	26	34,994	.07	99.98	75	34,912	.21	99.74
210,000–219,999	6	35,000	.02	100.00	65	34,977	.19	99.93
220,000–229,999	0	35,000	0	100.00	12	34,989	.03	99.96
230,000–239,999	0	35,000	0	100.00	9	34,998	.03	99.99
240,000–249,999	0	35,000	0	100.00	2	35,000	.01	100.00
Total	35,000		100.00		35,000		100.00	
Average	$120,535				$118,197			

CASE 17-2. FERGUSON MILLS CORPORATION

The management consulting firm with which you are associated has been engaged in a series of information systems projects at the Ferguson Mills Corporation over the past decade. Thus, it was not surprising when the executive vice president telephoned your management consulting firm and asked one of the senior consultants to join him for lunch. The executive vice president had read an article in *Business Week* explaining how simulation models had been used in another industry, and he saw many similarities to the problems in the textile industry. He is wondering how simulation models might be used at Ferguson Mills.

The Company

Ferguson Mills Corporation is one of the 15 largest corporations in the textile industry, and it is a company that has continued to make a reasonable profit while many of its competitors have been dissolved. For example, over 800 textile companies have been liquidated during the past decade, and 125 textile companies have been merged with other textile companies. The result of this general movement has been that the remaining larger corporations have increased their share of the market. For instance, the 10 largest corporations currently have about 25 percent of industry sales, whereas a few years ago they had less than 20 percent.

Technological Factors and Market Changes

Ferguson Mills has invested substantial funds in new laborsaving equipment utilizing technological advancements. Among these acquisitions are high-speed frames for spinning fiber into yarn that have increased productivity by over 50 percent. Improved looms for weaving fiber into cloth are also included in this equipment, and these looms permit the operator to produce larger strips of fabric in less time. This new equipment is augmented by changes in production procedures. For example, the computer system, utilizing operations research techniques, supervises the mixing of different colored dyes.

In recent years, Ferguson Mills has experienced significant

changes in market mix and in market demand. Some of these changes were the result of management's marketing and production activities; others were based on external factors. Management has intentionally shifted from natural fibers to man-made fibers, such as acrylic, polyester, and triacetate, which have supplemented the traditional synthetic standbys—nylon and rayon. Through the use of synthetic fibers, marketing management can be more sensitive to changes in consumer preferences.

The textile industry has experienced a general change based on three factors. First, garment manufacturers have perfected a new manufacturing process which permits delicate fabrics to be bonded with another substance and then manufactured on a mass scale production basis (the price of some finished items, for example, can be reduced by more than 50 percent). This change in the garment manufacturing process has resulted in shifts in the demand for certain products from the textile industry. Second, all domestic textile companies have benefited from the "Cotton Bill," under which these domestic companies are reimbursed at $6\frac{1}{2}$ cents per pound for the cotton they use. This reimbursement rate is supposed to approximate the difference between the world market price of cotton and the U.S. government price-supported level. Third, new types of management personnel have been recruited for the textile industry, and these individuals have utilized new management techniques and procedures. The innovations made by these new management groups have resulted not only in greater stability of earnings by individual companies, but in greater stability of earnings by the whole textile industry.

Information Systems

The management consulting firm with which you are associated has assisted Ferguson Mills personnel in the application of operations research and linear programming techniques to various problem areas, such as warehousing, transportation, production scheduling, and sales forecasting. The latter application consists of a system which relates sales forecasts by style, including the salespeople's confidence estimates, with production capacity and profitability factors.

These management consultants were also instrumental in the design and implementation of an inventory anticipation system for style goods. The basic sales pattern for each product line was determined, and experience data were accumulated regarding the probability of deviation from average by each item within a product line.

Prediction factors have been derived for estimating the duration of the season for each product. All of these insights and relationships have been incorporated into a set of tables which management can use in making day-to-day decisions.

These tables, for example, indicate the odds on selling enough goods to fill the looms' profitability objective, and these odds would vary based on the week of the season involved. Other tables show the odds on allocating various styles to different looms in order to have a good assignment for profit purposes. Management must continuously use these tables and others in making day-to-day decisions if a satisfactory profit level is to be achieved, which, incidentally, requires a zero level of style-goods inventory at the end of the season. (This latter comment is based upon statistical studies presented in the industry's professional literature.)

In the nonstyle-goods area, another type of system had to be developed. Orders are daily received for production with a three-month delivery date, and each of these orders is at a negotiated price. In the early part of each production season, the sales price per order is lower than it is later in the season. After numerous companies in the textile industry have committed their production capacity for three months ahead, then the remaining production capacity brings a premium. However, if management waits too long before accepting orders, there may be insufficient orders to satisfy full production; thus, the company will have unused capacity.

In coping with this general problem in the nonstyle-goods area, a system for setting refusal profit levels was established. The system shows the value per loom week for specific styles, taking into account the costs, loom speeds, and sales commissions. Thus, each style has a different refusal price in terms of cents per yard. Furthermore, this system provides an acceptance price based on the forecasted average profit level of the loom class. Separate refusal profit levels and prices are established for delivery in each future quarter.

Recently, the management consultants assisted management in the design and implementation of an information system which connects the various regional sales offices with the home office. This communication network is not only used in marketing management, but also permits an immediate response to sales orders. This immediate response is extremely important in the peak of each season.

REQUIRED:

1. Indicate how simulation models might be used at Ferguson Mills. Be specific and, if appropriate, attempt to relate one application of the simulation technique to the next application.
2. What are the advantages and disadvantages of employing simulation techniques at Ferguson Mills compared to the statistical techniques that they are currently using?

CHAPTER 18

Internal Control and Audit of Advanced Information Systems

THE MODEL of a series of formal information systems presented in Chapter 1 emphasized the choices that management has as to scope, content, and origin of the data within each network. There are also choices as to timeliness and currency of data. As these FISs increase in complexity, administrative arrangements are required for planning and coordinating these developments; in Chapter 4 the role, function, and membership of four committee structures for coping with these administrative arrangements were discussed. Approaches, methods, and procedures were examined in Chapter 5 for establishing, maintaining, and monitoring control over the computer center and computer-based operations.

Sophisticated computer-based networks have been designed and implemented in many organizations, and in most of these networks, there is some type of interactive inputs of data over keyboard or terminal facilities. While there are no source documents that the professional accountant can use in an attempt to "audit around the computer," the editing and screening phase is responsible for significant improvements in the quality of the processed data. When this editing and screening phase is directly interfaced with the systems processing phase, there is an improvement in the quality of data processed, sorted, and assigned to unique files.

On the other hand, there are numerous organizations which have interactive inputs with an editing and screening phase but which do not have an online systems processing phase. The reader might reflect on the generalized models of information systems presented earlier in this book; neither the TYPE 1 information system nor the TYPE 2 information system contained an online systems processing phase. The general model of a marketing management information system was the first discrete level of advancement in which a systems processing phase was presented as an online capability.

The availability of an online systems processing phase does not eliminate the need for audit of advanced information systems; however, it does change the focus of the review process in a given area. If the processing, sorting, and assigning capabilities are being performed offline (as is the case in a TYPE 1 or TYPE 2 network), then the professional accountant must make a special audit of these offline activities for purposes of determining both the consistency and appropriateness of these operations.

To some extent, the review of these offline activities is analogous to the auditor's special review in a manual system of those activities for which there are no written procedures. Where there are written procedures covering the manual system, the auditor will perform tests for compliance with the written procedures (that is, of course, after the auditor has reviewed the written procedures for appropriateness) ; however, a disproportional amount of the auditor's time is spent on the activities performed where there are no written procedures. Likewise, in the case of computer-based operations, a disproportional amount of time is spent in examining offline activities; the online procedures are reviewed for appropriateness and are tested for compliance.

We encounter problems when making additional analogies between the manual and the computer-based system. Critical areas in a manual system were subject to the separation of duties so that no one person had complete responsibility for a vulnerable area; collusion by two or more persons was required for misuse of the organization's assets. This same concept of separation of duties can be applied to the operation of the computer center and to organizational delegations of corporate responsibility; however, the interactive, online capabilities of advanced computer-based systems have created an array of new vehicles through which a misuse of organization's assets can occur. New types of examinations are required by the auditor in coping with these developments.

From the discussion in previous chapters, we have some appreciation of the magnitude of the changes that pertain to the internal control and audit functions in organizations with advanced computer-based systems. We have seen dominant management control issues in planning, designing, implementing, maintaining, and monitoring computer-based systems. Because of this dominant role of management control, attention is initially directed to management's participation in the control process. The other three issues examined in this chapter are (*a*) internal control, (*b*) auditor's participation, and (*c*) audit tools.

In this discussion the consideration of these issues is restricted to computer-based networks that are beyond a TYPE 1 information system. In addition, the four facets of control in advanced computer-based networks which was presented in Chapter 5 is not repeated in this discussion; the reader is encouraged to review this previous material on these four facets: (*a*) physical control as related to the computer center, (*b*) internal control associated with personnel management, (*c*) management control over computer-based activities including equipment control, input and output control, program control, editing and screening subsystems, and the day file monitoring subsystem, and (*d*) security controls and confidential data arrangements.

MANAGEMENT'S PARTICIPATION

If an organization has an advanced computer-based information system, then it is a tautology that the organization possesses critical assets in the form of *information* which must be controlled. These assets are in the form of online data about operations, plans, performance, goals, and objectives; there may be confidential data on customer profiles, products, competitors, and other specialized information, depending on the nature of the organization. But, overall, there must be critical, confidential data if the composite network is appropriately classified as an advanced information system.

The point of the above remarks is that an organization with an advanced information system has, by definition, critical, confidential assets which must be protected by a confidentiality of data committee. It is also important that members of management participate on the other related management control committees: (*a*) information systems coordinating committee, (*b*) data management committee, and (*c*) code structure identification and maintenance committee.

Confidentiality of Data Committee

It is important for security, administration, and control purposes that key members of executive management serve as active participants on the confidentiality of data committee. Active participation by selected members of executive management on the confidentiality of data committee's monitoring and analyzing functions is probably one of the most important control features in an advanced information system.

The Equity Funding scandal has widely publicized the ability of management personnel to use computer access to accomplish a multimillion dollar embezzlement. According to *The Wall Street Journal,* only a few weeks before the Equity Funding Case broke, the chief teller at a branch of the Union Dime Savings Bank in New York was charged with stealing more than $1.5 million from the bank's deposits.[1] A recent government list of bank embezzlers by position indicates that executives and managers are the key perpetrators. For example, there were almost twice as many presidents as cashiers who were identified as the principal perpetrator of reported bank embezzlements.[2]

We must guard against overgeneralization from a few instances. However, the recent events might suggest that members of management merit some attention in monitoring unauthorized access to computer-based assets. If attention is to be given to unauthorized access to confidential data by members of management, then it has to be a *peer review* to be effective.

One of the more critical functions of the confidentiality of data committee is to identify valuable assets in the form of computer-based data. Drawing upon their respective professional competences and experiences, members of the committee are in an informed position to identify critical information and to assign priorities to these data.

The confidentiality of data committee is the senior, management review committee for information systems activities throughout the

---

[1] N. R. Kleinfield, "Unsafe Combination: Crooks and Computers Are an Effective Team Business World Learns," *The Wall Street Journal* (April 26, 1973), pp. 1 and 14.

[2] Donn B. Parker and Susan Nycum, "The New Criminal," *Datamation,* vol. 20 (January 1974), pp. 56–58.

organization and, in this role, these committee members should be aware of the ongoing activities of the junior committees: (*a*) information systems coordinating committee, (*b*) data management committee, and (*c*) code structure identification and maintenance committee. One practical reason for this awareness is that there are many organizational variations as to where certain decision making occurs, and the confidentiality of data committee members have an organization-wide perspective from which to examine a given issue. Another reason is that there are variations by organization as to the precise separation of responsibilities among the four committees. For example, which committee approves a personalized data base for a member of executive management? The confidentiality of data committee members should at least be aware of the existence of a personalized data base for a member of executive management.

The external auditor is interested in the membership of the confidentiality of data committee and is also concerned with the nature of the participation by the individual committee members, the frequency of meetings, and the minutes of the meetings.

Information Systems Coordinating Committee

Management's participation on the information systems coordinating committee is an important control feature to the organization in (*a*) effective utilization of organizational resources, (*b*) assignment of priorities and (*c*) internal control over assets. The members of this committee serve in a similar role as those on the confidentiality of data committee. The diverse professional backgrounds and experiences of the committee members permit them to collectively analyze and evaluate complex relations and to make informed decisions.

The external auditor is interested in examining the scope of the committee's function, the committee membership, the frequency of meetings, and the minutes of the meetings. Some attention is given to examining the information systems project selection, project management, and project review functions; however, these are more from the standpoint of a management review than from the standpoint of an asset review.

Data Management Committee

The nature of management's participation on the data management committee is the critical factor. What issues were discussed and considered when a given software package was approved? What types of documentation are made of authorization for exceptional processing? To what extent do committee members review the detailed documentation for systems and programs?

The external auditor is interested in the specifics of committee meetings. The results of the data management committee's efforts are reflected in approved changes in the day-to-day systems operations. The external auditor is concerned with both the quality of the consideration and the degree of compliance.

Code Structure Identification and Maintenance Committee

The attitude of members of management serving on this committee is a critical factor. The consideration given by the committee members to suggestions of change is an important indicator of the quality of the lifeblood.

The external auditor is interested in the specifics of committee meetings. The effect of changes in the code structure will frequently have an impact on all facets of the organization. Failure to maintain adequate documentation and cross-referencing of changes is a key problem with this committee in many organizations. Frequently, the committee members do not have an appropriate perspective so they can appreciate the effect of periodic changing the code structure upon the subsequent use of these multipurpose data for long-range planning purposes. We have frequently found this type of committee in different organizations where their attitude toward documentation left much to be desired.

INTERNAL CONTROL

In the introductory statements to this chapter, analogies were made between the disproportional amount of time (*a*) that the auditor gives to offline operations versus online activities in a computer-based advanced network and (*b*) that the auditor formerly gave to operations for which there were no written procedures versus those activities covered by written procedures. There are similarities in the type of evidence that the auditor seeks in the unspecified areas.

The examination of internal control within an organization with an advanced information system (beyond a TYPE 1 network in which there is at least an online coordination phase interfaced with a control phase and a planning phase) begins at a rather sophisticated level. The auditor is immediately concerned with the operations and documentation for the editing and screening phase which filters the interactive inputs for the network. The quality of the results of the code structure identification and maintenance committee impacts the network at this point.

The auditor is seeking a quality level of specification and documentation for data. Detailed minutes of approved changes, matrices of cross-references of old specifications with new identifications, and flowcharts of major data flows are types of evidence the auditor expects from the editing and screening phase in an advanced information system.

As previously indicated, the auditor is especially concerned with analyzing the offline processing, sorting, and data assignment operations in a TYPE 2 information system. These offline operations are included in the systems processing phase of a TYPE 3 information system and in other networks which are more advanced than a TYPE 2 model. Where there is an online systems processing phase, there are other concurrent developments which change the focus of the auditor. In the latter case the auditor is concerned with the emerging importance of *confidential* data and the related issues of restricted access to these valuable assets.

Through the internal control examination of online operations, program controls, input and output controls, processing controls, documentation, flowcharts, code structure specifications, access controls, and day file management operations, an overview is sought of the environment surrounding the major information movements within the organization. Participation by members of management on the confidentiality of data committee, information systems coordinating committee, data management committee, and code structure identification and maintenance committee are an important part of this environment.

The auditor is especially concerned with the level of the examination that is made by the appropriate committee over new computer-based operations and programs. What types of tests are run? How thorough is the documentation? What type of security and administrative control is placed around the approved computer-based capability? How are online computer programs, data routines, assignment features, and retrieval specifications administered to prevent erroneous changes?

The auditor really looks for exceptions. There must be a manual override of online processing for handling unusual events, such as the classical situation of having no item of inventory at the reorder point in an online, integrated inventory control and production control scheduling system. What types of administrative controls are placed over manual override operations? What types of input and output controls are placed over rejects from the online system?

At a different level where the focus is on confidential data, is online access really monitored? By whom and for what purpose? Are the frequencies of online inquiries examined? What period is used for suggesting when online, confidential tapes, files or drums should be transferred to an online, physical controlled setting?

The auditor is aware that cash and cash-like items are more vulnerable than noncash items. However, the computer-based environment has added many complexities to the auditor's old focus on liquid assets. The online manipulation capabilities have created new avenues for asset misuse. Customer profile data may be the organization's most valuable asset. While access to product specifications and trade arrangements has always been controlled, access to customer profile data may not be viewed as a valuable asset by the organization.

AUDITOR'S PARTICIPATION

The major focus of the auditor's role in an advanced information system must shift from a *retrospective review* to a *concurrent examination*. Complex, online data manipulations must be concurrently reviewed while they are being processed. Frequently, there is no reasonable approach to recapture of these data at the precise, online environment. Concurrent review of sophisticated, online operations is the only reasonable approach toward understanding these data processing, data sorting, data assignments, and data manipulation operations.

Where the client organization has a rather sophisticated, advanced information system, then the auditor may need a controlled access for concurrent examination purposes. In most cases, this will mean that the auditor's special software, processing, and transmission capabilities are not owned by the client. The auditor needs the option of performing a concurrent review in accordance with his audit program and not at the convenience of the client organization's computer center. (Access during peak periods might be prohibited if the client's facilities were used.)

It is acknowledged that a significant financial investment may be required to provide a controlled access to these online capabilities for periodic, unannounced inquiry and analysis in accordance with the auditor's program of review. A significant part of this investment is special purpose computer programs for the specific client which permit access to complex, online operations without being disruptive. In this context it is important that the auditor thoroughly examines the review and monitoring program, including the elimination of any "dummy" transactions and companies which might have been created as a part of the online internal control examination.

In addition to the responsibility for concurrent examination, the auditor's active participation is needed in reviewing major systems design efforts. We hope that this active participation occurs before the systems efforts have been implemented and that the auditor will suggest control procedures and audit checks which flow through the data movement within the system. Through active participation at the systems design stage, the auditor is aware of the complexity of a proposed computer-based system *before* it becomes an online reality for managing organizational assets. It is possible that in some cases the auditor might suggest that additional internal controls, program controls, and audit checks should be incorporated within the proposed network before it is implemented.

AUDIT TOOLS

The use of test decks was one of the earliest computer control techniques employed by external auditors. A sample set of transactions for a particular organization was created, and data cards were prepared to reflect these accounting entries. Predetermined totals were calculated for various data files created by these entries, and, then, the data cards in the test deck were processed by the client's computer system. From analyzing the manner in which the client's computer system handled the test data, the auditor was able to gain some insight into the operation of the computer system. After applying the test deck to other versions of the client's program and to other related operations, the auditor was able to gain an overview as to how the accounting transactions were processed.

Later, the external auditors began using the computer system itself as an audit tool. Each of the computer equipment manufacturers developed general-purpose computer programs for retrieving and sorting data which were stored within the computer system. These utility programs were used by the external auditors to print data files from punched cards, tape reels, discs, drums, data cells, and other types of recording media.

Next, the external auditors began developing specific audit computer programs for each client which embodied these utility programs. Designing a tailor-made computer program for performing specific audit tasks was a significant personnel and financial investment. Moreover, it required a large staff of computer specialists who were conversant with the many machine languages used by the various computer systems.

Finally, the capabilities of utility computer programs and specific computer programs were integrated into a generalized form which could be immediately used in any organization. Gradually, the quality of these generalized audit packages for accessing and retrieving computer-based data has significantly improved, and the scope of these packages has been expanded to include statistical and attribute sampling, quantitative analysis, and special reporting operations on these selected data. These generalized audit packages were so designed that the auditor merely indicated by parameter cards the set of audit tasks that he desired the generalized audit package to perform.

The current generalized audit package contains an efficient miscellaneous report generator for retrieving and processing client's data and for assigning these abstracted data in the external auditor's common data file. There are other computer programs in this generalized audit package which are interfaced online with the auditor's common data file. These programs have expanded the statistical sampling activities to the point that the computer-based capabilities not only select the items for confirmation, but the system prepares the confirmation letters and establishes controls over monitoring responses.

In some of these generalized audit packages, a new capability has been added. Specifically, an online "working paper" selection process covering abstracted client's data has been interfaced with the other retrieval capabilities. These expanded capabilities permit the complete preparation of financial reports, governmental reports, income tax reports, special property tax reports, and other types of analytical reports.

In summary, these generalized audit packages permit the external auditor to retrieve and evaluate selected client data. Specific computer-based audit programs and routines for a given client permit the external auditor to examine the client's processing facilities. However, neither the generalized audit package nor the special purpose computer programs addresses the most critical auditing issue: the internal control review. The nature of the internal control review in an organization with an advanced information system was discussed earlier in this chapter.

TOPICS FOR CLASS DISCUSSION

1. Differentiate between a retrospective review and a concurrent examination as performed by an external auditor in an organization with an advanced computer-based information system.

2. To what extent must the auditor depend on nonclient computer facilities and software capabilities for a concurrent review in an organization with an advanced computer-based information system. Explain your response.

3. Management consulting firms often emphasize that there is a problem of conflict of interest when the administrative services department of a certified public accounting firm designs a computer based system which is later examined by the commercial audit department. Do you believe that this is a conflict of interest? Explain your position.

4. Regardless of your response to question #3, to what extent must the certified public accounting firm participate in examining a proposed computer-based information system in order to protect the organization's assets? Explain your response.

5. In the case of commercial banks, savings and loan companies, and insurance companies which are operating with online, real-time capabilities, executive management may desire duplicate records. For

628   *Information Systems for Management Planning and Control*

example, the original source documents are retained and stored so that they can be easily retrieved for internal audit and internal control purposes. It is assumed that the general public demands a high degree of confidence in all external statements and reports issued by these companies. On the other hand, the typical organization is not a bank, and members of management are not willing to spend the extra cost associated with duplicate records in order to increase the degree of confidence in the various internal and external reports.

Suggest some procedures that management might use in achieving a high degree of confidence in the data within the system without maintaining duplicate records. If necessary, please make extensive use of the library in coping with this question.

6. What is more important to the external auditor of an organization with an advanced computer-based information system: documentation or management's participation? Explain your opinion.

7. Explain the current retrieval features of a generalized audit package.

8. What problems may be encountered if a "manager-level" individual were appointed to the confidentiality of data committee? Explain your response.

9. Assume that you have just been selected as the auditor for a new client organization which has a TYPE 2 information system (an online editing and screening phase, coordination phase, control phase, and planning phase) and that the organization has *one* management review committee: code structure identification and maintenance committee. This latter committee has its usual set of responsibilities. How will you approach this audit? Explain your position.

10. The project manager of a large business organization notified the company's external auditors that management was planning an advanced information system, specifically, a real-time information system. The external auditors were invited to send representatives to observe the designing and implementation activities. The partner for the certified public accounting firm asked, "How can we subsequently audit a system that we have previously reviewed?" Therefore, the external auditors refused to observe the designing and implementation activities. Later, after the real-time information system had been designed, installed, and in operation for a few

months, the external auditors arrived to perform their annual audit. The external auditors were given copies of some of the original flow diagrams for the proposed system and were informed that the system was modified during the implementation phase.

The external auditors had an outside data processing service center prepare a test deck of cards that would check the real-time information system. To the embarrassment of all concerned, none of the test deck of cards was properly coded for the existing, modified information system. Thus, the computer system rejected each card in the test deck. Computer personnel in the company being audited worked overtime during the next month to develop test decks of cards which the external auditors could use in reviewing the real-time information system.

REQUIRED:

A. How can the certified public accounting firm verify the activity for the past few months while the company was operating under this real-time information system? Explain fully the problems involved in auditing this type of system under these circumstances.

B. Suggest alternative procedures that might have been followed by both executive management and the external auditors in the company. Justify each of your suggestions.

CASE 18–1. STATE HOSPITAL SERVICE, INC., AND STATE MEDICAL SERVICE, INC.*

Recently the management of State Hospital Service, Inc., and State Medical Service, Inc., began the transition to an integrated total information system by changing operations from a punched card data processing system to a large-scale computer system. The information flow provided by the punched card system closely resembled the information flow generated by traditional accounting procedures, and management was determined that the new system would not be the blind adoption of the present procedures on

---

* The author and Prof. Hershel M. Anderson of North Texas State University concurrently prepared separate case studies on the business process of the above corporations. Certain parts of this case study are reproduced verbatim from the original draft of Professor Anderson's case study and are used with his permission.

another kind of machine. Instead, each operation of the firm was carefully examined for the purpose of trying to determine (1) "What is it that the people in this operation are trying to do?" and (2) "What information is required for the performance of this operation?" From the consolidation of the findings for each operation, attention was focused on the total information requirements of the firm. Next, management attempted to determine the most timely and accurate methods consistent with low cost that could be employed to meet these total information requirements of the firm.

The most striking departure from traditional accounting procedures contained in the new system was the control over accounts receivable. A rigid system of internal control was imposed over cash receipts, and the system was extended to provide collection data by group of customer accounts. After the total cash receipts had been verified by group of customer accounts, punched cards reflecting the collection data were fed into the computer, and the information system was so programmed that the customer accounts maintained on magnetic tape were updated. If the balance in any customer's account reflects a credit balance, the computer will automatically process a check payable to the customer for this credit balance. On a cycle basis the computer prepares statements used for billing certain customers. Other groups of customers are under a different plan where they pay without being billed. Throughout all of these operations the primary point of control is on cash.

The new accounting procedures are not designed to "prove" that the balance in accounts receivable is equal to the beginning balance plus billings less collections. Instead, a physical inventory procedure is followed. The computer accumulates from the records in the magnetic tape unit the ending balance of accounts receivable, and no attempt is made to reconcile the beginning and ending balance.

As a result of these procedures and the unique information system that was established, the company's independent auditors have been faced with many new problems which will confront other auditors as more companies develop and install integrated total information systems. Currently, the independent auditors and management are arguing over the extent to which controls will be established over the operations of the computer. This matter is an outgrowth of a $1,500,000 difference between the detailed accounts receivable accounts maintained on the computer and the control account which is manually posted.

The Company

State Hospital Service, Inc., and State Medical Service, Inc., began in this midwestern state in the late 1930's for the purpose of providing, on a nonprofit basis, hospital and medical insurance for citizens of this state. The policyholders control the company through the annual election of a board of directors, and this board elects an executive director to serve as the chief executive officer. State insurance regulations provide for control over State Hospital Service, Inc., and State Medical Service, Inc.'s rates. Claim payments are regulated by periodic audits of hospital costs and by a committee composed of doctors, the state insurance agency, and the company. State laws and insurance regulations also set the company's statutory reserves. Thus, by design, the company's primary goal is to provide a vehicle for sharing the risks of sickness and accidents at minimum costs to the citizens of the state.

Both group and individual contracts are written. Currently, there are approximately 3,000,000 members, and 75 percent of these members are covered by group policies. Because of the number of members on family policies, the 3,000,000 members are covered by only 1,300,000 contracts. Of the 3,000,000 members, approximately 20 percent are over 65 years old. The increase in membership this year over last year was 340,000. The number of claims processed has now increased to 1,500,000 a year, representing over $160,000,000. Following are *selected* financial data:

Balance sheet, end of current year

Cash	$ 4,500,000
Investment in bonds	95,000,000
Premiums receivable	6,700,000
Total Assets	$109,000,000

Income statement for the current year

Premiums earned	$160,000,000
Claims incurred	160,500,000
Underwriting expenses	4,500,000
Net Loss	$ 4,000,000

Aside from several staff functions, the company is organized around two functional areas: (1) enrollment "sales," which is concerned with maintaining contact with members through district offices, and (2) operations. All departments in the operating division are involved in some manner in either the receipt of premiums or the payment of claims. The new system, therefore, vitally affects every operating department. (Note that divisional status for electronic data processing resulted from the new integrated system.) The organization chart for the operating division is presented in Exhibit A.

EXHIBIT A
Organization Chart—Operating Division

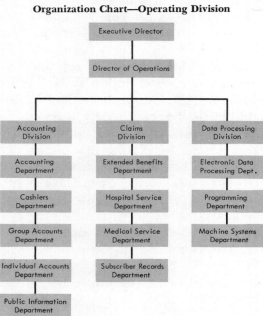

The New System

The director of operations, a very able and progressive administrator, has watched the evolution of electronic data processing. In the period following World War II, the company made effective use of punched card equipment; however, the records maintained on this equipment were nothing more than duplicates of the older manual records. Accounting records (such as premiums receivable) and statistical records (such as membership records) were separately maintained. Each operating department used the punched card processing equipment only to eliminate manual work. As the capabilities of electronic data processing equipment increased, the director of operations began to consider the feasibility of a completely integrated system which would avoid duplication of effort and provide the information needed by all operating departments. To this end a comprehensive feasibility study for an IBM 7070 was begun by the methods and systems group about three years ago, and its report was favorable. The actual transition began about two years ago.

The director of operations issued a statement of operating policy setting forth the objectives of the new system and the priorities to be assigned to different interests. Exhibit B represents this bold statement.

EXHIBIT B
Statement of Operating Policy

Our operating policy is to provide the subscriber, physician, and hospital the most timely and accurate service that is consistent with low cost.

The application of computer technology is designed to further this policy.

Designing an "integrated system" is a condition precedent to the efficient application of automation.

Our systems, programming and operating personnel are being guided by the following precepts.

1. We are developing a totally integrated system. This means that we are not attempting to "put present operations on another kind of machine."
2. We want to develop the *best way* to
   a. serve subscribers
   b. serve hospitals
   c. serve doctors
3. After the "best way" is determined, we then shall design as *by-products* of the system the accounting, statistical, and other internal needs for management.

This distinction is important. External orientation is primary, and internal orientation is secondary. It also follows that internal needs and reporting will necessarily undergo substantial alteration.

In case of conflict, the primary (external needs) will take precedence over the secondary (internal needs).

(Signed)
Director of Operations

This policy statement (Exhibit B) was used by the systems analysts and programmers as a basis for selecting data that would be reflected in the new integrated information system. As previously mentioned, the systems analyst in the previous step had identified the pertinent data required in each operation. Exhibit C is an example of the findings of the previous step; the data reflected in the application card are identified and the steps followed in the approval of a hospital admission are indicated. Schematically, the total integrated system is depicted by Exhibit D.

Given the director of operations' bold policy, the manager of the

EXHIBIT C
Examples of Systems Analyst's Findings
(subscriber history file)

Each application card contains the following data:
1. Hospital service, effective date.
2. Medical service, effective date.
3. Extended benefits date.
4. Certificate number.
5. Group number or direct payment or pending conversion register number.
6. Name of subscriber.
7. Date of birth of original subscriber.
8. Address (original changed if information received).
9. Employer (not updated and sometimes blank).
10. Sex and marital status (not updated).

On reverse side of jacket:
1. Adjustments with continuity of coverage:

Effective Date	Explanation (if any)	Group No.	Coverage B.C., B.S., Ext.	Clerk's initials & Posting date

2. Adjustments with noncontinuity:
Original effective dates are crossed out and remarks entered that the new dates are the effective dates of membership.

3. Claims:

Dr. or Hosp. No.	Admission Date	In or out Patient or D for Diagnostic	Name of Patient	Relationship 1. sub. 2. spouse 3. child	Clerk's Initials & Posting date

*   *   *

(hospital service admissions)

Approval of a hospital admission depends on the following:
1. Correct certificate number.
2. Patient must be included on the membership. If spouse or child:
   a. Coverage must be family type.
   b. Child must not be overage.
   c. Age of spouse must be within reasonable number of years of subscriber.
   d. If subscriber, check name and date of birth.
3. Correct status at time of admission.
   a. Group or direct payment
   b. Coverage.
   c. Must not be cancelled.
   d. Are there extended benefits?
4. Previous hospitalization.
   a. Check 2 previous admissions within past year.
   b. Check current admission for duplicate.
5. Waiting periods incomplete.
   a. Is there a waiver? Interplan, Medicare?
   b. Is it a 3XB deletion? (19 yr. old child deleted from parent's membership)
   c. Is it a state membership?
   d. Is there a cross-reference to another number?
6. Restrictions.
   a. Health waiver.
   b. Tabbed as delinquent.
   c. Flagged for department head.
7. Maternity information.

*   *   *

EXHIBIT D
Data Flow

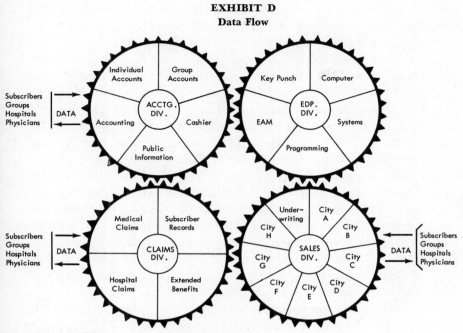

Input data originate in four external areas:
  1. Subscribers
  2. Groups
  3. Hospitals
  4. Physicians

They are introduced into the system and prepared for processing through three divisions:
  1. Sales
  2. Claims
  3. Accounting

All data are processed in one division:
  1. Electronic Data Processing

Output data are distributed to external areas (subscribers, hospitals, physicians, groups) through three divisions:
  1. Sales
  2. Claims
  3. Accounting

EDP (Electronic Data Processing) division began by training programmers and developing programs. First efforts were aimed at subscriber records for billing and receivable purposes—to serve the subscriber best by giving an accurate, timely notice of the premiums due. This part of the system, dealing with earned and unearned premiums, premiums receivable, and subscriber records, was in operation throughout the past year. The programs for claims, hospital, and other payment records are being developed; transition from the old system to the new one in these areas is presently in process.

In the new system there is a significant time lag. For example, individual (nongroup, direct payment) accounts are billed on a quarterly basis 35 days in advance. These subscribers are divided into 13 billing cycles, and one cycle is billed each week. The lead time for changes in the bills of each cycle is about 50 days. If a change is to be made in the cycle which pays for the first calendar quarter, notice must reach the data processing center by November 10.

The built-in lag is not restricted to adjustment to accounts receivable. There are unreported admissions and it is necessary to estimate the amount of such unreported claims at the time of preparing the annual report. Furthermore, individuals will have submitted a claim and possibly received payment on the claim even though they have not paid their premium for the quarter (this will be discovered later when the data in the magnetic tape unit are updated and the appropriate collection action will be initiated) .

The director of operations accepts the time lag as being an inherent aspect of an integrated information system. The director's objective is not to establish new procedures to try to eliminate the time lag, but rather to try to reduce the time element of the lag. The current goal is to try to reduce the time lag to 30 days. The director feels that 30 days will be about as far as she can profitably go in reducing the time lag. Any further reduction would cost more than the benefits derived from such efforts.

Under the current system, a general ledger (including control accounts for the group and individual accounts) is maintained in the accounting department. Charges to the accounts receivable control are based on the weekly totals of premiums billed as shown by the computer runs. Credits are based on the cashier's daily reports. Information on rejects, changes in coverage, additions, cancellations, and errors go directly into the computer runs. The accounting department does not maintain control over these items. Because these items do not go through the accounting department, the general ledger balance of accounts receivable does not agree daily with the balance in the magnetic tape unit. (Remember that even for the accounts on magnetic tape, no attempt is made to reconcile the beginning and ending balance by considering all of the adjustments, additions, cancellations, collections, and billings. Instead, a physical inventory is taken at the end of the year as to the ending detailed accounts receivable balance per the magnetic tape unit, and the general ledger account is adjusted to reflect this amount.)

The Auditor's Appraisal

The state insurance commission conducts an audit of the company every three years. However, members of the board of directors and the executive director believe that an annual audit by a certified public accounting firm more than pays its cost by increasing public confidence in the company's fiscal soundness. New auditors were selected at the time the computer was installed.

During the interim work, which the audit firm started in the 11th month of the fiscal year, the in-charge manager of the audit was disturbed to note that the total of the detailed accounts receivable was $1,500,000 over the balance shown by the control accounts. A closer look at the new system uncovered several unorthodox procedures which led him to prepare a memorandum for the company's consideration (Exhibit E). Investigation revealed an error in the program for group accounts which resulted in an understatement of the billed premium amount used to charge (debit) the control account. After the correction of this error, data for the first eight months of the year were reprocessed and the company's accountant arrived at a $1,000,000 increase in the control account. The auditor felt that the additional difference could be traced to the same source, but the company would only agree to an adjustment of $1,000,000. Furthermore, the load on the computer did not permit further inquiries.

The audit manager's concern goes beyond this single error. His questions center around three permanent features of the new system:

1. The accounting department has no control over the billed premiums. Amounts supplied by the computer cannot be checked to an independent source.

2. Rejected cash receipts are ignored by the accounting department. At no time does the cash credit to the control agree with the sum of the credits to the detail.

3. Time lags result in the reflection of some changes in the detail

Memorandum on Accounting Procedures and Internal Control of the Data Processing Department

As a result of our observations during the course of our recent review of the accounting procedures and internal control of the data processing department in preparation of our audit work for the current year, a number of ideas and suggestions were developed which we are presenting in this memorandum for your consideration.

We hope the suggestions contained in this memorandum will be helpful to the companies in improving operations and strengthening internal control in the data processing department.

Positive Controls of Information Processed

During the course of our examination of the financial statements of the companies, we noted that very substantial differences existed between the general ledger control balance and the total of the premiums receivable detail maintained on the computer. In our opinion, this situation has developed, in part, because adequate positive controls have not been established to provide assurance that the processing of information on the computer system is correct. Currently, the only means of checking the system are the reviews for reasonableness of the volume of data prepared and the time required to process it. While the monitoring of volumes by the test of reasonableness is important and should be continued, positive control should also be established.

We recommend that these controls include the following:

A. *Source Data Control*
1. New Business—Item counts of new subscribers should be made manually and these counts should be reconciled to the number of new accounts set up by the computer.
2. Miscellaneous Transactions (Dollar Adjustments)—Precomputer processing totals should be established of dollar amounts which should be reconciled to the amounts processed by the computer.
3. Nondollar Miscellaneous Transactions—Item counts should be reconciled to the count of nondollar transactions accepted by the computer.
Transmitting this data in batches of workable sizes with preestablished controls will help substantially in isolating errors and in locating missing data.

B. *File Control*
1. Receivable Amounts—Normal balancing procedures should be followed after each weekly processing as follows: Previous week's balance, plus billings, less cash received and adjustments equal present ending balance.
2. Policy Count—Normal balancing procedures should also be followed for these counts.
3. Billing Amounts—Independent control over the billing should be established. For example:
   a. Accumulate on the computer file run the number of policies to be billed the following week.
   b. Provide totals by groups of certificate numbers, for example, every 100,000 numbers, and compare these to the previous quarter's billing figures.
   The count prepared on direct payments should be monitored and double checked until the bills are actually put in the mail. Having the computer serially number these bills would be desirable.
4. Transfers between Billing Methods—Control the receivables, in dollars, and the item counts which are transferred between the group billing and the individual billing accounts.
5. Rejects—Totals of amounts rejected by the computer which are still pending should be controlled as a separate account. Weekly trial balances of the unprocessed detail should be made and reported as to the number of items and the dollar amount to disclose that an unusual buildup in rejected items has not occurred.

We noted that there are some reports containing the type of data indicated above which would facilitate the establishment of controls over rejects. The tie-in of the reprocessed items to that processed by the computer could be simplified to provide the basis of establishing the controls suggested.

General Ledger Control Accounts

The records of the accounting department should control the amounts as processed by the computer in each stage of operation in order to isolate computer errors. It is not adequate to accept computer amounts without the ability to independently verify the amounts on an overall basis as suggested above through batch controls. Control totals should be directly traceable to the detail supporting them.

A suggested setup of the accounts and a description of the journal entries relating thereto follows:

General Ledger Accounts
  Cash
  Cash Clearing
  Premiums Receivable—Computer
    Groups
    Direct Payment
  Premiums Receivable—Manual
  Rejects Receivable—Manual
  Rejects Receivable—Items Pending Investigation
Journal Entries
  (1) As deposits are made—
      Dr. Cash
        Cr. Cash Clearing
  (2) As the computer accepts cash—
      Dr. Cash Clearing
        Cr. Premiums Receivable—Computer

The balance in the Cash Clearing account would represent deposits which the computer has not processed. A trial balance of this account should be prepared at least monthly and reconciled with the actual unprocessed cash items on hand.

  (3) As the computer processes refunds, rejects, and sundry write-offs, an entry would be required to reflect the disposition of these items by the computer:
      a. Dr. Premiums Receivable—Computer
          Cr. Cash (Refunds)
          Cr. Rejects
      b. Dr. or Cr. Premiums Receivable—Computer
          Dr. or Cr. Write-off of Sundry Debit or Credit Balances
  (4) As items are processed out of the reject file:
      Dr. Rejects
        Cr. Premiums Receivable—Computer

The balance in the rejects account represents unprocessed items which should be in the trial balance weekly.

  (5) As writings are calculated by the computer:
      Dr. Premiums Receivable—Computer
        Cr. Premiums Billed (Income)

The detail listing of accounts receivable balances on the computer should be reconciled monthly with the general ledger control account for premiums receivable—computer.

Master Tape Routine

We believe the Company would realize substantial benefits by adopting a technique known as master tape routine. This technique facilitates more rapid correction to program instructions, and of greater importance, changes can be made only under strict conditions as established by the controls provided in the master tape routine. Another advantage of this technique is that the master instruction tape minimizes setup time and reduces the potential for operator error.

While we recognize that it would be a substantial undertaking to revise the existing programs to effectively insert control and linkage instructions, we believe the Company should seriously consider that as a project and schedule it for evaluation by its programming group. This technique, of course, could be used with little additional effort in developing programs for new applications.

Test Program

The Company should provide for a comprehensive and coordinated test program using test data monitoring a computer program in a test session. It is a major effort to prepare this material for testing purposes but it is imperative to identify as many error conditions as possible before processing actual transactons. In addition, this test program data would reduce computer time for debugging and it would facilitate revision and control changes to the program once the system has been put into operation.

Other

We suggest that the individual activity list be condensed to two items a line and that the list provide more "coverage" and "paid-to" information on all accounts. This would reduce printing time and would provide a complete listing of the file which could eliminate the manual maintenance of the card file.

before reflection in the control and vice versa. The records kept are insufficient to permit reconciliations.

The audit manager's recommendations are included in his memorandum. These recommendations are based on the position that internal check and control are essential in every system; an integrated system, like any other system, must be controlled to avoid errors. Furthermore, control does not mean that the company must "put present operations on another kind of machine."

The Company's Rebuttal

Generally, the director of operations and his division managers reject the auditor's recommendations. They contend that no important administrative decisions are based on accounts receivable balances, that the degree of accuracy indicated by the auditor's memorandum would not improve administrative action, and that tighter controls would not be worth their costs. The company depends on the audit of groups and individual subscribers to uncover major errors. Minor errors will eventually come to light as claims are filed and other changes made. The director of operations stated that implementation of the auditor's recommendations would result in as much manual processing (and costs) as experienced under the punched card system.

INDEX

Index

643

This book has been set in 11 and 10 point Baskerville, leaded 2 points. Part numbers are in 14 point Bodoni and 24 point Bodoni Bold; part titles are in 18 point Bodoni. Chapter numbers are in 11 point Baskerville and 24 point Bodoni Bold; chapter titles are in 18 point Bodoni Bold Italic. The size of the type page is 27 by 45 picas.

226738

HF
5548.2
.P7
1975

Prince, Thomas R.

Information systems
for management
planning and
control